, 2019

To Keep the Ball Rolling

To Keep the Ball Rolling

Anthony Powell was born in London in 1905 and was educated at Eton and Balliol College, Oxford. He worked for a London publisher from 1927 to 1935, and as a film scriptwriter from 1935 to 1936. In 1939 he was commissioned in The Welch Regiment and subsequently transferred to the Intelligence Corps in which he served as a liaison officer with the Allied Forces. From 1952 to 1958 he was Literary Editor of *Punch* and he has written reviews and literary columns for many newspapers and periodicals. He became an Honorary Member of the American Academy of Arts and Letters in 1977 and was awarded the C.B.E. in 1956 and C.H. in 1988.

His published works are *Afternoon Men* (1931), *Venusberg* (1932), *From a View to a Death* (1933), *Agents and Patients* (1936), *What's Become of Waring* (1939), *John Aubrey and His Friends* (1948), *Selections from John Aubrey* (1949), and his great twelve-volume sequence *A Dance to the Music of Time* which comprises: *A Question of Upbringing* (1951), *A Buyer's Market* (1952), *The Acceptance World* (1955), *At Lady Molly's* (1957, winner of the James Tait Black Memorial Prize), *Casanova's Chinese Restaurant* (1960), *The Kindly Ones* (1962), *The Valley of Bones* (1964), *The Soldiers Art* (1966), *The Military Philosophers* (1968), *Books do Furnish a Room* (1971), *Temporary Kings* (1973, winner of the W. H. Smith Annual Literary Award for 1974) and *Hearing Secret Harmonies* (1975). His latest publications are the novels *O, how the wheel becomes it!* (1983) and *The Fisher King* (1986).

To Keep the Ball Rolling is an abridged and revised edition of the four volumes previously published as *Infants of the Spring* (1976), *Messengers of Day* (1978), *Faces in My Time* (1980) and *The Strangers All Are Gone* (1982).

To Keep the Ball Rolling

The Memoirs of
ANTHONY POWELL

Foreword by
FERDINAND MOUNT

THE UNIVERSITY OF CHICAGO PRESS

The University of Chicago Press, Chicago 60637

Copyright © Anthony Powell, 1976, 1978, 1980, 1982

This abridged and revised edition copyright © Anthony Powell, 1983

Foreword © 2000 by Ferdinand Mount

University of Chicago Press edition 2001

Printed in the United States of America

05 04 03 02 01   6 5 4 3 2 1

Photographs used by permission of Lady Violet Powell.

Library of Congress Cataloging-in-Publication Data

Powell, Anthony, 1905–
  To keep the ball rolling : The memoirs of Anthony Powell / foreword by Ferdinand Mount.
    p. cm.
  Originally published : To keep the ball rolling. Harmondsworth, England ; New York : Penguin Books, 1983.
  Includes index.
  ISBN 0-226-67721-4 (cloth : alk. paper)
  1. Powell, Anthony, 1905– 2. Novelists, English—20th century—Biography. I. Title.

PR6031.O74 Z477 2001
823'.912—dc21
  [B]   00-050780

CONTENTS

for my grandchildren

To keep the ball rolling I asked Marlow if this Powell were remarkable in any way.

'He was not exactly remarkable,' Marlow answered with his usual nonchalance. 'In a general way it's very difficult to become remarkable. People won't take sufficient notice of one, don't you know.'

Joseph Conrad: Chance

Foreword

At three in the morning, Anthony Powell took a turn for the worse, and the doctor was summoned. He was new, youngish and he turned out to be called Powell too. While they were waiting, the novelist's elder son, the film director Tristram Powell, chatted to Dr Powell about what part of Wales his ancestors came from. It was a typical Powellian moment: unexpected, genealogical, comical, melancholy. Tony Powell died later that night, quietly, at a great age (94) after a long period of frailty, surrounded by his two sons and his wife Violet to whom he had been married for 65 years, with grandchildren and great-grandchildren asleep in the converted stables beyond the lawn.

He left instructions that his ashes should be scattered on the lake below the Chantry, his Regency house in Somerset. While the rest of us gathered on the bank, his sons rowed the ashes out to the middle of the water. As he scattered them, Tristram read "Fear no more the heat of the sun". The moment was, I think, less reminiscent of *Cymbeline* than of Tennyson's *Morte d'Arthur,* a favorite of Powell's. Snow was gently falling, as it does at the beginning and end of *A Dance to the Music of Time.*

Powell's death seemed a calm and graceful one. The huge obituaries all recognised him as the last literary lion of his generation, and his 12-volume novel series, *A Dance to the Music of Time,* as perhaps the greatest achievement in English fiction since the war. Yet almost at the same moment, the old chorus of detractors launched into their familiar catcalls: Powell was an incurable snob, obsessed with upper-class life, *Dance* was a soap opera for a closed society which was destined for the scrapheap of history—in fact, was already smouldering there. Vainly his admirers asked whether, on that account, Shakespeare was to be dismissed for his obsession with the life of the Danish court. Powell certainly was greatly interested in family trees, and the old green volumes of the Complete Peerage were always on a handy shelf, although he said that, if there was a Burke's of Bank Clerks, he would buy that, too. But the accusation of snobbery needs not merely rebutting, but standing on its head.

His admirers were certainly not confined to dyed-in-the-wool conservatives. On the Left, his fans included the playwright Dennis

Potter, the Marxist historian Perry Anderson, and the socialist fire-
brand, Tariq Ali. The truth has it that Powell's fascination was not
at all with the smug connections of a closed caste, but rather with
the remarkable anarchic openness of English life, its quirks and
eddies and, indeed, with the ups and downs of life generally—as
conveyed in the torrential quotation from *Burton's Anatomy* with
which he closes the twelfth and last volume of *Dance*. As a matter
of fact, his fiction was extraordinarily democratic in a way few other
writers of his time could claim. The light plays evenly on each personage—not merely on the beautiful, elusive Jean Duport, or the
charming, doomed Stringham or even the monstrous Widmerpool,
who has joined the fictional valhalla of Raskolnikov, Fagin, Sherlock
Holmes and Jeeves—but also on Alfred Tolland, the dim aphasic
relation who only appears at family parties, on Le Bas, the awkward housemaster with a weakness for late Victorian poets, on
Eleanor Walpole-Wilson, the dogbreeding dyke, on Uncle Giles,
who so memorably said in the 1930s, "I like the little man they've
got in Germany now." Indeed, it is these unremarkable,
unglamorous characters whom we are most pleased to meet again
and the sense of whose ongoing life Powell revives. The same is
true of places—the Ufford (the private hotel in Bayswater which is
the nearest thing to a home for Uncle Giles), or the upstairs room
at Foppa's restaurant, or Stonehurst, the Aldershot bungalow rented
by the narrator's parents.

It is not simply that these people and places are shabby or past
their best (if they had one). It is more that they simply exist as we
do, without necessarily having to take to drink or communism or
the priesthood (or, in the case of Graham Greene characters, all
three) in order to qualify for fictional attention. Perhaps the most
crucial of Powell's insights was that everyone, when you got to know
them, was equally extraordinary. It is this evenness of curiosity,
this utter lack of bedazzlement, which gives the world of his novels—particularly the middle volumes about the war—their unique
quality, a kind of shimmering solidity which both haunts you as
irremediably other, and yet breathes a familiarity which makes you
want to identify the original models—which are, of course, com-
posites. "If someone is good for being a 'character,' he is probably
good for many characters. You can form the basis of perhaps half a
dozen people from one human model" (Dickens certainly did with
his father), as Powell liked to say when maddened by admirers'
claims to have found "the real Widmerpool."

The technique behind the 12-volume series was not quickly or
easily arrived at. He wrote five novels before the war, while he was
working for Duckworth's the publisher: *Venusberg, Afternoon Men,
From a View to a Death, Agents and Patients* and *What's Become of
Waring?* They are light, crisp and funny (*Afternoon Men* was adapted

for the West End stage, rather effectively), and some people prefer them to the postwar series, but then these are usually people who prefer Evelyn Waugh to Powell. Like Waugh, he was interested by Firbank, and Hemingway too, but his interests stretched a good deal further, to include ee cummings, Dostoevsky and Stendhal. His circle stretched further too. His regular lunch companions were George Orwell and Malcolm Muggeridge, and of the next generation he was quick to spot the talents and gain the friendship of Philip Larkin, Kingsley Amis and VS Naipaul. He brought out four volumes of autobiography to forestall the biographers (although Hilary Spurling was not discouraged from producing a considered life after his death), and in his late eighties, to the consternation of some of his nearest and dearest, he published three volumes of quite unsuspected journals which contained not only some uninhibited judgements (of Virginia Woolf: "What a dreadful woman she was—humourless, envious, spiteful"), but also some acute and thoughtful literary criticism.

The style which he evolved for his great panoramic *roman-fleuve* was peculiarly his own, and seemed to have been long brewing during his war service with the Welch Regiment and in the Cabinet Office and his postwar researches into the world of John Aubrey (which bore fruit in two volumes of biography and selections from Aubrey's work). There was a 12-year gap between *What's Become of Waring?* (1939) and the first volume of *Dance, A Question of Upbringing.* The texture of the new style was much denser: in the length of the sentences, in the heavy adverbial structures, the adjectival impasto and, most remarkable and then unfashionable, the substantial participial clauses moored alongside the main sentence. At its most successful, the entire sentence would then convey something of a whole world, containing with it the awkward contradictions and slippery undermining in which real life abounds. Occasionally, in its efforts to include so much, the whole sentence would collapse into ponderousness. But then that is the risk you take (as you take it with Henry James, or even with Kingsley Amis, when he gives his serpentine syntactical second thoughts one twist too many). As Powell himself was fond of saying, with every writer there is always something you have to put up with.

Although he was not at all a performance wit like others of the same generation such as Maurice Bowra or Osbert Lancaster, some of his remarks linger in the mind. One often notices them being quoted without the quoter remembering where they came from, such as his remark that self-pity is the magic ingredient of all bestsellers.

Self-pity was certainly not his own failing. Although occasionally touchy (his friendship with Malcolm Muggeridge never recovered from the latter's supercilious review of *Casanova's Chinese Res-*

taurant), basically he was of an amiable and curious temperament, even when housebound in old age, remaining eager for gossip and ready to meet and form a view of a new visitor. His dedication to the craft of writing was unremitting, and while tolerant of most human vices and failings, he showed little mercy towards slapdash work (usually signing off his regular reviews for the *Daily Telegraph* by pointing out a couple of solecisms which had caught his eye).

His willingness to point out where celebrated authors had gone off the rails became an enjoyable mannerism, brilliantly parodied by the satirist Craig Brown—"*Hamlet* is a not uninteresting play, but the plot is flawed." Yet on rereading the journals and recalling our conversations over 40 years or more, since I first spent Christmas at the Chantry (he was my uncle by marriage, and after my mother died, the Chantry was almost a second home to me), I find that his sharp, practical criticisms are never to be wholly disregarded (to use another of his favourite double negatives).

Lying propped on a Regency settee, with one of his favourite, scrawny, Cornish Rex cats on his lap and talking in a drawl which even to my ears sounded a little old-fashioned, his conversation had an ample strolling tempo which might range from the horrors of the War Office to his fruitless sojourn in Hollywood, where he met Scott Fitzgerald. But then back to books. VS Naipaul said that he had never met anyone else except himself who was so utterly absorbed as Powell in the life of being a writer. Perfection of the work then was his preferred choice, but the life was by no means to be underestimated either.

I think his books will be read a long time hence, as, say, Fielding or Jane Austen (also an English upper-class specialist, one might think) are still read, and that my own pleasure in them has nothing much to do with the background we shared. Perhaps I shall turn out to be wrong, but what Powell's detractors fail to grasp is that the underlying argument is not that dreary one about class, but more about what a novel should be like: should it "privilege" kings and geniuses, or glamorous spies and drug addicts; should it feel a duty to tackle "great themes," or should it attempt to render life as it really looks and feels to most of us, trying in the process to satisfy Dr Johnson's test that a book should help us to enjoy life or endure it? It may seem odd to compare Anthony Powell to James Joyce (although Powell did admire Joyce as a great naturalistic writer, even if he thought *Ulysses* went off a bit), but I think they were ultimately engaged on the same task: to celebrate the light of common day.

Ferdinand Mount, April 2000

Note: A version of this essay appeared in *The New York Times Book Review.*

PART ONE

Infants of the Spring

Laertes Virtue itself 'scapes not calumnious strokes.
The canker galls the infants of the spring
Hamlet I 3

✳ I ✳

I was born in London, 21 December, 1905, the winter solstice ('' 'tis the year's midnight, and it is the day's'), feast of the sceptical St Thomas, cusp of The Centaur and The Goat; the hour, towards one o'clock of a Thursday afternoon; the place, 44 Ashley Gardens, Westminster, a furnished flat rented for the occasion in one of the several redbrick blocks in that rather depressing area between Victoria Street and the Vauxhall Bridge Road. My father, Philip Lionel William Powell, lieutenant in a regiment of the Line, had been married to my mother for a year and a day. She was second of the three daughters of Edmund Lionel Wells-Dymoke, barrister-at-law. Both her parents were dead.

Expected to survive at most two days, I seemed about to follow them, so christening took place without delay in the flat. Later, a more formal ceremony was held over the way at St Andrew's, a Gilbert Scott church destroyed in the blitz, its site now a car park. The names given were 'Anthony Dymoke'; the first, whim of my parents, no relation possessing it, nor special association invoked; the second, from my mother's surname. That was how things started. Why, one wonders, did it all come about? Like Gauguin's picture: *D'où venons-nous? Que sommes-nous? Où allons-nous?*; a journey in my own case tackled under the momentum of a slow pulse, lowish blood pressure, slightly subnormal temperature.

Like many Welsh families my father's has been documented from an early period, a line settling in what was to become Radnorshire in the 12th century. There some of them lived from the beginning of the 17th century to the 1860s in a house called The Travely up in the hills above the valley of the Wye. An offshoot from these Powells moved to Pembrokeshire for two generations, then drifted away from Wales and the Marches. The generation before my grandfather's had gone into the East India Company's army or naval service, and he himself had greatly wished to become a soldier. As only child of a widow circumstances prevented that. He became a surgeon at Melton Mowbray, married the daughter of a local wine-merchant, what time he could spare from fox-hunting being spent with the Leicestershire Volunteers of which he became colonel. My grandmother, a fantasist in a high class, was much devoted to such pursuits as occultism and fortune-telling.

My father, an only son, was in 1901 commissioned into the Welch Regiment, chosen not on account of the Powells' Welsh extraction (pretty well forgotten, and never sympathetic to my father personally), but because recommended as 'good' and cheap by a rather eccentric distant cousin Major-General Sir Alfred Turner. My father, posted to the Battalion serving in South Africa where the Boer War was in progress, was in The Transvaal a month or two after his nineteenth birthday.

My mother's predecessors, lesser landowners and parsons in Lincolnshire (where the surname, as Welles, was that of a powerful mediaeval family), appear to derive directly or collaterally from Thomas Wells of Horncastle, sequestrated as a Royalist under the Commonwealth. His descendant the Revd Thomas Wells married in the 18th century Elizabeth, daughter of Robert Dymoke of Grebby Hall, a small property near Spilsby. Mrs Thomas Wells's brother, the Revd Robert Dymoke, was heir to the main Dymoke estate Scrivelsby Court near Horncastle, to the manor of which the office of King's Champion had been attached since the reign of Richard II. Returning one night towards the precincts of Lincoln Minster after a glass too much he fell into the Chequer Wells and was drowned. Accordingly Scrivelsby went to another Dymoke cousin; Grebby came to the Wells family. My maternal grandfather, an easygoing figure, was much preoccupied with this Dymoke relationship and assumed the double-barrel on remarriage as a childless widower in his fifties.

A connexion through brothers-in-law made the Wells-Dymokes and the Powells honorary cousins. My mother, brought nearer by being daughter of a second marriage, in fact belonged to an earlier generation than my father's. She was well into her thirties when they became engaged. I do not know exactly when that was, but there had certainly been some sort of understanding when he sailed for The Cape.

If the Wells-Dymokes could be classified as a happy family, the same could hardly be said of the Powells, though discord was to some extent veiled. My father reversed the traditional psychoanalytical situation by being well disposed to his father; highly critical, not to say hostile, towards his mother.

My parents' marriage was a wholehearted success. My mother, throughout her life, had no other aim than to make my father happy – no easy assignment in the light of his untranquil temperament – and, however difficult he might at times show himself, whatever rows he made, or wounding things he was prepared to say (one of his worst failings), he was completely broken up when she died; altogether incapable of reconstructing any sort of life without her.

As in all forms of stepping out of line, when human behaviour is concerned, life exacted a price. This was not, I think it true to say, that my father seemed ill assortedly younger than his wife, although difference of age may have been more apparent when they were first married. In latter years there were times when he might well have been the elder of the two. In the main, the quittance was that my mother – who above all things detested having attention drawn to herself, even in a complimentary manner, or (though a very exceptional person) to seem in any way exceptional – was always acutely conscious of having taken a step at which the world might look critically. Of course I never knew this explicitly as a child, though always aware, in the manner that children are, of my parents' marriage being in some way 'different' from others.

My mother possessed none of her sister's (and mother-in-law's) fortune-telling flair, although in her younger days she too had not been at all averse from the Occult and its byways. She retained a life-long interest in Christian Science; though never taking those beliefs on as a religion – religion profoundly occupying her inner life – remaining always a devoted member (Broad to Low) of the Church of England. Several writers come to mind whose parents were to a greater or lesser degree involved with Christian Science. I have sometimes wondered whether emphasis on the unreality of 'matter' – as opposed to the omnipotence of 'Infinite Mind' – has the effect on a child of stimulating imaginative instincts, and, as in my own case, directing them into channels ultimately intellectual or aesthetic rather than religious.

During the first two years of my parents' marriage, my mother moved house nine times. The incessant dislocations of army routine, with attendant inconvenience, separations, expense, for the married of all ranks, are a commonplace of Service life, of which those whose professions keep them most of the time in one place are apt to be altogether unaware. Such displacements played a considerable part in the way in which I was brought up.

My earliest recollection is of snow descending in small flakes outside the window of an hotel bedroom. Several old women in black were scurrying round. That was the winter of 1907, or early months of the following year. I was therefore just about two years old. This was probably a short period of leave before my father took up duties as adjutant of The Kensingtons, a battalion of London Territorials; becoming the 13th (Princess Louise's Kensingtons) London Regiment, part of the Grey Brigade, so called because, instead of changing over to the scarlet tunics of the Line, they retained the grey uniforms of Rifle Volunteer days.

Seeking somewhere in London to live, my father inspected a flat in Albert Hall Mansions, which overlooked Kensington Gardens and the Albert Memorial. It turned out that the owner wanted a tenant for immediate occupation on almost any terms. He accepted an offer of about a quarter or third of the flat's market value. In consequence, 25 Albert Hall Mansions became our home for the next five years.

My nurse (nanny is too professional), Clara Purser, starting life as

parlourmaid, derived from before the move to London, when for a short
time my father had been stationed at Gravesend, a small garrison in
the Thames Estuary. Fascinatingly, one of Clara's brothers was not
only Purser by name, but by vocation purser on a vessel. She was a
sensible kindly intelligent young woman, to whom I became much
attached. I do not remember a great deal about early childhood, a season
that has never consciously obsessed me. The shining gilt serrations of
the Albert Memorial's spire; the great groups of white statuary –
Europe, Asia, Africa, America – the wide flights of marble steps leading
to the frieze of figures representing the arts and sciences throughout
history, the rich greenery of Kensington Gardens beyond, together
formed the central landmark of my first continuously remembered
existence. I enjoyed playing with other small boys in Kensington
Gardens, but did not as a rule greatly like children's parties, of which
I do not remember very many taking place. At home my main amusement was drawing – I cannot remember a time when I did not draw
– combined with deployment on the nursery floor of a respectably large
force of lead soldiers.

Clara and I were once walking through a tunnel beneath the road
in the neighbourhood of South Kensington Underground Station
(always a mild adventure), perhaps on the way to the Victoria and Albert
Museum. Suddenly Clara announced to a man hanging about there
that she would send for the police. Undersized, with a cap, and small
moustache, he looked like a workman. He was apparently a 'flasher',
who had just exposed himself. I saw only his embarrassed grin as he
sidled off. I think no attempt was made at home to disguise what had
happened, nor make heavy weather of the incident.

I was taken by my mother and Clara to watch King Edward VII's
funeral from the Mall. There was a lesser crowd than would assemble
today for such a procession; even so I could see nothing but the
bobbing plumes of the Household Cavalry. Behind the gun-carriage
bearing the coffin were led King Edward's horse, saddled and bridled,
and his terrier, Caesar. When this group passed the place we stood,
I was held up (I think by a good-natured man in the crowd), but failed
to discern Caesar – a great tear-jerker in the rôle of dog-mourner –
though, as easiest way out, I pretended to have done so.

I must, however, have glimpsed for a moment the officer of 2nd Life
Guards commanding the escort riding a short way behind the gun-
carriage. This was the 5th Earl of Longford, later killed at Gallipoli;
father of my future wife. We possess a photograph which includes my
father-in-law, as well as my father: Lieutenant-Colonel Lord Longford
on his charger just behind Caesar's kilted attendant; Captain Powell
among the group of regular army adjutants standing at attention with
drawn swords.

One afternoon – I was about five or six – we had returned from Kensington Gardens, and were waiting outside the door of the flat to be let in. After the park and the street the interior of the building seemed very silent. A long beam of sunlight, in which small particles of dust swam about, all at once slanted through an upper window on the staircase, and struck the opaque glass panels of the door. On several occasions recently I had been conscious of approaching the brink of some discovery; an awareness that nearly became manifest, then suddenly withdrew. Now the truth came flooding in with the dust infested sunlight. The revelation of self-identity was inescapable. There was no doubt about it. I was me.

> So rounds he to a separate mind
> From whence clear memory may begin,
> As through the frame that binds him in
> His isolation grows defined.

In contrast with what might be called my father's Sandhurst personality, he possessed, as a young man, certain *fin-de-siècle* leanings. In one form, these were expressed by delight in the drawings of Aubrey Beardsley, though this attraction for the *Décadence* was balanced by disapproval of much that it stood for.

Family legend embodied a night-out spent in the company of a Grenadier friend called Hermon-Hodge (later Lord Wyfold), Sandhurst contemporary or comrade-in-arms of South Africa. 'Hermon' was staying with his extremely rich father-in-law at a house in Grosvenor Square. On arrival back at this residence in the small hours, the front door was opened by an elderly man in black. Hermon-Hodge was fairly tight, and my father (representing himself in the story as far the more sober of the two) pressed a coin into what he supposed was the butler's hand; with the request that Mr (possibly Captain) Hermon-Hodge be conveyed to his room, and nothing said the following morning of this unsteady arrival home. The money was quietly accepted; the message evidently well understood. In due course my father found that he had tipped Hermon-Hodge's father-in-law, Robert Fleming (grandfather of the writers Peter and Ian Fleming), a banker as rich as any in the country. This P. G. Wodehouse episode, and its *dramatis personae*, would not have been at all typical.

In certain respects my mother's way of looking at things – no doubt owing to the generation to which her father belonged – was almost pre-Victorian. She would use 'Early Victorian' as a pejorative epithet for anything she thought absurdly prim. Hating remarks that suggested unkindness, she was at the same time capable of sharp observations, such as that it was 'the greatest misfortune to be the best looking in a plain family'.

Among the Territorial officers (tending to be stockbrokers) who used to visit the flat was one named Howard (perhaps killed in the war, as the battalion was early in action), who was a sculptor. He was shown a selection of my drawings. I remember laughter, and the words 'Post-Impressionism', which dates the incident to 1911, the year of the famous show, or soon after. One drawing depicted Mephistopheles, a diabolical figure who played a great part in my imaginative life of that time. Mephistopheles had been portrayed by me in profile, wearing a kind of glengarry cap, surmounted with a long feather. The sculptor, Mr Howard, remarked that the spine of the feather ran in a direct straight line with the devil's slanting eyebrow. 'That continuation of line is something only children do naturally,' he said. This comment made a deep impression on me (then probably about six) at the time, but seven years later, when Sidney Evans, the Eton drawing-master, pointed out the balanced pattern created in a picture, I had altogether forgotten about such conscious principles of design. The idea of a pattern in drawing returned as an entirely fresh revelation. What picture did Evans show? I seem to recall two separate groups of figures on one canvas in a book of reproductions, each group forming a kind of arch, one large, one small. Peter de Hooch? Watteau? Millet?

More adventurous social frontiers within my parents' purview are suggested by an encounter of my mother's when lunching with friends living on the outskirts of London. To reach the house entailed a journey by train. At the station my mother noticed getting into one of the compartments a man whose appearance made her feel a sudden sense of extreme repulsion. At her destination, this man reappeared on the platform. She found herself almost praying that he would not be her fellow-guest at luncheon. Needless to say he was. It was the magician, Aleister Crowley – to use his own preferred style – The Beast 666. Asked what he talked about at lunch, my mother simply replied: 'Horrors.' I don't think my father ever met Crowley, but he owned a set of *The Equinox*, and one or two of Crowley's other publications. The Beast's name would have been familiar, if in no other way, through an army friend, Captain (later Major-General) J. F. C. 'Boney' Fuller, a great Crowley adherent in those days. Fuller, regarded by his military superiors as able in professional matters, though too eccentric to be taken over seriously, was also an early partisan of the armoured vehicle in warfare.

It was to Albert Hall Mansions that James Gomme came as cook. An impressive figure, fond of making sententious remarks, James was said to cook superbly. He was, indeed, wasted on my parents, who did no more than the minimum of entertaining required by good manners or duty; neither of them at all greedy, my father always complaining about his digestion. When my mother was ordering the meals for the day, James once remarked: 'I should not wish to cross the Captain in any of his appetites.'

Albert Hall Mansions represents, I think, the happiest interlude of my parents' married life, a peace and coherence never quite achieved again. My father's military duties took a civilized form; my mother liked London, its largeness leaving her comparatively untroubled by social obligations, and giving opportunity for the unobtrusive 'good works' to which she liked mainly to devote herself. As stock subject for humour, or serials in boys' magazines, there was, of course, always talk of the impending German invasion.

In the early months of 1913, the tour of duty as Territorial adjutant terminated, my father rejoined his regiment, then stationed at Bordon Camp about a dozen miles from Aldershot. We lived in a large bungalow of Indian type, let furnished, its situation on the top of a lonely hill, surrounded by heather, gorse, pines, sandy hollows skirted with bracken. Here I must digress on a matter scarcely avoidable in the context.

The less novelists descant on their own works the better. Nevertheless, autobiographical material produced by a professional novelist is bound to raise speculation as to how much direct experience has found a place in his fiction. I will therefore, though unwillingly, make a few comments on a subject that can be tedious unless approached with businesslike severity. I choose this moment because a fairly close description of the bungalow (though not its domestic staff, except for certain aspects of James) appears in my novel, *A Dance to the Music of Time* (hereinafter abbreviated to *Dance*), in which the house is called Stonehurst; a name that will serve in these memoirs too.

Most novelists draw their characters and scenes in some degree from 'real life'. If a character in a novel bears no resemblance whatever to any human being one has ever met – nor could ever meet whatever the circumstances – there is likely to be something wrong; a principle just as true of fantasy (say *Alice in Wonderland*) as of 'naturalistic' writing. On the other hand, the images that present themselves to the mind of any novelist of more than amateur talent take an entirely different form when the same writer attempts to describe 'real people' known to him; the former altogether more complex, free-wheeling, wide ranging.

There are no doubt exceptions to this rule, especially minor figures in the background of certain novels, drawn directly from life, but playing little or no part in the development of the narrative. The 'real person' who sets going the idea of a major 'character' in a novelist's mind always requires change, addition, modification, development, before he (or she) can acquire enough substance to exist as a convincing fictional figure. These alterations come not so much from thought on a novelist's part as from the uncontrolled subconscious instinct that gives a 'character' life; while the smallest deliberate change made by a novelist to suit the story's convenience means, in truth, that all genuine dependence on the original model ceases – in contrast with traits (possibly inconvenient from a fictional point of view) that must unavoidably be chronicled about a 'real person' in Memoirs or Autobiography.

'Real people' who merge successfully into fictional 'characters' are comparatively rare; and much bad novel-writing can be laid at the door of the misconception that, because someone has an outstanding personality, he (or she) can be easily assimilated into a novel. In fact, strongly 'realized' persons simply move through a novel as themselves, not on the fictional plane demanded by 'art'. In Dostoevski's novel *The Devils* (*The Possessed*) the Russian historian, Granowski, is adapted to create one of the great comic characters of the European novel, Mr Verkhovensky. In the same book, the writer Karmazinov is admittedly modelled on the writer Turgenev.

Karmazinov, in contrast with Mr Verkhovensky, never quite comes off. This is in some part because Dostoevsky allows personal spite – a fatal ingredient in any novel – to enter into his representation of Turgenev; but the flaw is even more from the interest attaching to Turgenev existing in his being Turgenev; not Turgenev watered down to Karmazinov. Once you turn Turgenev into a character in a novel – even in what is perhaps the greatest novel ever written – no true life is left in him. Proust clearly recognizes this principle in his projection of Anatole France as Bergotte, omitting all sorts of comic aspects of Anatole France's true character that might have been included in an unfriendly portrait (or caricature) by a lesser novelist, but would, in the context, have ruined the purpose for which Bergotte is intended.

This rule – that 'realized' personalities are likely to be unsuitable as characters in novels – does not apply only to individuals who have made a name for themselves. The obscure 'realize' themselves just as much as the celebrated; and can prove an equal trap for novelists lacking the right instinct. In any case the example of Granowski (unknown as an historian to most readers outside Russia, possibly to many within) shows what an insignificant matter 'identification' is, so far as appreciating a novel like *The Devils*. Often, of course, no model exists to 'identify'; invention is total; yet naturally even invention too must be undertaken in relation to the observed, or inwardly understood, manner in which human beings behave.

I have paused – perhaps too long – on this subject, because Stonehurst was, indeed, much as suggested in *Dance*, even if not in every character and incident. Among the factual elements was the strange cult, with odd costumes and bearded leader, going for runs past our gate. James was our cook (until he left to get married), and some of his remarks as Albert are authentic. My father's soldier-servant was Thorne who would disparage the military policemen jogging through the heather. Thorne also took me to see an inter-regimental rugger match at Bordon; but he did not in the least otherwise resemble Bracey, the batman in the novel.

These small items would be scarcely worth mentioning, were it not for the Stonehurst 'ghosts'. The bungalow, built towards the turn of the century, looked the last place on earth likely to be 'haunted', but certainly various individuals (who could not have been in contact to discuss the matter) found reason to say there was something 'spooky' about the place. The appearances, such as they were, took two main forms; the more commonplace – if least easy to accept as genuine – a whiteish shape, misty, of no great density but some height, that materialized at the bedside of successive maids when they woke up in the morning. This apparition – most traditional of spectres, except in manifesting itself at morning instead of night – was laughed off as 'imagination'; never reaching a pitch where a member of the domestic staff even suggested giving notice on that account. The matter was treated as a joke, if a joke with a basis in possibility. This benefit of the doubt was allowed to some extent in the light of quite other unusual experiences undergone by my mother.

The Stonehurst household, as customary with my parents, included several animals. I make this point because, in order to convenience any domestic pet wanting to take a nocturnal prowl – then re-enter the house in the small hours – my mother was accustomed to leave the lower half of her bedroom window open to facilitate an easy return. When the domestic animals used this form of access, they were accustomed to sleep the rest of the night on her bed. I emphasize this arrangement, because in certain respects the story, as a ghost story, would be more convincing had we possessed no animals, my mother opened only the top half of her bedroom window.

One night my mother was awakened by the thud of a smallish animal jumping on to her bed. That, as I have said, was a happening not in the least uncommon. On this particular occasion, however, she suddenly felt a sense of awful terror. The thing landed near the foot of the bed, then slowly worked its way up, until pressing down the bedclothes just below her neck. This visitation took place several times, but I am un-certain of the length of interval between. Whatever these were, the normal animal population would recurrently turn up in the middle of the night without in the least disturbing my mother's nerves. She was not only very used to animals and their ways, but also, as explained earlier, on easy terms with anything in the nature of the Occult, which, so far from inspiring fear in her, she was inclined to seek out.

These manifestations must have come to something of a climax in the first half of 1914, the year of the outbreak of war; the less specific apparitions – supposed misty white shapes – probably spoken of earlier than that, indeed soon after we came to live in the house. Some parents would have tried to keep all this from a child of seven or eight. My father, left to himself, would probably have done so. My mother, on the other hand, regarded any such concealments as shutting off an essential aspect of life. Talk about 'ghosts' was never at all curtailed on my account, and did not in the least disturb me. I have fairly strong feelings about the 'atmosphere' of houses, but never, in fact, found that of Stonehurst in the least uneasy; though this was certainly a period of great imaginative activity – no doubt true of most children of that age – in which elaborate fantasies of all sorts occupied my mind to an extent that they seemed part of daily life.

There was a sequel to the Stonehurst ghost story. A year or more after leaving the house my mother met someone who knew the bunga-low, and spoke of 'rather an odd woman' who had lived there. The 'odd' lady – who was not one of the family from which we had rented the house – used to breed schipperkes, small black dogs from the Netherlands, with sharp ears and curly tails, at that period fashionable as pets. When one of her schipperkes died, so it was reported, the dog's photograph was hung in her bedroom, its individual eating bowl placed below. It looks a little as if my mother's great affection for animals had made her in some subjective manner a receptive medium. The fact that she should have been frightened was not only unlike her, but unlike most (though by no means all) documented accounts of such hallucinations, which often include animal apparitions.

The education of officers' children was undertaken by Miss Judkins, an easygoing figure of slightly droll appearance, who lived in a cottage about a mile away, and did her rounds on a bicycle. Miss Judkins, adequate at instruction, was, I think, no more than that; my impres-sion being that most of what I learnt at this period was in consequence of books my mother read to me, or such that I read myself. That view may be unjust. Certainly I was sufficiently equipped to cope with the usual subjects when, in due course, I arrived at a day-school. It had been supposed that I should go to boarding-school at nine and a half. What interim state, if any, had been contemplated between Miss Judkins and a preparatory school, had we remained at Stonehurst, I do not know. I should have found the change a drastic one if I had gone direct from one to the other. As things fell out, the war turned all plans upside down.

I have quite often come across persons of my own age, even a year or two older, both male and female, who say that as children they were scarcely aware of World War I taking place. Such is not my own experience. For me the impact of the war was menacing from the beginning. Within a few weeks of the Regiment's embarkation, the air was full of rumour of casualties – some true, some untrue – to be confirmed one way or the other later. The killed were often fathers of children who had come to tea, or subalterns remembered as chatting in the hall while they changed into tennis-shoes. Life seemed all at once geared to forces implacable and capricious, their peril not to be foretold. By the time we left Stonehurst I was approaching nine years old. Childhood, with its intensity of imaginative adventure that comes to an end with school – at least is greatly altered and modified there – had been allowed to linger on rather beyond its statutory limits. Mine had been on the whole rather a lonely childhood (though I never at all desired brothers or sisters), but not in the least an unhappy one. Now the condition was brought categorically to a close.

War was declared on 4 August, 1914. My father, a company commander, embarked on 12 August, and was engaged in the early open fighting of the campaign, before the armies settled down to trench warfare. My mother and I moved to London. Clara remained as an adjunct. We lived at different times in houses or flats of friends; furnished rooms; a boarding-house in South Kensington. The furnished rooms, where we did not stay long, were almost next door to Mr Gibbs's day-school, which I now attended.

Teaching was good, though not at all intensive. Mr Gibbs, an attractive personality, showed that it was perfectly possible for a headmaster to be also a nice man. Games were played at a sportsground in Barnes, to which a private bus travelled twice a week. I became aware for the first time of my own inability to play them; also of the unpleasantness of some boys – a necessary prelude to the unpleasantness of not a few men – but on the whole memories of Gibbs's are agreeable.

Towards the end of the year my father went down with dysentery. On recovery, he was posted as brigade-major to a formation in one of the newly raised 'Kitchener' Divisions. It was made up chiefly of recruits from the Midlands, especially Birmingham; troops he subsequently regarded as the best he ever came across throughout his services. Like Falstaff and his levies ('We'll to Sutton C'fil' together'), my father was ordered to report to a Brigade Headquarters at Sutton Coldfield in the environs of Birmingham. One of his first duties was to pick from several candidates a staff-captain to serve under him. He chose a temporary officer of The Gloucesters, Thomas Balston, within a year of his own age (then thirty-four). The Division moved fairly soon from the Birmingham area to Yorkshire; Brigade HQ at Leyburn in Wensleydale. I went up to Yorkshire for the summer holidays of 1915. August was as cold as winter. The steep dark wooded slopes, rocky tree-shaded streams, a dramatic even sinister country, has always remained in my mind. Brigade staff was housed in a small requisitioned hotel. Before the rest moved in, my mother and the staff-captain (whom she never found very sympathetic) undertook some of the initial domestic arrangements for living there. I must have come in contact with Balston at Leyburn, but cannot remember him at that period. He was to play an important part in my subsequent life.

Tall, spare, with short thick black hair that stood up like a flue-brush, Tom Balston had a jerky nervous manner, literary interests, a great obstinacy of purpose. A good staff-officer, he got on pretty well with my father in principle, though after the war each would complain about how difficult the other had been to work with. This is credible in each case; Balston, as subordinate, probably having the worse time. They must have had something in common, because, in an unintimate way, they remained friends for years; both neurotic, though in a different manner.

Balston was, of course, far the better educated of the two. In accounts of his own life, he always insisted on the bad terms existing between himself and his father, whom he represented as thoroughly unamiable, not least in being well off, but too cantankerous to spend anything on his children. Balston had more or less paid for his own education by scholarships: at Eton (of which his great-uncle had been headmaster); and later at New College, Oxford. Before the war he had kept himself by tutoring, and literary hack work, but his ambition had always been to be a publisher.

After Wensleydale, the Division moved south to Salisbury Plain. We lived at Boyton Cottage, dower house of Boyton Manor, the local 'big house', then let to Colonel (later Sir Martin) Archer-Shee, who was commanding a battalion of the Gloucesters. A lively Tory MP, Colonel Archer-Shee was half-brother of the naval cadet accused of stealing a postal-order; theme of Terence Rattigan's play, *The Winslow Boy*. Mrs (later Lady) Archer-Shee was American. On visits to their house I saw the four volumes of *Battles and Leaders of the Civil War*, which first aroused an interest I have never quite lost in the War between the States; rekindled on discovery of the distant Powell cousins who fought for the Union, and at least one of whom had Confederate brothers-in-law. From Boyton Cottage, in 1916, then ten and a half, I finally set out for boarding-school.

The school to which I went was in Kent, recommended by a fellow Territorial adjutant. At least eighty per cent of the boys were sons of regular army officers, a good sprinkling of the fathers being generals. At this period – even if I sometimes toyed with the idea of becoming a painter of huge subject pictures, or illustrator of historical novels in the manner of Cruikshank or Phiz – I quite seriously supposed that I should myself in due course enter the army. As the war showed no sign of ending, this seemed logical enough, and (with the navy) was the normal goal of most of the boys at the school. My own concept of a soldier's life was a purely romantic one; not at all encouraged by my parents, who – if inclined, then and later, to sheer off the more tricky problem of what on earth I *was* to do for a living – no doubt saw the army, even at that stage, as an inappropriate calling. I persisted until the age of about fourteen – when the incongruity of any such ambition dawned even on myself – in supposing that an army career lay ahead. The nature of the school, as such, did not therefore strike me as at all exceptional.

Before becoming a pupil, I was taken by my mother to see the school. It had been built for that purpose, conceding no architectural or decorative feature to attract the eye. We had tea with the Headmaster, in his sixties, recently retired, but returned to take charge again, both his sons being now in the forces. Although rather notably lacking in all literary appreciation, he strongly resembled the photographs of Kipling towards the end of his life; that hanging on the stairs of the London Library always a disagreeable reminder of the Headmaster's sparse grey hair, drooping tobacco-stained moustache, abnormally thick spectacles, eternal old thick tweed suit, worn whatever the climate. Cutting a loaf of bread at tea, he barked out: 'Crust or crumb?' The phrase was unfamiliar to me. He looked enraged.

After tea we were taken over the premises. In the gymnasium the junior boys were marching round. The Headmaster called one of them out, and questioned him. The boy, just about my own age, good-looking, dark, rather plump, gave his replies in a quiet manner. He was Henry Yorke (later the novelist, Henry Green), who was to be a close friend for many years. Indeed, being brought in touch with Yorke is the only outcome of any interest to be connected with the school. This preview of Yorke was one of those curious foreshadowings not uncommon in life. Yorke's own theory as to why he had been pulled out from the rest of the small boys doing gym was that comparative plumpness disposed the Headmaster to show him off to parents as an example of how sumptuously the boys at the school were fed.

Even for prep schools of the period mine would rank high in any

competition for dearth of cultural enlightenment. By this stage of the
war, competent teachers hard to come by, there was an ever rolling
stream of assistant-masters and mistresses: the males likely to be
ancient, shiftless, wounded, gassed; the females (at this school
uniformly charmless), often scarcely qualified academically to do the job
at all. Two fairly doddering veterans dug out of retirement (both, I
believe, Old Harrovians) were agreeable, and liked my essays. The
drawing-master, Mr Corke, also stands out as a well wisher.

The Headmaster taught classics, mathematics, and a language that
passed for French. He had cranky ideas about instilling the principles
of arithmetic, in consequence of which my own mathematical capacity,
at best frail, never wholly recovered; though the subject was well taught
at Eton, the change for the better staggering me when I went there.
I firmly believe in the value of Latin (quite apart from Stendhal's ten-
able view that 'le latin est bon parce-qu'il apprend s'ennuyer'), but
the classical syllabus of the top (Headmaster's) form might have been
judged a little old-fashioned by Dr Arnold himself. The whole of
Saturday morning (three or four hours on end) was consecrated to
turning complicated English sentences of five or six lines in length into
Latin prose. In the course of one of these sessions the Headmaster went
so far in commendation as to remark: 'If I'd had you earlier, I could
have done something with you'; but the regret was his rather than my
own.

There were frequent and remorseless promptings that the men in the
trenches were having a worse time than ourselves. In the music hour we
used to sing *The School at War*, a song with words by Cyril Alington,
headmaster of Eton; the tune (somewhat recalling *The Londonderry Air*)
composed by A. M. Goodhart, my future Eton housemaster.

> We don't forget you in this dark December.
> We sit in schoolrooms that you know so well;
> And hear the sounds that you so well remember,
> The clock, the hurrying feet, the chapel bell . . .

Orwell, Connolly, Waugh, Betjeman, Jocelyn Brooke, to name only
a few, have pungently described the disenchantments of schooldays of
that date, so that in the case of my own preparatory school there seems
no point in rehearsing once again a subject already exhaustively
treated. Nothing picturesquely horrible ever happened to me there,
though I should be unwilling to live five minutes of it again. At the
same time I do not wish to appear less competent than my contemporaries in making creep the flesh of the epicure of sadomasochist
school-reminiscence. A single small side-dish will suffice in adding to
this generously laid out feast.

The Archer-Shee postal-order case being prototype of an endemic category of school row, a boy at my prep school was similarly accused. Though such things are hard to judge, he was a boy who might have been supposed particularly unlikely to have done anything of the sort. Two senior boys, officious and half-baked, reported him. In consequence the Headmaster administered thirty-two strokes of the birch. The whole school was assembled to hear the victim's cries from the Headmaster's classroom (down two or three steps from the big schoolroom), where afterwards it was found that, in the course of this flagellation, the boy had urinated on the floor. His schoolfellows were forbidden to speak to him until further notice.

Some weeks later it turned out that a slip had been made. The boy in question had neither stolen, embezzled, nor forged. He was, in short, totally innocent. The Headmaster was put under the humiliating obligation of making public amends in the presence of the whole school (once more assembled in the big schoolroom), and (his father being on active service) the boy's mother. After recapitulating in an ungracious manner whatever shreds of explanation were available to excuse such a miscarriage of justice on the part of one set in authority, the Headmaster observed: 'Of course the licking doesn't matter in the least. What's important is that there remains not the smallest imputation of dishonesty.'

Henry Yorke, as opposed to Balston – almost literally carrying a spear when the curtain goes up on him – enters the stage with a speaking part. Close friends of early years are apt to be less easy to 'rationalize' to oneself, therefore less easy to describe, than those known more casually, and Yorke, in any case a somewhat enigmatic personality, is a forcible example of that. As Henry Green, he wrote an autobiography (*Pack My Bag*, 1940), which takes him to the age of about thirty-five; a book, at once reticent and revealing, that gives his own account of our preparatory school, and much else besides.

Pack My Bag opens with the arresting statement: 'I was born a mouth-breather with a silver spoon ...' This metaphor perfectly hits off one side of Yorke; the grotesque physical image invoked possessing a comic potentiality certainly recognized by him in offering an economic and moral definition of himself. The silver spoon refers to coming from a family reasonably categorized by him (in a press interview) as aristocratic. He was the youngest of three brothers. His father, a classical scholar who had made a prosperous career in business, was half-Dutch, an odd mixture of reserve and rather crude teasing (an amalgam Yorke to some extent inherited), not only characteristic of that generation, but perhaps also evidencing the Netherlands blood; which was laced with equally grand Austrian and Portuguese. These foreign strains were reflected in Yorke's own appearance, and (like George Orwell's quarter-French ancestry) should be taken into account in relation to temperament and approach to writing. His mother (a Wyndham, brought up at Petworth, accordingly regarding all other residences as small), in contrast with her husband a sparkling talker, had an inimitable style in anecdote, in which sporting vernacular would be deliberately decorated with the brilliantly pedantic phrase.

If one side of Yorke found the silver spoon a handicap to respiration, another accepted it as understandably welcome; and coming to terms with opposed inner feelings about his family circumstances, his writing, his business activities, his social life, was something he never quite managed to achieve to his own satisfaction. When we were young I had no idea how deep interior tumults must have lain. Then – and later – he always seemed pretty successful in whatever he put his hand to – writing, business, life in general – but success is not the criterion of whatever alleviates the stresses that his own self-examination suggests.

The eldest brother had preceded Yorke at our preparatory school, the other going elsewhere. Both elder brothers were unusually good at work and games, and Yorke records how his own fallings-short were invariably contrasted by the Headmaster with the eldest's glowing achievement. Yorke himself, if no dazzling star, was perfectly competent at the normal routines of school life, a skilful fisherman, and later to play billiards for Oxford. Nonetheless (even if left unspoken by anyone but the Headmaster), there was a tendency for him to be treated at home with affectionate but slightly amused acceptance that he was not quite the performer the other brothers had been at his age.

This situation is not to be exaggerated. When such a motif is set down on paper it can acquire an altogether undue weight. Yorke's family perfectly recognized that he had a line of his own, but his talents were not easy to define – and he was himself the worst possible salesman of them. No one, least of all his relations, could be altogether blamed for not immediately grasping the nature of his gifts. To myself, as guest in the house, he always seemed on the easiest terms with his own family – ragging his father in a manner I should never have dreamt of using towards my own – but he would often complain of tensions at home, and was certainly obsessed by a parental 'myth', especially where his father was concerned.

I do not remember when we first made friends at our prep school; not immediately; possibly only after moving into one of the two dormitories containing twenty or more boys. In these big rooms both Yorke and I – like professional narrators of the Orient – were recruited, during the half-hour after lights-out when talking was permitted, to entertain the company by telling stories. This folk-type of group culture was surprisingly popular. The stories were usually re-hashes of popular novels, or serials running in magazines. I occasionally offered a concoction of my own; here too (as with Shakespeare) derivative elements probably traceable. I remember establishing some sort of status for the narrator – a blow struck for art and letters – by refusing to continue if too much whispering, or other interruption, took place. All this sounds as if at an early age I had decided to become a novelist. That was not so; although, sitting on the radiators of the gym, Yorke and I did begin to write a novel together (a thriller), but it progressed no further than the first half-page of an exercise book.

Yorke, who himself never possessed the smallest relish for military mystique, had been sent to the school on the recommendation of an uncle by marriage, a general. I can't remember how he saw his own future at that age, but feel sure that he spoke of it – as of most things – altogether dogmatically. As a boy he was an unremitting talker, especially if not at ease, a compulsive flow, hit or miss in content, but, as often as not, funny, perceptive, entirely individual. He records that while growing up he would sometimes produce for the benefit of strangers in a railway carriage narratives of pure fantasy about himself. As a small boy he had an exceptional command of the mature phrase, but was otherwise a fairly conventional schoolboy, daring only in his spoken objectivity. When we were about eleven I was astounded in this respect by Yorke remarking: 'The fact is that both my parents are extremely selfish.'

He was always interested in words, repeating unfamiliar ones (e.g. hirsute) over to himself, laughing at them, discussing them. We must have been about twelve or thirteen (I don't think I was yet at Eton, though Yorke may have been) when we found, in an out of the way sitting-room in the Yorkes' country house, two volumes of Rabelais. The name even then conveyed unspeakable obscenities, and we set to work at reading them forthwith. Neither then, nor later, have I been able to make much headway with the great satirist, but at the time he seemed something of a milestone in varieties of literary experience.

Yorke, though he constantly reiterates the tyrannous nature of the Headmaster, relates that he was on the whole happy at our prep school. He writes of the Headmaster: 'We respected him until in my case I at least went further and came to reverence him.' The literary device of speaking collectively is open to objection, but (even if not my own view) Old Boys might well concur in the Headmaster being owed respect; even (Old Boys being what they are) reverence. What I find an interesting paradox, in this Kiplingesque praise of a famous man of little showing, is that (though coming to his work seriously only in middle life) I am a great admirer of Kipling; while Yorke found him wholly unreadable.

Yorke went to Eton at the end of the summer term of 1918. I stayed on two more terms. We used sometimes to exchange letters.

In 1917, my father was sent as instructor to the Staff College, then quartered at Clare College, Cambridge. The University was housing mostly officer-cadets. We lived in undergraduate furnished rooms at 4 Great St Mary's Passage. It was winter, Cambridge some of the time under snow. After some months at the Staff College, my father returned to France again (on the staff of the 25th Division); was then posted to the War Office. It must have been about this time that my parents took a house in St John's Wood. I remember air-raids on London after we went to live there; a bomb dropped on the pub at Lord's Cricket Ground, which was just round the corner.

Back at school, the Headmaster's form were construing Livy one November morning – he had just objected to the word 'voluptuous' as translation for some epithet applied to Capua, on grounds that boys did not know what the term meant – when at the back of the classroom the door opened. The Headmaster's wife ('Ma Baboon', her physiognomy to the life) came hurrying down the two or three steps. She went up to her husband, and began simian mumblings in his ear. The Headmaster removed his wire spectacles, contracted his eyes, closed the small blue-bound teaching edition of Livy. The news had just come through that an Armistice had been declared. He announced that there would be no more work that day. Instead, the morning was divided into playing football, and, for the top form, cutting wood in the miniature labour camp adjoining the Headmaster's garden. In the afternoon we played football again. That evening I was reading a book in the big school-room. The Headmaster tramped in. He had experienced an afterthought. There would be prep after all, notwithstanding the Armistice. Otherwise, he said, the next day's work would be disrupted.

The following term, the Easter one, I sat for the Common Entrance Examination for Eton. Some weeks later, having just slipped a cartridge into the breech of a ·22 rifle, I was lying prone on the mats of the rifle-range. The Headmaster would sit behind those shooting, registering with field-glasses the area of hits on the target. Suddenly he addressed me.

'You've taken Middle Fourth.'

A feeling of indescribable wellbeing flowed through me; a sensation I have experienced on one or two subsequent occasions on hearing good news. Middle Fourth, far from a triumph of scholarship, was a perfectly respectable level to achieve. My body had to remain a few more weeks where it was; the real me had already moved into another, and preferable, condition of life.

Until my late twenties I used to have a recurrent – if not very frequent – dream that I was back at my preparatory school. One night this dream took the shape of the Headmaster lying on a sort of chaise-longue; myself standing beside him. I don't know whether I had become a boy again, but he was speaking in the harsh tone he was accustomed to use when angry. Instead of answering him, I took one side of the piece of furniture on which he lay, and shook it. He protested. I continued to shake it with increasing vigour. The Headmaster's protests became weaker; then ceased altogether. I examined him. He was dead. So far as I can remember, dreams of the school never recurred after that night.

✱ **3** ✱

I went to Eton in the summer half of 1919. I could not have been more fortunate in my Eton house. A. M. Goodhart's was not merely a 'bad' house, but universally agreed to be far the 'worst' house in the school. Its record at every branch of sport was unimaginably low; its only silver trophy, the Lower Boy Singing Cup. Tolerant scepticism was the note struck. This was partly due to chance – the particular boys who happened to have been sent there – partly to the eccentric character of Mr Goodhart himself; in certain respects a typical schoolmaster; in others, an exceptional example of his profession.

Then in his fifties, Goodhart somewhat resembled photographs of Swinburne's friend, Watts-Dunton; the same high forehead, walrus moustache, look of slightly unreliable benevolence, an awareness of being always prepared for the worst, and usually experiencing it. He also looked like the novelist A. C. Benson, whose Eton house he had taken over. With the Eton master's uniform, black suit and white bow tie, he was old-fashioned enough to retain the starched shirt and cuffs of an earlier generation; often remarking that in his own time at Eton (in College) a boy who did not put on a clean stiff shirt every day was regarded as an 'absolute scug'. On the other hand, Goodhart equally deprecated modern extravagance in demanding all sorts of special clothes for sport; asserting that for the Wall Game (which, as an acknowledged star of all time, he would still sometimes play) an 'old tailcoat' was looked on as wholly appropriate.

Goodhart's sentences always began with a curious little purring sound, much parodied, but almost impossible to reproduce, far less describe; best indicated perhaps by a favourite quotation of his (from the *vers de société* of Frederick Locker-Lampson) referring to a race-horse of Lord Rosebery's:

> And the winner of the Derby
> And the Guineas
> Proudly whinnies,
> When e'er the Opposition takes a fall.

Classics was the subject Goodhart taught, but his real interest was music. When the day was over he used to compose in his study, which was situated at the end of a passage lined with boys' rooms. There were several bathrooms in the house by the time I went there, but only a few years before hip-baths used to hang outside every door. Riotous members of the House would sometimes emerge at night – having made sure the night-watch was on the upper floor – take one of the baths from the wall, and bowl it against their tutor's study-door; disappearing round the angle of the passage, to be found fast asleep when en-quiries were instituted. By my day a quieter mood characterized Goodhart's pupils.

The Captain of the House when I arrived there was Arthur Peel (later Earl Peel), for whom I fagged. My second half, Peel gave his fags the run of two or three shelves of quite readable books. Among these I found Alec Waugh's *The Loom of Youth*; greeted on publication two or three years before as a work of unspeakable depravity, owing to its references to public-school homosexuality. By the time I read the novel it was accepted, anyway by boys, as a reasonably accurate treatment of the 'romantic friendship', that might take in some cases physical form.

Naturally enough, Goodhart preferred goodlooking boys to plain ones, but not to excess, and one would suppose him a repressed bisexual. A touch of kinkiness was added by a fervid preoccupation with ladies' shoes (a fancy said to presage masochism), which Goodhart made no attempt to conceal. On the contrary he would from time to time hurry round the house after prayers, bearing with him for the admira-tion of his mostly indifferent pupils a huge volume illustrating *Feminine Footgear through the Ages*, or some similar saga of the Boot and Shoe.

The Saturday night sing-songs were a welcome change from the self-conscious attitude towards singing prevalent at my former school. One night – a carol suggests the Michaelmas half – when *Good King Wenceslas* was being sung, the verse was reached:

> In his master's steps he trod,
>   Where the snow lay dinted:
> Heat was in the very sod
>   Which the saint had printed.

At the moment when the third line was sung, Goodhart (perhaps not without all *arrière-pensée*), looking up from the piano, observed a boy, Elmley, I think (later Earl Beauchamp), laughing. When the sing-song was over, he told the boy, whoever it was, to wait behind. When the rest had left the room a confrontation took place.

'Why were you laughing, etc?'

The boy, not attending to what was being sung, had by then entirely forgotten the reason for his own amusement. He was completely mystified.

'I don't understand, sir.'

'You understand perfectly well, etc.'

The boy continued to show utter incomprehension, Goodhart growing increasingly angry. At last he burst out:

'You were laughing at the word *sod*. Do you know what it means?'

The boy gave some noncommittal reply. Goodhart was foaming by now. 'It is in vulgar use as short for sodomism – *the most loathsome form of dual vice.*'

I can't remember how this misunderstanding was eventually cleared up, but all ended relatively happily; though there was a certain amount of discussion throughout the House afterwards as to what Goodhart himself regarded as among the less loathsome forms of 'dual vice'. As housemasters went, he was no more obsessed about homosexuality than most, the problem never far from the minds of any of them; one without conceivable solution – but then what sexual problem can ever be said to have been solved? About a year before my arrival several members of Goodhart's had been sacked, at least one for sending an indiscreet note to a younger boy. I remember during my second half hearing an elder boy spoken of as being 'gone on' someone, and finding no difficulty in grasping the general implications; nor, for that matter, in understanding those aspects of *The Loom of Youth*. At the same time there were probably a few boys who passed through the school with scarcely an apprehension of the underground love affairs, or more brutal intimacies, that took place; boys having a keen instinct for what could be suitably spoken of in front of their own kind.

Certainly romantic passions were much discussed, but – on the romantic level – I should have thought physical contacts were rare, though contemporaries indulged at times in more knockabout performances together. I felt no disapproval, but never knew of these except by hearsay. The masters might look on the subject as one of unspeakable horror; the boys behaved much in the manner of public opinion as to homosexuality today; ranging from strong disapproval to unconcealed involvement. In between these extremes of sentiment existed an abstinence that was as much due to fastidiousness as morals; a sense that, at best, this was a very makeshift release for those who had other objectives in view.

An early incident suggested to me that such goings-on were not always taken too seriously by grown-up people. Out for a run with another boy one winter afternoon, we were making for the open country beyond the railway arches that link Windsor with the main line. Men were working at the top of the viaduct. One of them shouted something. We yelled back that we could not hear. He repeated his words, now borne down wind: 'It's a cold day for sodding.'

In the middle age-group of most houses there inclined to occur a cluster of fairly rackety boys, from whom the house-tutor might expect trouble. In this respect Goodhart's was no exception, but, about three-quarters way up the House, the mixture was seasoned by two or three boys with intellectual interests, notably David Cecil (for whom I fagged at one time), Robert Gathorne-Hardy, and Eric Dance; the last slightly older than the others, and, unlike them, in the House Library.

David Cecil, as a boy, was remarkably little different from the well-known author and critic he became, his demeanour very grownup (he behaved with great forbearance when I let his fire out), his interests already directed to literary matters. Gathorne-Hardy was later secretary to the American man of letters, Logan Pearsall Smith (employment in which he was followed by Cyril Connolly), about which he wrote an amusing book. Dance possessed quite unusual talents as an actor, though for some perverse reason his family would never allow him to go on the Stage, where he would certainly have made a name. Like several other gallant but unmilitary types known to me, Dance, serving in the Far East, met his death during the war.

These three were the hard core of something that made Goodhart's rather different from the run of the mill Eton house, even 'bad' house. They were, for example, foremost as organizers of Goodhart's House Dramatic Society. I was not personally involved in its productions (only just arrived, and without the smallest gift for acting), but, through the shows put on, had opportunity to see at an early age – among other works – Marlowe's *Doctor Faustus* (somewhat cut, but Helen of Troy played in the Elizabethan manner by a boy), *The Importance of Being Earnest* (I had already read *Lord Arthur Savile's Crime*, *Dorian Gray* soon after), and *Arms and the Man*, the only Shaw play I have ever found free from all tedium.

In principle, Lower Boys (a status lasting not less than three halves, nor more than seven) were not supposed to take Extra Drawing, but Goodhart approved of small boys who were interested in the arts (a type that often developed into the sort of boy he liked a great deal less), so that by exerting pressure I was allowed, from my second half, to attend the Studio, the scene of all but routine drawing lessons. The Eton Drawing Schools nowadays are a complex of red brick buildings set at one end of a rather cheerless open space, the whole looking like a military cantonment in India. The many rooms give greatly improved accommodation for instruction, posing models, holding exhibitions; premises in all respects more luxurious than in my own day. No doubt such changes were overdue, inevitable, beneficial. My nostalgias for the past are by no means automatic, but in this particular case I cannot help feeling regret. In fact not to insist that a great deal has been lost would be, on my own part, to betray an institution for which I always felt a deep affection.

The old Studio in Keate's Lane, at one end of a low-roofed house across the front of which trailed a purple wistaria, consisted of two moderate sized sky-lighted rooms opening into each other, which had probably once been part of the house itself. These rooms were always in a state of comfortable disorder; piled up with pictures, plaster casts, oddments of silver, china or glass, suitable for forming 'still life' compositions. Among the casts were a miniature Belvedere Apollo, and an impressive head of Mirabeau (pockmark on chin), the latter drawn at one time or another in charcoal on blue-grey paper by everyone who came to the place.

Over this nook of the Latin Quarter – Du Maurier's, or even Thackeray's – magically reconstituted among the byways of an English public-school, presided Sidney Evans, a drawing-master who might himself have been a hearty British artist in the Paris of the *Trilby* period. Bluff, good-natured, absolutely sure of himself (for instance, when a model looking like a retired burglar suddenly began to rave in the middle of a sitting of the School Drawing), Evans belonged to an Eton dynasty of some antiquity; among which his aunt had been the last 'dame' to reign over a boy's boarding-house. Evans himself combined a matter-of-fact manner with a tolerant, by no means badly informed approach to painting. His own pictures were somewhat in the tradition of Sickert and the Camden Town Group, but he had that facility for pastiche that can be a handicap to developing one sort of talent, useful to those who teach. It was from Evans, when I was still a Lower Boy, that I first heard views on Matisse and Picasso, painters whom he might regard with a certain degree of scepticism, but – unlike many of his age at that date – did not declare fit only for the gallows or the madhouse.

I had got off to a good start from the point of view of work, partly due to having been placed too low, and, throughout my time at school, Goodhart would quite often bestow a leatherbound book inscribed with some such precept as 'Improve the Best'. He was very generous in these gifts to his pupils. The first Goodhart communication (July, 1919) is entirely commendatory: 'He seems to be very happy here and gets on well with the other boys, no doubt because he is modest & unassuming and unselfish and goodtempered ... He certainly has character.' This approving tone continues for two halves; but a year later (July, 1920) a warning note is struck: '... quiet but effective industry ... gentleness and sense of humour ...' but 'He does not make friends very easily and I am at a loss to know the reason, but I could not wish for a more conscientious pupil.' In December of the same year things were still all right, but only just: 'He is a thoughtful and serious-minded boy though not very responsive at first.' There were still saving graces (March, 1921): 'He is a little apart from the other boys but I think they respect him', and (December, the same year): 'He will always have a good influence in the house owing to his sensible views and high principles.'

The clouds that had been threatening this hitherto comparatively sunny landscape now (August, 1922) become darker. The nature of the path downhill will be touched on later. 'He is a little different from the other boys and I feel that his quiet reserve and dignity may prevent him having any strong influence upon others when he gets to the top of the house. I hope this may not be so but I sometimes fear that they may regard him as superior and coldly critical. That is only an impression that may prove wrong ... He is the sort of boy that grown up people, as I know, find an attractive companion.'

This condition of things, however regrettable, had come to be pretty well accepted by the following December: 'Anthony has plenty of power even if misdirected at times. [This rather sinister comment refers, I think, merely to some school routine, such as concentration on biographies rather than constitutional history.] You will see that Mr Marten speaks favourably of his work & advises that he should try for a Balliol scholarship next half and matriculate that way ... I don't think he gets on very easily with other boys in the house. It may be due to his moodiness, which Mr Bell mentions & a way of speaking which may give offence to some because it seems to imply a cold superiority or frame of mind too judicial. It may of course be simply due to shyness.'

Henry Marten (later Provost of Eton), senior history master, could claim a goodish record among his specialists for scholarship winning. E. A. Bell – who seems to have complained, no doubt justly, of my own moodiness – also an excellent teacher of history, was an altogether different type from Marten, as well as being younger. A fat bespectacled little gnome in his late thirties, he used dramatic methods of his own, a form of instruction that was much less formal than Marten's. When a boy said: 'But that was a matter of luck, sir', Bell replied: 'If you haven't got luck, you might just as well go away and hang yourself.' When I was up at Oxford, Bell attended an undergraduate luncheon party (I was not myself present), where he got so tight that some of his former pupils had to put him to bed for the afternoon. I never came across him again after this Oxford visit. In due course he became a headmaster, and turned to Moral Rearmament.

The Goodhart letters continue into my penultimate half, like a dog with a bone, to worry away at my isolated condition (April, 1923): 'It so happens that he is rather aloof from the others in the house – though he is a great friend of my captain Duggan of which I am glad.' This was Hubert Duggan, of whom more later, but it may be remarked right away that such an axis might not always have met with Goodhart's approval; Duggan having been associated with fairly turbulent elements, when less high up in the House. In fact there may have been a touch of apprehension commenting on this association, which in any case undermined the thesis of my friendlessness.

In my own memory the situation seems to have been no worse than that I got on well with some, less well with others; a situation that maturity has left altogether unchanged. Goodhart's view, understandably, rests on observation made within the *House*, rather than within the *School*. About 1922 – the beginning of the period when the letters become less well disposed – various things happened which may well have made me seem different, not so tractable as at an earlier period.

✳ 4 ✳

In general I associate holidays with 1 Melina Place, St John's Wood, the first house, rambling with a small garden, where my parents had their own furniture again, since all had gone into store after leaving Albert Hall Mansions. At one moment Melina Place was let, no doubt while we were at Camberley, where my father (student now, instead of instructor) was attending the Staff College course. There was also a period when he was back with his regiment, then stationed in Ireland, where the 'troubles' preceding the Treaty and Irish Civil War were in full swing.

The group photograph of 1920 Staff College students shows an almost solid phalanx of World War II generals; among the army-commanders, Major B. L. (Field-Marshal Viscount) Montgomery. My father did not care for his fellow-student – 'His jokes ...' he used to say – and would have been stewed alive in later days rather than refer to the Field-Marshal as 'Monty'. He did not by any means always denigrate successful contemporaries, for some of whom, like Alanbrooke and Dill, he early prophesied brilliant careers. In fact he pointed out the former to me once when lunching at his club (The Rag), saying: 'You'll hear more of the young fellow looking at the papers over there – he's called Captain Brooke.'

As a child I saw little of my father, but fully accepted my mother's propaganda to the effect that he was greatly to be admired. She genuinely regarded him, anyway in their earlier days, as a man of enormous intelligence; among the two or three most remarkable in the country. He was certainly unusual, possessing various *aperçus* and powers of expression that in most men would have led to some sort of personal philosophy of life. In him, they seemed merely to serve as cause of a perpetual inner conflict and anxiety. He was himself dimly aware of this paradox. It was a conflict he never contrived to resolve. His temperament could not be called a happy one; age and disappointment finally imposing an overwhelming cantankerousness.

Basil Hambrough (of whom I shall speak later), had been a subaltern in The Welch Regiment before transferring to the Welsh Guards at their formation in 1915. I once asked if he remembered my father. Hambrough thought for a moment. 'I seem to see something going wrong at an exercise, and a fellow standing in the middle of the road speechless with rage – almost literally foaming? Would that have been him?' That was the picture to the life. This lack of self-control never went further than saying regrettable things, but these were often regrettable enough. The state was likely to be followed by dreadful depression and inertia; no doubt psychologically definable as a condition. Alternatively, he would enjoy bursts of great cheerfulness, when everyone else had to fit in with his mood. He would, for instance, sit happily for hours going through his book collection (never reading much, but looking at the pictures); these buoyant patches not to be entirely relied on, confidences offered during them always liable for use as damaging evidence later. My father kept his favourite books locked up, but inevitably forgot at times to turn the key; in consequence of which I glimpsed at a comparatively early age a couple of volumes of Havelock Ellis's *Psychology of Sex*, and a certain number of illustrated books which art did not always salvage from the realm of erotica.

My mother, coping skilfully with my father's framework of nerves, in general able to bring about peace after an outburst of temper, never seemed to suppose that her married life might be other than it was. She had chosen that state, and was perfectly prepared to take its disadvantages. In the last resort she was in command, but things rarely came to that. She too had an uncommon way of looking at the world; expecting little from it, though not at all in a cynical way.

St John's Wood (Swinburne's 'Grove of the Evangelist', district of his Marlborough Road brothel), was only just emerging from Victorian disrepute as bower of love-nests and houses of assignation. By the time we went to live there blocks of flats had already begun to disfigure the outskirts, but a wide area still consisted of Regency villas with gardens (dwellings designed for keeping a mistress), their structure by then likely to be in need of repair, but of extraordinary quiet and charm for London of that day.

Literary life was brought closer soon after our arrival in Melina Place by Arthur Machen taking a house at the end of its *cul de sac*. I did not know then that Machen's short story *The Bowmen* (September, 1914), had given birth to the legend of the 'Angels of Mons', but Beardsley had designed the cover for his Keynotes Series novel, *The Great God Pan*, and his then fame as a writer of eerie tales is exemplified by John Betjeman's line in *Summoned by Bells*: 'Arthur Machen's *Secret Glory* stuffed into my blazer pocket'. We never knew this mysterious neighbour, but the occasional sweep of an Inverness cape, surmounted by a black broadbrimmed hat, with the sound of a throaty cough, made him seem all a bohemian author should be.

In the summer of 1920, *The Beggar's Opera*, by John Gay, was revived at the Lyric Theatre, Hammersmith; costumes and sets by Claud Lovat Fraser. This was an exciting experience for far more persons of my own age than I was ever aware of at the time. The style of Lovat Fraser was pillaged by imitators so immediately, so freely, that its originality is now hard to appreciate. That his art, especially in lesser designs, is not without a touch of whimsy, must be admitted. The implications of irony, disillusionment, cruelty, that add force to Bakst's Russian Ballet décor, for instance, are toned down to what is at times no more than a goodnatured cynicism. Nevertheless, Lovat Fraser brought about something of a minor revolution in his own line. The influence of *The Beggar's Opera* quickly entered every branch of daily life. When (possibly still a schoolboy) I was first taken by an Eton friend, John Spencer, on a round of nightclubs, among them that inconceivably squalid haunt, The Forty-Three, at least one of the tarts present was wearing a bedraggled version of the close-fitting bodice and panniers of a Beggar's Opera whore.

If Lovat Fraser's decorations opened up new ideas, so too did Gay's libretto. First produced in 1728, its wit and economy of language remained – and remain – altogether untarnished after two hundred and fifty years. The Opera's mood was perfectly adjusted to that of the Twenties; sentiment that seemed about to spill over into sentimentality (*cf*. Michael Arlen), suddenly cut short by a call to order demonstrating the absurdity, savagery, pointlessness of life; for example in such scenes as Macheath's idyll with the whores who betray him. I cannot remember when I first saw the show – fairly early on, I think – but I was already old enough to find some of the songs at once sexually and romantically exciting in a way that was altogether new.

This fervour of mine for Lovat Fraser's work linked up with an odd encounter of the Melina Place period. For Christmas or birthday present, my mother was likely to give my father some addition to his book collection, possibly a Nineties volume suggested by himself.

A secondhand-book catalogue turned up one day emanating from an address, rather a peculiar one, in St John's Wood itself: 'The Bungalow at 8 Abercorn Place.' This was a street not much more than ten minutes' walk from where we lived. I cannot remember how contact was first made with the bookshop, but certainly my father was away, probably serving in Ireland. My mother may have ordered a book from the catalogue, which the bookseller, noticing the distance was small, had brought round himself by hand. Anyway, relations were opened up by my mother with the occupant of The Bungalow, and she herself visited the focus from which these books were sold. It turned out to be just the sort of unusual nook for which she had a *penchant*; for, without strong intellectual or aesthetic interests, as such, she had a certain taste for the out of the way and eccentric.

The houses in Abercorn Place, characteristic 19th century stucco residences with basements, turned out to have small gardens in front; slightly larger ones at the back. Access to the basement was gained by an area, but at 8 Abercorn Place, if you crossed the little front garden and went down the area steps, you found, instead of a kitchen door at the end of the passage, a narrow alley leading past the house itself to the back garden beyond. On the far side of this grassed yard stood a miniature two-roomed wooden bungalow. From this strange place the bookseller who had sent out the catalogue conducted his business; in principle, entirely by correspondence.

'There's something odd about him,' my mother reported, after her first visit. 'I didn't at all dislike him – with his deep voice – but there's something odd.'

There certainly was something odd. This was Christopher Millard, a man considered odd by people far more inured than my mother to odd manners of living.

The standard account of Christopher Sclater Millard (b. 1872) is given in the opening pages of A. J. A. Symons's book, *The Quest for Corvo*, which briefly outlines the career of this prodigal son of an Anglican canon. Millard had been educated at Bradfield (he sometimes talked of the Greek play the boys performed there), and Keble College, Oxford; the latter suggesting that he too was originally destined for the Church. At an early age he developed a hero-worship for Oscar Wilde, though they never met; Millard becoming (under the pen-name 'Stuart Mason') historian of Wilde's three trials, and bibliographer of his works. He had earned a living by teaching, working in bookshops, acting as clerk in the War Office (during the war), and assistant editor to the *Burlington Magazine*. Setting up his own bookselling business had been made possible by a legacy of £100 a year left him by Wilde's friend, Robert Ross, to whom Millard had been for a time secretary.

I do not remember my first visit to The Bungalow at 8 Abercorn Place, nor how often I used to drop in there; perhaps a couple of times a holiday. Millard transacted his business, entertained his friends, lived his life in one of the minute rooms; in the other, he slept. There was an exiguous kitchen-bathroom. The whole place must have been dreadfully cold in winter. Books were everywhere: on shelves; on tables; stacked on the floor; stored away in boxes; all neatly arranged, because Millard was intensely methodical.

Tall, greyhaired, handsome in a rugged way, with the deep musical voice my mother had remarked, Millard had an appearance and personality to make him an impressive even overawing figure. I was at an age when thirty seems the threshold of declining years, and, in one sense, he seemed more than fifty, which must have been about his age when we met; in another sense, he appeared far younger, because he was the first grown up person to treat me in conversation on absolutely equal terms. The melancholy of his demeanour was accompanied by a complete ease of manner. Although steeped in the Nineties, he was entirely without the mannerisms that Nineties relics subsequently encountered (Arthur Symons, Ada Leverson the Sphinx) displayed in one form or another. On the contrary, Millard always talked with a directness refreshing compared even with the affectations of my own generation.

Millard always wore an old tweed coat, flannel trousers, a faded blue-grey shirt. The elegance with which he carried off these ancient garments somehow gave no hint of the grim poverty in which he lived; the extent of which I had then no idea. He was much too undaunted to allow any such suspicion to take shape; and, in fact, one always imagined that he was doing pretty well out of his business. Sometimes, no doubt, he did do reasonably well, but his system of bookselling was designed to suit his own convenience, rather than the humdrum exigencies of the trade. He existed most of the time in the most frugal manner, but, after disposing of an expensive item from his catalogue, would celebrate with some sort of bust in the way of food and drink.

In the course of these visits to The Bungalow I infected Millard with my own Lovat Fraser enthusiasm. He used to write to me sometimes at school on this subject, and about other books that he thought of interest. One letter (22 February, 1922) says: 'It wasn't till I went to the Leicester Galleries show that I was badly bitten by the Lovat Fraser craze'; another (15 March, 1922): 'You say you "expect" I know ... but I assure you I know very little about Fraser's work save from what you tell me.' In the end, as for Wilde, Millard compiled a Lovat Fraser bibliography.

There were often interesting items at The Bungalow. Millard showed me the manuscript of *The Ballad of Reading Gaol* (for some reason in transit there), written in purple ink, inscribed across the top in Wilde's hand: 'For those who live more lives than one, more deaths than one must die.' On another occasion, two framed drawings by Simeon Solomon, female classical figures in chalk on tinted paper, were propped up against a stack of books. They were said to have hung in the Wildes' drawing-room at 16 Tite Street. Millard also had on offer at one time a full-length portrait of Wilde in oils, showing him as a young man wearing a frockcoat. This picture had been refused (something unlikely to happen today) by the National Portrait Gallery. 'I should have thought they might have been able to find space for it in the lavatory,' Millard said.

Millard (20 February, 1922) refers to 'six of Max Beerbohm's letters (1895–96) to a married woman with whom he seems to have been having an affair. I have promised not to catalogue these last ... It's a sordid business selling books, but very amusing.' These Beerbohm letters are perhaps of the same lot described (5 April, 1922) as: 'Very interesting, about 20 or 30 of them'. In view of the usual judgment that Beerbohm was not very active in the field of sex, one would like to know if Millard's surmise was well-grounded.

Millard himself was, of course, homosexual; had, indeed, been in prison at least twice for getting the wrong side of the Law. Once, when we were having tea at The Bungalow, he said very casually: 'You know, you're a great temptation.' Although by then school had made me thoroughly familiar with the idea of such things, the implications seemed altogether absurd in the circumstances. I made some light remark in return, passing the words off as a joke. I don't remember Millard's comment being more than momentarily embarrassing at the time, nor was it an embarrassment to future visits. Looking back, it seems to me strange that I took the remark with such complete lack of seriousness – otherwise it would certainly have discomposed me – and, so far as I can remember, thought no more about it. Nothing of the sort was ever spoken again.

This hobnobbing with Millard occupied, I suppose, at most a period of eighteen months, perhaps less. At fifteen or sixteen – in fact well into one's twenties – incidents that take up a few weeks or months seem of far greater extent in memory. In due course my father came back to London. I do not know how he was employed. He may have been at the War Office again. Nor can I remember whether he ever saw Millard. I think some brief meeting did take place; possibly Millard coming to tea.

By this period Tom Balston (my father's former staff-captain) was a comparatively frequent guest at Melina Place. He had been working in publishing for some years, and was now installed as a director of Duckworth's. There may already have been suggestions that I should join the firm. Balston had persuaded my father to become a member of a rather shadowy institution called the First Edition Club, founded and run by A. J. A. Symons, author of the Corvo biography mentioned above. I don't think the First Edition Club ever played much part in my father's life. Nevertheless, he certainly went there once or twice, and it may have been in those surroundings that Millard's name cropped up.

Balston told my father that Millard had been in prison, and that he thought it unwise that I should frequent The Bungalow. This was a tiresome thing to do, though in line with the way people behaved at the time; Balston himself suffering an obsession that he would be blackmailed, and everlastingly telling stories of men or women who accosted him in the park in order to ask the way; a form of nervousness that suggests a deep-rooted fear of sex. Edith Sitwell used to say that she always saw Balston's gold spectacles flashing under the peaked cap of a Salvation Army officer (he was, in fact, a fanatical atheist), and these inhibitions may excuse such interference in someone else's life.

My father (speaking of the matter, if it had to be adumbrated at all, in comparatively reasonable terms) told me I must cease to see Millard. It fell out that this injunction exactly coincided with his own posting to a new appointment outside London. Quite how I should have otherwise dealt with the Millard problem, I do not know. I was unwilling to drop the visits; at the same time their imputations were painted in such forbidding light that I felt a trifle intimidated; although such menace as might have existed was already past. Balston himself represented in my life another important link with a more inviting world. I was brought face to face with the difference between schoolboy sentiment and sensuality – something with which to tease the masters – and the whole force of society lined up to threaten a reputation. It was hard to experience no misgiving.

As matters turned out, the move from London made the break with Millard natural enough. One of his letters (5 April, 1922) shows that no suggestion of an awkward severance took place: 'I was passing Melina Place a few days ago and saw furniture vans outside, to my regret. I looked in to see if your mother was at home by any chance, but found she was out: she very kindly wrote to me the next day ... If the "candle" is available for the enlightenment of a non-Etonian, please put me down as a subscriber, a subscription implying that the paper will be sent to the subscriber until one of the three expires.' I am glad to think that my mother, who understood things by instinct rather than by other means, behaved as she did.

Millard's last sentence refers to *The Eton Candle*, a magazine to which I shall return. I never met him again. He died in 1927. By then I had already come to work in London, but not yet found my feet in a world where he might be met.

Millard had worked on the *Burlington Magazine*, which C. J. Hope-Johnstone ('Hopey' or 'Hope-J' of many anecdotes of Augustus John/Bloomsbury provenance) had at one time edited. I am not sure whether they were on the magazine contemporaneously. Hope-Johnstone, a figure every bit as eccentric as Millard, though in a different genre, said: 'He was the sort who couldn't resist, when out on a country walk, leaping the hedge and raping a ploughboy. I remember talking about him with Clive Bell in the *Burlington* office one day. Clive said he'd rather have a female gorilla than the most beautiful boy alive.'

Another of Millard's affiliations in this latter stage of his life was The Varda Bookshop, which must have come into being about 1926. In terms of bookselling, The Varda Bookshop was a venture at least as out of the ordinary as The Bungalow at 8 Abercorn Place. Its small premises were situated a few doors down the street, where High Holborn curves south into Shaftesbury Avenue. Millard merely looked in there from time to time to give professional advice to Varda, who presided over the bookshop named after her.

Varda, who had not long before been billed (no misnomer) as 'The Beautiful Varda' in one of C. B. Cochran's shows at the Pavilion Theatre, productions renowned for their lavish stagings and the good looks of the cast, owed her name to an odd circumstance. She had been married for a short time to a Greek surrealist painter, Jean (Janko) Varda, a lively figure sometimes described in those days as the 'uncrowned king of Cassis', keen on the opposite sex but not the marrying sort. On parting company with her husband, she had somehow managed to appropriate to herself (though christened 'Dorothy') his surname without prefix.

As well as beauty, Varda possessed a sharp and witty tongue. 'The only woman I know with a male sense of humour', Constant Lambert used to say. Lambert lived in one of the two small flats (the other inhabited by Peter Quennell) above The Varda Bookshop. This gift – or burden – of astringent wit was not always appreciated by those in contact with Varda, especially in the world of the Theatre. She did not follow up her appearances at the Pavilion (where she had been only required to walk across the stage), and the question of what to do with her life became one she was herself never tired of discussing in an entirely objective manner.

Among those who attempted to solve this problem was Michel Sala-

man, who set Varda up in the bookshop. Salaman, usually type-
cast as a rich foxhunting art-fancying friend of Augustus John at the
Slade, was all those things; also romantic, able to enjoy a joke, happily
married, father of a lot of children. His notion was that having a bookshop to look after would allow a margin for intellectual life (regarded
by Varda herself as a necessary element in anything she did), while
regular employment might modify a too wayward manner of existence.

Salaman did this out of a disinterested admiration for beauty and
wit, combined with his own kindness of heart. This is far the most
interesting aspect of the whole Varda Bookshop enterprise. If Salaman
had been 'keeping' Varda, there would have been nothing much to it,
but (so far as anything sexual can be certain in this world) she never
became his mistress. This may seem extraordinary – in a sense both
parties always seemed surprised about it themselves – but there it was.
One effect of their platonic relationship was that Salaman and Varda
always remained on good terms.

As impresario of The Varda Bookshop, Salaman proved no more
successful than C. B. Cochran, where finding a permanent niche for
Varda was in question; but for a time the shop was a place where friends
bought their books and congregated for a gossip. Varda herself was
by no means always available to serve her customers, if something better
to do offered, when a stand-in of one sort or another would be
nominated. This was occasionally Lambert, who complained that he
always struck a day when all the lunatics in London had been let out
to buy their books. One afternoon, when a friend was understudying
Varda in the shop, a customer asked if they had Shelley's *Prometheus
Unbound*. The works of the Romantic School were then not much in
fashion, and the proxy replied: 'No, but I'm sure I've seen a bound
copy on the shelves.'

Millard (by some arrangement of which I am ignorant) used to drop
in from time to time to instruct Varda in the art of bookselling, and
bring some order into this chaos. He and she seem to have got on well
together, though the clash of temperaments must have been considerable. Varda, when I asked her about him, seemed chiefly impressed
by Millard's strong views about the preservation of health, a subject
on which he was something of a crank, it appeared, though I never
remember that arising. One evening, after shutting up the shop, Varda
and Millard had gone into a baker's, where he wanted to buy a loaf
of bread. Whoever served him had blown into a paper-bag to open
it. Millard was outraged. 'When you've quite done spreading germs
and disease, etc.' Even Varda, no stranger to rows, was taken aback.

The Varda Bookshop died not much more than a year later than
Millard himself. Perhaps it was better that his unique personality
should remain an isolated vignette of my growing up; rather than

remembered as one of the thousand strange facets of that early London life when I came to it.

5

At Goodhart's, I eventually settled down to mess with Denys Buckley and Hugh Lygon. Lygon, fairhaired, nice mannered, a Giotto angel living in a narcissistic dream, was a year older than Buckley and me. He left after a couple of halves to travel abroad before Oxford; his place at tea taken (perhaps not immediately) by Hubert Duggan, also a year or more older; by then Captain of the House. That combination – Duggan, Buckley, myself – is my most remembered Eton life, out of school hours, or the Studio. Once, when the three of us were walking down town, a small boy in jackets, afterwards identified as named Laycock (later Major-General Sir Robert, who arranged for Evelyn Waugh to be transferred from the Royal Marines to the Royal Horse Guards), muttered 'Goodhart's bloody trio.' Duggan was delighted. 'Excellent' he said. 'Excellent. That's what we are. Goodhart's bloody trio'.

Hubert Duggan's demeanour at school – though not in later life – contributes something to Stringham in my novel. On the other hand, Buckley bears no resemblance whatever to Templer, represented as the Narrator's other companion at tea. Templer (if such things must be established) is – again only at school – a trifle like John Spencer, a friend at another house, one of the several temperamentally unmilitary figures known to me who died in action.

Denys Buckley (later Lord Justice Buckley) is one of the few incontrovertibly well behaved friends of my early days. Equipped with dark good looks, quick at his books, not at all bad at games, Buckley neither indulged in bad behaviour, nor was particularly interested in it in others. He accepted good behaviour as a natural way of life, not something imposed from the outside. In another house he would probably have ended in Pop. As it was, he was committed to being a component of Goodhart's bloody trio.

Hubert Duggan had an elder brother, Alfred, who was at another house. They were of Irish–Argentine stock, their father – both were never tired of reiterating – having died of drink in his early thirties. Their mother, an American beauty and heiress, was by then second wife of Lord Curzon (Marquess Curzon of Kedleston), a public figure celebrated not only as a member of the Government, but, since his Oxford days, prototype in the popular imagination of an aloof and pompous English aristocrat. Curzon deliberately propagated this 'image' of himself. The Duggans were well disposed towards him, saying that (provided his own opinion was not called into question) he was perfectly able to appreciate a joke; and only possession of a modicum of humour could have seen him through some of his elder stepson's goings-on.

When – thinking of Hubert Duggan's appearance – I wrote that Stringham looked like Alexander the Great receiving the children of Darius, as represented in Veronese's picture in the National Gallery, I assumed that Alexander (rather than Hephaestion, as stated in the National Gallery hand-out) was the central figure in crimson. I shall continue to do so until convinced by overwhelming iconography. Anyway, Veronese's man in crimson, with slightly receding dark curly hair, is the one like Hubert Duggan. This may be checked by reference to a photograph in Harold Nicolson's *Curzon: the Last Phase*, in which Duggan, in hunting clothes, stands by his stepfather under the colonnade of Hackwood. His short upper lip (faintly scarred), and the shape of his forehead, also recalled portraits of Byron; though it was his brother, Alfred, who inclined to a consciously Byronic stance.

As with all persons living very much in the moment, Hubert Duggan's qualities are hard to convey. In some ways unexpectedly tough, in spite of indifferent health, he had wit, a strong vein of melancholy, a kind of natural dash and elegance, altogether untouched with 'showing off'. Without being good at games he could keep his end up, and he was a stylish rider in point-to-points. At school he spent a lot of his time reading (though exiled in the wilderness of Army Class), would quite often introduce books hitherto unknown to me, but he never in the least became part of the Eton (or Oxford) intellectual world.

I did not know Alfred Duggan at Eton, but he may be introduced at this point, if only on account of his characteristic exit from the school. Shorter, more thickset than his brother, Alfred was far more rackety than Hubert at his most exuberant. His hook nose, and (when sober) somewhat assertive manner (when drunk he became genial) made him a trifle Napoleonic. Notwithstanding being always in trouble, Alf was very much his mother's favourite.

Towards the end of his time at Eton, Alf Duggan had formed the habit of leaving the house by an unfastened window between the hours of lock-up and prayers; a period he would spend with a girl from the town, with whom he had established some sort of relationship. To avoid identification as a member of the school, he would naturally change from tailcoat and white tie into ordinary clothes. Inevitably these absences were noticed. His housemaster, rather an unpleasant man, instead of simply taxing him with the offence by circumstantial evidence, locked the door of Duggan's room so that he was forced to come down to prayers in a lounge suit, thereby drawing everyone's eye to him. It might be added that, as a Roman Catholic, Duggan would not have been compelled to attend house-prayers (an option in which Catholics varied), but probably, like his brother, he preferred not to seem 'different'.

The Duggan brothers, under the resplendent wing of Lord Curzon, and affluent international connexions of their mother, moved – not entirely without protest – in a decidedly grand world. Alfred, although professing himself a Communist in those days (given to singing the *Internationale*, a tune for which tone-deafness presented no handicap), was not at all indifferent to smart society. His undoubted abilities were then thought to presage a parliamentary career, even his stepfather apparently sharing the view that Alf would end in the Cabinet, and accepting wild oats as established ingredient of great men in their youth. In the event, it was Hubert Duggan (who used to grumble about his mother's efforts to turn him into a conventional young man) that went into the House of Commons, thereby to some extent fulfilling her ambitions for her sons.

The grandiose life surrounding the Duggans certainly did not exclude all dissatisfactions with the *beau monde*, even all lack of social precariousness. I remember my own surprise when Hubert Duggan angrily dissented from my describing as amusing Maugham's comedy, *Our Betters* (1923), which satirizes Americans married into aristocratic (mainly British) families. The satire may not be of a very subtle order, but it must have got home at Carlton House Terrace and Hackwood.

Hubert Duggan did not finish the course at Eton. His health went wrong (he was tubercular), and he left school earlier than intended. There was a long visit to Argentina. We corresponded, but did not meet again until my third term at Oxford.

I cannot exactly recall the earliest stirrings of the Eton Society of Arts, but, when the Society was formed, the Studio became its centre for Saturday evening meetings; thereby bringing in there several boys not necessarily associated with drawing, though likely to have some claim to practise one or other of the arts. Some of the members were also contributors to the magazine produced not long after the Society's inception, *The Eton Candle*, to which Millard had referred. The clearest method of considering both the Society and the magazine is perhaps to give a list of the former's foundation members, saying a word about each rather than attempt to deal with everything that pertains to these interwoven matters in a more chronological fashion. The foundation members of the Eton Society of Arts (list dated February, 1922) were as follows: W. S. Evans, *President*, B. C. de C. Howard, *Vice-President*, H. V. Yorke, *Secretary*, H. M. Acton, W. M. Acton, R. Byron, A. F. Clutton-Brock, KS, H. Lygon, A. D. Powell, R. L. Spence, C. S. Anderson, C. E. Minns, KS.

Evans was, of course, ultimately in control. The other names, apart from officers of the Society, might be expected to run alphabetically – school order would certainly have been regarded as too stuffy an approach – but, in fact, the gradation probably followed Brian Howard's own whim as Vice-President; settled as if he were captain (in Eton phraseology 'Keeper') of some game, choosing members of a team for special aptitudes; the number eleven perhaps settled on for the reason that a printed list pinned to the wall would resemble precisely that. The list did not, of course, represent anything like the total of boys in the school addicted to the arts. There was, however, a kind of homogeneity of membership, though one hard to define; some individual always seeming to run counter to any generalization attempting to cover all members of the Society. It would at least be true to say that everyone there had been prepared to come out in the open as belonging to a newly formed association bound to excite a good deal of ridicule among the boys; unlikely to be very popular with a fair number of masters.

On one hand, inclusion avoided masters' pets, conformists already belonging to established societies approved by the authorities, members of which were likely to be in any case higher up in the school than most of the Arts Society. On the other hand, Arts Society membership rose above (anyway in our own eyes) devotees of art and letters of too seedy a bearing, or too abject a pi-ness; of which there existed in the school a fairly considerable underworld. It was, indeed, something of an embarrassment to the Society that the uninstructed were often unable to tell the difference between such outcasts and ourselves. In terms of school order, membership stretched from a boy just below Sixth Form, to one who had only just reached the lower remove of Upper School. A suggestion of raffishness, here and there observable in the list, was not looked on amiss.

Brian Howard and Harold Acton (later Sir Harold) were most active in the foundation of the Society; certainly in influencing the shape it took. Howard did not do Extra Drawing, consequently was not a frequenter of the Studio in the ordinary way, though he had at least on one occasion entered a picture (mildly 'modernistic' in design) for some drawing prize. I never liked Howard, nor found his performances in poetry or painting of interest. He seemed to me the essence of that self-propagation for its own sake which has nothing whatever to do with creative ability. At the same time, if some of his antics were likely to obstruct, rather than encourage, an interest in the arts at Eton, his self-confidence and sophistication were both startling in a boy of that age. It was overwhelmingly Howard's drive that brought the Society of Arts and *The Eton Candle* into being; something that must be fully acknowledged.

In the manner of the Twenties (belaboured by Wyndham Lewis,

himself a claimant in the same line, not without all reason), Howard supposed himself a 'genius'. Like the Actons and the Duggans, he was American on his mother's side. His father's origins, enigmatically imprecise, seem to have been largely American too. The surname 'Howard' had been adopted in preference to that of 'Gassaway'; the latter understandably regarded as having too richly Dickensian a ring for an art-dealer and professional critic.

Tall, a dead white face, jet black wavy hair, full pouting lips, huge eyes that seemed by nature to have been heavily made-up, Howard had the air of a pierrot out of costume. He was immediately noticeable among any crowd of boys, but I never came across him at school until the Arts Society was under way. There was something of Bloch (in *À la recherche*) about him, but a far more aggressive, violently behaved Bloch, prepared to make a scene on the smallest provocation; less well educated too, for in spite of modish intellectual fireworks in conversation, Howard found difficulty in passing into Oxford at a time when the University's scholastic requirements were not excessive.

Once their son was up at Oxford, Howard's parents are said to have exercised some influence in persuading him to abandon intellectual ambitions and friends in favour of the more socially advantageous world of hunting and steeplechasing. Howard courageously took on the physical hazards of these pastimes, and it is hard to feel that much pressure was required in making the change. He had brought off a triumph at school with *The Eton Candle*. Competition in that sort of line at Oxford was keener. Howard's equipment would have been put to considerable strain to attempt anything of the kind. As it happened – university generations varying in such respects – an eminently available cluster of young lords arrived to get to work on in Howard's second year; an objective he successfully attained. The rest of his career does not make cheerful reading: notoriety as giver and disrupter of parties; nomadic homosexual wanderings over Europe; lowly duties in the ranks of the RAF during the war; drink in excess; drugs of the hard sort; suicide in his early fifties.

Henry Yorke, the Arts Society's Secretary, had entered Eton at the same level as myself, but, arriving two halves before, was a couple of forms higher up. We did not see very much of each other at first, but began to meet more later on. We used to talk a lot about books, Yorke's literary tastes already beginning to diverge from my own. I don't think he ever went through a Nineties period, though in due course he became much addicted to George Moore. I remember enjoying *Lewis Seymour and Some Women* (Moore's first novel, *A Modern Lover*, published in 1883, revised with the new title, 1917), a book anticipating some of the Nineties tone. Yorke may have produced Moore's novel in the first instance, but I chiefly remember laughing with Hubert Duggan (its possible originator) about a long conversation there between a man and a woman, which turns out to be taking place while they are in bed together.

Quite early on, Yorke was accustomed to take the line that he did not like Shakespeare (not a good sign as a rule), one characteristic of a standpoint equally uninfluenced by convention or fashion. At Oxford, perhaps before, he had a passion for Carlyle (an author tolerable to myself only in small doses), and (a taste I have never acquired) Doughty's *Arabia Deserta*; both indicating a congenial leaning towards obscure diction. Yorke was later a Jamesian, traces of ihat influence to be seen in his own work. His preference for an 'experimental' approach in his own writing was not (like Joyce's) founded on a wide range of reading, and general interest in styles of every sort. On the contrary, Yorke was extremely eclectic in the books he read. He had begun writing a novel at Eton, its nature unrevealed, though the fact admitted; an undertaking not regarded over seriously by relations and friends.

Yorke complains in *Pack My Bag* of having allowed himself to become Secretary of the Arts Society, of which he speaks rather condescendingly; asserting that no one would have bothered with such things, if they had been in a position to make their mark in the school by more conventional paths. This seems not only a kind of ingratitude towards what was a considerable enhancement of school existence, but an attitude altogether surprising in Yorke himself, who throughout life – when he had much else on his plate – toiled away in his spare time at writing novels that were unlikely ever to bring him more than *succès d'estime*. Again the deep split in his feelings is revealed; half a despising of the arts; half a dedicated writer. It would also be hard to guess from *Pack My Bag* that its author, as a boy and young man, was a gifted witty companion, refreshing in many of the ways he looked at life; rather than the figure presented thus as eternally hesitating between a stuffy conventionality, and scarcely less tiresome revolt against convention.

Harold and William Acton (both at the same house as Alfred Duggan) belonged to a ramification of the Shropshire family of that name that had become Italianized; one of its offshoots virtually ruling the kingdom of the Two Sicilies in the 18th century. The two Actons, brought up largely abroad, familiar from childhood with the arts as a professional adjunct of everyday life, viewed the Eton scene very differently from the average boy there. Their father (represented by his sons as a formidable figure, fighting duels in middle age, and behaving somewhat oppressively to his children) had been intermittently a painter, but his energies were chiefly devoted to La Pietra, the splendid Renaissance villa outside Florence where they lived. I paid a visit there at fifteen, when travelling in Italy with my parents; then fifty years later saw the garden altogether changed by the yew hedges that had grown up.

The Acton brothers looked unEnglish, totally unschoolboyish, an impression increased by talking with them; their manner dramatic, formal, courteous, seasoned – especially in the case of Harold – with a touch of impishness. Harold Acton's high forehead, eyes like black olives, slightly swaying carriage, created an ensemble perfectly to fit the conventions of the Chinese artist who later painted him in Chinese dress. William, no less unusual, was more heavily built, in fact quite muscular, exuding energy, words pouring from him in a torrent that made almost a language of his own.

William Acton (a shade younger than me, his brother a shade older) had not yet arrived at Eton, when I first met Harold at the Studio, on one of my earliest evenings there. We must both have been Lower Boys. Acton was showing Mr Evans a book of Picasso reproductions; probably my own introduction to the painter's name, certainly to his work. While Evans turned the pages, Acton remarked that the previous evening the Headmaster, dining with his housemaster, had been taken round some of the boys rooms after dinner. In Acton's room he had picked the Picasso *cahier* from the bookshelf, and glanced through it.

'What did the Headmaster say?' asked Evans.

Acton gave one of his most impish laughs.

'He smiled rather sourly, sir.'

Evans laughed heartily at that too. The drawings (Picasso's early 1900s period) included the drypoint of Salome kicking up her leg high before Herod. Even a sour smile did credit to a headmaster of that day.

Harold Acton (as will be seen in connexion with *The Eton Candle*) made his début as a poet, but soon moved on to other forms of writing; appropriately becoming historian of the Bourbon kings of Naples. His two volumes of Memoirs (to which his book in memory of Nancy Mitford might be regarded almost as an extension) are written in an easygoing style that sometimes cloaks a good deal of shrewd objectivity on the subject of individuals mentioned there. With regard to his own contemporaries in general, he makes the sage observation that, so far from being a flight of frivolous butterflies, as sometimes labelled, they were a collection, most of them, of hardheaded and extremely ambitious young men.

William Acton's painting at Eton tended to vary between 'still lifes' severe as Cézanne's, and costume designs more exotic than Bakst's. At Oxford, he too, rather unexpectedly, rode in the hunting-field, and at 'grinds' (university point-to-point racing) – for excitement rather than social reasons – totally disregarding headlong falls. One of these falls took the form of descent from his own second-floor window in Meadow Buildings at Christ Church; a mishap that did permanent interior damage. He became a professional painter.

Since the fall from the window his health had never been good, and, when war came, he saw it through in the ranks of the Pioneer Corps; resolutely rejecting all efforts to transform him into a Camouflage Officer. In 1944 he was sent to Italy as interpreter for Italian prisoners-of-war. Rundown and depressed, he was found one day dead in his bath.

Robert Byron, in certain respects every bit as flamboyant a personality as the Actons or Howard, was also in quite another mould. His character is more of a riddle. I never knew him at all intimately, but he was a close friend of Yorke. His house at Eton, nearly as exotic as Goodhart's, accommodated Clonmore, Oliver Messel, his cousin Rudolph Messel, John Spencer, and several others with claims to unconventionality and raffishness. A connexion with the Poet's family has been suggested possibly through Byrons who had gone over to Ireland. His father was a civil engineer. Although not at all keen on Lord Byron's poetry or legend, he found himself from the outset of his career associated with Greece, where his surname was one to stir the blood.

Stocky, very fair, his complexion of yellowish wax, popping pale blue eyes, a long sharp nose, Byron looked thoroughly out of the ordinary. His husky insistent manner of speaking demanded immediate attention, a way of talking that could be attractive, even when protesting, which it usually was. He was energetic, ambitious, violent, quarrelsome, with views in complete contrast with those of the typical precocious schoolboy of the period. Anti-Nineties, the very words 'intellectual' or 'good taste' threw him into paroxysms of rage. He was in any case habitually in a state of barely controlled exasperation about everything.

Byron drew with facility (his subtly pornographic frescoes chalked on the walls of The Hypocrites Club at Oxford are, alas, no more), but he may not have been one of those to frequent the Studio. It would have been in his manner to operate independently, to enter (like Howard) for prizes, without participation. I am unsure about this. Byron's vitality was of the kind other people live off. What appeared on the surface undoubtedly hid much that was unguessable beneath. There was a great deal of toughness, mental and physical, both camouflaged by wild buffoonery and exotic behaviour. Always hard up, Byron was also always generous, while making the most extraordinary supposed economies, like finding some purveyor of grotesque tweeds, who would tailor for him suits of unheard-of cheapness. Not at all averse from going out of his way to make himself agreeable to rich or influential people likely to be of use, Byron would always be the first to draw attention to any such comparative genuflexions on his own part; at the same time prepared to have a blood row at a moment's notice with any-one whomsoever, no matter how inconvenient to his own interests.

Like Yorke, Byron was anti-Shakespeare ('Hamlet that emotional hoax') and in due course his passion for all things Byzantine overrode any other consideration, where art or antiquity was concerned. If taken *au pied de la lettre* Byron's literary judgements are as unreliable as those on painting and archaeology, but a determination to be always on the look out for a new approach – anyway one individual to himself – makes a great deal of what he says worthy of attention; if only for the light cast on his own personality. At school, and as an undergraduate, he used to express horror of 'abroad' and 'foreigners', but his life was largely spent making adventurous journeys, and his best book, *The Road to Oxiana* (travels in Persia and Afghanistan), shows his blend of persuasiveness and aggression dealing with alien persons and situations.

In Byron's books an obsessive repugnance for cliché sometimes leads to overwriting; complicated mosaics of private reference, or semi-facetious pedantry, piling up in a manner to obscure the issue. This is particularly true of *The Station*, a visit to Mount Athos in a party that included David Talbot Rice and Gerald Reitlinger. When Byron's style comes off there are splendid images and literary parallels, but it is a hit-or-miss method. D. H. Lawrence (in his days of reviewing for *Vogue*) gave a word or two of condescending but authentic Laurentian praise to *The Station*. One regrets that the two of them never met. The impact would have been considerable.

Byron's ambitions undoubtedly extended beyond a mere wish to be known as a writer, action and power playing a prominent part in his inner needs. He carried in him something of the genuine 19th century Englishman – a type even in those days all but extinguished in un-mitigated form – the eccentricity, curiosity, ill temper, determination to stop at absolutely nothing. Notwithstanding the old fashioned British-ness of his nature, Byron might have found easier expression of his gifts in another country. We do not much run here to the d'Annunzio type, the writer who is also a man of action (Malraux, Koestler, Mishima, Mailer), personalities drawn to politics, striking public poses, but also desiring to excel in the literary field; Disraeli perhaps our sole notable example at both levels; with Orwell in a different manner. It is somewhere there that I think Byron belonged.

Byron remained a friend of Yorke and Harold Acton, to some extent kept up with Howard, but after early London days (when Duckworth's published *The Station* in consequence of my knowing Byron) I never saw a great deal of him. The comparatively elaborate production requirements for his subsequent works on Byzantine art (collaborating with Talbot Rice) caused the books to go elsewhere. Byron was an author not easily satisfied. He wrote in my copy of *The Station*: 'Tony, with bitter remorse for his sufferings, Robert.'

By the time the war came, Byron was working (doing well, it was said) with an oil company. Unhappy at failing to get himself into uniform – though the Services would have exacerbated him beyond belief – he joined a news-section of the BBC. His varied connexions, reputation for enterprise, nervous energy, would certainly have brought a more picturesque job sooner or later; even if his employment was not already 'cover' for something adventurous. When, in 1941, he sailed for Egypt as special correspondent, the ship was sunk on the voyage by enemy action.

Byron had by no means finished all he was likely to do in life. The force of his personality, quality of his talk, his powers of extensive imagery, taste for the macabre, can be caught only in snatches from his writings. Explosions were frequent. When someone tediously enquired what he would like best in the world, Byron snapped back: 'To be an incredibly beautiful male prostitute with a sharp sting in my bottom.' This love for the perversely grotesque would have taken pleasure in the prophetic nature of a passage he wrote about himself in *The Station* a dozen years before his own end. The monks of Athos had told a story of one of their deacons, drowned at sea, later found whole in the carcase of a shark. Byron comments: 'Having long arranged, in the case of natural and accessible death, to be buried in a mackintosh and manure the garden, I was appalled by this prospect of leaving my vile body, not even digested, in the body of a fish.'

In the Arts Society, Alan Clutton-Brock, a colleger (whom I hardly knew), was more staid. Through his father, a professional art-critic, he was closely associated with painting; both father and son appearing together in the pages of *The Eton Candle*. Like Harold Acton, he served during the war as an officer in the RAF Intelligence Reserve. While undertaking these duties a situation occurred which parallels one in *Dance* that has been condemned for being too coincidental. Brian Howard, posted to Clutton-Brock's RAF station, was employed there serving teas. I had not heard of this surprising reunion of two members of the Eton Society of Arts, when I wrote of Stringham turning up as a waiter at the Narrator's Divisional Headquarters.

Hugh Lygon was younger brother of Elmley. They were sons of Lord Beauchamp, then Leader of the Liberal Party in the House of Lords, who, like Lord Curzon, was celebrated for his own brand of pomposity; indeed, considered by the Duggans (and Yorkes, who were neighbours) an unsurpassed exponent of that propensity. He eventually had to retire to the Continent under the shadow of homosexual scandal, leaving the family home Madresfield as playground for his children and their friends. Lygon made no pretensions to practise the arts. It is possible that his inclusion was to be accounted for by a *tendresse* (probably un-voiced) felt for him by one of the more influential members, like Howard or Byron.

Roger Spence (at the same house as the Actons) was one of the essentially well-behaved members of the Society. Son of an Indian

Army colonel, Spence, tall, dark, quiet, always a little worried in demeanour, had appointed himself a kind of unofficial guardian of the Acton brothers, especially Harold; a buffer between them and un-appreciative elements in the school. When *The Eton Candle* was published, Spence was business-manager; that side of the magazine accordingly conducted with cool efficiency. In those days bound for the Diplomatic Service, Spence decided he had not enough money for the career. To the surprise of his friends he went into the army, becoming a brigadier.

Colin Anderson (at the same house as Henry Yorke) was a refutation of Yorke's opinion that membership of the Arts Society necessarily aroused conventional disapproval, because Anderson, in spite of this association, was elected to Pop; thereby certainly adding to the Society's prestige. Large, sandyhaired, quiet voiced, the only member of undoubted athletic distinction (Byron possessed certain claims as a long distance runner), he used to draw at the Studio. Family connexions took Anderson (later Sir Colin) into the shipping world, where he became youngest President of the Chamber of Shipping. He was also a trustee of the National Gallery and the Tate.

Finally, the other colleger on the list, Christopher Minns. By then within sight of Sixth Form, he was at the same level of the school as Cyril Connolly, who speaks of Kit Minns (*Enemies of Promise*) as a friend; a boy who refused to be bullied. (Incidentally, Orwell uses the name 'Minns' in *Coming up for Air*.) This Connolly affiliation is not without interest, because it shows Minns as prepared to take on the Arts Society, regarded by Connolly as too dubious in character to get mixed up with. At the time I had no idea that any likelihood existed of Connolly's membership, but from what he himself wrote later, he seems to have toyed with the possibility. Minns, dark skinned, very quiet, scarcely spoke at all at meetings. I could not imagine why he was there, unless nearness to Sixth Form was regarded as an impending benefit for the Society. Then, years later, Harold Acton revealed to me that Howard had a 'crush' on Minns. Acton's recollections of Howard's asides on these warm feelings bring their speaker convulsively to life: 'He *definitely* has a certain something ... So subtle, of course, *you* wouldn't see it ... still waters run *deep*, my dear ... Pure Hymettus *honey*, my dear ...' Minns seems to have been altogether unaware of having inspired this passion.

He passed top into the Diplomatic Service, but after a few years, not liking the life, resigned. The rest of his life was spent in a somewhat desultory manner doing odd jobs: journalism of a rather nondescript kind; 'selling strange drinks to clubs for wine-merchants'; a certain amount of teaching. Minns married, had children, but as member of the Arts Society with undoubtedly the highest academic qualifications of a conventional sort, his days were passed comparatively in the shadows.

Looking back now, the Eton Society of Arts seems essentially the group expression of certain individuals rather than a general need for the school. So far from Yorke's implications of hatred and derision, my own enquiries suggest that, among contemporaries and near-contemporaries, only a few boys had ever heard of the Society and its activities.

A month after the Arts Society's foundation *The Eton Candle* was published in March, 1922. The magazine, quite a handsome production bound in pink cardboard, with superlatively wide margins to the page sold at half-a-crown. The cover was boldly inscribed *Volume I*. The tradition of magazines edited by boys – usually known at that time as 'ephemerals', since they appeared on one day only, probably the Eton Festivals of the Fourth of June, or St Andrew's Day – went back as far as Canning, Praed, and Gladstone, while boys there.

A feature of *The Eton Candle* was its Old Etonian Supplement of writers and painters. The O E painters represented (only one of whom could be regarded as in the least *avant garde*) were an irretrievably *pompier* crowd, but Modernism was loudly proclaimed by the names of Osbert Sitwell and Aldous Huxley; the second of whom had been employed at Eton as an assistant-master the half before I arrived. The *bonne bouche* of *The Candle*'s Old Etonian Supplement was an 'unpublished' poem by Swinburne, to whose 'illustrious memory' – in spite of a lengthy opening article by Howard insisting on the pre-eminence of free verse – the magazine was dedicated.

Inevitably, the O E Supplement swamped the schoolboy contributions, of which by far the major part consisted of poems by Howard himself and Harold Acton. What remained at the literary end was fairly typical of juvenile *belles lettres* of the period; the graphic arts being represented by a promising if unadventurous *Nature Morte* by William Acton, and a not very interesting drawing (influences of Beardsley and Lovat Fraser unconcealed) of my own. The latter had been felicitously captioned by Howard (off the cuff) *Colonel Caesar Cannonbrains of the Black Hussars*.

The Swinburne lyric of four stanzas, entitled *Love*, had been handed over to Howard by Edmund Gosse, then at the height of his fame as man of letters of the Old Guard. I have a high regard for Swinburne as a poet, but to say that they are not Swinburne at his best is a very considerable understatement. They are, in fact, so awful that, on rereading them after many years, I had serious doubts that Swinburne could ever have written the lines. Nevertheless, Mr John S. Mayfield, the American authority on Swinburne, confirmed that *Love* was one of the four poems privately printed by the forger, Thomas Wise (with whom Gosse had always remained on friendly terms), in 1918; and that they

Colonel Caesar Cannonbrains of the Black Hussars: drawing by AP in
The Eton Candle, 1922.

also occur (without reference to previous publication or printing) in the Bonchurch Edition of Swinburne's Collected Works.

What were Gosse's motives for producing – like a rabbit from a hat – this Swinburne item for a schoolboy magazine? People, especially people like Gosse, usually have a good reason for performing conjuring tricks of that particular kind. From the moment when Wise issued the privately printed edition of these verses, there is a dubious air about the whole undertaking. Did Swinburne ever write them at all? It is an interesting question. Gosse, as it happened, turned up at Eton about this time as judge, or one of the judges, of the Loder Declamation Prize. After the grander recitations had taken place, two Lower Boys in jackets who were in for the final of the junior prize, read from the Bible. One of them was Alan Pryce-Jones, my first sight of the later editor of *The Times Literary Supplement*. Gosse, the essence of self-assured self-satisfied literary men, made several sagacious remarks about not stressing prepositions when reading aloud.

❊ **6** ❊

At some stage towards the inauguration of the Arts Society, and *The Candle*, Howard asked me to tea in his room, a form of hospitality not unique to himself, but with distinct implications of style. After issuing the invitation, he added as an apparent afterthought: 'Connolly may be looking in'.

I was impressed. Connolly was in Pop, and – although to walk arm-in-arm with Connolly would not, in snobbish terms, have rated anything like as high as with the Captain of the XI, Keeper of the Field, or Captain of Boats – to run across him in this informal manner would nevertheless grade as a manifest social success. I hardly expected such heights, nor, in the event, was there any sign of Connolly at tea, taken tête-à-tête with Howard, who may genuinely have credited the possibility. Neither Howard nor I knew at the time that any hope of such patronage had gone overboard through Howard's too vainglorious display on the mantelpiece of Connolly's Pop-headed postcard accepting a previous invitation. This was the only occasion when I nearly came across Cyril Connolly at Eton; no contact between us ever taking place there.

I knew him, of course, by sight. It was impossible not to notice Connolly as he passed in the street, or loitered in School Yard. He looked like no one else. Even so, his personality made no very definite impression until one afternoon when I was walking back from the tree-shaded playing field called Upper Club. The picture remains a clear one in my mind. Connolly himself mentions that, after becoming a member of Pop, he experimented in wearing a dinner-jacket (instead of blazer or tweed coat) with flannel trousers, 'a fashion that was not followed'. In this guise I first took him in as a formidable entity. Arm-in-arm with another colleger (one not in Pop), he was strolling towards the elms of Poets' Walk. Connolly was laughing and talking a lot. I felt conventional misgiving at the dinner-jacket as an innovation in schooldress.

In later life, when – in Praed's apt phrase – Connolly had matured into an 'Eton boy grown heavy', his outward appearance was not in a general way unlike that of Sainte-Beuve in some portraits, the same used-up sulky expression of one burdened with too many books to review. There was also slight suggestion – an identification he himself would have welcomed – of a beardless uncarefree Verlaine. When younger, Connolly's features are not so easy to describe. He speaks of his own 'ugliness', and it is true that, when news broke of the Pop election, Hubert Duggan rather brutally enquired: 'Is that the tug who's been kicked in the face by a mule?' Nevertheless, if Connolly's face was not in the common or garden sense his fortune, it was certainly one of his several means of imposing a fascination on people.

One searches for some parallel in similar facial contours. They were of the kind required for admission to the Pavlovski Guard, recruited (in memory of Tsar Paul) only from applicants with retroussé noses. Puck of Pook's Hill comes to mind, but, in Connolly's case, amused malice took the place of the hobgoblin's air of age-old understanding. A comparison with Socrates has also been made (I remember the suggestion greatly irritating Henry Yorke), and to come suddenly on a sculpted head of the philosopher in a museum might easily call Connolly to mind. If antiquity is to be invoked at all, the lineaments were perhaps more those of the formal masks worn in Greek drama – Comedy or Tragedy equally suited – an expression at once mocking and uneasy. The antique mask analogy would not, I think, have displeased Connolly himself.

Since the days of his 18th century forebear who had served with my own Powell great-great-grandfather in the Marines, the Connollys had been soldiers and sailors; usually attaining respectably senior rank. Connolly's father had retired as only a major, but was also an authority on conchology, and had compiled a cookery-book. He and his wife were estranged. Sea shells and gastronomy might have been thought to offer a life-line, but relations were not warm on his son's side; though perhaps rather less hostile in private than publicly proclaimed. Very little is said about the author's parents in *A Georgian Boyhood* (satirically titled sub-section of *Enemies of Promise*), a wonderfully vivid account of upper-class schooling of the period. Unlike most records of its kind, *A Georgian Boyhood* develops a coherent narrative, with a beginning, middle and end. In fact the 'plot' is so good that a summary far from does justice to its many subtleties, but some outline is required to understand the Connolly myth, one which regulated all its creator's subsequent standpoint and career.

A bright little boy, an only child, is sent to a preparatory school specialising in winning scholarships. The headmaster's wife, dominating, capricious, prone to favouritism, worshipping success, induces in the boys a combined burden of ambition and guilt. Among the other pupils are Eric Blair (later to be known as George Orwell); and, for good measure, Cecil Beaton (later Sir Cecil, photographer and designer). Connolly and Orwell became close friends. Both win scholarships to Eton. (The age ratio all important in schooldays, was: Orwell b. 23 June, Connolly b. 10 September, 1903; Orwell, taking the examination a year before Connolly, therefore always three forms above him at Eton.)

After a novitiate of comparative hell in College, the hero emerges in the ascendant. Beyond all reasonable expectation, he is elected to Pop; also gaining the blue riband of history scholarship, a Brackenbury at Balliol. But life is over. Oxford falls short; London shorter. After the Eton triumphs, all is anti-climax, dust and ashes. The rest of existence is spent in a state of suspended animation, idleness and apathy inhibiting any true release of intellect and talent.

The Connolly myth, therefore, is that of the oppressed hero who wins through, only to find the Fates have stacked the cards against him. The circumstances are, of course, special ones – it might not unreasonably be asked, who on earth is interested in the particular customs of Eton or any other school – but in a sense the circumstances of all effective autobiographers are special, only a few individuals possessing the powers required to assemble and assess their situation; as Connolly himself says: 'writers who can analyse their own environment'.

Factually true, the Connolly myth cannot be accepted in all its implications. In school terms, Connolly does not at all exaggerate the extent of his achievement, though perhaps overestimating the executive powers of Pop, which chiefly rested with individual members holding specific offices. That is not to discount the prestige of the body as a whole, probably as high as ever in the school's history. For a boy without athletic distinction to be elected was not unknown, but Connolly's handicaps as a starter in the race included not only being outside Sixth Form (a status likely for any colleger in the running, simply because that meant the top ten of the seventy), but not even among the next half-dozen collegers, who enjoyed certain minor privileges.

Where the myth burgeons into over elaboration is in Connolly's insistence on his own unproductivity. Even if the work produced was not, on the whole, the sort for which he himself would have most wished to be remembered. *Enemies of Promise* is a remarkable book; *The Unquiet Grave* has many admirers; much of the literary journalism retains its sparkle; *Horizon* was something of a beacon during the war; the *Letters to Noel Blakiston* have a stamp of their own. Evidence, in fact, points to Connolly enjoying his journalism more than he would ever admit. His neuroses ('cowardice, sloth, vanity, *Angst*', on all of which he was never tired of harping) certainly led him to refuse jobs and cut appointments, but that was in a sense a form of action; greater firmness of purpose often required to turn down some offer from an editor, or the BBC, than resignedly to accept.

Conviction of his own 'genius', that virus of the Twenties, had infected Connolly, too, at an early age. He wanted, in his own words, to be 'Baudelaire and Rimbaud, without the poverty and suffering'. He would also quote with ironic regret the bitter law laid down by his sometime master, Logan Pearsall Smith: 'You can't be fashionable and first-rate.' Something of a prodigy of assorted literary knowledge as a boy, a natural writer, an acute (if limited) critic, a gifted satirist, Connolly was not a poet or novelist. Novels, in any case, came a bad second to poetry in his literary affections, and his ruminations in print as to how they should be written reveal profound lack of appreciation of what it feels like to be a novelist.

By the time I was at Oxford the Connolly myth was already pretty well established in his own mind, even if other people still saw 'promise' that he had himself ostensibly (anyway in retrospect) jettisoned. One speculates as to what might have happened had a few additional blackballs found their way into the Pop ballot-box; a bloody-minded Balliol don taken against the Connolly interpretation of history. In the latter event, Connolly might well have found himself – King's, Henry VI's sister foundation, more traditional for a colleger – an under-graduate at Cambridge, with its different ethos. Would the plea then have been – like Scott Fitzgerald's failure to make the Princeton football side or achieve an army posting overseas – that (Pop and the Brackenbury missed by a hair's breadth) not success, but dire dis-appointment, had paralysed the will?

In one of the letters to Blakiston, Connolly writes: '... just as one imagines Narcissus looking into the pool, not with vanity but with troubled curiosity and flower-like absorption ...' I suspect that any alteration in the mere narrative shape of the Connolly myth would have made little ultimate difference to its dramatic overtones, their inspira-tion deriving not so much from the author's relative success or failure in early life, as from a passionate interest in himself. True interest in yourself is comparatively rare, sharply to be differentiated from mere egotism and selfishness; characteristics often immoderately developed in persons not in the least interested in themselves intellectually or objectively. Indeed, not everyone can stand the strain of gazing down too long into the personal crater, with its scene of Hieronymus Bosch activities taking place in the depths.

In self-inspection, Connolly could endure more than most. Not unnaturally, he tends to concentrate on specific areas below, in preference to others not necessarily less worth analysis, but from his chosen angles he can be absolutely ruthless in drawing attention to what many persons would be very willing to leave concealed. The sheer intensity of this self-interest makes everything Connolly writes about himself interesting; even when, as in some of the later book reviews (much of his literary criticism being a branch of autobiography), touches of self-fantasy from time to time obtrude.

As a writer, he paid for this gift of self-examination by possessing no deep interest in other people as such, unless they were immediately orientated on himself. Even then, those concerned were likely to be romanticized or denigrated, without too much attention being allowed to their circumstances. This did not prevent brilliant flashes of caricature like Brian Howard as de Clavering in the squib *Where Engels Fears to Tread*, or Ian Fleming in *Bond Breaks Camp*. A lack of interest for individuals in what might be called the Proustian sense was perhaps characteristic, too, of the whole of the Arts Society. There were several champion egoists, but none among them was capable of taking his own machinery to pieces, and scrutinizing its workings in the Connolly manner.

Yorke had leanings in that direction, *Pack My Bag* making confessional references to physical and moral cowardice, parsimony, snobbishness, sexual shyness, and so on. These glances lack Connolly's objective treatment; an agonized self-consciousness being something different from self-revelation treated clinically yet understandingly. One of the most peculiar aspects of autobiography is the way in which some authors are acceptable in their sexual and suchlike intimacies (Proust masturbating in the lavatory), others are without great interest in those rôles, at worst only embarrassing. At first sight, the simple answer seems to be that some write 'well', others less well; but in the field of self-revelation the altogether uninstructed can produce a masterpiece of apt expression; the seasoned writer, at times a cliché. I can find no literary explanation other than that only certain personalities are appropriate to dissection; others not.

Connolly, like Yorke, though in a different vein, is inclined to insist that what he thinks supplies the rule for what those around him thought, but he always writes with clarity, whereas Yorke will often blur the picture with deliberate obscurantism. Connolly's current assessment of an individual or way of life (even books and authors) was inclined to move up and down like mercury in a thermometer, he himself at times scarcely able to keep up with the speed of his own quicksilver's rise and fall. Nevertheless, any Connolly rating, even when it readjusted yesterday's estimate, was likely to be invested with its own kind of force; if only desperate fear that he might himself be in some way inconvenienced and bored, rather than benefited and amused.

A Georgian Boyhood emphasizes two overwhelming factors in what its author calls 'the background of the lilies' (emblems on Eton's coat of arms), both elements examined by him with much understanding: first, the 'monastic intensity' of life as lived in College; secondly, the 'romantic' preponderance of all Eton education. To the former, Connolly brought his own natural intensity of feeling (his 'sloth', as has been remarked, almost as much an expression of a strong personality as participation could be), a condition which so to speak doubled the intensity dose. The pressurized romanticism also stimulated something already within him, Eton education merely indicating the channels that a purely personal romanticism should best take.

No doubt all public schools of the period attempted to inculcate at least some of the 'romantic' influences Connolly so well describes – Homer metamorphosed into a preraphaelite poet, Plato seen as a great headmaster, Greek homosexuality merged into heroic comradeship – but Eton, historically and architecturally, was unusually well placed to indoctrinate the romantic mystique; her antique towers, beside the still unpolluted Thames, offering a dreamlike sanctuary for the antithetical deities presiding over that particular romantic vision: Honour and Discipline; Success and Sacrifice; Death and Victory; in a school of eleven hundred boys, after four and a half years of war, eleven hundred killed, fourteen hundred wounded. If the prizes offered were splendid, the oblation was no less unstinted.

Those who resisted these pressures often ended up more deeply imbued than the conformists, and it is part of Connolly's thesis that he had thrown himself into school life so wholeheartedly that there was no disintoxication from its opium dream. On this myth of personal experience he superimposed another of personal aspiration: self-identity with Palinurus, pilot of Æneas voyaging to Italy after the sack of Troy. Palinurus, overcome by sleep at the tiller, and falling into the sea, gained the shore, but was murdered for his clothes by the savage inhabitants of that coast.

Connolly's Palinurine symbolism is never altogether clear, but I take his meaning to be, broadly speaking, that as a young critic he had undoubtedly led the way in trying to get rid of what was out of date, also in drawing attention to new writers. This elaboration of his own personal myth – in the manner of extended myths – runs somewhat counter to the version earlier propagated, the frustrated creative writer who has taken only unwillingly to criticism; but there seems no other explanation. As Palinurus was never ritually buried ('the unquiet grave'), his shade had to wait the prescribed time to cross the Styx. Here the image of a restless dissatisfied soul can be accepted. Even if Connolly was not actually murdered by the literary barbarians on whose coast he was cast, his presence there was associated with drowsiness. There was also a case for regarding his critical raiment as having been to some extent pillaged, especially in relation to the immediacy with which he had appreciated the importance of American writers like Scott Fitzgerald (then scarcely at all known in England), and, to a lesser degree, Hemingway.

That Connolly missed some of the credit for these reconnaissances was largely his own fault. The account of the situation of English writing at the beginning of *Enemies of Promise*, in many ways acute, is also far less adventurous in tone than Connolly's early reviewing. He gets bogged down in self-pity about the difficulties of a writer's life – his King Charles's Head – showing some uncertainty whether it is better for a writer to be a success or a failure. There are hedgings of bets, and genuflections to Bloomsbury. Scarcely anything is said of trails he had once begun to blaze. There is, I think, a reason for this loss of confidence.

Connolly inscribed my own copy of *The Unquiet Grave* with a four-line portrait of himself:

> An artist he of character complex;
> Money he loved, and next to money, sex.
> No roses culled he from the Muses' garden;
> Neurosis held him in the grip of Auden.

The unserious tone of the verse embodies in the last line an important and interesting confession. After Connolly had written a good deal of *Enemies of Promise* (of which he would sometimes talk before it was finished) he came in contact with the Left Wing poets of the Thirties. Little as Communism – the great *trahison des clercs* of the Thirties – accorded with Petronian hedonism he was carried away. It was, indeed, a moment when, for a while, W. H. Auden and his troop swept all before them; briefly extinguishing almost everything else in their literary age-group. This flavour is particularly noticeable in *Enemies of Promise* towards the end of the critical pages, where the author's newfound Left Wing enthusiasms form a kind of superstructure that sits somewhat awkwardly on the book's original foundations.

Connolly (compared with, say, Orwell) had no flair whatever for politics, and, as the years rolled by, changes took place in many viewpoints; not least in those of Auden and his associates. Accordingly, *Enemies of Promise*, so far as it expresses political opinions, shows its author as marooned on an island of somewhat vicarious commitment; an uneasy Prospero whose spells, in which he himself only halfheartedly believes, have become vitiated by the passing of time. *The Unquiet Grave*'s inscription suggests that Connolly – aware of so much about himself – was aware of that too.

Much admired when it appeared during the war, *The Unquiet Grave* seems to me a far less effective work than *Enemies of Promise*. Some of its *obiter dicta* date back to a Commonplace Book kept by Connolly since his earliest days, which 'with a view to publication', was shown to me, perhaps as far back as 1927, when first at Duckworth's. It was characteristic of Connolly that, after handing over the Commonplace Book for publisher's reading, he added: 'If your firm doesn't like it, make some excuse when you give it back to me. Say the Autumn List is already full, or something like that. Not just that they don't think it good enough to publish.'

The Unquiet Grave's self-portrait, more impressionistic than *A Georgian Boyhood*'s, less unguarded than the Letters, emphasizes the author's love of pleasure, sensual and intellectual. That pleasure was as much in pretension to being expert as in the thing itself. Connolly loved the concept of scholar, dandy, bibliophil, gourmet, connoisseur. He knew more than the average about many things, but aspired to know all there was to be known about everything. This desire to lay down the law could result in howlers about such matters as marks on china or silver. Friends who produced (for attribution) a bottle of Australian champagne in a napkin were told it was Krug 1905 (or some such vintage); in consequence, losing their nerve, and assuring Connolly that he was miraculously correct.

That did not mean Connolly lacked all knowledge of wine. On the contrary, he could talk convincingly on the subject, and I drank some of the best claret I have ever tasted in his house. At the same time I have seen him apparently altogether unaware that he was drinking something specially good. What was at fault was the claim to omniscience. He could be very generous (especially in giving presents), but could show himself less than grateful for generosity in others. Superlatively competitive, he had to give a one-man performance. Somebody else's anecdote or artefact was always a challenge. He was jealous, rather than envious; whatever was in question, he must always go one better. Unlike such good talkers as Constant Lambert or Maurice Bowra (anyway up to a point), Connolly had no great liking for being entertained by talk, and as a rule himself no flow of conversation. His flair was for the unexpected comment or elaborate set piece.

What, in short, was the point of Connolly? Why did people put up with frequent moroseness, gloom, open hostility? Why, if he were about in the neighbourhood, did I always take steps to get hold of him? The question is hard to answer. The fact remains that I did; though never coming under his sway to the extent he expected of friends; unless – for which he was prepared in certain cases – he was the one to submit. He was rarely at ease with an equal relationship. I never avoided being under slight suspicion of not accepting all his sides with equal serious-ness. Nevertheless, I knew well that, if it suited Connolly to flatter, I was an easy victim. He was a master of flattery; flattery of the best sort that can seem on the surface almost a form of detraction. There was undoubtedly something hypnotic about him.

In Connolly's collected literary criticism it is rare to look up a given subject, and find nothing of interest. Some point is almost always made, if only a subjective one. Logan Pearsall Smith used to advocate the principle of limited literary objectives, rather than taking in writers perhaps not sympathetic to the critic himself, and Connolly inclined to accept that lesson. His own personality, pervasive, mutable, is less easy to pinpoint than his writing. He was one of those individuals – a recognized genus – who seem to have been sent into the world to be talked about. Such persons satisfy a basic human need. Connolly's behaviour, love affairs, financial difficulties, employments or lack of them, all seemed matters of burning interest. He had, so to speak, taken the sins of the world on himself. Some rebelled, refusing to be drawn into the net of Connolly gossip. They were few in number, and perhaps missed something in life. From the moment when he burst through the Pop-barrier (no doubt before that too, on a smaller scale), he was the subject of profuse anecdote; his interest in himself somehow com-municating its force to other people.

Connolly – like others of his generation – recalls Laertes' comment that 'the canker galls the infants of the spring'; and, as Hamlet remarked of Laertes himself, 'To divide him inventorially would dizzy th' arithmetic of memory.'

It was through Connolly that I first heard about George Orwell. At Eton, Orwell's face eludes me. Looking at photographic groups of boys in College, I can remember – anyway by sight – most of those sitting round about, in many cases their names. Orwell himself I do not remember; nor even the name 'Blair, KS', spoken aloud or seen on lists. This is strange because his platoon in the Corps – one of two made up of collegers – was in the same Company as Goodhart's; so that for at least two halves we must have seen each other hurrying across Cannon Yard on the way to Monday morning parades. By that time Orwell was in Sixth Form, myself just in Upper School, a large gap therefore stretching between us. Nevertheless, it seems best to speak of Orwell here, while Eton is surveyed, rather than leave him to a later period. He was, in his way, very much an Etonian, however greatly in apostasy, but was of course altogether uncompromised by Oxford.

When *Down and Out in Paris and London* appeared in 1933 Adrian Daintrey recommended the book to me, adding; 'You'll never again enjoy *sauté* potatoes after you've heard how they're cooked in restaurants.' I read Orwell's book, and was impressed by its savagery and gloom, but cannot claim to have marked down the writer immediately as one we should hear a great deal more of; still less, that here was someone who would become a close friend. A year or two later, seeing *Keep the Aspidistra Flying* in a secondhand bookshop, I bought it. Again I liked the novel for its violent feelings, and presentation of a man at the end of his tether, rather than for form or style, both of which seemed oddly old-fashioned in treatment, as did many of the views expressed in the story.

I spoke of the book dining one night with Connolly in about 1936. He was then married to his first wife, Jean Bakewell, an American, and living in a flat in King's Road, Chelsea. By that time I too was married. Connolly revealed – something of which I had no idea – that Orwell was one of his oldest friends. They had recently been in touch again, and Connolly gave a sobering account of Orwell, his rigid asceticism, political intransigence, utter horror of all social life. Connolly emphasized Orwell's physical appearance, the lines of suffering and privation marking his hollow cheeks. The portrait was a disturbing one. Connolly was at the same time enthusiastic about Orwell. He urged me to write him a fan letter. This I did, thereby making my first Orwell contact fifteen years after he had himself left Eton.

Connolly's picture of a severe unapproachable infinitely disapproving personage was not altogether dispelled by the reply I received to my letter. Orwell, with his first wife Eileen O'Shaughnessy, was at that time running a small general shop near Baldock in Hertfordshire. His answer, perfectly polite and friendly, had also about it something that cast a faint chill, making me feel, especially in the light of Connolly's words, that Orwell was not for me.

I was so sure of this that, when opportunity arose of meeting him in the flesh, I was at first unwilling to involve myself in so much frugal living and high thinking; more especially in wartime, when existence was uncomfortable enough anyway. This was in 1941. I was on leave from the army. Violet and I were dining at the Café Royal. Inez Holden came across to talk to us from a table on the far side of the room. Writer, author of several novels, miscellaneous journalist, she was at that time doing war work in an aircraft factory operating the house-cinema. She said that the man and woman with her were George and Eileen

Orwell, suggesting that we should join them after we had finished dinner.

To make the evening rather more of an occasion, as one did not 'go out' much in those days, I had changed into 'blues', patrol uniform, an outfit with brass buttons and a high collar. I felt certain Orwell would not approve of such a get-up. It was no doubt bad enough in his eyes to be an officer at all; to be rigged out in these pretentious regimentals, at once militaristic and relatively ornate, would aggravate the offence of belonging to a stupid and brutal caste. Notwithstanding these apprehensions – made light of, I admit, by Violet – we moved over in due course to the Orwells' table. Orwell's first words, spoken with considerable tenseness, were at the same time reassuring.

'Do your trousers strap under the foot?'

As the uniform had belonged to my father, they were indeed 'overalls' (rather than trousers), though I was not wearing the regulation spurs on the heels of the wellingtons beneath.

'Yes.'

Orwell nodded.

'That's really the important thing.'

'Of course.'

'You agree?'

'Naturally.'

'I used to wear ones that strapped under the boot myself,' he said, not without nostalgia.

'In Burma?'

'You knew I was in the police there? Those straps under the foot give you a feeling like nothing else in life.'

His voice had a curious rasp. I thought at the time that its note was consciously designed to avoid vocables that could possibly be regarded as 'public school'; though equally the tone made no concession whatever to any other 'accent' known to me. When later I commented in print on Orwell's way of speaking – suggesting the delivery was intentionally to escape any class-label – a postcard arrived from Orwell's former 'classical tutor' at Eton, A. S. F. 'Granny' Gow (by then a Cambridge don), saying: 'Well, G. O. had little need to "avoid consciously a public school tone" for he croaked discordantly already in 1917 when he reached Eton.' Gow (who also briefly taught me Greek), had also been a good friend to Orwell.

Connolly and Beaton, both from the same preparatory school, shared this slight rasp (in Connolly's case approaching without exactly resembling Duke of Windsor cockney), but Orwell's way of speaking has twice at least been brought back to me when talking with former forestry officials from India and Africa. The intonation perhaps derived from Orwell's father, who had been in the I C S, possibly a recognisable official delivery, something occasionally suggested in descriptions of

Kipling who could have picked it up. Nevertheless, however he talked, Orwell had, as it were, resigned from the world in which he had been brought up; while never really contriving to join another.

Tall – as has been more than once remarked, closely resembling Gustave Doré's Don Quixote – Orwell also looked uncommonly like Cézanne's portrait of Monsieur Choquet, the painter's friend in the Custom House. The deep grooves in Orwell's cheeks, of which Connolly had spoken, were at once apparent on either side of his mouth. He wore a narrow moustache, neatly clipped, along the lower level of his upper lip. This moustache, as long as I knew him, was always a bit of a mystery to me. I never had quite sufficient courage to ask about it. Orwell's approach to life was always strictly controlled, so that this feature must have possessed some special meaning for him. Perhaps it was his only remaining concession to a dandyism that undoubtedly lurked beneath the surface of self-imposed austerities – a side momentarily revealed by the enquiry about strapped-down trousers.

Indeed Orwell, in certain respects, was far closer to the moral concept of a 'dandy' than Connolly, who liked talking about dandyism as a philosophy, but was himself burdened with the essentially undandyish trait of intermittent lack of social self-assurance. Orwell's contemporaries at school even speak of a tendency in those early days towards the mannerisms of a P. G. Wodehouse hero, the moustache – in itself somewhat un-Wodehousian – possibly partaking of this 'dandyism à rebours' in Orwell's nature. Perhaps, on the other hand, it had something to do with the French blood inherited through his mother, which caused him to resemble the Cézanne portrait, or one of those fiercely melancholy French workmen in blue smocks pondering the meaning of life at the zinc counters of a thousand *estaminets*.

Certainly this last image was the nearest Orwell ever achieved in the direction of even faintly proletarian appearance. It was the moustache that provoked thoughts of France, because nothing could have been more English than his consciously tattered old tweed coat and trousers of corduroy or flannel, an outfit that always maintained exactly the same degree of shabbiness, no worse, no better. In much the same manner as Millard, Orwell always looked rather distinguished in these old clothes.

'Does it matter my coming in like this?' he asked, before entering the room at a party we were giving, when we lived in Regent's Park.

The question is an example of the unreality of much of Orwell's approach to life. By that time he and I knew each other well. The clothes were the clothes he always wore. Why should I have invited him, if I thought them inadequate? It was hardly to be expected that he would turn up in a brand new suit. Did he half hope for an unfavourable answer?

'Yes, George, it does matter. They won't do. You can't come in. We'll meet another time.'

In justice to Orwell, some of his suppositions regarding social behaviour were so strange that he might not have been surprised had I
replied in those terms. I am certain that denial of entry on such grounds
would, on his side, have made little or no difference to our friendship. It
would merely have confirmed his worst suspicions; perhaps even
pleased him a little to find his views on the tyranny of convention so
amply justified.

A year or two after the meeting at the Café Royal, when I had been
posted to the War Office, Orwell and I arranged to lunch together. For
some reason we failed to make contact at the small but very crowded
Greek restaurant in Percy Street he had suggested for luncheon. Each
thought the other had not turned up, and ate alone at a table. On his way
out, Orwell passed me.

'Come back and sit for a moment,' he said. 'I ordered a bottle of wine.
I'm afraid I've drunk most of it, as I thought you weren't going to arrive,
but there's still a drop left, as I couldn't get through it all.'

Wine, at that period of the war, was hard to obtain and expensive. It
was characteristically generous of Orwell to have provided it, when beer
would not have seemed at all close-fisted. At that time he was employed
in some BBC news-service, not in want, but certainly not particularly
well off. None of his books had yet begun to sell. With all his willingness
to face hard times – almost welcoming them – Orwell was by no means
a confirmed enemy of good living, though always tortured by guilt when
he felt indulgence was overstepping the mark. This sense of guilt is, of
course, generally attributed to Orwell's 'social conscience'. He himself,
at least by implication, would have ascribed such feelings to that cause.
My own impression is that guilt lay far deeper than roots acquired
merely by politico-social reading and observation. Guilt had, I think,
been implanted in him at an early age, no doubt inflamed by the
preparatory school experiences, shared with Connolly, about which
Orwell himself wrote in *Such, Such Were the Joys*. He may – like
Kipling, for whom as a writer he possessed a vigorous love/hate – have
contrasted those grim days with a happy early childhood; for, although
Orwell himself was inclined to imply that he had been brought up in a
home of Victorian severity, his sister's memories suggest that, on the
contrary, he had been rather 'spoilt'.

When, in the latter years of the war, Violet and Tristram were living
at Dunstall (her uncle, Lord Dunsany's house, which we had been lent)
at Shoreham in Kent, George and Eileen Orwell came down for the day.
Going for country walks, Orwell would draw attention almost with
anxiety to this shrub budding early for the time of year, that plant
growing rarely in the south of England. He was, it is true, very fond of
flowers, but there was something about this determined almost
scientific concentration on natural history, or agricultural method, that

seemed aimed at excusing the frivolity of mere ramblings. 'Interesting to note the regional variation in latching of field gates,' he would remark. 'Different sometimes, even in the same county.'

In this was something of Connolly's love of being an expert, also some of Connolly's omniscience. Guilt, naturally enough, harassed Orwell in matters of sex.

'Have you ever had a woman in the park?' he asked me once.

'No – never.'

'I have.'

'How did you find it?'

'I was forced to.'

'Why?'

'Nowhere else to go.'

He spoke defensively, as if he feared condemnation for this 'cold pastoral', as Connolly used to call such *plein air* frolics. It was a Victorian guilt, and in many ways Orwell was a Victorian figure – though of very different sort from Robert Byron, to whom I have also applied the label. Like most people 'in rebellion', he was more than half in love with what he was rebelling against. What exactly that was I could never be sure. Certainly its name was legion, extending from the turpitudes of government to irritating personal habits in individuals.

For example, Orwell complains (in the essay *How the Poor Die*) that English hospital nurses wear Union Jack buttons. This used to puzzle me, because, even at the period of which he wrote, if – in an access of chauvinism – you had wanted to sport a Union Jack button, I do not believe you would have been able to procure one for love or money. The button in question probably indicated the hospital at which the nurse had qualified; some such insignia resembling the design of the flag. To see such a badge as an emblem of flaunting jingoism comes near a mild form of persecution-mania. Many of Orwell's prejudices seemed equally to belong to this world of fantasy. That may be unjust. Mental and moral surroundings are subjective enough. It is largely the way you look at things. At least no one would deny the nightmare world envisaged by Orwell round about, if a true one, was drastically in need of reform.

'Take juries now,' he would say. 'They're mostly drawn from the middle-classes. Some fellow comes up for trial on a charge of stealing. He's not wearing a collar. The jury takes against him at once. "No collar?" they say. "Suspicious-looking chap." Unanimous verdict of guilty.' What would he think of juries these days?

Orwell himself was not at all unaware of the manner in which his own imagination strayed back into the Victorian age, nor, for that matter, of the paradoxes in which some of his enthusiasms involved him. Indeed, he liked to draw attention to the contradictions of his own point of view.

He was also fond of repeating that, if some formula for agreement were reached by the nations, world economics could be put right 'on the back of an envelope'; but never revealed how this solution was to be achieved.

To his Victorianism he constantly returned, both in conversation, and, so far as possible, in life; the latter chiefly represented by the places he inhabited. He was delighted, for example, with the period flavour – certainly immense – of a small house in Kilburn, where, during the war, he rented the basement and ground floor. Its terrace had been built about 1850. The house conjured up those middle-to-lower-middle-class households (Orwell put himself in the lower-upper-middle-class) on which his mind loved to dwell; particularly as enthroned in the works of Gissing, whom he regarded as England's greatest novelist.

'They would probably have kept a Buttons here,' he said, enchanted at the thought.

We dined with the Orwells in Kilburn one night, prior arrangements being made (in the Jorrocks manner, himself employer of a Buttons) for sleeping there too, owing to the exigencies of wartime transport. The sitting-room, with a background of furniture dating from more prosperous generations of bygone Blairs, two or three 18th century family portraits hanging on the walls, might well have been the owner's study in a country house.

'When George went to the Spanish war,' said Eileen Orwell. 'We panicked at the last minute that he hadn't enough money with him, so we pawned the Blair spoons and forks. Then some weeks later his mother and sister came to see me. They asked why the silver was missing. I had to think of something on the spur of the moment, so I said it had seemed a good opportunity, Eric being away, to have the crest engraved on the silver. They accepted that.'

I never knew Eileen Orwell at all well. My impression is that she did a very good job in what were often difficult circumstances. At the same time it was, I think, an exception for her to tell a story like that. She was not usually given to making light of things, always appearing a little overwhelmed by the strain of keeping the household going, which could not have been easy. Possibly she was by temperament a shade over serious for a man falling often into a state of gloom himself. Orwell might have benefited by a wife who shook him out of that condition occasionally. He was fond of emphasizing his own egoisms.

'If I have a dog, I always think my dog is the best dog in the world,' he used to say, 'or if I make anything at carpentry, I always think it's the best shelf or bookcase. Don't you ever feel the need to do something with your hands? I'm surprised you don't. I even like rolling my own cigarettes. I've installed a lathe in the basement. I don't think I could exist without my lathe.'

The night we dined at Kilburn I slept on a camp-bed beside the lathe. There was just about space. It was an unusual, though not entirely comfortless room, and by that stage of the war one had become accustomed to sleeping anywhere. At about 4 a.m. there was a blitz. The local anti-aircraft battery sounded as if it were based next door. The row the guns made was prodigious, even by normal blitz standards. Orwell came blundering down in the dark.

'I'm rather glad there's a raid,' he said. 'It means we shall get some hot water in the morning. If you don't re-stoke the boiler about this time, it runs cold. I'm always too lazy to leave my bed in the middle of the night, unless like tonight there's too much noise to sleep anyway.'

The bad health that prevented Orwell from taking an active part in the war was a terrible blow to him. He saw himself as a man of action, and felt passionately about the things for which the country was fighting. When he heard Evelyn Waugh was serving with a Commando unit, he said: 'Why can't somebody on the Left do that sort of thing?' As a sergeant in the Home Guard he always spoke with enjoyment of the grotesque do-it-yourself weapons issued to that force, ramshackle in the extreme, and calculated to explode at any moment. Goodness knows what Orwell would have been like in the army. I have no doubt whatever that he would have been brave, but bravery in the army is, on the whole, an ultimate rather than immediate requirement, de- manded only at the end of a long and tedious apprenticeship. It is possible that he might have found army routine sympathetic. He was not without love of detail, in fact was very keen on detail in certain forms. His own picture of military life was apt to be based on Kipling.

'Did you ever handle screw-guns?' he asked me.

At the time the phrase struck me as scarcely less obsolete than the pikes issued – and strongly recommended – at the beginning of the war, when invasion seemed likely to take place. I found that was in- correct, and screw-guns were indeed used in Burma and elsewhere. In the Spanish Civil War Orwell had served with a force designated POUM, chiefly Anarchist, which he joined not on account of special political affiliations, but because that unit seemed to offer the best chance of getting into action. Wounded in the throat, in danger of being arrested, perhaps executed, by the Communist Secret Police, he had to get out of Spain in a hurry. I once enquired how discipline was maintained in such an army. 'You appealed to a man's better nature,' Orwell said. 'There really wasn't much else you could do. I took a chap by the arm once, when he was being tiresome, and was told after- wards that I might easily have been knifed.'

Orwell was in his way quite ambitious, I think, and had a decided taste for power; but his ambition did not run along conventional lines, and he liked his power to be of the *éminence grise* variety. That preference was no doubt partly owed to a sense of being in some manner cut off from the rest of the world; not allowed, as it were by an irresistible exterior influence, to enjoy more than very occasionally such few amenities as human existence provides. This did not prevent his strong will and natural shrewdness from making him an effective negotiator. Indeed, his genuine unworldliness – in the popular sense – was used by him with considerable effect when handling those who were rich or in authority. He would somehow unload on them the whole burden of his own guilt, until they groaned beneath its weight. He was not at all afraid of making himself disagreeable to persons whom he found, in their dealings with himself, disagreeable. 'If editors, or people of that sort, tell you to alter things, or put you to a lot of trouble,' he used to say, 'always put them to trouble in return. It discourages them from making themselves awkward in the future.'

It is interesting to speculate how Orwell's life would have developed had he survived as a very successful writer. The retirement to Jura, even at the preliminary warning signs of financial improvement, was probably symptomatic. Orwell, I suspect, could thrive only in comparative adversity. All the same, one can never foresee the effect of utterly changed circumstances. Prosperity might have produced unguessable alterations in himself and his work. It would inevitably have invested him with more complex forms of living; complications which, in accordance with his system, would have to be rationalized to himself, and weighed in the balance.

Orwell's gift was curiously poised, as suggested earlier, between politics and literature. The former both attracted and repelled him; the latter, close to his heart, was at the same time tainted with the odour of escape. He once said that he could not write a line without a specific purpose. On the other hand, so far as day to day politics were concerned, he could never have become integrated into any normal party machine. His reputation for integrity might be invoked; his capacity for martyrdom relied on; his talent for pamphleteering made use of. That was all. He could never be trusted not to let some disastrously unwelcome cat out of the political bag. With literature, on the other hand, in spite of an innate 'feeling' for writing and criticism, he always had to seek the means of attacking some abuse or injustice to excuse himself. This did not prevent books from being, in my opinion, his true love.

In his own works Orwell returns more than once to the theme that, had he lived at another period of history, he would have written in a different manner. I do not believe this to be a correct judgment. I find his talent far removed from that objective sort of writing which he saw as an alternative to what he actually produced. His interest in individuals – in literature or life – was never great. Apart from various projections of himself, the characters in his novels do not live as persons, though they are sometimes effective puppets in expressing their author's thesis of the moment. Orwell had a thoroughly professional approach to writing, and a finished style. His critical judgments are sometimes eccentric, and his dislike for all elaborate methods of writing, whatever they might be, seems to be an altogether untenable form of literary puritanism.

He was easily bored. If a subject came up in conversation that did not appeal to him, he would make no effort to take it in; falling into a dejected silence, or jerking aside his head like a horse jibbing at a proffered apple. On the other hand, when Orwell's imagination was caught, especially by some idea, he would discuss that exhaustively. He was one of the most enjoyable people to talk with about books, full of parallels and quotations, the last usually far from verbally accurate.

The adoption of a child, the sudden death of Eileen, the world wide success of *Animal Farm*, the serious worsening of his own health, all combined within the space of a few months to revolutionize Orwell's life. The loss of his wife, just after the much contemplated acquisition of the baby, especially created a situation that would have caused many men to give in. No doubt some arrangement for re-adoption could have been made without too much difficulty. That would have been reasonable enough. No such thought ever crossed Orwell's mind. He had enormously desired a child of his own. Now that a child had become part of the household, he was not going to relinquish him, no matter what the difficulties. In fact one side of Orwell – the romantic side that played such a part rather enjoyed the picture of himself coping unaided with a small baby. Let this point be made clear; Orwell *did* cope with the baby. It may have been romanticism, but, if so, it was romanticism which found practical expression in that way. This was characteristic of him in all he did. His idiosyncrasies were based in guts.

He would still go out at night to address protest meetings – '... probably a blackguard, but it was unjust to lock him up ...' – and the baby would be left to sleep for an hour or two at our house, while Orwell harangued his audience.

'What was the meeting like?' one would ask on his return.

'Oh, the usual people.'

'Always the same?'

'There must be about two hundred of them altogether. They go round to everything of this sort. About forty or fifty turned up tonight, which is quite good.'

This mixture of down-to-earth scepticism seasoned with a dash of self-dramatization formed a contradictory element in Orwell's character. With all his honesty, ability to face disagreeable facts, refusal to be hoodwinked, there was always also about him a touch of make-believe, the air of acting a part. Connolly mentions that at their prep school he, no doubt Orwell too, used to read the poems of Robert W. Service (chiefly memorable for the verses about Dangerous Dan McGrew), and Sir Anthony Wagner (herald and genealogical scholar, later Garter King of Arms) told me that, when he was Orwell's fag in College, Orwell, on his departure, presented him with Service's *Rhymes of a Rolling Stone*. 'He was a kind and considerate fagmaster,' said Wagner, 'but he did not talk much.' The parting gift is not without interest in consideration of Orwell's character.

Orwell came to see me in London one day when our younger son, John, was lying, quiet but not asleep, in a cot by the window. I went out of the room to fetch a book. When I returned Orwell was assiduously studying a picture on the wall the far side of the room. John made some sign of needing attention. I went over to the cot, straightening the coverlet, which had become disarranged, my hand touched a hard object. This turned out to be an enormous clasp-knife. I took it out and examined it.

'How on earth did that get there?'

For the moment the mystery of the knife's provenance seemed absolute. Orwell looked away, as if greatly embarrassed.

'Oh, I gave it him to play with,' he said. 'I forgot I'd left it there.'

The incident, infinitely trivial, seems worth preserving because it illustrates sides of Orwell not easy to express in direct description: his attitude to childhood; his shyness, part genuine, part assumed; his schoolboy leanings; above all, his taste for sentimental vignettes. Why, in the first place, should he want to burden himself, in London, with a knife that looked like an adjunct of a fur-trapper's equipment? Echoes perhaps of Dangerous Dan McGrew? Why take such pains to avoid being found playing with a child, a perfectly natural instinct, flattering to a parent? If some authentic masculine sheepishness made him hesitate at being caught in such an act, why leave the knife behind as evidence? It was much too big to be forgotten.

I think the answer to these questions is that the whole incident was arranged to create a genre picture in the Victorian manner of a kind which, even though he might smile at the sentimentality, made a huge appeal to Orwell's imagination, and way of looking at things. He was, so to speak, playing the part of a strong rough man, touched by the sight of a baby, but unwilling to confess, even to himself, this inner weakness. At the same time, he had to be discovered for the incident to achieve graphic significance.

Orwell would not, I think, deny that sentimental situations had a charm for him. I can imagine him discussing them in relation to another favourite theme of his, 'good bad poetry', and 'good bad novels'. In his own books Orwell is too practised a writer to be betrayed into presenting sentimentalities in their crude form, though he is fond of showing them, so to speak, brutally in reverse; for example, his taste for such episodes as lovers' assignations ruined by forgotten contraceptives or the curse.

In due course the trouble with Orwell's lung became so serious that he had to take to his bed. It was fairly clear that he was not going to recover; only the length of time that remained to him in doubt. 'I don't think one dies,' he said to me, 'as long as one has another book to write – and I have.'

During these last months he married Sonia Brownell, first met by him some years before, when she had been on the staff of Connolly's magazine, *Horizon*. In spite of the tragic circumstances of Orwell's failing condition, marriage immensely cheered him. I saw a good deal of him when he was in hospital. In some respects he was in better form there than I had ever known him show. There was now and then a flicker to be seen of the old Wodehousian side.

'I really might get some sort of a smoking-jacket to wear in bed,' he said. 'A dressing-gown looks rather sordid when lots of people are dropping in. Could you look about, and report to me what there is in that line?'

War shortages still persisted where clothes were concerned. Nothing very glamorous in male styles was to be found in the shops. Decision had to be taken ultimately between a jaeger coat with a tying belt, or a crimson jacket in corduroy. We agreed the latter was preferable. It was a small concession to an aspect of human frailty that Orwell had for years strenuously denied himself. Sitting up in bed now, he had an unaccustomed epicurean air – only, unhappily, his conviction that an unwritten book within preserved life proved untrustworthy. I have often wondered whether he was buried in the crimson coat.

The Orwell myth, now substantially launched in a shape scarcely amenable to modification, presents on the whole a tortured saint by El Greco (for whom Orwell would certainly have made an admirable model), a figure from whom all human qualities have been removed. Periodically fierce arguments rage as to precisely where he stood politically. I am not here concerned with that side of him, although it is worth remembering that it took courage – in that now largely forgotten post-war period, when Stalin was still being held up by the Left as a genial uncle – to fire an anti-Communist broadside like *Animal Farm* that placed a permanent dent in the whole Marxist structure; especially courageous on the part of a writer, himself of the Left, laying his professional reputation open to smear and boycott, which those he so devastatingly exposed hastened to set about.

Early in 1922, my father posted to Headquarters Southern Command, we moved to Salisbury, there inhabiting at different times two furnished houses: 16 The Close, just within St Anne's Gate; 35 The Close, on the green opposite the Cathedral. Even at that period much of Salisbury was already marred by unsightly building, though far less than today, a few of the streets then comparatively unspoilt. The Close remained – and remains – a precinct of immense beauty, a quiet dignity not easily rivalled. Unfortunately quiet dignity in architecture does not stave off adolescent gloom. The muggy climate, somniferous social ambience, my own inability to keep myself amused in conventional ways, made the city a powerful toxin to inflame that endemic distemper of growing up, during late holidays from school, and early Oxford vacations. In fact Salisbury represented – still recalls when I pass through its now traffic-infested streets – unfathomable depths of adolescent melancholy and boredom.

About the end of the time that I was at school *The Morning Post* ran a John Galsworthy Competition. I won it. I still possess the prize, a pocket set of Galsworthy's Collected Works (leather, 7s 6d each), volumes damaged by damp when our house in London was left un-occupied (and bombed) during the war, but *The Man of Property* still comparatively intact, inscribed: 'A. D. Powell, with the wonder and admiration of John Galsworthy'. One day in School Library I came across a magazine (I suppose *The Criterion*) which contained a long account of James Joyce's *Ulysses*. I was very interested by what was said, but this interest seemed quite separate in itself; causing, so to speak, no conversion or repentance as to middlebrow reading matter. Such forms of intellectual double-harness are perhaps characteristic of literary self-education. When *Antic Hay* came out almost the same week as I went up to Oxford, I was prostrated by its brilliance. Huxley's novels, even the early ones, seemed disappointing when reread in middle life, but now the originality of *Antic Hay* is apparent to me again; though the note goes flat when erudite frivolity is abandoned to teach a moral lesson. In those days I was quite unaware that from time to time a moral lesson was being taught by the author.

When I left Eton, at the end of the summer half, 1923, I was ready to go, though life had been pleasant enough in the House Library. I spent a day or two in Oxford for the Balliol Scholarship examination; in that way matriculating for the college. The *viva* on this occasion was my first contact with Kenneth Bell, subsequently my Balliol history tutor. 'You're the fellow who liked *The Beggar's Opera* so much,' he said; but I do not remember what question in the papers could have elicited this conclusion. At Eton, the July Examinations took place. From the results of these the marks of all Specialists were brought down to a percentage; everyone then arranged in order, no matter what their subject. I came 9th in the school, and 3rd oppidan, thereby winning an Oppidan Prize, regarded as a laurel of reasonable distinction.

An encounter that took place my last half should be recorded; perhaps as a mystic example of persons suitable for inclusion in novels instinctively offering potential novelists an opportunity for looking them over as appropriate material. A young woman known to my parents – possibly she had worked as a secretary in the War Office – was passing through Eton by car. As a friendly gesture, she called on me. She had a man with her, not himself an Old Etonian, but who behaved rather as if hoping to be taken for that. Why the girl and the man knew each other, I have no idea, but, years later, I was able to identify the girl's companion as Evelyn Waugh's model for Captain Grimes. I feel grateful to fate that I was thus – almost magically – privileged to meet Captain Grimes in the flesh.

My father, between spasms of grumbling about school bills, and occasional resistance to attitudes of mind inevitably acquired at Eton, had taken a fair amount of vicarious pleasure in my being there. When, rather tentatively, I first raised the possibility of proceeding to a university, he was less well disposed; remaining always suspicious of Oxford, and everything for which the academic principle might be supposed to stand. The relationship of father and son is never less than exacting, but there is no avoiding for either this particular climacteric brought on by the years; the metamorphosis of boy to man. I may myself have handled that critical period without special adroitness, but my father's exceptional dislike for any change or development in life, his own or anyone else's, did not lessen the strain of a traditionally delicate evolvement. He was never able to make up his mind whether success or failure in a son was the more inimical. As Balston remarked later: 'It's an entirely unphilosophic mind.'

Chiefly on Balston's recommendation, Balliol was singled out as the most fitting college; my father half-fascinated, half-repelled by its reputation for arrogant brilliance. The usual syndrome of Dreaming Spires, Lost Causes, Zuleika Dobson, Sinister Street, together with the general drift of most of my friends, made me prefer the idea of Oxford to Cambridge, but I did not feel strongly as to which college harboured me. Balliol's effortless superiority sounded as good as anything else.

The best thing about Balliol was a tradition of tolerance. Everyone did what he preferred. There was little or no pressure – as at some smaller colleges – as to playing games or other types of conformism. No one was expected to live the same sort of life as other members

of the College simply because they were members of the College; and
many Balliol men, even of the same year, never exchanged a word with
each other during their Oxford residence. At the same time there was
plenty of college-spirit for those who liked college-spirit. It was not
forced on those who did not.

My Oxford generation was the first of that decade to inhabit a university untinged by the ex-soldier and his ways. Persons who had been
'in the war' might seem a million to us, yet only the previous year there
had been undergraduates in residence liable to speak of hall as 'Mess',
and otherwise indulge in obsolete barely decent locutions derived from
military service. Such jargon was naturally deplored by the more
sophisticated ex-campaigners, but even these latter were inexpungibly
branded by war-service in the eyes of the oncoming waves of school-
boys. This 'age-gap' of the Twenties was a chasm to make all subsequent ones of its sort seem inconsiderable. Men and women grown
up before 1914 were not only older, they were altogether set apart;
and thus they remained throughout life. You never caught up with
them.

Evelyn Waugh (*A Little Learning*) speaks of three hundred a year
as an average undergraduate allowance for that period. In his own case,
he says, a scholarship, with various additional subventions from home
sources, made this sum up to about fifty pounds more. I was in much
the same case. I had a basic three hundred; my father (not without
all protest) showing himself, when it came to the point, open to putting
up fifty pounds more for foreign travel during the Long Vac. It would
probably be true to say that most Etonians at Oxford had four hundred;
a few, fifty or a hundred in addition to that. On the whole undergraduates who graded (in Oxford terms) as 'very rich' were not Etonian;
most Eton parents, however well off, holding strong views about discouraging extravagance in their sons; any extra money being provided
with a view to keeping a horse, rather than for lavish entertaining.

I found myself receiving (through whose offices I do not know) cards
for evenings at the house of the Slade Professor (Sir Michael Sadler),
at which some notability in the arts would from time to time speak.
I am surprised now by the comparative lack of interest I took in these
invitations. This indifference seems explained by a kind of intellectual
recession undergone while I was at Oxford. Perhaps something of the
kind is less uncommon than might be expected; the potentially bright
schoolboy, pressures of school relaxed, becoming a slightly dazed
undergraduate. Up to a point, I suppose, I continued to pursue interests
possessed at school, but they seem to have lost much of their former
force; a falling off of intellectual vitality that was characteristic, it now
seems to me, of my three years at the University.

I had at least the good sense to attend the Slade Lecture at which

Sickert spoke, though I remember only a little of what he said. Tall, grey-haired, crimson in the face, wearing a thick greenish loudly-checked suit, he chatted in a conversational voice, humorous and resonant, while he flourished a cigar. His personality filled the room. Half a century later, I learnt that Sickert (his second wife having died three years before), was still sunk in the deepest depression. No one could have guessed that. On the contrary, he appeared in the best of form, delivering his direct no-nonsense art criticism to an audience of not much more than twenty, most of whom, like myself, probably had little idea what good stuff they were listening to; what safeguards against swallowing whole the doctrines of Bloomsbury (of which I was equally uninformed), by then beginning to dominate the critical scene so far as painting was concerned.

When I came up to Balliol in October, 1923, A. L. Smith was Master of the College. He was well spoken of, but I never saw more of him than to attend, with a batch of other freshmen, a routine tea party at The Lodgings. Smith died the following year. He was succeeded as Master by an ambitious politician, A. D. Lindsay (later Lord Lindsay of Birker), with whom I also had little contact, beyond being taken by him for one term in Political Theory. I found him unsympathetic as a theorist and a man.

The tutor to conduct me through History Previous was C. G. Stone, known as 'Topes'. In principle regarded as a 'good man', Stone, then in his late thirties, was rather unusually deaf, with an illimitable stutter. To these two obstructions in communication between us he added inability to read my already regrettably illegible handwriting. An awareness of these barriers made him seem shy and gruff. In spite of intermittent difficulties in conveying the substance of my essays, he perfectly caught the opening sentence of the first, which began: 'The close of the Dark Ages fell on Christmas Day in the year 800, when Charlemagne was crowned in Rome as Emperor of the West.' Stone articulated a comment: 'Don't start your essays with that sort of metaphorical clearing of the throat.'

A week or two later I forgot some textbook required. Stone managed to get out: 'You must try and remember you are no longer a schoolboy.'

I found such admonitions galling at the time, but the former made me think about writing in a way I had never done before. Christmas Day in the Dark Ages had seemed, if not the happiest day in the epoch (as in the Workhouse), at least the most picturesque. I now saw in a flash the importance of structure. Stone's words did nothing but good. His particular brand of donnishness was in any case suitable foundation for a very different sort of tutor – one possibly best not encountered at first onset – Kenneth Bell, by whom I was taught for several terms after surmounting the first History School hurdle.

Kenneth Bell was one of the two outstanding Balliol dons of that era; the other being F. F. Urquhart, always known as 'Sligger' – not 'Sligger Urquhart', as now sometimes altogether incorrectly rendered, either Sligger or Urquhart – Dean of the College; responsible, with the administrative support of a Junior Dean, for undergraduate discipline. Urquhart and Bell (judged to be on not specially good terms with each other) were a contrast in every respect: Urquhart, then in his middle fifties, mild, monkish, whitehaired, withdrawn, elusive in manner: Bell (as a Balliol undergraduate Urquhart's pupil) still under forty, wartime Gunner major with an M C, militarily moustached, bluff in demeanour, apparently a hearty of hearties, but in fact full of unexpected powers of discrimination.

It is convenient to speak of Urquhart first. In earlier days as a don he had gained the reputation of operating an undergraduate salon. By the time I came up to Balliol anything to be so called had fallen into abeyance. Callers in the evening were not discouraged (lemonade always on offer), but Urquhart was usually alone. The term 'Sliggerite', for an habitué, was almost always attached to those of an earlier Oxford generation than my own. I was on good terms with Urquhart, who tutored me (not very effectively) for a term or two, but was never in the running for being a Sliggerite; feeling even unable to face the alleged rigours of the châlet in Switzerland, where he conducted annual reading-parties.

At least half-a-dozen Oxford dons possessed claims to run a salon; no doubt as many at Cambridge, because, when reviewing my book *Dance*, two Cambridge papers said that the don there called Sillery was obviously modelled on a wellknown Cambridge figure. Nevertheless, Sillery has time and again been 'identified' with Urquhart. Here seems an opportunity for stating that Sillery and Urquhart, apart from both being dons, were persons of altogether different sort. Perhaps it is tedious to labour the point. I do so only for the sake of truth. Urquhart has undoubtedly been portrayed in more than one novel about Oxford. Had I wished to do so, I could have offered my own projection of an unusual personality. Such was not my aim, and Urquhart, far from being (like Sillery), a talkative power-seeking Left Winger, was a devout Roman Catholic, hesitant in manner, conversationally inhibited, never pontificating about public affairs, nor addicted more than most dons to the habit of intrigue. Somebody once said with truth that a typical 'Sligger remark' was, after a long pause: 'Have you ever noticed how, the higher you get in mountainous country, the more the sheep begin to resemble goats?'

At noisy college festivals Urquhart was likely to slip away early to his rooms, while Bell remained to get tight. At one of these dinners (the year before I came up) a disaster had nearly taken place on this account. Urquhart had reappeared in the quad, probably because of the row that was being made, and Bell, in a burst of high spirits, threw some coal at him from an upper window. It was not immediately clear who was responsible for this bombardment, and, by the time Urquhart (more probably the Junior Dean) reached the place from which the fusillade had been launched, undergraduate friends (including Alf Duggan) had concealed Bell under the bed, or otherwise disposed of the body. Had they not done so there might have been serious consequences for Bell, possibly loss of his Balliol Fellowship – finally removed in quite other circumstances.

Drunken uproariousness was only one side of Bell, the avatar in which he was a beer-swilling devotee of the college boat. In another, he was the great promoter of Balliol's 'clever man', champion of any undergraduate he thought intelligent, especially one in difficulties of some sort with the authorities. Bell's support was not in the least limited to those of academic promise as such. The undergraduate in question might easily belong to a type Bell could be expected to reprobate. He approved of success, but he recognized that there were different sorts of success. He was prepared to stand up for ability concealed by an awkward manner, rackety behaviour, absurd clothing.

Bell's own pupils were expected to work hard. He was a most stimulating teacher, but it was best to go in the first of the three morning sessions, during each of which four undergraduates would in turn read aloud their essays. Like all who function on nervous energy, Bell, at the start, would give unsparingly of himself, pouring out acute comment; some of the fire dying down by the third hour of the morning. He had his own views on history, but liked to be amused and surprised by what his pupils wrote; especially, for example, in attacking high-minded muddleheadness, and the clichés of the Whig historians.

Bell paid attention not only to history, but to the manner in which an essay was written. 'But what a portentous length!' he would protest, at the end of a long screed by an over-diligent student. He was always anxious to show that history was about people, human beings, not a cluster of well arranged political and economic theories. Somebody (possibly myself) made some priggish judgment on the policies of the Holy Roman Empire. Bell commented: 'Yes, that may well be true – but we shall never know what Charles V felt like in the early morning.'

If I had been made to think of the structure of writing by Stone, Bell carried the lesson much further. The price his pupils paid (myself willingly enough) was that he taught history for itself, not as medium for acquiring a good degree in the Final Schools. The History syllabus, as laid down, was obviously impossible to cover with any thoroughness in three years. Bell took the line that it was better to know some of the conspectus well, rather than attempt superficial acquaintance with the whole. His methods (and their results) exemplify an eternal anti-thesis in education – and almost every other branch of existence – the inner good, as opposed to the immediate practical advantage.

Kenneth Bell's own career ended rather sadly. In the early years of the war his marriage broke up. In those days official academic attitudes towards the sex-life of dons were very different from what they were to become. The fact that Bell had left his wife for another woman (who died tragically only a few months later) was not countenanced by Lindsay, who, as Master of Balliol, was instrumental in having Bell's Fellowship removed from him. That was, of course, Bell's daily bread. A man like Bell was able to find other employments (he made a new career for himself, in due course becoming a parson), but Balliol had been his whole life. The College was in the end the loser. Kenneth Bell was in his way rather a great man.

Three or four days after arrival in Oxford, one evening after hall, I was sitting in my room wondering if it were too early to go to bed, when the door began to open very slowly and jerkily. A figure stood on the threshold, supporting itself by a hand on the door-knob, the body visibly trembling, the face of ghastly pallor. It was Alfred Duggan. He was all but speechless with drink. Words came at last, but only with great effort.

'Can you – lunch with me – Hypocrites – Friday?'

'I'd like to very much. Won't you come in?'

Duggan smiled kindly, but did not answer, or enter the room. Very slowly, very jerkily, the door closed again. The sound of much staggering and crashing came from the staircase. I was flattered by the visit, and the invitation. I had, of course, heard of The Hypocrites Club. There would be no great difficulty in discovering its whereabouts. I did not know Duggan at all well. We might have met a couple of times when he had driven over to Eton to see his brother. Once he had brought with him another Balliol Etonian of his year, John Heygate, and the four of us had gone down to Tap. There was a slight sense of Hubert Duggan being determined not to be high-hatted by his elder brother. Heygate barely spoke. In due course I was to know Heygate well, but – in the Balliol manner – I don't think we ever exchanged a word during our overlapping Oxford period. He was not of The Hypo-crites world.

The Hypocrites Club has often been described; two or three rooms over a bicycle-shop in an ancient half-timbered house at the end of St Aldate's, not far from where that long street approaches Folly Bridge, a vicinity looked on as somewhat outside the accepted boundaries of Oxford social life. The Club had been founded by a group of Trinity and Oriel men, relatively serious and philosophy-talking, so the legend ran, an orientation of which traces still remained at the stage of its evolution when I lunched there with Duggan. David Talbot Rice, and John 'the Widow' Lloyd, had been among its foundation members, and the former may have been responsible for bringing there Acton, Byron, and more frivolous elements. When I first set foot in the Club transmogrification had gone a long way, though still short of the metamorphosis, on the whole regrettable, into a fashionably snobbish undergraduate haunt; before final closure by the authorities, ostensibly for being outside the University licensing area, but in effect for rackety goings-on.

The Hypocrites was staffed by a married couple called Hunt, with an additional retainer, Whitman. Mrs Hunt did the cooking (simple but excellent), her husband and Whitman acting as waiters. Hunt was clean-shaven, relatively spruce: Whitman, moustached, squat, far from spick and span. Both Hunt and Whitman were inclined to drink a good deal, but, in their different ways, were the nearest I have ever come across to the ideal of the Jeevesian manservant, always willing, never out of temper, full of apt repartee and gnomic comment. Evelyn Waugh (intermittently a prominent Hypocrites member, though excluded at this period for having smashed up a good deal of the Club's furniture with the heavy stick he always carried) had been served with a drink one evening just before closing time.

'But, Whitman, I told you, when you asked, that I did *not* want another drink.'

'I thought you were joking, sir.'

I can't remember who else were guests at Duggan's luncheon-party, but, among other members of the Club present, were John Lloyd (called 'the Widow' possibly on account of a shaving preparation styled *The Widow Lloyd's Euxesis*), a great mainstay of The Hypocrites, and joint host, with Byron, of the fancy-dress party given there the following year; Graham Pollard, of revolutionary bearing and sentiments, already earning a living while an undergraduate by selling rare books; E. E. Evans-Pritchard, the anthropologist, grave, withdrawn, somewhat exotic in dress. Pollard lived over the main gate at Jesus, where he later asked me to tea to see his books. He said that, judging from the finger marks, he concluded *Love and Pain* to be his scout's favourite volume of Havelock Ellis, whose works he also possessed. With John Carter (a colleger I had known slightly at school, who had gone on to Cambridge) Pollard was to be the first to expose the Wise forgeries.

I recall some difficulty (soon mastered) in getting through a pint of the Club's dark beer, powerful for one still unaccustomed to alcohol. Duggan himself was inclined to drink a pint of burgundy out of a tankard at lunch. He may have done so that day. His head was not specially strong, and he was often tipsy, though an amusing companion when not overdoing his Byronic swashbuckling in such ways as playing poker for absurdly high stakes. Duggan used to hunt, and ride with the Drag, thereby making one of the few links (in my first year) between sporting spheres of Oxford life, and the very different crowd, its character not easy to define, that made up The Hypocrites' Club.

This was about the peak of the social division in the University (in a sense, the larger world too) crudely covered by the labels 'aesthete' and 'hearty'; both only very relative terms to distinguish certain antithetical attitudes of mind and body. A Ninetyish aestheticism of a musty sort was by no means defunct in Oxford of those days, but on the whole, with one or two exceptions (another subsequent anthropologist, Francis Turville-Petre, could scarcely be excluded from the category) aesthetes of a type unrevised since the turn of the century were not Hypocrites material. The Club was equally far from the soberly dressed, well behaved undergraduate intelligentsia (L. P. Hartley, David Cecil) of a year or two before.

With the exception of Duggan, I can remember no early intermingling of Hypocrites types with the Bullingdon (hunting, plus an admixture of golf) such as took place later, in the way that there was overlapping with the Union or OUDS. Another link with a different sort of Oxford was Romney Summers, recently down from Brasenose (where he had rowed), a pre-eminently 'hearty' college, where Summers retained several friends. Redfaced, beefy, with a lot of charm, and passion for social life, Summers had been unable to tear himself away from Oxford. Not enormously rich in the wider sense, he was very comfortably off for a young man, combining fast cars, bridge-playing, large parties at Commem, with Hypocrites life. He was one of the two or three in my first year who would give dinner-parties for, say, thirty guests (sometimes one would literally not know the host by more than name), a form of hospitality that – like a particular kind of party in London later – withered away completely after about a year.

In the main sitting-room of The Hypocrites stood an upright piano, which Byron (occasionally others, but predominantly Byron) would play, contorting his features into fearful grimaces, while he sang Victorian ballads in an ear-splitting alto.

> Rose a nurse of ninety years,
> Set his child upon her knee –
> (*f*) Like summer tempests came her tears –
> (*fff*) Like summer tempests came her tears –
> (*ppp*) 'Sweet my child, I live for thee.'

About three weeks after I had been in residence at Balliol, Alf Duggan arrived in my room, this time about ten o'clock in the morning. His manner was brusque. He said: 'I was in London last night, and omitted to take any precautions about my bed not having been slept in. The scout reported me. I was sent for by Sligger. I've just seen him. I told him I lay drunk on your floor all night. Will you confirm that, if Sligger asks you about it.' He went away without further words on the subject.

Duggan used to talk a good deal about his 'mistress' (a night-club hostess), whom he would visit in London from time to time. Absence from rooms in college at night was normally covered by arranging for a friend to untidy the bedclothes, and urinate in the chamber pot, the night before; thereby giving an impression that the owner had risen early, and (when the scout called him with a jug of hot water) was already up and abroad. Alternatively, it was possible to climb into college before dawn, though by that method Balliol was a college not particularly easy of access. In due course I was sent for by Urquhart, and questioned. I corroborated Duggan's story. Urquhart accepted it, but I felt I was not making the best of impressions as a freshman.

Among Balliol freshmen of my first year were Matthew Ponsonby, Arden Hilliard, Peter Quennell, and Pierse (then more usually 'Piers') Synnott. Ponsonby (who later inherited the peerage his father, the Labour politician, Arthur Ponsonby, was given about this time) was brother of Elizabeth Ponsonby, already something of a gossip-column heroine of what came later to be looked on as the *Vile Bodies* world of London. Ponsonby himself liked parties, but had none of his sister's taste for publicity, even if he could be rampageous at times, but was best known as a sympathetic friend, and great recipient of confidences. This made him an expert on the interior life of the College, but, immensely goodnatured, altogether without ambition, he liked the information entirely for its own sake.

Ponsonby was a friend of Arden Hilliard (son of Balliol's bursar), who had come up to Oxford from Winchester, with a Balliol Exhibition, and an unmanageable burden of good looks. Handsome, nice mannered, mild in demeanour, Hilliard, at first meeting, conveyed not the smallest suggestion of his capacity for falling into trouble. The variety of ways in which he got on the wrong side of the authorities during his period of residence (prematurely cut short) was both contrarious and phenomenal. He was one of the nicest of men, in certain moods content to live a quiet even humdrum existence; at other times behaving with a minimum of discretion, altogether disregarding the traditional recommendation that, if you can't be good, be careful.

Prudence was even less known to Hilliard than to Alf Duggan, though Hilliard was entirely without Duggan's taste for swagger. Nevertheless, one evening (on his way to The Hypocrites fancy-dress party) he passed through the main gate of Balliol dressed as a nun. After going down there were periods of farming before becoming a captain of infantry during the war; later an erratically charted course that had something of Jude the Obscure in reverse; erstwhile scholar who transformed himself into a rustic swain. A vignette that remains in my mind of this early Balliol period is of being woken up one night to find Hilliard and Ponsonby standing by my bedside. Without a word, one of them held out a brimming glass of sparkling burgundy. I drained it, equally in silence.

The attitude of the University authorities of those days towards the question of 'women' (they were indifferent to homosexuality) is shown by an incident involving Ponsonby and myself. We were returning to Balliol one night (dead sober), when in the High we met a waitress called Nelly, on her way home with another girl, who also worked at The George. Nelly, rather a famous Oxford figure, was known as much for her niceness and good nature in the restaurant, as for her prettiness. We talked to the girls for a minute or two, wished them goodnight, and returned to college. The following day Ponsonby and I were both sent for by the Proctors. 'You were seen talking to women at a quarter to twelve last night in the High.' A Proctorial spy had followed us, enquired our names at the Balliol gate, then shopped us. We were not fined, but given a stern warning.

Peter Quennell, arriving at Oxford with an already respectable reputation as poet, also on easy terms with celebrities like Gosse and the Sitwells, was somewhat alarming in his freshman sophistication. His pale yellow hair, attenuated features, abstracted demeanour, seemed all a young poet should be; an appearance that could mislead those who did not expect a businesslike attitude towards literature, and down-to-earth approach where the opposite sex was concerned; the second of those particularly rare in the Oxford circles here described.

Quennell's poetic exterior as an undergraduate led to an outstanding example of the birth of legend. During wartime military liaison duties it came my way to attend a dinner-party given for King Haakon of Norway and the Crown Prince Olaf. Prince Olaf (later King of Norway) had come up to Balliol my second year. I had not known him there, but was presented at this dinner as a fellow Balliol man. After dinner the Crown Prince talked of Balliol days. He said: 'And do you remember that fellow Quennell, who used to walk through the quad holding a lily in his hand?' I admitted that I had never had the good luck to witness such an occasion. The Crown Prince was plainly surprised. 'Yes, I assure you –' turning to those round about he demanded attention: '*The man walked through the quad holding a lily! Would you believe it?*' Quennell was rather justifiably indignant when I told him the story, because, far from walking Piccadilly (more literally Balliol quad) with a poppy or a lily, his fullblooded tastes had brought an abrupt end to an Oxford career.

Connolly had exchanged his school impetus for a strangle-hold on Urquhart. For him the Hypocrites was not even to be thought of. Even by Balliol standards he lived a life apart; one more resembling the 'correct' intellectual undergraduates of two or three years before, but without their smooth social gambits. One summer afternoon in my first year, he asked me to come on the river with him. On the way down to where a canoe was to be hired, he enquired: 'Do you like adventures?' Uncertain what exactly he meant (probably still rather awed by his school prestige) I gave a tempered reply in favour of adventure; one not to be taken as involving anything too wholesale. When we were afloat Connolly directed the boat up a side stream, where flowed some mild rapids evidently already known to him. The adventure consisted in paddling violently against the current, so that the stones were at last surmounted while travelling upstream.

The incident illustrates a side of Connolly not widely recognized; the fact that, although the first in any company to become bored, he retained keen pleasure in certain childish activities. This taste for canoeing against rapids is referred to in the *Letters* (together with one for cutting sticks, and throwing them as assegais); and, fifteen years later, staying with Connolly, and his first wife, Jean, in a small house they had rented in Sussex, he repeated (this time Violet the passenger) his performance of paddling a boat upstream against some minor hazard.

In my second year there came up to Balliol a future friend, of whom I never saw a great deal at Oxford, but often visited later, who, up to his death in 1969, would read the proofs of my books, never without making improvement. This was Wyndham Ketton-Cremer, who, like Quennell – in a manner more traditional, less sophisticated, though scarcely less assured – arrived with already some name as a poet. An odd mixture of shyness, humour, obstinacy, shrewd judgment, literary sensibility, love of country life, Ketton-Cremer was always well behaved. He never seemed to need the mildest form of saturnalia. To the end of his days an additional glass of sherry before dinner, one of port after, represented the height of his indulgence. At Balliol he did not always avoid rowdy companions. His friend John Bowle (historian and Marlborough crony of John Betjeman), with others, would sometimes become impatient at Ketton-Cremer's staidness. One longed for him to get drunk, swear, fall down, smash a window, even if he remained (as he always did) uncommitted as to sex. No such outbreak ever took place. Probably he knew what was best for himself.

In his early twenties Ketton-Cremer inherited Felbrigg (a mansion now in the National Trust) near Cromer in Norfolk. The house had come down to him in a curious manner. Original seat of the Wyndham family in the middle 1400s, the estate passed in the 18th century into the hands of owners who took the name of Wyndham, without Wyndham blood. These pseudo-Wyndhams going downhill, the house, with all its contents, was sold in the 19th century to a Norwich merchant called Ketton. Ketton's son died without issue, but his daughter had married a Mr Cremer (Wyndham Ketton-Cremer's grandfather), who was himself half a genuine Wyndham. Accordingly, house, portraits, furniture, in the end passed back to one of Wyndham blood in the female line. (The name was sometimes spelt Windham.)

Here he lived as squire, producing works – notably *Horace Walpole* and *Thomas Gray* – which, in unshowy brilliance, put him in the top class of historical biographers. His recommendations when reading my own proofs sometimes indicated that, anyway inwardly, he was not as innocent as some might suppose.

To round off these Balliol fragments: Alfred Duggan, although he escaped retribution on the occasion when he had supposedly passed out on my floor, was sent down a term or two later for spending a night out of college. At this period Duggan's stepfather, Lord Curzon, was Chancellor of Oxford University, a circumstance that may have played a part in the sentence being reduced from total dismissal to mere rustication. Possibly Smith was less inflexible in such matters than Lindsay. By the time Alf Duggan returned to Balliol, Hubert Duggan had come up to Christ Church, and (at his own wish) gone down; the two brothers never being at Oxford simultaneously.

On his reappearance in Oxford, Alf Duggan was at first in a somewhat chastened mood, working hard, drinking comparatively little, not gambling at all, apparently a changed man. Then, for some minor offence like not attending enough roll-calls, he was 'gated' during a week when some party was taking place which he particularly wished to attend. To do this it was necessary to leave Balliol by some route other than the main gate; later return by climbing in. In consequence, Duggan asked me to lower him from his first-floor window, which looked out on to St Giles. There was some difficulty in finding suitable tackle for this operation, eventually effected by use of a long woollen Old Etonian scarf. Just as Duggan was suspended from the window, the scarf split in two, causing him to land with a heavy bump on the pavement. He seemed none the worse, threw back the other half of the scarf (which, repaired, survived to keep my younger son, John, warm during an upstate New York winter at Cornell), and proceeded on his way. Unfortunately Duggan drank too much at the party to make feasible climbing back into college. This time his exit from Oxford was final.

Alfred Duggan's subsequent story was an unexpected one. For twenty years (during which we met briefly not more than a couple of times) he existed as a spectacular drunk. All sorts of attempts were made to cure him. None had the smallest effect. During the war he pulled himself together sufficiently to serve in the army for a year or two, taking part in the Norwegian campaign. Then, after the war, in his late forties, he made a tremendous effort of will, not only giving up drink, but opening for himself an entirely new career. In 1950, when I was editing the novel-review pages of *The Times Literary Supplement*, a publisher asked that a first novel by an unknown writer should not be overlooked on the grounds of belonging to an obsolescent genre of literature. The author was called 'Alfred Duggan'. I remarked how strange that I should have known someone of that name; the last man on earth to attempt an historical novel. The book was clearly well done, and went out for review. Only appreciably later did I learn that the un-believable – as so often – had taken place. Alf Duggan had begun a new career.

On my first or second Sunday in Oxford, I had been taken to a morning gathering, regularly given at his rooms in Beaumont Street, of an odd fish called George Kolkhorst. Kolkhorst (who for some reason encouraged his friends to address him as 'Gu'g') held an unexalted position in donnish hierarchy as Lecturer in Spanish. He was fairly well off; an income believed to be derived (though grave doubts have been cast on this legend) from shares in the Lisbon tramways. At these Sunday morning parties, Kolkhorst, who spoke in a reedy voice, always articulating with great care, used to wear a silk dressing-gown, and eyeglass hanging from his neck by a broad black ribbon. Sherry or madeira was dispensed in small glasses. In a little secret book Kolkhorst would record from time to time his own epigrams; hatched with herculean effort.

Just as The Hypocrites had been taken over by Acton, Byron, and their friends, Kolkhorst's Sunday mornings were similarly invaded; though I think that was a Byron enthusiasm which Acton did not share. Even within the host's own Oxford terms of reference some of the more faithful Kolkhorst frequenters were of an extraordinary dimness. John Betjeman (who came up my third year, and I met at Oxford only once) has impishly stated that Kolkhorst and Bowra were in rivalry. This pronouncement is not to be taken too seriously, Bowra moving in a donnish empyrean, compared with the seedy salon of Beaumont Street.

Nevertheless, each would speak disparagingly of the other: Bowra always referring to Kolkhorst as 'Kunthorse'; Kolkhorst, to 'that fly in the ointment on the seats of the mighty', or the 'Twelfth Man of the Upper Ten'.

Among other people met for the first time at this *après midi de Kolkhorst* was Evelyn Waugh, then (having come up in a by-term) technically in his third year, and a famous Oxford figure. I was introduced by Clonmore, who said: 'I'm glad to see you put on a suit for Sunday, Evelyn.' The suit in question was dark blue double-breasted, the coat open. Small, rather pink in the face, his light brown wavy hair not far from red, Waugh nodded severely, at the same time giving utterance to a curious little highpitched affirmative sound, a mannerism that always remained with him. He showed no disposition to chat. His air then – and when we met in Oxford later – was of a man disillusioned with human conduct, a man without ambition, living a life apart from the world. This was in any case what one was inclined to feel in one's third year, but Waugh (as described in *A Little Learning*) had consciously withdrawn from earlier University activities of a popular sort, undergraduate journalism, the Union, the OUDS.

I do not remember where I next came across Waugh (possibly with Quennell, with whom he had pre-Oxford acquaintance), but that was quite soon. We never knew each other at all well as undergraduates, though always on good terms. I was invited at least once, if not more, to an 'offal' luncheon at Hertford, where about half-a-dozen of Waugh's cronies, mostly from his own college, would eat 'commons' in his rooms. These lunches were highly enjoyable, without any of the self consciousness apt to attend more pretentious undergraduate luncheon-parties. Waugh himself seemed to enjoy them. His moods were always unpredictable. He could be disagreeable to persons he took against, weaving grotesque fantasies about them, but he was the most generous and compelling of hosts; though innate melancholy was never far away.

At this date Waugh did not at all identify himself with Oxford's rank and fashion as conventionally understood; in fact (as the opening pages of *Decline and Fall* indicate) he was, if anything, hostile to the smart ethos of the Bullingdon or anything resembling that. His own earlier celebrity had also been at a level on the whole inimical to the nihilistic side of Hypocrites life and culture, which was not well disposed to what were regarded as more commonplace undergraduate activities. Waugh was a contributor to The Cherwell, doing the magazine's illustrated headings. Some of my own drawings appeared in that magazine, as well as a few reviews.

It was still relatively an Age of Innocence for most of those concerned with this aspect of the Oxford scene, one greatly to alter in the next two years; become less rackety, more political, more snobbish. So far as *Brideshead* presents a naturalistic picture of the University of that epoch (some contemporaries, myself not among them, think it does), the novel is closer to the times when Waugh used to come up to see old Oxford friends (of which he has left a pungent account in the Diaries) during his purgatorial interlude of schoolmastering.

When not suffering from melancholy, Waugh had extraordinary powers of improvising – and carrying through – antics on so extensive a scale that a great professional comedian seems to have been lost in him. In those days he had the gift, by no means universal, of being intensely funny when drunk. The sessions he devoted to ragging ('mocking', to use a Waughism; another favourite Waugh term, 'zany') were likely to take certain routine forms, for example, to sing under Urquhart's sitting-room that looked out on St Giles, – to the tune of *Here we go gathering nuts in May* – the (certainly unjust) jingle: 'The Dean of Balliol lies with men'.

Hubert Duggan came up to Christ Church in the summer term of 1923; and immediately took a dislike to Oxford. No aspect of under-graduate life, drunk or sober, appealed to him. Unlike Alf, variously prepared to hunt, play poker, drink at The Hypocrites, impress his tutor with an essay, Hubert – who spoke highly of girls in Argentina – had no taste for any of those things. He went down at the end of the term; later joining The Life Guards. While he was still at Oxford we used to see a good deal of each other, but, after going down, he disappeared, naturally enough, into a different world from my own, which swallowed him up, producing perhaps no great happiness.

While Hubert Duggan was still at Oxford, we were both involved in an absurd, and not very creditable, incident that began by an Eton friend of Duggan's driving over from Sandhurst with another cadet. We may all have met at Reading, as halfway house, and lunched in the neighbourhood. As well as the two RMC cadets, Duggan and my-self, the party included Byron, with another Oxonian, identity now for-gotten. The penultimate stage of the excursion was dinner in or near Camberley, to which we finally returned with the Sandhurst couple. No doubt a fair amount was drunk. After dinner it was decided that the visiting party should take a look at the Royal Military College. This venture was a hazardous one, Sandhurst regulations (in precise contra-distinction to Oxford's) being comparatively liberal about 'women', but rigorously severe as to 'drink'.

The RMC consisted of two buildings, the Old and the New, to some extent separate from each other in administration, so that cadets who saw us assumed that we were also cadets from the other building. A dance was in progress – a weekly affair – and couples were moving in and out from the ballroom to the grounds. Byron, who never did things by halves, threw himself into this adventure with his usual enterprise. He had somehow become possessed of a roll of lavatory paper, and, stationing himself at the door of the ballroom, handed a few sheets to every couple as they left the room. I saw this happening momentarily, but Duggan and I, both relatively sober, were in some manner occupied elsewhere; perhaps saying goodbye to the Etonian friend, who, foreseeing trouble, had decided to lock himself in his quarters. The other cadet had disappeared. I do not know what arrangements had been made for a rendezvous to return to Oxford – perhaps the car had been hidden – but, when Byron appeared there, it turned out that he had – not without all reason – been thrown in the Sandhurst lake. On the homeward journey, still dripping torrentially, his teeth chattering because it had turned rather cold, Byron, in his exacerbated voice, though sometimes unable to speak with laughter at the thought of all that had happened, described how he had been put on 'a sort of gun-carriage', trundled down to the lake, then quite gently propelled into the water. He suffered no after-effects from this immersion. The other cadet, less prudent than Duggan's friend, or less lucky, allowed himself to be seen in a supposedly intoxicated condition, for which he was court-martialled and sacked.

Quite a long time after this happened, I was told that two versions of the incident had taken shape in Sandhurst legend: one, that a raiding party of several hundred Oxford undergraduates had come over, and, after a pitched battle lasting several hours, been repulsed; the other, that the whole story was absolutely imaginary, an invention that had somehow grown up over the years, a neurotic fantasy, perhaps a solar myth.

A final vignette of my first year: I went round to Hubert Duggan one morning, probably between nine and ten o'clock. On entering his sitting-room, I saw the bedroom door was open. A middle-aged man, wearing a grey homburg, was standing by the bed talking to Duggan, who had not yet risen. I thought possibly a tradesman had come to deliver some goods, measure the window for curtains, possibly press that a bill should be paid. A don, wearing a hat, would be unlikely to be holding a conversation with an undergraduate in bed at that hour. As the two continued to talk, I decided to return later in the morning. By the time I came back Duggan was up and dressed.

'I overslept this morning,' he said. 'When I woke up, who should be standing by my bedside but the Chancellor.'

The man in the grey hat had been Curzon.

My first Long Vacation I planned as a Grand Tour of Europe. That autumn, 1924, my father was sent to Finland as staff-officer to the major-general heading a British Military Mission requested in an advisory role by the Finnish Government. Accordingly, I spent two Oxford vacs at Helsingfors (the Swedish, rather than Finnish name,

Helsinki, then in general English use); thereby experiencing a new entirely unfamiliar mode of life that was certainly a contrast with Salisbury or Camberley.

Venusberg recalls some of these Finnish interludes, though much of the novel's background, especially the political circumstances, are altogether imaginary, with no bearing on what was happening in Finland at the time; nor, for that matter, in the neighbouring Baltic States, not yet overrun by the USSR. The town described in *Venusberg* is a mixture of Helsinki and Reval (as Tallin was still apt to be called), the Estonian capital across the Gulf of Finland, where I spent a weekend. The architectural admixture of this ancient Hansa city, with the modernity of Helsinki, apparently produced an approximation to Riga, capital of Latvia, which I did not visit.

Finland, ruled for six hundred years by Sweden, possessing a Swedish–Finn 'ascendancy' class not without all parallel to the Anglo–Irish, was absorbed by Russia after the Napoleonic wars. In theory Finland was to remain a semi-independent grand duchy, with its own political institutions, but throughout the 19th century an increasing policy of Russification resulted in much unrest there. In 1919 Finland became independent, following civil war in which the Swedish–Finn, General Mannerheim, defeated the Bolsheviks. After independence, a strong nationalist movement curtailed Swedish–Finn influences in all branches of the country's life, in favour of those exclusively Finnish; a process under way when we were there, though not yet run its full course.

Most Finns detested the Russians, Tsarist or Soviet, but their social life, to a considerable extent Scandinavian, had inevitably been influenced too by Russian domination. One entered a social world, familiar in Russian novels, of which there was no precise English equivalent: diplomatic; official; military; professorial; everyone knowing everyone else; no one at all rich; everybody inhabiting flats. Dinnerparties took place at the mid-Victorian hour of five-thirty in the afternoon – sometimes advanced to six-thirty as concession to foreigners' taste for dinner at a late hour – and, if the occasion did not merit a white tie, the older generation of men would wear (rather than the modern dinner-jacket) a black tie and black waistcoat with a tailcoat. The considerable colony of White Russian refugees augmented the sense of living in a 19th century Russian novel or Scandinavian play.

Finland then had a Prohibition law, only thin beer allowed, though something stronger was almost always available at parties. The triennial ball given by the nobility – that is to say the Swedish–Finn gentry, a class living very modestly – took place on one of my visits. After the President had arrived, a fanfare of trumpets announced the entry of Marshal Baron Gustav Mannerheim (to whom I was presented in in the course of the evening), whose personality dominated the room.

At the invitation of the Military Mission's interpreter, Captain Hameen-Antilla, I spent a weekend at Viborg (Viipuri, now annexed by the USSR), an old border fortress with a castle. Hameen-Antilla's regiment, the Karelian Guard, was stationed there, and (to celebrate some national event) a big party was taking place. We dined in Mess at five or five-thirty, prelude to one of the longest jollifications I have ever attended. First was a theatrical entertainment at the townhall; then dancing until midnight in another part of the same building; after which a second show took place in the theatre. When the later performance was over, dancing continued until dawn. We walked back at six through the streets of Viborg after an enjoyable party that had taken up just about twelve hours.

These Finnish trips brought vividly alive the societies described, on the one hand, by Strindberg and Ibsen; on the other, by Dostoevski and Chekhov.

When the Mission's tour of duty was at an end, we travelled back over Sweden, Norway, and Denmark, to Hamburg, where the streets were littered with the torn posters and scattered pamphlets of a recent election. Hindenburg had just become German President.

Romney Summers was always planning elaborate journeys and with another friend and myself he drove his car to Vienna the summer of 1925. Towards the end of that same year, a few weeks before my twentieth birthday, my father took some leave in Paris. I accompanied my parents there. Marcus Cheke, an eccentric Oxford friend at Trinity cramming French for the Foreign Office examination, was living in Paris with a French family. Failing to become a regular diplomat, Cheke settled down as an honorary attaché and was absorbed into the regular Foreign Service during the war. He rose to be Deputy Marshal of the Diplomatic Corps; then Minister to the Holy See.

In Paris, Cheke and I used sometimes to go out together. One afternoon he took me to a place he knew in the Avenue des Champs-Elysées, combination of tea-shop and dance-hall, where you could take tea (or a drink), and foxtrot all the afternoon. Everyone was dancing-mad at that epoch, the *thé-dansant* all the rage. We had no one to dance with – the place (as also Cheke) was of the utmost respectability – but the scene was enjoyable to watch from a table. Amongst a predominantly French clientèle, a tall grey haired man was clearly wearing a London-cut suit. This middle-aged rather elegant Englishman was dancing with a small decidedly pretty girl, obviously French. Whenever the couple passed our table the girl cast unmistakable *œillades* in my direction. I felt elated by this notice – my then inexperience with the opposite sex was beyond belief – and I could not think why anything of the sort should be happening.

Finally it was time to go. Cheke retiring to the *Messieurs*, I was left standing in the large foyer, or anteroom, to the dance-floor. Suddenly I noticed the girl of the *œillades* also standing by herself on the other side of the room; her partner no doubt absent for the same reason as Cheke. With an enterprise I should almost certainly have lacked a few years later – what Surtees calls, in another connexion, 'the daring pleasure of youth undaunted by a previous fall' – I went quickly across the hall, and, in halting French asked if we could meet. The girl smiled, and said: 'Ici, demain.' We parted before Cheke or the grey haired Englishman returned.

That night, dining with my parents at the hotel, I could hardly believe what I had done; though the incident was confirmed in my dreams. The following day I said that I was again going out with Cheke, with whom I should also be dining. In the afternoon, overwhelmed with apprehension, I turned up at the *thé-dansant* place at five o'clock, or whatever the appointed hour. A minute or two later the girl arrived. She was undoubtedly pretty. We found a table. The girl said at once that she was called Lulu, and worked at Zelli's; well-known *boîte de nuit* of that era. I grasped for the first time that I had picked up a tart. What on earth else I supposed could possibly have brought about the situation in which I found myself is hard to imagine, but, at the time, such was not what I had thought or intended.

We had something to drink – Lulu a grenadine, myself a *fine* – and danced a bit. She told me she was twenty-six. Certainly she looked no more. I felt far from sure of myself, and ordered another *fine*; which Lulu rightly deplored. Obviously we could not stay at the dance place for ever, though I was not altogether anxious to move on to the next stage of the adventure. Finally a taxi was summoned, and Lulu gave the address of a *maison-de-rendezvous* on the slopes of Montmartre. By this time the unwontedness of the occasion, the two *fines*, most of all the unhappy gift of seeing oneself in some sort of perspective, had removed almost all the right feelings of crude sensuality. The preparatory traditions of the bedroom did not help. The best to be said was that total fiasco was evaded.

Afterwards we dined in a small crowded restaurant known to Lulu, and not far away. This dinner was really the most enjoyable aspect of the whole episode. Lulu, a great talker, made jokes about a couple at a neighbouring table: the man, not a Frenchman, with a beard ('certainement bolchevik'), and his vis-à-vis, a lady with a straw-coloured bob ('une femme troublante'). After dinner we kissed goodbye: Lulu making for Zelli's; myself for my parents' hotel. I felt considerable nervous exhaustion, though in principle better able to face the world.

In the summer term of my first year at Balliol, Synnot brought Maurice Bowra, then Dean of Wadham, to my rooms in college. I had, of course, already heard of this famous young don, but without gaining much idea of what he was like, nor why he was famous. Noticeably small, this lack of stature emphasized by a massive head and tiny feet, Bowra – especially in later life – looked a little like those toys which cannot be pushed over because heavily weighted at the base; or perhaps Humpty-Dumpty, whose autocratic diction, and quickfire interrogations, were also paralleled. As against that, the short ringing laughs likely to accompany Bowra's comments were not at all characteristic of Humpty-Dumpty's rather sour resentment, though their tenor could be equally ominous.

Bowra possessed a considerable presence. As a don, he habitually wore a hat and suit; the last, during festive seasons like Commem, sometimes varied by flannel trousers, light grey, though never outrageously 'Oxford' in cut. My memory of the suits is of different shades of brown, but some say they tended, anyway later on, to be grey; whichever colour, they were very neat, always seeming a trifle tight over the outline of a figure essentially solid rather than plump.

This exploratory call went off pretty well. Conversation turning to the poet Byron (rather a favourite topic of Bowra's), he remarked that, in his hearing at the Gilbert Murrays' recently, a visiting notability had asked: 'Are you interested in incest, Professor Murray?', to which the Regius Professor of Greek had rather brusquely answered: 'Only in a very general sort of way.'

After the Balliol meeting I was to some extent included in the Bowra *monde* – or rather one of them, for there were not a few – a world which partook of various others in Oxford, avoiding the extremes of either 'hearty' or 'aesthete', although in itself a little apart from any of the worlds of which it might be said to partake. Immensely generous, Bowra entertained a good deal at Wadham; in my own experience, always undergraduates. I can never recall meeting a don in his rooms. No doubt that was simply a matter of segregation. The dinner parties were of six or eight, good college food, lots to drink, almost invariably champagne, much laughter and gossip, always a slight sense of danger. This faint awareness of apprehension was by no means imaginary, because the host could easily take offence (usually without visible sign, except to an expert) at an indiscreet word striking a wrong note – anyway one personally unpleasing – in dialogues which were, nevertheless, deliberately aimed at indiscretion. Bowra's reaction was likely to be announced a day or two later.

'What so-and-so said the other night has just come back as Bad Blood.'

The rooms themselves were simply furnished, with few pictures; what pictures, I cannot remember. Later, at the Warden's House, there was a drawing of Bowra himself by Henry Lamb, which almost certainly dated from a visit to Pakenham in the early Thirties, when he and the Lambs (Henry and Pansy) had been staying with the Longfords at the same time. The larger surfaces of wall to be regulated in the Warden's House underlined this taste for austere interior decoration; a characteristic worth mention as reflecting Bowra's energetic practical nature, concerned with action, rather than amelioration of his own surroundings; an aspect of himself in contrast with his other – if you like 'poetic' – side, and one he would perhaps have preferred more evenly balanced.

The impact on me, as an undergraduate, of Bowra's personality and wit is one not easy to define, so various were its workings. If the repeated minor shocks of this volcano took many forms, their earliest, most essential, was a sense of release. Here was a don – someone by his very calling (in those days) suspect as representative of authority and discipline, an official promoter of didacticism – who, so far from attempting to expound tedious moral values of an old fashioned kind, openly praised the worship of Pleasure.

Of course everybody who had got as far as the Nineties at school was familiar with 'older people' (in my own case, Millard), who represented, even recommended, a romantic paganism, but Bowra went much further than that. He was totally free from anything approaching Oxford 'aestheticism' of the Kolkhorstian order. Everything about him was up-to-date. The Bowra innovation was not only to proclaim the paramount claims of eating, drinking, sex (women at that early stage somewhat derided, homosexuality and autoerotism approved), but to accept, as absolutely natural, open snobbishness, success worship, personal vendettas, unprovoked malice, disloyalty to friends, reading other people's letters (if not lying about, to be sought in unlocked drawers) – the whole bag of tricks of what most people think, feel, and often act on, yet are ashamed of admitting that they do, feel, and think.

In the field of personal hates – Bowra made no bones about these – was his suggestion of the Bête Noire Club. Subscribing members of the Club were each allowed one name to put on its list, to be circulated to all other members, who, irrespective of whether or not they personally had anything against the individual concerned, would secretly persecute him on every possible occasion. Not only was the Bowra gospel sustained with excellent jokes, it was seasoned with a sound commonsense and down-to-earthness, distinguishing it not only from pretentious high-thinking, but also from brutal pursuit of self-interest divorced from all good manners. 'You don't get the best value out of your selfishness, if you're selfish all the time.'

Perhaps some analogy might be drawn between first coming in contact with Bowra, and an initiatory dip into the works of Nietzsche; although, so far as I know, Nietzsche's altar was not one where Bowra burned much, if any, incense. No modern philosopher, alone the Ancient Greeks, supplied all he loved and stood for. That, at least, was the impression he chose to give.

The Bowra delivery, loud, stylized, ironic, usually followed by those deep abrupt bursts of laughter, was superlatively effective in attack. I have heard it suggested that another alumnus of Bowra's school (Cheltenham), one a few years older than himself, was reputed to possess a somewhat similarly detonative form of speech – thereby suggesting a common Cheltonian source, probably a master there – but no details were available, and this rumour has never, so far as I know, been authenticated. It is rather the sort of thing people invent about a much talked-of personality like Bowra. Even if a foundation had already been laid, Bowra himself had undoubtedly perfected the mechanism, formidable, succinct, earsplitting, in a manner that could only be regarded as his own. Its echoes are still to be heard (1983) in the tones of disciples, who, in an unfledged state, came heavily under Bowra's influence.

One felt immediately, on meeting him for the first time, that Bowra was a man quite different from any met before. This awareness was certainly true of myself, also I think of most other undergraduates, whether they liked him or not. Some very definitely did not. He was prepared – for an acutely sensitive man, as he himself always pro-claimed, far too prepared – to make enemies. To any question about drawbacks in his own nature from which he had suffered, he had an invariable reply: 'A skin too few – yet one continues to go out of one's way to court hatred.'

I am, of course, speaking of the young Bowra. As in the Beer-bohm cartoons of Old and Young Selves, there was modification – though not all that modification – with increased age and fame. No doubt sides had been always hidden away from what was revealed to undergraduates, who were simply admitted to an astonishing vision of forbidden things accepted as a matter of course; and with appropriate laughter. Kenneth Bell used to say: 'The wall round the Senior Common Room is a low one, but there is a wall'; a remark not only metaphorically but literally true of Balliol. Bowra, most of the time, ignored this barrier altogether. I remember the unexpectedness of a sudden reminder of his own professional status, sense of what was academically correct, when, after a noisy dinner party at Wadham, someone (not myself) wandering round Bowra's sitting-room, suddenly asked: 'Why, Maurice, what are these?'

Bowra jumped up as if dynamited.

'Put those down at once. They're Schools papers. No indeed . . .'

A moment later he was locking away in a drawer the candidates' answers, laughing that such an outrageous thing had happened, but for a second he had been angry. The astonishment I felt at the time in this (very proper) call to order shows how skilfully Bowra normally handled his parties of young men. One used 'Maurice' as a form of address, but a note from him (usually an invitation) would always be signed 'CMB'.

Even in those early days it was from time to time apparent that Bowra himself was not immune from falling victim to Bowra doctrine, a fact that he – anyway in later life – was far too intelligent not to recognize, and ironically to acknowledge. The showmanship, usually brilliant, was never in the least fraudulent, but only the more naïve of the spectators could fail to grasp that a proportion of it was purely defensive. There were less well fortified Bowra positions to be considered with the well fortified ones. The former sometimes proved vulnerable, not so much to deliberate assault, as to undesigned incursions on the part of disciples speaking too frankly; indeed speaking in the manner Bowra had taught them. They would, for instance, report back painful things other people had said about Bowra himself, which, very naturally, he did not always appreciate. Nevertheless, in spite of such occasional boomeranging, he would stick to his guns, and usually come out on top, or not far from that.

Bowra, less than eight years older than myself, must have been just twenty-six when I first knew him. The fact now seems altogether incredible. Certainly, as indicated, he navigated with perfect ease the waters dividing undergraduate and don. Beyond that stream was a flood not to be crossed; an intangible sense of experience, which – then and for ever – set those who had been 'in the war' apart. Belonging to the strange fascinating brood of survivors, Bowra had come up to New College not only older than the average pre-war or post-war freshman (and far more intelligent), but, with others of his species, already on familiar terms with sex and death. He often spoke of the former; of the latter, very rarely.

So far as sex was concerned, when I first knew him, Bowra always talked as if homosexuality was the natural condition of an intelligent man. I think it extremely unlikely that, as a don, he ever had physical relations with an undergraduate, but he would gossip much of such goings-on, and tease friends like Yorke and me for being 'heterosexual'. His stories about women were rarely obliging, but his own tastes began to run less consistently very soon after this period. He was certainly attracted by women in the course of his life, and actually engaged to be married more than once.

The war was another matter. When he spoke of army experiences it was always with mimicry and laughter. ('Got a boil on your cock, old boy, then crash along to the MO, who'll soon put you right with a Number 9'; or his own battery commander's commendation of *Artillery Training*: 'A book written by far cleverer men than me or you.') All the same, I am sure that the comparatively short (though not unadventurous) time Bowra spent in the army played a profound part in his thoughts. I believe it possible that even at those Wadham dinner parties, when the uproar was at its height, not least on the part of the host, the days and friends of the war were never far away; a shadow falling like Cynara's.

There existed a Bowra system of social terminology which the neophyte had to pick up, and adhere to. That was not at all difficult on account of its convenient terseness, and manner in which it had been designed to cover most human types to be found at Oxford, and elsewhere. Indeed, its total adoption was hard to resist; one of the forms of power Bowra exercised. In this special phraseology, 'presentable' was not merely an important label, but *sine qua non* for being accepted into the Bowra system of things. There existed certainly Bowra acquaintances – kept well in the background – who never quite made the grade, yet were (Bowra being kindhearted as well as ruthless) still allowed some access to the sanctuary; but the status these occupied, even if low, never went so far as the very damaging absolute antithesis, 'unpresentable'. Those who had 'unpresentable' pinned on them were likely to be remorsely barred.

'Able' (or 'able, I'm afraid') probably did not signify personal approval, but was at worst a fairly high commendation. 'Upright', also not lightly accorded, might be held in its way equally complimentary (if you cared about oldfashioned honourable dealings), but was likely to carry overtones a shade satirical, with also no guarantee of friendliness. 'Nice stupid man', hardly flattering to the object of its designation, was at the same time well disposed, and accorded relatively sparingly. 'Shit of hell', a status in the severest degree derogatory, was in practice inclined to imply, as well as hearty dislike, an element of uneasy suspicion, sometimes amounting to acknowledged fear.

Bowra made great play with these categories, which were an established part of his verbal barrage. There were other important phrases, such as 'make bad blood' (referred to earlier), and 'cause pain'. 'Bad blood' might be used in two different senses. Bowra would remark: 'I made splendid bad blood between so-and-so and so-and-so over such-and-such a matter the other night'; laughing at the thought of what he had brought about. He would also, as has been said, speak despondently of 'bad blood' made in relation to himself. This latter might be deliberate vilification, or a casual phrase later conceived as having snide bearing on himself. 'Cause pain' was likely to refer not to specific attacks of his own, or other people, but the success or good luck of individuals, which brought pangs of envy or jealousy on hearing the news. 'Cause pain' may have had its origins in a favourite saying of the hero of R. L. Stevenson's *The Wrong Box*, also much quoted (and acted upon) by an Eton master, E. V. Slater: 'Anything to cause a little pain.'

These Bowra approaches to life, jocular yet practical, provoking both laughter and trepidation, are hard to preserve on paper. That is true of his – and all other – wit. Bowra's wit could be of the carefully perfected order (none the worse for that), setpieces produced with a flourish for social occasions, many examples of which remain on record; good talkers being apt to be remembered chiefly for their comparatively elaborate *mots*. Excellent as those could be, Bowra's throwaway lines, and comebacks, often surpassed them; thereby marking him out (which cannot be said of all good talkers) as a wit who neither required previous preparation for what he said, nor saved up all the best stuff for smart company. The ephemeral nature of such good remarks prevents them from passing into history, since they ornament conversations too trivial to remember or reconstruct: for example, someone (perhaps myself) commented on a story just told: 'On earth the broken wind ...', to which Bowra added without a pause '... in the heaven, a perfect sound.' On another occasion a recent graduate spoke of the uncertainty of some job put forward by the Oxford Appointments Committee's secretary, named Truslove; Bowra replying at once: 'How shall I my Truslove know?'

The Bowra world was one where there must be no uncertainty. A clearcut decision had to be made about everything and everybody – good, bad – desirable, undesirable – nice man, shit of hell. This method naturally included intellectual judgments, and taste in works of art. In one sense, nothing is more expedient in approaching such matters than lucid uncompromising thought, well expressed; in another, the arts inhabit an area in some degree amorphous as their means of creation; in short, a good deal of latitude required for experiment. In the Bowra world there was little or no concession to uncertainty – latterly that was perhaps less true – and, when I first knew Bowra, he always seemed to show a slight sense of uneasiness at activities in art and letters of a too independent sort. That was, of course, within the sphere of Bowra being, in principle, always well disposed to what was *avant-garde*.

With all his intelligence and spoken wit, Bowra himself remained throughout his life curiously unhandy at writing. He was a capable, if rather academic and uninspired, literary critic. His comic poems were comic, no more. They possess no unique quality. Any field in which he did not excel was a distress to him, the literary one most of all; one of the reasons why, for young men who wanted to develop along lines of their own, it was better to escape early from Bowra's imposed judgments. There was a touch of something inhibiting. It was preferable to know Bowra for a time, then get away; returning in due course to appreciate the many things he had to offer.

Henry Yorke came up to Magdalen in my second year. He did not find university life sympathetic, though he disliked it less than had Hubert Duggan. I underrated his neurotic pressures. Yorke has written, for example, that when (in the manner of all sports secretaries) a visit was paid to ask if he wanted to play rugger, he replied that he could not do so, because he suffered from a 'weak heart'. This begins to suggest persecution mania of a positive sort. Magdalen, a small smart self-contained college in those days, might in a general way be classed as 'hearty', but Yorke, quiet in demeanour and dress, with no reason whatever for being unpopular, was not in the smallest danger of being, say, debagged on the night of a bump-supper. If he possessed undoubted eccentricities, these were not of a kind to excite popular disapproval.

Legend (partly his own) has somewhat overstated the extent of these eccentricities; also Yorke's drinking, which, as an undergraduate, I should have thought on the whole more moderate than that of many of his friends. He did, however, make a point of watching a film every afternoon, and every evening, of his Oxford life; change of programme at the city's three cinemas making this just possible without repetition. He also, without exception if he had control of the matter, ate fried fish and a steak every night for dinner. Another of his idiosyncrasies was to shave with ordinary washing soap.

Through connexions of his own Yorke had almost immediately registered as a Bowra friend, and we used obsessively to mull over together Bowra parties and Bowra lore. Yorke also had an introduction (probably through his mother, who must have been just about a contemporary) to Lady Ottoline Morrell at Garsington; a house to which he soon brought me too. Bowra was already a Garsington habitué, and great retailer of Garsington stories.

Garsington conditions have often been described, emphasis usually laid on the exotic appearance and behaviour of the hostess, both of which certainly had to be reckoned with. The worst perplexities always seemed to me to lie rather in the utter uncertainty as to what level of life there was to be assumed by the guest. A sense of 'pre-war' constraint – or rather what one imagined that to be – always prevailed, in fact probably more characteristic of contemporary Bloomsbury than the *beau monde* of earlier days. There was also, I can now see (Harold Acton's memoirs bear out), a war between the generations; young men from Oxford welcome as much to be overawed as encouraged.

At Garsington one more or less wild man was likely to be present, a bohemian exhibit (in Wyndham Lewis's phrase, an Ape of God), making appropriately bohemian remarks. To have these comments addressed to oneself, especially during the many silences that fell, was something to be dreaded. Alternatively, you might be caught out, in quite a different manner, by forgetting, say, the date of Ascot, or the name of some nobleman's 'place'. On the whole the legend of imposing intellectual conversation was the least of Garsington's threats. The arts, if discussed at all, were approached in a manner that – if such can be said without offence – might reasonably be called middlebrow; though none the less alarming for that. It was like acting in a play – or rather several different plays fused together – in which you had been told neither the plot, nor your own cue: sometimes a drawing-room comedy; sometimes an Expressionist curtain-raiser; sometimes signs loomed up of an old-fashioned Lyceum melodrama.

On my first visit to Garsington the other guests were David Cecil (by then a don), and L. P. Hartley, who at that time had written only his first novel, *Simonetta Perkins*, a story of a middle-aged spinster, who fell in love with a gondolier. Leslie Hartley and I made no contact on this occasion, but subsequently, as a critic, he gave my early novels encouraging notices, and twenty or more years later, as a country neighbour, we used to see a good deal of him. A somewhat Jamesian figure (a writer he much admired), Hartley had a mild manner that concealed a certain taste for adventure. This took the form of thoroughly enjoying extraordinary *contretemps* with members of his own domestic staff. He loved entertaining – and being entertained – and was the most generous of hosts, but would go out of his way to find cooks or butlers of literally alarming eccentricity. If he had kept a day-to-day record of some of the consequences of this hobby, it would make extraordinary reading. One of his favourite anecdotes was of a cook who worked for him for a short time, mother of a small daughter. Some row took place, and the cook gave notice. Just before her final exit she brought the little girl into Hartley's sitting-room, and said: 'Take a good look at him, Emily, an Oxford man, and a cad.'

Even Bowra was prepared to recognize that an invitation to Garsington was not a matter to be treated lightly. For the most experienced in salon life, it represented moving up to the front line; for a nervous undergraduate, an ordeal of the most gruelling order. Bowra, staying once in the house, coming down to breakfast early, had inadvertently eaten the toast (possibly Ryvita, even if toast, toast of some special sort) found in the toast-rack. A short time later Lady

Ottoline arrived. She looked round the table. Something was wrong. She rang the bell.

'*Where is my toast?*'

Lady Ottoline's very individual way of speaking, a kind of ominous cooing nasal hiss – often imitated, but, like Goodhart's whinny, never altogether successfully – was at its most threatening. The parlourmaid (also a formidable figure, addressed by name, which I do not remember) fixed her eyes on Bowra.

'The toast was there when *he* came down, m'lady . . .'

Garsington was one of those educational experiences of which, like many of that date, one appreciated the value only much later. The visits belonged, I think, chiefly to my third year, by when Yorke and I had moved from our respective colleges to rooms side by side on the top floor of 8 King Edward Street, the corner house; lodgings in the robust music-hall tradition kept by the redoubtable redhaired Mrs Collins, who herself rarely appeared. In general, undergraduates remained two years in college, and I do not now understand why Yorke went into rooms in the town after his first year. Possibly Magdalen was short of space, and glad for anyone to do that; Yorke's apprehension about being attacked may have also played some part.

Yorke and I used sometimes to give luncheon and dinner parties together at King Edward Street and one of these, which seemed an amusing experiment at the time, I now recognize as a piece of reckless tight-rope walking. We invited both Kenneth Bell and Maurice Bowra to dinner. There were several other guests, and the occasion appeared a great success at the time, even though Bowra, first to arrive, had commented without enthusiasm when he heard Bell was to be there. Throughout the evening, Bell, in his own bluff erratic manner, let fly a coruscation of amusing remarks; Bowra for once keeping relatively quiet. Such a dinner-table combination was not a very tactful one, both from general principles as to the unwisdom of mixing too strong personalities – overseasoning the dish – and, in this particular case, playing tricks with Bowra's own very delicate relationship with the other dons of that day; some of whom were inclined to raise an eyebrow at the ease with which he moved among undergraduates. Bell moved easily among undergraduates too, but in a very different manner. In fact the two of them belonged to such disparate categories of don that no great harm was done; but the risk had been great.

That dinner party gave an opportunity to learn, which I did not take. Had I been quicker to comprehend its intricacies, later events might have been less gauchely handled; although, the way things fell out – so far as I myself was concerned – could have been for the best.

After returning from Finland, my father went back to his regiment, then stationed at Tidworth, my parents living for a time a few miles away at Andover, in a 'private hotel'. This residential hotel was a depressing spot. One afternoon – I do not remember the season, but summer rather than winter – an obviously hired car turned into the short drive leading to the hotel, and stopped at the entrance. Out of the car stepped Bowra and Synnott. Synott (later a civil servant at the Admiralty) was much about with Bowra at this time. They said they had dropped in to tea. My parents were out, but arrived back later, and were introduced.

It appeared that Synnott had been staying up for some weeks of the vac and, he and Bowra coming over to this part of the country for a jaunt (possibly to visit the sights of Winchester), had decided to pay a call. I cannot imagine how they knew where I was living. This was an unprecedented excitement in the cheerless Andover day. When it was time to return to Oxford, Bowra put forward the suggestion (which may even have been represented as the object of the visit) that I should come back with them; stay for a day or two with Bowra at Wadham.

I accepted this proposal in the manner one accepted so much at that age, just as something that happened – rather like being taken to Garsington, or the drive to Vienna – an adventure, more or less. I was very glad to get away from Andover even for a short time. I did not give much thought to what might be expected of me at the receiving-end; which was, I suppose, to make myself reasonably agreeable for a day or two; return home without overstaying my welcome. I remained at Oxford for two or three days, then came back to Andover; but, entirely owing to my own fault, the visit was not a success. This was due to a lack of discernment that goes with immaturity. There was also little to do in Oxford out of term (Bowra himself naturally occupied with his own academic duties during the day), and I was scarcely less bored pacing the High than back at the Andover hotel.

One evening, dining tête-à-tête with Bowra in his rooms, I spoke of how little I liked being at Oxford, and how I longed to get it over and go down. The lack of finesse in voicing such sentiments in the particular circumstances was, of course, altogether inexcusable. The concept that Bowra himself was a young man with a career still ahead of him, about which he no doubt suffered all sorts of uncertainties, even horrors, never crossed my mind. Bowra seemed a grown-up person for whom everything was settled. In a sense that made my gaffe even worse. One learns in due course (without ever achieving the aim in practice) that, more often than not, it is better to keep deeply felt views about oneself to oneself. In any case a little good sense – a little good manners even – might have warned me that such a confession was not one to make to a slightly older friend, who, even then, was rapidly becoming one of the ever brightening fixed stars of the Oxford firmament. Bowra's own hospitality had no doubt played a part in inducing such plain speaking, but I make no attempt to put forward wine in extenuation.

Such sentiments towards Oxford – though shared by Hubert Duggan and Henry Yorke – were uncommon for an undergraduate of my generation, most of whom regarded – still regard – those days as the happiest, etc. I do not in the least wish that I had never been up at Oxford. I owe an enormous amount to my three years there. Nevertheless, although reminiscence of the University has here largely been in the shape of chronicling rackety goings-on, a great deal of my time was spent in a state of deep melancholy. All this burst out at Bowra's dinner-table.

It took some thirty-five years for my relationship with Bowra to recover from that evening in Wadham. I was not put into anything like the worst disgrace possible, condemned to the unmitigated outer darkness to which some might be liable; especially those to whom the phrase 'treading on other people's corns' had been used – and not at the time understood – although Bowra himself did not merely tread on corns, he deliberately stamped on them, as most appropriate treatment. Beyond the adoption of a somewhat tarter form of address, and a falling off of invitations, no spectacular censure took place. We continued to meet while I remained up at Oxford, later sometimes running across each other in London. Although I regret my maladroitness in causing this rift, I am not sure whether for my own good it was not just as well to be withdrawn from Bowra influence before the grip became all but irremovable. Probably disjunction would in any case have taken place, seeds of variance existing at the stage each of us was approaching, some sort of a temporary break inevitable.

The Bowra story, so far as I am concerned, may be brought to completion out of chronological order. In 1941, while I was awaiting a posting at the Intelligence Corps Depot at Oxford, Bowra lunched with Violet and myself at the Randolph. All went well, even if things were not quite on the footing they once had been. Professor Lindemann had just been raised to the peerage as Lord Cherwell.

'Don't mind that at all.' Bowra said. 'Don't mind that at all. Causes pain. You'd hardly believe the pain it's caused.'

About 1948, I met a young man who turned out to be an undergraduate of Wadham, of which Bowra was by then Warden. I asked him how he got on with the head of the house. His praise was abounding. He could not sufficiently commend a man of such distinction, for whom no member of the college was too humble to be noticed, none too geographically remote to be lost touch with after going down; understanding, amusing, hard working, the Warden was a don in a million. 'But', added the young Wadhamite, 'I've heard he's an absolute fish out of water when he's away from the academic world he's accustomed to.'

I cannot imagine any typification that would have annoyed Bowra more; nor, indeed, one that was on the whole less true, though I believe he did find himself not much at ease, towards the end, with certain academic developments in which he had to be involved. The words are, however, of interest in illustrating how easily one can make that sort of mistake at an early age (not necessarily only then), and by showing how profoundly Bowra threw himself into the Warden's rôle. This capacity for taking on with enthusiasm forms of life comparatively alien to those with which he was commonly associated (though in a sense perhaps still possible to call academic) was well illustrated by Bowra on Hellenic cruises.

Never to have seen Bowra on an Hellenic cruise was to have missed an essential aspect of him. The ship would contain close on three hundred passengers, of whom more than half might come from the United States. Bowra (now Sir Maurice) would from time to time lecture, and in general propagate, sometimes in an indirect manner, the archaeological sites to be visited. His lectures at Oxford were not – anyway in the eyes of his colleagues – regarded as Bowra's forte. Those he gave on the cruise were another matter. No one who heard him in the museum at Olympia could be anything but richly stimulated. It might be supposed that a man by this time famous as a scholar, and personality, might have become a trifle unapproachable for the run-of-the-mill tourist. Nothing could have been further from that, nor from his former pupil's assessment of Bowra removed from a conventionally academic setting; at least one very different from Wadham. Bowra was just as likely to be seen at a table of delighted greyhaired matrons from the Middle West or West Kensington, as exchanging cracks with Mortimer Wheeler (or whatever might be snobbishly regarded as the tourist élite) over a *raki* at a bar.

In 1960 Violet and I went on one of these Hellenic cruises, which included putting in at Sardinia, Sicily, Malta, North Africa, as well as Greece. When, with the rest of the party, we met at London Airport, there was a second of wondering how things were going to go, so far as the Bowra relationship was concerned. The plane flew to Milan, then came a longish bus journey to Genoa. Bowra and I sat next to each other on the bus. We talked a lot. Old contacts were re-established. The détente was complete.

At Malta, Bowra asked us (including our son, John, then fourteen years old) to dine with him at a restaurant he knew on the island. This restaurant was situated on the higher levels of Valletta. We reached it on the way out by taxi; Bowra explaining that we could more easily return by public lift, which operated at regular intervals, grounding its passengers only a short way from the harbour, and our ship. We dined enjoyably, and strolled to the place of the lift. A notice indicated that we had missed the last descent by ten minutes, and were faced with a long and steep journey back on foot.

Four-letter words have been rather overdone of late years, but, when the ex-Vice-Chancellor of Oxford University, President of the British Academy, holder of innumerable honorific degrees and international laurels, expressed his feelings (and the feelings of all of us), it was intensely funny.

'Fuck!'

The monosyllable must have carried to the African coast.

On another cruise that included Bowra the ship passed through the Dardanelles. As we sailed by the shore of Gallipoli, in a brief quite unemphasized ceremony, a wreath was committed to the sea. Some days later I remarked to Bowra that, although the best part of half a century had passed, the moment of the wreath's descent to the waves had been moving, even rather upsetting. I was not prepared for the violence of agreement.

'Had to go below. Lie down for *half-an-hour* afterwards in my cabin.'

After this second cruise, Bowra asked me to be his guest at the Wadham 'Dorothy' Dinner. We stayed with him in college. On the morning we left, I was with him in the hall of the Warden's House, when an undergraduate (bearded) arrived to ask a question or obtain some permission. Bowra fired out a question in the old accustomed explosive manner. The young man did not at all react. One knew that an amused – even a naïve – reflex would immediately have achieved a favourable result, but no reaction was visible at all. The undergraduate went away. 'I don't understand them at all nowadays,' Bowra said.

Later in the same year Bowra came to us for a weekend. It was during this visit that something (in addition to Gallipoli) convinced me how much the first war had meant to him. We took him to dine with neighbours. There was certainly plenty to drink, but that did not altogether explain what happened after dinner. Bowra insisted – he really did insist – on the whole party spending the rest of the evening singing 'There's a long, long trail a-winding' and 'Pack up your troubles in your old kitbag'. Perhaps by then he did not often find himself in company where such behaviour was even conceivable. I suppose it is just possible that an evening might have ended in the same way in days when I had first known him, but I never remember anything of the sort; and in any case it would then have been somehow different.

Two additional cruise incidents should go on record. Violet had been dancing *The Blue Danube* waltz with Bowra, the sole dance he recognized, first of all (she reported) pawing the ground like a little bull entering the ring. When we were sitting together afterwards, speaking of invitations, domestic arrangements – some trivial matter, its subject forgotten – she let fall a quite thoughtless comment.

'But surely that's easy enough for a carefree bachelor like you, Maurice?'

Bowra was suddenly discomposed.

'Never, *never*, use that term of me again.'

He laughed immediately after, but for a second it had been no laughing matter; perhaps a sudden touch of what he himself, in the old days, had named 'creeping bitterness'.

The other matter arose one afternoon sailing past Samothrace. Kipling's name had cropped up. Bowra said: 'Have you ever played the game of marking yourself for the qualities listed in *If* –? It's a good one.'

We set about playing the *If* game at once. Rather unexpectedly Bowra knew the poem by heart. I now greatly regret that I did not immediately afterwards write down the attributes Bowra claimed (he was very modest about them), and also the correct system of marking. My impression is that you clocked up half a mark for possessing a quality in principle, another half for improving on the situation; that is to say, trusting yourself when all men doubt you, scoring additionally for making allowance for their doubting too. It is, however, possible that you were assessed out of five for each combined condition. The second system is less likely, because I seem to recall that Bowra gave himself a total of three-and-a-half out of a potential fifteen, or thereabouts. His own comments greatly augmented the pleasures of the game.

'Being lied about, don't deal in lies – that's absurd of course. Next one.'

We came to Triumph and Disaster.

'Can't say about Triumph. Never experienced it.'

'Maurice, what nonsense.'

But he was adamant. He had never known Triumph. All the same he had liked playing the *If* game, and was in very good form after it.

I once calculated that nine of my Oxford friends left the University (mostly sent down) by the middle of my second year. I can now bring the total up to seven only; even that number leaving a distinct gap. The names of two others may well have slipped my memory. To some extent in consequence of this elimination, my last year was passed in a comparative retirement. Perhaps, as I have said, that is often what a final year feels like. By that time there had also been a shift away from the old sort of Oxford life represented by The Hypocrites. It would be impossible – to take a couple of lords as examples – to imagine undergraduates less snobbish than Elmley or Clonmore; but an influx of rather a different sort had followed them, resulting in something of an *entente* between the smarter 'aesthetes', and a 'hearty' world centred on the Bullingdon; while a sprinkling of rich Americans also showed preference for rather self-conscious little cocktail parties. These things are hard to map, but the old knockabout styles were at an end, replaced by attitudes perhaps no more ambitious (because plenty of ambition had been about before), but less happy-go-lucky.

Meanwhile Yorke had placed his novel, *Blindness* (1926), with a publisher; a stroke that demanded from certain people a sharp new assessment of the position of someone who might have seemed well on the way to posing the unanswerable question (set at the start by so many bright young men) of what, when it came to the point, was he going to do. A published novel could not altogether be laughed off. It also dignified our comparatively withdrawn life in King Edward Street.

In the spring of my last year, 1926, Hubert Duggan, by then in The Life Guards, came up to Oxford to ride in a 'grind'. He brought with him a young American, of whom both the Duggans had sometimes spoken, usually with such phrases as 'he hangs round my mother, and helps do the flowers, that kind of thing'. This was Chips Channon, then in his late twenties. He did not come to the point-to-point, and, when we were alone together, Duggan explained that Channon was now more or less accepted as a friend by himself and his brother; adding that Channon had made himself very useful to Alf after the final sending-down from Balliol; and, Hubert Duggan admitted, had also been good at supplying books, etc., at the time of his own illness. I met Channon again when we came back from the grind. He seemed very friendly, easy to get on with, not at all what I had imagined from the picture painted by the Duggans of what a social climber was like.

I did not see Channon again until twenty years later; the icebound winter of 1947. Violet Wyndham (daughter of Ada Leverson, The Sphinx) gave a dinner party, something by then rather rare in immediately post-war London. Channon was among the guests. Now a comparatively veteran member of the House of Commons, he was greatly changed from the *beau jeune homme*, who had received letters (which he says he destroyed, thinking them of no great interest) from Proust. I reminded him of our former meeting. The effect was almost startling. He began an impassioned attack on the Duggan brothers, speaking with great bitterness of the way they had treated him. I was prepared for Alf having given Channon a rough ride, and being unpopular, but his deep resentment of Hubert's behaviour surprised me. 'And their drinking!' Channon added. It was one of those spells when Channon was not keeping his Diary, so no record remains, as it might have done, of past vexations recalled by this conversation.

When the General Strike took place in 1926 the country was divided up into areas administered by Civil Commissions designed to deal with emergencies. Most of the personnel of these Commissions was drawn from the regular civil service, each including an army officer to act in liaison with troops stationed in the neighbourhood. One of these Civil Commissions was situated at Reading, where my father was appointed liaison officer. The universities were more or less closed down during the strike, and it was arranged that I should come over to Reading to work in the Commission. I had a small office through which passed the letters brought in, and sent out, by motor-post. This episode (apart from giving some experience of what working in a government office was like) would have possessed no great interest had not the Commission itself been housed in Reading Gaol. The prison had been out of use even then for many years. Those temporarily working there were shown round. Wilde's cell was naturally the chief exhibit; the 'foul and dark latrine'.

During the summer term that year, my last at Oxford, I had to visit London. It was arranged that Hubert Duggan and I should dine together. He was then living in quarters at the Household Cavalry barracks in Albany Street, Regent's Park, only a short way from Chester Gate. In Duggan's quarters, that evening, took place the scene which suggested the episode in *Dance* where Stringham puts off the Narrator for dinner; and, at the time, it was indeed true that I grasped a parting of the ways had come. The occasion represents the last moment in the novel when Duggan might be said to have any direct bearing on Stringham's doings as described. After that evening Hubert Duggan and I scarcely met again before running into each other during the war in White's Club (then accommodating my own, which had been bombed), and having a talk. We were both captains. 'Of course you don't get into the big money until you're a major,' Duggan said. That was our last meeting. He died about a year later.

Before the Oxford Final Schools, a Balliol examination was held called Collections. At this college try-out I was judged to have done reasonably well. Kenneth Bell said: 'When you go up for your *viva*, they'll recognize you're a fairly bright chap, and ask you about what you know.' Schools took place; the day of the *viva* came. Nothing could have been further from Bell's prophecy. I was long cross-questioned as to a period of English mediaeval history at which I had hardly glanced. I had also been unwise in choice of 'special subject'; for some inexplicable reason insisting on doing the Congress of Vienna, its material largely in French, and – a language of which I was altogether ignorant – German. All I can remember from it are unconvincing descriptions of his love of natural landscape in Talleyrand's dispatches.

I took a Third without the satisfying conviction that I had never done a stroke of work. On the contrary, I had worked quite hard, though without the least sense of direction. As things turned out, nothing could have mattered less than a Third; but a good degree might have been important. Bell wrote: 'It will be all the same in four or five years' time.' It was pretty well all the same then and there, even if I expected a Second. My father – who perhaps feared a First – did not seem greatly disturbed. Henry Yorke stayed on for a term or two, then decided he would not take a degree. Instead, he planned to spend some time (in the event two years) working as an operative in the family business at Birmingham.

Yorke usually defined his family's engineering firm as making lavatories, though sanitary fittings were subsidiary in the production to such equipment as beer-bottling machines. His decision to work there has been represented (to some extent by himself in *Pack My Bag*) as ideological, but I remember no suggestion of that at the time – though there always existed deep and secret recesses in Yorke's mind that were not revealed – the motive specifically given as wish to write a novel about factory life from first-hand experience. In *Living* (1929), though trade unions are not mentioned, and (for my own taste) the 'experimental' style threatens at times to become laboured, he brought this off with as great force and originality as has probably ever been achieved. Whether or not it occurred to Yorke from the start that experience 'on the floor' would be ideal foundation for working as executive in the office, I do not know, but that certainly turned out. His remaining elder brother, traveller, scholar, student of esoteric beliefs, chose a path in life far from the world of business; Yorke himself becoming in due course head of the firm (from which he retired at the age of about fifty), while continuing to write his books.

In one sense novelists are unsatisfactory critics of other novelists' work, because they always feel that they themselves would have written any given novel another way. At the same time they are probably the only individuals truly aware of the interior images that haunt the novelist's imagination. Yorke has the novelist's fascination with the casual phrase (especially that), the exceptional situation, the oddly adjusted human relationship. He has a deep interest in the eternal contrast between everyday life's flatness and its intensity. At the same time, there is always something in Yorke's writing – an unassimilated vein of feeling in which whimsicality and sentimentalism seem to be fighting it out with bareness of diction and moral austerity – that suggests better accommodation in poetry. So far as I know, he himself speaks only once of writing poetry; doing so when staying with a French family before coming up to Oxford. I never saw this, or any other verse, by him, but the images in his novels, together with certain aspects of his temperament, strike me as those of a poet rather than novelist.

In 1959 I went to a large party given by the American Institute in a house on the south side of Grosvenor Square. There were a few chairs round the walls, but almost everyone was standing up, and, acoustics being not of the best, the noise made by concentrated literary conversation was even more resonant than usual. A long way off I saw a hand feebly waving from a chair, but could not discern, from where I stood, who was sitting there. It turned out to be Yorke. He began to speak excitedly. He was not in very good shape. We talked for a while, the row going on round about making his words hard to catch. In one of his old bursts of volubility, he began to pour out a lot of memories of the past experienced together: our prep school; how his uncle, the General, had shown him campaign maps of France; names of people we had known at Eton, whom he now never saw. In the end he was almost in tears of emotion. 'I'm not well,' he said. 'People say it's drink. It's not that. I'm not well. I think I'm going to die.' I felt rather upset after this encounter. It was the last time I saw him. He died in fact in 1974.

Yorke's Memorial Service was at St Paul's, Knightsbridge. I was at the back of the dark church, with several empty pews behind me. Half-way through the service an old man with white woolly hair and a brownish-yellow skin came in. He might have been a Mexican by his appearance. He knelt down in the back pew, and began muttering prayers half aloud, as he told some beads. After a while, before the end of the service, he left. It was an incident Yorke himself would have greatly relished.

Looking back on my own coming down from Oxford, I am surprised at how little I remember about it, how vague are the circumstances in my mind. The occasion seems to have lacked all drama. At some stage that summer I went with Arden Hilliard for two or three weeks to Corsica; an enjoyable trip though without great adventure. We crossed from Marseilles to Ajaccio, toured the island, returned to France by Bastia then to Nice. We were in a café a day later when Hugh Lygon came in. Seeing us, he established at a table the girl who was with him, and made for where we were sitting.

'I'm staying at Willie Maugham's villa,' Lygon said. 'I've been stuck for the afternoon with this terribly boring Rumanian. May I sit and talk to you for a minute or two? She'll be all right on her own for a bit.'

The subjective interest I find in these words is that I felt not the smallest curiosity – as I should have done a few years later – at the possibility of hearing about Somerset Maugham and his houseparty. Maugham seemed to me then an irretrievably third-rate author, and I could well believe that staying with him was boring, shunting his guests round, an unenviable way of spending a Riviera afternoon. I am now astonished at such simplicity, literary and social. Maugham has his failings as a writer, but *Rain, The Outstation, Cakes and Ale*, are pretty good in their own genre; while the happenings at the Villa Mauresque always offered at least one good anecdote. In a month or two's time, enveloped in this fog of naïvety, I was to dive headfirst into the opaque waters of London life.

. My mother.

2. My father.

. AP with Pekoe, Christmas 1908,
a Holland Walk, Kensington.

4. AP aged twelve; first passport photograph.

5. AP at Eton, just before fifteenth birthday.

6. A.W.A. Peel and R.W.E. Cecil, with Lower Boys who fagged for them at Goodhart's. AP front row left.

7. Shepherd Market, Carrington House (9 Shepherd Street) on corner, AP's rooms marked X.

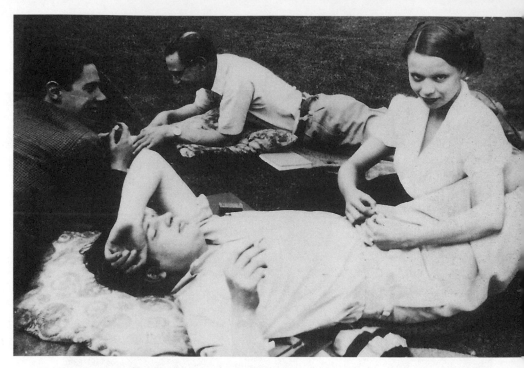

8. Constant and Flo Lambert at Woodgate, with AP and Gerald Reitlinger in the background

9. Pakenham Hall, Co Westmeath.

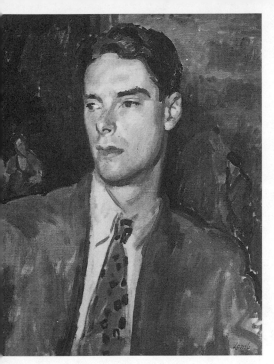

10. AP, oil painting by Henry Lamb, 1934.

11. Drawing of AP by Augustus John, 1960.

12. The Tranby Croft case at Woodgate: Violet (as Mrs. Wilson), John Lloyd (Prince of Wales), AP (Sir William Gordon Cumming), Francis Watson (Capt. Wilson), about 1938.

13. AP reading outside, about 1927 or 1928.

14. AP and Violet, near the time of their marriage in 1934. Photograph taken by Barbara Ker-Seymer.

15. Field-Marshal Montgomery puts the Military Attachés in the picture: Gen. Peabody (hidden), Col. Schoonenberg (hand to face), Gen. Regulski (just hidden), Col. de Almeida (spectacles), F-M Montgomery, AP, Gen. Noiret, Col. Carlisle, Comdt. Lechat (just hidden).

16. The Chantry.

7. AP with Col. Carlisle in Normandy, 1944.

8. Allied Military Attachés at Field-Marshal Montgomery's Tactical Headquarters,
1 Army Group, near Roermond on the Netherlands/German frontier, November, 1944.

19. Leslie Hartley and AP at The Chantry, 1959.

). Violet and AP (scene like a movie "still") in Cairo night-club, 1964.

. Congress in Sofia, 1977. AP (reading) in back row, Gore Vidal in dark spectacles,
dian delegate, Peter Elstob.

22. AP at Royal Wedding celebration aboard
MTS Orpheus, 1981.

23. Violet, at Royal Wedding celebration
aboard *MTS Orpheus*, 1981.

PART TWO

Messengers of Day

Decius Here lies the east: doth not the day break here?
Casca No.
Cinna O, Pardon, sir, it doth; and yon grey lines
That fret the clouds are messengers of day.

Julius Caesar II 1

In the autumn of 1926 I came to work in London. I should be twenty-one in December. Clichés, says Jarry, are the armature of the absolute, and no figure is more tritely familiar, at the same time more truly arche-typal, than the young man setting out on a metropolitan career. Balzac and Stendhal especially love his situation. I had read no Stendhal then, only dipped into Balzac's *La Fille aux Yeux d'Or* (Dowson's transla-tion, acquired by my father for the Conder illustrations), where the hero is a fully fledged man-about-town; the lesbian and transvestite scenes largely lost on me at the age of sixteen. Accordingly, I was not inspired to identify with Rastignac or Rubempré, and their high standards of ambition. The best I could do in the way of Balzacian (or Stendhalian) ambition was that of every reasonably literate young man of the period; vague intention to write a novel myself one of these days.

The first thing to do was to find somewhere to live. As to *quartier* I had my own ideas, though I might not have admitted to everyone that the Shepherd's Market seduction scene which opens Michael Arlen's novel, *The Green Hat* (1924), chiefly caused me to set my sights on that small village enclave (also described in Disraeli's *Tancred*), so unexpectedly concealed among the then grand residences of Mayfair.

(By an odd chance I found myself giving luncheon to Arlen tête-à-tête thirty years later, and was able to reveal what had prompted my first London *garçonnière*. Small, slight, neat, infinitely sure of himself, yet somehow set apart from other people, he twice repeated at the table a personal definition: 'I, Dikran Kouyoumdjian, an Armenian'. Dikran is the equivalent of Tigranes, the name of several kings of Armenia in classical times. Arlen talked entertainingly of books and sexual relationships, saying among other things that, unlike most men he knew, he did not believe in sleeping with friends' wives.)

Even today (1983), in face of ruthless knockings down, scarcely less ruthless smartenings up, Shepherd Market – more frequently called Shepherd's Market by those who lived there – has kept vestiges of an old stylishness. At that period all the traders were 'little shops'; the pubs, down-to-earth pubs; the prostitutes, as such, differentiated from the merely raffish by segregation in one large forbidding block of flats. Even a few years later – soon after the initial demolitions – this primi-tive innocence had begun to dwindle, but, when I arrived with the object of trying to find somewhere to live, the Market's air of seedy chic perfectly suited my own post-Oxonian mood. Chiefly on grounds of price I had not much hope of achieving this aim. On the contrary, the first door bell rung supplied an answer.

Shepherd Street crosses the lower levels of the Market east and west, from which, at right angles, the short cul-de-sac of Carrington Street runs south, terminating even at that date in a busy all-night garage. A pub, The Old Chesterfield Arms, still remains on the north-east corner of Carrington Street; on the opposite corner then stood Carrington House, a building going back at least to the 17th century. Reputed former town mansion of the Earls of Sefton, Carrington House could never have been of inordinate size. The courtesan Kitty Fisher is said to have lived there; later, Lord Nelson. At some time not at all recent the structure had been divided into two houses. These traditions, true or untrue, were all unknown to me, when I rang the bell of Carrington House's easterly wing, by then simply 9 Shepherd Street.

The door was opened by a lady, handsome, full of attack, who wore a rather dashing hat. She turned out to be the wife of the owner, Commander Williamson, an ex-naval officer employed at the Air Ministry. Mrs Williamson (I suppose in her forties, though she looked younger), undeterred by a dilapidated exterior, had made that half of Carrington House their London home, letting off a couple of rooms on the ground-floor, one above. The former were vacant; with breakfast, someone to make the bed, two pounds a week. In a matter of minutes they were engaged.

It should be emphasized at once that my suite was neither large nor luxurious. In fact, as an airing-cupboard divided into two compartments, the extent would not have been thought excessive, even in a moderately sized house. Nearly half the tiny sitting-room was taken up by a vast glass-fronted bookcase reaching almost to the ceiling. A miniature sofa set against this elephantine piece of furniture allowed just space for a chair and folding table, the table kept in a corner when not in use. An outdated set of the *Encyclopaedia Britannica* took up most of the bookcase, the upper shelves of which were stocked with technical manuals of inconceivable dryness. The bedroom, even smaller than the sitting-room, was an irregular pentagon (otherwise unmagical in character), three of its walls on the street. In one of these outside walls a nailed-up door, perhaps former tradesmen's entrance, had been made partially draught-proof, though retaining within and without the appearance of offering additional ingress to the house.

It had been arranged through my father's friend, Thomas Balston, that I should learn the business of publishing – a mystery to be attained within the span of three years – at the firm of Gerald Duckworth & Co. Ltd, of which Balston was now a director. I was perfectly amenable to becoming a publisher; indeed could conjure up no more plausible means of attempting to earn a living. During the years of apprenticeship I was to receive a certain allowance from my father, a certain salary from Duckworth's. I do not remember the precise proportion each party was to pay, but, as year succeeded to year, my father contributed less, the firm more; the amount I received, three hundred pounds annually, remaining a constant. Finally, I think, my father was paying half that sum, which he continued to do later as an allowance.

Duckworth's, one of the smaller London publishing houses, had been founded in 1898 by Gerald Duckworth himself, a man at this time in his middle fifties. The firm's offices were at 3 Henrietta Street, the Covent Garden end of what still remains a publishers' alley. Dingy without, only a few finely ornate door-fittings recalled better days within. The three directors of the firm were Gerald Duckworth, George Milsted, Thomas Balston. Gerald Duckworth, himself not specially rich, came from a decidedly well-to-do family. His widowed mother had married a widower, Sir Leslie Stephen (founder of the *Dictionary of National Biography*), producing further children, who included Vanessa Bell and Virginia Woolf. This last circumstance has caused chroniclers of 'Bloomsbury' to focus attention on the two Duckworths, Gerald and his elder brother, George (knighted civil servant of the official art world), both of whom being accused by their half-sister of indulging in unbecoming fumblings with her as a little girl.

Such imputations on the part of a person of Virginia Woolf's mental condition are to be accepted with a certain degree of caution, but there can be no doubt that her relationship with the Duckworth brothers was a complex one, arousing all her own ambivalent feelings about sex, money, and the social life to which, when old enough, her more affluent half-brothers introduced her. She always stigmatized them as 'clubmen', but, notwithstanding forebodings on that score, submitted a first novel, *The Voyage Out*, to Gerald Duckworth, who published it in 1915; her second, *Night and Day*, four years later. These two books (straightforward in style, arguably her best) were ceded to The Hogarth Press when set up by Leonard and Virginia Woolf; a sense of relief probably felt on both sides at this rearrangement.

Gerald Duckworth had some reputation as a rackety Edwardian bachelor, and the varied sexual promiscuities of Bloomsbury were generally known. Nevertheless, the notion (true or untrue) that either of the Duckworth brothers had indulged in erotic scufflings with Virginia Woolf – at any age – would in those days have seemed grotesque beyond words; my own generation regarding Bloomsbury as no less elderly, stuffy, anxious to put the stopper on rising talent, than the staunchly anti-avant-garde Duckworths.

Gerald Duckworth (who remained childless) had married and settled

down only a year or two before I came into the firm. I do not remember
a first presentation to him. I dined at his house in De Vere Gardens,
Kensington, only once, I think, when, without any strong sense of conviviality, a memorable amount was drunk. He was a big burly man,
slight grey moustache, small rather baleful eyes behind steel spectacles,
a vaguely dissatisfied air. Some suggestion of a love affair gone wrong
was hinted (which late marriage might endorse), but I never heard any
details of his personal past. Like Marley's ghost in more gastronomic
guise he moved gloomily through the office, a haze of port-fumes and
stale cigar-smoke in his wake; probably showing greater amiability
among cronies at The Garrick, where – reputed on a good day to dispatch a bottle of claret at luncheon – he undoubtedly earned his half-
sister's label as clubman.

Though I have heard a literary agent describe him as devious in
negotiation, the truly extraordinary thing about Gerald Duckworth was
that he had chosen to become a publisher at all; much less founded
a firm for that purpose. His interest in books, anyway as a medium
for reading, was as slender as that of any man I have ever encountered,
though he had some liking for the Theatre, a milieu where the legendary
love affair was by tradition placed. If the virus of bibliophobia is
dormant in the blood there is nothing like a publisher's life for aggra-
vating the condition.

Nevertheless, the firm's earlier lists contained conspicuous names.
This vigour on the editorial side had been almost entirely due to
employing Edward Garnett as Duckworth's reader between 1901 and
1920. I never met Garnett, but by an odd chance was familiar with
his name before joining the firm. When we were both still undergraduates I had suggested to Yorke that he might show the manuscript
of the novel he was writing to Balston. Balston, not greatly impressed,
turned it down. Somehow it reached Garnett, then working for another
publisher. *Blindness* was not issued by Garnett's then firm, but, liking
the book, he carefully went through the manuscript with Yorke, who
would often talk of 'old Garnett's' attractive character, odd mannerisms,
invaluable hints about novel-writing.

George Milsted, second on the mast-head of directors, had been with
the firm since its early stages of inception; though away in the army
during the first war, while Gerald Duckworth kept things going on
his own. Small, thickset, white-moustached, Milsted's turn-out was
always intensely sporting. Together with a brown bowler, he wore,
all the year round, tweeds of the loudest check, most uncompromisingly
horsey cut; in winter, as for hacking, a short fawn covert coat. I could
not imagine who this figure from the race-course might be, when I
first caught sight of Milsted pottering about the room in which I
worked. He was examining the file-copies with apparent surprise, as

if never seen before, and he were browsing round a secondhand book-shop. The ensemble, suggesting a prosperous bookie on the way to Newmarket (his air perhaps too grave for a bookmaker's), was not un-like one of Evelyn Waugh's favourite outfits in latter days; though Waugh's bowler was grey, his tweeds apt to be spongebag, or that Household Troops pattern, intended by the designer in the first in-stance for tweed caps, rather than complete suits. In Milsted (contrasted with Waugh) these outwardly aggressive garments did not in the least denote a rebarbative nature.

In legend, Milsted is said occasionally to have arrived at the office driving a phaeton – no easy undertaking among the also horse-drawn fruit wagons of Covent Garden – but I never witnessed the ribands in his hands. He and his wife lived modestly in a house they had built for themselves somewhere south of London, only a jump or more ahead of the suburbs. They too were childless. Milsted would sometimes remark: 'As long as a man owns a horse, and a gun, and a dog, he has no cause to complain of his lot in this world.' Unless devoting himself to some such demanding labours as proof-reading *The Collected Works of Ronald Firbank*, Milsted did not very often show up at Henrietta Street; indeed scarcely averaging once a week. His general knowledge was considerable. So much so, that – like Brougham and the Law – he might have been said to know a little about everything except the business side of publishing.

When, a few years before my own appearance there, Thomas Balston became the junior director of Duckworth's, that (so he told me) had been on the strict understanding that Milsted would be dead in six months. What (or who) was to finish Milsted off, I do not know, nor how he so unexpectedly escaped imminent mortality. Milsted's later career has no particular relevance here (he lived, in fact, well into his eighties, seeing the firm through another war, showing interest in its doings within measurable distance of his own end), the point being merely that, when Balston took on this directorship, he supposed the business was his for the asking: Gerald Duckworth, if allowed to hobnob with the two or three authors he found possible to tolerate, would show little or no interest in what names were added to the firm's list; Milsted, if not soon dead, would at worst live on as a moribund colleague, seen at the office with increasing rarity. After a few years of the hard work Balston was only too anxious to bestow, Duckworth's could reasonably be envisaged as an over-ripe fruit about to drop into his lap.

If Gerald Duckworth came close to detesting books with all his heart, Milsted to regarding them as no more than a pleasantly civilized adjunct to stables, kennels, gun-room, Balston felt a passionate dedication to the publishing trade and its manifold obligations. He had always wanted to be a publisher, and at last some fortunate circumstance – possibly demise of a brother – had put him in the way of sufficient capital to invest in the Duckworth partnership. He was unmarried – his sexual proclivities always remained enigmatic, apparently non-existent in physical form, though he was capable of being stirred by emotional attachments of a sentimental sort towards both sexes – so that all his energies could be freely devoted to building up what was undeniably a thoroughly tumbledown concern.

Tall, thin, black moustached, jet black hair standing up on end, Balston, who was in his middle forties, gave expression to a mass of nervous tensions. He moved with jerky precipitancy, never closing a door without slamming it. Something of a classical scholar in his youth, other literary tastes were less easy to define. A delight in argument and contradiction required such preferences to be varied from one hour to the next; sometimes total reversal of his normal point of view on any given subject. On the one hand, he favoured modernism, being attracted by any chance of shocking the oldfashioned or straitlaced with perverse philosophic, political, above all anti-religious views; on the other hand, too much sexual frankness could provoke in him embarrassed giggles.

In the former mood, when in the same month (January, 1928) Hardy and Haig both died, Balston liked to tease literary people by saying that unquestionably the soldier would be remembered by history as a greater man than the writer. He was, indeed, an admirer of the Field-Marshal, whose words he had found on some occasion during the war deeply moving. In this same connexion, Balston approved my own proposal that – to avoid recurrent controversy as to whether or not such-and-such a poet or novelist should be buried in Westminster Abbey – an Unknown Author might be interred there once and for all.

To get some practical experience of publishing himself Balston had worked for a time in the office of T. Fisher Unwin. Fisher Unwin graduates often cropped up in the publishing world, the acceptance of trainees probably a recognized policy. In Balston's case that had not been a success; terminating in a letter from him to The Fishy Onion – as he always designated his former boss, giving at the same time an imitation of Unwin pulling at his goatee beard, while considering some monetary saving – a communication of his own departure, which included the phrase 'reducing your staff to the duties and emoluments of the office-boy'.

Nevertheless it was at Fisher Unwin's that Balston came across, on the managerial side there, a future henchman, who was to mean a great deal to him, also to Duckworth's. This was A. G. Lewis – I believe his christian name was Abbot, but to have called him that would have been unthinkable, or indeed anything but 'Mr Lewis' – whom, when in a position to do so, Balston installed as Duckworth's manager. Balston possessed for Lewis a kind of hero-worship that (in business terms) approached passion, causing Lewis to become a preponderant figure in the office, especially my own corner of it, as we shared a room.

I am not, unlike many people I know, a great fan of *The Diary of a Nobody* (1892), but I recognize the Grossmiths' book uniquely pinpoints a certain level of life in its day. Lewis himself was not in the least like Pooter, but Pooter's background was entirely Lewis's, making him prototype of a race all but departed even at that date, anyway in so unmodified a form; the oldfashioned middle-class, when the term really had some meaning. Slight in build, skeletally thin, with a small toothbrush moustache, Lewis always wore a black coat and striped trousers, the jacket fastened in the Victorian manner by only its high top button. A deep reddish complexion in all weathers made him seem either flushed by drink, ominously dehydrated, or just come into a warm blaze from an outside climate below freezing. In point of fact no one could have been more moderate in eating and drinking. Lewis liked an occasional glass of wine, but told me that he could never eat game when served at trade banquets.

At times rendered irritable by the vexations of publishing life, particularly exacerbating on the production side – suffering too from digestive troubles, probably why game was to be avoided – Lewis was a very nice man, straightforward, kindhearted, absolutely reliable, who knew his job exceedingly well within certain terms of reference. At the same time he had his limitations. Where the editorial side was concerned, the most unassuming of managers – in the sense that he would stick word for word to Balston's, or my own, description of a given book, when dealing with, say, an American publisher – Lewis would also, if to some extent waggishly, always bemoan anything taken on that had the air of being highbrow, or required presentation in what he regarded as a highbrow manner.

This was a standpoint that caused a kind of chronic attrition. Naturally Lewis was Balston's subordinate, but Balston, if not exactly afraid of Lewis, never liked to cross him too far. Accordingly, compromises were made that might at times have been better unmade. That was especially true in the way Duckworth books were produced. Lewis, quite rightly, was always keen on economy in printing and binding; occasionally a trifle parsimonious about the number of review copies sent out. Such things are all very well in principle; moments come when exceptions must be allowed. Some highbrow books, especially when well produced, turn out to sell very well.

That the picture in my mind of Lewis – particularly as belonging to a species all but extinct even in the Twenties – was not an exaggeratedly subjective one was confirmed forty years later.

Towards the end of the 1960s, in an old-established bookshop off Piccadilly, I came across first editions of two early novels of mine. A gratifying price was being asked. Both were inscribed to Lewis. I enquired if anything was known of their provenance. It turned out that the bookseller to whom I spoke had himself negotiated their purchase. He was eager to tell the story. He seemed scarcely to take in that I had once known Lewis well.

Although a middle-aged man himself, the bookseller had been astounded by the antique air of this veteran, from whom he had apparently bought several 'collectors' items' in the past. For some minutes he spoke animatedly about the house (in Streatham, I think), its lace curtains, oldfashioned atmosphere, above all the clothes of its owner, recalling an antediluvian epoch. Lewis must then have been in his late eighties. These two books, the bookseller said, had long been refused. He added that times were hard for those on fixed pensions, so that in the end he had persuaded the obstinate old fellow to part with them. I felt very touched.

The premises at 3 Henrietta Street to which young writers were to be lured were not outwardly inviting. The front door, kept open during the day, gave on to a shabby uncarpeted passage with a staircase at the end. On the left was another door inscribed with the name of the firm; possibly followed by the word ENQUIRIES, though I am not sure about that. If so, the hope was not one to build on. Within stood simply the trade-counter, no focus beyond that barrier existing to which an enquiry might specifically be directed; nor, for that matter, was any one individual responsible for answering the telephone. Three or four breezy young men, invoice clerks, would be engaged in caustic conversation among themselves at their long high desk on the far side of the room, and their attention had to be caught. That was not always easy. Out of sight to the right lay the (one man) packing-department, from which a Dickensian ancient kept up a fusillade of cockney banter with the invoice clerks, with whom he was perpetually at war.

In theory all arrivals at Duckworth's came to this bar of judgment: authors; visiting American publishers; literary agents; book-jacket designers; travellers in printing, binding, papermaking; sellers of advertising space; not least, the steady flow of the mentally deranged, whose routine was – no doubt still is – to call regularly on publishers. If clients had to wait, there was nowhere for them to sit. Later a kind of hutch was constructed between counter, wall, and window, furnished with a couple of hard chairs. Writers familiar with the severities of ground-floor conditions would not bother to be announced on the house-telephone (a concession to modernity), but come straight up to the room of whomever they wanted to see.

On the first floor, a small room at the top of the stairs was occupied by Balston. Cramped, austere, there was just room for two visitors. Balston's room overlooked Henrietta Street, where it approached the south-west corner of Covent Garden. The considerably larger room next door, with a small view of the market, was shared by Gerald Duckworth, and, when on duty, Milsted. Their roll-top desks were set back to back, so that each had a window from which to watch what was happening outside, but they were hidden from each other by a towering wall of dust-covered books, accumulated on the space between since the foundation of the firm. More books and manuscripts, usually a newspaper or two, littered the floor round Gerald Duckworth's seat, beside which, for the use of a potential caller, stood an armchair in the last stages of decomposition. Dust was everywhere, disorder infinite.

Order was only a little more apparent in the room behind this one (its outlook on to the backs of houses), occupied by Lewis and myself. Lewis's roll-top desk faced the door, but he could not see who entered without craning round a stack similar to that set between the two partners; in this case, recently published books, proofs of books, 'dummies' of books, estimates, invoices, letters currently to be considered; everything else that could find no other place to rest than the top of the desk. Further into the room stood my own smaller (non-roll-top) desk, beside it another crumbling armchair, unearthed from some cubby-hole, after energetic efforts on my part, and installed – not without all opposition – for visitors. Formerly authors had been required to stand in the presence of their publisher's staff. This room was lined from floor to ceiling with the dust-wrapped file-copies of the firm's output since the beginning; a record not too scrupulously kept over the years. Beyond the office in which Lewis and I sat was a tiny closet, where a succession of secretary-typists lived out their usually disgruntled being.

At Carrington House, when I returned there, Mrs Williamson was the quintessence of goodwill; sending down a cup of tea and slice of cake 'last thing', which I had to countermand, because – so it seemed – strong tea kept me awake. Tea and cake probably had nothing to do with insomnia, because I continued to sleep badly for years, and have never achieved anything like an Abou Ben Adhem standard of deep dreams of peace. Nor could I eat the hearty breakfasts Mrs Williamson provided. I had not learnt then to ask for one piece of toast in the Continental manner, even in those days perfectly normal behaviour, though perhaps less common than nowadays. These things disturbed Mrs Williamson. I, on my side, felt embarrassed by her extrovert kindnesses. I was going through a period of ineptitude at dealing with people. She must have thought me a very odd young man.

An excellent pub dinner was to be had at The New Chesterfield

Arms, opposite Carrington House to the north; three courses for half-a-crown, where a dozen or more persons sat round a large table on the first-floor. I would sometimes try to settle down to a book after dinner, but my sitting-room was not a place to encourage reading; still less writing. When, after the best part of a year, I took down one of the faded Encyclopaedias, a crumpled French pornographic paperback, concealed and forgotten by some former tenant, lurked behind them. It was a work of no great merit even in its own genre. In order not to seem its furtive owner (if someone looked up an article in the Britannica when I was out, or after I had moved to other accommodation), I passed the volume on to some friend. Said to be haunted, Carrington House certainly projected that heavy overcrowded atmosphere common to most very old inhabited dwellings. Nothing spectral ever came my way, though in the night bemused drunks, or tarts hoping to make contact, would knock on the illusory door of the bedroom that gave on to the street.

The local tarts were themselves inclined to drink a good deal. It was not unknown to find one of them, surrounded by sympathetic colleagues, totally passed out on the pavement in White House Street, the narrow alley flanked by huge buildings, which linked the Market with the tarts' nightly beat on Piccadilly. After midnight, two small male prostitutes would linger, humming gently to themselves, at White Horse Street's Piccadilly end. The mansion-block on the opposite side of Carrington Street was a kind of tarts' barracks. It contained at that period only one male inhabitant, but that a distinguished figure, Sir Ronald Waterhouse, the Prime Minister's Principal Private Secretary. This eminent public servant (who in similar capacity had worked under several other administrations) must have required all his official *sang froid* to cope with the neighbours, in general not at all well behaved. One night, a rumpus in progress at the flats, the landlord or manager, who, perhaps wisely, lived not on the premises but round the corner, came to see what was amiss. One of his tenants, looking down like Jezebel from her window, exclaimed: 'Why, there's that little bugger so-and-so! He's had every woman in the block, including myself.'

I look back on the period without nostalgia. Perhaps embarkation on life in the Balzacian manner is a kind of shock to the system, which different individuals sustain in different ways. I had wanted to come down from Oxford, begin the great experiment. Now things appeared difficult to organize. At the University, whether you liked them or not, people were just round the corner. In London, special arrangements had to be made to see the most casual acquaintance. When I came out of the office I was often at a loose end, unable to decide what on earth to do with myself. Balston, a very hospitable man, would quite often issue invitations to dine at his flat; occasions likely to have a business basis. Decorated with Staffordshire figures (on which he wrote the first major book), pictures by Mark Gertler and Ethelbert White, Balston's service-flat in Artillery Mansions, Victoria Street (close to the scene of my birth) was more than a trifle claustrophobic.

Recurrent guests were G. S. Street, the (in effect) censor of plays; Rose Macaulay, a writer not published by Duckworth's; Charles Ginner, Camden Town Group painter; G. U. Ellis, who worked in Lloyds bank, in his spare time writing novels for Duckworth's. George Street (another bachelor inhabitant of Artillery Mansions) was in his sixties, deaf and grumpy. His name was associated with the Nineties, but – as one of W. E. Henley's circle – in an anti-aesthete capacity. Among Street's various books, *The Autobiography of a Boy* (1894) had some success in its day; a satire on Wilde and his friends, which I have never read. I see now that, tackled in the right manner, Street could have produced interesting information about the past. At the time I did not have the good sense to grasp that. I remember inadvertently shocking him by saying 'about half the people one knows are homosexual'.

Ginner, middle-aged, worthy, inarticulate to a degree, painted the sort of pictures I now recognize as capable work; then judged not very exciting. I don't think Ginner would ever have risen to anecdotes.

G. U. Ellis, Balston's discovery as an author, was always hoping to make enough by writing to enable him to leave the bank, work he disliked. He hovered on the brink of producing a popular novel, in what was even then a somewhat old-fashioned genre, but never brought off that ambition. Ellis's critical tastes were more go-ahead than his own novels. After he left Duckworth's (in circumstances he was to feel rather bitter about) he wrote *Twilight on Parnassus: a Survey of Post-War Fiction and Pre-War Criticism* (1939), the first study of that sort to devote an appreciable amount of space to my own early novels; something for which I have always felt grateful.

By the time Rose Macaulay used to visit us at Chester Gate, Regent's Park, in the late 1940s (chaining her bicycle to the area railings) I greatly liked her. In those early days at Balston's dinner-parties she seemed prim, chilly, forbidding, the embodiment of academic spinsterhood. Such a judgment was inept, though true that she enjoyed emitting an impression of Cambridge severity.

In fact, prepared to consider all human behaviour in the coolest most objective manner, Rose Macaulay was unusually flexible in revising her own statements. Referring to some recently published novel – possibly Waugh's *A Handful of Dust* (1934) – she said to me: 'I have not read it yet. Not a very interesting subject – adultery in Mayfair.'

'Why should you think that an uninteresting subject?'

'You are quite right,' she said. 'It was a silly thing to say. Subjects are entirely a matter of how they are treated by the writer.'

It was Evelyn Waugh, in about March of the New Year (1927), who cheered up what remains in my mind as a rather dreary introduction to London life. We had not seen each other since his sporadic visits to Oxford eight or nine months before; quite a long gap in acquaintance when you are that age. In principle still earning a living by working as a schoolmaster – which he had been doing on and off by then for two or three years – Waugh had just been sacked out of hand from whatever was the school of the moment. Finding himself in the lowest of water financially did not in the least impair his spirits outwardly, though no doubt there were gloomy moments when alone. He took the line that he was an adventurer, prepared to do anything; and that sooner or later the right opportunity would turn up.

Waugh possessed one substantial advantage. Although he might speak condescendingly about the world of his novelist elder brother, that world was always open to him. Alec Waugh's affiliations – roughly speaking, competent middlebrow professional writers, and the less stage-bound end of the Theatre – were quite lively ones. Nevertheless, even if freely available, like everywhere else they demanded a certain amount of money for overheads. This was the period when I knew and liked Waugh best. We must have met at times elsewhere, but I chiefly remember invitations to cold supper on Sunday nights at his parents' house in North End Road; even then still a comparatively unbuilt up locality, linking Hampstead with Golders Green.

I can think of no other notable writer of Waugh's generation who came from so unequivocally 'literary' a background; books – their writing, editing, printing, advertising, marketing – the normal way of life. His father, Arthur Waugh (always called Chapman & Hall, from his chairmanship of that publishing company), is naturalistically outlined in *A Little Learning*; more fantastically projected in several of his younger son's novels.

Waugh *père* was not only a 'man of letters' of somewhat old-fashioned sort, as described in these projections, but, having a taste for self-dramatization, played that rôle with considerable verve. Although he kept his firm quite successfully afloat almost singlehanded, and must have possessed a vast literary acquaintance dating back to the Nineties, he, the whole Waugh household, gave an agreeable sense of remoteness from modern life. Arthur Waugh, as a publisher, made Gerald Duckworth seem more than ever clubmanlike; Balston, a thrusting youngster of alarmingly modernistic tendency. This Pickwickian *persona*, assumed with such determination, was at once irritating to his younger son, yet also in a manner sympathetic to the side in love with Victorianism.

If Waugh – as he himself records – was sometimes on bad terms with his father, no sign of any such awkward relationship ever appeared during North End Road visits. On the contrary, the two of them seemed to agree uncommonly well. Arthur Waugh's air of mildness was perhaps a little too good to be true, and he was apt to begin sentences with the jocose opening: 'Speaking as a member of the lower-middle classes ...', but, if a fancy for exaggerated humility sometimes grated on his younger son's nerves, that was more for its implied lack of adventurousness, than on account of any explicit social ambition at that date.

Where smart life was concerned, Waugh himself would speak with a love/hate not unlike Thackeray's; a state of mind not in the least averse from receiving chic invitations, if any were going, but always flavoured with a certain animus against what was grand, rich, fashionable. In due course, when he adopted quite another approach, something always remained beneath the surface of a kind of social resentment.

I think there is nothing mysterious about either standpoint. Waugh was, in his way, an extraordinarily uncomplicated man; so uncomplicated that even in those days – far more so later in life – it was often hard to accept that some of his views and attitudes were serious. That was mistaken. They were perfectly serious to himself; within the limits that, possessing his father's powerful taste for self-dramatization, all Waugh's energies were concentrated on any rôle he was playing, however grotesque or absurd.

This simplicity of approach was particularly true in Waugh's manner of looking at social life. He really did believe in entities like a 'great nobleman', 'poor scholar', 'literary man of modest means'. Of course, in one sense, such stylized concepts may certainly exist, but at close range they usually require a good deal of modification. At the same time their acceptance – allied to gifts like Waugh's – can be by no means a disadvantage to a novelist, clearing the air automatically of extraneous detail that can clog a narrative. Hardy, for instance, is prepared to employ positive lay-figures to simplify telling a story; no less Dickens, a strong influence on Waugh's early style.

The 'high-life' of *Decline and Fall* is mostly depicted from imagination, hearsay, newspaper gossip-columns. Later, when Waugh himself had enjoyed a certain amount of first-hand experience of such circles, he was on the whole not much interested in their contradictions and paradoxes. He wished the beau monde to remain in the image he had formed, usually showing himself unwilling to listen, if facts were offered that seemed to militate against that image. This taste for stylization is somewhat modified in *The Ordeal of Gilbert Pinfold*, the most searching of Waugh's works, a book unmatched for its combination of funniness and horror.

On these pleasant North End Road evenings, Arthur Waugh would tell literary anecdotes at the dinner-table; Mrs Waugh (whose quiet exterior suggested much inner firmness of purpose) scarcely speaking at all, slipping out at the first opportunity. One night Waugh asked if I would like to hear the opening chapters of a novel he was writing. Waugh's embryonic novel – then called *Picaresque: or the Making of an Englishman* – was the first ten thousand words, scarcely at all altered later, of *Decline and Fall*. The manuscript was written with a pen on double-sheets of blue lined-foolscap, the cipher EW printed at the top of the first page of each double-sheet. There were hardly any alterations in the text.

In his early days Waugh would write all his books straight off, then make one fair-copy for the publisher, which was not, I think, typed; though I could not be certain about that. I found this overture extremely funny, but did not in the least guess the *popular* success *Decline and Fall* would eventually achieve. Some months after the reading aloud of these chapters – probably a moment towards the end of the same year – I asked Waugh how the novel was progressing. He replied: 'I've burnt it.'

On the evening of the reading, or another, Waugh gave me an inscribed copy of *P. R. B. An Essay on the Pre-Raphaelite Brotherhood 1847–1854*. Bound in blue-grey boards, printed on handmade paper, slim, elegant, this essay had been specially written for Waugh's close Oxford friend, Alastair Graham, who at that time owned a small printing-press. Graham had issued it privately the previous year. Waugh himself dismissed *P. R. B.* as a mere trifle, but, even if the author clearly needs more room in which to manoeuvre, the instinctive ability of the writing, feeling for words, unusual point of view, are all immediately apparent. *P. R. B.* also puts on record for the first time Waugh's lifelong pleasure in mid-Victorian culture. He was proud of his own family connexions with the PreRaphaelites; Holman Hunt having married successively (then against the law) two Waugh sisters. In the essay Waugh makes the comment that Holman Hunt's *The Awakening Consciousness* (called by a slip *The Awakened Conscience*, a picture by William Henry Hunt, confusingly so titled) 'is, perhaps, the noblest painting by an Englishman'; a startling opinion within the aesthetics of 1926.

At the time simply a spontaneous gift, *P. R. B.* turned out to have bearing on what Waugh was in due course to write for Duckworth's. A month or two earlier, discussing potential biographies that might be commissioned by the firm, Balston had remarked that an up-to-date account of Dante Gabriel Rossetti's life was already overdue. Various names were put forward to undertake that; nothing decided. In the course of these North End Road meetings with Waugh, it had been arranged that he should come to Henrietta Street to talk over the possibility of authorship. Waugh brought a copy of *P. R. B.* with him as evidence of literacy. Balston, on the strength of the essay, immediately suggested Rossetti as a theme. So far as I can remember, Waugh had no particular plan to deal further with the PreRaphaelites – he may even have had some other subject in mind – but the combination of *P. R. B.* and Balston's already existent leanings towards a book about Rossetti, resulted in *Rossetti: His Life and Works* being commissioned in May, 1927.

On one of Waugh's visits to Henrietta Street as a future Duckworth author he suggested that we should lunch together at a Soho club he had just joined, The Gargoyle, founded a year or two before with an eye on the intelligentsia; even if Constant Lambert was later to complain that the dance-floor on Saturday night was 'packed with the two hundred nastiest people in Chiswick'. I had already heard of The Gargoyle, which was on the top floor of an alley just off Dean Street, but had never been there. In principle a night-club, it was one of respectable kind, drinks not likely to be available 'after hours'. On the way to The Gargoyle (possibly on its premises) we met a girl Waugh had recently come across at *The Daily Express*, a newspaper on which he was himself employed for a few weeks at about this time; later contributing items for its gossip-column. This was Inez Holden, one of several figures belonging to this early stage of my London life, whom I was to meet on and off for forty years or more.

The three of us lunched together under the large picture by Matisse that hung in The Gargoyle's dining-room, lending an air of go-ahead culture to the club. I feel pretty sure that Waugh, with his usual generosity, paid for Inez Holden's lunch, though the advance on *Rossetti: His Life and Works* was probably not more than twenty or thirty pounds. Afterwards I was put up for the club, of which – though never a great frequenter – I remained a member for some years. It would have been logical for Waugh to have put me up, Inez Holden to have seconded me, but I have an idea that for some reason the process was vice versa. The appearance of Inez Holden in later life was sadly altered by some glandular condition. In those days she was very pretty, with the fashionable type of beauty Lambert used to call 'consumptive charm' (he thought her attractive but too *difficile* for involvement), a fragility of feature well suggested in two drawings by Augustus John, though neither a striking likeness.

Inez Holden was a torrential talker, an accomplished mimic, her gossip of a high and fantastical category; excellent company when not – as sometimes in later life – obsessed by some 'story' being run by the papers, of which she was a compulsive reader. At this period she too was trying to find her feet in London. Later she became a writer, erratic, though never without wit and originality. Very much a figure of the Twenties and early Thirties, she moved from High Bohemia to the extreme political Left, possibly as far as Communism. Her later passionate hatred of the Communist Party suggested close knowledge of its methods.

Born Old; Died Young (1932), probably Inez Holden's best book, contains something of a self-portrait; the heroine described as an 'adventuress', daughter ('left homeless and penniless') of an Edwardian beauty. That was more or less her own case (her father a retired cavalry-man), and, sometimes desperately poor, she lived fairly dangerously in a rich world of a distinctly older generation. This makes her sound like a *poule de luxe*. She was certainly not that, no one seeming to know (outside the fantasies she projected about herself) whether she allowed these shadowy love affairs to take physical shape. 'There was a period of my life,' she told me years later, 'when I knew only millionaires. That was when I was working on the *Express*. They were always asking me to arrange for them to buy the paper for a halfpenny, instead of a penny.'

For a couple of years after this Gargoyle luncheon I scarcely saw Inez Holden, but in 1929 Duckworth's published her first novel, *Sweet Charlatan*, a manuscript not steered there by me (unconvinced of its merits), nor, I think, by Waugh. She had met Balston somewhere, and brought pressure to bear on a nature altogether unused to adventuresses. It would not be going too far to say that for a time she made hay of him. After her interlude as a Duckworth's author, I did not see much of her again until the late Thirties. By that time I was married, and we were living at Chester Gate. Inez Holden had rooms in Albany Street, just round the corner. Then the war came, and I have described how she introduced me to George Orwell, to whom she was always greatly devoted.

The story of the row between Orwell and H. G. Wells (the coolness had taken place when Inez Holden was living in Wells's garage) has often been told, its climax in Wells's famous note to Orwell saying: 'Read my early works, you shit'.

I spent one or two weekends in Birmingham during the two years Yorke was working in his factory there. He boarded with a family in the manner of an ordinary engineering operative, and seemed happy;

more so than when at home, or travelling in America with his father, a journey that at one point interrupted this Birmingham reclusion. Yorke said that he never followed up occasional temptingly frisky invitations to join groups of factory girls roaming the streets after work, though they would sometimes shout after him. My impression is that he was as content during this Birmingham period as I ever knew him to be.

At one moment I decided to become a Territorial (Royal Artillery), but was not much enjoying the period of probation, when Duckworth's issued a fiat that I should undertake a course of printing at the Holborn Polytechnic.

Other people have told me they too experienced a monochromatic twelve-month before London had much to offer, then all at once new vistas opened up. How exactly that took place in my own case I have never been able to establish. Suddenly at the same moment there seemed fresh paths to explore. That was, I suppose, in the best Balzac tradition.

Spring and early summer brought through the letter-box a few invitations to débutante dances. Deb dances have often been described, usually disobligingly. At the moment they were acceptable, indeed I could have done with more cards for them. In their most intrinsic form the hard core was made up of two or three hundred girls, whose parents were expected to give a similar dance on the 'coming out' of a daughter. The net for young men was cast far wider. This was before the depression, a period when young men wore white gloves as a matter of course; as often as not there was 'taking in' to dinner. Three years later a young man wearing gloves was an elegant exception; to go into dinner on a partner's arm fallen altogether into disuse. At the time it seemed not at all odd that, apart from people already met, an entirely unknown hostess should invite one to a dinner-party, where not a soul at the table was previously familiar.

Deb dances included, of course, girls not débutantes in the strict sense of having been presented at Court that year; the number of 'seasons' at which a girl would appear varying according to taste and temperament. I tended to meet girls I knew at dances only at dances, a watertight compartment of my life. There were exceptions to this rule, for example, the charming Biddulph sisters, Adèle (Dig) and Mary (Miss), cousins of the Yorkes (the former of whom was to marry Henry Yorke), and several more. I continued to go to deb dances, on and off, until 1930, when – at what appears to be the last attended – my future wife, Violet Pakenham, was also present (one of her first), but we failed to meet.

3

I was all the time aware that a more invigorating, less staid, world existed, than that to which I possessed a somewhat hand-to-mouth access. Those other parties – in their specifically Late Twenties/Early Thirties sense – burned phosphorescently for a few years only, dying away as randomly as they had flamed into being. Most of those present at a 'typical' party would be likely to possess some connexion with the arts, however marginal, but never enough of any one calling to make the assembly a painters' party, an actors' party, an ad-men's party, though several painters would be likely to be present, the stray actor and ad-man. Indeed painters would be more in evidence than writers. There would be occasional musicians; architects; photographers; in the theatrical contingent, the Ballet likely to outnumber the Legitimate. The girls, largely drawn from the all-inclusive (one avoids the word all-embracing) vocation of model – both artists' model, and one who 'modelled' clothes, the latter then quaintly known as mannequins – usually showed an altogether exceptional standard of looks.

Like Augustus John and Bloomsbury, the three Sitwells had created a world perceptibly their own, though its affiliations, differing in the case of each individual Sitwell, seemed less immediately recognizable. One of Balston's earliest publishing ambitions was to take over the Sitwells' work; his first capture, Edith Sitwell, whose volume of verse, *Bucolic Comedies*, had been published by Duckworth's as far back as 1923. In the month I began employment with Duckworth's, the firm brought out both Osbert Sitwell's first novel, *Before the Bombardment*, and Sacheverell Sitwell's 'autobiographical fantasia', *All Summer in a Day*.

The triune nature of the family cartel – fatally effective at the time as vehicle of publicity – has not otherwise been advantageous to the Sitwells as individual writers. Their striking physical resemblance, a taste (in at least two) for polemics that was excessive, even for the chronic literary skirmishes of that date, the whole nature of the family's myth and its propagation in their own writings, have in different ways helped to obfuscate the picture for separate consideration.

Edith Sitwell was the first of the family I met; almost certainly dining at Balston's. She got on well with Balston, whom she unremittingly teased. Lacking her brothers' easy flow of conversation, unless in company familiar to her, she could be a little alarming at first, and was never really at ease in large gatherings. With people she knew and liked, no one could be gayer, though controversial topics were even then to be avoided. At this period, to some extent throughout Edith Sitwell's life, she was not at all well off. She lived in a tiny flat at St

Petersburg (eccentrically written 'St Petersborough' on the street sign) Place, Bayswater, where she would give tea-parties; the sitting-room on such occasions filled to capacity – and beyond – with guests invited for a thousand incongruous reasons. Notwithstanding the literary rows in which she was so often enmeshed, Edith Sitwell was a person of the kindest instincts; indeed to a fault, in a manner that could involve her with worthless hangers-on. She was altogether unsuited for the virulent public squabbles in which she found herself for ever caught up; scrimmages often her own fault, but really an extraneous part of her existence.

Much later than this period, Dylan Thomas, at one of Edith Sitwell's parties, said: 'If poetry was taken away from Edith she mightn't die, but she'd be bloody sick.' This characteristic uttering, gnomic and earthy, was a fair estimate of the case. Edith Sitwell's judgments were always clearcut. Her critical faculties might be arbitrary, they were never narrow. She said of Virginia Woolf and V. Sackville-West: 'I don't like what Virginia writes, but she knows what writing is about – Vita doesn't know what writing is about.' Describing how she herself had refused to dine with some literary bore (I do not remember which), she added: 'After all, I only have one dinner a day.' When a sudden warm friendship sprang up between Siegfried Sassoon (then in his forties, of melancholy saturnine appearance) and Stephen Tennant (at that moment the prettiest of young men), she used to call them The Old Earl and Little Lord Fauntleroy.

I first came across Osbert and Sacheverell Sitwell in the office, where the former especially would spend most of the morning or afternoon – sometimes a fair proportion of both – if he had a book to be published. After leaving Balston's room, Osbert Sitwell would gossip, discuss other authors (he could feel competitive about the most insignificant of writers), rag Lewis, who enjoyed Sitwell leg-pulling, however time-wasting. Osbert Sitwell thought Gerald Duckworth a *faux-bonhomme*, but at this stage nothing worse than an armed neutrality existed in that quarter.

The 'portraits in verse' of *England Reclaimed* (1928), village people known to Osbert Sitwell as a child, sometimes bring an odd reminder of sequences in novels by Henry Green; not only as affectionate, almost romantically yearning, pictures of a different world, viewed (notwithstanding both writers' efforts to minimize that angle) through aristocratic eyes, but, more essentially, on account of certain parallels in style, arrangement of words. If Henry Green's paragraphs were cut up into short lines like verse, Osbert Sitwell's poetry set continuously as prose, without too much adjustment either might be presented as the alternative art-form. I don't think the two ever met one another; if so, only superficially.

Excellent company tête-à-tête, Osbert Sitwell's wit was best adapted to the set-piece with an audience, rather than the kind that instantaneously grasps – then brilliantly caps – the implications of a conversation. He dominated a dinner-table with geniality, but essentially as protagonist. That does not mean that he lacked repartee. On some occasion he and Harold Nicolson were together filling embarkation forms on a Channel crossing.

'What age are you going to put, Osbert?' asked Nicolson.

'What sex are you going to put, Harold?'

Like his sister, Osbert Sitwell was by nature very kind; at the same time far better equipped than she, or his younger brother, for the dusty encounters of the arena. In these gladiatorial shows Sachie Sitwell loyally, but perhaps not very profitably, seemed at times carried along at the chariot wheels of the other two. His variety of interests make him the most complex of the three Sitwells, possibly the most gifted, the one who has always reaped least advantage from collective attack, handicapped, rather than sustained, by antecedent family influences thrust upon him.

William Walton, whose musical inspiration Sachie Sitwell first recognized, when both were undergraduates at Oxford, had been taken on by the Sitwells more or less as a member of the family. Willie Walton (later Sir William, OM), quiet, well organized, faintly satirical in manner, also lived at Carlyle Square, and was usually present at any party held there. He was very much one of the household (together with another occupant, Osbert Sitwell's close friend, David Horner called by Constant Lambert 'The Captain's Doll' after the D. H. Lawrence short story), yet also in a curious way somehow separate from it.

Walton (like the poet, Roy Fuller, also with musical affiliations) came from Oldham, Lancashire, and was physically of much the same North Midlands type as that to which the Sitwells themselves belonged. Walton, as protective colouring, naturally acquired other Sitwell resemblances and tricks of speech. In consequence (so Constant Lambert asserted), foreigners, at musical occasions attended by both Walton and the Sitwell family, would smile at English hypocrisy in pretending that this manifest Sitwell was not a by-blow of their father, Sir George; though, in fact, nothing could be less Sitwellian than Willie Walton on a night-out with Lambert or other uninhibited cronies.

At the Private View of the London Surrealist Exhibition in 1936 (oldest of old hat to anyone with the least claims to avant-gardism), Walton, to rag the whole affair, arrived at the Exhibition with a bloater in a paper bag. This, at a suitable moment, he removed from its covering, and, as a piece of active surrealism, hung on one of the pieces of sculpture. There, so far as I know, the fish remained throughout the run of the show; perhaps returning with the exhibit to whatever gallery or studio was its home.

After publication of *Before the Bombardment* Osbert Sitwell arranged for his next work to be a collaboration: *The People's Album of London Statues* (1928), thirty-two drawings by Nina Hamnett, to which he would provide an Introduction and Commentary. Nina Hamnett has recorded her own life in two volumes of memoirs, a trifle breathless in tone, but essentially first-hand in what they say about painters, sculptors, writers, nondescript bohemians, met at one time or another in the course of an adventurous career. Her father, an Army Service Corps colonel, cashiered for taking a bribe in South Africa, landed his dependents in fearful straits by this indiscretion, but his daughter's gift for drawing had somehow got her to the Slade; later to Paris, in a luxuriant epoch. Sickert, whose pupil she had been, wrote in praise of her drawing (the painting, never less than competent, is not so stylish); Augustus John too, with the literary flourish he loved: 'A slight French accent adorns a perfectly original talent.' Now in her late thirties, short haired, a good figure, rather belligerent manner, Nina Hamnett had become an alcoholic, a condition not affecting her gift, but restricting continuous work to a few months at best; human relationships to equally fragmentary associations.

The Sitwells admired Nina Hamnett's work, Osbert Sitwell (with an unaccustomed seriousness that throws light on himself too) once remarking: 'Of course Nina is the sort of person one couldn't possibly imagine doing a mean thing.' That integrity, founded on an unshakeable, if not always very judicious, confidence in her own myth, together with an undiminished response to life, no less inconsequent, kept her going through the hardest of hard times, to what was inevitably a tragic end.

In the course of delivering the drawings of the London statues to Duckworth's, Nina Hamnett suggested doing a drawing of me too. Her studio was off Fitzroy Street, one of two on the ground-floor of Thackeray House (some reputed connexion with the novelist), a small dilapidated but not inelegant façade (now no more), among the otherwise undistinguished dwellings of Maple Street. The opposite ground-floor studio belonged to another painter, Adrian Daintrey; a larger one, taking up the whole of the first-floor, occupied by an inventor and his mistress. These three studios made up the whole house. As neighbours some sort of a *modus vivendi* had been established, but Nina Hamnett and Adrian Daintrey never cared much for each other. I first met Daintrey there, when the drawing was being undertaken (he also drew me later), and we have remained friends to this day.

The Charlotte Street restaurant and pub, which, each in its own kind, dominated the remainder, were the Restaurant de la Tour Eiffel

(The Eiffel), at the west end of Percy Street looking north towards Fitzroy Square; The Fitzroy (Kleinfeldt's), on the corner of Charlotte Street and Windmill Street. In Windmill Street also existed a strange establishment, The Windmill, where nocturnal bacon-and-eggs – served by a grave butler-like personage in a tailcoat, whom a duke would have been proud to employ – could be obtained at any hour of the night until dawn. The celebrated Vicar of Stiffkey was said to patronize The Windmill for the entertainment of prostitutes; who in any case provided a proportion of its midnight clientèle. This pub world was peopled by transient shapes, some in due course to make a mark, others disappearing into heaven knows what depths. There were many painters, and it was not long before one encountered Augustus John; based on Chelsea, but spending a good deal of his time in this neighbourhood.

Among the many lesser figures, John Armstrong, a lank cadaverous but genial kobold, was then occupied with classical compositions that veered towards Surrealism, and John Banting (who executed the décor for Lambert's ballet, *Pomona*), also Surrealist in tone, his shaved head, curious laugh, recalling the madman playing with the piece of rope in the ballet of *The Rake's Progress*. Oddly enough, short lengths of rope often figure in Banting pictures.

The Eiffel was treated almost like a club by those *abonné* there, as more or less notable representatives of the arts, or otherwise looked on as desirable customers by Rudolph Stulik, the proprietor. The restaurant being relatively expensive as a haunt, I never had much to do with Stulik, a Viennese with a brusque manner, who talked Comic Opera broken English. He was very conscious of being a famous restaurateur, on easy terms with the great, but, while naturally preferring his clientèle to be as renowned as possible, nevertheless behaved accommodatingly to the less prosperous in the art world; indeed finally ruined himself by too generous addiction to bohemian life at all levels.

The literary side of John was perhaps a handicap to his painting. The subtraction of 'pure painting' from a Sickert picture leaves, in general, a 'literary' comment at once mordant and witty. The same process, when applicable to a John picture, runs the risk of discovering a residue of the wrong sort of bravura, even downright sentimentality. Any excursion into 'literariness' on the part of painters requires, in addition to the disciplines of painting, those normally imposed on a writer. This fact may sound obvious, but the additional burden, as such, is an aspect often forgotten.

In those days one used to be warned never to introduce the names of Sickert or Picasso into any conversations with John. Years later – only a year before his death in 1961 – he undertook some drawings of me. They were probably the last portrait drawings he executed, because he was then working most of the time on his triptych, *Les Saintes-Maries*. I used to drive over to Fryern for sittings. John would place himself at the end of a long narrow dining-room table. I would be in a chair at the side. On these occasions he would repeatedly bring in the names of both Sickert and Picasso, deriving obvious pleasure from reminiscence about both of them. Sickert he had known well; Picasso once invited John to his studio.

One day I remarked that, passing through Fordingbridge in the car, the girls had seemed pretty. John grunted, but made no comment. Later, Dorelia John brought in his mid-morning whisky. John took it from her.

'He says the girls in Fordingbridge look pretty.'

His wife glared at him.

'You'd better go out and pick one up then.'

By that time John, in his eighties, was very hard of hearing. He sometimes wore a deaf-aid. This caused chronic dissatisfaction. In the midst of an interchange of conversation that had interested him, he would suddenly wrench the appliance from his ear with an exclamation of strangled rage, and throw it to the end of the refectory table. There the deaf-aid would come to rest, its mechanism ticking ominously, like a bomb about to explode, until the close of the sitting.

Both Augustus John and Wyndham Lewis had painted convincing likenesses of Thomas Earp, an indispensable drinking companion of Charlotte Street.

Sometimes crimson, sometimes waxen, Earp's large face was set off under a cloth cap, probably relic of a former Oxford fashion, rather than claim to a proletarian manner of life. Ineligible for military service in World War I, he had stayed up at the University, becoming secretary, sometimes sole member, of every conceivable Oxford club; handing on in apostolic succession these secretaryships, representing continuous existence of the clubs themselves, when hostilities came to an end. Now living modestly (though the Sitwells, who did not like him, alleged more money than admitted), Earp was reputed to have got through a fair amount as a young man. His remarks, much bandied about, were uttered in a thin trembling voice. Working intermittently as an art-critic (in spite of resolute detestation of all pictures about equally), Earp would from time to time produce a volume of belles-lettres. In youth there had been a book of poems. His *Who's Who* recorded *Recreations* were: 'as many as possible'. When drunk, a condition not infrequent, Earp showed little exterior sign of intoxication – certainly none of exuberance – sooner or later falling into a stupor. Returning from comparatively far afield one night, he felt that state coming on, and took refuge under the tarpaulin cover of a Covent Garden barrow;

waking up the following day at an early hour to find that he had been wheeled to a distant part of London.

Even if not at all outwardly fitted for home life in many of his habits, Earp had his own preferred domestic rhythms. When an affluent friend invited him to luncheon one day, Earp shook his head: 'No – going home to lunch – apple-charlotte'. On another occasion, seeing Earp at midday in a pub, in front of a pint of beer and large hunk of bread-and-cheese, an acquaintance commented: 'I thought you said you were lunching with Lord Ivor Churchill [patron of the arts, brother of the Duke of Marlborough] today?' Earp, in his shaky treble, replied: 'I am – but I believe in being on the safe side.' On one of these occasional forays into upper-crust life, spending a weekend at some country house, Earp brought with him to read in bed a work entitled *The History of a Pair of Drawers*. He had not foreseen that his bag would be unpacked, this volume set out on the dressing-table beside his hair brushes. It was possibly on the same visit that the butler, helping Earp into an overcoat in the hall at departure, slipped his hand underneath the topcoat to adjust the lower part of Earp's jacket, but, missing the jacket's edge, seized the habitually baggy seat of Earp's trousers, jerking them down.

C. J. Hope-Johnstone would also appear in Charlotte Street from time to time. Although not 'of Bloomsbury' in anything like the strictest sense, Hope-J was accepted in Bloomsbury circles as an equal, for his Cambridge education, learning, eccentricities. He belonged more to the Augustus John world, though not in the least confined to John's court either. Spare, bespectacled, dry in speech, Hope-Johnstone had some of the air of a well turned-out don. Notwithstanding chronic money difficulties – he claimed he could live in fair comfort on £150 a year – he was always prepared to discuss the best tailor, where a man should buy his shirts.

When I first knew him Hope-Johnstone's chief means of support (he no longer edited the *Burlington Magazine*) was picture-dealing. He was likely to be in possession of a minor work by some master – a small Gainsborough, say, or a Renoir (in those days to be bought for a couple of hundred pounds) – on which he hoped to make a quick turnover. In excess of that canvas, he probably controlled a working capital of thirty shillings or less in his pocket. He said: 'A fortune-teller once told me I'd got the temperament of a civil servant – liking for routine, detail, what is meticulously arranged – yet lived dangerously, always on the brink of an abyss.'

This antithesis of action and character in Hope-J was well put. He seemed to have read most books, was always familiar with (usually to demolish) the latest thing in aesthetics or philosophy. He much recommended Rimbaud to me; also Restif de la Bretonne, an author I did not attempt until years later, nor got on at all well with, beyond noting signs that Restif had perhaps influenced Stendhal. Not having read *Les Liaisons Dangereuses* at that time, I never discussed Laclos with Hope-Johnstone, but I am sure he knew the book well, as he loved analysing the character of women. Indeed the general view was that Hope-J preferred theory to practice in that field. Certainly his own marriage in middle life (to a beautiful dancer) was almost imperceptible, so quickly ended, and never referred to by himself. He used to say: 'Those very fair ethereal virginal-looking girls are almost invariably nymphomaniacs.'

An interesting assertion of Hope-Johnstone's, which I have never confirmed, was that Wyndham Lewis, in early days, wrote many poems strongly influenced by Browning. These, he said, had appeared in obscure magazines. It is certainly true, vice versa, that Browning's *Soliloquy of the Spanish Cloister* has more than a touch of Lewis in its tone. Hope-Johnstone liked children: they him. At an Augustus John party I was watching him blow smoke-rings from his cigarette for the amusement of one of the sons of Lady Cynthia Asquith (painted by John some years before), and, after watching the rings slowly floating through the air, the small boy said: 'Now blow square ones.'

By the time I arrived in London the name of Rosa Lewis's hotel, The Cavendish, had been long familiar from stories told by my father. He regarded the place with a certain amount of awe, as haunt of various dashing contemporaries of his own. I do not know whether he himself ever went there, but imagine he must have crossed the threshold at one time or another. He would hint at orgies, but gave no clue to their nature. I did not like to ask.

I think I first entered The Cavendish with Richard Plunket Greene (an easygoing figure, known through many Oxford connexions), whom I ran into one evening in Jermyn Street. He suggested stepping into the hotel, which we were just passing. Plunket Greene was a friend of Rosa Lewis, but we struck a night when she was absent, accordingly nothing at all going on; all Cavendish life completely dependent on the proprietress.

The atmosphere of The Cavendish, unforgettable, is at the same time not easy to convey. Evelyn Waugh's picture in *Vile Bodies* is pretty close to life in some respects, but, among other things, omits the air of melancholy that hung like a pall over the place. I do not know who first took Waugh there, probably Alastair Graham, very much *ami de la maison*, but Plunket Greene was also a friend of Waugh's, and the introduction may have been owed to him.

At the time of which I speak the hotel was already in its decadence, a silver period, but I suspect that even in more palmy days lightheartedness was always tempered by a touch of something a shade macabre. I never stayed there, which must have been an interesting experience. A small but steady proportion of the clientèle was drawn from people who came up from the country from time to time, and knew nowhere else round the Piccadilly area so 'reasonable' in its terms; remaining totally unaware of the hotel's less prim side.

Rosa Lewis's legend is well known. Renowned in her early days as cook for Edward VII (when Prince of Wales) and his circle (plenty of lesser households too), she was reputed to have been the future monarch's mistress. The story is unconfirmed, and has all the air of myth, but (b. 1867) she gave the impression of considerable beauty in days gone by. She talked that old fashioned cockney now passed almost as far into oblivion as the speech of the Etruscans. Tall, stately, white-haired, Rosa Lewis was formidable to a degree. It is often said that she possessed a very aristocratic mien. If she had looked like a rackety duchess, or minor royalty who was no enemy to the bottle, she would have seemed less exceptional in appearance. Rosa Lewis, so it seemed to me, showed far more the utterly unexpected exterior of the statuesque wife of a senior civil servant, or President of the Royal Academy; a lady who had suddenly decided to have the most reckless of nights-out, rather than attend a reception at the Guildhall, or Ten Downing Street. Perhaps that is hair-splitting, but social hairs are the most enjoyable ones to split.

People went to The Cavendish fairly late, after 11 o'clock, probably after midnight, when drinks had in general ceased to be procurable in public places. Round the large drawing-room on the first-floor (done up in the manner of a somewhat decayed country house, but nice pieces of furniture there, and throughout the hotel) one or two persons – perhaps more – might be sitting. It is impossible to say who these figures would be, or what particular circumstances caused their presence in the room. One thing The Cavendish very decidedly did not represent was a place where anyone who felt so disposed could get a drink 'after hours'. It would have been a very determined man or woman who, if personally unknown to Rosa Lewis, brought that off. On the other hand, the loiterers to be found in that drawing-room would often defy definition; sometimes appearing themselves scarcely aware why they were there. A couple of pink-faced Guards ensigns would not be unexpected; nor an American, perhaps a couple of Americans, drawn from almost any of the widely varying types of the US, the extreme 'Western' not to be ruled out. Augustus John, sitting drinking alone in the corner, was always a possibility.

Rosa Lewis herself tended to wander about her domain, ever restless, passing through the drawing-room from time to time, rather than playing any static part as hostess. She was excellent company if in good form, but had her gloomy moments. 'Lights on all over the house,' she would complain despairingly. 'It'll be the ruin of me. I'm too old now to keep an eye on things. I'm turning the front into shops as quick as I can. That'll bring something in. I'll go bankrupt otherwise.'

Possibly someone might be playing the piano in the corner. A little man in a dinner jacket was strumming jazz one night. After a time he left the piano and came across the room. Rosa Lewis, occupied with her reflections, was lying back in an armchair. Noticing the music had ceased, she looked up sharply.

'Go back and play *Ole Man River*,' she ordered.

The pianist began to protest. He was an American, and obviously played very well. Probably he was a wellknown performer.

'Do as I tell you.'

'I'm not going to be treated like a servant.'

'Don't be a bloody fool.'

'I won't be spoken to like that.'

'Don't talk so much. Let's have another bottle of wine. Go back and play *Ol' Man River*, and do as you're told.'

He gave in, of course. It had been foolish to rebel. The champagne arrived. It was poured out all round. At The Cavendish 'a bottle of wine' always meant champagne. It was as if champagne was the only wine anyone had ever heard of there. The American obliged again with *Ol' Man River*. Rosa, Lewis went fast asleep in her armchair. The faithful Edith, Rosa Lewis's lady-in-waiting (who was herself to rule The Cavendish in the years that remained of its existence after the death of the proprietress), appeared in the doorway for a moment, pale, tired, but ever watchful, saw all was well, disappeared again.

The most affluent person present – often American – was in general expected to pay for champagne. He would probably be staying at the hotel, the wine put down on his bill; in any case the legal fiction always observed that drinks were served for hotel residents only. It was by no means unknown for Rosa Lewis herself to 'stand' a bottle, especially if those present were notoriously hard up. There was usually someone on the spot to accept the acting of host as a privilege; more or less so, according to temperament. Rosa Lewis's famous pie – like Frau Sacher's chocolate cake – might be produced at unexpected moments.

As an impecunious young man, the question of being suddenly faced with a bill for a dozen bottles of champagne did not arise, though persons of more mature years, less exiguous means, could feel extremely apprehensive as to such a possibility. This sense of financial anxiety had perhaps something to do with the tense menacing atmosphere of The Cavendish, an oppression that only more beakers of champagne could wash away. As Douglas Byng, incomparable singer of his own comic songs, neatly put it:

The bridegroom's with Rosa,
She's saying he owes her
For millions of magnums of Mumm.

It has been asserted that Rosa Lewis was a great snob. The indictment is undeniable if the word – one of many meanings – is used merely in the sense of being interested in the ramifications of aristocratic life: who engaged to whom; who running away with someone else; who blessed with grandchildren; who forced to sell their estates; who resigning from the Brigade of Guards after matrimonial disaster. On the other hand, Rosa Lewis could not have been less of a snob in the sense that she liked only the grand or successful; nor would she have hesitated for a moment to order from her hotel anyone of whatever rank or station, if bored or otherwise displeased by them. When she found people amusing, or they otherwise took her fancy, neither class, race, colour nor tongue, would create a barrier. She liked the feeling of belonging to a huge family, the sort of gossip too subtle to reach the ears of the professional gossip-writer.

In her day she must have been a kind of nanny, a faintly sinister one, to a lot of rich raffish, but perhaps ultimately rather lonely young men, whose photographs in bearskin cap, or frogged military frockcoat, covered the walls of the downstairs office. Nevertheless, whatever her rôle of nanny to some, Rosa Lewis could feel strong dislike for others. She never forgave Evelyn Waugh for *Vile Bodies*, and would often – for what reason I don't know – vilify the name of Mark Gertler, who would seem an improbable frequenter of The Cavendish. In any case all question of sentimentality should be rigorously excluded from any account of Rosa Lewis and her hotel, both apt to become blurred with nostalgia over the years. An aroma of toughness permeated the place; the fact never forgotten that dissipation must be paid for.

* 4 *

I must undoubtedly have met Constant Lambert in the autumn of 1927. Lambert was within a few months of my own age, and from the start we got on well. His painter father, George Washington Lambert (born in Russia, son of an American engineer of first-generation emigration), was a great admirer of Bronzino, and, as the Bluecoat portrait of his younger son shows, managed to impose a distinctly

Bronzino type of looks on his own offspring. Lambert *père*, whose work – more romantic, less brassy – was somewhat in the manner of William Orpen, lived mostly in Australia. He was quite prosperous as a painter, but took small interest in his family, his wife remaining in England most of the time with her two sons. Mrs Lambert (whom I always found a little daunting) was a most devoted wife and mother, keeping her household going, never deviating in admiration of her husband, in the face of untold worries and difficulties.

The elder son, Maurice Lambert (also musically talented), was a sculptor, relatively academic in style. Tough, bearded, ungregarious, he had a reputation for morosity that might suddenly erupt into rudeness, but I always liked what little I saw of him. (He was at Augustus John's funeral, but, beard removed, I did not recognize him, and we made no contact before he died not long after.) In contrast with his younger brother, Maurice Lambert was devoted to pursuits like boxing and sailing, committed to spheres of physical action, while being at the same time personally inward-looking. Constant Lambert would have rows with his brother, but was fond of him too; liking to compare what he regarded as the extrovert life of a sculptor with that of a musician: 'The amount of work my brother does is limited only by the hour he gets up in the morning. If you speak to him of constipation, he asks you what you mean.'

A story Maurice Lambert used to tell seems worth preservation. A year or two before the period when I met him he had taken a studio from the widow of another sculptor, James Havard Thomas. Havard Thomas's bronze, called Lycidas, used to stand in the forecourt of the Tate Gallery; a young shepherd, naked, conceived in the sculptor's imagination as having just caught sight of nymphs disporting themselves in the stream below. Havard Thomas was a friend of Norman Douglas, who writes amusingly of him in *Late Harvest* (1946), alleging that he himself suggested the name Lycidas to the sculptor, as vaguely classical, without too close affiliations with any well-known legend. The bronze of this work was in the Tate, but the original wax model for the statue had been consigned to the Manchester Art Gallery.

At Manchester, Maurice Lambert said, embarrassments had arisen because mill-girls, enjoying a Sunday afternoon's stroll through their city's Art Gallery, would playfully snap off the male organ of Lycidas, and bear it away with them. Accordingly, Havard Thomas was required to travel by train to Manchester, with three waxen 'spare parts' in his overcoat pocket; thereby anticipating further spoliation on the lines of the Mutilation of the Hermae. I used to come across Norman Douglas occasionally in the 1940s, when he was in London, and greatly regret I then did not know of his acquaintance with Havard Thomas. It was a story Douglas would have enjoyed.

Goodlooking in a boyish but distinguished way, Constant Lambert was already getting a trifle fat, though Christopher Wood's picture (National Portrait Gallery) shows the emaciated figure Lambert had been only a very short time before. With regard to his own weight, a favourite theme with him was the lean, rather than well covered personage, as typical butt of 18th century jocosity. He would defend this standpoint vigorously.

Although his clothes were ordinary, Lambert never looked ordinary. He usually wore an oldish brownish London suit, a shirt of one fairly deep colour, blue or orange without a pattern, a plain tie of another shade; latterly an open collar, if the weather was hot. His habit of hatlessness (followed also by Walton), slightly unconventional at that period, persisted from Christ's Hospital schooldays. Getting into a stiff shirt or 'morning clothes' for conducting, one or other form of 'tails' required most days, was always likely to threaten apoplexy. Lambert tied by hand the bow of white evening ties, but once caught Sir Thomas Beecham standing before the looking-glass of a Covent Garden dressing-room, while he adjusted a made-up one; for which, to Lambert's great satisfaction, the famous conductor muttered some sort of rather embarrassed apology, a rare reaction in him.

Soon after we first met, I suggested Lambert should contribute something of musical bearing to a series of essays by young writers (Waugh, Byron, Connolly, Green, *et al*), contemplated at my suggestion by Duckworth's, though never brought to birth. I addressed the letter to 'Constantine Lambert, Esqre.', thinking Constant an abbreviation of the longer name. Lambert used to affirm – the Russian composer, Modest Mussorgsky, always excepted – that no one had ever been given a less appropriate forename than himself. (He was, I think, never christened for moral reasons, his parents being strict atheists.) I am not sure that was absolutely true. In one sense, as things turned out, constancy may not have seemed the most conspicuous trait in Lambert's character. In another, there was a consistency about his life, even his 'love life', that had something of constancy about it.

At this period Lambert was in professional doldrums, though not long before he had been experiencing tempestuous times with Diaghilev, then at the height of his fame, and for a variety of reasons anxious to commission a ballet by a British composer. Lambert, only eighteen at the time, had been chosen for that rôle.

Dealings with Diaghilev had been volcanic, reaching a pitch when Lambert, who would not be bullied, threatened to withdraw his music. One of the reasons for this explosion had been Diaghilev's decision to use Surrealist painters, Max Ernst and Joán Miró, in place of the English artist, Christopher Wood, to whom the work for Lambert's ballet had been in the first instance assigned. This change made

Lambert exceedingly angry. Over and above his liking for Wood's designs, Lambert was a personal friend of Wood, for whom (in a quite unhomosexual manner) he had a certain hero-worship.

Wood (whom I met perhaps a couple of times), a talented performer in the *faux-naïf* manner, was goodlooking and self-assured. He was the only British artist found acceptable in the Paris *monde* of Picasso and Cocteau, a convenient bisexuality being no handicap in that sphere. Understandably, this professional success as a painter, popularity in other respects with *les deux sexes et autres*, had made Wood more than a little *tête-montée*, causing him to give the outward impression not so much of an artist, as of a young stockbroker, who has made a pile before the age of thirty. The going proved too fierce. Two years later, tensions of life complicated by drugs, Wood, returning from his parents' home, threw himself under a train coming in at Salisbury station platform.

Lambert's row with Diaghilev was eventually patched up, but ever afterwards (according to Osbert Sitwell), when crisis threatened, Diaghilev would beg: 'Surtout – pas de Lambert.' On his side, Lambert bore little ill will, though he always insisted that one of the great impresario's highest claims to fame was in being the only known Russian, of either sex, to restrict himself to only one sex. Lambert would also complain that Diaghilev's habit of greeting a newly arrived guest with the words: 'Will you have one [a] drink?' always got the evening off to a bad start.

Intellectually speaking, Lambert moved with perfect ease in the three arts, a facility less generously conferred by nature than might be supposed from the way some people talk. Appreciation of two arts in a discerning fashion is not at all uncommon; where three are claimed, more often than not grasp of the third shows signs of strain. With Lambert there was no strain. Although he himself had scarcely any talent for drawing (beyond playing a creditable game of heads-bodies-and-legs), he had been brought up in close contact with the technicalities of painting and sculpture, always retaining his own equally penetrating line also on any matter that arose which had to do with writing. He had a natural gift for writing, a style individual and fluid, that brisk phraseology so characteristic of those musicians able to express themselves on paper.

Lambert loved discussing painters, Böcklin to Braque, Breughel to Brangwyn, especially enjoying to put forward subjects for Royal Academy pictures in the sententiously forcible manner of Brangwyn – once much imitated – of which two proposed canvases (titles in which perhaps Maurice Lambert too had a hand) were: *Blowing up the Rubber Woman*, and *'Hock or Claret, Sir?': Annual Dinner of the Rectal Dining Society*. Lambert once described the work of the Russian painter, Pavel Tchelitchev (a great favourite of Edith Sitwell's) as looking like the winning exhibit in the *Daily Mail*'s annual prize for the season's best design in the sand at Margate.

We used to meet fairly regularly, drinking in pubs, going for walks, attending the sort of parties described earlier. Lambert was the first contemporary of mine I found, intellectually speaking, wholly sympathetic. The fact is not easy to explain even to myself. I lack musical sensibilities, and although, when it came to books and pictures, we had tastes in common, we differed greatly too. Lambert (in the taste of that moment) detested the High Renaissance, loving the arts of Asia and Africa. Admirable as the two last can be, I should never wish to surround myself entirely with their artefacts, and, whatever its undeniable excesses, I enjoy the High Renaissance in all its glorification of the individual.

It was, however, Lambert's general approach to the arts (for that matter, in many respects, Daintrey's) which was in such contrast with that of my Oxford generation. With them there seemed always an amateurishness, a narrowness of view, a way of treating the arts as if they were a useful social weapon. Again explanation eludes me, because several of my Oxford contemporaries were gifted enough. The crux was perhaps that the people I knew at Oxford who practised the arts did so with a self-consciousness of which Lambert – and many others I now met – was totally free. This difference of outlook can be gauged by comparing, say, *Enemies of Promise*, *Pack My Bag*, *A Little Learning*, with *Music Ho!*; though admittedly all these books were produced by their authors at different ages, with different ends in view.

Richard Shead's biography, *Constant Lambert* (1973), firmly identifies its subject with Moreland in *Dance*. Moreland, musician, wit, sometimes exuberant, sometimes melancholy, has the Bronzino-type features already described as Lambert's. There the resemblance fades, invention, imagination, the creative instinct – whatever you like to call it – takes over. If I have been skilful enough to pass on any echo of Lambert's incomparable wit, then Moreland is like him; in other respects, the things that happen to Moreland approximate to the things that happened to Lambert only within the extent that all composers' lives have something in common. Here and there, as often falls out when writing a novel, a chance bull's eye is registered. For example, I was ignorant – or had altogether forgotten – that Lambert was specially interested in Chabrier. Perhaps I had inwardly stored that fact away in the manner characteristic of the novelist's latent machinery. To those aware of Lambert's liking for Chabrier's music and personality (subject of Lambert's first published article), Moreland's talk about the French composer must have seemed deliberate, possibly even including snatches of quoted speech. That was not so, and in a dozen ways Lambert's career differs from that assigned to Moreland.

Towards the end of his life especially, the laughter and talk of Lambert's lighthearted moods had an obverse side of periodical grumpiness and ill humour. Even in his palmiest days there were good friends who could stand only limited stretches of the Lambert barrage of ideas, jokes, fantasy, quotations, apt instances, things that had struck him as he walked through London, not because these lacked quality, on the contrary because the mixture was after a while altogether too rich. The world prefers on the whole, if not simple, at least less nourishing conversational fare. As with every known 'good talker' there was also a modicum of repetition. Speaking for myself, I very rarely felt the show had gone on too long, but I could see what others meant when at times they complained.

Lambert was prodigal of his wit. He never dreamt of postponing a joke because the assembled company was not sufficiently important for a witticism to be used on. Another point should be emphasized. Impatient, at times intolerant, Lambert was also an unexpectedly good listener. He did not in the least insist on holding the floor. In fact he liked nothing better than being entertained by the talk of others. He had a mind of extraordinary quickness (equalled, I think, for sheer speed in seeing the drift of a given story, only by my later friend, Alick Dru, met in wartime), beginning to shake with laughter before most anecdotes of any merit were halfway through, simply because he saw how they were going to end.

Lambert himself always disparaged those social milieux – again Oxford of my day comes to mind – where the conventions of a supposedly 'amusing' society disallows any development of a narrative. That was true, for instance, of Sitwell life. In such a world anything like a long story must, by definition, be regarded as a bore. Lambert used to point out that the best, the funniest, stories can rarely be told in a sentence. I should not wish support of this view to be perverted into the appearance of exonerating purveyors of prosy *histoires*, but there is a case for unprosy ones that may require a comparatively extended build-up for their punch-line. The wit of the Twenties, often tempered with self-consciousness and narcissism, even a rather childish buffoonery, was on the whole not well disposed to that view. Iago, on the other hand (even if he may have meant something rather different), remarks that 'wit depends on dilatory time'.

If Lambert possessed a different approach from Oxford contemporaries, he was even less like the group then spoken of as the 'new poets', to whom he was not at all drawn. He used to complain of their metre, rhymes, subject matter, the last of which he epitomized as 'like reading back-numbers of the *New Statesman*'. The fact that several of them were school-masters caused Lambert to picture them as discouraging their pupils from all poetry in traditional style, and (himself quite a performer in complicated verse forms) he produced several squibs on this theme. One began:

> W. H. Auden whips a kiddy on
> His bottom for reciting *Epipsychidion*.

Lambert possessed, I think, a touch of genius. The word is unsatisfactory. One envisages a row of lifeless effigies stretching back in time, mysterious unapproachable beings emitting a suffocating leakage of something that inspires awe; lay-figures carousing in cafés, or lying overcome with despair on truckle-beds in garrets. Another label is required. One tries again. Lambert inwardly inhabited, often outwardly expressed, a universe in which every individual, every action, was instantly appreciated in terms of art. Once more the concept threatens to fall flat. It could be even worse than 'genius', if the words suggest a pompous self-conscious aesthete, laboriously evaluating every trivial experience. Lambert could hardly have been further from that too. All the same, those are perhaps the lines along which to explore him as an entity.

That October – the Territorial riding-school exchanged for the Holborn Polytechnic – I used to turn up several evenings a week to study printing at Southampton Row. The girls flitting about the Polytechnic corridors seemed to offer exciting suggestions of co-educational student life at some foreign university. I dreamt of all sorts of romantic encounters, fantasies that never throughout the course showed even the remotest sign of taking shape. Instruction in the craft of printing was scarcely more fruitful, Union restrictions limiting guidance to what might easily be picked up, with a little experience and commonsense.

One night, on the way down the passage to my printing-class, a male student came hurrying from the opposite direction. He seemed deeply preoccupied. His appearance had the familiarity, coupled with complete improbability, which one associates with dreams. Notwithstanding, identification, however hard to accept, was equally hard to deny. There could be no doubt whatever that here was Evelyn Waugh. We saw each other at the same moment. Mutual astonishment was expressed at meeting in such a place at such a time; reasons compared for finding ourselves at this hour in the corridors of the Holborn Polytechnic. My own explanation was simple enough. When I asked what subject Waugh was studying, his reply was less easily comprehensible.

'Carpentry.'

'Why on earth?'

'Oh, Tolstoy and all that.'

This was the moment when Waugh had decided to give up school-mastering, and earn a living with his hands. Carpentry seems always to have held a fascination for him, over and above an interest in the craftsmanship side of the PreRaphaelite Movement. For example, at King's Thursday (the country house in *Decline and Fall*) the 'estate carpenter' is described as holding 'an office hereditary in the family of the original joiner'; while in middle life, when living in a prosperous but hardly grandiose style in Gloucestershire, Waugh would some-times refer to his own employment of a retainer thus designated. Waugh was determined to take up cabinet-making as a profession; though invocation of Tolstoy's name (recently suggesting itself to me, too, in the Russian novelist's rôle of artilleryman) obviously implied that writing need not be absolutely barred as a sideline. When our re-spective classes were over we ate something together at a pub-restaurant in Southampton Row, discussing the progress of Waugh's book on Rossetti, commissioned by Duckworth's earlier that year. Waugh was full of enthusiasm for this latest excursion into manual labour.

Not long after the Polytechnic encounter with Waugh, Balston, who had been talking about giving a party, finally decided to do so. The occasion was to be primarily for the Sitwells, but would also include the less stick-in-the-mud Duckworth authors – and potential authors – seasoned with a small but hardy nucleus of relatively bohemian friends Balston himself had acquired over the years. Waugh's Diary seems to refer to Balston's party, but I do not remember him being at the flat. Perhaps (for reasons later apparent) he slipped away early to more seductive commitments.

Among other guests was Robert Byron (recently signed up with Duckworth's for his Mount Athos book, *The Station*), who showed no exceptional behaviour throughout the evening, until it came to going home. The several blocks that made up Artillery Mansions were approached from Victoria Street through a lofty arch that stood above high iron gates. These gates were kept open during the day, but (like the portals of a college) closed at a certain hour of the night; persons coming in and out then using a small side-door. While the rearguard of Balston's departing guests was crossing the courtyard, Byron, letting out a series of blood-curdling war-whoops, rushed at the closed gates and began to climb them at a great rate. Reaching the top, he achieved descent into Victoria Street without impalement.

Whether or not Waugh attended Balston's party, he and I had not met for some weeks when, probably towards Christmas, we saw each other in the same compartment of a Tube train. Waugh was in the highest of spirits. Before a word could be said on any other subject he made a statement.

'I'm going to be married.'

At first I supposed a joke was intended. Marriage, as already emphasized, was something unthought of among contemporaries at that date, an undertaking well outside the consideration of the possible; or so it seemed to me. The next two years were to demonstrate the fallacious nature of that opinion, but at the moment matrimony was something particularly inconceivable in connexion with Waugh.

'Who to?'

'She's called Evelyn Gardner.'

The name was not wholly unfamiliar owing to a chance meeting in the street not long before with Waugh's elder brother, come across once or twice, always very agreeable. I had run into Alec Waugh one evening in the neighbourhood of Sloane Square. I cannot quote verbatim, but roughly speaking Alec Waugh's words were on this occasion: 'Do you know two delightful girls who live just round the corner from here called Evelyn Gardner and Pansy Pakenham? We're always reading newspaper articles about the Modern Girl putting on too much make-up, drinking too many cocktails, being brassy, bad-mannered, gold-digging, but these two couldn't be nicer, prettier, quieter, more intelligent.'

It was not at all uncommon for Alec Waugh himself to write the sort of article typified, so that he spoke with authority on the subject. I knew the name of Pansy Pakenham from debs who talked of her (though she herself had abandoned the deb world), but this was the first time I had heard of Evelyn Gardner. Alec Waugh had not mentioned either girl as friend of his younger brother's, and (Evelyn Waugh always emphasizing the difference of their lives) I had in no way connected him with this exemplary couple.

Evelyn Gardner, like Pansy Pakenham, had outgrown deb dances. She was the youngest daughter of the 1st Lord Burghclere (deceased without heir to the title some years before), himself illegitimate son of the last Lord Gardner, a family of naval distinction in the past. Evelyn Gardner's mother (*née* Lady Winifred Herbert, daughter of the 4th Earl of Carnarvon) was sister to Lady Margaret Duckworth, wife of Sir George Duckworth, Gerald Duckworth's brother. This Herbert connexion was to be not without all publishing (and other) significance at a later date. Pansy Pakenham, eldest daughter of the 5th Earl of Longford (killed at Gallipoli), worked in an architect's office. She and Evelyn Gardner shared a flat over a tobacconist's shop at the west end of Cliveden Place, a few yards from Sloane Square.

For girls of that sort to set up house together was in those days an unconventional thing to do; in this case made possible by both being not only of age, but possessing a little money of their own. The Dowager

Countess of Longford, somewhat autocratic in dealing with her children, having, perforce, agreed initially to her daughter leaving home to work, could only accept the situation. Lady Longford had also, as it happened, fallen victim to Evelyn Gardner's charm. In this she was by no means alone, though a notable captive on account of her position vis-à-vis the girls' household. Lady Burghclere, no less opposed than Lady Longford to girls leaving home, judged Pansy Pakenham – although the younger of the two – a potentially steadying influence on her own daughter, perpetually being proposed to by young men, none of whom her mother found ideal as a potential son-in-law.

I do not remember the circumstances of my first introduction to Evelyn Gardner by Evelyn Waugh (from the start they were known as 'the two Evelyns') – possibly a brief exchange at The Gargoyle – but, not so very long after the meeting with Waugh on the Underground, I was asked in for a drink at the flat shared with Pansy Pakenham.

Waugh was not present when I arrived at Cliveden Place. I think he turned up much later. He was probably busy with his now rapidly expanding professional life (writing once more in the ascendant over carpentry), or making the endless arrangements consequent on an engagement, even an unofficial one; the news, once it broke, that he and Evelyn Gardner were to get married, causing a considerable commotion. The welcoming atmosphere of Cliveden Place bore out all Alec Waugh had implied, and he was probably not far from the truth, given the circumstances, in describing the girls as a unique couple.

The warmth and charm of Evelyn Gardner – who remains a friend to this day – were, on the one hand, in direct contrast with the supposedly brassy traits of that ominous figure, The Modern Girl, while at the same time she seemed in her person to exemplify all thought of as most 'modern'. She possessed the looks and figure of the moment, slight, boyish, an Eton crop; that simplicity of style more often to be found breaking hearts at the rackety parties outlined earlier, than in the ballrooms of Mayfair and Belgravia, however pretty the debs; and (Pansy Pakenham among these) some debs were very pretty indeed. The only other person present, apart from the two girls, was Henry Lamb. I was familiar with Lamb's painting, particularly his quite famous portrait (in the Tate) of Lytton Strachey, and had just caught a glimpse of the painter himself at the party of Augustus John's where Hope-Johnstone had blown the smoke-rings. Indeed, it was Hope-Johnstone who had pointed Lamb out to me.

'They say Lamb has got hold of an aristocratic young girl, and is trying to marry her,' Hope-Johnstone said, adding a disparaging view of Lamb.

The first story was no less than the truth, though not so sinister in realization as import of the words sounded at the time. There was no way of guessing that a future brother-and-sister-in-law, with both of whom I was to have long and happy relations, were thus defined. Lamb and Hope-Johnstone, men with strong likes and dislikes, did not get on at all well.

Henry Lamb was then in his middle forties. Regarded when younger as devastatingly handsome, he was thin, unrelaxed in manner, with a searching air that gave the impression you were expected to prove yourself before he easily accepted you. On varying terms with John himself, Lamb moved to some extent within the John orbit; more so, in fact, than among the Bloomsburies, in spite of Lytton Strachey's passion for him. Indeed Lamb, fairly irascible in temperament, lived a comparatively segregated life at Poole in Dorset. Among his friends was George Kennedy, an amusing and agreeable architect, with certain Bloomsbury affiliations. It was in Kennedy's office that Pansy Pakenham worked, and there she and Lamb met.

Lamb had set out in the first instance on the career of surgeon, a profession for which he showed great promise; a touch of the medical man always remaining with him. During the first war he had won an MC as doctor with a battalion in the field, and by now he had made a name for himself as a painter, earning a respectable if not abounding income. Marriage to a celebrated beauty of the bohemian world had gone wrong many years before, but, long parted from his first wife, Lamb had never bothered to sever the union by law. He was now taking steps to obtain a divorce in order to marry Pansy Pakenham.

The Cliveden Square household at that moment had some of the air of a play: the two charming girls; the two detrimental but gifted suitors; the very situation come into being most dreaded by the two dowager mammas.

Notwithstanding his relative fame as an artist, a gallant war record, ability to support a wife and family, Henry Lamb, divorced (if he brought that off, not absolutely assured, as the Law then stood), long committed to the bohemian life, more than twenty years older than Pansy Pakenham, could not be looked upon by Lady Longford as ideal *parti* for a pretty and talented daughter of twenty-three; even if the brothers and sisters were keenly in favour of the match, as likely to add an exciting dimension to family life.

In a different manner, Evelyn Waugh, though younger, could be regarded, in the circumstances he found himself, as even less eligible by Lady Burghclere. If Lamb was too old to be immediately acceptable, Waugh, only just twenty-four, was, in the eyes of the parents of those days, too young as aspirant to marriage. Apart from the potential royalties of *Rossetti: His Life and Works* (due to appear in the spring), he possessed no visible means of support, while nothing popularly known of his life was of a nature to inspire confidence in an aristocratic mother-in-law of admittedly straitlaced outlook.

It was, indeed, one of Waugh's most endearing characteristics at this period not to care in the least what anyone thought of his goings-on. To a large extent that contempt for public opinion remained with him throughout, but, the style of his own life altering, those who disapproved of his attitudes in later days, did so for quite other reasons. One need hardly add that, as soon as the engagement became known, rumours of Waugh's supposedly dissipated habits were hurried to Lady Burghclere's ears.

The two mothers concerned took the impact of a daughter's engagement in a differing spirit. Lady Longford, who at that time lived, with the rest of the Pakenham family not yet grown up, at North Aston Hall, Oxfordshire, had already met Henry Lamb at tea in the girls' flat. She received a letter one morning from Pansy Pakenham announcing the engagement; containing the added information that Lamb was being brought down to the country to renew their acquaintance. If Lamb wished to make himself agreeable, no one was more capable of doing so. The second meeting was an unqualified success. All had gone admirably, the engaged couple were just leaving the house, when Lady Longford drew Lamb behind a pillar.

'I have to be father and mother both,' she said. 'It *is* a clean sheet, Mr Lamb?'

Lamb, having absolutely no idea what was meant, was struck dumb for the moment. Lady Longford, like Pilate, did not wait for an answer. She spoke at once of other things. The car drove away. Afterwards, Lamb would often speculate with his in-laws on the bearing of the question. Illegitimate children? Venereal disease? Forgery? Murder? There the matter rested. The enigma of Lady Longford's enquiry was never solved. No sort of obstruction was offered, and Lamb was soon welcomed by a large circle of new relations, many of whom he was to draw or paint in the years that were to follow.

In connexion with the Lamb/Pakenham wedding (which took place in August, 1928) only one matter made Lady Longford cross – very cross – which was that Waugh (by that time married himself, and contributing items of social gossip to the *Daily Express*) fed in several paragraphs, which were printed in the paper, to the effect that 'the wedding of Lady Pansy Pakenham and Mr Henry Lamb had been almost secret'. It had, of course, been nothing of the kind.

On the other hand, there was truth enough in calling Waugh's marriage to Evelyn Gardner 'secret', since he had experienced with Lady Burghclere no such easy passage as that encountered by Lamb with Lady Longford. There had, indeed, been several unhappy inter-

views. Waugh told me that on one occasion he called on Lady
Burghclere (whom, from the locality of her house in Mayfair, he always
referred to as 'the fairy of Green Street') wearing a top-hat and tailcoat,
even in those days rare except for weddings and Ascot. I am uncertain
whether he chose this turnout for the initial visit to ask her daughter's
hand in marriage, or on a subsequent call at the Green Street house,
when the match was already meeting with considerable discouragement.

Lady Burghclere was no enemy to intellectual life as such (indeed
had herself written several books), but, as mentioned before, she had
already raised objection to several other young men as suitors, some
of them – from a conventional point of view – more eligible than
Waugh; of whom she was reported to have used the phrase *les moeurs
atroces*. Accordingly, when the wedding took place in June, 1928, that
was without Lady Burghclere's knowledge.

This disapprobation, involving as it did parent and daughter, might
not be entirely unexpected, but all sorts of other people, with little or
no business to concern themselves about the wisdom or unwisdom of
the marriage, expressed their views loudly on the subject. Among those
feeling something well short of approval (so Balston revealed) was
Gerald Duckworth, who, on the one hand, a sort of uncle by marriage
of the bride (his brother having married Lady Burghclere's sister), on
the other, publisher designate of the bridegroom, regarded himself as
in a position to speak out.

Henry Lamb and I got on pretty well at our first meeting, and so
things remained until his death in 1960, but after introduction at
Cliveden Place I scarcely came across him until early in 1934, the
year I married Violet Pakenham, his wife's younger sister.

Lamb, who, as well as being a painter, was a musician of more than
ordinary attainment, held opinions very much his own. Witty, unpredictable, fractious, he wrote vigorously articulate letters, especially
to people who rubbed him up the wrong way. When William Rothenstein sent what Lamb deemed patronizing criticism from a fellow
painter of a recent Lamb picture-show, in which the phrase 'a tendency
to tightness' had been used, Lamb sent a letter to Rothenstein in reply,
saying that he used to be loose, but nowadays he was always tight.

When he remarried, Lamb threw himself into family life with the
same sort of energy and enthusiasm that he brought to everything else
he did, behaving as if no one else had ever produced children – at least
none like his own – confounding all who had shaken their heads about
his reactions to domesticity.

Lamb, wounded or sick during the first war, had been for a time
in an army hospital. One day the RAMC officer doing the rounds
turned out to be the then bestseller novelist, Warwick Deeping (author,
among many other works, of *Sorrell and Son*, describing an ex-officer,

a widower, who has to take a job as an hotel porter); Deeping having himself begun life as a doctor. Lamb was lying in bed reading Milton. Deeping, after making routine medical enquiries, looked over Lamb's shoulder at the book. 'Strange old-fashioned stuff,' he said.

After this or another spell in an army hospital, Lamb came up for examination before a medical board. Seeing from the report that he was a fellow medico, the members of the board treated him as a colleague who knew the ropes. Just as everything was over, Lamb leaving the room, one of the board said: 'Perhaps we'd better see your Rhomberg, old boy.' (The Rhomberg Test is with feet together, eyes closed, to see if subject sways.) Lamb, absent for many months from medical practice, his mind filled with thoughts of painting, music, Milton and his old-fashioned stuff, had forgotten the meaning of Rhomberg. Making a guess, he began to undo his fly-buttons.

❋ 5 ❋

During the three years of my novitiate at Duckworth's, 'learning the business', I did not make much headway in the technicalities that The Complete Publisher should master. Lewis, not a born instructor – in any case much too busy with immediate problems to give lessons that could be easily understood – would from time to time mutter a few traditional watchwords about typefaces, flourish the wooden rule marked out with 'ems' (the unit for measuring printed matter), but he did not care for the routines of production escaping from his own direct control, and would become a little sulky if even Balston took too close a hand in that field.

Balston, for his part, would occasionally remark: 'You ought sometimes to get the books [the account books] down and have a look through them.' If I ever attempted to extract 'the books' from the accounting department, every sort of difficulty was put in the way; usually the simple and effective answer that work was being done at that very moment on whatever author's sales I hoped to examine. The accountant himself, a stunted troglodyte, neither young nor particularly obliging, caused concern at about this time by uttering strange animal cries from behind the closed door of the tiny cell where he totted up the royalties, and, long years at Duckworth's having affected his brain, he had to be removed in an ambulance.

Early resolution, perhaps never as vigorous as it should have been, to gain prosaic skills, withered away under passive resistance. There were in any case plenty of other things to do. Once I had left invoicing behind, I read MSS, composed ads, interviewed callers (those to be got rid of in no other way), made up the bi-annual illustrated catalogue of new and already published books, designated (in one of Balston's more puckish moods) *Spring Buds* and *Autumn Leaves*.

I had first pick at the five hundred or more MSS (once in a way written by pen) that arrived every year, mostly through the post or via agents, a few delivered by hand. Of these perhaps fifty had to be more than cursorily examined; thirty fairly seriously read. It is, of course, not necessary to ingest the whole of a manuscript to know that the reader's firm will not wish to publish the work, but incipient authors find that hard to believe. They will often complain if they receive the parcel back by return of post, or even within a few days of submission. That is why MSS are sat on by publishers for months at a time. Trouble can also be caused by a special demon, who arranges that the reader's report should be accidentally included in the back pages of a rejected manuscript. So far from treating lightly what is sent to them, publishers are only too anxious to find something to sell; even a few coherent sentences raising hopes in a desert of literary ineptitude.

This reading and tinkering about with manuscripts is not, I think, to be underestimated in the opportunities such work gives for picking up the rudiments of 'writing'. When some experience in that art has been undergone, it is possible to see, anyway to some extent, how 'good' books are written – the breaking down into elementary essences of the writer's method – but, when you are without the rough-and-ready self-training acquired by writing a book or two yourself, it is possible to read the classics over and over again without being able to see how a great writer brings off effects. On the other hand, the faults of a 'bad' book can immediately spring to the eye.

Where new blood was in question, my own introductions to the firm included Evelyn Waugh, Robert Byron, the historical biographers Wyndham Ketton-Cremer and Roger Fulford; quite a few more. Duckworth's did not manage to retain all of these. I also pressed the claims of Ronald Firbank, whose novels at this period were all out of print. The directors showed no overwhelming enthusiasm for Firbank, but, in consequence of making enquiries as to where the 'rights' lay, it was disclosed that Firbank had left a sum of £800 to be devoted to guaranteeing the republication of his books at some future date. Among manuscripts brought in by me, or marked for special attention, then turned down, were Antonia White's novel about a convent school, *Frost in May*, Christopher Isherwood's *The Memorial* (which came, I think, through an agent); and (among American books of 1933 seeking a publisher in England) Nathanael West's *Miss Lonelyhearts*.

One or two of the Old Guard of Duckworth authors would turn up at the office from time to time. Elinor Glyn, a neat figure, redhaired, smartly dressed, once disappeared through the door of Gerald Duckworth's room, when I was coming up the stairs. Belloc, wearing an Inverness cape, Wellington boots under his trousers, grumpy, bad mannered, would look in from time to time to collect a copy or two of his volumes of comic verse, which the firm still published.

One hot summer afternoon, feet on the desk in front of me, I was reading a manuscript, when the door opened quietly. A tall man, dressed in the deepest black, stood there in silence, clothes and bearing suggesting a clergyman. He smiled – to use an epithet he might well have employed in his own writing – 'quizzically'. I withdrew my feet from the desk, but he seemed to expect more than that; indeed instant acknowledgment of something in himself. A further survey convinced me that here was John Galsworthy. He gave off the redolence of boundless vanity, a condition not at all uncommon among authors, in this case more noticeable than usual. I was about to alert Lewis, bent double at his desk over a sheaf of estimates, which, according to habit, he was examining at a range of about two inches off the paper, but Galsworthy, making the conventional gesture of finger to lips, indicated silence. He was just within sight of Lewis round the corner of the desk, the implication being that by sheer personality Galsworthy would send out rays which would compel Lewis to look up.

We both awaited a respectful burst of recognition. For some reason the magnetism did not work. Galsworthy stood there smiling with benevolent condescension; the smile becoming increasingly fixed, as Lewis continued to ponder the estimates. Finally Galsworthy gave it up as a bad job. He announced his presence abruptly by word of mouth. He was evidently disappointed in Lewis's lack of antennae, where famous writers were concerned. Lewis raised his head to see who had spoken, then, taking in at a glance one of the firm's most lucrative properties, jumped up full of apologies, and hurried the Great Man into the Senior Partner's room.

Another Duckworth author, though only intermittently, was Ford Madox Ford. As the work of an old acquaintance, Gerald Duckworth was prepared to publish Ford's books from time to time, but they were not popular with Balston, who did not regard their small sales as redeemed by the author's undoubted interest in literary experiment. Ford's novels usually deal with a similar social level to those of Galsworthy, though Ford is far more aware of the paradoxes of human nature, the necessity, at that moment, of exploring new forms of writing. An immense self-pity – in general an almost essential adjunct of the bestseller – infected Ford adversely as a serious novelist, while at the same time for some reason never boosting his sales. His misunderstandings and sentimentalities on the subject of English life (half-German himself, he very nearly opted for German nationality just before 1914) make him always in some degree a foreigner, marvelling at an England that never was.

Much canvassed as an underrated writer, Ford undoubtedly brought off something in the war tetralogy, which shows signs of brilliance in the treatment of the earlier sequences. Notwithstanding that, when, late in our lives, Cyril Connolly, a Ford fan, gave me *The Good Soldier* (one of Ford's best constructed novels, and written with great attack), he failed to convert me.

At Duckworth's I remember reading the typescript of a novel by Ford, which began about a man who had fought in the Carlist War. I think this never appeared – anyway as the story then stood – in print, but another Ford novel, placed at the period of the Hundred Days, was being discussed at a moment when I was about to spend a day or two's holiday in Paris, and it was arranged that I should get in touch with him. Ford invited me to luncheon at a favourite restaurant of his, the Brasserie Lipp in the Boulevard Saint-Germain. He was then in his middle fifties, walrus moustache, puffy face, half-open mouth. I saw what the novelist, Mary Butts, meant, when she had said: 'It's extraordinary what a fuss is always being made about who is to get into bed with old Ford', but he seemed amiable enough in a somewhat bufferish genre. Drinking in those days either what was probably too much, or scarcely anything at all, I refused a pre-luncheon apéritif. Ford was surprised. He said: 'You're going to be a very cheap young man to entertain.' I don't remember being in the least grateful for his hospitality, though Ford was chronically hard-up (no doubt he signed the bill), and, as representative of his publisher, I might reasonably have been expected to do the paying myself.

Duckworth's, an impecunious firm, were, in fact, not at all forthcoming in allowing expenses for entertaining authors (though Balston certainly did a good deal of that himself in his flat), and it never occurred to me that quite often it would have been reasonable for my employers to shell out for meals and drinks produced by myself to get some promising writer on the hook. The only occasion when I remember being specifically told that the firm would pay, if I took someone out to luncheon, was in the case of Hilda Harrisson, former girl-friend of Henry Herbert Asquith (1st Earl of Oxford and Asquith); the Liberal Prime Minister having deliberately written a sequence of chatty letters to this lady to provide some sort of a small dowry for her after his own death.

A friend of a slightly older Oxford generation, Alan Harris (who just missed a Balliol Fellowship, and later himself worked at Duckworth's), produced Mrs Harrisson, who was then seeking a publisher for the Asquith letters. I gave her lunch at the Savoy Grill. She looked the part in every respect; reddish hair; evasive manner; air of carrying within her bosom all sorts of state secrets. Unfortunately, after these *billets doux* reached Henrietta Street, disagreement about terms resulted in their appearing under the imprint of another publisher.

Duckworth's used occasionally to make a little on the side by issuing books 'on commission', that is to say paid for by the author. One of these, a novel, accepted rather unwillingly as not quite up to the firm's standard (called *Impetuous Betty*, one reviewer wrote: 'There is humour as well as pathos in a tale that never flags in the telling') confounded everyone by selling quite well. At about this moment three unusually well-off young men decided almost simultaneously that they wanted their poems to appear in book-form. Duckworth's was prepared to oblige. Lambert suggested that these separate volumes of verse should be reprinted as an omnibus under the title *Poor Poems by Rich Poets*.

A somewhat bizarre work which I was responsible for Duckworth's publishing – not without some trepidation on Balston's part – was *Tiger-Woman* (1929), the autobiography of Betty May; a title highly coloured, if not wholly indefensible, as designation for the author, one of the many professional artists' models from time to time making an appearance in the Charlotte Street pubs. Betty May dated back to pre-1914 Café Royal days (when she must have been very young), and had been represented on canvas by many painters, though best known for the bronze portrait-head by Jacob Epstein.

Even allowing for a good deal of journalistic exaggeration, Betty May must have experienced fairly hair-raising adventures in various underworlds of one kind or another. For some time she had been anxious to have certain newspaper articles (bestowing the sobriquet 'Tiger-Woman') cobbled into a book. A young journalist with whom she was then living was prepared to take this job on.

Betty May, as it happened, linked up with a story much talked of during my first Oxford year, which had involved the magician, Aleister Crowley, and an undergraduate of St John's College, Frederick Charles (renamed by himself Raoul) Loveday. Loveday, an early member of The Hypocrites Club, like the Scholar Gypsy – though with far more baneful results – had abandoned Oxford halls to learn the secrets of Crowley's magic lore. In the first instance he had met Crowley in London, but, soon after an association between them had been struck up, the Mage moved to Sicily, where he established an abbey (in fact, a whitewashed farmhouse of characteristic local type) at Cefalù. There, having first married Betty May, Loveday followed him. While engaged in practising the magical arts, Loveday died at Cefalù; quite how and why, no one seemed to know. That happened in 1922, the year before I came up to Balliol.

The earlier forms of the Loveday myth had centred on a projected undergraduate expedition to rescue this Oxford friend from Crowley's clutches. I think the party was to have included Alfred Duggan and several other members of The Hypocrites. By the time the story was retailed to me Loveday himself had died the previous year; Crowley been ejected from Sicily by the Italian authorities. Nevertheless the circumstances were remembered for their sinister climax.

When, not without some difficulty, Betty May managed to get back to England, she sold to the press a fairly lurid account ('ghosted', of course) of her Cefalù experiences. The routines of daily life at Crowley's abbey sound thoroughly unpleasant, making the official expulsion of the magician not in the least unreasonable. Among other disagreeable ceremonies, Loveday had been required to sacrifice a cat by decapitation, then ritually drink the animal's blood. This cannot have been good for anyone's health, but – in spite of digestive consequences of such an act, and rumours that he had been strangled by Crowley – Loveday's end seems to have been brought about by the banal indiscretion of quenching thirst by water from a polluted mountain stream.

Betty May, who described herself as of East London costermonger origin, looked like a gipsy, the two elements not at all incompatible. With her hair tied up in a coloured handkerchief, she would not have seemed in the least out of place telling fortunes at a fair. I believe she did undertake a little soothsaying when in the mood. The remarkable modelling of her features, exotic formations somewhat oriental in suggestion, had appealed to Epstein in sculptural terms, but, when asked if she might dedicate the book to him, he refused in a cross letter.

In spite of a reputation for turbulence, Betty May, diffident in conversation, articulating with the utmost refinement, always behaved with complete decorum on the few occasions I met her. Most of the arrangements about the book were made by correspondence with the 'ghost', and, when Betty May herself once came to the office to arrange about illustrations, so far from behaving in a tigerish manner, she was overcome with terror in dealing with Lewis.

Lewis himself, paralysed with shyness at the sight of this figure from the fortune-telling booth on the pier, had taken refuge in a flood of publishing technicalities, uttered in the severe tone that merely meant he was ill at ease. When I saw Betty May down the stairs to the front-door, she said: 'Please, please, never, *never*, make me talk to that *thin* man again. I fear him. I *fear* him!' Used as she was to artists, gangsters, magicians, drug-fiends, Lewis had proved altogether too much for her.

Since everything said in *Tiger-Woman* about Crowley had appeared years before in the newspaper articles, when no legal action had been taken, trouble about libel – an aspect of statements about himself in which Crowley always maintained keen interest – was not much feared. At some stage, however, whether before or after publication, I do not remember, Crowley telephoned to the office, inviting me to lunch with him at Simpson's in The Strand. I had never met him in person, but his celebrated near-cockney accent grated at once on the ear, as familiar from stories.

'You will recognize me from the fact that I am *not* wearing a rose in my button-hole.'

The ring of the old-time music-hall comedian in this observation was much Crowley's style. On the way to Simpson's I wondered whether I should be met in the lobby by a thaumaturge in priestly robes, received with the ritual salutation: 'Do what thou wilt shall be the whole of the Law'; if so, whether politeness required the correct response: 'Love is the Law, Love under Will.'

The reality at Simpson's was less dramatic. Instead of a necromantic figure, sonorous invocation, a big weary-looking man rose from one of the seats and held out his hand. He was quietly, almost shabbily, dressed in a dark brown suit and grey Homburg hat. When he removed the hat the unusual formation of his bald and shaven skull was revealed; so shaped as to give the impression that he was wearing a false top to his head like a clown's.

This Grock-like appearance was not at all unbefitting the steady flow of ponderous gags delivered in the rasping intonation. Crowley's ancestral origins included more than one dissenting sect (Quaker, Plymouth Brethren), and I wondered whether his cadences preserved the traditional 'snuffling' speech ascribed to the Roundheads. There was much that was absurd about him; at the same time it seems false to assert – as some did – that his absurdity transcended all sense of being sinister. If the word has any meaning, Crowley was sinister, intensely sinister, both in exterior and manner.

Sylvia Gough, a raffish South African beauty of the first war period, once remarked: 'Crowley, you've got such a kind face.' The countenance that had thus struck her was dull yellow in complexion, the features strangely caught together within the midst of a large elliptical area, like those of a horrible baby, the skin of porous texture, much mottled, perhaps from persistent use of drugs required for magical experiment.

We lunched off Simpson's traditional saddle of mutton, Crowley drinking a glass of milk, his guest a pint of beer. He began to complain at once about Betty May's book (which suggests it must have been published by then), though not at all violently, almost as if he expected nothing in the way of response. Crowley kept up this monologue for some little time, then gradually moved away from Betty May, her in-accuracies and vulgarities of phrase, to more general consideration of the hard life of a mage, its difficulties and disappointments, especially in relation to the unkindnesses and backbiting of fellow magicians.

Crowley was full of resentment at the injustice with which the world had treated him. His demeanour suggested that of a general relieved of his command for dropping shells into his own trenches; a mixture of explanation, apology, defiance, self-pity. Throughout luncheon it was never quite clear what he had really hoped to gain from our meeting; perhaps merely hungering for a new listener. I heard him out, and, though no conclusions were reached, we parted on good terms. I did not mention that my mother had met him with friends years before, an experience she had not at all enjoyed.

Several years after this period, Nina Hamnett, who had known Crowley for a long time both in Paris and London, produced a volume of memoirs. What was said of him there might have been thought well within his own accepted terms of self-reference, but he brought a libel action against the publishers. Had Crowley won that case (which he spectacularly failed to do), he would certainly have instituted another suit regarding *Tiger-Woman* against Duckworth's. Accordingly, I was sent to court to observe the proceedings.

Betty May, one of the witnesses for the defence, was effective in the box as an innocent young wife, who, on her honeymoon, had been trapped into enduring the aberrations of behaviour then taking place at Cefalù. Crowley, on the other hand, giving evidence on his own account, was altogether futile. He seemed unable to make up his mind whether to attempt a fusillade of witty sallies in the manner of Wilde (a method to which Crowley's music-hall humour was not well adapted), or grovel before the judge, who had made plain from the start that he was not at all keen on magic or magicians. Crowley's combination of facetiousness and humility could hardly have made a worse impression. An increased element of knockabout was added to the proceedings by the stage-Irish accent of Counsel for the Defence.

'Mr Crowley, is ut thrue that ye crucified a toad on therr basilisk's abode?'

To counteract cross-questioning in that vein, Crowley's Counsel read out a poem of inordinate length, written by his client as a young man, each verse of which terminated with the lines:

> Ashes to ashes, dust to dust,
> So let it be, in God we trust.

It was of no avail. The reiterated moral sentiment of the refrain did not establish in the mind of the judge or jury any conviction of Crowley's innate goodness. On the contrary, the case was not argued to an end, the foreman of the jury sending up a note to the judge expressing their view that Crowley was a man impossible to libel. Much of the evidence had certainly pointed to that conclusion.

Our tête-à-tête luncheon at Simpson's was the only occasion when I met Crowley in the flesh (perhaps one should say The Beast 666 incarnate), but about a year after the publication of *Tiger-Woman* (and before the libel case) a letter headed with a Berlin address, written in Crowley's hand, arrived at the office:

My dear Powell,
     I am the beautiful German girl for whose love the infamous Aleister
     Crowley committed suicide ...

The gist of this not always very lucid communication seemed to be that Duckworth's was offered 'the story of our elopement' – entitled *My Hymen* – for an advance of £500 on a 15% royalty. The signature, a woman's name, was followed by the words: ' "Blue Eyes" only to Horace Cole [the wellknown practical-joker].'

Soon after I joined the firm, Duckworth's took over the books of William Gerhardi (later Gerhardie), including *The Polyglots* (1925), an outstanding novel, particularly in the rare gift of making child characters come to life. I never had more personal contact with Gerhardi than to meet for a moment or two in the office, but through him Duckworth's also published several books by his close friend, Hugh Kingsmill, whom I met for the first time at this period, but did not know at all well until many years later.

Kingsmill's books never quite do justice to him as wit and critic. His journalism was composed with care, but he was too lazy to write at book length. Although in revolt against Victorianism, Kingsmill (b. 1889) remained very much a Victorian himself in the complacency of his judgments. In his own field he possessed powerful attack, founded on exceptional familiarity with certain standard writers: Shakespeare; Boswell's Johnson; Wordsworth; Tennyson; Dickens; a few more. These he knew almost by heart. He was not at all interested in authors who fell outside his chosen scope. He had a passion for the novels of Stanley Weyman, which, it has to be admitted, reflected in some degree Kingsmill's own view of history.

Good talk, however, is not a matter of pedantic accuracy. The very opinions that might lay Kingsmill open to criticism on paper were often the most illuminating when spoken extempore. From the limited number of writers he had canonized, he could keep up a flow of brilliant and apposite quotation. He was anti-Nineties, anti-Kipling, most of all anti-Freud and anti-Jung.

One of Kingsmill's literary categories (adapted from Horace Walpole) was the 'inspired imbecile', the writer whose books do not stand up to 'serious' examination, perhaps are not even intended to do so, but remain alive, readable, even poetic. Kingsmill put the Sherlock Holmes stories in this class, a useful one, critically speaking. He was always adept at defending his own critical position. He had, for example, expressed dislike on some occasion for the weekly articles the novelist, Charles Morgan, was then writing for a Sunday paper. I asked Kingsmill what he would say if, the following Sunday, Morgan's piece was devoted to praise of a Kingsmill book. 'In that case,' said Kingsmill. 'I should consider the whole question of Morgan's status as critic reopened on an entirely new basis, bearing in mind the fresh evidence to be considered.'

A favourite saying of Kingsmill's was that *No Exit* always means *Exit*. There is a certain truth in this view, as most people must have discovered, but, in his own style of setting about things, Kingsmill was apt to carry to extremes the principles of this paradoxical conviction. As a writer he never quite made the mark he should, but, in spite of existing in a state of acute financial crisis, he managed somehow to keep himself and a family afloat, while never in the smallest degree deviating from his own rule of living.

Kingsmill's vision of the world is well illustrated by a remark he made on hearing my account of an investiture at the Czechoslovak Embassy at the end of the second war. I had been awarded a decoration and, when the ceremony was at an end, refreshments handed round, the occasion became a party. The sparkling stars and crosses seemed reasonably appropriate on the uniforms of the soldiers, however threadbare the khaki; on the shiny lounge suits of one or two senior civil servants from the War Office, who were also decorated, they looked more than a little strange. I described to Kingsmill this incongruous scene. He said: 'I always think moments like that are when the poetry of life has gone wrong.'

6

After our first meeting, Adrian Daintrey and I used often to see each other in those early London years; and have continued to do so, on and off, ever since. Even when first encountered, Daintrey had set out on a pattern of life that veered between the pinnacles of the beau monde, and social circumstances of a far more down-to-earth order. At both ends of the scale, Daintrey (a notable admirer of women in their many forms of attraction) has always been a master of spoken reminiscence, on that subject and many others. He has written memoirs (illustrated by his own drawings), but more fantastic experiences than any told there have sometimes come his way, reserved for the ears of friends.

In his memoirs, Daintrey, the least political of men, mentions my name in connexion with a matter perhaps worth brief expansion here. In 1935, the year after I married, he had a studio in Oakley Street, Chelsea. In the same house lived a young man from the Foreign Office called Donald Maclean. Finding Maclean very agreeable, Daintrey asked me to meet him. So far as I can remember, Daintrey's account of Maclean approximately ran: 'Donald's not a bit like what people imagine someone in the Foreign Office to be. He's always very shabbily dressed, and is more or less a Communist. Apparently he was walking back from Whitehall the other evening with von Ribbentrop [recently appointed by Hitler German ambassador to the Court of St James's], and made Ribbentrop absolutely furious by stopping in the street to buy a copy of *The Daily Worker* [the current name of the Communist Party's official newspaper] from a man selling them on the kerb.'

When the meeting with Maclean took place at Oakley Street – there were just the three of us at the studio – I did not at all share Daintrey's view of this Foreign Office young man. He seemed to me vain, pompous, and in his own particular way, notably snobbish. These are no doubt venial enough imperfections in themselves, but, in Maclean's case, so it seemed to me, was an emanation of shiftiness positively creepy. I reported these reactions at home, so am on record in the matter. There was no reason to see Maclean again. I forgot about him until the later 1940s.

By the time Maclean reappeared, to a small extent, in our lives (an occasional meeting at dinner-parties or in a club), he had become quite a talked-of personality. His drunkenness and violence were referred to with awe as example of what you could not only get away with, as member of the country's diplomatic corps, but actually turn to good account in augmenting your reputation as a rising man. Such antics belonged, of course, to Maclean's lighter moments. In a more serious vein, he was reputed to decline invitations to official dinners (which after all he was paid to attend) from moral objection to expenditure of that sort in a country with Egypt's low standard of living. Maclean's superiors (blind to political affiliations that Daintrey, a painter without the least interest in politics, had noticed as far back as 1935) not only took these whims in their stride, but showed themselves positively impressed by such humanitarianism.

On the several occasions when I met Maclean on his return to London – though we got on perfectly well – I saw no reason to change my earlier opinion of him. He still struck me as inordinately conceited, unreliable, drunken, bisexual, yet remaining in his own way a typical civil servant; the *fonctionnaire* who wishes to be 'different', a not unfamiliar category, carried to its logical conclusions; the complete reversal of conventional behaviour, while remaining in conventional circles. That was, of course, only the exterior.

At the moment of the Maclean/Burgess decampment (1951), we were in France. The French press was understandably elated by such a story about 'English diplomats', especially the homosexual angle; while even in England the couple were written of as if they belonged to the same official level. Such was, of course, far from the case. Maclean, however protracted his wild oats, was an authentic member of the Foreign Service, who had passed the required examinations, was supposedly destined for a routine career, ending as an ambassador. The same was by no means true of his confrère, Guy Burgess, of whom a word may also be said in passing.

Burgess, taken on as a temporary wartime governmental employee, was well known in London as a notorious scallywag, to whom no wholly baked person, among those set in authority, would ever have dreamt of entrusting the smallest responsibility, or access to secrets of even a low grade classification. In London circles of a kind that could not possibly be censured as puritanical – even fastidious, about sexual goings-on – Burgess was regarded as a man to steer clear of. Indeed, it might be said of him, as Churchill is alleged to have remarked of the Labour MP, Tom Driberg (later created life-peer as Lord Bradwell): 'He has the unenviable reputation of being the only man in this House who has brought buggery into disrepute.'

When the row broke, my impression was that I had never met Burgess. Years later, sorting letters written to Violet in the early months of the war (she was out of London expecting a baby) I came across the following (4 October, 1939), describing dinner at the house of Dennis Proctor, official of the Treasury: 'There was a man called Anthony Blunt who is an art critic but now in M[ilitary] I[ntelligence]. He was quite nice in a very Cambridge way. After dinner an absolutely nauseating character called Guy Burgess came in, a BBC fairy of the fat go-getting sort.'

The Varda Bookshop, mentioned earlier in connexion with Christopher Millard, was at 189 High Holborn; its sign (painted by Edward Wadsworth) hanging outside, simply announcing in the idiom of the Twenties, without definite article or capitals, *varda bookshop*. The business was still (1928) being conducted by the beautiful and stormy Varda. I probably met Varda through the fact of Lambert living in a flat above the shop, but she had first manifested herself by writing to me at Duckworth's, putting up a project for translating *Le Diable au Corps* (1923), the first of the two novels written before his early death by Jean Cocteau's protégé, Raymond Radiguet.

Varda, whom I was to know for years (until the terrible devils of self-destruction took their final revenge, when her life seemed at last well ordered), was both a beauty, and a personality not to be disregarded. Her taste for strife caused trouble in the lives of a lot of men, several women, at one time or another, but, when in good form, no one could be wittier, or show greater appreciation of wit in others. She was unfortunately incapable of finding tolerable any known pattern of existence. She would racket round London; retire in complete solitude to a country cottage. Neither simple nor complex paradigms of life suited her, nor were effective in casting the devils out.

Notwithstanding that, Varda could be wonderfully funny about her own troubles; other things too, but desperation with life was her accustomed theme. She was, indeed, unique in her kind. One of her favourite stories was of a former charwoman of hers, who had remarked to a subsequent employer: 'That Mrs Varda wore herself out thinking of others.'

Lambert was pretty comfortably situated at the Varda Bookshop flat, but at an early stage of our knowing each other would complain that he had been kept awake until a late hour by Varda's friends carousing in her sitting-room, especially by prolonged singing of 'The Hole in the Elephant's Bottom'. The names Lambert cited as causing a disturbance with this chorus were those of John Heygate and Bobby Roberts. Roberts I had not heard of till then; Heygate, familiar by sight from having been only a year senior to me at Balliol, I had never come across at that time in London.

Bobby (in fact, Cecil A.) Roberts was an acquaintance of Evelyn Waugh's at about this period (often mentioned in the Waugh Diaries), but I don't think Waugh had ever spoken of him to me. He was a figure to crop up often, usually in farcical circumstances, during the next twenty or thirty years; and, of course, like most persons of his sort, must have fought against a desperately melancholy side, though that was rarely if ever revealed. Although far from military in background or outlook, Roberts had been to school at Wellington, where the poet-journalist, J. C. Squire (then editing *The London Mercury*, a fairly stodgy literary monthly), had come to lecture. Even as a boy Roberts clearly possessed a measure of that devious persuasiveness that distinguished him later, because, after hearing how much Roberts loved books and poetry, Squire, in an unguarded moment, offered him, when he left at the end of the term, a job on the staff of *The Mercury*.

Roberts – who would gaze benevolently through huge spectacles set in a moonlike face, while he recounted some startling act committed in his cups – proved competent to cope with the work on a literary monthly only so far as the heavy drinking was concerned, a *sine qua non* among Squire's entourage. Squire, a man who had kept afloat by dexterous manipulation of his own talents, grasping the extent of his mistake, unloaded this still outwardly plausible assistant on to the BBC. The Corporation, come only recently into being, was then established at Savoy Hill, just south of The Strand. Among several other young men working there, inimical to the prudish overlordship of Sir John Reith (later Lord Reith), was Heygate. I don't know which arrived at the BBC first, but Heygate and Roberts soon became friends.

Although a little of his company went a long way, Roberts was a richly comic figure, and, as I have suggested, possessed also an element of tragedy. He always wore the same suit (a restrained Glen Urquhart check), which never seemed to grow any older; Heygate attributing the suit's apparent agelessness to the care Roberts expended on it; however drunk always remembering to fold the coat and trousers before he himself passed out. After a few drinks Roberts would indulge in protracted monologues, usually devoted to the meaninglessness of life. His undoubted success with women was assigned by many of his friends to the fact that the objects of his desire found less trouble in going to bed with him, than in sitting up all night listening to an inexhaustible flow of Joycean streams of consciousness.

At a certain stage of intoxication Roberts would become a compulsive telephoner. Attending a party in a house where there was a nursery, a fellow guest, who knew about this fever for telephoning, found a toy telephone (reasonably like the actual instrument), and put it within reach of Roberts. When in due course the lust for telephoning descended upon him, Roberts seized the toy telephone (these were pre-automatic days), and tried to 'get through' to the exchange. He made many complaints about the London Telephone Service, but this kept him out of mischief for the rest of the evening.

One night I was with Roberts and some others at a fairly seedy night-club, The Blue Lantern, in Ham Yard just behind the Piccadilly end of Shaftesbury Avenue. Like The Gargoyle, though at a lower level, The Blue Lantern could claim a faintly intellectual tinge. On this occasion a party at the next table included Tallulah Bankhead, then at the height of her fame as embodiment of the Twenties, an unusual star to appear in that place.

Tallulah Bankhead was on the right; the table on the left dominated by a man with one of those peculiarly resonant voices, who for some reason was telling a long story about the sterling qualities of his mother. Customers are said to visit brothels largely to talk about their wives and children; perhaps some night-club habitués find the atmosphere congenial for working off their Oedipus Complex. Halfway through this undoubtedly rather tedious narrative, Tallulah Bankhead, who seemed bored with her own companions, suddenly turned away from them, leant forward with elbows on my knees, projecting herself towards the man reminiscing about his mother.

'Do tell me whom you're speaking of?' she asked.

The mum's boy looked startled by the question from such a source, though it was put in the most formal tone.

'I was talking about my mother, as a matter of fact.'

'Oh, I see,' said Tallulah Bankhead. 'I thought you *must* be describing Sybil Thorndike.'

Having never shared the almost universal admiration for Sybil Thorndike as an actress, I enjoyed this exchange. Tallulah Bankhead levered herself off my knees. As she straightened up, this seemed an opportunity not to be missed.

'Will you dance?'

She looked me up and down.

'Do you dance well?'

'Very badly.'

'In that case I will.'

She moved with incredible lightness, holding her was like holding nothing at all, a contact with thistledown, which at the same time controlled my own steps, as she glided across the floor. The story, I'm afraid ends there. It was not the start of a great romance. We never met again, but the impression remained of much fun and charm, as well as a very decided toughness. The period flavour of the incident must excuse its triviality.

At a somewhat later stage of acquaintance with Bobby Roberts, he was appointed assistant-manager at Sadler's Wells (built by Lilian Baylis to present opera, ballet, the drama, on the site of the old 18th century theatre there, a stage in north London to work in conjunction with the Old Vic on the south bank), where, as 'front of house', Roberts, in a dinner-jacket, relatively sober, was to be seen every evening. This high standard of conduct was hard to maintain, and a day came when it was clear to his friends that Roberts was in no state to attend the Theatre, undertake his 'front of house' duties. An excuse must be found, that quickly, to propitiate the formidable Miss Baylis, who ruled Sadler's Wells and the Old Vic as a dual despotism, absolute in character. If Roberts did not turn up, he would certainly get the sack.

Then some man of genius remembered that the date was the 11th of August, the day before grouse-shooting opened on 'The Twelfth'. Roberts had probably never discharged a shot-gun at a bird in his life, but Miss Baylis was nevertheless asked by telephone 'if it was all right for Mr Roberts not to come to the Theatre that night, as he wanted to sit up late cleaning his guns'. This plea (which might be held to imply an overnight journey to Scotland, brief blaze away at the grouse, return for duty the following evening), although one of the most fantastic that can ever have been offered in comparable circumstances, was at once accepted.

'Front of House' at Sadler's Wells included the concession of hiring out camp-stools for use of those who would queue for hours outside the Theatre to buy seats in the pit. Much later, after he had left the job at Sadler's Wells, Roberts retained dominion over these camp-stools (possibly available at other theatres too), an increment brought to an end, I think, only by the outbreak of war in 1939.

In due course finding himself in the Public Relations Branch of the RAF, Roberts was posted to India and Ceylon. There, as usual, difficulties arose with those higher up. One night, travelling down the subcontinent to Colombo in a railway sleeping-compartment from Madras, Roberts was assailed by a Pinfold-like hallucination that his Commanding Officer – with whom he had often been in trouble – was repeating a complaint already made: 'Roberts, you are sycophantic.' This was not to be endured. Roberts, opening what he took to be the office door behind him, backed out to the plains of the Carnatic. Although the express was travelling at 50 m.p.h., he was discovered some hours later, hardly at all damaged, but so great was his persecution mania when he returned to the Colombo office that he habitually arrived each morning by way of the fire-escape.

After marriage, the Evelyn Waughs moved into a maisonette in Canonbury Square, Islington, where George Orwell was to occupy a flat twenty years later. For anyone with a taste for going to parties, especially smartish parties, the district could not be called handy.

It has often been suggested that, after his first marriage foundered, Waugh turned to social life as consolation. Undoubtedly certain social objectives became more outwardly explicit after matrimonial disaster, but I think the process of change that took place was only hastened by the parting of ways. A transformation of some sort was inevitable, both in the light of Waugh's energetic ambitious character, an early success that necessarily, and suddenly, widened the scope of his life. The old Waugh – in my view – was already fading into the past that night we met on the Tube, when he said: 'I'm going to be married.' It was gone for ever, such is my belief, by the time he moved into Canonbury Square.

There can be few persons, whatever their place in life, who, as their own situation changes, expanding or contracting, have not shed a few early friends, or been shed by them. As an example of this process, Waugh was very positively no exception. Indeed, even before marriage, his Diaries reveal a fairly steady sloughing off of acquaintances who had become uncongenial; sometimes a jettisoning that no one could look on as unreasonable. On settling down as a married man, he made no secret that he wanted his life in some ways to alter, expressing a desire to know 'only the intelligent and the smart'; even in those days highly amorphous concepts, and an ambition hard to satisfy in its very simplicity of definition.

The Waughs' Islington flat, looking out on to a wide quiet 19th century square, was transformed by the hand of Evelyn Gardner (so it seems simplest still to call her), a light but accomplished touch, which then and later made every place she inhabited comfortable and attractive. Brought up in an aristocratic world, she was perfectly prepared to accept that world's most notable characteristic (as remarked in the very different case of Rosa Lewis), its vast panorama of relationships, but, so far as she herself was concerned, she wanted to diminish, rather than increase, those aspects of aristocratic life that become tedious if taken too seriously.

In short, Evelyn Gardner liked to enjoy now and then what was conventionally offered by her former background, without burdening herself with too much of its ironmongery. Waugh, on the other hand, so far as could be managed on a limited – if expanding – income, was not in the least averse from taking up the Smart Man's Burden.

From the start there was much hospitality at the Waughs' flat. Among those who reappeared in my life, if he can be said previously to have figured there at all before, was John Heygate. It was at Canonbury Square that Heygate and I effectively met; for, when Alfred Duggan, visiting his younger brother, had brought Heygate over from Oxford to Eton, I had not at all demurred at Hubert Duggan's complaint about the dullness of his elder brother's Oxford acquaintances. When Heygate turned up at the Waughs', on the other hand, he seemed a different person. We became friends almost at once.

John Heygate's father (younger brother of a baronet, to whom Heygate himself was heir, though never on good terms with his uncle) had retired as an Eton housemaster just before I arrived at the school. Heygate's mother, a woman of rather uncomfortably dominating personality, having lost an eldest son in childhood, doted on this younger one, though barely agreeable to her daughter. She was proud of her descent from John Evelyn, the diarist, and Heygate was nearly named 'Evelyn' after this distinguished ancestor; something which would have added additional confusion to future events.

As a young man, Heygate *père* had gained a reputation for such oppressive social correctness of demeanour and dress that Edwardian society had coined the verb 'to heygate' or 'do a heygate', meaning to act in a manner uncompromisingly conventional, bordering on the priggish. In principle, Heygate got on well with his schoolmasterly father, rather less well with his adoring imperious mother. Tall, good-looking, with an easy rather lounging carriage, John Heygate, so far as outward appearance was in question, tended to be well dressed, as the word was popularly used, with the addition of some slight eccentricity in colour or cut. He had been through the routine of deb dances, and, so to speak, come out the other end. Waugh was very much taken with Heygate – whom he knew through Bobby Roberts – in the early days at Canonbury Square.

In a piece of self-analysis that illustrates his own brand of wit, Heygate used to say that his tragedy was that stupid people thought him intelligent; intelligent people found him stupid. This drastic definition of a personal predicament was not without all acuteness in its attempt to pinpoint relations with others. Heygate himself would often refer to his own lack of sparkle at school and university, for which he was inclined to blame – an element not to be denied – the stuffiness of his family. Release from inhibitions imposed by parents seems to have been brought about at the age of twenty-three, when, just down from Oxford, in preparation for the Diplomatic Service, he was sent to Germany for three months to learn the language.

The Diplomatic Service was never attained, but Heidelberg always remained the great romantic experience of Heygate's life, fundamentally affecting him for good or ill. He lived with the family of a former Prussian cavalry officer, impoverished by the war, and postblockade Germany – the Germany from which arose the legend that ultimately brought Hitler to power – made an impression that was never effaced, nor even modified, in Heygate's mind.

After this Heidelberg idyll (possibly on failing the Diplomatic Service examination), Heygate experienced some sort of breakdown (called by him 'when I was mad'), which had included the illusion that everyone round him in a London club was talking German. His account of this condition (like Roberts falling out of the train in India) conveyed something strikingly like the hallucinations of Evelyn Waugh's alter ego, Gilbert Pinfold, when Pinfold heard voices addressing him from the void. Certainly, in all three cases, much had been drunk at an earlier stage.

Heygate drank a good deal without being an alcoholic, even if at moments he was within hail of that condition, notably at the time of the breakdown. He had a flat in Cornwall Gardens, South Kensington, when a homosexual man-servant was employed (merely by chance, not for erotic reasons), who disapproved so strongly of Heygate's drinking that he came into Heygate's sitting-room holding a tumbler of neat whisky in one hand, a piece of liver in the other. Dropping the liver dramatically into the whisky, he paused for a moment while the meat shrivelled up. 'That,' he exclaimed, 'is what is happening to your liver all the time you drink as you do.' Heygate, who was undoubtedly startled by this action, reported himself as replying: 'What a shameful waste of liver and whisky.'

Agreeably successful with women, Heygate remained well short of being anything like a professional womanizer. He rather enjoyed admitting to hypochondria, and suffered from occasional black moods, when he was fairly unapproachable; these last rare in those early days. None of his friends guessed how deep-seated was a neuroticism that began to take a grip in middle life; eventually, after frequent bouts of melancholia, precipitating his own end. On the contrary, Heygate then seemed to most of his friends – among them myself – a man who had solved many of the pedestrian problems some contemporaries were still unable to face.

If Lambert, intellectually speaking, came as a refreshing draught after Oxford self-consciousness about the arts, Heygate, in quite another manner, offered a different freedom of movement in his acceptance, if not on its most obvious terms, of everyday life. That was an attitude equally unOxonian. He was familiar with the conventional social world (the snobbish social world, if you like), aware of its amenities, but quite undazzled by them. If grand invitations came his way, he did not refuse them; they were never pursued for their own sake. Heygate to some extent revolutionized my London existence; among other things inciting me to save up, and buy a car, which materially affected my way of life. He was stimulating in the sense of providing something that had not been there before. Quite soon after we met, Heygate and I arranged to make a trip together in his car, which was to take us to Berlin the following summer.

Much myth has circulated on the subject of Duckworth's failing to publish Evelyn Waugh's first novel, *Decline and Fall*. Some of these legends appear to have emanated from Balston himself. At least one version that gained some acceptance, which has no basis whatever in fact, was that Gerald Duckworth turned down Waugh's novel out of hand, while Balston was taking a holiday abroad.

In its pristine state, when *Decline and Fall* arrived at the office, the manuscript contained a sprinkling of phrases, mostly in the dialogue, to be regarded in those days as falling into an equivocal category. At that time, where an 'outspoken' book was concerned, the publisher ran not only risk of prosecution – often on absurd grounds – which might result in a heavy fine, even imprisonment, at best landing the firm in heavy legal expenses, but also, at an unofficial level, the additional censorship exercised by booksellers and librarians.

Evelyn Waugh, brought up from birth in the shadow of the publishing trade and its traditions, was well aware of these obstructions, notwithstanding his impish side, and the conviction he shared with every other serious writer of the day, that literary censorship should be resisted so far as possible. At the same time, Waugh held extremely practical views on encouraging sales. When demur was made at Duckworth's about some of the things he had written in *Decline and Fall*, Waugh did not, as sometimes implied, immediately walk out. On the contrary, had not a special problem arisen, tactful handling would probably have resulted in mutual agreement about a small amount of discreet trimming before publication. This unlooked for complication was vested in Gerald Duckworth himself as semi-uncle of Evelyn Gardner.

Not particularly well disposed towards Waugh from the start as a writer, Gerald Duckworth liked even less the prospect of having him as a semi-nephew. It might very well be urged that Waugh's marriage, even to a semi-niece, was no business of his. That was not the way Gerald Duckworth looked at the matter. In short, *Decline and Fall* gave an excellent opportunity to be awkward. Waugh might be an already published Duckworth author; that did not prevent him from being an undesirable character to have in the family. People like himself, who had always feared the worst – such was Gerald Duckworth's stance – were now proved quite right. Here was Waugh, a blatant adventurer, not only married by stealth to his publisher's semi-niece, but trying to foist on the firm an obscene novel.

Balston, for his part, not at all opposed to a touch of impropriety, at the same time suffering chronic fear of sexual scandal, found himself between the Scylla of losing a promising young writer, and the Charybdis of having a stand-up row with his partner, regarding a matter about which he himself harboured mixed feelings; while his adversary held the comparatively trump card of protesting that this connexion by marriage added family insult to business injury. Accordingly, Balston set about doing what he could to arrange a satisfactory compromise. He went through the manuscript of *Decline and Fall*, marking everything he judged risky; Waugh showing himself perfectly prepared to await the result of this picking over. In the event, fussed by the circumstances, Balston may well have lost his head, queried more than was necessary, but even so, without Gerald Duckworth's specialized intrusion, some sort of agreement could almost certainly have been reached. As it was, Waugh considered the suggestions, then turned them down.

One of the classical situations of the publishing business is the process of a publisher requesting certain alterations in a book, the author refusing to make these; afterwards agreeing to do so for a subsequent publisher. Waugh, as he records in the foreword to the reset edition of *Decline and Fall* (1962), took the manuscript up the street to his father's firm, Chapman & Hall (a publishing house certainly, in principle, no less stodgy than Duckworth's), where they too demanded certain excisions. These were made.

The 1962 Edition of *Decline and Fall* replaced words and phrases removed or altered for Chapman & Hall. In his brief preface Waugh implies that the chief emendation was the Welsh station-master pimping for his sister-in-law, rather than his sister. Those with the curiosity to compare the two texts will find about a dozen other changes to indicate Chapman & Hall's determination to be on the safe side. Nevertheless, severance was probably inevitable in the light of Gerald Duckworth's feelings about Waugh's first marriage. He did not live to see the second one; also to a Gerald Duckworth semi-niece.

From this time on, Chapman & Hall published Waugh's novels; Duckworth's, his travel books. The first of these travel books was to be Waugh's next work to appear. The Waughs were to take a cruise, free of charge, in a Norwegian ship touring the Mediterranean. In return for this trip Waugh was to write a book giving publicity to these holiday cruises. The prospect was additionally acceptable, because at the outset of married life, Evelyn Gardner had not been at all well; a combination of physical illness and nervous exhaustion. It was hoped that the voyage, which was to begin in January, last about three months, would set her health right again.

❋ 7 ❋

In the spring of 1929 I moved from Shepherd Market. I took the first flat inspected, the self-contained basement of 33 Tavistock Square, Bloomsbury, three rooms for £110 a year. In one of the flats of the house above lived Thomas Burke, poet of London's Chinatown, whose mild exterior did not suggest the title of one of his works, *Limehouse Nights*. We never met.

Once settled in Tavistock Square, I began to get my life into better order, if one can ever be said to make any headway in that process. Plans to write a novel, never in practice advancing in the least at Carrington House, had in any case been held up by work on another book, which, quite fortuitously – indeed, rather pointlessly – I had taken on. This was the editing of a volume published by Duckworth's under the title *Barnard Letters* (1928), a collection of late 18th century and early 19th century correspondence, preserved by a family of that name, with whom I was friends.

The novel I planned was to express in contemporary terms all sorts of feelings about life and love. These themes, as first conceived, were to have a background of dances and country houses, as well as the

parties, nightclubs, pubs, which, with a modicum of office life, eventually provided most of the scenario. In the event, the deb side, proving
unassimilable within the scope of seventy-five thousand words, was
cut out. The original design for my first novel was, in other words,
not without resemblance to the initial framework of *Dance*; and, allowing for inexperience, the treatment is perhaps less different from the
long novel than has sometimes been suggested by critics. Abrupt
dialogue certainly predominates, but comparatively elaborate description and commentary are also to be found.

The year 1928 was an *annus mirabilis* of books that made an impact.
It was then, for example, that *The Enormous Room* (1922) by E. E.
Cummings reached England. Cummings was the man who opened my
eyes to a new sort of writing, putting out of date the style of authors
like Norman Douglas and Aldous Huxley. *The Enormous Room* received
an unfriendly notice in the *Times Literary Supplement*, which made
me pretty sure – the *TLS* being what it was in those days – that I
should like the book. This turned out a correct guess; incidentally high-
lighting an aspect of unfavourable notices to be borne in mind both
by writers dispirited at receiving them and reviewers hoping to do
damage. Ernest Hemingway's *The Sun Also Rises* had appeared in
England as *Fiesta* in 1927. I had read the novel with a fair amount
of enjoyment as a picture of American expatriate Paris life, but without
noticing anything revolutionary about the method; by no means a
triumph of critical perception on my own part. Then someone spoke
of Hemingway's style (whether in praise or blame, I'm not sure), and
I read the book again. Perhaps rereading *Fiesta* had been stimulated
by a brief meeting with Duff Twysden (model for its heroine, Brett,
Lady Ashley), because I do not recall more than mild interest at being
brought face to face with what was then a much favoured brand of
heroine in novels of the period, the lost lady. Boyish in appearance,
emaciatedly thin, decidedly battered, Lady Twysden (by then possibly
married to the young American with whom she was travelling through
London on the way back to the States) seemed a type from the bar
of a Surrey golf-club, rather than what I supposed appropriate to Montparnasse.

If E. E. Cummings, rather than Hemingway, was the revelation in
throwing overboard a good deal of Edwardian literary débris, Hemingway systematized a treatment of dialogue in a manner now scarcely
possible to appreciate, so much has the Hemingway usage taken the
place of what went before. It was an approach explored by Firbank
(influenced, it seems to me, by Hardy's renderings of Wessex peasant
talk), the naturalistic vocable, banal, even inane; purposeless exchanges
that are their own purpose, on account (especially in Firbank) of an
undercurrent of innuendo and irony. Rather surprisingly (*The Great*

Gatsby published in England 1926), I did not hear of Scott Fitzgerald until recommended by Connolly six or seven years later.

On returning from Paris on one occasion I undertook the breach of the law required from anyone who hoped to keep up in literary circles by smuggling back a copy of *Ulysses* (9th printing, May 1927), but did not find Joyce in general at all a tempting model. Wyndham Lewis's *Tarr* (1918, revised 1928) was another matter. Hitherto I had thought of Lewis as a Vorticist painter. Now his luminous brutal prose, blocked in with a painter's eye, was at once immensely exciting. On the first round, I accepted *Tarr* at Lewis's own estimation as a deliberate gesture in writing a novel of a new sort – which up to a point *Tarr* undoubtedly was – not noticing Dostoevskian borrowings; the 'privileged' manner with which Tarr himself is treated by the author; the haphazard change of gear in the narrative, all at once removed from the hero's point of view. These things can grate a little on later readings; nevertheless – together with several of the short stories collected in *The Wild Body* (1927) – for instance, *Bestre, The Death of the Ankou* – *Tarr* remains for me Lewis's most striking work as a writer. Its characters (belonging of course to a pre-war Montparnasse) were a good antidote to those of *The Sun Also Rises*; though *Tarr*'s opening sentence – splendidly poetic, however satirically spoken – would be equally appropriate to the Hemingway novel: 'Paris hints of sacrifice.'

When no more manuscripts remained to be reported on, all current book production in the pipeline – sometimes simply when other occupations palled – I used to read the less ephemeral file-copies on the shelves of the room at Duckworth's where I worked. Among other writers, those shelves introduced Henry James. In 1898, Duckworth's had published *In the Cage*, my first James, which stimulated getting *The Awkward Age* and *The Turn of the Screw* out of the London Library. James, with an exceptional eye for situations, unmatched as example of a novelist capable of dealing in his own particular way with any subject, however unmentionable at that day, is at the same time too niggling, too full of inhibitions, for me to regard myself as a Jamesian. At the same time James must be given the credit for forcing, almost singlehanded, the English novel into the status of a work of art; together with the sometimes forgotten corollary, that all works of art require an effort at the receiving end.

I was early familiar with Joseph Conrad, because my father had bought a secondhand set of Conrad's Collected Works at some auction-room. In those days I liked several (such as *Romance*) which I am no longer able to read, but only much later took in the innovatory nature of certain Conrad techniques. Jamesian influences are not happy in Conrad's dialogue, especially in love scenes. Nevertheless, if naturalism is the aim (which of course it need not be), Conrad, oddly enough,

laid down a precept I came across about this time, in one of his autobiographical books, that I found very helpful: that characters in a novel,
shown as engaged in conversation, should not usually be represented
as replying to each other's questions. The extent of his technical virtu-
osity is of a kind to be easily missed on first reading. Lambert was
an admirer but, on the not uncommon though really indefensible
grounds that he 'did not like books about the sea', Yorke was no
Conradian.

A file-copy, too, probably first put me on to the plays of Strindberg
(whose second wife's night-club, The Golden Calf, was still in those
days sometimes talked of by its former frequenters). Lambert recommended Strindberg's autobiographical writings, perhaps less well-
known in this country than they should be. He is very conscious of
the importance to be attached to the coincidences of life, things that
happen all the time, yet seem to be magic.

An uncharacteristic pre-war Duckworth venture among the file-
copies was Robert Burton's *The Anatomy of Melancholy* (first issued
1621) in a three-volume edition. There are worse places to read about
Melancholy than a publisher's office. I have never developed the habit
of making at all copious notes for use in potential books, but had already
(1927) begun to jot down occasional ideas, quotations, scraps of dialogue
(invented or overheard), viable names for characters in a novel; all sorts
of odds and ends of that kind. They were inscribed in an octavo
'dummy', one of those volumes of bound blank pages made up by the
binder for publishers to check the correct size of a book's paper-
wrapper. To this day these notes take up only about a hundred pages.
One of the earliest entries is a longish passage from Burton, which
begins 'I hear new news every day', and ends 'one runs, another rides,
wrangles, laughs, weeps, &c.' For the novel I was then trying to write,
The Anatomy of Melancholy soon suggested a title (I don't think *Afternoon Men* ever had an earlier name), and its epigraph: '... as if they
had heard the enchanted horne of Astolpho, that English duke in
Ariosto, which never sounded but all his auditors were mad, and for
fear ready to make away with themselves ... they are a company of
giddy-heads, afternoon men.'

On the principle that the Narrator of *Dance* should be a man who
had shared some (though not necessarily all) of my own experiences,
he is represented as writing a book about Robert Burton, therefore
undertaking researches that would have something in common with
my own work, when engaged on a biography of John Aubrey; historical
research having a particular bearing on a writer's life, with which no
other literary activities are exactly comparable. The passage from
Burton entered in the notebook (with several others, and quoted more
fully) occurs in the closing sequences of the twelve-volumes; Burton

– quite by chance – spanning the opening of my first novel to the ending of *Dance*.

Yorke and I had shared the discovery of Proust at Oxford, where we spent a good deal of time discussing *À la recherche*, of which I read the first half as an undergraduate; finishing the remaining volumes on coming to London. I followed that up by attempting to improve a not very extensive knowledge of other French writers, beginning with Flaubert. *Madame Bovary* required a certain effort to get through. I have always preferred *L'Éducation Sentimentale*, although, notwithstanding the great to-do made about Flaubert's technique, its treatment (for example, in relation to time sequences) is perhaps not above all criticism.

I found longueurs too in *Le Rouge et le Noir* and *La Chartreuse de Parme*, though Stendhal was soon to establish a firm grip. The *Chartreuse*, vigorous in its opening, still remains obscure to me after two hundred pages. The unfinished *Lucien Leuwen* would be my choice among Stendhal novels. It is the Diaries and autobiographical works (among which *De l'Amour* should be included) that I find absorbing; notably *La Vie de Henry Brulard*.

In due course Stendhal took hold with sufficient force to cause contemplation of writing a book about him. This project, carried far enough to assemble a few notes, was in the end whittled down to representing the Narrator of *What's Become of Waring* (1939) as at work on a study to be called *Stendhal: and Some Reflexions on Violence*. This title at once recalls George Sorel's *Réflections sur la violence* (1908), a book I had probably read about somewhere, the phrase sticking in my head. I knew nothing of Sorel or his views. On becoming aware of this duplication – in order not to confuse the issue – I altered the Narrator of *Waring*'s projected study to *Stendhal: and Some Thoughts on Violence*. I now rather regret the change, also my then ignorance of Sorel, an interesting figure of his period, who believed (as things came about, more than a little mistakenly) that, in the political world, violence was on the way out.

Balzac arrived for me only in middle-age, then wholeheartedly. Proust, a great admirer of *La Comédie Humaine*, observes somewhere that Balzac is vulgarer than life itself, and there can be no doubt that the dedicated Balzacian must accept not only a torrent of vulgarity, but, in matters of situation and behaviour, a great deal of improbability too. Never mind. Balzac's improbabilities do not prevent many of his least likely climaxes from being also the best ones. Besides – something never to be forgotten – with all novelists the reader has to put up with something.

More immediate Continental benefactions came, not from the French, but from the Russians; though from neither of the two most prominent Muscovite performers. Tolstoy, with all his genius, has never been an all transcending idol of mine (not least for his ludicrous views on Shakespeare), and I remained comparatively lukewarm towards Dostoevski (whom I now incline to put top of the league, Russia or elsewhere), until David Magarshack's translation in the 1950s of *The Devils* (*The Possessed*), *The Idiot*, *The Brothers Karamazov*. Dostoevski's characters and situations have one of the qualities I prize highest in a novelist, the ability to be at once grotesque yet classical, funny and at the same time terrifying. It seems incredible, having once discovered the Russians, that I should take so long to appreciate Dostoevski.

At Oxford I had not been able to get on with Turgenev. Now I saw his virtues. Goncharov's *Oblomov* (translated 1929) also gave pleasure, perhaps pointing the way to Gogol, whom I think I read later. *Dead Souls* is, of course, a far richer work than *Oblomov*, though both tail off disappointingly towards their close. Gogol and Surtees have something in common, Chichikov's tour of country houses comparable with that of Mr Sponge.

There was, however, a more overwhelming Russian revelation than any of these, also owed to the year 1928, when a new translation appeared of Lermontov's *A Hero of Our Time* (1840). I had vaguely heard of this Russian classic when I picked up a quickly sold-off circulating-library copy. As with *The Sun Also Rises*, more than one reading – in fact three – was required for *A Hero of Our Time* to mesmerize me. At Lermontov's first impact I could not in the least understand why this disjointed collection of short stories, loosely linked only by the appearance in different rôles of the 'hero', Pechorin – bored, heartless, Byronic – should be regarded as one of Russia's seminal works. Notwithstanding this feeling of being let down, something about the book caused me to read it again – and immediately. On the second reading I found myself better disposed, even a trifle haunted by some of the incidents, though still far from being persuaded. Again I applied myself to *A Hero of Our Time*. The third reading convinced me that here was a writer, and a book, in a very high class indeed; an opinion I strongly maintain.

While speaking of books that left a mark, I should mention one that came much later, in fact not long before the outbreak of the second war, by which time I had already written five novels myself. The *Satyricon* of Petronius, a name long familiar, was still unread, until, in a manner that seems to have become endemic with favourite works, I picked up a copy in a secondhand bookshop. It was the first English translation, 'Made English' in 1694 by 'Mr Burnaby of the Middle-Temple, and another Hand': *The Satyr of Titus Petronius Arbiter, a Roman Knight, with its Fragments recover'd at Belgrade*. The edition (undated), an inexpensive one, rebound also inexpensively but with an eye to style, has only the 17th century publisher's imprint, with head-and-tail pieces of sub-Beardsley design. The 'fragments recover'd at Belgrade' (the text in one place says Buda) was fictitious, a recent forgery in William Burnaby's day, too trivial to affect the rest of the *Satyricon*, especially that masterpiece of characterization and racy dialogue, Trimalchio's Feast. After a few pages of Petronius I was captivated by the genius of Nero's more intellectual Brummell (forced to suicide on falling from favour); the writer of what can reasonably be looked on as the first modern novel. Petronius, so far as I was concerned, was probably the last writer to help form a taste still open to development.

The move to Tavistock Square required some sort of house-warming. In any case a project had occasionally been discussed that one day Lambert and I should work off various social obligations (his largely musical) by giving a party together. The new flat, with its three rooms and back yard, was suitable for that, but nothing was done until the end of June. By that time various things were taking shape in the worlds round about both of us, one of which was foreshadowed by a remark made by Lambert on a Sunday when we were lunching together. 'I have the most boring afternoon ahead of me you can imagine,' he said. 'I have to go and play the piano to a Russian female pianist, who lives in St John's Wood. Can you think of anything one less wants to do on a Sunday afternoon?' I expressed conventional sympathy. He went off on his mission, which I thought no more about.

At our next meeting, quite soon after the lunch, Lambert was in a state of some excitement. He said: 'You never know what's going to happen in this life. You remember the dreary prospect ahead of me in St John's Wood? I arrived on the doorstep of the Russian's flat, and the door was opened by the most beautiful creature you ever saw in the world.' This superlative, in Lambert's terms, essentially implied the features of Africa or Asia, rather than Europe, even if not necessarily a beauty belonging by birth to one or other of the first two named continents. Where ideal good looks were in question, no Nordic types were permitted in Lambert's canon; particularly not blondes. There had been examples of this rule being broken, but in principle it was a rigid one.

Lambert was too stricken to convey any detailed description of the vision that had opened the door, beyond invoking the name of Florence Mills, the star of *Blackbirds*. This famous musical, recently played in London, had been a great hit, its cast invited everywhere; so much so, that Evelyn Waugh, on issuing a minor invitation, would add: 'It's not a party – there won't be a black man.' On being pressed to reveal more, Lambert enlarged further to the extent of suggesting that the genre of beauty was perhaps Javanese or Malayan, rather than African or Creole. I asked if he had made a date. Lambert was a little put out in having to admit that he had attempted no assignation. He said that he was determined to do so on his next visit to the flat; the Russian lady's stock having steeply risen.

Most of one's friends (not to mention oneself) suffered from these *coups de foudre*, some (Daintrey, for example) in a more or less permanent state of declension from the sight of some desirable phantom. I did not take Lambert's romantic experience in St John's Wood too seriously at the time, but, perhaps as much as a month or more later, remembering about the exquisite Javanese, made some casual enquiry as to whether he had seen her again. Lambert, though his manner might have been thought in the smallest degree furtive, seemed to have forgotten about her too. I attributed what could have been a touch of embarrassment at my question to regret at having allowed himself to speak of the encounter at all; which, on reconsideration, had probably proved to threaten too many complications of one sort or another, if followed through. There for the moment the matter rested.

In about May, the Waughs had returned from the Mediterranean. So far from the trip having set Evelyn Gardner on her feet again, she had fallen ill – seriously ill – while abroad. When Waugh, renewing publishing contacts, brought her with him to Henrietta Street, she still looked rather pale, even if in good spirits. Waugh himself seemed in the best of form, full of plans about future books. That, at least, was how things appeared to me. Probably the two of them dined with Balston a day or two later. If I were present, I remember nothing of the dinner-party. I did, however, note a comment of Balston's, made either after this visit to the office, or subsequent to an evening spent by the Waughs at his flat.

Balston remarked that he thought the marriage was showing signs of strain. I don't recall how he put that – probably less bluntly than the phrase sounds on paper – but certainly he expressed some such opinion. In general Balston was not specially intuitive, but, as a middle-aged man, he had undoubtedly noticed indications of matrimonial tension not apparent to myself. I attribute this lack of insight on my own part in some degree to the already mentioned unfamiliarity of my generation with the whole condition of young marriage. There were also few, if any, of the Waughs' friends in England – certainly not I – who grasped how exceedingly ill Evelyn Gardner had been in the course of the cruise.

Almost immediately after coming back to London, Waugh went off to an hotel in the west country to write *Labels* (1930), the travel book dealing with the cruise. Segregation was his habit when working on a book, but this the first occasion when, as a married man, he had followed the practice. Evelyn Gardner remained in London, where, after their comparatively long absence, she began to reassemble friends at the Islington flat. Among those who returned to the hospitality of Canonbury Square were John Heygate and myself.

By that time Heygate and I had arranged that our holidays should coincide in July, when the trip by car to Berlin was to be undertaken. We were seeing a good deal of each other, and, within the group of friends known to all three of us, we now saw a good deal of Evelyn Gardner. Towards the end of June, I dined with Balston. The other guests were Rose Macaulay, Evelyn Gardner, Heygate, an obscure male Duckworth author, whom I remember being furiously disapproving of Firbank. There had been a party on the *Friendship* (a boat moored on the Thames where parties were given) the night before, at which Heygate (more resolute than I) had stayed till dawn. In consequence, such was his fatigue at Balston's dinner-table, that quite quietly like a child he went to sleep between courses.

I record this dinner-party, Heygate's unconventional behaviour at it, for two reasons: first, because Balston, a man quite peculiarly prone to fear of scandal, would never have dreamt of inviting Evelyn Gardner and John Heygate together had he seen anything approaching a threat to the Waugh marriage; secondly, because the ludicrous incident of Heygate slumbering in his chair at dinner displays the lighthearted atmosphere at this stage.

In the same week as Balston's dinner-party Lambert and I gave our cocktail party at Tavistock Square, which began at six o'clock; in the event, lasting until three in the morning. When the list of guests had been drawn up, there had been no question on Lambert's side of inviting the vision of the St John's Wood piano-playing afternoon. That caused no surprise to me, as the incident was ostensibly closed. It was only some eighteen months later that friends, attending concerts where he was conducting, began to ask who might be the exotic beauty, sometimes to be seen in the audience, sometimes waiting for the conductor in the foyer at the end of the performance.

The Waughs turned up at Tavistock Square separately, neither staying long, nor seeming greatly to enjoy what they saw of the party; Evelyn Gardner having a brisk disagreement with Heygate. This was the first public occasion when there was a sense of something being wrong between the Waughs. Quite how wrong I did not even then take in. Heygate, one of the first to arrive at the party, was present until the most final moment of its extended revels.

Some months before both the Waughs and I stayed at Salt Grass, the Heygate house on the Hampshire coast. From the undercurrents at Tavistock Square it should perhaps have been clear that a fairly serious situation was blowing up. At the time, Waugh away from home except for weekends, there seemed nothing very extraordinary in Heygate, or anyone else, seeing something of Evelyn Gardner, when she was on her own in London; entertaining both husband and wife, when both were available for a weekend together in the country. That was no doubt a naive point of view, but one all three parties shared in the first instance.

During the Salt Grass weekend, neither of the Heygate parents was particularly easy; Heygate *père* schoolmasterish to a degree; his wife fond of laying down the law on all subjects. I remember no special tensions throughout the visit, though Waugh subsequently complained of Mrs Heygate's snobbishness; particularly in drawing attention to the fact that 'dukes are mentioned in the Bible'.

Heygate and I set out for Germany after the party. It might be thought that a lot of conversation was devoted to the embroilment in which Heygate now undoubtedly found himself, but in fact we hardly spoke of that at all. I knew no more than that a tricky situation existed. How deeply those involved were committed, what each proposed to do about it, were subjects not at all discussed, and I was in the dark as to the larger issues.

Germany, in the summer of 1929, seemed on the surface all that was most free and easy. This relaxed atmosphere was in general attributed by British tourists to what they regarded as healthy reaction from German attitudes that had certainly played a part in launching the first war. Few people in England were aware of the sinister vapours seething beneath the surface. That ignorance did not equally persist – as has sometimes been alleged later – after Hitler came to power. When Hitler arrived many persons in Great Britain saw at once that the international situation had become very dangerous indeed. The change of balance was still to come.

In the light of Heygate's never more than irrational and undecided leanings towards National Socialism (sentiments with their foundation in happy if confused memories of Old Heidelberg, congenital ineptitudes where anything in the nature of politics was concerned, a temperament that was far from stable), it might be thought that he held forth about Hitler, but I have no recollection of Hitler's name being mentioned during the trip. I remember Stahlhelm marches, Communist marches, but no Nazi marches, and, on this visit, not even many Brownshirts in the streets. It was, however, true that Heygate – as he told me later, after Hitler had made an unpleasant stir in the world – had carried with him on a former holiday (in Bavaria, I think) a letter written by some British journalist of his acquaintance beginning: 'Dear Hitler, this is to introduce John Heygate, a young Englishman interested in your movement'; a presentation he had never bothered to use.

Berlin was then at the height of its Isherwood phase: top-booted tarts equipped with riding-switches; transvestite bars and nightclubs; naked cabarets; all the sexual freedoms that now seem so humdrum. Nevertheless, infested with prostitutes of both sexes, beggars, pimps, freaks, eye-glassed duel-scarred ex-officers, this macabre city presented a monstrous vision of life, the cast peopling the cartoons of George Grosz, the artist who has memorialized for ever the Berlin of that epoch.

Munich was the first destination to which it had been arranged that mail should be forwarded poste-restante. After establishing ourselves we went to see if any letters were to be collected. There were, indeed, letters; a pile of them; cables, too, addressed to both of us. The first I opened read: *Instruct Heygate return immediately Waugh*. Heygate's own communications were no less pressing. It was clear that our trip together was at an end. The blow had fallen; crisis come. I now see the Tavistock Square party as something of a showdown.

Taking the car, Heygate set out the following morning from Munich, heading for whichever port was to ship him back to England. During the week of holiday that remained to me I made my way by train from Munich to Frankfurt; Frankfurt to Cologne. On one of these journeys, the train very full, I had to travel standing in the corridor. A friendly young German, with a girl, got into conversation – no doubt wanting to practise English, but such amiability was a common experience at the time – and insisted on standing me ham-and-eggs in the restaurant-car. I think he and his girl only drank beer. I mentioned the Berlin nightclubs. He shook his head. 'The shadow of life,' he said.

That year several more friends were married; the Evelyn Waughs the first couple known to me – though by no means the last – to be divorced. The place the Waugh divorce was to take in the mythology of the period was at the time not at all to be foreseen. The older generation, in principle discouraging marriage, found in divorce (especially this divorce) complete justification of that attitude. A few worldly persons expressed the view that it had been incautious to leave a young lively newly married wife (only recently recovered from a grave illness) in a comparatively out-of-the-way flat all the week, but on the whole those who had inveighed against the marriage, inveighed equally against separation as inexpiable.

In short, then and later, a good deal of humbug was talked on the subject. I have no doubt whatever that it is, in general, far better to remain married when at all possible, but during the next few years plenty of other marriages were to break up. If this one was to come adrift, that was surely better taking place when there were no children, giving opportunity for both parties to build – as they did – new lives. Waugh's second marriage was successful, but no one reading his Diaries could doubt that an exceptional staying-power was required in any woman who remained married to him.

The inevitable consequence of the circumstances in which I now found myself – committed to Heygate by the trip to Germany, in any case by being by then a friend of Evelyn Gardner's – was that I saw no more of Waugh for some years. No immediate awkwardness took place, partly because Waugh himself was often abroad during the period following the divorce; partly because he had largely ceased to inhabit the sort of world in which we had formerly met. No doubt my own paths were changing too. I was less aware of that at the time than on looking back. Even after I was married (1934), I don't think I came across Waugh more than a couple of times; when we dined on one occasion with the Connollys; at a party of Alice (Astor) von Hofmann-stahl's.

Waugh's irascibilities have been much dwelt on. He took the termination of his first marriage very hard. In a less vengeful character than he, to sever all social contacts with one who had perforce remained Heygate's friend – indeed close friend – would not be unexpected; equally, to avoid all mention in print of a fellow writer who found himself in that position. On the contrary, so far from adopting any sort of professional boycott, Waugh (in an article not mainly about books) went out of his way to write enthusiastically of my third novel, *From a View to a Death*, when it appeared in 1933.

The manner in which Waugh and I were again to become associated may be described out of chronological order, the better to appreciate those coincidental juxtapositions that are such a feature of human experience. In 1937, he married as second wife Laura Herbert; through the Herbert connexion, half first-cousin of Evelyn Gardner. Four years later than that, I found myself working at the War Office with Alick Dru, who, in 1943, had married Gabriel Herbert, Laura Herbert's sister. By that time Dru, as well as military colleague, had become a personal friend.

In the days when we first knew each other in London, Waugh, not caring in the least what details he broadcast about his private life, told me things of a fairly intimate kind, but I am sure that he would have revealed them no less to almost anyone else he found momentarily sympathetic; the point being that we were never close friends in the sense in which young men sometimes deeply confide in each other. I think

Waugh was perhaps not temperamentally given to friendships of that kind. I may be wrong about that. Nevertheless, in those days, and in middle life, we always got on well together, though on terms that would never have sustained the sort of behaviour that, in certain moods, Waugh, especially in his latter years, would impose on friends far closer to him than myself. He always delighted in teasing, to which I was as much exposed as anyone else, but, in my own experience, there was never a moment when he attempted to display the savage disagreeableness of which he was at moments so regrettably capable.

After his move from Gloucestershire to Somerset, Waugh lived about fifty miles away from us. He would sometimes arrive without warning on a visit; and at least on one occasion we did the same, looking in on the way to dine with one of his neighbours. For example, one morning while working I heard a car arrive at the door about midday, then go away. This turned out to be the Waughs, accompanied by one child. Waugh (who did not drive a car) was to lunch in our neighbourhood with Katherine Asquith at Mells, where his wife would deliver him; then take more of the Waugh children out from school for the afternoon, putting the one with them on the train to London. Meanwhile, we were to collect Waugh himself from his luncheon at about three o'clock. His wife would return to us for tea. The two of them would then go home.

All fell out according to plan, but after tea it became clear that the Waughs had nothing ahead of them. They stayed for dinner, leaving about eleven o'clock that night. Eight hours on end, without warning, can impose a certain strain on almost any conversation with the same company, let alone someone as cantankerous as Waugh. Nothing worse took place than a fairly sharp argument (brought up by Waugh, then abandoned by him) as to what members of what clubs were homosexual. He had been under the mistaken impression that no names could be quoted from his own. There is not any particular point in this story, except to show, notwithstanding a good deal of evidence to suggest the contrary, that Waugh was perfectly capable of spending an afternoon and evening without making a scene. On another occasion – only about eighteen months before his own death – we met him at Paddington on a train travelling west. Like ourselves he was on his way home. I suggested he should detrain at our station, dine, spend the night. (Though oddly, when writing to Katherine Asquith on 14 September 1964 he represents Violet rather than myself as extending the invitation.) This he did, ringing up his home (though usually an unwilling telephoner) with a message that he had been kidnapped. The evening was an enjoyable one. Again, Waugh is presented so rarely in an easygoing state that the incident seems worth recalling.

In November, 1965, at a country wedding, we found ourselves in the queue to greet bride and bridegroom with Waugh, his wife, one of their daughters. Waugh did not look at all well. For some time he had been too fat to be in good health; now he seemed at the same time portly, yet wasted. He walked in a very shaky manner. One could never be sure such staggerings were not the pretence of being an old man. that he had begun in middle-age, together with the ear-trumpet, but, if the ear-trumpet itself remained always something of a game, the deafness and unsteadiness on his feet were now genuine enough.

'Do you think there's any whisky?' he asked at once.

'I'd forgotten you drank whisky.'

That was true enough. A great consumer of wine, especially port, Waugh's favourite spirit had always seemed gin, drunk with Italian vermouth, or orange; though no doubt a whisky-and-soda last thing.

'One must at an affair like this. I'll have a look round the house.'

He broke off from the queue; reappearing a minute or two later, before we had anything like reached the newly married couple.

'I'd very much like your opinion on two decanters I've found. I'm not sure either is whisky. My sense of smell isn't what it used to be.'

He led me through the back parts of the house into a kind of scullery. On a tray, with a bottle of barley water, stood two all but empty decanters. Whatever they contained could have dated back some days, if not weeks. It was evident they had been put out of the way for the party that was taking place. I diagnosed port residues in each case. Waugh sighed.

'Just what I thought myself.'

We returned to the queue. The main part of the reception was taking place in a marquee, to reach which a ramp had been placed, leading down to the tent from the higher level of the lawn. The slope, though perceptible, was not a specially steep one.

We happened to leave the party at the same moment as the Waughs. Laura Waugh went first, Waugh following, holding his daughter's arm for support. Suddenly, from sheer physical weakness, he could not manage the ascent. His daughter had to call for her mother to return and help. Together they got him up the ramp. This was the first time I grasped quite how bad was his state of health by that stage.

At the top of the slope the three of them paused. Waugh smiled as we passed, making a faint gesture of his hand to say goodbye. That was the last time I saw him. He died about five months later.

I had heard nothing of Rosa Lewis, nor her hotel, for a long time, when in 1941, in Piccadilly, by chance I ran into a former fellow-student of an army course we had both attended. I was, I think, by then actually employed at the War Office; he passing through London on the way to a new army posting.

On the course, I had exchanged an occasional word with this quiet slightly eccentric lieutenant, like myself rather old to be of subaltern rank, but we had not known each other at all well. At our meeting in the street, almost his first words were: 'You know, I felt I simply must have a woman before taking on this new job, so I went to see Rosa, who made all sorts of difficulties, said she didn't do much in that line now, was interested in other things, but I absolutely insisted, so in the end Rosa said: "Well, all right, I'll try and get Ivy Peters to meet you in the bar of The Dorchester tomorrow", and I'm hoping everything's fixed.'

I can't imagine why the middle-aged lieutenant unburdened himself to me in this way about his sexual needs, as we had never discussed that sort of thing, nor why he had instantly assumed that I should know who 'Rosa' was. I never discovered the reason for this candour, because he went on to speak of military matters, but, by an extraordinary chance (never to be accepted in a novel), passing The Dorchester in a bus or taxi the following evening, I saw him entering its doors. I hope all went well. The curious thing was that I was again to hear the name of Ivy Peters (as I have fictitiously called the lady in question) pronounced by Rosa Lewis herself in my own house.

1 Chester Gate had been somewhat knocked about during the blitz, but, by 1945, in a sufficient state of repair for us to live there again. The Drus at one moment came to live at Chester Gate too. Gabriel Dru's brother, Auberon Herbert, unable to get himself accepted by the British forces owing to his low medical category, had with considerable enterprise managed to join the Polish army in the ranks. In due course Auberon Herbert was commissioned by the Poles as an officer, and it was probably to celebrate this promotion that he gave a party at The Cavendish.

As sequel to this party, Auberon Herbert arranged for Rosa Lewis to lunch at Chester Gate. Violet was away (lying up for the birth of our second son John), but Gabriel Dru cooked luncheon, and there was probably Algerian wine, one bottle of which, with luck, could be procured most weeks. Only the two Drus, Auberon Herbert, and I, were present.

At first it was like entertaining any elderly lady of the Edwardian zenith, who had begun to feel her age a little; a flood of civilities about the eternal wartime topic, the difficulties of getting hold of food and drink. Then, beginning to warm up at the table, Rosa Lewis set off on a monologue in her old style, in the midst of which she touched on the fascinating subject of 'Lewis', her butler husband, whose personal history was long lost in the mists of time.

'I took The Cavendish on because I was sorry for him,' she said. 'After he went bankrupt, that was.'

Unfortunately, in the course of a fairly long peroration, the name 'Lewis' turned almost imperceptibly into 'Lois'; that is to say Lois Sturt (by then deceased), formerly wife of Evan Morgan (2nd Viscount Tredegar), both of these two last well known at the bohemian end of the beau monde. With the new name Rosa Lewis's narrative swerved, too, in a new direction. The anecdote, which had begun about her husband, became dovetailed into a story about Lois Sturt. I tried to get conversation back on to the right lines, but it was no good. The subject had changed irretrievably. An attempt to salvage in tranquillity some of what had already been said about Lewis was later equally un- successful; impossible to distinguish for certain where Lewis ended, Lois began. Potentially absorbing information was lost for ever. 'Some- body ought to write it all down properly,' said Rosa Lewis. 'After what that man put in *Vile Bodies*.'

I felt pretty sure she did not know, at best had long forgotten, that Evelyn Waugh had a sister-in-law, two brothers-in-law, present sitting at the table.

'People repeat all sorts of bad things about me,' she said. 'They never remember all the good I've done. You don't know how much I've helped some of these young men. Look at the way Jack Fording- bridge wanted to marry Ivy Peters. He wanted to *marry* her. Set on it, he was. The Duke was almost off his head about his son and heir. I introduced Fordingbridge to Frieda Brown, and he dropped Ivy Peters like a hot potato. People forget all the good I've done.'

In spite of the apparent paradox in such an illustration of the virtuous deeds a society indifferent to moral values allows to pass unregarded, it was probably true that Rosa Lewis, not at all malevolent in the manner of many of her power-loving kind, had played a comparatively beneficent rôle in that and similar entanglements. The vignette of the middle-aged lieutenant on his way to his assignation with the seductive Ivy Peters – who might have become a duchess – added a piquant footnote to the story.

The confusion of 'Lewis' and 'Lois' is a good example of the 'time- travelling' in which Rosa Lewis would indulge during her declining years. The war, if not over, was quickly drawing to a close, when, on the way back to work after lunch one afternoon, I saw her approaching from the far end of Jermyn Street. She was smiling to herself. I saluted as we came level. Rosa Lewis stopped me. 'Well, *you're* a ghost from the past,' she said, though certainly she had no idea who I was even after a name was given. We talked for a minute or two.

'Come in and have a drink this evening,' she said.

I got away from the War Office soon after seven, and went along to The Cavendish. Four or five persons, male and female, none known to me, were in Rosa Lewis's downstairs sitting-room. I was the only one in uniform. The others, youngish, belonged to the unplaceable Cavendish category spoken of earlier. Since our afternoon chat Rosa Lewis herself had moved a considerable distance along the road of vagueness. I told her my name again, why I had turned up. She seemed quite happy about that; something upon which one could not wholly rely after such a chance invitation. A 'bottle of wine' no longer a practical proposition, I was handed a stiff whisky. Then Rosa Lewis took my arm and introduced me round the room.

'This is Bimbash Stewart,' she said.

At first I thought a joke was intended. The designation, attracting by its exoticism, conveyed nothing. Then, when several more persons arrived, she repeated the name to each one of them, apparently in all seriousness, no more than her usual air of moving in a dream. After a while, deciding the party was not my sort, I said goodbye, and slipped away.

Not much less than a dozen years later (possibly in a book to be reviewed) I came across the name Bimbash Stewart again. He was described in a note as an 'Edwardian man about town'. This tantalizing piece of information was a spur to further enquiries. These revealed that Henry King Stewart (1861–1907), an officer in the British Army, had also served in the rank of bimbashi (captain, commander) with the Egyptian forces. On retirement he had become a King's Messenger.

Then, quite by chance, an incisive picture of Bimbash Stewart was drawn for me by Lady Diana Cooper. He had lived in a flat, she said, just opposite her parents' house in Arlington Street, Piccadilly. Clearly that address had been convenient for The Cavendish. Bimbash Stewart used to sport a black fur cap, said Lady Diana, and his life was believed to be full of romantic undercurrents. As a child, she added, she had been madly in love with him; when he died in the flat over the way, for some time wearing a chain round her neck as reminder to pray for him.

All this might be gratifying to self-esteem, but, even in uniform, I cannot flatter myself that the resemblance to Bimbash Stewart can ever have been a very close one. Mine must have been one of those arbitrary identifications brought into being to invest the rooms of The Cavendish with relics of the old days. Nevertheless, it was pleasant to feel that one had found some sort of a niche, even if an incongruously shared one, in Rosa Lewis's vast tapestry of memory; rather like becoming an element in that larger consciousness, which some think awaits us when individual existence fades.

On the subject of mortality, as on all other matters, Rosa Lewis had few illusions. After suffering a severe illness not very long before final abdication of her reign over The Cavendish, she is reported to have remarked: 'I've seen the Gates of Heaven and the Gates of Hell – and they're both bloody.'

✳ 9 ✳

In the London Library, works devoted to the subject of Love are classified under the heading *Science and Miscellaneous*. Not long after I moved to Tavistock Square, I was taken by John Heygate to a party in Chelsea, to which he had been invited by some little piece, met casually in a similar milieu a few nights before. It turned out to be a fairly unstimulating gathering (with slightly lesbian undertones), and, Heygate having already left, I was preparing to go home too. I was hanging about in an almost empty outer room, when a girl came through the door from the hall. She stood there for a moment inspecting what could be seen of the mainstream of the party, which was taking place in the room beyond. She looked as if she were a little unwilling to join it.

Small, dark, elegant, this girl was of ravishing prettiness, the looks then most fashionable, though at the same time somehow not at all those of a fashion-magazine. I don't think she was twenty. I spoke to her, and we talked for a minute or two. She said she was not going to stay at the party, because almost immediately she had to move on somewhere else, but, mentioning her own name, she asked me to look in at her flat (which was in the King's Road) on a date a day or two later that week. She added an unexpected comment: 'I'll tell them you're my new young man.' I did not know who 'they' might be, but this was a promising opening.

When I made enquiries (probably from Lambert) as to who this, almost literally, enchanting new acquaintance might be, I was – as it turned out very reasonably – greeted with considerable amusement at confessing to such naively ambitious enthusiasms. This girl (with her younger sister, or half-sister, at that moment abroad) turned out to be one of the reigning beauties of the already touched on party-world. 'Modelling' clothes, doing odd jobs on the edges of the arts, the two sisters were quite famous figures, the name of each associated with men somewhat older than myself and decidedly richer.

Lambert added that Peter Quennell used to call them (from Villiers de l'Isle Adam's story in *Contes Cruels*) 'Les Demoiselles de Bienfilatre'. This caustic pleasantry carried an undeniable sting in the tail. The Bienfilatre sisters of Villiers's short story are two little professional Paris tarts (with *spécialités* inscribed on their visiting cards) pretty, elegant, demure, devoted to each other, models of behaviour to their clients and colleagues. Suddenly they separate from their shared household. It appears that one has been deeply shocked by the conduct of the other. Her sister has committed the unpardonable offence of falling in love without mercenary motive. The renegade Bienfilatre is taken ill. In spite of the shame she has brought on the family, the other goes to see her. On her deathbed the lovelorn Bienfilatre manages, with her last breath, to gasp out that honour is saved – her lover has paid up.

Once you have decided that you are in love (unless an accomplished trafficker in that element) the whole situation is likely to change vis-à-vis the other person, not only for yourself, but for her too. It is the difference of the recruit and the Recruiting Sergeant; before taking the shilling; afterwards in barracks. I was for some time an ineffective admirer of the girl I met that night. Even a year or more later, that condition was probably what caused Cecil Beaton – negotiating at Henrietta Street about Duckworth's publication of his *Book of Beauty* (1930), an album restricting itself and its photographs to beauties of only a well publicized order – to note in his diary that he had dealt at the office with a 'young man of Dickensian gloom'. Painful as love can be, I cannot pretend to have abandoned all attempt at finding consolation. In fact that very situation became largely the theme of my first novel.

Although slightly lame from a childhood's illness – his characteristic movement in walking closely resembling descriptions of the manner in which Lord Byron appeared never to set the heel of one foot to the ground – Lambert was a great walker. One Sunday afternoon in the summer we had tea together, probably in his flat over The Varda Bookshop, afterwards, I can't imagine why, strolling east to have a drink at The Tiger on Tower Hill, a pub of attractive interior standing opposite the main gate of the Tower itself. Licensed premises opening only at seven in the evening on a Sunday, it must have been towards eight, perhaps later, when we left The Tiger, and continued to press eastward. The immediate object was to inspect the bas-reliefs of the Seasons, supposedly executed by Caius Cibber (Danish-born father of the 18th century dramatist, Colley Cibber, much derided by his own contemporaries), then to be seen on the exterior walls of a house in Wellclose Square, some way beyond the Mint. The sculptor himself is buried nearby in the former Danish–Norwegian Church.

Having inspected these elegant plaques we moved on through the twilight into Wapping and Shadwell. Dinner was eaten rather late at a Chinese restaurant in Limehouse. In general I found Chinese food tolerable only in Lambert's company, because (his cult for the Orient particularly biased towards China) he justly regarded himself as an authority on Chinese food procurable in London. He had formerly claimed a taste for Chinese wine, but, becoming disillusioned with celestial vintages (examples of which had been given him), made over his Chinese cellar to Tommy Earp. After the first draught, Earp enquired in his piping voice: 'Rather an aphrodisiac effect?' Lambert replied he had never noticed that. Earp thought the matter over. 'Perhaps it coincides with my annual erection,' he said.

Continuing our journey, there was almost certainly a visit to The Prospect of Whitby, and several other riverside pubs were included in our survey. Skirting the Isle of Dogs we crossed the River by the Blackwall Tunnel in order to make a return journey along the South Bank. By this time it was past midnight, the domes and towers of Wren's Greenwich illuminated by the moon. This is a sight worth seeing, but it would be hypocritical to pretend that the walk back did not become a little exhausting. Between Rotherhithe and Bermondsey a miracle took place. There was a rattle of wheels along metal lines, and, altogether unaccountably, a tram drew up beside us. Perhaps it was a ghost tram. No one else seemed to be using it as a means of transport, and, even at that date, its outlines and method of locomotion appeared noticeably antique in the gloom. Nevertheless we were grateful, entering the tram, and riding as far as possible. It turned south just before one of the bridges. We alighted. The spectral tram disappeared southwards into the night. I do not recall where the River was recrossed. The hour was past four when, rather footsore, I descended the steps of the area in Tavistock Square.

Lambert took me once or twice to see his friend, Philip Heseltine (Peter Warlock, the composer), who lived with a mistress in what was then a very rundown area of Pimlico. Heseltine, in his early thirties, had by taking thought turned himself into a consciously mephisto-phelian figure, an appearance assisted by a pointed fair beard and light-coloured eyes that were peculiarly compelling. His reputation, one not altogether undeserved, was that of *mauvais sujet*, but I always found him agreeable and highly entertaining; though never without a sense, as with many persons of at times malignant temper, that things might suddenly go badly wrong.

Heseltine had been model for Halliday in D. H. Lawrence's novel, *Women in Love*; for Coleman in Aldous Huxley's *Antic Hay*. Coleman (a name perhaps chosen from the Victorian pornographer) is given Heseltine's beard, taste for composing limericks, intellectual anarchism. If exact portraiture of an existent individual is what the reader requires from a character in a novel (and many novel-readers seem interested in little else), Coleman conveys quite a good idea of what Heseltine was like to meet. Halliday, on the other hand (much reduced in scope after a libel action brought by Heseltine himself), is chiefly to be identified (before legal pruning of the novel) by Heseltine's habit of speaking of his girls as if they were cats; animals for which – like Lambert – he had a passionate affection. As a character in a novel, Halliday embodies that overheated unrealized air that envelopes so many of Lawrence's projections of his own acquaintances, especially if he had fallen out with them. In that connexion the generalization might be risked that envy hatred, and malice (of which Lawrence must have had at least his fair share) can build up a reputation for journalism, but in less ephemeral writing, especially the novel, are almost always disadvantageous.

In December, 1930, choosing a moment when his mistress was away from the flat (they had possibly had a slight quarrel, but not a serious one), Heseltine put the cat outside the door one night, so that it should not be a fellow victim, and turned on the gas. He was hard up at the time, though not desperately so; simply tired of the business of living. This climax, which came about just before our planned Christmas jaunt to Paris, greatly upset Lambert. Heseltine was the first person known to me, as an acquaintance of that sort, to do away with himself.

Heseltine's short unhappy but not unproductive life was recorded by another of Lambert's friends, the music-critic, Cecil Gray. Gray had also belonged to the D. H. Lawrence circle and was Lambert's chief link with Wyndham Lewis. A plump bespectacled rather unforth-coming Scot, Gray possessed considerable acuteness over and above musical matters. He was comfortably off, married (in the event, several times), with a small neat house in Bayswater facing the Park. Unfit for military service, he had inhabited a Cornish cottage near the Lawrences during the first war. He was (as indicated by his marital career) a thorough-going heterosexual, indeed somewhat intolerant of inversion, but was fond of telling the story of how, one afternoon in Cornwall, a knock had come on his cottage door. He opened it to find Lawrence standing there. 'Gray,' asked Lawrence. 'How long have you been in love with me?'

Another story of Gray's that turned on the opening of his own front-door, very different from the Lawrence one, took place at the Bayswater house. Sitting in the window one evening reading, he saw Wyndham Lewis turn in from the street, mount the steps as if to pay a call. Gray waited for the bell to ring. He continued to read for some moments, no sound coming from bell or knocker. After allowing several minutes to elapse Gray went to the front-door and opened it. Lewis, apparently unable to nerve himself to knock or ring, was standing on the doorstep. Lewis said nothing. He did not look at all at ease. Gray said: 'Won't you come in?' Lewis still did not speak, but slowly entered the house. In the hall he broke his silence. 'Lambert has got something against me,' he said. The matter of whatever Lambert supposedly had against Lewis was, so far as I know, never further ventilated.

Tendencies in Lewis not far from paranoiac (doing him grave damage as a writer) were well on the way by the time of the publication of *The Apes of God* (1930). Notwithstanding the brilliance of much of the language, the unrelieved subjectivity of *The Apes of God* defeats its own specifically satirical ends. If the prototype of the 'ape' in question is known personally to the reader, the description, however unjust in omitting all redeeming features, is at the same time so vivid that the victim might almost be in the room. On the other hand, if Lewis is dealing with a personality the reader has never encountered in the flesh, there is a total breakdown in communication.

I did not come across Wyndham Lewis himself until about twenty years after this period. I had written a piece about satire in the 1920s for the *Times Literary Supplement*, then edited by Alan Pryce-Jones This article had spoken in praise of *Tarr*, but some sort of a correspondence followed, Lewis denying that he had used the phrase (which occurs in the preface to the novel's 1928 edition) 'the first book of an epoch'. As nothing had been printed that was not entirely favourable to Lewis (except his own forgetfulness of what he had written), Pryce-Jones, thinking this might be an opportunity to persuade him to become a *TLS* contributor, invited Lewis and myself to luncheon *à trois* at the Travellers' Club.

Big, toothy, awkward in manner, Lewis behaved with an uneasy mixture of nervousness and hauteur. In his white shirt and dark suit he looked like a caricature of an American senator or businessman, causing one to remember that his father had been born a citizen of the US, and that, during the war, Lewis had described himself in books of reference as 'of American parentage'. In fact his forebears were mostly Canadian. There was also a touch, if only a faint one, of Crowley's moments of thaumaturgical majesty of demeanour, though Lewis was, of course, a considerable artist, not a sinister if gifted buffoon. The comparison seems worth making simply because some aspect of a shared megalomaniac egotism may have accounted for a sort of resemblance. From time to time in the course of the meal Lewis swallowed what were presumably digestive tablets. I had come prepared to admire, but found some difficulty in doing so.

In consequence of the civilities offered by Pryce-Jones, Lewis was induced without too much difficulty to write a 'front' for the *TLS*, the subject of which I do not remember. In those days *Times Literary Supplement* articles were unsigned, as indeed they remained long after that date. Lewis had apparently never noticed this essential rule of the paper, in his own piece using the first-person throughout, a method obviously inappropriate, if the reader has no idea who 'I' may be. Pryce-Jones, as editor, naturally had to return what Lewis had written for alteration; at the same time, wishing to save Lewis as much trouble as possible, pencilling in a few suggestions as to where, without change of sense, the first-person could easily be altered to a general statement.

The effect of Pryce-Jones's letter on Lewis was utterly unforeseen. A reply came back expressed in scarcely sane terms. Legal action was threatened from Lewis's solicitor, interspersed with personal abuse, and bitter complaint of the way he had been treated. This explosion was brought about simply by a request to make at most half-a-dozen minor variations of phraseology in an article of four or five thousand words. The impression of some years past that all was not well with the balance of Lewis's mind could not be avoided.

John Heygate married Evelyn Gardner in August, 1930. They continued to live for a time at the Canonbury Square flat, the lease of which belonged to her. The first act of the Heygate parents on hearing that their son was involved in a divorce had been to cut off his allowance; while the baronet uncle (somewhat impotently, since the Ulster property was entailed on the heir to the title) declared that he would disinherit his nephew out of hand; proceeding to do so in whatever manner lay within his power. Sir John Reith, on his pontiff's throne in Langham Place, did not recognize divorce (nor was there any form of BBC annulment to be sought), so Heygate resigned from the Corporation before pressure was applied to enforce that. Shortage of money brought about by these two eventualities, loss of his job, cutting off of parental supplies, caused Heygate to set about writing a novel, with the object of earning at least a little, while he looked about for something to do.

Heygate's novel, *Decent Fellows* (1932), had an Eton background, and was first published as an experimental paperback. The book made a certain stir on account of its supposed impropriety, though why, even in those days, anyone should have been at all shocked, is hard to understand. References to public school homosexuality – a subject by then treated comparatively openly for at least fifteen or twenty years – were of the mildest. Nevertheless, *Decent Fellows* outraged certain people, and very silly things were written and said of it. Lambert read Heygate's novel simultaneously with *The Enormous Room*, alleging that he got the two books hopelessly confused in his mind, causing perpetual surprise at how uncomfortable were circumstances at Eton.

Disapproval of *Decent Fellows* did no harm to Heygate professionally, indeed probably helped in finding employment later as writer of film scripts, a vocation he undertook for a time with a certain amount of success. He worked with the German film company, UFA, at Neubabelsberg, outside Berlin, where he was engaged on trilingual pictures (with the English actress, Lilian Harvey, as star); continuing to write books, when these employments came to an end. I visited Germany in 1932, and some relics of this glimpse of the film industry, experienced through Heygate, found a place in *Agents and Patients*.

In contrast with earlier attempts, *Afternoon Men*, once begun, moved fairly steadily forward. Some of this first novel was written in Toulon, a delightful place in those days, impressions of which occur in *What's Become of Waring*. Lambert had recommended the Hôtel du Port et des Négociants, where he had himself stayed several times, though we were never in Toulon together. The hotel, far from luxurious, very reasonable in price, was placed conveniently for cafés and paddle-boat. No doubt the local *négociants*, to whom the Hôtel du Port was partly dedicated, made use of its facilities; French intellectuals also stayed there for summer holidays that included opium smoking and chasing sailors.

I set out alone for Toulon, intending to work hard, but in the event undertook little more than a few pages of revision. That was because of the company found at the hotel. At the Tavistock Square party the year before, guests had included several of the Ballet, among them the two dancers, Frederick Ashton (later famous choreographer, knighted, OM), William Chappell (later stage-designer and theatrical director). Chappell turned out to be spending a holiday at the Hôtel du Port with two cronies from art-school days: the painter, Edward Burra, and Irene Hodgkins ('Hodge'), an extremely pretty girl, who was also a painter and model. After meeting in the hotel, we all used to have meals together, bathe together at Les Sablettes. Hodge, whom I may have come across rather vaguely at parties, was to be collected in about ten days' time by the middle-aged publisher, C., to whom she was engaged; for whose sake she had joined the Jewish faith. I knew Ed Burra hitherto only by name. Burra never sunbathed (then the rage), his skin retaining its constitutional tint of parchment, appropriate to an air of having just stepped out of a Cruikshank engraving. Like the rest of the party he was in his middle twenties, but seemed prematurely old; truer perhaps to say that he resembled a prisoner just brought out into the sunlight after years of confinement in a pitch-dark subterranean dungeon. He spoke rarely, but always with devastating aptness.

Burra spent a great deal of time at Toulon working. His method was one of the most unusual I have ever observed in a painter. He would sit in an hotel bedroom on a rickety hotel chair at an equally rickety hotel table – possibly even a dressing-table – dozens of extraneous objects round about him (including the remains of petit déjeuner), while he executed his pictures. What was always an immensely compli-cated design would be begun in the bottom right-hand corner of a large square of paper; from that angle moving in a diagonal sweep upward and leftward across the surface of the sheet, until the whole was covered with an intricate pattern of background and figures. If not large enough, the first piece of paper would be tacked on to a second one – in fact would almost certainly be joined to several more – the final work made up of perhaps three or four of these attached sections. At this period Burra's pictures were likely to be brightly coloured grotesque images of Firbankian fantasy, often Negroid, the forerunners of those 'bulging husky leathery shapes' described by Wyndham Lewis in a much later critique. In middle age Burra was also to explore in his own disturbing fashion a very unnaturalistic English countryside; a sphere where he was perhaps finally at his best.

Burra was reputed to engage in no sexual activities at all, nor to feel emotional attachments of any kind; a view of himself to some extent confirmed from his own lips, when (I think) Hermione Baddeley, a great comic star of those days and frequenter of parties, crossquestioned him on the subject.

'Have you ever loved a man?'

'No.'

'Have you ever loved a woman?'

'No.'

'Not even your mother?'

There was a short pause while Burra considered the matter. A conclusion was reached.

'No.'

This singularity in his own affections did not prevent Burra from making apt comment on the sexual behaviour of others. His remarks, in any case, had a quality all their own. Once, at a party, the sound of such frightful retchings and vomitings came from the lavatory that the host, disturbed that one of his guests should be in such an unhappy condition, tapped on the door to ask if first-aid was needed. From the far side Burra's voice faintly answered: 'It's *only* Madame.'

About a week had passed at the Hôtel du Port in this tranquil manner, when half-a-dozen persons, some known, some unknown, appeared by boat from Cassis – then a centre for artists – for a night out in Toulon. One of the girls who turned up was the heroine (or anti-heroine) of *Afternoon Men*. She was known to Hodge – who supported life in much the same manner – but I don't think Hodge had previously met any of the men, two of whom were painters. We all joined up for an evening at the *bal-musette*, during which it became clear that Hodge was having a success with one of the painters. In due course, the night having clearly nothing to offer from my own point of view, I returned to the hotel, leaving some of the others to seek yet further haunts to dance. The following day, by the time I was up and about, the Cassis group had shipped themselves back to base. That afternoon, or the next, Hodge's middle-aged publisher, C., appeared by train in Toulon. The morning after C.'s arrival I found him at a café table on the *rade*, where it was customary to have breakfast, rather than in the hotel. We talked of this and that. I asked when he and Hodge were to return to England.

'I'm leaving tomorrow,' he said. 'Hodge isn't coming with me. She's going off to live with this fellow who came over from Cassis the other night.'

It was not easy to know how to reply. This was not (as I knew) the first rough ride C. had experienced in matters of love; nor, as it turned out, was it to be the last. There is no particular point in the anecdote, except, like others recorded here, to convey the atmosphere of the period. It also adds force to C.'s recipe for writing a good Jewish novel: write a good novel; then change all the names to Jewish ones.

The following year, again with the object of working (on *Venusberg*), I set off once more alone, this time going to Sainte-Maxime. Becoming bored by myself, I moved up the coast again to Toulon, where I knew various friends were to take a holiday. This time there was quite a crowd at the Hôtel du Port; with several more from both sexes, Billy Chappell, Freddy Ashton, their great crony, Barbara Ker-Seymer, then an avant-garde photographer. Other friends of mine present were Wyndham Lloyd; Beatrice 'Bumble' Dawson, another photographer in those days, later a successful stage-designer.

Also staying at the hotel on this occasion were Cocteau and his entourage. I never met him personally, though they were all to be seen playing about together at Les Sablettes. It was said that the bitter-sweet fumes of opium were discernible on the staircase of the hotel, but I was myself not able to distinguish the scent among a variety of others hanging about there.

I left Toulon with a week in hand, wanting to travel back slowly through Provence, stopping at Arles and Avignon. The Arlésiennes are spoken of as particularly attractive. Sitting alone in an Arles café one evening, my attention was riveted by the appearance of a girl strolling through the crowd. I thought how true was what had been written about this tradition of local beauty at Arles. Then, as she looked straight at me and waved, I became aware that here again, passing through the town by car – ratifying once more the inexorable law of coincidence – was the girl of *Afternoon Men*.

During these years I stayed twice with the Sitwells in Derbyshire. Osbert Sitwell's account of his father in *Left Hand, Right Hand!* does not at all overstate the case. Indeed, in depicting the figure of Sir George Sitwell, 4th baronet – always known among his children and their friends as Ginger – less pleasant sides are toned down, rather than exaggerated. Sir George sailed at times uncomfortably close to the condition of madness. That did not prevent him from mustering an exceptional array of abilities in many different fields – a fact he himself was never tired of affirming, modesty not being one of his handicaps – gifts manifested through a nature equally likely to express itself in the wildest prodigality, with shrewd business sense, or a grinding stinginess that would have shamed Scrooge. By this period Sir George had been built up by his children as a supremely comic creation. In a sense he certainly was a comic personality, one of the most notable of the day, but that was by no means the whole picture.

Nevertheless, notwithstanding a tone that seemed on the whole to avoid the deeper notes of tragedy, not much more than a dozen years before a disaster of Dostoevskian dimensions had occupied this same stage; a calamity that goes far to interpret need to escape from too grim a realism, into the stylized glitter of the harlequinade. Lady Ida Sitwell (daughter of the 1st Earl of Londesborough) had been married off to Sir George at the age of seventeen. Utterly imprudent about money, a compulsive gambler, deep in debt, she found herself caught in the snare of a professional swindler. This man trapped her into signing papers that led to a prison sentence. The circumstances are set out in Osbert Sitwell's memoirs, but no judgment is passed on his father, whose behaviour was perhaps equivocal. Certainly some people thought so at the time; others asserting that, the papers having been signed, the Law could take no other course.

Sir George's manner was abstracted, distant, not much short of hostile. He might have been an accomplished actor playing for a laugh among the more subtle of his audience. It was an exterior that made one think of Osmund in *Portrait of a Lady*. There was something 'wrong' about Sir George Sitwell, badly wrong, and for me he always lacked the air of distinction possessed by his children; indeed also by his unhappy wife. The eccentricities were certainly genuine enough, not in the least assumed to make an impression; yet he was in some manner an actor dressed up to play a part; that part perhaps a not very pleasant one.

Among the guests at Renishaw on my first visit was Arthur Waley, invited with his maîtresse en titre, Beryl de Zoete, also a fairly formidable figure and accomplished translator. Waley, now famous for having translated and promoted the literature of Japan and China, worked in the Print Room of the British Museum. Though not one of Bloomsbury's highest inner praesidium, he ranked as an authentic Bloomsbury of the next grade; in Waley's case perhaps appropriately to be described as a Mandarin of the Second Button. Slight, sallow, among other accomplishments an expert skier, Waley spoke always in a high clipped severe tone, as if slightly offended, quiet, but essentially smacking-down. He habitually refused to make the smallest compromise in the way of momentarily lowering intellectual standards in the interests of trivial conventional courtesies; demeanour that could produce in a room an extraordinary sense of social discomfort.

It has been suggested that Waley himself was unaware of his disconcerting manner. I do not believe that to be true. I think he was perfectly conscious of its impact. Waley possessed his fair share of aggression, even if that was also to some extent a barrier of rather agonized self-defence against people who might underrate his own abilities. Tête-à-tête, Waley was an amusing talker, who loved gossip. At the same time one never knew when a friendly tone would be withdrawn, and he would re-enter his carapace of disassociation. After our meeting at the Sitwells' he rang me up once or twice, asking me to dine with him, though himself never apparently available for playing a return. On one of these occasions he took me to see Patrick Hamilton's play, *Rope* insisting on paying for both tickets. When we left the theatre I expressed a word of thanks for his gesture. Waley listened for a second, as if to find out what I was talking about, then, without replying, quickly turned away and withdrew into the night.

How far, if at all, Sir George apprehended the extent to which, behind what was undoubtedly a barrier of fear, his children made fun of him, is impossible to guess. Certainly he found their literary activities in many respects a mystery, but, adapting his own behaviour accordingly, he was possibly aware of more than they supposed. He would from time to time utter a protest. On reading a poem written by his daughter which included the line 'the poxy doxy dear' (*Rustic Elegies*), he remonstrated: 'To anyone conversant with Elizabethan idiom, or the low speech of our own day, etc. etc.' Not long before the publication of *Before the Bombardment*, he observed to Lambert, when staying at Renishaw: 'It would be a strange novel that Osbert would write – there will be no love and no buried treasure. I fear it may not find great favour with the public.'

On one Renishaw visit I was strolling with Walton on the lawn before luncheon. Sir George approached. 'I have just been reading about mediaeval painted chambers ... strange ... very strange ... rather horrible at times ...' He paused, contemplating the horror of mediaeval painted chambers. Taken off our guard, Walton and I gave way to involuntary nervous laughter. Sir George showed no sign of noticing this response, inadequate, not very well mannered. Nevertheless he said no more on the subject, striding moodily away.

Sir George Sitwell felt a strong prejudice against drink, so that at Renishaw was none of the vinous plenty to be found at Carlyle Square. A house-party of perhaps twenty persons sitting down to dinner would be individually lucky to get more than a glass of white Bordeaux that certainly did not startle the connoisseur by its pretensions. When the ladies withdrew, the men would sit gloomily round the white tablecloth, draining the dregs of their coffee, while Sir George, who did not consider want of port or brandy a reason for cutting short the traditional male interlude spent in the dining-room, held forth on one of his favourite topics, such as Nottingham in the Middle Ages.

Such austerity was not at all to the taste of the rest of the family, and picked guests would be secretly bidden to assemble before dinner in Lady Ida's upstairs sitting-room, where, unknown to Sir George, a clandestine apéritif was provided for those deemed worthy. Traces of Lady Ida's former beauty remained, but, never wholly recovered from her ordeal, she would disconcertingly address one as 'Osbert' or 'Sachie', during a dinner-table conversation. She said to me: 'I love Paris so much, but I daren't ever go there, because I spend so much money.' She always pronounced *Façade* with a hard 'c'.

Osbert Sitwell liked to describe how on some occasion, no guests at Renishaw, he and his mother decided one afternoon to sample a bottle of Maraschino together in her sitting-room. Suddenly, altogether unexpectedly because in general he never showed himself there, Sir George stood in the doorway. Seeing the bottle he started dramatically back.

'*Not* Maraschino!'

His voice was agonized. Lady Ida answered her husband in a fashionable Edwardian drawl.

'What djer mean – Maraschino?'

If *Left Hand, Right Hand!* does not exaggerate the peculiarities of the author's father, neither does it overestimate the remarkable qualities of the Renishaw butler, Henry Moat, of whom many stories are told there. Moat, who looked like pictures of the traditional John Bull, and seemed rarely in less than the highest spirits, once observed to Lambert: 'Sir George is the strangest old bugger you ever met, and as for poor old Ida, she doesn't know whether she's coming or going.'

Nevertheless, the final word on the subject is perhaps owed to Cecil Gray. Travelling by himself in Italy, staying for a night in a small provincial hotel, Gray had been kept awake all night by maniacal laughter from the bedroom next door to his own. When he paid the bill the following morning, he enquired at the hotel desk who his neighbour might have been. '*Inglese.*' The clerk pointed to the register. The name inscribed there was that of Sir George Sitwell.

During the war, Violet and I stayed at Renishaw for my week's leave. Only Osbert and Edith Sitwell were there. Contrary perhaps to the popular picture of her, Edith Sitwell loved feminine chat, clothes, shopping, where to get your hair done, if that chat was carried on with a sympathetic woman friend. Discussion of the last of these matters led to the arrangement of an expedition to Sheffield. The Sitwells recommended that I should accompany the party in order to see a towr with its own particular fascination. As the Sheffield group was leaving the house, Osbert Sitwell drew Violet aside. 'We're a little short of food,' he said. 'Don't bother Edith about it, but should opportunity arise, visit Mr So-and-so, the fishmonger, who sometimes gets hold of a salmon. He might have one today.'

When we were in the car Violet put forward this possibility. Edith Sitwell – who left all the housekeeping in the competent hands of her brother – asked how best to cook the salmon, if the fish proved available, so that it went as far as possible. Violet offered some sort of an exposé on this subject, ending with the words: 'Then you make the tail into kedgeree.'

In one of the high-banked streets that give Sheffield its unique character we stopped at the fishmonger's. A queue, not one of great length but perceptible, waited on the pavement outside. For this foray into town Edith Sitwell had gone to some trouble in her outfit, which included a high cylindrical hat, something between an archimandrite's and that of a Tartar horseman in *Sohrab and Rustum*. She was a person who would never have deliberately jumped a queue, but, her head full of her brother's instructions, Violet's words on the culinary uses of salmon, she swept forward, disregarding the people waiting patiently outside, and seized the fishmonger – who was wearing the traditional straw boater of his trade – by the hand.

'Mr So-and-so, what a long time since I have been in to see you. How are you? How are your family? You are looking well yourself. Mr So-and-so, I have come to ask something, whether by any chance you have a salmon? *We want a salmon for making kedgeree.*'

The fishmonger went pale. Had the days of the Bourbons returned? Lucullus himself might have thought twice before devoting a whole newly caught salmon to kedgeree; anyway while Rome was at war. Notwithstanding, a salmon was produced.

One of the essential drop-scenes of my early London life was Castano's, an Italian restaurant in Greek Street, Soho, where in principle I used to lunch every day. I was introduced there, when still an undergraduate, by John 'The Widow' Lloyd. It was then called Previtali's (presumably after the Bergamesque painter), a name that occurs quite often in the Waugh Diaries during the period 1924/25, though I don't think I ever heard Waugh mention eating there. It appears in *Dance* as Foppa's.

Castano's served only *espresso* coffee, the deposit of which some find distasteful, so that a tradition grew up of drinking *café filtre* at Legrain's in Gerrard Street which provides the opening scene of *Agents and Patients*. When I married in 1934, Castano, in ironic reference to my rarely if ever drinking coffee in his restaurant (though I have, in fact, no particular objection to *espresso*), presented us with a self-straining coffee-pot as a wedding-present.

Gerrard Street included Maxim's Chinese Restaurant, to some small extent model for Casanova's Chinese Restaurant, in the volume of that title. The street, something of a centre for itinerant musicians, at times echoed with the marvellous voice of the very pretty blonde crippled girl, with whose singing *Casanova's Chinese Restaurant* (1960) opens, though she is there represented as passing through another area of London, since she might suddenly appear in almost any neighbourhood. The blonde singer would certainly have been heard in opera had she not been lame. At the east end of Gerrard Street, in the open space behind the Shaftesbury Theatre was a street market where could be found the two performers in chains and padlocks, who also figure in *Agents and Patients*.

As a London Italian, Castano certainly did no more than flick the minimum pinch of required annual incense at the shrine of Mussolini but that minimum included his daughter's ownership of a black tasselled Fascist cap, on her head cute in effect, which she would sometimes assume for fun in the restaurant. Some member of the Sadler's Wells Ballet borrowed this paramilitary headgear for Ashton to wear as The Officer in Rieti's *Barabau*, revived at The Wells in 1936. At this performance of *Barabau* (a choral ballet originally composed for Diaghilev), costumes and décor were by Ed Burra, but some sort of dress had to be laid down for the female choir, which appears on the stage for occasional bursts of singing. Someone suggested they should wear hats. The redoubtable Miss Baylis showed her accustomed flair for combining improvisation with economy by saying she herself could produce the hats. Years before, so it appeared, Miss Baylis had been presented with a collection of old hats – some possibly going back to Edwardian days – for use in the Theatre's wardrobe. In these hats the *Barabau* choir was fitted out. This antique headgear was meant to be a joke, but one music-critic wrote in his notice: 'The choir was in good voice, but wore rather depressing mufti.'

I have spoken of Gerald Reitlinger; then painter, writer, editor, collector; later historian of Hitler's extermination of the Jews, and oracle of the economics of aesthetic taste. He belonged to a slightly earlier Oxford generation than my own. Reitlinger appears in *The Station* as Reinecker, a profile not wholly complimentary (there had been differences with Robert Byron on the Holy Mountain), which defines Reinecker as 'financially independent; and emanating from a large house of his own in Kensington filled with rare and austerely disposed Oriental potteries'. This pen-picture, so far as it provided a rough outline for Reitlinger too, was no less than the truth. We did not know each other at the moment when Duckworth's published *The Station*, but (probably brought together by the Lloyds or Daintrey) must have met soon after that, because I visited the large Kensington house, with its austerely disposed pots, an inherited residence, shared with an elder brother, and sold by its owners soon after the appearance of Robert Byron's book.

The brother with whom the Kensington house had been shared, appreciably older than Reitlinger himself, was also a collector, something of an eccentric. I probably met him at least once, but he remains a memorable figure not on account of that so much as for the stories his younger brother would tell. The best of these gave rise to the nickname 'Captain Teach', by which the initiated always referred to him. According to Reitlinger, he was sorting family papers on some occasion – possibly on leaving the Kensington house – when he came across a letter from a Swiss publisher, rendering a royalty statement for a book written by Reitlinger's brother, and complaining that sales had been disappointingly small. The book itself seems to have been a work of dubious tone, entitled *Slavey*, the author appearing pseudonymously as *Captain Teach*.

This might have been thought a piece of pure (or impure) fantasy, a story invented or exaggerated by a younger brother to entertain the company at dinner. The tale was, however, borne out in a curious manner. Lambert – describing the act as a moment of weakness – disclosed that, when in Paris on some occasion, he had himself bought a copy of *Slavey* from one of the bookstalls along the quays of the Seine, which – with other more humdrum works – used to display a good many publications of that genre.

This authenticated purchase of his brother's book by a friend might have been thought sufficient embellishment to Reitlinger's story, but additional flavouring was added by Lambert.

A few minutes after buying *Slavey*, Lambert ran into Lytton Strachey, also on a visit to Paris, and taking a stroll along the quays. Lambert, understandably, did not wish this recent acquisition to his library to fall under Strachey's satirical eye, and make a good story for spreading about Bloomsbury. Concealment was fairly easy in the street, where he tucked the book well under his arm. Strachey now complicated matters by inviting Lambert back to wherever he was staying in Paris. Even then *Slavey* might have been kept hidden without too much difficulty, had not something not at all bargained for by Lambert taken place; the making by Strachey of a determined physical pass. Nevertheless, all was well. Lambert managed to repulse Strachey – too concerned with his objective to think of other things – and escape without the detection of what appears to have been Captain Teach's sole publication under that pen-name.

When I first knew Reitlinger he had a country cottage at Iden, not far from Rye and the coast. It was called Thornsdale, and stood well away from the road, beyond several fields, on the edge of where the country sloped down to the Romney Marsh; a romantic spot, not another building in sight. Later he moved a short way into Sussex; Woodgate House, Beckley, a redbrick farmhouse in the local tradition, to which a stucco Regency façade had been added. Soon after this rather more impressive change of address, Reitlinger became widely known among his friends as The Squire.

The entertaining at these country seats was very much *sui generis*, free and easy, without being outstandingly luxurious. Lambert used to complain that, no looking-glass in the bedroom, he had to shave round his face in the glass reflections of a framed watercolour by Meninsky; The Widow Lloyd, that one of the beds caught the inmate's shoulder, when turning over, in an iron grip between its springs, from which it was impossible to obtain release.

Daintrey used to say that, when driving a car, Augustus John always kept to the right, except in France. Reitlinger's driving could also discompose nervous guests, and he himself recalls some altercation on this subject with Lambert, who suddenly snapped out: 'Well, I've dismantled a chain transmission drive, and that's a damn sight more than you've ever done'; thereby revealing an altogether unexpected knowledge of mechanics, particularly surprising in one who did not drive a car himself, and always denied, in his own case, the supposed connexion between musical and mathematical abilities.

After dinner at Woodgate the game of *bouts-rimés* was often played. It will be remembered that each player writes down a line of heroic verse, which (after a single line by everyone has been passed to the next player in the first instance) rhymes with the verse above; then turns down the paper, so that the verse cannot be seen, only a second new line visible, which has to be rhymed; and so on. This *bouts-rimés* playing was the basis of a squib of mine, which occasionally comes on the market nowadays, and requires a word of explanation. It may even have begun with lines composed during these after-dinner games.

At about this period several books written in a somewhat self-applauding tone by Scotchmen on the subject of Scotland (or condescendingly humorous about the rest of Great Britain) had been published. A counter-satire in the 18th century manner seemed required. I used to compose verses in this vein during hours of insomnia, from which I suffered in those days. They would be repeated, sometimes improved, at the Castano luncheon table; Lambert writing the section on Scotland's music. *Caledonia*, as this pastiche came to be called, knocked about as a rough typescript for a time; being read aloud – in the Elizabethan manner of publication – to anyone who might want to hear it. When I married (at the end of 1934), Desmond

Ryan, a friend who possessed control over a small printing-press, said he
would pull off some hundred copies as a wedding present. He arranged
for the production, which was bound in tartan boards, to have a black-
and-white frontispiece by Ed Burra. Like Ryan himself, the printer was
somewhat given to the bottle, and *Caledonia*, a treasure-house of long
forgotten topical references, is also notable for its misprints.

In 1931, probably after a celebration of the appearance of *Afternoon
Men*, Lambert had gone down on one knee in my Tavistock Square flat,
and proposed marriage to the beauty he had found on that Sunday in St
John's Wood. In August of the same year (when I was in Toulon) they
were married; in due course going to live in the top flat of 15 Percy Street,
where I often used to visit them. They were frequent guests at Woodgate. Another was Basil Hambrough. Outwardly, a typical Guardsman,
brushed-up moustache, Brigade tie, indefectible turnout on all occasions, Hambrough concealed under this stylized exterior not only a
genius for mimicry and improvisation, but an essentially individual
manner of attacking life. His stories, especially those about himself, were
likely to merge into fantasy, but, so odd had been his genuine experiences,
the point at which fantasy took over was always hard to establish.

Hambrough claimed to be half – in some moods, three-quarter –
Russian. One of Hambrough's stories described his expulsion from
Sandhurst after some escapade, but as mentioned earlier he had been in
1913 a subaltern in The Welch Regiment, who had entered the army
through the Militia. This was perhaps not wholly incompatible, as, after
being sacked from the R M C, he might have approached a regular commission through the Militia. In any case Hambrough transferred from
The Welch Regiment to The Welsh Guards on their formation in 1915.
During the first war Hambrough (before the Revolutionary Government
made peace with Germany) had been attached to a Cossack unit or formation in Russia. How much Russian he knew was never clear, but his
rendering of an Orthodox priest entoning the liturgy could be altogether
convincing. Hambrough was far from impressed by the manner in which
the Cossacks had looked after their horses, negligence that would never
for a moment have been tolerated in the British Army.

Hambrough also served with the Guards in France, and, after the
war, as assistant-military-attaché in Greece. He hoped to follow up
this Greek appointment with a similar one in Rumania (where the
Queen was known to have a penchant for British officers), but did not
bring that off. Not long after returning to England and his regiment,
financial embarrassments (he was something of a gambler, with
atrocious luck, I have seen him hold four kings under four aces) led
to his resignation from the army.

During the period when I first knew him, a characteristic Hambrough
incident took place in the Bosham neighbourhood, when he was return-

ing from a pub-crawl. Prudently deciding that he had consumed more drink than made it fitting to drive a car, he drew up by a church (as it happened, an undistinguished late 19th century edifice), and, with the object of resting for a time, sobering up, entered the building. Sitting in one of its pitch-pine pews, he went to sleep. When he woke night had fallen. Surrounded by darkness he could not at first remember where he was, and, possessing no watch, or unable to see its face in the dark, did not know the time. He had the impression of having slept for several hours. He groped his way to the door. It was locked. He found another door. That was fastened too.

By now quite sober, Hambrough saw he must devise some means of avoiding a night spent in the church. There seemed only one possibility. He looked about for the belfry. While Hambrough tolled away, for a long time nothing happened. Then a key turned in the lock. Hambrough went to the door. It was the vicar. He was white with fear. When he saw Hambrough, fright turned to anger.

'What are you doing here?'

Hambrough thought from the tone that he was going to summon the police.

'I saw your beautiful church, and stopped to look round it. Then I sat down to meditate for a moment or two. In the atmosphere of peace I must have dropped off to sleep. I can only offer my deepest apologies for having had to summon you from your bed in this manner.'

The vicar did not look at all convinced. Hambrough quickly said good night, and made off towards his car.

It may have been at Woodgate that Hambrough met his fourth wife, Monica Nickalls, whom he married – this time with resounding success – at about the time of the outbreak of war in 1939. Monica Nickalls, a charming young woman then making a career for herself in advertising, had been staying with Reitlinger on one occasion, when a mother and daughter were 'doing' for him; the mother as cook, the daughter, Cath, undertaking the housework. Cath, of fairly mature age, somewhat woebegone appearance, suffered from 'nerves', the reason why mother and daughter sought employment together. One day, Monica Nickalls alone in the sitting-room, the mother approached her in a somewhat conspiratorial manner.

'Miss Nickalls, may I ask you something?'

'Of course, Mrs So-and-so.'

'Miss Nickalls, I hope you won't mind my speaking about this, I wouldn't do it only it's such a worry to Cath. She wants Mr Reitlinger to do something for her, and she doesn't like to ask him herself. You don't mind my mentioning this, Miss Nickalls?'

'No, no, please go on.'

Cath's mother braced herself to speak of her daughter's need.

'Miss Nickalls – Cath wants Mr Reitlinger to give her a little goblin.'

Monica Nickalls was too startled by this announcement to make any answer. Cath's mother mistook astonishment for disapproval.

'Oh, Miss Nickalls, do tell him. It isn't all that of a thing to ask of Mr Reitlinger, and Cath does want it so. It would make all the difference to Cath's nerves, it really would. If *you* speak to Mr Reitlinger, I'm sure he'll listen – he'll give her a little goblin, he really will.'

Only later in the conversation did it turn out that financial action, rather than physical or magical, was required; a Little Goblin being a make of vacuum-cleaner, wellknown, but, as it happened, unfamiliar to Monica Nickalls.

❋ I I ❋

In its opening stages the scheme agreed between my father and Balston had been that, if the three years' apprenticeship at Duckworth's proved fruitful, my father would invest a modest sum (not precisely specified) to constitute some sort of partnership for myself in the firm. It was never stated that the shares were to be made over to me, my father, in fact, probably envisaging them as remaining in his own hands; from his point of view an ideal focus for making trouble; from Duckworth's, a risky disposition in the light of his unforeseeable permutations of mood.

The question did not arise, because, when the time came, my father refused to produce any money at all. He gave no reason for this change of tactics, beyond objection that the security offered was insufficient; although, as a publishing house, the status of the business, as such, was certainly better than when things had been first talked over. By this time, of course, my father had left the army, and was becoming at a rapid rate increasingly cantankerous. I am inclined to think my father never intended to go through with the deal. The plan had at first seemed a good one for settling my future, and goodness knows what otherwise would have happened to me, had not its initial framework been, so to speak, delivered on the doorstep by the existence of the Balston link. Now the original project had at least to some extent taken shape, my father wished to carry matters no further; certainly not in the form of parting with money.

It was convenient for Balston to have on the premises a young man more or less capable of reporting the literary activities of his contemporaries; one of the things unforeseen in early life being the near impossibility in middle-years of keeping in touch with the writing of a younger generation. Over and above that aspect, Balston, I suspect, even if momentarily put out by failure to increase the firm's capital, wished as little as my father for any such alteration in my own status quo. A useful subordinate was one thing; an additional director to meet on more or less equal terms, quite another.

To my own relationship with the firm was now added the fact of becoming one of its authors. *Afternoon Men* was published in the spring of 1931. In the course of several years spent interviewing a steady stream of diversified callers at Henrietta Street, I had been impressed by the portfolio of a rather tousled young man, looking like an art student and even younger than myself, whose designs for book-jackets included several schematized through the medium of photography; then rarely used except in a straightforwardly representational way. He was called Misha Black (in due course knighted, architect and industrial designer of some fame), to whom I unfolded the theme I had in mind for the jacket of my novel. This was an artist's wooden-jointed lay-figure posed drinking a cocktail against a plain background. Black executed this subject to perfection. He was to carry out similar designs for my next three novels. *Afternoon Men* was, on the whole, not at all badly received. I had been infected by Cummings – to some extent also by Wyndham Lewis and Hemingway – with the then fashionable antagonism towards capital letters, so that proper names used adjectivally were (as in France) printed in 'lower case' lettering. This innovation, which proclaimed at the time an aggressive modernity, agitated a few reviewers, a race with strong resistance to the most trivial mutations of habit.

I have touched on the extent to which *Venusberg* (1932) owes – and does not owe – material to Oxford vacations spent in Finland. Some years ago I read Maurice Baring's novel, *Friday's Business* (an Eton phrase), which appeared in the same year as *Venusberg*, and also deals with a small diplomatic society. Baring's novel is founded on the story of J. D. Bourchier, an Eton master, who gave up teaching because he could not keep order among the boys, became *Times* correspondent in the Balkans, where, especially in Bulgaria, his influence was much revered. It was interesting to note how many period similarities existed in a novel written about a small imaginary country (Balkan rather than Baltic), by a man thirty years older than myself, who had himself been a professional diplomat. *Venusberg* also received for the most part well disposed notices.

From a View to a Death (1933), the scene laid in the English country-side, fuses a mixture of experiences, varying from the 'Orphans of this Town', street-musicians drawn from life in the streets of Salisbury to a day's hunting in Northern Ireland (a field where I had not distinguished myself) that must have taken place while the book was actually being written.

The title and epigraph of *From a View to a Death* required, on publication, establishment of the authentic words of *John Peel*, a song of several versions. The most correct rendering of the relevant lines, historically speaking, seemed to run:

> From a drag to a chase, from a chase to a view,
> From a view to a death in the morning.

When the book appeared, the kibitzers – to use that expressive Yiddish phrase for those (particularly familiar to writers) who offer gratuitous advice – questioned the pedantry of this choice, persuading me to alter the first line to the more accustomed wording:

> From a find to a check, from a check to a view,
> From a view to a death in the morning.

Nowadays, the term 'drag' – meaning a man wearing woman's clothing – is to be seen in newspaper headlines, but forty years ago it was used only in the theatrical world, or the sort of intellectual society that included a high proportion of homosexuals. 'Drag', in that sense, would have been incomprehensible out of those milieux; liable, at best, to be taken as deliberate indication that the speaker himself was homosexual. In short, by substituting 'find' for 'drag' (the latter restored to recent reprints of *From a View to a Death*), I had also eliminated an undesigned, but now generally intelligible, reference to Major Fosdick's taste for transvestism. This point seems worth noting, if only as an example of the manner in which what is initially written in a novel can develop, with the passing of time, changing of language, other things, in an altogether unexpected manner.

A rather rackety young White Russian woman (whose father had been in Kerensky's brief Cabinet), met with Reitlinger at Thornsdale, introduced me to Carl Bechhofer Roberts, an amusing adventurer, who should not go unrecorded. When he heard I lived in Tavistock Square, Bechhofer Roberts said I must meet Theodore Besterman, then secretary of the Society for Psychical Research, the premises of which were also in the Square, only a few doors from my flat. Later Besterman became an authority on Voltaire, and Director of the Voltaire Institute and Museum at Geneva. The Society of Psychical Research, an organization of the highest respectability, undertook its experiments in a manner to give every facility for those present at a 'sitting' to detect anything that might even hint at the possibility of a medium contriving faked effects. To get the best results, reasonably large sittings – at least seven or eight persons – were considered preferable, and, after meeting Besterman, I would sometimes be invited to attend the

Society's rooms simply in order to make up numbers. Some of these psychical odds and ends found their way into *What's Become of Waring*.

Not long after the publication of *Venusberg*, that is to say later in the summer of 1932, I received from Balston, at my private address, a letter, written in his own hand, that was unambiguously menacing. It was to the effect that recent sales at Duckworth's had been very disappointing; the directors had agreed to halve their own fees; severe retrenchment was to take place all round at Henrietta Street. Publishing is always apt to be a precarious business, but, in spite of the depression, the firm had until then not being doing too badly, at one moment my wage having been even slightly raised. Now, where money was concerned, two alternatives were presented: that I should return to £300 a year, for the continuance of which no guarantee could be offered; be reduced to an annual £200, attendance at the office required only in the morning.

The veiled threat, implied by the statement that fulltime employment might not be possible to maintain, underlined the prudence of accepting the halftime proposition. Less money would at least mean less office hours. I had by now written two books. The new arrangement would give additional time to write more; strike out into journalism. A reorganization of life therefore took place. In point of fact I found in due course that I hardly ever worked in the afternoon, not as a rule a fruitful time of day to write a novel; while literary journalism was at that period far from easy to come by.

In the same year, having overstayed by a few months the original three-year lease of Tavistock Square, I decided to move. The flat was sympathetic, but existence had gone on long enough in a basement. In the course of looking about for other accommodation, an opportunity was offered which I have always a little regretted not to have tried out, anyway for a time.

I spoke earlier of Michel Salaman, one of the most goodnatured of men, whom I did not see very often, though he was known to a great many people I knew. He had a Lutyens house – the first, I believe, built by that architect – in Surrey; Ruckman's, a secluded place not far from Leith Hill. Salaman's circumstances were comfortable, and he was fond of describing how, when he first sought her daughter's hand in marriage, his future mother-in-law's opening words had been: 'Of course, Mr Salaman, we can never forgive you for crucifying Our Dear Lord.' Later, hearing how agreeably he was situated, she agreed to overlook this culpability. Ruckman's combined homelife of a most domestic sort with an atmosphere not unlike that of the house-party represented in Noël Coward's *Hay Fever*, with its recklessly assorted guests invited by various members of the family. In spite of his domesticity, Salaman liked plenty of girls about the place whom he found attractive: Varda; Juliet and Helen Wigan; many of the corps de ballet; an occasional star like Gertrude Lawrence.

Salaman owned a flat (possibly the whole building) on the top floor of the north-east corner of Haymarket, which brought in £100 a year from an advertisement hoarding set in front of its windows. He said, if I wanted to occupy the premises at the same rate, he would be glad to remove the hoarding. To have lived in that flat would have meant looking steeply down on to Piccadilly Circus; a kind of watch-tower, from which one could find endless entertainment. Indeed, a good deal too much time might have been spent gazing out of the window on to the scene below. There were objections too. Thought of an almost perpetual clatter of traffic, the inconvenience of parking, the miles of stairs to be climbed, in combination caused me to reject Salaman's offer, and instead to remain in Bloomsbury.

I found a slightly more expensive two-room flat at the top of 26 Brunswick Square. In the flat below mine lived E. M. Forster (a writer whose books have never greatly appealed to me), but we never met. He once sent me a note to apologize for repairs being made to his ceiling, which, Forster said, might involve workmen coming up through my sitting-room floor. This did not happen, and there were no further contacts. Another resident in the Square reported that Forster was to be seen at his window each morning first thing, waving to the policeman setting out on his beat.

In August 1933, after the publication of *From a View to a Death* earlier in the year, I had the offer of a holiday in a car driving through Spain, where administration was breaking down everywhere, people already hinting that violence could not be long delayed. No doubt such is the impression Spain has given to the newcomer for centuries, but certainly the air at that moment seemed loaded with menace of the conflict that was to come in less than two years' time.

A year later, in August 1934 (after a summer holiday of which more in a moment), an altogether unforeseen upheaval took place at Duckworth's. Balston's hints as to the uncertainty of my own position there had made me feel its balance more than a little precarious, but, in the event, things turned out otherwise. If not precisely a situation in which the dog it was that died, the dog was voted off the board, a circumstance for him almost as disastrous. At a meeting of the firm's directors to reconsider the still rickety condition of the business, there was a sudden explosion. I think the question at issue was a further cut in directors' fees. Whatever the cause, all Gerald Duckworth's barely pent up rage over the years on the subject of the Sitwells, Waugh, Beaton, other modern abominations forced on him by Balston, broke out; while at the same instant Balston gave voice to his equally powerful resentment of what he had long regarded as Gerald Duckworth's obstruction and inertia. Both directors seem to have expressed their feelings in the plainest possible terms.

Balston's passing from Henrietta Street could hardly be said to have improved my own chances there, in one sense leaving me more insecure than ever, since at least in theory he was a personal friend. In another aspect, King Log, a very genuine one, was taking over again from what was, in contrast, broadly speaking King Stork; Gerald Duckworth's preference for making no change whatever in any circumstances including by this time lack of any active inclination to get rid of me. In any case editorial and other odd jobs had to be done by someone.

PART THREE

Faces in My Time

Kent Sir, 'tis my occupation to be plain:
I have seen better faces in my time
Than stands on any shoulder that I see
Before me at this instant.

King Lear II 2

In the spring of 1934, the world heading for trouble, my own existence, personal and professional, had showed no immediate prospect of organic change. I should be thirty the following year, more than eighteen months to go, but that ominous milestone looming into view. A current love affair still possessed charm, though – as ever – a charm tinged with anxiety.

> ... it's half past six she said – if
> you don't like my gate why did you
> swing on it, why *didja*
> swing on it
> anyhow –

Even if Hart Crane's lines, so often applicable, did not altogether meet the case yet, there was a shared awareness that things could not go on like this indefinitely.

The new literary fashion then in the ascendant dominated by what Jocelyn Brooke (himself homosexual, but detached from 'committed' writing) used to call The Homintern, was unsympathetic to me; at the same time the fourth novel on which I was now at work – to have the title *Agents and Patients* – did not entirely satisfy my own standards in breaking fresh ground.

I was engaged on my novel – much more likely lying at full length on the long rickety blue sofa – in my Brunswick Square flat one April evening in 1934 when the telephone bell rang. The voice, a woman's, gave in tone the impression of a slightly disgruntled parlourmaid, not best pleased at being made use of as secretary by her employer. Whoever it was announced herself as 'speaking for Lady Pansy Lamb', pausing slightly after that statement, as if requiring assurance from the receiving end. On the reaction proving positive, the intermediary asked if I would come in for a drink a day or two later at 12 Rutland Gate. I unhesitatingly accepted, requesting that thanks be conveyed to the hostess, whom I had not seen for some little time. Such were the first words exchanged between my future wife and myself.

The Knightsbridge address to which I was invited was unfamiliar; the formality of a third-person telephone transmission of the invitation most uncharacteristic of the Lambs, though I did not give much thought to that at the time. An oblique approach had in fact been decided upon with the object of ascertaining whether my Bloomsbury address in the telephone-book housed the right man. Violet Pakenham, the third sister (just twenty-two), had volunteered to implement the enquiry in the rôle of secretary or maid; assuming that character-part with all the verve of oldfashioned music-hall.

The house in Rutland Gate, so it appeared in due course, had been rented as tail-end of a lease by the Pakenhams' mother, the widowed Countess of Longford, who had died five or six months before. The eldest son, Edward Longford, by now married for eight or nine years, rarely emerged from Ireland; his younger brother, Frank Pakenham, also married, was a don at Oxford; the Lambs lived in Wiltshire, not far from Salisbury. During the few months before the lease of Rutland Gate fell in, the three unmarried Pakenham sisters – Mary, Violet, Julia – were getting a good deal of fun out of continuing there on their own, while other members of the family found Rutland Gate a useful base for such a round-up of friends as the present one.

At the Lambs' party, not knowing her to have been the heroine of the innominate telephone-call, it fell out I scarcely spoke to Violet Pakenham herself after being introduced. She was, in fact, undergoing the disembodied state of one about to collapse with the pneumonia which overtook her a day or two later. I did, however, have a long conversation with Frank Pakenham's wife (also met for the first time), who, as Elizabeth Harman, had been a celebrated belle of the undergraduate generation following my own at Oxford. When we met again by chance at another party a few weeks later, Elizabeth Pakenham suggested that in the summer I should come for a week to the Longfords' house Pakenham Hall (now Tullynally) in Co Westmeath. Although attracted by this invitation, I was contemplating a usual routine of crossing the Channel for a holiday in August.

Elizabeth Pakenham swept such pretexts aside. The answer was an easy one: make it an Irish holiday; stay at Pakenham for a fortnight; in fact, stay as long as I liked. She herself returned to England at the end of August, but the Lambs would not arrive until the first week in September – and of course I should want to be there for the Lambs. I am now a little appalled at the ease with which Elizabeth Pakenham overcame any doubts that may have arisen in my mind as to the seasonableness of imposing myself for a fortnight on her brother-in-law and sister-in-law, two persons I had never met. I had some slight preconception of the household to be expected, though not at all a clear one. I assumed, for instance, that to have written a book or two would not be considered abnormal (my hostess having written several), and that probably an agreeable element of eccentricity might be looked forward to in my host.

At Eton I had known Edward Longford and Frank Pakenham by sight, but, apart from the Rutland Gate party, only once, at a dance, exchanged a few formal words with the younger brother. Both, like myself, had been born in December, one three years older, the other the same age. All I knew of Frank Pakenham was that he moved in political as well as academic circles. I could, however, recall an occasion at school when Edward Longford had stood out as more than just another boy passing up and down the road outside my window. Very fair, not bad-looking, with a rather petulant air, he was even as a school-boy getting decidedly plump, though not yet unduly troubled with a glandular disturbance, which caused him in quite early manhood to grow fat beyond even the tendency to that condition for some reason oddly prevalent among Irish landowners. He had come into his inherit-ance at the age of thirteen on his father's death in action in the first war.

One evening in the Studio Mr Evans, the drawing-master, was laugh-ing in his goodnatured way, while offering advice regarding a large composition in charcoal on blue-grey paper at which Longford was at work. The picture on the easel, plainly symbolic, showed a female figure loaded with chains. Ambitious in conception, the emphasis on subject rather than medium, the lady evidently personified Hibernia, Dark Rosaleen, the Spirit of Ireland. This remembered vignette (which must have taken shape before the Irish Free State came into being) could not have been more apposite. Irish Nationalism was then Edward Long-ford's most passionate enthusiasm.

At Oxford, a speech made by Edward Longford at the Union (con-doning the murder by Irish terrorists in London of Field-Marshal Sir Henry Wilson) had proved unacceptable to contemporaries at Christ Church, leading to immersion in Mercury, the fountain dedicated to such expressions of undergraduate disapproval. This ducking was the great event of Longford's career, ever afterwards a gratifying memory, his favourite set-piece. I don't think I have ever been in his company for more than a couple of hours without his making reference to the occasion. According to himself the ceremony had been mildly – even courteously – performed, leaving him on a warm summer night lying in his pyjamas slightly submerged in a few inches of water.

The Mercury incident had taken place the year before I came up to Oxford, where my sole recollection of Longford – again characteristic owing to his devotion to the Theatre – was seeing him arrive, accompanied by a girl, in the front row of the stalls at some per-formance of the Oxford Players. I thought the girl might be from one of the women's colleges, then remembered being told that Edward Longford was unofficially engaged to Christine Trew, whose widowed mother lived at Oxford, and had been up at Somerville. She had also figured as one of the protégées of Lady Ottoline Morrell.

Her eldest son's early marriage was welcomed by his mother as a lucky escape from the scheming débutantes of Mayfair and Belgravia.

Hitherto the family had lived most of the year in Oxfordshire, but the young Longfords naturally decided to settle for good in Ireland. Dublin's two theatres of intellectual flavour – known locally as Sodom and Begorrah – were The Gate and The Abbey; the former casting a net wider than merely Irish drama; the latter traditionally dedicated to plays of essentially ethnic complexion. The Gate had fallen into financial difficulties soon after Edward Longford's marriage, and, at short notice, he came to the theatre's rescue.

These theatrical activities naturally demanded fairly prolonged residence in Dublin, *villeggiatura* in Westmeath becoming increasingly reduced to a month or so in the summer, even such interludes punctuated by occasional flying visits to the capital to keep an eye on plays and players. In short, the Longfords had begun to make little or no secret of the fact that they themselves were becoming heartily sick of these exiles in the country, with the deprivations entailed of all The Gate meant to them. Guests from other worlds provided no sort of compensation.

Christine Longford's first book had been a study of the Emperor Vespasian, followed by several novels. She also wrote occasional plays, which were performed at The Gate. I had taken particular interest in the first of these novels, *Making Conversation* (1931, republished 1970), since it appeared in the same year as my own first novel, *Afternoon Men*. Both books were docketed by reviewers (often apt to confuse satire with comedy) as satirical.

Making Conversation observes the Oxford scene of an undergraduate generation just preceding my own, through the eyes of Martha Freke, a girl of dutiful behaviour, if somewhat haphazard background. This sense of having more or less shared a common experience of Oxford, combined with both of us later receiving similar treatment at the hands of reviewers, made me feel I had almost met Christine Longford already. Nevertheless I had not been in the house long before I began to suspect that, so far from being accepted as a colleague of much the same approach, I was in fact not far from being regarded as personifying something little short of those specimens of unwarrantable sophistication and intellectual worldliness so neatly burlesqued in the pages of *Making Conversation*.

London literary patter would be playfully dismissed as much too grand to be valid currency in these wilds. Edward Longford, whose temperament was not easily geared to interests other than his own, did from time to time display bursts of curiosity about sides of London life, social or intellectual, of which he seemed by then to have felt a trifle starved, though making such enquiries with a kind of implied guilt, as if a betrayal of his principles. The two Longfords were perfectly friendly, perfectly hospitable, but deprecatory laughter often suggested that I was rambling on about a society which, even in its more bohemian expression, was painfully overcivilized for those with simpler cultural tastes.

One's impressions can be misleading to oneself. My hostess saw things from quite another angle, later presenting her own view in one of her plays performed at The Gate, by good fortune included in the Company's repertoire on a London tour. The picture given there, at variance with what remains in my own mind, is also a far more bracing one. This allegory of my visit is built round the embarrassments of a noted London theatrical-director, who turns up in an Irish country-house, the owners of which are for some reason unknown to him. Emphasis is laid on his appearance being 'very English'. Among those already assembled there are various ladies, married and unmarried, who see this as a situation of which to take advantage. One girl is drawn in the Irish fictional tradition of extreme harum-scarumness. For example, she becomes involved in a brawl which includes chasing another member of the cast with a broken umbrella. In choosing from this rich assortment of rivals, the theatrical-director opts for the rampageous tomboy.

Before the real-life dénouement could be even anticipated, I had (un-like the theatrical-director, so far as to be judged) developed those inner uneasinesses mentioned earlier, doubts to some extent counterbalanced by the energy and gaiety Elizabeth Pakenham brought to the household. Notwithstanding, as the second week of my stay approached, prospect of a change-over in the party imminent, I began to wonder whether her boundless optimism had not for once overstepped itself in arranging for my installation in her brother-in-law's house over quite so long a period. All was buoyant enough while she was there. How would things be after she and her family returned to England?

I shall not attempt to describe how my personal problem was (to borrow a favoured Jamesian idiom) beautifully solved, when Violet Pakenham arrived at the house in the company of the Lambs. She her-self has in any case touched on that in her own autobiographical volume *Within the Family Circle* (1976). It was at once clear that the situation had been saved; or – if the imagery of my future sister-in-law's play is to be retained – the curtain had gone up on the final Act, with its (apparently) unexpected climax.

Lamb, so it turned out, regarded himself equally suspect as purveyor of an alien culture. As he enjoyed a touch of conflict in life, this rôle was perhaps not wholly misprized by him. Clandestine visits to neigh-bouring pubs became one of the changed patterns of behaviour, and Lamb immediately established a studio in one of the bedrooms, into which he moved a large 18th century screen for the background he preferred.

In connexion with this last matter, Lamb had a story of his sole meeting with Henry James, which had taken place at Lady Ottoline Morrell's house in Bedford Square. That, as he put it, had been in the days when he was 'the sort of person who didn't own an overcoat'. Lady Ottoline, who had been one of Lamb's patrons, had accompanied some departing guest down the stairs from the drawing-room to the front door. Lamb and James were left alone together. There was a dreadful silence. Lamb did not feel he should speak first; James, visibly agitated, agonizingly gestant with an ideal sentence. The words came out at last: 'I hear you are the *fortunate* possessor of a studio?' There is much to be said for James's opinion. Studios have their own particular intimacy. To keep his hand in at work Lamb suggested painting a portrait of me. We used to have sittings every morning. After an hour or two in the chair, models, becoming stiff in their joints, develop a lifelessness inimical to the painter's vision. Accordingly, Violet Pakenham used to attend these morning sessions, enliven them with conversation to keep the model alert.

My scheduled stay at Pakenham ended. Violet was committed to a short round of other visits. We were not able to meet again until she came back to Rutland Gate in the latter half of September. That gave time for adjustments in certain spheres, which – something by no means to be dismissed as negligible – were brought about *sans rancune*. On the last day of September 1934 I invited myself to tea at Rutland Gate. The condition of being engaged was in those days allowed more attention than today. It was one in which we now found ourselves. If time apart from each other is subtracted from the span of days dating from our meeting at Pakenham (the Lambs' Rutland Gate party scarcely counting, still less the earlier telephone conversation), we had known each other about three weeks.

The decision could hardly be regarded as less than rash on both sides. Undoubtedly it was rash. On the other hand, there is absolutely no knowing what being married to someone is going to be like, short of marriage to that person. Nothing else will do. The state is quite different from any other relationship. People can be close friends for years; cohabit, sometimes under the same roof, for decades; meet and marry on sight. All are equally chancy once the knot is tied. Even in marriage at least twenty or thirty years are required to test the implications of a given partner; both parties, in the nature of human beings, changing in the Hegelian manner all the time. On this delicate question it might be added that, by the age of close on twenty-nine, I had never asked another woman to marry me – nor indeed thought much about marriage – and, after nearer fifty than forty years, to speak unequivocally, have never wished to be married to another woman. In consequence, taking a risk in the matter seems something not always to be condemned.

During the next two months we began to look for a flat, something slightly larger than Brunswick Square though in the same neighbour-hood.

An upper-part was advertised at 47 Great Ormond Street. Facing the Children's Hospital, a redbrick building of unmatched hideousness, the house was divided into three flats. The tenants were not at home the afternoon we called, but the name under the bell was that of a couple – the B's – whom I had come across when guest at the sittings of the Society for Psychical Research. I knew neither of the B's at all well, the husband better than the wife. She, somewhat older, gave the im-pression of keeping a strict eye on him, particularly when the assembled psychical researchers held hands and sang, while the medium 'went under'. It was agreed that Violet should try to gain access again the following morning (I should be at the office), reporting later on the flat's possibilities.

When Violet rang the bell in Great Ormond Street the next day, the door was opened by Mrs B in person. Violet said her piece, re-hearsing the fact of my acquaintance with the B's, together with the news that we were getting married, and looking for somewhere to live. Mrs B's reaction was disconcerting. 'Well, I hope your married life will be happier than mine,' she said. 'I've been married for nine years, and my husband's just left me with a woman he's known for five weeks.'

Notwithstanding this unpromising reception, Violet spoke favour-ably of the flat itself. We decided to make a further inspection, this time together. Mrs B showed us round, divided between despondency regarding the prospects of all marriage, and hope to get the flat off her hands. The panelled sitting-room looked out over the street. There was a much smaller room at the back, beyond it a minuscule kitchen. Bedroom and bathroom were on the top floor of the house; above the bedroom, in a loft, the water-tank; a fact of ill omen. In the bathroom, Mrs B drew attention to the rowing-machine she and her husband had installed for daily exercise. This contraption was now for disposal, she said, speaking nostalgically of the rhythmic creak made by its sliding seat, to be heard in the bedroom. She did not effect a sale of the rowing-machine, but we arranged to move into the flat early in the New Year.

We were married at All Saints', Ennismore Gardens, parish church of Rutland Gate, on 1 December, 1934. There was no formal reception after the service, but a party had been given in the house the night before, which, beginning at 5.30 and extending to past 10 o'clock that night, had included every form of friend and relation. On the following morning Wyndham Lloyd, my best man (an old friend, reliable for such an occasion), arrived at Brunswick Square with half a bottle of champagne to ease the journey to the church. Constant Lambert had arranged the music, but was himself too incapacitated by the party to attend the service. The honeymoon was to be in Greece, a country neither of us had then visited. The first night was spent at The Orleans Arms, Newhaven (booked by John Heygate, then living nearby), the room King Louis-Philippe had occupied on arrival in England as a refugee. December seas were rough the following morning, a stiff gale blowing, great green waves, clouds of white spray, bursting over the jetty of even the inner harbour. Neither of us is a bad sailor, but that was the most malign crossing I have ever experienced. The old Orient Express, a different *cuisine* at every frontier, gave three nights to re-cover. In those days Athens, archaeological glories apart, was a small Balkan capital, dispraised on the whole by tourists, though by no means without charm. The view from Sunium's marbled steep had scarcely changed since Byron's day. At Delphi, no more than a village, we were the only guests at the small inn, the slopes of the eagle-haunted mountain as deserted as the ruined shrines. The climate of Athens can be unsympathetic. Friends, on our return, hastened to explain that everyone feels ill on their honeymoon, but subsequent visits have convinced me that the capital is the one place in Greece where one is apt to suffer malaise.

On return to London there was a short interim at my old flat. On the first morning at Brunswick Square, when Violet went out to do the shopping, the front-door of the flat below (something quite unusual) had been left open. The tenant, E. M. Forster, was not personally known to me. The novelist was standing in a room beyond the small hall, thoughtfully arranging his ties. He gave a quick glance over his shoulder as Violet passed down the stairs, curiosity having apparently overcome an avowed distaste for the opposite sex.

We took over Great Ormond Street in about February. Below, on the first floor, lived a bachelor in the Treasury; a German refugee on the ground floor. The Treasury official, small, consequential, pre-occupied with his own affairs, was not much in evidence, except for one unhappy occasion, when the photographer come to take a picture of Violet for an illustrated paper, managed to fuse all the civil servant's lights. The German refugee, quiet and sententious, also rarely ap-peared. In the basement lived a caretaker, whose duties included stoking the furnace for the boiler, the landlord providing hot water for the whole house. Various families or single individuals presided over the caretaking at different times; one couple, a middle-aged chef and his much younger wife, doing a midnight flit with all their belongings on a barrow, which we watched from our window. They were never seen again. These last black sheep were replaced by an elderly window-cleaner, a widower.

Soon after the window-cleaner's installation in the basement we were woken in the small hours by the sound of dripping water. It was soon revealed that a steady stream was pouring through the ceiling, and down the walls of the bedroom. Clearly all was not well with the storage tank at the top of the house. I quickly descended to the lower regions, where the caretaker slept. Blundering about there in the dark, I at last found a door and an electric-light switch. When the light was turned on, a bed was to be seen with two heads on the pillow: one that of the old man; the other, a boy of eleven or twelve years old. The boy woke, uttered a piercing cry, disappearing at once under the bedclothes. This disturbance aroused the other occupant of the bed.

I explained what was happening about the water, but felt I must hurry back upstairs to Violet as soon as possible to give an account of the grotesque scene below. The bed-sharing was, in fact, as likely to have been a consequence of hospitality (possibly even temporary accommodation of a grandchild) as an occasion of pederasty, which was my immediate assumption, and certainly the boy seemed deeply embarrassed at being discovered in these particular circumstances.

Meanwhile boiling water had begun to course down the walls of the main staircase and flats below our own. When I returned to the hall, after telling Violet my story, the other tenants were assembled in a state of some disquiet. The Treasury, in the best tradition, could offer no easy solution nor practical wisdom, but the German refugee – perhaps a scientist or engineer – pedantically explained in his slow precise English that the answer to our problem was to turn on all the hot-water taps in the house. This was done. The deluge slowly abated. Everyone went back to sleep.

The elderly window-cleaner vacated the post of caretaker after this débâcle, whether or not on account of it, I am uncertain. He remained, however, in our own lives, continuing to clean the windows when we moved later to Regent's Park. During the course of our association (ended only by the war) Violet paid for him to be fitted out with a new set of false teeth.

At one time or another we had various cooks at Great Ormond Street (none of whom lived on the premises), far the most remarkable and accomplished of these being Clara Warville. Mrs Warville never spoke of her husband, who seemed to belong to an infinitely distant past, though I think 'Mrs' was probably not, as the case with some cooks, a courtesy title. She had been cook-housekeeper to George Moore during the writer's Ebury Street period. In theory now retired, living in Chelsea on a pension, she preferred to have some not too demanding job, rather than doing nothing, but it was essential that she should be the sole member of the staff.

We were indeed lucky to find such a cook, not only an admirable exponent of the art at its simple English best – a *cuisine* by no means to be despised – but also a person of quite unusual gentleness and niceness of character. She used to wear a cap reminiscent of Falstaff's Mistress Quickly, though her temperament was far other.

Clara Warville had contributed a chapter to Joseph Hone's biography (1936) of George Moore, in which she gives a most convincing account of the writer and his quirks. She inscribed this book for us. While she was at Ebury Street cooking for Moore he paid a visit to Paris, on his return bringing a present for the parlourmaid, but either forgetting Clara Warville or unable to find one for her. In consequence he asked Lady Cunard to get something suitable the next time she was in Paris. Lady Cunard bought an exceeding pretty oval broach, ivory with a motif of flying birds, which the Empress Eugénie might well have envied, the piece belonging very much to what was worn at that day. Moore also gave his cook a photograph of himself, a picture that had once included Edmund Gosse, whose hand was resting on Moore's shoulder.

'I had Mr Gosse's arm painted out,' said Clara Warville.

At an early stage while living in Great Ormond Street we became possessed of a Siamese cat, Bosola, who was a strong feline personality, intelligent, serious, noting such things as Violet tying an unaccustomed ribbon in her hair, but also a trifle neurotic. We thought a companion of his own breed might steady Bosola's nerves, give him a friend to confide in, so a year or two later, after we had moved from Bloomsbury to Regent's Park, acquired another Siamese neuter. This was not a success. Paris, younger than Bosola, was hearty, carefree, bouncing, not unfriendly, but Bosola could never get used to his extrovert ways, was indeed a little afraid of him. Nevertheless, although not developing truly fraternal feelings towards each other, Bosola and Paris would occasionally enter into a temporary alliance to exclude from what they regarded as their own territory any cat they both looked on as a social inferior. I do not record the names of these two Siamese cats from mere sentiment. They were to play a decisive rôle in my own life.

I continued to work at Duckworth's, and Violet (together with occasional articles on horses and equitation) wrote the 'Mary Grant' column for the *Evening Standard*. This was a feature dealing with shops and their current stock, one inherited from her sister, Mary Pakenham, who had originated it. Among weekends out of London some were still spent at Woodgate, Gerald Reitlinger, 'The Squire's', house in Sussex where fairly consistent discomfort blended with a good deal of random fun. All sorts of stories centred on subterfuges to increase the flow of alcohol. On a certain Monday morning, driving back to London, Basil Hambrough quite simply made off with a bottle of champagne (used as prop in a posed photograph the night before), which the three of us drank at luncheon. Constant Lambert, lying on the lawn, accidentally upset a glass of sherry, at which the Squire had rapped out: 'Wasteful beast.'

Reitlinger, even if some of his statements were to be accepted with caution, possessed an extraordinary fund of information on all sorts of unlikely subjects. His collection of pictures and artefacts was equally varied, including the large assortment of Oriental pots kept in glass cases. Some of these pieces had been varnished – deemed undesirable by experts – and he would wander abstractedly about the house, scraping away with a sharp instrument at one or other of them; a process Violet named de-sharding. No one guessed for a moment that Reitlinger's ceramics (bequeathed on his death to The Ashmolean) would turn out to be one of the finest collections of its kind ever brought together, worth today nearer two than one million. When fire destroyed Woodgate in 1978 fortunately all the best pieces survived.

This disaster, bringing about The Squire's own end within sight of eighty from shock at his loss, had come about in a characteristic manner. One winter afternoon the chimney of the room in which he was sitting caught fire, the flue, in the tradition of the house, probably unswept for immemorial ages. With typical stubbornness Gerald Reitlinger, having managed to extinguish the blaze, lighted the same fire again in the evening, the calamitous consequences of which took place that night. It was a suitably tragic climax for a figure whose strange nature, macabre humour, disconsolate appearance, might fittingly have found a place in the pages of Dostoevski.

Cyril Connolly was then married to his first wife, Jean Bakewell, one of two sisters from Philadelphia, though for some reason Connolly preferred to emphasize their upbringing in Baltimore. The other sister, Annie Bakewell, and her American husband, Bill Davis, lived much of the time in Spain. We did not know the Davises at this period, but after the war used to stay with them at La Consula, an attractive Italianate house, a touch of English Regency about its exterior, near Malaga.

A perpetual flow of variegated guests passed through La Consula, scene of continuous hospitality. Ernest Hemingway (whom I never met) on one occasion had been at La Consula at the same time as Lord Christopher Thynne, then an almost painfully emaciated-looking young man, who had just completed his National Service with the Household Cavalry. Hemingway used to swim a regulation number of lengths in the swimming pool every day, marking each length by removing a pebble from a pile kept at one end for the purpose. Thynne entered the pool while this rite was in progress. Hemingway at once challenged him to a race of two lengths. There was absolutely no means of guessing from Thynne's outward appearance that he had represented the British army's swimming team a short time before. Hemingway's defeat was so unexpected, so overwhelming, that the writer confined himself to his bedroom for the next twenty-four hours.

Connolly's keenness on food, much propagated by himself, was usually beneficial for his guests, the wine always, but at the King's Road flat the succession of cooks went up and down in quality, sometimes sharply. Whether or not the proprietor of a mobile coffee-stall got wind of this, one of these was certainly parked every night in a strategic position just opposite the house. There Connolly dinner-guests would sometimes end the evening with a sausage-roll or two. I had first met Elizabeth Bowen with Connolly and after one of these somewhat unfulfilled dinners we left in her company. The coffee-stall had perhaps been suggested, but Elizabeth Bowen, with that slight hesitation in her speech, said: 'Come back with me to Regent's Park. I've got a h-ham.'

As Mrs Alan Cameron she lived with her husband in Clarence Terrace, as it happened, next door to my parents. When we arrived at the house she led the way to the kitchen in the basement, and began to look about for the ham. Elizabeth Bowen rarely wore spectacles, and perhaps did not see very clearly without them, the possible explanation of her next remark. 'Some people complain of cockroaches in the basements of these Regent Park houses,' she said. 'Your parents do, but they say their cook doesn't mind a bit. She just stamps on them. I never seem to see any here.' In one of the Dr Fu Manchu stories (I quote from memory) the sinister Chinese doctor, by the use of hypnotism, causes the wallpaper of a room to appear to be writhing with huge beetles. That was just how Elizabeth Bowen's kitchen floor looked at that moment.

Connolly (who always remained an encourager of young writers) spoke of a Welsh poet recently come to London, whom he judged to have talent. His name was Dylan Thomas, and he was, so it seemed, an agreeable young man. New blood always welcome, we suggested that, when the Connollys next played a return at dinner, they should bring this young Welshman with them. In due course a party of the five of us took place at Great Ormond Street. Much that is disobliging has been written of Dylan Thomas, the chip on his shoulder, his boorish behaviour, his drunkenness. No doubt all these could be trying enough at a later date. The evening he came to dinner should be recorded as one of perfectly normal drinking and talking, even if a good deal of both took place. Odd as the judgment may now sound, Thomas gave the impression of being quiet, amusing, good-natured.

As an example of the last, Thomas spoke appreciatively of Richard Church, a middle-aged man of letters of somewhat prim exterior, easy to make fun of, who helped Thomas to publication, an act which had not been received at all ungratefully.

Thomas talked for the most part about such things as his recent brief employment as reporter. He had been sent to interview Charles Laughton, an actor who excelled in explosive parts like Captain Bligh of the *Bounty*. Perhaps not very tactfully, Thomas had asked: 'How do you act, Mr Laughton?'

Laughton's reaction had been violent.

'How do I act? How do flowers grow? How do birds sing?'

Thomas had attended a party in Paris a week or so before, where, feeling very drunk and seeking respite, he had gone upstairs and crawled under a bed. Soon after withdrawing to this retreat he heard two lesbians, unaware of his presence in the bedroom, come and recline on the bed above him. Sounds took place of unsuccessful efforts to achieve a physical relationship. For a while he listened, then sleep overcame him. He passed out utterly. Hours later, so it seemed, he came to. He felt awful and could not remember where he was. Then, as consciousness slowly returned, stirrings took place somewhere above his head, the sound of voices. The lesbians were still there, still unable to realize their mutual passion, conveying an awful sense of unremitting yet fruitless human exertion.

Thomas inscribed a copy of *18 Poems* (1934) at this dinner, and we met again quite soon after at the Connollys', a biggish dinner-party round which a certain amount of legend, largely spurious, seems to have grown up; for instance, that the party was given specifically for Dylan Thomas, and that he caused offence there by telling bawdy stories. I have no recollection, when invited, of even being told that Thomas would be present. I was not at his elbow all the time, and, when drink has flowed, few can claim never to have attempted a lurid anecdote that missed fire. Apart from that local possibility, certainly no atmosphere of failed jokes on Thomas's part at any stage dominated the evening. One of the guests was Desmond MacCarthy, in his late fifties, more than twenty years older than anyone else. The rest of the party included Evelyn Waugh, Robert Byron, and – so far as I remember – ladies representing on the whole fashion rather than literature. Waugh, who seemed depressed, left early. Jeanie Connolly thought he had been made melancholy by some remark, possibly Byron's, to the effect that Thomas's looks resembled Waugh's own when younger. In *A Little Learning* Waugh speaks of a Welsh great-grandfather claiming descent from the Glamorganshire chieftain, Cadwgan Fawr. There was certainly an outward impression shared with Thomas of reddish hair, small stature, steeply banked fires within.

I had met MacCarthy, a link with a much older world of writers, but we knew him much less well than his daughter, Rachel, married to David Cecil. That night, the women having left the dining-room, conversation turned to Swinburne and the poet's exuberant correspondence, some of which MacCarthy had seen, on the subject of flagellation, and kindred erotic topics, with his friend George Powell of Nanteos (Gorge of the Nightingales), an ancient house in Cardigan, alleged repository of the Holy Grail. Speaking of these letters, MacCarthy asked if I were any relation (George Powell's was a different family) to Swinburne's correspondent, all of whose letters (by then in the National Library of Wales at Aberystwyth, not far from Nanteos) are believed not to have been released to this day. Thomas questioned MacCarthy about them.

'What are they like? Oh, bloody bottoms, all that.'

Thomas pondered.

'I wonder whether one could pretend to be writing a book about Swinburne. Take a look at those letters some day when in the neighbourhood.'

I ran across Dylan Thomas again only a few times, once at one of Edith Sitwell's parties at the Sesame Club; then after the wedding reception given at the Savoy on John Heygate's second marriage. Violet and I walked up Kingsway on our way back to Great Ormond Street. Two young men strolling just ahead of us were revealed to be Thomas and a companion. Rather full of champagne, I caught Thomas from behind with the rolled umbrella I was carrying. As he was dead sober this seems a mild instance of *Man Bites Dog*, or rather bites artist as young dog. The other young man was David Gascoyne, poet, and historian of the Surrealist Movement. I had not met Gascoyne before, though he had sent some poems to Duckworth's I had thought well of. The firm showed no enthusiasm.

The Surrealist Exhibition of 1936 at the New Burlington Galleries, scene of Walton's bloater-hanging, was the last occasion I saw Thomas. We were talking to him when a young woman wearing over her head what appeared to be a fencing-mask covered with red roses, accompanied by a *quadrilla* of associates, entered the gallery holding the model of a female leg high in the air. The object must have been one of those furnishments for displaying women's stockings in shop-windows. This 'happening' – to use a modish term of later date – fell uncommonly flat to all appearances on the assembled company. Thomas explained that the Surrealist significance of the gesture was vested in the surname of the bearer (whom he designated by a rather rude phrase) being Legge. Although Thomas was friendly, I had the impression that some degree of success had not improved him. There was sense of his having coarsened as a person. We never came across each other during the succeeding years when his name became increasingly well-known, and his behaviour proportionately declined.

In the autumn of 1935, after a trip to Portugal, there was a disaster. Violet suffered a miscarriage. The following year we brought off a project much discussed, a trip to Russia to see the architecture and galleries; also the home-ground of the great Russian writers. No one was then aware how sinister a juncture that moment was for the world, the Stalinist immolations just about to gather momentum. The year, 1936, was indeed the last of the routine InTourist visits then in operation.

At that period the ambition of most young novelists, many elder ones too, was to find employment scriptwriting for a film-company. In the autumn of 1936 my agent arranged some weeks of probation with one of these, with any luck to be followed by a six-months contract. Accordingly, I resigned my job at Duckworth's (the firm having published *Agents and Patients* earlier in the year, last of my novels to appear under that imprint), bringing to an end an association of close on ten years. I was not sorry to leave, feeling by then that my days in Henrietta Street had lasted long enough. Nevertheless, such early experiences of life are never quite rivalled in sharpness of outline by most of what follows, and, after fifty years of authorship, I find difficulty in not looking on even my own books from a publisher's point of view. Gerald Duckworth himself accepted my departure with composure, indeed a more than oriental impassivity.

The work to which I now transferred myself, one of the humblest categories of 'The Industry', was known colloquially as 'quota quickies'. At that era in order to assist British films a protective tariff had been imposed, laying down that for every foot of foreign film, a proportion of film made in the UK must be shown in British cinemas. This was called The Quota. Some of the larger Hollywood studios conformed with this measure by establishing their own subsidiary companies in England, where the pictures produced would be technically British, written on the whole by British screenwriters, while so to speak officered by American executives and scenario-editors. Naturally such American companies did not want to compete with their own parent company in Hollywood, so that this was not a milieu in which to find the art of the film at its most dextrous and imaginative.

The American company in question was Warner Bros, then renting a studio in Teddington. The pay offered was the dazzling sum of fifteen – rising to twenty – pounds a week, but the six-months contract laid down that the writer worked from ten to six every day, including Saturday. In practice, Saturday afternoons were not usually exacted (though there were exceptions), but this oppressive threat was always a possibility, and a reprimand was issued to any writer who arrived more than five minutes late, or departed more than five minutes early.

The two other aspirant scriptwriters with whom I was teamed up were in marked contrast to each other: a middle-aged Irish journalist and a *beau jeune homme* in his very early twenties, whose charm and goodlooks seemed the chief assets. I found these labours profoundly unsympathetic; indeed, during later uncomfortable moments in the army, I used to buoy myself up by thinking that at least I was not trying to compose quota-quickies. Teddington seemed to combine some of the dreariest aspects of office-life with making demands on the machinery of creative invention in a manner that was at once superlatively exhausting, yet wholly unsatisfying. The regimentation was as futile as it was irksome. Few writers would be able to sit six or seven hours on end, working six days a week, incarcerated in a small strip-lighted whitewashed cell, producing the desired product of their own imagination. It could be argued that the banalities prescribed for that sort of film make, in one sense, less demands than truly imaginative work. Even so, the writer must possess the appropriate instinct – which certainly quite a few good writers have shown – for turning out what is required.

The higher echelons of the Teddington set-up, not a particularly prepossessing crew, were accustomed to eat together at a kind of road-house in the neighbourhood, where a heavy luncheon, formidable in its number of courses, was provided. Scriptwriters anxious to make a good impression (a harsher image comes to mind) on the senior executives of the Studio would habitually eat there too. A fair number of drinks would be consumed before sitting down at a long table in a private room, where, throughout the meal, a spelling game was played. I can't remember the precise rules, but everyone present put down a pound, the object of the game being to avoid the word's last letter terminating at oneself; upon which one's money became forfeit. I dislike all parlour games (except as otherwise specified in these memoirs), but, above all, I hate parlour games which involve spelling. This is not so much from inability to spell, as on account of their tedium and profanation of language, but even spelling games, detestable as they can be, are not normally played at meals. A more barbarous form of disturbing the pleasures of eating and drinking, such as they were in that place, while at the same time debasing the dignity of words, would be hard to conceive; not to mention adding a further hazard to an indigestible menu and overplus of midday aperitifs.

I attended this macabre feast not more than a couple of times. There appeared to be no snack-providing pubs of the right sort in the vicinity, but I nosed out a Cranfordian tea-shop, where refined spinsters laid on some form of light refreshment at the luncheon hour, a repast infinitely preferable. I learnt later that the chief executive – who was in the habit of circulating fiats couched in some of the strangest prose I have ever read on such weighty matters as writers not allowing wet umbrellas to drip on the floor of their rooms – suffered from chronic dyspepsia, and had been advised by his doctor to rest every afternoon for ten minutes after the midday meal before beginning to work anew. His daily indigestion caused me neither surprise, nor, to tell the truth, great regret.

The youngest member of our syndicate, Thomas Wilton Phipps, an Etonian, had recently eloped with a pretty American girl even younger than himself. He was three-quarters American too, his mother (separated from his father and living in the US) sister of Lady Astor, the MP. Tommy Phipps's own sister, Joyce Grenfell, was already becoming known as a *diseuse* in very much her own manner. These connexions made Phipps a rich source of gossip, not only from Cliveden's proud alcove, but cutting a wide swathe through both sides of the Atlantic, anecdotes brightening an otherwise sombre scene.

Phipps owned a secondhand (nearer twentieth-hand) car of daunting ramshackleness, which seemed operated by will-power, since neither gears, brakes, nor engine, reacted with the smallest conviction of reliability. Notwithstanding this vehicle's crumbling body, the alarming sounds that issued intermittently from under the bonnet, it conveyed him daily from Chelsea to the Studio, sometimes accommodating me too. One night Phipps was giving me a lift back to London, when (at a point on or near the Great West Road) the highway narrowed sharply, probably owing to repairs on the surface taking up most of the width. Suddenly three high-powered cars of considerable size, travelling at a great rate almost abreast of each other, bore down from the opposite direction. Seizing the hand-brake as we sped towards what seemed imminent collision, Phipps muttered to himself: 'This is just going to be a question of upbringing.' Even at the time I thought that a suitable title for a book, but fifteen years passed before I found an opportunity to use it.

Moving at a more elevated level in the Studio than people like Phipps and myself, since he had written a play which had been performed, albeit one in collaboration, was Terence Rattigan, who now had another work soon to be put on in the West End. This new play, staged a month or so after I came to work at Teddington, was *French Without Tears*, which turned out a resounding hit at the Criterion. In consequence of the immediate success of *French Without Tears*, Rattigan naturally wanted to escape from film hack-work as soon as possible, settle down to the profession of dramatist, but his contract with Warner Bros ran on for at least six months, possibly an option existing for an even longer period. One of the most oppressive of Hollywood's methods imported into the UK (like working on a Saturday afternoon) was that an actor or writer, under contract to one studio, might be hired out to another. In the case of stars large sums could be involved, but even a scriptwriter making twenty or thirty pounds a week, might be loaned at, say, sixty, the company pocketing the difference. I believe Rattigan, as a promising newcomer, had already suffered one of these exchanges. His present good fortune made a repetition of such borrowing probable. At first Warner Bros refused to release him on any terms, but compromise must finally have been reached, because he disappeared from Teddington.

Although he had sidestepped his father's efforts to put him into the Diplomatic Service, Rattigan was outwardly very much like the popular notion (as opposed to the usual reality) of a young diplomat; tall, good-looking, elegant in turnout, somewhat chilly in manner. He had been a cricketer of some eminence at Harrow. His homosexuality, of which he made no particular secret, probably unswerving, was not at all obvious on the surface. Over a period of about three weeks Terry Rattigan and I were immured together with the purpose of producing a story between us. This brief collaboration added no classic to movie history, indeed professionally speaking, was totally barren, but we laughed a lot over preposterous subjects discussed as possibilities. One was already aware in Rattigan of a deep inner bitterness, no doubt accentuated by the irksome position in which he found himself at that moment. In the Theatre good publicity such as he was enjoying is something to be taken advantage of without delay. He had a touch of cruelty, I think, and liked to torment one of the male executives of the Studio, who showed signs of falling victim to Rattigan's attractions.

Rattigan would talk entertainingly about the mechanics of how plays are written, always consciously from a 'non-artist' angle, though in a manner never to bring in doubt his own grasp and intelligence. One of his favourite formulas was: 'Take a hackneyed situation and reverse it.' His own natural abilities always seemed to me to conflict with this disregard for more than popular success, even if a popular success that designed to be a cut above run-of-the-mill banalities. Nevertheless, Rattigan's freely accepted approach in this respect poses the question to what extent any writer can control what emerges, or, put in another form, whether escape from too much 'popular' writing, once indulged, is ever possible.

The last task undertaken for Warner Bros – like the final labour imposed by an enchanter into whose power one has fallen through imprudent search for hidden treasure – was to produce a 'treatment' for a film about the life of the Victorian philanthropist, Dr Thomas Barnardo. No other scriptwriter being associated with this project in the first instance, I was allowed to work at home. When submitted to those who made such decisions, this 'treatment' of the Barnardo story was considered sufficiently satisfactory for the scheme to be followed up. The question now arose of how to make sure that surviving representatives of the Barnardo family would raise no difficulties about an exceedingly free and easy version of the philanthropist's biography. On enquiry it turned out that Barnardo had left only one child, a daughter, Syrie Barnardo, who, after marriage to a pharmaceutical tycoon, had abandoned her first husband for the writer, W. Somerset Maugham. The marriage with Maugham had also broken up about ten years before this, and, under her second married name, Syrie Maugham now ran a fashionable interior-decorating business, often mentioned in the gossip-columns.

How best to tackle the problem of obtaining Mrs Syrie Maugham's clearance for the intended Barnardo picture much exercised the Studio executives concerned. As London based, they were perhaps less at ease than in Hollywood, and – so it seemed to me – they now showed an artless lack of aplomb in handling the matter. My own view was that, even if the precise sum was not specifically stated at this stage, a hypothetical subvention should at once be adumbrated as preliminary for permission to go ahead. That might well save much beating about the bush. Those in authority, however, possibly from mere parsimony, showed an extraordinary coyness about mentioning money to someone they regarded as a lady of quality.

After various comings and goings, it was finally agreed that Mrs Maugham should be invited to luncheon, and, during the course of the meal, I should read aloud to her my (preponderantly fictional) account of her father's rise to fame, trimmed up in such a way as to make a saleable motion-picture. The scenario-editor thought a *partie-carrée* preferable to a trio. This would obviate his having nothing better to do at the luncheon-table than follow Mrs Maugham's changes of expression as I unfolded my largely imaginary narrative of her father's life and good works. Violet, though she had not otherwise met her, had once attended one of Mrs Maugham's parties, so she too was invited to make a fourth.

The scenario-editor rented a flat in Whitehall Court. He had written a play produced in New York some years before, but failed to follow up, and was a bachelor, a decidedly gloomy one, the antithesis of traditional American high spirits. His flat, where the party met, monastically austere, was in key with its owner's temperament. When Mrs Maugham arrived she remarked rather grimly that, having lived in Whitehall Court with her first husband, she knew the journey from where we sat to the dining-room took twenty minutes. Her estimate proved no less than accurate; the restaurant itself, catering for the convenience of residents rather than professional gourmets or those who liked a chic atmosphere, not warming up our party by a sense of riotous conviviality. The tables had, however, the supreme merit of being set far apart, particularly merciful for an audition likely to require a good deal of carrying off. Mrs Maugham herself maintained a demeanour of inscrutable severity throughout my embarrassed recitation, entoned between gulps of the Whitehall Court table d'hôte. There was, indeed, no earthly reason why she should dissipate her energies, on which there were no doubt many demands, in conventional courtesies or an engaging manner. She wisely attempted neither. I felt considerable relief when the macabre performance was at an end.

Back at the Studio, the whole question of the Barnardo picture was allowed to remain in the air. No one seemed to know what to do next. Further action in the matter never took place, and not long after this my own contract with Warner Bros ran out.

This passing encounter with Mrs Syrie Maugham (whom her husband in his old age handled, at least on paper, rather roughly) gives excuse for saying a word about Somerset Maugham himself. I had met him perhaps three or four times over a quarter of a century before exchanging anything but a conventional sentence on reintroduction. We sat next to each other in the mid-1950s at a luncheon party given more or less in his honour at *Punch*. He was then far less publicly revealed than later as an undoubtedly tragic, if sometimes not very attractive figure, whose immense popular success in one area of his life contrasted with ghastly interior misery at the other. The stutter – referred to so often by Maugham himself, as well as those who have written about him – was in ordinary conversation far less in evidence than I had expected. No doubt the impediment was a recurrent personal annoyance in disturbing the climaxes of his own anecdotes, the delivery probably deteriorating when he was angry (apparently no uncommon condition), but otherwise the slight hesitation had charm rather than the reverse. He took charge of the conversation at once, detonating a few near epigrams in the Nineties manner, which seemed to indicate a desire to keep matters at a formal rather than easygoing level. Then he began to discuss young writers, saying that he admired, for instance, John Lodwick.

It happened that, while employed on the *Times Literary Supplement*, I had reviewed John Lodwick's two last novels. Perhaps not now much remembered, Lodwick was then making some name, but, in consequence of a car accident in Spain, died soon after this in his early forties. I had thought Lodwick's writing competent, in places a trifle undisciplined, and gave Maugham a guarded answer, saying I liked what I had read, but thought there was not yet sufficient work to judge Lodwick's staying power. Maugham replied rather huffily: 'He writes a book a year. I don't know how many more you expect.' Years later,

I found that my friend and publisher, Roland Gant, had been also Lodwick's friend and publisher. I mentioned this conversation with Maugham. Gant was able to add a footnote. He described Lodwick as an adventurous type with a lively war record, a man always involved in love affairs and travel. Maugham, on account of his approval of Lodwick's books, had extended a rather vague invitation to come and see him as Lodwick then lived in the south of France. Some time later, Lodwick, fairly dishevelled and somewhat drunk, turned up at the Villa Mauresque allegedly leaving outside the gates a gipsy girl he had picked up on his wanderings. The visit, so Gant understood from Lodwick, who was unnerved by Maugham's icy politeness, had not gone with a swing.

The snobbish overtones of the next stage of my conversation with Maugham need no apology, since one of the best of his short stories, *The Outstation*, turns on that very theme; while in *Cakes and Ale*, Alroy Kear (prototype of Hugh Walpole) is specifically described as a novelist in whose works 'You will never find any of those solecisms that disfigure the productions of those who have studied the upper classes only in the pages of the illustrated papers.' Having found me wanting in my attitude towards John Lodwick's writing, Maugham now moved back to Victorian times. He remarked: 'It's amusing in Trollope's novels how the Duke will address his son by his courtesy title.'

One should always reflect, however briefly, before answering. I spoke thoughtlessly. I was influenced by the knowledge that, when their father was killed, the younger Pakenhams had been sent for by their mother, and told that in future Silchester would be called Edward. Indeed I could remember at least half-a-dozen boys at school to whom that convention (probably now fallen into disuse in a more down-to-earth world) equally applied. Without the need of anything like Alroy Kear's expertise, the practice could, in fact, probably have been gleaned from the illustrated papers themselves. Incautiously, I said: 'But surely that quite often happens in these days too?' The moment the words were out of my mouth I saw I had blundered. Maugham did not reply. He simply turned to his other neighbour and conversed with him throughout the rest of luncheon.

In the course of my scriptwriting interlude, temporary increase in earnings seemed to make this a good moment, if we were to have children, for moving into somewhere rather less restricted in space than Great Ormond Street. The man from the Treasury had expressed a wish to take the top-floor flat if vacated, so there would be no trouble in finding a new tenant. We acquired the lease of a small house in Regent's Park, 1 Chester Gate, situated in a short turning leading into the east side of the Park from Albany Street. To our great regret Clara Warville left us, but wrote Violet a letter saying that the previous year had been the happiest in her life.

Meanwhile some other employment had to be sought. Plans were known to be on foot in Hollywood for making a picture to be called *A Yank at Oxford*. There seemed hope of getting a job in this production, since I could now be deemed to have scriptwriting experience (though in fact no syllable written by me had even been spoken from the screen), and had spent three years at the university which was to be the background of the story. Negotiations were opened up between my agent in London and the firm's collaborator in Hollywood. Some hope of a deal was held out if I were on the spot. The next thing to do was to get to 'the Coast'. Deciding to approach California by sea, we set out in May, 1937, on a voyage due to take four weeks. The *Canada* (a Danish vessel sunk a few years later by a German mine) put into harbour only three or four times.

At Jamaica we visited the Mona House (in Jamaican terms, we were told, not unlike Rosa Lewis's Cavendish Hotel) in the company of an American married couple, part of that flow begun some years before of American expatriates no longer able to afford life in Paris. These two, so it appeared, had been lucky enough to find an inestimable *bonne* for their Montparnasse household. When they planned to return to the US they put an advertisement into the local paper of the *arrondissement*, stating that this maid's services were available, and that she could be interviewed in their flat any afternoon. The following day two ladies arrived on the doorstep. They turned out to be no less than Gertrude Stein and Alice B. Toklas. The famous couple were in search of a maid. The employers, overawed by such eminence under their roof, summoned the unparagoned *bonne* – among whose other qualities was a total self-possession – and themselves retired from the sitting-room to the kitchen. The murmur of interrogation could be heard through the wall. Suddenly the door between burst open. White and trembling, almost in tears, the maid burst in.

'No, madame, no! I cannot go to those two sorceresses!'

There is nothing specially welcoming about Hollywood, rather the reverse, especially as I was greeted by the news that my agent had died while we were on the high seas. The replacement, as an individual, was wholly antipathetic. This was getting off to a bad start. After a day or two at the Beverly Hills Hotel, money – of which there was not an inexhaustible supply – seemed to be disappearing at an alarming rate. In fact, so one fairly soon discovered, Hollywood, if you kept your head, was not necessarily expensive for those who designed to enter The Industry, provided they had not yet found a job. Indeed, certainly in relation to availability of passable accommodation, Hollywood was cheaper than London; at least for those prepared to live as Untouchables 'on the wrong side of the track'. In that far from chic area we found a self-contained furnished flat in a two-storeyed house, 357 North Palm Drive, Beverly Hills. There were two quite sizable rooms, another much smaller one, kitchen, bath, for sixty dollars (about the then equivalent of twelve pounds) a month, including one day's cleaning. The next necessity was a car. A secondhand one was acquired for two hundred and fifty dollars.

The car, an Oakland, deserves a word. The model had been only briefly produced (two years, I think), then withdrawn from the market, perhaps (a purely British phrase I was recently told by an American) because too 'good value for the money'. It came from a used-automobile lot, personal property of the salesman, a sympathetically inscrutable Missourian, and served us well. At first, when asked by parking-attendants: 'What make?', I would reply: 'An Oakland.' Later, even when row upon row of shining new automobiles stretched far away to the horizon and beyond, I changed the answer, not without pride, to: '*The* Oakland'. That was enough. By this time it must have been the sole example still on the road. I returned the Oakland to the Missourian, who, on its resale quite a long time later, forwarded to England a very respectable proportion of the car's cost in the first instance.

Now began the depressing round of being interviewed by executives for a job. I soon became increasingly tired of retailing my life-story in pursuit of what was revealing itself as a mirage, so far as any clarity could be distinguished through that utter stagnation of movement, total inanition where action is concerned, characteristic of almost all theatrical negotiation, perhaps most of all apparent in the film-world's dealings. No one would say; 'We haven't got a job for you', while at the same time no summons came from those visited, who were supposedly looking into the matter.

While trying out the Oakland for the first time in some secluded neighbourhood of Beverly Hills, I all but collided with an infinitely larger and grander vehicle containing two celebrated stars of that period, Ronald Colman and his wife, Benita Hume, but in general film stars were not greatly in evidence, except at certain restaurants or night-clubs currently fashionable, where naturally prices were high. At that moment the favoured bar was The Cock n' Bull. On our sole visit there, film-stars stretched as far as the eye could reach, among them Marlene Dietrich, perhaps the only one I had any wish to see in the flesh, who did not at all disappoint.

This recognized concentration of celebrities of one sort or another in a given public place is – even apart from Hollywood – a phenomenon more Continental and American than English. At the Café de Paris, then and much later, Douglas Byng, with an ineffable sparkle, sang his own songs for the piano, to what was usually a conventionally smart world. Nearer the mark as an 'amusing' place demanded by foreign visitors was the Café Anglais in Leicester Square, where, for a very brief period in 1928, Rex Evans put on a similar, though individual, entertainment, to a large audience, lions in reasonably high proportion, evening dress optional, prices not high. Rex Evans was to be one of our supports in Hollywood.

Our only Hollywood contact of a non-professional sort was an American-born great-aunt of Violet's, Mabel Leigh, who with her husband, Rowland Leigh (seventy-eight and fairly shaky) had come to visit their son, also called Rowland, who was making a successful career as a scriptwriter and librettist. Mrs Leigh, an altogether delightful person (whose father, a professional soldier, had fought for the Confederacy with unhappy results for their fortunes in Savannah) had married a younger son without prospects. Mabel Leigh had travelled to America on the same boat as the sister of the current Mrs Douglas Fairbanks Sr (formerly Lady Ashley), in consequence of which we were taken to see Douglas Fairbanks, even then regarded as a giant (in fact, almost dwarf) from Hollywood's Heroic Age, at his Santa Monica beach-house, a residence bolted and barred like a fortress. The atmosphere of the Fairbanks household was not easy. On other occasions we met the exuberant comedienne Sophie Tucker, who at once started up a flirtation with old Rowley Leigh, and the Mexican vamp, Lupe Velez, but stars played no real part in our Hollywood life. Rex Evans, a friend of young Rowley Leigh's, had left England to settle in Hollywood. Evans's songs proved too English, perhaps too subtly of their passing moment, for export, but he had found plenty of other things to do. Huge, plump, goodnatured, always heaving with giggles, he took Hollywood's suburban atmosphere less seriously than most of its phrenetically inward-looking residents, a refreshing attitude.

Another couple who kept their heads in relation to their surroundings, very hospitable to us (a quality by no means so universal in those parts as elsewhere in my own experience of the US), were Stanley and Odette Logan. He was an English actor, now turned director; she French (having enjoyed theatrical success in London too), not only charming but an excellent cook. Logan had many stories of the Theatre, such as the producer of a 1920 revival of a wartime musical by Bruce Bairnsfather and Arthur Eliot called *The Better 'Ole* saying: 'It can't fail – there's not a new thing in it'; or recalling a night-out with C. B. Cochran: 'At the end of it CB was in a dilemma – he wanted to borrow his fare home, but he also wanted to try and sleep with Odette.' The veteran English actor C. Aubrey Smith (created Sir Charles Aubrey Smith in his eighties, no doubt one of the stately Hollywood knights pictured in the opening paragraphs of Evelyn Waugh's *The Loved One*) who was to appear in Kipling's *Wee Willie Winkie* in 1937 (of which more later) teamed up with Shirley Temple. Prototype of the Gentleman of the Old School, Carthusian, cricketer, Aubrey Smith was already getting very deaf. He had recently been present at an actors' dinner-party also attended by Stanley Logan. Conversation had turned on the subject of homosexuality. Seeing talk become animated, assuming the merits of some sport were being argued, Aubrey Smith suddenly leant forward and spoke with authority: 'Well, whatever you say, give me three stumps, a bat, and a ball.'

Through Mabel Leigh we met Freddie Bartholomew, whose laurels as Little Lord Fauntleroy had not long before been conspicuously renewed in Kipling's *Captains Courageous*, copies of which fans would bring the boy-hero to sign. Freddie Bartholomew lived with his aunt, a splendidly sensible and unassuming English woman, at that moment assailed with law-suits instituted by her nephew's parents, who, previously content that she should take on the expenses and responsibilities of their son's upbringing, now hoped for a larger slice cut from the cake of his fame. Miss Bartholomew remained quiet, firm, unfussed, entirely dedicated to what she looked on as best – not solely with an eye to professional advancement – for her nephew; a lady of whose bearing in the circumstances any country might be proud.

Throughout these commotions, theatrical and legal, pleasant and unpleasant, Freddie Bartholomew himself remained in private life an attractive little boy, quite 'unspoilt' by all that was going on round him. With charming candour he insisted on revealing to me the complex cat's cradle of delicate wires and filaments installed in the furthermost caverns of his jaw, purposed to remodel the back teeth in whatever form was regarded as most appropriate for a child-star of his eminence.

Once in a way we would go to a film or play. The Mayan Theatre in Los Angeles, a low terracotta-coloured building, designed inside and out to resemble a temple in Yucatan, stood near the intersection of South Hill Street and West Eleventh. The WPA (Works Progress Administration, a governmental organization for dealing with unemployment) had mounted *Macbeth* at the Mayan Theatre with an all Black cast of over a hundred. This performance has always remained in my mind as an example of the fluidity characteristic of most great art. The play was also notable for the manner in which actors relatively obscure or even unsuccessful can sometimes put on a show scarcely at all short of the best.

The curtain went up on a tropical forest. A thunderous storm raged, giant cactuses spreading their spikes in a manner to make the luxuriant undergrowth all but impassable. The trembling foliage parted. Two big Blacks in ostrich-plumed head-dresses, carrying exotic broadswords and wicker shields, stepped through into a clearing. A sudden green glare above the warriors lighted up the three witches, cackling horribly in a neighbouring eucalyptus tree where they seemed to be practising the rites of Voodoo. Most of the action had the same palace or castle for background, the interior of an African mud fort, in the centre of which was set a deep archway leading to a gate and turret. In this tower Duncan, a short thickset Black, whitebearded, crowned with a high cylindrical cap hooped with gold, was murdered with his grooms. On either side, staircases led up to the ramparts, and the massive wooden door on which Macduff and Lenox knock from without. This was one of the best moments of the play, for the porter was a fine actor, although his lines had been shamefully bowdlerized. He was the only member of the cast to allow himself the traditional accent of the Old South.

Lady Macbeth was small, slight, a good actress, but here perhaps the metamorphosis of presentation seemed not quite right. Macbeth and his wife are so essentially a British couple, her lines, especially, not intended for the favourite of the harem. In the torrid zone, one felt, weak-willed husbands and strong-minded wives would behave differently from the Macbeths, so Nordic in their moods. The banquet, on the other hand, had with good effect been turned into a wild Harlem party, in which first dancers, then guests themselves, the thanes of Scotland and their ladies, palpitated backwards and forwards in frenzied rhythm, which, but for its peculiarly African grace, might have been a reel. When the dancing had subsided Macbeth and his Queen circulate among the company. Drinks were handed round.

At that moment came a blinding flash, Banquo's head, some twenty times larger than life, appeared in the form of a giant mask, grotesque and terrifying, peering over the castle walls. This happened several times, throwing Macbeth into paroxysms of terror, which seemed to infect the rest of the party; indeed was frightening enough for the audience.

In the scene where the three witches (with their Voodoo men and Voodoo women) preside over the burning cauldron, American sensitiveness to such things – even at this period – omitted the lines:

> 'Liver of blaspheming Jew,
> Gall of goat, and slips of yew
> Sliver'd in the moon's eclipse,
> Nose of Turk, and Tartar's lips,'

With the exception of Duncan's murder, all violence in the play was acted out with fire-arms, Young Siward's failure – because 'born of woman' – to slay Macbeth being represented as missing with a pistol shot. There was a final admonitory footnote to this excellent show: *The Federal Theatre project is part of the WPA Program. However, the viewpoint expressed in the play is not necessarily that of the WPA, nor any other agency of the government.*

We went to hear Ernest Hemingway speak a commentary to *Spanish Earth*, the documentary about the Spanish Civil War made by Hemingway in collaboration with Joris Ivens, a professional movie-man. The film was to be shown at the Los Angeles Philharmonic Auditorium in Pershing Square, gardens where the bums clustered in the twilight under sub-tropical boscage. We called up in the morning to reserve seats for the performance, billed for 8.15 p.m. but were told booking was unnecessary. Nevertheless, on arrival at about seven, a brisk sale was in progress. Outside the hall neon lights shone:

HEMINGWAY AUTHOR
SPANISH EARTH

After what subsequently proved an indiscreet dinner of clam chowder, seafood à la Bernstein, Sonoma Valley Chablis, we took our seats. There must have been 3,000 or more people in the hall. Some committed socialists – with one gentleman announcing himself as a Cuban fascist – had to be unwillingly removed from seats reserved for other people. It was nearly nine o'clock before these dissident elements were sorted out. Two kinds of pamphlet, red and yellow, lay on the seats. After reading the former (advertising the Soviet film *We from Kronstadt*), the man next to me handed across the yellow pamphlet, with the words: 'This should be good too.' It announced a meeting of protest on the anniversary of the outbreak of the war in Spain.

'Did you come last night?' he asked.

'No, what was it like?'

'Well, they had a Loyalist flying ace.'

He returned to reading *The Western Worker*, a paragraph headed: STOOGES OUTGAG UNIONS IN SACRAMENTO. The audience was getting restive. Occasional outbursts of clapping settled down to a regular tattoo. A compère of some sort came on the stage and begged for a little patience. It appeared there were still people trying to get in.

'Are you Canadian or English?' asked the man in the next seat.

'English.'

'I like the English. I've been to London several times. Woolwich is the part that appealed to me. I've been in the East too. To your face – to your face, mark you – the Japanese are the politest race in the world. And after them the English. A Camel?'

'Thanks.'

We just had time to strike a match before the compère appeared again, and requested everyone to stop smoking. My friend threw his cigarette away. With the country's reputation for politeness in my hands I could not do otherwise than follow his example. Then the lights went out, and the show began. *Spanish Earth* seemed to me scrappy, either too corny, or not corny enough, good shots of air-raids, troops training or on the march, but a continuous cutting back to impassive peasant faces, backbone of propaganda films all the world over. A close-up of art treasures being rescued from bombardment showed some indeterminable odds and ends that might have been on sale among the stalls of the Rastro.

At the close of the performance Hemingway himself came on the stage, the fulfilment which had brought us to the Philharmonic Auditorium that evening. Wearing a dark blue suit he leant against the lectern, straddling his left leg awkwardly outwards at an angle. He read aloud an account of the war and its progress, appealed for money to buy an ambulance. What he read had no very personal touch, except when he referred to a direct hit on a train: 'Two persons were taken to hospital, the rest removed with shovels.' Hemingway spoke with dignity, but was clearly in a highly nervous state. The audience received him with loud applause.

Spanish Earth may not have been the outstanding documentary of film history but Hemingway's visit to Los Angeles might have been thought a local event of some interest. Certainly he and his film were so regarded by several thousands who had turned up to hear him speak the commentary. Nevertheless the local press barely mentioned the event. In contrast, when Jean Harlow died some weeks before, the newspapers devoted half-a-dozen pages or more to her life-story, her films, her loves, dwelling much on the massed crowds standing in awed reverence before the celebrated blonde star's residence, never designated as less than 'vast' or 'gorgeous'. As it happened, Jean Harlow had lived, like ourselves, in North Palm Drive, though naturally at the smart end of that avenue, miles away from the 'wrong side of the track'. Quite by chance, on the day of her funeral, we drove past the house, which was far from the palace described in the papers. On the lawn in front a bored policeman (who bore a remarkable resemblance to a self-portrait by Wyndham Lewis) lolled back on a kitchen chair. The road was empty each way as far as the eye could see.

I found myself unable to write a line of a new novel, while at the same time had no great relish for parties, where everyone talked movie shop all the time. Nevertheless there were Hollywood subcultures that would undoubtedly have repaid investigation by a novelist of the right sort; sides which remained wholly unexamined, anyway by British writers who had lived there. It was probably at a party given by Rex Evans, or one to which he had taken us, that a chance interchange suggested the possibilities at hand. I had fallen into conversation with a rather tough-looking young American, whose name I did not know.

'That was a very beautiful girl who went out of the room just now,' he said.

I agreed.

'And your sister is a very beautiful girl too.'

'As a matter of fact she's my wife.'

'I didn't think you looked alike – except your noses a little – but I saw you were close. I am very close to my sister, so I thought maybe she was your sister.'

The view that Violet's nose and mine, structurally speaking, had much in common, showed an unacademic approach to significant form, but I did not offer to dispute the matter aesthetically, especially as the young man seemed disposed to enlarge on his own relationship with his sister.

'I was so close to my sister at one time,' he said, 'that I used to suffer just the same sort of pains when she had her periods.'

'Did you really?'

'Sometimes when we were apart, for no reason, I would have cramps and headaches. Then I'd write to her and enquire, and that was always when she was having her period.'

Somebody came up and spoke to one or other of us at that moment, so we drifted apart, and I heard no more of this unusual, even fascinating, physiological phenomenon. Afterwards, when I tried to find out who the young man was, no one seemed to know anything about him, except that he belonged to the U S Marine Corps, and had been bought a suit to appear at the party by whoever had there introduced him.

Through Rex Evans we met Elliott Morgan, a young man employed in the research department of Metro-Goldwyn-Mayer. Morgan's family, emigrants from Wales in his father's generation, was now settled in Los Angeles, and, apart from himself, unconnected with the movie business. The Morgans were wine drinkers, a habit marking them out, and they were kind enough to ask us to dinner. Elliott Morgan turned out to be 'researching' *A Yank at Oxford*, the film which I had once hoped would provide my own entrée into Hollywood scriptwriting. These activities had quite recently brought him into contact with Scott Fitzgerald, just arrived in Hollywood in an attempt to repair his fortunes, and assigned to work on that very script.

In these days it is hard to remember that in 1937 the name of F. Scott Fitzgerald as a novelist was scarcely at all known in the United Kingdom. *The Great Gatsby* had appeared in England in 1926, making no stir at all. Indeed, when *Tender is the Night* followed in 1934, the London publisher did not even bother to list *Gatsby* opposite the title-page. Fitzgerald's reputation, such as it was, rested on the recommendation of a few critics, of whom T. S. Eliot was one (though not, so far as I knew, in print), Cyril Connolly being responsible for drawing my own attention to a novelist for whom I at once felt enthusiasm. In the US, though in quite another manner – an essentially American manner – Fitzgerald's position as a writer was almost equally unsatisfactory. This once famous figure, golden boy, prototype of the 'Jazz Age', was all but forgotten. That is not quite true, for when we reached New York on this same trip, at least one Fitzgerald first-edition, in a tattered paper wrapper, was on display in his publisher's (Scribner's) window, positively emphasizing how much its author belonged to the past; Fitzgerald's book confirming the historic traditions of the firm, like the ancient headgear on display in Lock's hat-shop in St James's Street.

There are several reasons for this collapse into oblivion. Fitzgerald – that rare phenomenon, a 'bad' writer who made himself into a 'good' writer – had lost much of his former appeal simply because he had begun to produce immeasurably better novels than his early work. In the years of prosperity he had lived recklessly, drunk too much, involved himself in acute financial embarrassments, which would pursue him, while in addition had suffered unforeseeable and tragic blows through the mental breakdown of his wife. At the same time Fitzgerald had always managed to keep afloat by writing short stories, some accomplished, some less so. He had outlined his own sad tale in *The Crack Up*, a collection of autobiographical pieces which I had not read as the book was still unpublished in England. One could not fail to notice the tone in which people in Hollywood spoke of Fitzgerald. It was as if Lazarus, just risen from the dead, were to be looked on as of somewhat doubtful promise as an aspiring scriptwriter. 'Meet him? Of course Scott will be very pleased indeed to find an Englishman who knows his work. He says he's never gone over in England, and never will.'

So all was arranged. Elliott Morgan was to bring Scott Fitzgerald to lunch with us. For convenience this lunch would take place at the MGM commissary. I noted the engagement in my book for Tuesday, 20 July, 1937; as it turned out, a date of some consequence to Fitzgerald himself.

After undergoing the customary formalities demanded for entering the premises of a film studio – security precautions that might be deemed excessive for gaining access to a nation's most secret nuclear plant – we met Morgan standing outside the commissary, a hangar-like restaurant of no great charm. He found a table by the wall. The luncheon break for the subordinate employees of the film world, such as writers, was not yet due, but a sprinkling of loiterers of one kind or another had begun to congregate in the neighbourhood of the commissary, most of them in ordinary clothes. Through this crowd was suddenly led a girl in a blue Louis xv dress, her make-up bright yellow, powdered and curled hair enclosed under a transparent bag, her sunburnt hands suggesting the beach at Santa Monica, rather than the parterres of Versailles. Meanwhile, at the central table of the dining-room, the senior executives, the 'moguls', to use a popular term, were beginning to gather.

These magnates looked just as might be imagined, a picture by some Netherlands master of the moneychangers about to be expelled from the Temple, or a group of appreciative onlookers at a martyrdom. In the manner of most people in Hollywood, they seemed to be passionately acting the part life had assigned to them, movie moguls to the point of inartistic exaggeration exemplified in one of their own films. It should be added that a legend of the period representing every Hollywood waitress or usherette as a failed film-star of unimaginable beauty was without foundation. One might even have hesitated to affirm with any conviction that the Hollywood standard of looks, female or male – the moguls steeply diminished the average of the latter – sustained a good working average; certainly nothing to be compared with the likelihood of seeing a lot of pretty girls in the course of a morning's walk through (to mention a couple of cities at random where such abound) Cardiff or Madrid.

Suddenly, all coming into sight at exactly the same instant, a vast throng of employees emerged from the MGM offices, and surged in spate towards the commissary. I immediately recognized which figure was Scott Fitzgerald's. In an inexplicable manner he was quite different from anyone else. Then for some minutes he was lost to sight, re-emerging near our table from somewhere in the background. Morgan jumped up.

'This is Mr Fitzgerald.'

He was smallish, neat, solidly built, wearing a light grey suit, light-coloured tie, all his tones essentially light. Photographs – seen for the most part years later – do not do justice to him. Possibly he was one of those persons who at once become self-conscious when photographed. Even snapshots tend to give him an air of swagger, a kind of cockiness, which, anyway at that moment, he did not at all possess. On the contrary, one was at once aware of an odd sort of unassuming dignity. There was no hint at all of the cantankerous temper that undoubtedly lurked beneath the surface. His air could be thought a trifle sad, not, as sometimes described at this period, in the least brokendown. When, years later, I came to know Kingsley Amis, his appearance recalled Fitzgerald's to me, a likeness photographs of both confirm.

Food and drinks were ordered. Talk began to flow at once. That is certain. Scarcely an instant was required for conversation to warm up, adjustments all but instantaneous. Fitzgerald, off alcohol at that moment, drank milk, ate 'cold cuts'. The rest of us had beer, and – Violet's fairly convinced memory – pork chops with spaghetti. Naturally *A Yank at Oxford* cropped up almost immediately. The question of dialogue: would an English undergraduate say a 'shiner' for a black-eye? Could the American public be made to understand that 'the Prog' and his 'bullers' meant the Proctor and his bowler-hatted 'bulldogs', the University police?

This opened up a delicate theme, obviously a favourite topic of Fitzgerald's, the differences between the American and British ways of life. It was a subject upon which he had reflected a lot, one felt, and loved discussing. I said – what I have so often thought – that Americans allow other Americans such small powers of comprehension. Surely, if American policemen are sometimes termed 'bulls', only a minimum of imagination would be required in the context to guess the meaning of 'buller'. After all, the British public, in days when all films were American, had been expected to essay far greater feats in mastering alien language and customs. Fitzgerald seemed delighted to find some-one with whom to argue that sort of thing. In a moment he was well away with what Americans were like.

'At a party, some time, I used the word *cinquecento*. Donegall – do you know who I mean? – was present. He said how unexpected it was to hear that word on the lips of an American.'

From the way Fitzgerald spoke I had the impression that the party in question might have taken place a year or two before. Lord Donegall, a professional gossip-writer for the London papers, was a very un-surprising person for Fitzgerald to have run across. I did not know that Donegall was then in California, therefore the comment had almost certainly been made the previous Wednesday. The dating is not without interest. Fitzgerald explained how this assumption – that an American was unlikely to employ the term *cinquecento* – had brought him up with a start. In the past, in his own grandfather's day, even in his father's, Americans had been noted in Europe for being well educated, properly informed, culturally aware; possibly even too much so. Fitzgerald said he did not deny Donegall's imputation that Americans of the present age were often none of those things, nevertheless the conjecture saddened him.

Fitzgerald took a pen from his pocket, and a scrap of paper. On the paper he drew a rough map of North America. Then he added three arrows pointing to the continent. The arrows showed the directions from which culture had flowed into the United States. I am ashamed to say I cannot now remember precisely which these channels were: possibly the New England seaboard; the South (the Old Dominion); up through Latin America; yet I seem to retain some impression of an arrow lancing in from the Pacific. The point of mentioning this diagram is, however, the manner in which a characteristic side of Fitzgerald was revealed. He loved instructing. There was a schoolmasterly streak, a sudden enthusiasm, simplicity of exposition, qualities that might have offered a brilliant career as a teacher or lecturer at school or university.

We talked of his books. Fitzgerald dismissed the notion that they would ever be read in England. Certainly there seemed small chance of that then; a good example of the vicissitudes of authorship, for within ten years (true a world war had taken place) everything Fitzgerald had written would be in print in a London edition of his works. Among other things he mentioned that the American diplomat in *Tender is the Night*, who wore a nocturnal moustache-bandage, was drawn from life; and it turned out we had met the rackety lady whose rescue of a British compatriot from arrest in Switzerland had suggested a similar incident in the novel.

Fitzgerald's *Collected Letters* reveal him as not at all averse from the beau monde, in his own phrase 'dukes'. He possessed a writer's love for categorizing people, but, his own experience of life in the UK limited, some judgments were less than wholly reliable. After praising the aristocratic picturesqueness of Napier Alington (a peer with claims to be so designated), he spoke of a lady (whose name, correctly or not, had been coupled with that of a Royal Duke) as 'the wrong sort of English aristocrat'. Fitzgerald was disinclined to accept that, whatever other characteristics the lady in question might possess, she could not by any stretch of terminology be thus defined. This trivial talk is recorded only on account of its repercussion. An interruption took place at that moment in the shape of two film stars, Spencer Tracy and James Stewart, moving round from table to table in the dining-room. James Stewart had come to rest not far away from us. Fitzgerald indicated him.

'A Princeton man, I believe.'

That was to move into a more tangible realm of social surmise. Fitzgerald watched Stewart with the fascination of one Princeton man examining another; then (synthesis perhaps suggesting antithesis) he remarked that 'Ernest' was in Hollywood. At that time, unaware of the complicated love-hate relationship which professionally raged between Hemingway and Fitzgerald, I was interested to know that they were on first-name terms. We talked about the *Spanish Earth* performance, which I think Fitzgerald had not seen.

It has to be admitted that all this time Fitzgerald and I had been hogging the conversation, hardly allowing a word to Violet or Elliott Morgan. Fitzgerald must have become aware of this. In a good mannered effort to adjust the balance, make conversation less of a monopoly between the two of us, he brought back the subject of American and British degrees of difference. The Morgan parents, as mentioned earlier, were first generation in the US. Fitzgerald posed a question:

'Now what about Elliott? British or American?'

Eliot? I made a great mental effort. At that time I had never met T. S. Eliot. My knowledge of his works was limited to no more than the poems anyone living in a fairly literate world was likely to know. The Sitwells talked of him sometimes, but I couldn't remember other friends in common. I had given little or no thought to the question of Eliot's nationality. That was something not much bothered about in so accepted a figure, who, even if born an American, was now an essential feature of the British intellectual landscape. This was certainly an occasion for a lucid exemplification. The brilliant phrase utterly failed to materialize.

'You mean his poems?'

'Does Elliott write poems? I wasn't aware of that.'

Fitzgerald found the revelation amusing. I felt myself getting into increasingly deep water. Were there sides of T. S. Eliot that made his poetry a comparatively minor matter? I played for time.

'*The Waste Land*, and all that ...'

A good deal of laughter followed the clearing up of this confusion in identities. Its echoes sounded loud, even embarrassing, in the silence that had now fallen on the commissary. A change had come over that grim room, which was now all but empty. Time had passed so swiftly, talk been so animated, that I was unaware of the transformation – noted by Violet – that had taken place round about us.

First of all the lesser executives had hurried back to desks or sets. Then some of the scriptwriters, probably uncertain about renewal of their contracts, made some pretence of showing keenness on their job. One by one executives of a somewhat superior sort, though not the highest, had drifted away. Gradually even the most undisciplined slaves of The Industry returned to their labours. In short, except for the exalted, the group of 'moguls', only our own table remained occupied.

Worse than that, not only was the luncheon-break being grossly extended, but we were talking and laughing as if nothing mattered less than the making of commercial films. A gloomy silence had fallen on the moguls' table, as they puffed at their cigars. Like the patrolling cops glaring at an unexpected picnic among the yuccas, the same fishlike stare was beamed towards us. The moguls looked puzzled; not so much angry as hurt. Perhaps some of them had heard tell of Fitzgerald, even spelled out his early books. It was unlikely that any of them would know him by sight, but one never could tell. This climax was undoubtedly an indication that our party should break up, that we should all make a move.

I had brought with me to Hollywood one copy of each of my published novels. I asked Fitzgerald if I might send him *From a View to a Death*. That was the sort of question he knew how to answer very gracefully. I posted the book that afternoon. A couple of days later a reply came. The reference is to those British social categories adumbrated in the commissary.

> Metro-Goldwyn-Mayer.
> Corporation Studios.
> Culver City.
> California.
> July 22, 1937.

Dear Powell:

Book came. Thousand thanks. Will write when I have read it. When I cracked wise about Dukes I didn't know Mrs Powell was a duke. I love Dukes – Duke of Dorset, the Marquis of Steyne, Freddie Bartholomew's grandfather, the old Earl of Treacle.

When you come back, I will be in a position to have you made an assistant to some producer or Vice-President, which is the equivalent of a Barony.

> Regards,
> F. Scott Fitzgerald.

Scott Fitzgerald's good manners, a niceness that went side by side with less attractive traits undoubtedly on record, had been notably shown by finding time to acknowledge *From a View to a Death*. I discovered only much later that a lot was happening in his own life which would have excused forgetfulness. Some of this is set down in *Beloved Infidel*, the autobiography of Sheilah Graham. On Wednesday, 14 July (the night before the Hemingway film, when we had ourselves been watching the Black *Macbeth*), a party had been given to celebrate the engagement of Miss Sheilah Graham, a renowned Hollywood gossip-columnist, and the Marquess of Donegall, equally celebrated in London for the same vocation. This was no doubt the occasion when Donegall had been surprised by Fitzgerald using the term *cinquecento*. Here, too, Fitzgerald had first been introduced to Miss Graham. They had liked each other. Meeting somewhere else in Hollywood two or three days later, Fitzgerald had asked Sheilah Graham to dine with him on Tuesday, 20 July, the day he was lunching with us at MGM. That same afternoon, so it appears, a telegram from Fitzgerald's daughter was delivered to him, announcing her own imminent arrival in Hollywood. Fitzgerald, accordingly, sent another telegram, excusing himself from keeping his dinner-date with Sheilah Graham. On receipt of this she telephoned, holding him to the invitation, and suggesting that he should bring his daughter too. The evening, so Sheilah Graham reports in her book, was not a success. At the end of dinner Fitzgerald drove Sheilah Graham home. That night was the beginning of their love affair. It lasted throughout the years, not many by this time, which remained to him. Fitzgerald was forty-four when he died. I heard of his end, nearly two months after, on 21 December, 1940 (my birthday, as it happened), when I was in the army. By that time Fitzgerald, Hollywood, films, writing itself, all seemed a long way away, but that luncheon at Culver City Studios came back very clearly to my mind.

Two or three days after this meeting with Fitzgerald we drove down to Mexico ('south of the border', a phrase sung by marching men to reverberate on the ear in a couple of years' time), before making for home via New York.

❋ 4 ❋

The Hollywood expedition set a demarcation across the pattern of early married life. On return to England one settled down to the fact that sooner or later there would be a war. If war came I knew that, however inadequately adapted to the military profession, I should feel dissatisfied with myself unless in the army. In any case the Services, for a writer in times of war, seemed to offer infinitely the most advantageous viewpoint. Nevertheless, thought of all the tedium of military training, especially demands made on spare time, brought reluctance to join the Territorials straight away with a view to getting a commission, so that when the Territorial Army was doubled soon after Munich (September, 1938) I was a few months too old. I had, however, been accepted on the War Office's register of an Army Officer's Emergency Reserve, made up of those (over thirty, I think) possessing certain rather vague civilian qualifications. We prepared a gas-proof room in the basement at Chester Gate, and both of us enrolled in the Air Raid Precaution Service, attending lectures twice a week on that unentertaining subject. I was one of those deputed to take an ARP census of the neighbourhood for distribution of gas-masks, a duty irksome in itself, though not without all reward through the insight thereby acquired into how people live. Those answering a door-bell are apt to assume confrontation will mean either a demand for money, or threat of sexual assault.

Professionally speaking, I was in lowish water at this period. I had returned to London without even the germ of a book in my head; nor had I a job. In due course I managed to procure a novel-reviewing column once a fortnight for *The Daily Telegraph* (a book page then edited with less enlightenment than in later years), also doing notices of autobiographies and memoirs fairly regularly for *The Spectator*.

So far as getting to work on my own fifth novel was concerned, some sort of a recovery took place – though perhaps three mornings a week might be spent gazing at a typewriter – *What's Become of Waring* reaching completion towards the end of 1938 or beginning of the following year. The manuscript was first offered to Duckworth's, who (on the whole to my satisfaction, because I wanted a change) refused to pay the modest increase of advance asked. The novel was published by Cassell (why I can't now remember), a firm with which for some reason I never managed to establish at all a close relationship, and published no subsequent book of mine. Since *Waring* has been described in print as a more or less blow-by-blow account of my own days as an employee of Duckworth's, it is relevant to add that Duckworth's former director, Tom Balston, read the manuscript (commenting that the plot was 'most ingenious and amusing, beautifully worked out', together with a hope that the novel would sell 'like hot cakes'), while the current directors of the firm raised no objection to the theme, merely showing disinclination to offer more money.

What's Become of Waring finally appeared in March, 1939, just at the moment when Hitler was sending troops into Memel (then governed as an international free port), a juncture at which many people, not without reason, supposed that the war, due in September, had already arrived. With such vibrations in the offing, the Spring publishing season that year was not a favourable one for sales. *Waring* achieved a circulation of just 999 copies, resembling hot cakes only later, when, like King Alfred's, the remaining stock was burnt to cinders in the blitz.

For some little time before we left London for Hollywood plans had been set on foot to launch a new comic weekly to be called *Night and Day*. Graham Greene, who was closely involved in this venture, had suggested that I might become a contributor. In the event the paper did not appear until we were in California, from where two pieces of mine were sent under the heading *A Reporter in Los Angeles*. A few very minor odds and ends followed on return to England.

Although Greene had been only a year senior at Balliol, in the Balliol tradition of everyone living his own sort of life, we spoke together there only once, I think. At least I have a sole memory of Sligger's (F. F. Urquhart's) rooms, Greene one of a crowd of undergraduates in dinner-jackets, no doubt a Balliol dining-club ending the evening by a call on the Dean. We had come to know each other in 1933 or 1934, when Greene was editing a volume by various hands called *The Old School*,

and used occasionally to dine together. The Greenes were then living
on Clapham Common, one of the fine 17th century red brick houses,
later, he told me, destroyed in the blitz.

Night and Day was designed to dislodge *Punch*, long regarded by
the Young Turks of Fleet Street, many people elsewhere too, as the
quintessence of tameness, tapering off into an insipid philistinism. The
New Yorker format was rather too much in evidence when the first
number of *Night and Day* was put on sale in July 1937, though the
contents showed an undoubted freshness and style, which was kept
up during the brief six months that the magazine was to survive.
Graham Greene was not, I believe, in fact an editor of the paper
(which was marketed by the publishing house of Chatto & Windus),
but one had the impression that he played an active part in its life.
Peter Fleming wrote the opening editorial notes (signed Slingsby), and
his younger brother, Ian Fleming (later to beget Bond) may have helped
to raise money for the enterprise in the City. Glancing through a bound
copy of *Night and Day* in its entirety I am struck by Fleming impact
on its tone.

At this time I had not met Ian Fleming; Peter Fleming only very
casually. After the war I saw something of both of them, though never
knew either at all well, the elder brother the better of the two. Ian
Fleming was one of the few persons I have met said to have announced
that he was going to make a lot of money out of writing novels, and
actually contrive to do so. Peter Fleming used very obligingly – always
most valuably – to read the proofs of the war volumes of my own novel
before publication to check correctness of military detail and army
jargon. At the *Night and Day* period Peter Fleming, already renowned
for explorations in Brazil, with more recent adventures in Tartary, was
a great favourite with retired generals and the like, as almost singlehanded consoler of all who shook their heads over the decadence of
Youth. In his own person he demonstrated that unquestionably the
Younger Generation was 'all right'. He was often tipped as future editor
of *The Times*, but I think any such routine would have irked him;
besides, he was not really interested in politics. A brave man both in
peace and war, prepared to take on bleak feats of endurance, as well
as flashy acts of daring, Peter Fleming had a preoccupation, almost
an obsession, with not appearing to 'show off'. This self-consciousness
about avoiding anything in the least resembling Hemingwayesque
bluster, might in itself have become a form of showing off, had not
the characteristic been balanced in Fleming by a profound inner melancholy. A strong sense of duty also went hand in hand with a certain
puritanism. Peter Fleming's conversation, as befitted a man of action,
was laconic yet pithy, ornamented with his own individual figures of
speech, such as when he was heard excusing himself from some invita-

tion with the words: 'Got to help a friend give a hot meal to the Queen.'

Night and Day's book review 'lead' each week was written by Evelyn Waugh, on the whole less testy than might have been expected, anyway than he became after the war, Aunt Sallies of the Left being knocked about from time to time, but in a balanced manner. Waugh's opening review in the first number of the paper begins with praise of the painter (his pictures 'by no means bad'), David Jones, whose war autobiography, *In Parenthesis*, had just appeared, describing service in the ranks with the Royal Welch Fusiliers, with whom Jones was in action and wounded. Waugh speaks highly of *In Parenthesis*, a book which did not make a great stir at the time, though now recognized as not much short of a classic. 'Not a novel', Waugh said, so much as a 'piece of reporting interrupted by choruses ... as though Mr T. S. Eliot had written *The Better 'Ole*'.

Graham Greene reviewed films, his approach in marked contrast with the man-about-townish understating Fleming manner. Greene, on the other hand, fulminated like a John Knox of movie-criticism, sometimes demanding maiden tribute, sometimes denouncing the sins of the flesh. Every phrase was forged in a white heat of passionate feeling, emotive images abounding, such as von Stroheim 'climbing a ladder in skintight Prussian breeches towards an innocent bed'. This calling of fire down from heaven – and up from hell – on the cinema and all its works, did not remain unanswered, but retribution was still several months ahead.

Among other regulars in the critical columns were Elizabeth Bowen's rather staid notices of plays; sometimes varied by Peter Fleming's (who had dramatic status himself as an ex-OUDS actor), and the novelist Antonia White's. Osbert Lancaster (whose drawings would have suited the *Night and Day* style, but was perhaps inhibited by other contracts) wrote on Art. I did not know Lancaster in those days, though we were to become friends soon after the war. John Hayward (of whom more later), scholar and bibliographer, cast an eye over Broadcasting in those pre-Television days. Constant Lambert wrote an occasional article on Music. Architecture was given more of a look in than usual by Hugh Casson (later President of the Royal Academy) and John Summerson (who would rehabilitate the Soane Museum). A. J. A. Symons (*The Quest for Corvo*, Wine & Food Society) discussed Restaurants. Less expectedly, the poet Louis MacNeice wrote on the Dog Show; the literary critic, Walter Allen, on Football.

There were several serial features: John Betjeman's compendium of his own aversions, Percy Progress; Cyril Connolly's middlebrow family of Arquebus, viewed through their daughter Felicity's diary; pilgrimages by Hugh Kingsmill and Malcolm Muggeridge (HK & MM) to former homes of Victorian writers. Among the novelists and short story writers also occurring in *Night and Day* were Rose Macaulay, Christopher Isherwood, Pamela Hansford Johnson, T. F. Powys, V. S. Pritchett, R. K. Narayan, Gerald Kersh, Dennis Kincaid, Nigel Balchin, Hans Duffy (pseudonym of Mary Pakenham). Poets included Walter de la Mare, Stevie Smith, William Plomer, Herbert Read, William Empson, the last three contributing, in fact, prose pieces.

Gerald Kersh, at this period occupied with gamy novels about the London prostitute/ponce world, made some name when the war came with *They Died With Their Boots Clean,* and other novels about service in the ranks of the Coldstream Guards. Kersh, bearded, rampageous, immensely prolific, eventually emigrated to the US, where he died at no great age. When I met him once at El Vino's in the 1950s I had the impression that a little went a long way, but he was certainly funny teasing a pompous journalist (using the pseudonym Cassandra, and obnoxious to P. G. Wodehouse at the time of the unhappy wartime broadcast), Kersh pretending to bite Cassandra in the leg, while both were drinking in the bar.

Contributors to *Night and Day* from abroad included Paul Morand and James Thurber. Morand, who was to be French Minister Plenipotentiary in London in 1940, later became one of Vichy's ambassadors, but he rode the storm, and Violet found herself sitting next to him at a luncheon party in 1968, given at the Ritz in connexion with the French 18th-Century Exhibition at Burlington House. Morand was then in his eightieth year, but unsubdued. We talked afterwards of English friends eternally taking him to the Thames-side pub, The Prospect of Whitby, as somewhere he would never have heard of. Thurber, who wrote and drew for *Night and Day,* did both without any loss of quality in change of public, but his presence undoubtedly emphasized the paper's already over-close similarities to *The New Yorker.* A good comic artist, more or less ushered into prominence by *Night and Day,* was Roger Pettiward (drawing, quite why I don't know, under the name Paul Crum), Eton and Brazil pal of Peter Fleming, his pictures absolutely in the mood of the paper. Pettiward was later killed serving with the Commandos. Had he survived (though in quite a different manner from either), he would have been a cartoonist in the company of Osbert Lancaster and Mark Boxer (Marc).

I met James Thurber, not through *Night and Day,* but the year following the magazine's demise at a party given by Alice (Astor) von Hofmannsthal, as she then was. Thurber was in London with his second wife. They lunched with us at Chester Gate, the other couple present being Tommy and Betty Phipps. There seems no doubt that Thurber was sometimes an awkward guest, drinking too much, and insisting on singing 'Bye-bye, Blackbird' at inappropriate moments. He certainly put back a fair amount of wine at luncheon, but could not have been more agreeable, leaving behind him in our Birthday Book a tiny example of one of his dogs. Just twenty years later, in 1958, we met again, when Thurber was invited to the *Punch* 'table'. By this time, possessing at best throughout most of his life the use of only one eye, he was now blind. Those present at the luncheon were led up and individually introduced. It is hard to express how immediately Thurber took in – gaily replied to – the word of explanation as to our having met ages before. Thurber's method of dealing with his food was masterly. He would lightly touch the contours of what had been set before him on the plate. Once that was done no one sitting round the table would have guessed for a moment that he was a blind man. One grows to respect in the highest degree such self-management.

In October, 1937, *Wee Willie Winkie*, a film distantly based on a story of Kipling's, a tale his admirers prefer to pass over quickly, came to London. In it the small boy originally hero underwent a sex change, the little girl he became being played by Shirley Temple, in later life pillar of the U S Diplomatic Service, then, aged nine, among the top child film stars of the era. The cast also, as it happened, included C. Aubrey Smith, mentioned earlier. In reviewing *Wee Willie Winkie* for *Night and Day*, Graham Greene commented with even more than his usual verve. The film evoked in him a string of striking images. The article is good reading even to this day. Lawyers' letters were by no means unknown at the *Night and Day* office, but the one which arrived after the *Wee Willie Winkie* notice was of quite exceptional protest. A libel action ensued.

The case came up before the Lord Chief Justice, Lord Hewart, in March, 1938, Sir Patrick Hastings, K C representing Shirley Temple. Sir Patrick (less sanctimonious at his own table, where I had dined as a young man) described the libel as one of the most horrible that could be imagined; he would not read aloud the words complained of, as it was better that those who had not seen them should remain in ignorance of what was hinted. Lord Hewart (author of a sage book about civil service encroachment on personal liberty, but evidently a man for whom Freud had lived in vain) agreed as to the depravity of the review. He asked if the whereabouts of its writer was known. The answer – Greene being by then in Mexico – was in the negative. The Lord Chief Justice observed: 'This libel is a gross outrage, and I will take care to see that suitable attention is drawn to it.'

I suppose in those days a case might exist for considering Greene's notice 'bad box-office', but, even at that distant period, the notion that children neither had nor could express sexual instincts was, to say the least, an uninstructed one. The puritan's obscurantisms of one period provide the pornographer's extenuations of the next. The magazine was already in a parlous financial condition. Shirley Temple delivered the *coup de grâce* – what a scene for her that would have made in a film. A six months' run concluded in December, 1937. Nothing became *Night and Day*'s brief existence as a comic paper better than the exquisitely comic climax which terminated its publication.

Not long after the passing of *Night and Day*, Gerald Reitlinger, meeting us with his car at Robertsbridge station for what was always a perilous drive to Woodgate, where we were spending the weekend, suggested making a detour to call on the Muggeridges, recently come to live at Whatlington, a village a couple of miles away from Battle. I do not recall how, if at all, Reitlinger characterized these new neighbours, but (earlier than the *Night and Day* literary pilgrimages written with Hugh Kingsmill) I had been struck by an article on Russia in the *Evening Standard* with Malcolm Muggeridge's name as by-line. This piece, full of wit and acuteness, had been quite different from what was usually reported about the U S S R at that period. I felt curious as to the personality of the writer.

First sight of the façade of the Muggeridge house called to mind pictures of the home of the Old Woman Who Lived in a Shoe, children swarming all over the steps, children's faces looking out of every window, yet more children one felt, concealed in the garden at the back. In fact there were only four Muggeridge children, possibly reinforced at that hour of the morning by auxiliaries from the village, but the effect was as of a dozen or more. Kitty Muggeridge, welcoming, though plainly overwhelmed by domestic duties, dislodged two boys grappling together on the floor, so that we could pass into the house; then, her husband appearing, hastened away to further duties in the kitchen. Although we had called without warning (probably not at the most convenient moment on a Saturday morning), Malcolm Muggeridge displayed all the air of having been impatiently awaiting our arrival.

'Come upstairs,' he said. 'We'll have a talk.'

Years later, on my asking a girl whether she knew Malcolm Muggeridge, she replied: 'Yes – He always looks *blue* with cold.' There was, anyway from time to time, a certain felicity in this image. Muggeridge, then in his middle thirties, had the physical trait of sometimes appearing much older than his age (a man already getting on in life), sometimes much younger (almost a boy still). These transformations, which could take place from one minute to the next, were no doubt one of several outward expressions of an inner duality quite exceptional in the violence of its antitheses. As he began to talk, I felt here was a man I should like.

So pervasive is the latterday Muggeridge public *persona* that it seems extraordinary – even to myself – that we did not already know about him; extraordinary that there should ever have been a time when the

Muggeridge 'image', Muggeridge *obiter dicta*, were not familiar literally to millions. Yet such celebrity was in those days not merely an un-accomplished fact, but – so at least the circumstances seemed to me, something I cannot too strongly insist on – very few people seemed ever to have heard of him. No doubt the impression that Muggeridge was so little known rested to a large extent on my own ignorance of the byways of Fleet Street, where plenty of editors and others must have been by then alerted to the existence of a journalist of such pro-mise. Even so, journalistic reputations are precarious, made one week, forgotten the next, and Muggeridge's whole approach to life seemed remote from those determined to achieve that sort of ephemeral fame as quickly as possible. Obviously he had strong convictions (at least that seemed obvious, even if definitions might be less easy), but, except so far as such convictions had to be reconciled with earning a living, he showed not the least concern with personal ambition. To this was added an utter self-confidence.

I can think of no close parallel among my other contemporaries in this particular respect. Several of these moved from being comparatively unnoticed into the condition of having made some name for themselves. None in quite the same manner straddled the gap between an early personal privacy, more or less deliberately chosen, and an equally volitional relinquishment of that privacy in exchange for publicity on a multitudinous scale. In short, I find an almost complete contradiction in Muggeridge as he appeared to me when we first met; Muggeridge as the generally accepted end product. Muggeridge has himself, with brio, related the outlines of his own career. His memoirs contain no particular suggestion of making a change of direction in middle-life; on the contrary, if anything emphasis is placed on continuity. I do not demur at this, experience convincing me that individuals do not greatly change in character, though they may modify or develop what is there already. In other words I am struck (as not seldom) more by the im-perfection of my own early judgments, especially in relation to people known fairly well. Muggeridge was to play some part in my professional as well as personal life, yet I am not at all sure that I ever got the hang of him.

In happening first on his name in connexion with Soviet Russia, I had struck Muggeridge's chief preoccupation of that moment, one to some extent always so to remain. India, Egypt, Fabianism, other current infections, might be examined by him under the microscope for their morbific bacilli; the USSR remain the favourite tissue for expert if intermittent research. Disillusionment with Communism, dismay at the methods of the Soviet Union, are nowadays such familiar themes that the force of Muggeridge's virtually one-man onslaught in the 1930s is hard to grasp for those who did not experience those years.

The Muggeridge impact, for its cogency to be appreciated, must be understood in relation to the intellectual atmosphere of the period. At that time many people were apt to think of what was happening in Russia as no worse than a few rich people being relieved of their surplus cash, a proceeding of which some approved, some disapproved. True there were awkward stories about executions, torture, forced labour, government-engineered famine, but the analogy of omelettes and eggs would often be invoked by those who approved; while those who disapproved were suspected of doing so for the wrong reasons, that is to say desire to keep their own money. When, from time to time, those now called dissidents, having escaped to the West, described what was happening in Russia, no great impression was made on Left Wing intellectuals, who by then had invested too much moral capital in Soviet collectivism to adjust their portfolio without considerable loss of face; compassion being unevenly balanced against *amour propre* in most branches of life.

Muggeridge has some claim to be the first writer of his sort to disturb this Left Wing complacency in a lively manner. Hitherto detractors or reassessors of the 'Russian Experiment' had caught the ear only of those already interested in Russian affairs. Muggeridge, informed, readable, witty, convincing, was also an authority on the vulnerable side of Left Wing intellectuals themselves. Not only had his father been a Labour MP, but Kitty Muggeridge was niece of the Sidney Webbs, main British apologists for what Muggeridge denounced as a ghastly tyranny, an evil way of life, deserving abhorrence as much from the Left as the Right.

If a distinction is drawn between 'having politics' (as most people do, of one sort or another), 'being interested in politics' (as quite a lot claim to be), 'knowing how politics work' (comparatively rare, even among political commentators), Muggeridge, so it has always seemed to me, 'knew how politics work'. This is a gift altogether separate from how its possessor may lean politically, or the ultimate value of such leanings. Politics had permeated the manner in which Muggeridge had been brought up, become an integral part of him, in the manner that others might be musical, mechanical, have an instinct for horses or jewels. He could make the most prosy parliamentary measure sound an absorbing topic. In contrast, Muggeridge was altogether indifferent to the arts. Like most journalists, he might from time to time invoke a famous name in painting or music to hammer home a point, but in private he made no bones about being unable to distinguish one picture from another, and existing quite happily in that unacquaintance. Indeed, he was not merely indifferent, but possessed an active puritanical dislike for any approach remotely to be described as aesthetic. Writing was the only one of the arts which he was forced up to a point to recognize as such – having himself exceptional fluency and ear for phrase – but even in writing he would become impatient when emphasis was laid on form for form's sake, or over much to-do made about polishing up an article, or even a book. This disapproval of the arts (which went so far as reprobating the idea of a house too pleasing architecturally) may, in the first instance, have been vested in a need to excel in whatever Muggeridge himself touched, the arts not offering in that respect a congenial field. It was essentially different from, say, the execration aroused by suspicion of pretentiousness in aesthetic areas (in fact sympathetic to the writer himself on his own terms) to be found in some of Kingsley Amis's books. Muggeridge was the only close friend I have known over a longish period of years to be thus orientated. After this first meeting we soon began to see a good deal of each other.

There had been domestic anxieties too, as well as those caused by the becalmed state of professional employments, overcast skies of international affairs. In August, 1938, Violet suffered another miscarriage, this second mishap suggesting something might be physically amiss that needed to be put right by medical means. To other stresses were therefore added those connected with gynaecological superintendences aimed at improved hopes of having a baby. In spite of disquietudes, we were determined, while circumstances still allowed before the storm broke, to enjoy for the food and wine, if possible at least one holiday in the Bordeaux area, one in Burgundy. We had intended to make the journey to Bordeaux by sea, but troubles about the miscarriage prevented that. We had the Bordeaux holiday during the weeks terminated by 'Munich'.

By now fairly inured to the day-to-day business of novel writing, I felt clear about at least one aspect of the work: if war came, and I myself survived, that would not be in the state of comparative inner calm required for writing a novel. A thorough reintegration of essential elements would have to take place. Even before war arrived working conditions were already becoming less than tolerable owing to recurrent crises, so that it seemed wise to abandon the Novel for the moment – perhaps no bad thing to give those faculties a rest – and set out on a book which would require application rather than invention; one not likely to be finished before war broke out, and – should one still be extant – providing a nucleus to play about with on return to normal routines.

Possibly even as far back as undergraduate days I had been interested in John Aubrey (1626–1697), antiquary, biographer, folklorist, above all writer in whom a new sort of sensibility is apparent, the appreciation of the oddness of the individual human being. Aubrey's real originality in this respect is often dismissed as trivial observation, dilettantism, idle gossip, by those who have skimmed through his writings superficially. This mistaken view is not only on account of Aubrey's own extreme modesty and unpretentiousness, but because, in the case of Aubrey's *Brief Lives*, readers often fail to grasp that most of what is now published was intended only as rough notes.

Aubrey, it is true, was incapable of running his personal affairs in a coherent manner, accordingly, as he himself pointed out, never had an opportunity to work consistently for a long period at any of the subjects which preoccupied his mind. That did not prevent him from contributing to English history a very fair proportion of its best character sketches and anecdotes; or, by first drawing attention to the magnificence of the prehistoric temple site of Avebury, laying the foundation of that branch of archaeological research in this country. Aubrey's essentially new approach was vested in the manner in which he looked at things with an unprejudiced eye; an instinct for what his contemporaries, or historical figures, were like as individuals; his mastery of the ideal phrase for describing people.

No adequate biography of Aubrey had ever been put together, only a few scrappy summaries of his life, often full of inaccuracies of fact. When *Waring* was finished I began to assemble Aubrey notes with the idea of writing a book about him, which might see me through a war. There was a good deal of material, both in his own manuscripts and elsewhere. An additional circumstance which made Aubrey's background sympathetic to work on was that his family, like my own, was associated with the Welsh Marches, and he himself had passed some of his days in Wiltshire, a county where I too had lived at one time or another. In February, 1939, Violet and I undertook a tour through what Aubrey calls the 'campania of North Wilts', looking at the place of his birth, the villages and country from which he drew so many examples in his writings. In spite of the troublous times, as Aubrey himself remarks somewhere, *juvat haec meminisse*.

That August we set off once more for France. The announcement of the Molotov/Ribbentrop Pact burst in Bourg-en-Bresse. Soviet Russia had become the ally of National Socialist Germany. Hitler and Stalin were one in facing the rest of the world. War now seemed certain. We set off for England immediately, 24 August, St Bartholomew's Day. The following week was spent making hurried provision for coming events. At the time it was popularly supposed that on declaration of war (possibly even before that) London would be assailed by heavy air-raids. Members of the Emergency Reserve like myself thought – as it turned out mistakenly – that they would be called up forthwith for military training. Violet was a volunteer nurse in the Port of London Authority River Emergency Service (where the standard of female looks was unusually high), a body designed to undertake evacuation by water of casualties suffered during anticipated attacks from the air. It seemed possible that Violet was pregnant again. Medical tests were being taken. If these proved positive, she would leave London, and, in an attempt to avoid another miscarriage, lie up throughout the whole of the nine months. This eventuality had been foreseen. Violet's aunt, Lady Dynevor (her mother's elder sister) had suggested, should this precaution be necessary, that Violet should come to stay in Carmarthenshire.

Finally remained the problem of what to do about Bosola and Paris, a world-war postulating no future on which to set out with two Siamese cats as part of one's entourage. Enquiries were instituted as to catteries, so that they might be at least temporarily accommodated. We were recommended to a Mrs Perkins (with whom, in the event, Bosola and Paris were to reside permanently), whose establishment was not far from London.

On Sunday, 3 September, 1939, Neville Chamberlain made an announcement over the air that war with Germany had been declared. The day was spent undertaking a thousand last minute arrangements, packing things away as best that might be done. At last, pretty tired, far from cheerful, we retired to bed. Some time not long before midnight the telephone bell rang. Violet answered it. The call was from her doctor. He had completed the pregnancy test. The findings were positive. She was with child. The following day Violet left for Wales. It was a sad and upsetting moment when the train steamed out at Paddington, one I don't care to dwell on.

I remained at Chester Gate. The next three months constituted a strange unreal interlude, combination of the remnants of pre-war life, working on Aubrey, unwonted routines like ARP duties. There was still no sign of the Emergency Reserve call-up. Fellow members of the AOER, making enquiries, were told the War Office envisaged no immediate need of their services. Some of the time Wyndham Lloyd, as a doctor now working with the Health Service, stayed at Chester Gate for company. Constant Lambert reported that he had received a long patriotic poem from Aleister Crowley (engaged during the first war in making pro-German propaganda in the US), entitled *England – stand firm!*, for which he requested from Lambert a musical setting. A dream Lambert described may also belong to this period: he and I were at a party, where Virginia Woolf (whom I had never met, but Lambert might have known slightly) was also present; I went up to her and said: 'How now, bluestocking, what about the booze?' During the first week in October the telephone rang one evening. A man's voice asked for me.

'Speaking.'

'This is Captain Perkins. We haven't met, but my wife is looking after

your Siamese cats. I thought you would like to know they are well.'
    'That's very kind of you.'
    I was overcome with fear that he might go on to say that his wife
was unable to undertake further care of the cats, but he continued to
another subject at once.
    'I'm at the War Office, in A G 14 [or whatever the Section was],
the branch dealing with the A O E R. I've just seen your name there.
Do you want to be called up?'
    'Very much indeed. That is what I most want.'
    'You'd like me to put your name forward?'
    'Certainly, if you can.'
    'What regiment would you like to join?'
    I had not thought about that, expecting the whole Emergency Reserve
process to be quite other than this.
    'My father was a regular officer in The Welch – why not them?'
    'Easily get you into a funny regiment like that,' said Captain Perkins.
'Everyone wants to go into London units.'
    My father would not have been pleased by Captain Perkins' estima-
tion of The Welch Regiment (made up of the old 41st and 69th Foot),
with its long roll of Battle Honours, phenomenal record for winning
the Army Rugby Cup. Wellington had been an officer in the 69th, the
Regiment who had served as marines on Nelson's *Agamemnon* at St
Vincent, but this was no occasion for taking offence. I suggested that
Captain Perkins should lunch with me, when he could give if possible
further details of what might be in store. When we met, Captain Perkins
(who wore ribbons of the first war) said I should be called up within
the next week or ten days, medically examined, gazetted, probably sent
a week later to the Regimental Depot at Cardiff, trained for about a
month, then posted to one of the Welch Regiment battalions short of
an officer. A condition of this candidature was possession of Certificate
A, a military diploma, acquirable usually at school or university,
attesting the holder's sometime proficiency in a few elementary
principles of drill and tactics.
    I mention this because it often used to be said that 'Cert A' would
be of no value whatever, if war came, since the army would require
all potential officers available, whether they held Certificate A or not.
In this case the qualification was *sine qua non* of being accepted, and
(although I could have falsely claimed it without much likelihood of
being detected), as things turned out, I should have been in an extremely
awkward position later, had I never drilled a squad on a parade-ground.
Another requirement for immediate call-up was to be passed as
medically A.1. The examination necessitated attendance at Millbank
Military Hospital, a gloomy redbrick accretion of buildings behind the
Tate Gallery. All went well until the ocular test. I had a long-sighted

eye and a short-sighted eye. A young RAMC officer set me in front of the usual row of letters descending in size.

'Put your hand over your right eye and read the smallest letter you can.'

I did so.

'Now do the same with your left eye.'

Without thinking, I had pressed so hard on my short-sighted right eye that, with a hand over my left, all ahead was blurred. I could hardly see at all.

'I can't pass you A.1. You're almost blind in one eye.'

I tried to explain. He seemed doubtful, but yielded under persuasion.

'All right, put your reading spectacles on, and try again.'

This time I got through. Uniform and equipment had to be acquired. My father, who showed no particular enthusiasm about the whole undertaking (being unable to attain re-employment himself), handed over two well-worn khaki service-dress uniforms, blue patrols of even earlier date, a Sam Browne belt and revolver-holster, both of which had been through the South African as well as First World War. He was a shade larger than myself, but after trifling alterations the uniforms fitted tolerably well. About three weeks after my first contact with Captain Perkins on the telephone, an order arrived from the War Office instructing me to report for regimental duty on 11 December, in the rank of second-lieutenant, not to the Depot at Cardiff, but to the 1/5th Battalion, The Welch Regiment, at Haverfordwest, Pembrokeshire; as it happened, a familiar name, the Powell family having been associated with that neighbourhood at the end of the 18th and beginning of the 19th centuries.

Monday, 11 December, was a brisk winter morning. The train to Haverfordwest (a matter of two hundred and fifty miles from London) left Paddington at some such hour as 8.44 a.m. There were five other second-lieutenants in the compartment, all bound for different units and destinations. No one talked much, so far as I can remember. It was a long journey, one leading not only into a new life, but entirely out of an old one, to which there was no return.

❊ 5 ❊

At Haverfordwest an army truck was waiting, driven by a white-haired lieutenant, one of those veteran military types, leading a more or less freelance existence, to be found all over the place at the beginning of the war.

The 5th (Glamorganshire) Battalion, The Welch Regiment had known a unique distinction in the first war, on Turkish surrender of Jerusalem, having mounted the first British guard in the Holy City since the Crusaders. Territorials in Wales were very much a family affair, sons following fathers, father and grandfather of the 5th Welch's Commanding Officer having held that same command. The Colonel himself was a solicitor, but by long tradition nearly all the rest of the officers came from banks, few living more than a few miles from Cardiff. The 'other ranks' were from the Valleys, coalminers whose connexion with regiment and neighbourhood was no less close. At all levels of rank brothers-in-law and cousins abounded.

This strongly regional background, close consanguinity, did not result in the faintest expression of coolness towards someone like myself coming in from outside. I cannot imagine being received with greater cordiality that night. The Commanding Officer, more than a little appalled at being sent an untrained second-lieutenant in his middle thirties, could not at the same time have been nicer about my manifest drawbacks. It came at first as rather a surprise to be regarded as elderly to the point of senility, but with many other unaccustomed things, I soon became used to that rôle, one not without all validity in the circumstances. Three or four days after joining the unit I was changing guard as Orderly Officer; the second Sunday I had to march the Company to church, back past the Brigadier's saluting-base. There was no disaster, but I had not shouted out commands such as were required for more than sixteen years. I would find myself sometimes in charge of two platoons, forty or fifty Welsh miners to be taken into the country and taught how to attack a hill.

A powerful factor in this new existence was the ambience of the South Walians (as distinguished from the North Walians almost a different race), a people by nature talkative, goodnatured, witty, given to sudden bursts of rage, unambitious, delighted by ironic situations. The South Walian's lack of desire for promotion made the finding of NCOs difficult, hesitation almost always existing as to accepting authority which meant giving orders to relations and butties, thereby arousing not so much antagonism as derision. As I never served at regimental level with an English battalion I cannot speak with certainty, but my impression is that Welsh officers, close temperamentally to their men, probably understood their men's predictability better, while at the same time were utterly without what might be termed an Orwellian sense of guilt in being set above what was in general an overwhelmingly different class.

In South Wales the Williamses probably outnumber the Joneses. An officer I ran across, who had served with one of the battalions of The Welch Regiment in the first war, told me that his unit, then stationed in the United Kingdom, was required to furnish a draft of two hundred men for another unit of The Welch at, I think, Dieppe or Boulogne. Some regimental vendetta existed, so, to cause the maximum of administrative trouble, the two hundred men sent were all named Williams.

When I wrote about Welsh troops in *Dance* some demur was made among reviewers as to the phrasing of the Welsh-English spoken by certain characters. Since my own method had been adversely criticized, I consulted the Welsh actor and dramatist, Alun Owen (whom I did not know personally), asking if, as an impeccably authentic Welshman, he thought revision was required. I record Alun Owen's reply because I believe it to embody an important, perhaps essential, principle in writing dialogue in a novel. Owen agreed that a tape-recording of Welsh soldiers talking with one another might give a rather different result. At the same time, he found nothing inherently wrong in the interchange of talk, nor in the rhythms and inversions of speech. Above all, he said, the dialogue reproduced 'what the Narrator heard'. Owen's definition seems to me to embody a required precept for novelists aiming at naturalistic dialogue, one always to be borne in mind.

Just before Christmas, 1939, the 53rd (Welsh) Division was ordered to Northern Ireland, a move I did not at all welcome. The Battalion was first stationed in Portadown, a town politically reliable, if scenically unromantic. In February I was sent from there to a course at Aldershot, 169 OCTU, a training unit designed to give elementary instruction to those who had already become officers but needed polishing up in such matters as square-bashing, trench-digging, barbed-wire erecting, together with more theoretical sides of army training. On return from Aldershot to Northern Ireland, I found the Commanding Officer was replaced by Lieutenant-Colonel W. G. Hewitt, a somewhat younger contemporary of my father's in the Regiment. Bill Hewitt had a high reputation for personal courage in the first war. He is mentioned in Robert Graves's autobiography, *Goodbye to all that* (1929). Soon after this change in Commanding Officer the 1/5th Welch marched out of Portadown on the road to quarters in Newry, a town twenty miles south, nearer the Border. Unlike Portadown, most of the Newry people were anti-British. Corner-boys used to sing: 'We're going to hang out the washing on the Maginot Line'. Their friendly feelings for Hitler might well have been carried a stage further, as a German attack on Southern Ireland was officially regarded as very much on the cards. At Newry Hewitt began getting rid of older less efficient officers, promoting the younger and livelier to command Companies.

The requirements of a Company Commander are simple in the sense that they demand almost every good quality a man can possess: energy; initiative; conscientiousness about detail; capacity to delegate authority;

instinct for retaining the liking and confidence of subordinates, while
at the same time making them work hard, and never develop the least
doubt about who is in command; all these combined with a sound grasp
of handling weapons, and practical application of the theory of small
scale tactics. Off duty the Company Commander must spend most of
his spare time coping with the personal problems of his men, such as
having got a girl with child, or receiving news that a wife is being un-
faithful at home; not to mention minor matters like being reduced to
one pair of socks too shrunk to wear.

I list these ideal qualities in a Company Commander, because very
few civilians give much thought to the matter; certainly not because
I had the smallest claim to them myself. Indeed, even as a Platoon
Commander, though I came back from the Aldershot course with a
goodish report, it was clear to me that, unless I soon found myself
some other employment, I ran the risk, with other middle-aged
subalterns possessing no great turn for leading men (the absolute
essential in an infantry officer), of exile to the Regiment's Infantry
Training Centre; whence one might only too easily descend to the *bas
fonds* of the military ant-heap.

One morning in April, 1940, I was crossing the parade-ground at
Newry when two subalterns came out of the Orderly Room together.
They advanced towards me. At range of about thirty yards one of them
shouted: 'It's a boy.' That was the announcement of Tristram's birth.
Leave was granted for such occasions, and I got off right away. All
had gone well. There was a day or two of a new sort of domestic life.
I found that becoming a father had a profound effect upon the manner
in which one looked at the world.

On return to Northern Ireland my Company was sent 'on detachment' to the Divisional Tactical School, to provide 'security' and a
demonstration platoon.

The Tactical School was quartered in Gosford Castle, Co Armagh,
an 1820 neogothic pile, surrounded by a fine park. The castle replaced
a former burnt-down Georgian mansion belonging to the Earls of
Gosford, the house and grounds having associations with Jonathan
Swift. An air of inexorable gloom hung over Gosford, undissipated
by the crew of seedy bad-mannered middle-aged officers who made
up the staff of the Divisional School. The place figures as Castlemallock
in *Dance*. Later that summer a change took place in my army circumstances, which, as things turned out, removed me for good from
the Battalion. Headquarters, 53rd Division, at this moment stationed
in Belfast, required an assistant Camp Commandant. This is one of
the least distinguished jobs in the army, but its holder is required to
be less than utterly uncouth in habits, being responsible, among other
duties, for the Defence Platoon guarding the Divisional Commander's

Tactical HQ in the field, accordingly a member of the Major-General's Mess.

Variation of North Wales and South Wales temperament was well illustrated my first morning at Division inspecting breakfasts. The Orderly Sergeant, a Royal Welch Fusilier, remarked: 'The porridge is very good this morning, sir.' I was by this time so acclimatized to the irony of the South Welsh that, at once supposing some fearful slop full of cockroaches had been served up, I asked with apprehension: 'What's wrong with it, Sergeant?' The North Walian (not one of the dour sort, and an excellent soldier) meant no more nor less than what he said; the porridge was indeed very good.

Meanwhile the Battle of Britain was being fought out over the south of England. Sussex, where Violet, with Tristram, was now living, represented one of the most vulnerable areas. Wives were in certain circumstances allowed to join their husbands in Northern Ireland.

Accommodation was far from easy to find in Belfast, especially as army duties gave little or no time to search. It was also possible that Div HQ might at any moment be transferred to some more or less inaccessible spot in a part of the country without housing for camp followers. Notwithstanding these uncertainties the increasing vehemence of the blitz in the south of England seemed to make a move advisable for a mother with a young baby. Violet arrived in Belfast before any very satisfactory arrangements could be made to receive her there, putting up for a time at a boarding-house in fairly dispiriting surroundings. In the end, after a good deal of searching about, we managed to rent a small house.

Up to this time Northern Ireland had been free from air-raids. Now, as if planned to coincide with the new presence of one's family, they began with some heat. The Luftwaffe's visits, unlike those to London, where a stray plane would sometimes make a lone flight, were usually in force, if Belfast was thought worth the journey at all. For a time I had orders to turn out the Defence Platoon, mount brens as practice for anti-aircraft cover, but, no dive-bombing taking place, this routine was after a while abandoned. The only promise my army future held was that, after expiration of eighteen months, all second-lieutenants became lieutenants, automatically promoted. The prospect was not inspiring. Then an altogether unexpected thing happened. In January, 1941, a War Office telegram arrived instructing me to attend the 3rd Politico-Military Course at the Intelligence Training Centre (Cambridge Branch).

The Politico-Military Course, each one of which comprised about twenty officers, and lasted eight weeks, did credit to British self-assurance as to the eventual outcome of the war. At that moment victory did not seem very probable. Germany, having overrun Europe, would soon feel strong enough to attack the Soviet Union, her own ally in the devastation of Poland; while Pearl Harbour, bringing about US declaration of war on the Axis Powers, was still nearly a year away. The blitz was in full swing; invasion of the British Isles apparently imminent. Notwithstanding the sunlessness of the strategic horizon, the Politico-Military Courses had been organized with the object of training a nucleus of officers to deal with problems of military government after the Allies had defeated the Axis.

The concept was mainly due to Colonel (later Brigadier) K. V. Barker-Benfield, then Commandant of the Intelligence Training Centre. The principle of these Cambridge courses was that the greater part of the instruction should be undertaken by the University, officers living more or less as undergraduates, billeted in Trinity, most of the lectures in St John's. Other army courses were also taking place in the colleges at this time, notably one for languages.

The teaching side of the PM Course was organized by Professor (later Sir) Ernest Barker, Emeritus Professor of Political Science, in his late sixties, a fairly famous Cambridge figure and exuberant personality. Barker, in an era when claims to humble birth were less widely boasted than today, was always determined to emphasize the extreme modesty of his beginnings. Cheerful, dominating, egotistical to a degree, he had lost none of the Victorian optimism, sense of a career open to talents. As another Balliol man, he was predisposed towards me.

Notwithstanding the supposed frigidity of Cambridge manners, the dons were exceedingly hospitable. Among my Cambridge hosts was A. S. F. 'Granny' Gow, a former Eton master, now Fellow of Trinity. Andrew Gow (who died in 1975 at the age of ninety-one) could hardly have been in greater contrast with Ernest Barker. Barker was the sort of don who would these days be familiar on the 'media', while Gow, with his muted humour, somewhat Jamesian manner, taste for cultivated bachelor life, preferred an absolute personal privacy; tempered with great concern for the arts, expressed through the National Art Collections Fund. He left 'my French things' to the Fund for presentation to the Fitzwilliam Museum. Gow's 'French things' included a couple of dozen drawings by Degas, perhaps fifty more by such masters as Boudin and Toulouse-Lautrec.

The Eton instinct for penetrating nicknames had not gone astray in appending 'Granny' to Gow's name, in spite of the fact that he was by no means an old woman, and had been firm rather than the reverse in school. He had taught me Greek for one term at a lowish level, and been George Orwell's 'classical tutor'. When Gow kindly sought me out at Cambridge, and asked me to dinner, we did not talk of Orwell, who had not yet come into my life, but I believe Connolly had already mentioned to me that Orwell kept up to some extent with his former tutor. Such discriminating dons of the old tradition had no doubt always been something of a rarity with their collecting (though Gow was not a rich man), and good claret. A few years before this, Gow had produced a memoir of A. E. Housman, whose friend he had been, a book with moments of dry humour, but chiefly bibliographical in aim. Gow gave me his Housman book, inscribing it. In return, at the first opportunity, I sent him *Agents and Patients*. He wrote in acknowledgment that he 'found its frivolities a suitable solace for the weary hours spent this week at the [air-raid] warden post where it alternates with professional matter and a book on the equally frivolous habits of the cuckoo'.

One night, dining I think at Jesus high table, I found myself next to Sir Arthur Quiller-Couch, 'Q', sometime Professor of English Literature, another celebrated Cambridge figure. Q's books are now not much remembered, but he left an indelible mark on two generations by editing *The Oxford Book of English Verse* in 1900, 1910 and 1939, thereby netting three miraculous draughts of wartime readers of poetry, war producing conditions when the gauge of poetry consumption rises steeply. For forty years Q pretty well laid down what verse ought to be given a chance to survive. Quiller-Couch, then approaching eighty, extremely spry, gave the impression of thinking not too badly of himself. He told me he had just received a letter from Marie Stopes (apostle of birth-control), trying to enlist Q's help in keeping Lord Alfred Douglas off the rocks financially. I had met Douglas when John Heygate and Evelyn Gardner were married and living at Brighton, and not been greatly taken with him. He had curious movements, entering a room almost as if about to turn a cartwheel.

Among us was a whitehaired captain, whose appearance struck me at first sight as indefinably strange. He wore first war ribbons, and was rather incongruously listed with his Oxford degree on the roster of names: 'Captain G. P. Dennis, MA, Intelligence Corps'. It immediately struck me – by a means which he himself would certainly have looked on as occult – that this officer might be Geoffrey Dennis, author of a couple of novels I had read years before, *Mary Lee* (1922) and *Harvest in Poland* (1925). Captain Dennis, then about fifty, agreed almost with emotion that he had written these two novels. He seemed quite startled. His manner suggested that no one had ever heard of these early works of his. 'I'm a very *highbrow* writer,' he said. 'You understand that, don't you? A much more *highbrow* writer, for instance, than Aldous Huxley.' This comment was made in a tone not in the least conceited, in fact almost apologetically, with a note of anxiety in his voice, nearly chronic, so I discovered, when Dennis spoke about himself. His novels had seemed not so much highbrow (whatever that epithet, undoubtedly at times convenient, might be held to cover), as outpourings of an exceptionally uninhibited personality, highly strung, even tortured, obsessed with a sense of aggression against himself on the part of those around him.

Dennis himself, who possessed a gift for picking up languages, had lived for many years at Geneva, working in the Secretariat of the League of Nations. An amusing talker when not oppressed by anxiety, he had many stories of incidents at the League. On one occasion, the Japanese delegate spoke for several minutes in an utterly unknown tongue. When the Japanese had made an end, each supposing himself responsible for the translation, both English and French interpreters leapt simultaneously to their feet.

Dennis said he had a patent medicine in his room to cure some minor ailment (named, but now forgotten), and this pot or tube had caused someone to approach the Assistant-Commandant (not a regular officer, but rather aggressively keen to maintain a high standard of military discipline in the relaxed atmosphere of a university) with a complaint that Dennis was treating himself for venereal disease. Dennis had a strongly developed capacity for self-justification, and for some time the rumblings of this unpleasantness beneath the surface disturbed the harmony of the Course. Finally peace was restored. I never knew the name of the supposed troublemaker, nor what amends, if any, were made to the outraged Dennis for an unwarrantable allegation. Malcolm Muggeridge told me that years later the Assistant-Commandant was still complaining of the hell Dennis had given him on the subject. If this incident could easily have come out of one of Dennis's novels, I have to concede that another one, in which Dennis was also involved, pertained to my own books, at least to the extent that I subsequently made use of it. The scene in question took place on the last night of the PM Course, after a dinner at which no doubt a certain amount had been drunk.

Just as I was about to retire to bed, a fellow-student told me to come with him up another staircase to see some practical joke that had been played on Dennis. I had been in no way associated with this prank myself, probably expression of a general feeling that Dennis was an odd fish; a conclusion that may have been further interpreted – wholly erroneously – as indication that he was therefore homosexual. I could be paying the organizers a compliment in conjecturing anything so comparatively thought out, however wide of the mark. The joke, such as it was, consisted in having arranged a dummy in Dennis's bed. The mock-up of the dummy was quite well done. In the company of its constructors I was admiring the body's convincing outlines, when Dennis himself appeared. The scene then took place which is reproduced in *Dance*, where brother-officers plan to rag Bithel (a character in every respect unlike Dennis), a drunken middle-aged subaltern of dubious sexual tastes. The manner in which Bithel turns the tables on the raggers might be thought implausible in a novel, but Bithel's behaviour, and its consequences, exactly coincided with Dennis's at that moment in the Trinity bedroom.

No doubt Dennis, like the rest of us, had drunk a certain amount, but he was in complete command of his wits. He glanced at the recumbent dummy, at once grasping the inferences. Without the least warning he began to perform a complicated dance round the bed. While he danced, hands raised above his head, he sang. This stately pavan continued for a minute or two, at the end of which Dennis collapsed on the bed, clasping the dummy in a passionate embrace. A consciousness of awful embarrassment descended on all around. In spite of having myself taken no part in the planning of the affair, I had not been immune to a touch of inner uneasiness while Dennis went through the formal evolutions of his dance. The perpetrators of the frolic were altogether discomforted in their own terms. They crept off silently to bed. I don't think I have ever witnessed a similar hoax carried off by the intended victim with such unexpected éclat.

Among those who had withdrawn from the London blitz to work in Cambridge, where air-raid warnings were heard only rarely, was John Hayward, who had himself been up at King's. Hayward, bibliographer, editor of such poets as Rochester and Donne, attacked by the incurable muscular disease which brought an end to his life in 1965, now for years had been confined to a wheelchair. Suffering had left its grim marks on his features, turbid lips, and an expression of implacable severity, making him look like a portrait of Savonarola. In fact nothing could have been less puritanical than Hayward's lively talk, always expressed in carefully chosen phrases, somewhat Augustan in diction. A cluster of pretty women were usually standing round about his wheelchair at parties, doing their best to entertain him. In dealing with wellwishers of both sexes (men would push his chair, otherwise attend to his physical needs), Hayward, whose temperament was at once nervous and dominating, could at times approach the positively tyrannical. Indeed, holding court at a party, he had much about him of Ham, the seated autocrat in Samuel Beckett's *End Game*, regal yet immobile, continually dispensing a rich flow of comment, imperious, erudite, malicious.

Hayward was sharing Merton Hall (an ornamental house belonging to Lord Rothschild) with another notable figure unwontedly in Cambridge, Lord Gerald Wellesley. Lord Gerald, by profession an architect, was now a major in the Grenadiers, instructing at one of the army's courses for languages. Hayward could comfortably continue his literary work at Cambridge, and he also taught once or twice a week at a girls' school in the neighbourhood. Anthologies of verse were immensely popular during the war years, and, not long before my own arrival in Cambridge, Hayward had produced one of these: *Love's Helicon*, a volume arranged under headings to illustrate the myriad aspects of Love, ranging from successful seduction to hopeless despair.

After the war John Hayward, who had long been not only a close personal friend of T. S. Eliot, but a valued critic of his poetry before publication, set up house with Eliot in Carlyle Mansions (where Henry James had lived at the end of his life) on the Chelsea Embankment; a household which continued, until brought to a close by Eliot's second marriage in 1957. During this period Eliot might often be seen pushing Hayward's chair, sometimes as far afield as Battersea Park. Their companionship under one roof was looked on as an undoubted success, though one of its anomalies particularly remarked was that suggested by Hayward's boundless relish for stories, contemporary or historical, with a strong tang of sex about them; Eliot's notorious distaste for anything of that kind.

So far as was known, contretemps had never arisen over this disparity of humour; the same antithesis in what might be thought amusing certainly not arising during his co-tenancy with Lord Gerald Wellesley. Wellesley was to become 7th Duke of Wellington within two years, on his nephew's death in action serving with the Commandos, and it will be convenient to call him by the title he was soon to inherit. Gerry Wellington, then in his middle fifties, distinguished in appearance, a connoisseur in the arts, a courtier, possessed a keen sense of his own exalted position, which made him the subject of many stories even before his unexpected accession of rank. Indeed, his touch of haughtiness was scarcely, if at all, augmented by becoming a duke. No amount of ragging on the part of his own contemporaries, say, Osbert Sitwell, Harold Nicolson, Malcolm Bullock (long in the House of Commons, great purveyor of badinage), could undermine this lofty demeanour, maintained as much in bohemian circles – where Gerry Wellington did not at all mind making occasional forays – as in the beau monde. Mere pomposity, however splendid, would never have brought Gerry Wellington his fame if he had not possessed many other qualities too, one of which was a powerful capacity for counter-ragging his raggers. In that respect he could perfectly well look after himself. His preoccupation with the mystique of his great ancestor, the 1st Duke of

Wellington, might cause jocular friends to refer to him as the Iron Duchess, but he was a personality to be reckoned with, whose amalgam of gifts and idiosyncrasies are not easy to outline with justice to both.

As a younger son, who had to make his own way in the world (a starting point which, as much as Ernest Barker, he liked to emphasize), he had been in the Diplomatic Service, to the end of his days capable of making a stylish speech on any public occasion in French or German. He retired from Diplomacy as a comparatively young man to become an architect, the profession he had always wanted to follow. Devoted to ceremonial, Gerry Wellington equally disliked fuss, making a habit of carrying his own suitcase downstairs at hotels, perfectly prepared to do the washing-up, if circumstances imposed that liability. He possessed energy, kindliness (allied to a hot temper), an immense sense of personal obligation in performing duties he regarded as incumbent on his position, and, sixty in sight, was to leap into the sea with the British invading force undertaking the Sicilian coastal landings.

Gerry Wellington (who had two strikingly good looking children) was separated from his wife, Dorothy Wellesley, a poet much admired by W. B. Yeats. According to Osbert Sitwell, the two chief causes of marital discord had been Dorothy Wellesley's impatience with her husband's incessant plugging of the glories of the first Duke, together with his taste for highly spiced stories, cited above as a bond with John Hayward. Osbert Sitwell asserted that, at an attempted reconciliation between husband and wife, the former had arrived carrying an enormous brown-paper parcel, a present. While Dorothy Wellesley was undoing the string her husband had time to recount an anecdote of startling pungency; when the paper was removed, the gift turned out to be a gigantic bust of the 1st Duke of Wellington, executed in terracotta.

After the war we came to know Gerry Wellington quite well, often staying at Stratfield Saye in Hampshire, once at La Torre, the Wellington property in Spain, granted when the 1st Duke was created Duque di Ciudad Rodrigo. Gerry Wellington's great literary passion was for Jane Austen, a novelist on whom Violet is expert. He liked Violet to check some of his family papers (the First Duke having married Kitty Pakenham), and a tradition grew up for us to come to Stratfield Saye once a year to attend the annual meeting of the Jane Austen Society.

By happy chance for one so preoccupied with that epoch, Gerry Wellington, as a young diplomat, had been *en poste* in St Petersburg in 1912, the year of the centenary celebrations for the battle of Borodino. He possessed a photograph of a Russian peasant, aged one hundred and four years, alleged to have been held up as a child when Bonaparte and his staff had made a public appearance on the balcony of some building. The old man in the photograph, standing between two officers or court officials, had been questioned.

'And what did the French Emperor look like?'

'A very tall man with a fair beard.'

Gerry Wellington had himself appreciably added to the relics of the First Duke at Stratfield Saye, the interior of the house belonging wholly to that period. The place had at times suffered neglect, but luckily not the sort of renovation to destroy the atmosphere. One of its owner's keenest convictions was that his ancestor had never uttered the opinion that the battle of Waterloo had been won on the playing-fields of Eton, offering a standing remuneration of a hundred pounds to anyone who could prove its authenticity; the First Duke having been by no means a dedicated Old Etonian, the earliest coupling of the names of Waterloo and Eton (recorded by a Frenchman in 1855) making no mention of playing-fields.

A fellow-guest of Stratfield Saye was usually the novelist L. P. Hartley, a younger contemporary of Gerry Wellington's, friend of ours too and country neighbour. Hartley did himself – and his guests – extremely well so far as drink was in question, the wine always first-rate. One butler made a point of refilling a guest's glass after every sip, moderation thereby difficult for the most abstemious. The food at Stratfield Saye was always in the best tradition of good English cooking, but neither wine nor spirits by any means flowed. The host was himself not interested in wine, such as provided coming from the Spanish estate and in no great abundance at that. To remedy this alcoholic deficiency Hartley used to bring his own supplies, sufficient to see him through the weekend – or, as Gerry Wellington would have insisted on terming that efflux of time, Saturday to Monday.

During one of those two days, sometimes on both, there was likely to be a largish luncheon-party, followed invariably by a personally conducted tour of the house. This included the principal bedrooms, but, after inspecting these, did not usually stray from the main upstairs passage to an area somewhat further on, where bachelors were likely to be accommodated, and, in fact, Leslie Hartley was generally given a bedroom. For some reason on one occasion, when even more guests than usual had been at the table, Gerry Wellington, contrary to habit, altered the routine.

'You don't mind if we see your room, Leslie?'

Hartley, always somewhat involuted in speech, uttered a faintly deprecatory affirmative. The long crocodile of guests trooped into his bedroom, too many to be included all at once. The chief object for envy and admiration in the apartment was a newly opened half-bottle of gin, standing in front of the looking-glass on the dressing-table. The sightseers gazed round and withdrew. The tour continued. 'Gerry didn't see, thank God,' Hartley muttered to me, as we proceeded to another wing of the house.

To return to wartime Cambridge, the PM Course: John Hayward, as I have said, used to teach once or twice a week at a girls' school. Not long after work had begun he was horrified to receive a letter one morning, signed by the Headmistress of this school, saying she must at once terminate his employment. She could not possibly expose her pupils to contact with a man responsible for editing a book of verse which had just fallen into her hands, a farrago of lascivious obscenity, a collection altogether unfit for the eyes of a young girl. Hayward's presence must never again pollute the precincts of her school.

Hayward, who could be easily rattled, was not unnaturally very upset on reading this onslaught, the intemperance of the phrasing particularly disturbing him. It was true that *Love's Helicon* contained poems not specially adapted to a school textbook, but he had never attempted to introduce the anthology to the attention of any of the girls, nor included even a selection of the poems in their instruction. Much disturbed, he set the letter aside to read again later in the morning, while trying to think out what would be the best answer. A renewed reading of the Headmistress's letter some hours later revealed a certain familiarity in the handwriting, at the same time one he did not somehow connect with earlier letters received from the same source. Examination of previous correspondence showed, in fact, that the writing was quite different, nevertheless still encountered not long before. Then the truth was apparent. The letter was a forgery, plainly the work of Gerry Wellington.

Hayward took no action immediately, neither did he mention the matter to his housemate. He merely put the letter away in some private place. A day or two passed. Then a telegram arrived at the house: *Lord Gerald Wellesley* stop *Am in rather a fix* stop *Coming to stay next week* stop *Paddy Brodie*. Of Paddy Brodie (now deceased) it is necessary to say no more than that his surname had been made use of by Evelyn Waugh to create the composite character, Martin Gaythorne-Brodie (whose other two ingredients were also not far to seek), who appears in the first edition of *Decline and Fall*, but, owing to threat of legal action (from Brodie himself, I think), was reissued in subsequent printings as The Honourable Miles Malpractice, a figure who also occurs in *Vile Bodies*. After receiving this ominous telegram Gerry Wellington mentioned to John Hayward that, very inconveniently, urgent family business had forced him to put in for a week's leave. This request had been granted. He would therefore be absent from Cambridge the following week. There, so far as I know, both the matter of the Headmistress's letter and the Brodie telegram rested; neither subject being ventilated to each other by the two occupants of Merton Hall.

Barker-Benfield recommended my application for exchange into the Intelligence Corps. As a matter of routine all students were for the moment posted back to their units. Divisional Headquarters now moved from Belfast to Castlewellan in Co Down, another neogothic pile. When transfer from The Welch Regiment took place, I was sent as a preliminary on the War Intelligence Course, a six weeks' affair at Matlock in Derbyshire.

For some weeks after I was consigned to the Intelligence Corps Depot at Oxford. During this period took place the interview (described more or less word for word in *Dance*) when I was considered for the job of liaison officer, at battalion level, with the Free French in the Near East, turned down on account of insufficiencies of language. That was rather a blow to me, as I was told that otherwise I was what was being looked for, but I recognized the decision as just. A short time later I was posted, on probation, to a Section in the War Office.

Military Intelligence (Liaison) had a room on the first floor of what is now known as the Old War Office. Work was concerned in principle with most of the army's foreign contacts in Great Britain. These were made chiefly through the military attachés resident in London (not British military attachés in foreign capitals, who were separately administered), both Allied and Neutral. MIL was very decidedly not involved in any activities of the Secret Service (MI 6), nor Special Operations Executive (SOE). When, very rarely, administrative dealings with these organizations were in question (for example, transfer of Allied personnel for secret duties) negotiations were kept to a stringent minimum, so that liaison relations with Allies should be recognized as existing only in the sphere of open dealings.

Vichy, although naturally without an embassy in London, was recognized as the legal government of France (unlike the puppet régimes set up in German occupied territories), the Free French under General de Gaulle being approached through a special mission, an officer of which had interviewed me for the battalion liaison job with the Free French overseas. When, after invasion by Germany, the Soviet Union perforce joined the Allies, a special mission also came into being to deal with Russian military affairs. After the United States entered the war they too had a special mission. Among the Allies only Poland had a sizeable concentration of troops in the UK, the 1st Polish Corps numbering some 20,000 men, mostly stationed in the Lowlands of Scotland. When Stalin agreed to release the (still brigaded) units of the Polish army, held prisoner in Central Asia after the Soviet Union's invasion of Poland in 1939 (to become the 2nd Polish Corps), MIL was concerned with the arrangements made, and on certain other occasions with Allied overseas matters. The Free French, Czechoslovakia, Norway, Belgium, Holland, each had a few thousands, Luxembourg (the Grand Duchy's military personnel at first cadred with the Belgians, later a separate entity), a few hundreds. These were the foundation members of the club, of which Greece, Jugoslavia, other Powers, were in due course to become members.

Some – though not all – of the military attachés who appeared as characters in *Dance* are drawn directly from life. The Commanding Officer of the Section, instead of bearing some approximation to Lieutenant-Colonel J. C. D. Carlisle, DSO MC, is Lieutenant-Colonel Lysander Finn, VC, who (apart from certain invented civilian associations) is a fairly authentic portrait-sketch of Major A. E. Ker, VC. In practice Ker never exercised the seniority that made him second-in-command more than by deputizing in the Colonel's room when Carlisle himself was on leave or sick. In no other sense did Ker take charge or give orders. A Writer to the Signet before the Court of Session in Scotland, he was one of the nicest of men. He had often been offered promotion, but preferred to remain in MIL, where, with two captains to assist him, he looked after the Neutrals, some of whom from time to time were elevated into Allies. Deafness was a handicap from which Ker suffered, but was prepared to put to good use when that suited him. He was smallish, immensely broad, with a huge nose like Punchinello.

Jack Carlisle, in his early fifties, tall, slim, goodlooking, with candid blue eyes that looked straight at you, possessed a charm of manner of which he was himself not at all unaware. He worked immensely hard, found delegation of duties difficult, indulged in a good deal of intrigue, especially as to his own longed-for promotion. Imbued with an overwhelming respect for his superiors in rank, he rapturously longed for the red capband and red tabs of a full colonel; even a 'local' unpaid full colonelcy.

The officer to whom I was apportioned as assistant in Polish liaison was listed on the door of the MIL room as *Captain A. Dru, Intelligence Corps.* He wore spectacles, General Service badges, a blue side-cap. His manner was precise, perfectly agreeable, but not in the least forthcoming. Alexander Dru (who married Gabriel Herbert, sister of Laura Herbert, Evelyn Waugh's second wife) has already made a brief appearance in these memoirs, though nothing is said of a friend of extraordinary brilliance and subtlety, met not through any of the many people we turned out to know in common (until then I had never heard Dru's name), but quite fortuitously when thrown together in the army. Dru, about eighteen months older than myself, not yet married, had been up at Cambridge, afterwards briefly at the Sorbonne in Paris. His father was French (a family to have provided *présidents* of the pre-Revolutionary *parlements* of the Franche Comté, the province on the Swiss frontier); his mother (who had been dead for some years) coming from one of the Lancashire Roman Catholic families.

I never met Dru's father, who lived in England, but I believe remained a complete Frenchman to the end of his days. His son, an only child, had been brought up as an Englishman, but an Englishman habituated from the start to Continental life. Alick Dru could remember a birthday in pre-Revolutionary St Petersburg, had been guest at shooting-parties in remotest Ruthenia. France was known as a second country, together with an abiding attraction towards Swiss intellectual life. Speaking French as easily as English, he was only a shade less fluent in German. To say that one met in him a Frenchman translated into an Englishman is tempting, but not wholly true. In some ways he could be very English. He was always irritated by the cliché that English education produces a type; French education an individual. He insisted that precisely the opposite was true. English education did not bother with 'ideas' as such; 'ideas' in French education being regarded as of the very first importance. Accordingly, an English boy leaving school might or might not be adequately instructed, but he had an open mind. Dru asserted that a French boy was not only taught 'what to think', but – if judged the sort of boy likely to be 'in opposition' – what to think 'in opposition'. Nevertheless Dru always loved the French mind, and would comment on the pleasure of returning to Balzac after much reading of the Russian novelists, the clarity of the Latin after the obfuscations of the Slav.

Perhaps one might compromise by describing Dru as looking at things from an English standpoint, while pondering them in a French manner. His jet black hair (never grey even in later life), powerfully lensed spectacles (not inhibiting an air of elegance), something about the suits he wore (though unquestionably cut in London), contributed to an exterior in some manner distinctly French, but it was the line along which Dru's thought moved which made the inner Frenchness most manifest. His mind (in my own experience equalled in speed at reaching the essential point only by Constant Lambert's) was of lethal quickness. This instantaneousness of energy in speech – and action – was sometimes counterbalanced by bouts of *je m'en fichisme*, these contrary elements warring within him perhaps recognizable as a not unusual French amalgam. After coming down from Cambridge he worked for a time in an oil company, spending a year or more in the

US, a sojourn he hardly ever spoke of, one which seemed to have left surprisingly little impression on him. The work (which he described as 'easy') had bored him. He disengaged himself from oil. When I asked if no parental objection had been made to this abandonment of all visible means of support, Dru had laughed a lot, agreeing certain pressures had been brought to bear. Finally his father (with whom he was on the best of terms) made no great difficulties about allowing his son to go his own way.

In the years before the second war Dru represented to most of his friends the ideal 'spare man' for concert or dinner-party (Violet, who had met him then, says he danced beautifully), attending musical evenings (he played the piano rather well himself), reading much and promiscuously, with a leaning towards works in French and German on the subject of religion and philosophy. A Roman Catholic of profound – though incessantly searching – belief, he was on the whole inclined to frequent Catholic circles (no doubt one of the reasons we never met), a relatively enclosed world; though Osbert Sitwell, who knew Dru slightly, told me he associated him with the T. S. Eliot environment. Such amorphous studies as might seem to engage Dru's attention in this pre-war period were not taken with undue seriousness by most of his friends. Throughout his life it would have been possible – though perhaps not very perceptive – for a fellow-guest to have spent an evening in his company without carrying away much more personal impression than an uncontrollable *fou rire* when amused, and (though Dru was no wine snob) a taste for vintage claret. A certain aura of mystery – not wholly dissipated even when one knew him well – was vested in Dru's unwillingness, indeed almost total inability, to be explicit about himself or anything that had happened to him.

In the course of all this apparently desultory pre-war reading Dru had come on the works of the Danish philosopher and theologian, Søren Kierkegaard (1813–1855), by then translated fairly widely into German. In the English-speaking world Kierkegaard was still little known and to Dru was a *coup de foudre*. Dru's Catholicism did not at all preclude being carried away by a Protestant theologian, who, though greatly dissatisfied with the Lutheran Church of Denmark in his day, had himself planned to become a pastor. Dru at once set about learning Danish with a view to translating Kierkegaard's *Journals* (Dru's selection from which appeared in 1938), later also the satirical essay, *The Present Age*, in other respects pioneering the philosopher's recognition in English. He remained absorbed in Kierkegaard all his life, writing about him intermittently, though never producing the major study probably once planned.

Dru often complained that critics insufficiently emphasized Kierkegaard's aesthetic side. He insisted that the philosopher should be thought of in terms of a poet or novelist, say Baudelaire or Dostoevski. All the same one has to admit that Kierkegaard never managed to weld into any supreme form of literary expression the three archetypal figures that obsessed him: Don Juan (sensuality), Faust (doubt), Ahasuerus the Wandering Jew (despair). Kierkegaard, like Blake, is claimed as an early Existentialist, and Dru, believing passionately in individual choice, shared existentialist distaste for abstract thought, philosophies advocating what is outside ordinary human experience. Like Kierkegaard (in whom religious life was the aim), or Nietzsche (with a very different goal), Dru held that mysticism could be approached – was perhaps best approached – through the arts. To non-Christian Existentialists, religion, philosophy, ordered morality, are merely methods of avoiding the issue in solving the disastrous predicament in which man finds himself, and – as I understand it – their sense of absurdity, their despair, is all they have in common with the Christian Existentialism attributed to Kierkegaard. Dru would have enjoyed the American poet Delmore Schwartz's observation: 'Existentialism means that no one can take a bath for you', and I should have liked to hear Dru's judgment on Schwartz's short story in which a character remarks: 'Kierkegaard ... thinks there are three fundamental attitudes to existence – the aesthetic, the ethical, and the religious. Probably as good an illustration as any other would be a situation in which you wanted to kiss the wife of a friend. If you were aesthetic you would kiss her without compunction, and like it very much. If you were ethical, you'd take a sedative ... if you were religious, you'd neither kiss the lady nor take a sedative.'

In fact, Kierkegaard's own sole involvement with a woman was a painful broken engagement, an experience to make him victim of much psychological investigation. Dru found that side intensely boring, the very term 'subconscious' irritating him. Nevertheless, many of the writers in whom Dru was himself interested were close to the sources of modern psychology. Dru's own attitude towards sex was an enigmatic one. He was not in the least averse from bawdy jokes – would laugh a lot over them – but, where he himself was concerned, possessed an armour-plated withdrawnness, a way of being aloof from the small-change of army badinage in that respect which seemed to be granted in a surprisingly universal manner as if by common consent. Although Dru could scarcely have been less Scandinavian in outlook (differing from Kierkegaard in many other ways too), he did perhaps accept a touch of self-identification in concentrating on this peculiar and tormented figure, who, in the popular mind, has become prototype of intellectually pretentious name-dropping. In fact, so far from being an austere hermit, Kierkegaard (inheriting some capital when a young man) was for a time (in the Baudelairean sense) a dandy, a wit, a gourmet, a tease, who liked leg-pulling and getting tight. He himself says somewhere 'the humorist, like the wild animal, walks alone', and there is perhaps no real paradox in the fact that Kierkegaard was also desperately exercised about his own spiritual state. I do not suggest that Dru existed in any such agonized condition (nor was he, as in Kierkegaard's more worldly aspect, a tease), but something was shared in love of religious contemplation, while at the same time being regarded by those round about as a *flâneur*.

Dru's outward attitude to his own Catholicism differed considerably from that of many of his Communion, especially most of the converts who were contemporaries. He agreed that it might be said of himself *Yes, we have no Bernanos*, and would remark: 'Of course it's quite absurd to suppose that some sort of Reformation would not have taken place sooner or later', or 'I find such-and-such as difficult to believe as in a Future Life.' I once asked Dru if he had ever thought of going into the Church himself. He laughed, and said: 'No – but perhaps I wouldn't have minded being a very political bishop.'

Even those of Alick Dru's friends with clearer notions than others of his intellectual potential never guessed that the war would transform him into a staff-officer of exceptional ability. Something of the sort must, however, have crossed the mind of the major-general (an acquaintance through some merely social contact) responsible in the first instance for recruiting him into the army a few months before the outbreak of war. This senior officer answered a request for an additional assistant at the British military attaché's office in Paris by causing Dru to be gazetted an immediate emergency commission and posted to the appointment. In the ever varying, sometimes quite delicate, duties of MIL, Dru was habitually good mannered, taking immense pains to sort out intricate and tedious liaison problems, but, not at all given to military brusquerie, he was equally free from too much of that English liking to be thought a good fellow. In the War Office the vast majority were efficient and courteous, at worst grumpily correct. If Dru, in matters that seemed to him of prime importance, came up against obstruction or blockheadedness in an officer (or civil servant), he could be inflexible, use the sort of phraseology that got home. He did not at all mind making people angry, which he certainly contrived to do from time to time, and was not in the least impressed by rank.

The Poles, high spirited, gallant, ever unfortunate, were stimulating to work with. By the time I arrived in the War Office there was already great uneasiness as to whereabouts of 15,000 Polish officers deported after the Russian invasion of Poland to the Soviet Union, and not identified as among those Polish units known to have been transferred to Central Asia. At this period it was thought by the London Poles that the missing officers had been exiled to distant camps within the

Arctic Circle. Their atrocious massacre by the Russians at Katyn was
to emerge only later.

Dru and Carlisle had a complicated relationship. Carlisle's respect
for Dru's judgment made him unwilling to incur his subordinate's
displeasure, but, if up to a point Dru dominated Carlisle, Carlisle's
manner of looking at things (and implementing them) was in such
absolute contrast to Dru's approach to life that sheer philosophic
bewilderment at such deviousness would momentarily cause Dru to
lose his hold. Dru could be shrewd enough, but what he thought and
did was always based on strong principle. Carlisle could astonish by
a perpetual willingness to abandon principle for the pragmatic. As
already remarked, Carlisle did his job uncommonly well, working
unremittingly, taking decisions (as indeed did even majors and captains
of the M I directorate) exceeding what might be thought normal to his
rank. At the same time his obsequiousness to superiors (he would
enrage Dru by a grotesque habit of addressing senior civil servants as
'sir'), his extreme resilience under setback, were all things to be discussed unendingly. He became a kind of cult to Dru and myself, and
one could feel a real affection for him. Carlisle was, indeed, a near-
Shakespearian figure, who would have been superb proclaiming in
blank verse, like Polonius, his personal rules of conduct in life.

There was one free day a week, which most people saved up to make
two at the end of a fortnight, so that if possible they could get away
for the weekend. After a certain amount of moving about in an effort
to find a place to live, Violet, with Tristram, finally went to Shoreham
in Kent, about twenty miles south of London, a house called Dunstall
Priory belonging to Lord Dunsany, the writer, who had married her
mother's younger sister. The only occasion during the war when I
descended to a cellar during a raid was at a Dunstall weekend. We had
managed to get hold of an onion or two, and, a great treat, just sat
down to a curry. Then a fierce raid began, which went on just above
the house. This continued for at least forty minutes. It seemed wise
to move Tristram from the room upstairs, and, following Sir George
Sitwell's advice to Osbert Sitwell, then in the army during the first
war, if a bombardment took place, 'retire to the undercroft', for the
moment abandoning the curry.

One reads of 'literary life' in wartime London: Connolly and *Horizon*;
a younger generation, mostly on leave from the Forces, dredging the
Soho and Fitzroy Street pubs for cultural contacts. These last ports
of call were in general off my own beat even in leisure hours, and,
although more than once Connolly exhorted me to produce something
just to 'get my name into the Index' of his magazine, I never found a
moment (or theme) to do so. The image of Connolly's editorship in
the closing years of *Horizon* was of a kind of Pentheus in reverse, a

King held together by Maenads, rather than torn asunder by those dedicated ladies.

After my first meeting with George Orwell we used to see each other on and off, but, drink in short supply, anything like a night out was a rarity. In any case fairly chronic fatigue at the end of the day kept one from seeking out those with whom something of the sort might have been envisaged. Soon after my arrival in the War Office, which coincided with Malcolm Muggeridge's preferment from Field Security to the Secret Service, Muggeridge, after we had dined together, took me to see an old friend of his from Cairo University days, Bonamy Dobrée, a Regular soldier turned Eng. Lit. professor, now, like the man in the Kipling poem, back to the army again. Dobrée produced several bottles of Algerian wine. Muggeridge and I left at a late hour, both able to walk, but got lost in the blackout in the wilds of Camden Town. No one was about. Then miraculously – or we should have perished utterly – a car came out of the darkness and slowed up.

'Are you a taxi?' Muggeridge asked.

'No,' said the man. 'I'm a taxi-driver.'

One night Alick Dru and Osbert Sitwell dined with me at the Travellers Club, afterwards both of them witnessing a will I had just made: Dru recording his profession as 'Major, General Staff'; Sitwell as 'Poet and Justice of the Peace'.

It may have been the same evening that Osbert Sitwell related a story about the Duke of Cambridge, Queen Victoria's first cousin, who, as Commander-in-Chief, had for many years opposed all change in the army; expressing the opinion (according to my father) that 'he saw no reason why one gentleman should not command a regiment as well as another'. News had come to the ears of the Duke that an outbreak of venereal disease had taken place at Sandhurst. He set off for the Royal Military College at once, *en civil*, carrying as ever a rolled umbrella, to deliver a rebuke. When the cadets were all assembled, the Duke of Cambridge waved the umbrella above his head. He thundered: 'I hear you boys have been putting your private parts where I wouldn't put this umbrella!'

If Dru was an unusual brother-officer, so too in quite another manner was Major E. C. Bradfield. Bradfield, who some called Ted, some Charlie, was on the whole known to most of the Section as Bradders. He worked with the Norwegians, with whom he communicated in fluent Danish, the two languages being sufficiently similar to make no great matter. Now in his middle fifties, Bradfield had been awarded a Military Cross on the Western Front in the first war, a Bar to it in the War of Intervention against the Bolsheviks, 1918/19. Smallish, wiry, quite bald, Bradfield's features, anyway the upper part of his face, resembled that of the Emperor Vespasian, oddly enough a Roman head to be seen in Bradfield's adopted capital, Copenhagen. Bradfield was a man of notable good nature where his colleagues were concerned (if not handled carefully could be at first suspicious of officers from other Sections), and, highly strung not to say neurotic, would yell with wild laughter in which always lurked a sense of the deepest melancholy. On one occasion, when the general in charge of the Intelligence Directorate arrived in the MIL room early one morning to make some enquiry, he found Bradfield (demonstrating that he could perform that gymnastic) standing on his head. As well as this exuberant side, Brad-field had an obsession with personal cleanliness, Dru alleging (something not denied by Bradfield's complexion) that he scrubbed himself all over every morning with a wire brush.

An altogether phenomenal egotist when it came to talking about himself, Bradfield would treat his own past history as something with which everybody in the room should be thoroughly conversant. At the same time a few matters in that respect always remained obscure in a life story recited at the length, somewhat in the manner, of a Norse Saga. Bradfield's history was as out of the way as his personality. Ostensibly the son (youngest child by several years in a comparatively large family) of a Norfolk farmer and his wife, he seemed from his earliest days to have been under the wing of a Danish margarine tycoon named Horniman, who had formed the habit of making an annual visit to East Anglia for the fox-hunting season. Finally Mr Horniman (always referred to as 'my guardian') more or less adopted Bradfield as his son. Speculation was irresistible as to whether a blood relationship did not indeed exist between them, an ambiguity by no means diminished by Bradfield's own features. In fact Dru – familiar with clerical aspects of Danish life from Kierkegaard studies, and producing book illustrations to prove his point – used to say: 'All Bradders needs to make him look a typical 19th century Danish pastor is a black gown and ruff round his neck.'

When Bradfield left home at sixteen or seventeen employment had been found for him at the Danish Consulate in London. There his first duty had been to escort an intoxicated Danish sailor from the Consulate to the Docks en route for his ship. During their longish journey in a horse-cab the sailor had spent the whole time masturbating, an incident Bradfield could never banish from his mind, and would repeatedly iterate. Later Bradfield was transferred to Copenhagen with a view to initiation into the operating of the margarine business his guardian controlled. Mr Horniman also presumably arranged the lodgings which his ward now occupied in Copenhagen. These were kept by the Danish widow of Paul Gauguin, the French post-Impressionist. Gauguin, in his days on the Paris *bourse*, had picked up two Danish girls in a restaurant, and subsequently married one of them. Madame Gauguin – Madame Gau*guing*, as Bradfield always called her – was one of the major figures in the Bradfield Saga. She must have been in her sixties when he lodged with her, plainly a formidable lady, both from his own account and surviving photographs. Bradfield's anecdotes were hard to piece together for preservation, as he laughed so much while telling them, but a recurrent one was how a fellow-lodger, a Danish young man, being one day too lazy to visit the lavatory, relieved himself into a piece of brown paper, made up a parcel tied with string, which he then threw out of the window. Unfortunately a caller *chez* Madame Gauguin was at that moment approaching the front-door. The package, bursting on impact, scored a direct hit. Understandably, there was a colossal row; a Scandinavian incident worthy of Strindberg at his grimmest.

Mr Horniman owned a castle in Jutland, Nørlund, which he left to Bradfield for life; would indeed have bequeathed the property absolutely, had Bradfield agreed to go into the margarine business. I am not sure what Bradfield himself wanted to do, possibly become a musician, since he was a pianist of sufficient accomplishment to give public recitals from time to time. Before the war he had farmed the Nørlund estate, an occupation he thoroughly enjoyed, living most of the time in a small house nearby the castle. Though not badly disposed towards women, Bradfield always spoke disparagingly of his own powers in attracting them, and he never married. At the time of the German invasion of Denmark, April, 1940, he was lending a hand at the much overworked British Embassy in Copenhagen, since he was a passionately patriotic Briton in spite of domicile abroad. Having no diplomatic status he was held by the German authorities, the question of internment arising. No doubt partly owing to his age, he was told he would be less trouble, administratively speaking, if he proceeded to England, where German troops would in any case arrive within three weeks. Bradfield immediately rejoined the army on return to London, and was at once posted to MIL.

In the summer of 1949 Bradfield invited Violet and myself to Nørlund. The Castle, though much reconditioned, dated from the 12th century. Dominated by an onion-domed tower, stood two wings at right-angles to each other, one used as an orphanage, the other inhabited by Bradfield only during the months of the year when he entertained guests. On the chimney of the orphans' wing storks appropriately nested. The Castle had been used by the Germans as some sort of military school. When Bradfield returned to Nørland to get his home into working order again the moment came to light the stove in the Great Hall. The fuel was about to be put in, when an old retainer counselled the wisdom of making a thorough examination before that was done. A long iron bar was thrust into the deepest recesses of the stove. Right at the back of the fire-place floor, deliberately concealed, was found enough high-explosive to have blown up at least one wing.

Among other Jutland neighbours we were taken to see was Bradfield's Danish friend, Ole Benson, who had played a courageous part in the Resistance. Mr Benson's lifelong hobby was miniature railways. He had spent many years in perfecting a railway system in one of the rooms of his house, not only an impressive toy famous in the neighbourhood, but the superstructure under which the munitions of the Resistance fighters had been concealed. During the German occupation Benson's underground activities had never been discovered by the German authorities, though there had been some bad moments. The worst of these had been when an officer of the Gestapo had called to say that the Chief of the Gestapo in Denmark wished to talk to Herr Benson himself. The officer had come to arrange an appointment. Benson thought that now all was up. There was no alternative but to name a day. The Chief of the Gestapo arrived in due course and was shown in. At first he only made conversation. Benson became increasingly uneasy. The German seemed in some way embarrassed about getting to the point. At last with an effort he brought out what he had come to say. All was revealed. The Chief of the Gestapo was a railway buff. He had made the visit in person in order to ask whether Herr Benson would be kind enough to allow him to come round one afternoon a week to play with Herr Benson's model railway. Benson agreed, but only on condition that the Chief of the Gestapo wore plain clothes. This he did, while he sent the miniature engines rattling over a cache of Danish Resistance arms.

In wartime London, owing to the blitz, houses and flats were easily found, large scale sharing of these a commonplace of the times. Dru had belonged to such a commune in a relatively large and luxurious flat in Arlington Street, Piccadilly, but by the time I first met him, his co-tenants had sunk to one, a Treasury official seconded to the Cabinet Office. This Arlington Street accommodation becoming expensive even in war-time for only two persons, they moved, remaining together as a matter of convenience, to one of the blocks surrounding the Roman Catholic cathedral in Westminster, a flat Dru eventually took over when he married. One of the earlier temporary inhabitants of the Arlington Street flat had been a former Cambridge undergraduate acquaintance of Dru's, a barrister in civil life, then a major (perhaps already lieutenant-colonel) on the military staff of the Cabinet Office. Dru (combining play on this friend's double-barrelled name, creed, demeanour, personal appearance) used to speak of him as The Papal Bun, regarding him as a never failing source of laughter, even if a useful contact in the lofty governmental sphere in which The Bun now operated.

Apart from that last practical potential of The Bun, I myself never quite saw his point, while at the same time wholly accepting that, from Dru's field of view, special rules might apply. Where early contemporaries are in question, school, university, anywhere else before the age of twenty, the essences and memories of adolescence, with all their intensity, are largely untransmittable in primitive meaning to those who have never shared them.

'Believe it or not,' Dru used to say, with much laughter, 'When The Bun went down from Cambridge people used actually to *worry* that he would not be able to earn a living.'

That certainly seemed a misplaced valuation of someone evidently proving himself unequivocally successful in wartime, but I could not see precisely why Dru thought that so funny. On the two or three occasions when we met (always with Dru) The Bun had been – to use a favourite Edwardian expression – perfectly civil, no more. I did not find his personality particularly sympathetic; indeed rather the reverse. In such circumstances I was not much less than staggered when one day The Bun announced that he required an assistant for his Cabinet Office job, and would like me to fill the appointment. I can't remember throughout life anything of a similar kind having come my way as quite such a surprise.

This proposed change of employment signified something a little different from a move within the War Office. Military Assistant Secretaries at the Ministry of Defence and Cabinet Office, ranging in rank from major to full colonel (possibly higher), were, Assistant Secretary being a civil service grade, in theory equal with each other in their work. The Cabinet Office – often loosely referred to as the Cabinet Offices – represented not only the focus of government of the country, but also fount of war strategy, expressed in the persons of the Chiefs of Staff of the three Services, the War Cabinet, the Prime Minister himself.

I very much liked working with Dru, the whole Section was agreeable, Polish liaison rewarding. Nevertheless these duties had continued for some fifteen months. Unless the officer establishment of M I L was increased (at that moment no prospect) little likelihood existed of what used to be called in old fashioned army parlance a 'step'. Hubert Duggan, a fellow captain, had remarked: 'Of course you don't get into the Big Money until you're a major.' Apart from what would be a very acceptable rise in pay (majors in the Cabinet Office usually not long before becoming lieutenant-colonels), the prospect of viewing the war from this dizzy altitude (in actual practice, from the bowels of the earth) seemed a chance not to be missed. Carlisle was by no means pleased when informed of this proposal, though he could not very well stand in the way of one of his officers' promotion. He played a delaying tactic, brought abruptly to an end by the arrival of a signal from the Ministry of Defence stating that, unless I reported forthwith to the Cabinet Office, Great George Street, the order would come over at Adjutant-General's level. This awful threat, particularly fearsome to Carlisle, seemed to underline the importance attached to my setting about this job as soon as possible. That was in February, 1943.

To forestall the least suggestion of appearing to make excuses for myself, let me emphasize at once that, to put it mildly, I was not at all a success at my new employment. At the same time – so it seemed to me – I was confronted with a set of circumstances which have cropped up more than once in my life (Balston at Duckworth's providing a slightly similar example), that is to say someone going out of their way to involve me in undertakings of their own, then, that accomplished, showing an extraordinary unwillingness to concede a minimum of initiatory instruction in what was required; indeed almost displaying satisfaction in consequent shortcomings. Perhaps in this, and other instances, I am being unjust. As remarked earlier, probably no job is done well unless done instinctively.

The Joint-Intelligence Staff (Navy, Army, Air Force, Foreign Office, Economic Warfare) included a group of committees, hierarchical in ascent, reaching their apex in the Chiefs of Staff, the last reporting to the War Cabinet and Prime Minister. These committees produced a continuous flow of 'papers' devoted to every conceivable aspect of how the war was, or might be, waged. The main duty assigned to me was to act as secretary (usually two in number, of whom the other was The Bun) summarizing the findings of one of these committees. Arrival at the office was soon after nine, the meeting began at eleven, its sessions as a rule running on to at least half-past seven or eight in the evening. Two or three hours later than that was far from uncommon, though only occasionally did discussion close with midnight. When talk was ended its substance was boiled down by the secretaries (such as myself), a typed copy of the summary being made for each member of the committee to go over first thing the following morning, before returning to register approval or disapproval (in the latter case revision required) at Great George Street. The process would then begin all over again on a new subject.

In short, a fourteen-hour day was quite normal, occasionally an extension of that, protracted effort being expected of the higher echelons in wartime. Such working stretches required considerable physical as well as mental resilience, particularly if the blitz had extinguished sleep the previous night. No doubt the principle of utmost effort was good, though it was possible to wonder whether the best results were always achieved by weary men poring over complicated documents night after night into the small hours. The duties of a secretary recording minutes of a meeting need a certain flair even at a quite humble level, if they are to be discharged with skill. Where the often conflicting view of the three Services and two government departments were in question, agreement was not always easily arrived at. Much argument could arise over the difference between what had been said, what set down in the 'paper'. The Bun was preternaturally gifted in bringing about acquiescence.

I lasted about nine weeks, relinquishing the appointment without regret, though not without a sense of having fallen abysmally short in failing to give satisfaction in the job. This inadequacy was rubbed in on receiving my *congé*. All ranks of an emergency-commission were temporary, but, if a rank were held down for three months, the rank below became 'substantive'. Thus a major for three months could not go below the rank (and pay) of a captain. A request that I should be allowed to hang on for the tailend of my three months, a fortnight or so to go, was refused. Another appointment as major would certainly have been sought for me by the War Office branch concerned, no doubt found, but, anyway in theory during the interim of unemployment, I should sink from major to lieutenant. It happened just at this moment that Carlisle required a replacement in M I L. Hearing I was *en disponibilité* he at once applied for me by name. Acceptance would mean a return to the rank of captain, a demotion in principle not well looked on by the appointments branch; nevertheless, as I myself was willing to descend, no serious difficulties were raised. An immediate posting to duties already carried out satisfactorily seemed a great deal preferable to a potential period of unemployment, followed by something out of the lucky dip, which might well prove even more thankless than my recent assignment.

Kenneth Bell, my Balliol tutor (probably recalling his own less than happy publishing experiences before returning to Oxford as a don) used to say: 'Only after a series of ghastly humiliations does one begin to learn the extent of one's own capabilities.' There is much truth in that opinion. The interlude in the sub-basement of Great George Street, however ill-omened, made for clarity in that particular sphere. It brought other advantages too in glimpses of how government worked, what the individuals were like who controlled the machine, much else in the way of previously unfamiliar elements calculated to stir the imagination.

In 1945, not long after the surrender of Japan, the United Nations Charter was signed at San Francisco. Certain members of the Cabinet Office Secretariat were flown to California for duty at this conclave, among them the officer who had in the first instance suggested I should be his assistant. On the return journey to England the plane never reached London. All were lost. How that happened I have never heard, but I could not help reflecting that possibly greater ability in performing the duties required of me might have led – perhaps as a special treat owing to the prestige attached – to being included in the San Francisco party.

I returned to MIL duties with Czechoslovakia (henceforward referred to for brevity as Czech) forces, and the Belgian; liaison with these two Allies being handled by one officer. As well as their military attaché, the Belgians employed a major supervising affairs of the Congo, a colony possessing an army of its own, somewhat comparable with that of the former Honourable East India Company. The Czech military attaché, Colonel Kalla, appears in *Dance* more or less 'as himself' under the name of Colonel Hlava; the Belgian military attaché, Major Kronacker, also not much altered, as Major Kucherman; but the Belgian Colonial Officer, Major Offerman, is a composite picture in Major Clanwaert.

Pleasant relations with Kalla and his staff were brought to a melancholy end, when, by now aware of the tragic turn political circumstances were taking in his country, he went back to Czechoslovakia. Kalla himself had been one of the most determined champions of the Soviet Union throughout the war. Now, seeing the way things were shaping at home, his last words to me were: 'We can only hope for the best.' Not long after his return, by then under house arrest (some of the Czech officers who had fought with the Allies were shot out of hand by the Communists), Kalla died of heart failure.

If the Slav Allies preferred, so far as possible, to keep their political differences to themselves that was far from the habit of the Belgians (or, indeed, the French), who possessed no such inhibitions. The Belgians (as they themselves were always assuring me) are a nation much given to internal quarrelling, saying what they think about each other in the plainest possible terms. Indeed, their military attaché, Major Kronacker, told me that, when woken in a wagon-lit by the sound of a fearsome row going on in the next compartment, he knew he was back in his beloved country. Belgian circumstances at that moment offered scope for rows. One delicate matter, rivalling perennial discords between Flemings and Walloons, was the Royal Question. When in May, 1940, after a brief but stiff resistance, the Belgian forces had been compelled to give way before the invading German army, King

Leopold III – automatically Commander-in-Chief on outbreak of war – had been faced with an impossible choice. If he went into exile with the Belgian Government, headed by the Prime Minister, Hubert Pierlot, the King laid himself open to the charge of deserting his kingdom; if he remained in Belgium, there was no alternative to becoming prisoner of the Germans.

Belgian determination not to appear over respectful to their own authorities was well illustrated when, on some official occasion, I had to attend the showing of a Belgian propaganda film. The main picture was preceded by a short British satirical documentary called *Yellow Caesar*, constructed from shots pasted up from old news programmes about Mussolini, done in such a manner as to guy the Duce's pretentious public appearances. Several Belgians were sitting immediately behind me. When the title *Yellow Caesar* was flashed on the screen, one of them said: 'César jaune – mais c'est qui? Pierlot?'

At the outset of my new liaison job the relationship of the War Office with the Belgian military attaché's office was a far from happy one. Major (later Baron) Paul Kronacker, a Reserve officer just old enough to have served in the first war as lieutenant of Horse Artillery, commanded a battery at the time of the German invasion of Belgium in 1940. After various campaigning ups and downs he had been taken prisoner, but, soon released, managed to escape to England in 1942. Since then things had not gone too smoothly with him. Kronacker, scientist, businessman, politician, was a wellknown figure in Belgian life. He had received high academic honours for chemical research, was an industrialist whose concerns, Belgian and foreign, included the presidency of the big Tirlemont sugar refinery, and, in becoming a Senator not long before the outbreak of war, followed his Belgian maternal grandfather. His German-Jewish father had begun life as a German subject, only later taking Belgian nationality. Kronacker himself had retained certain German business interests even after the advent of Hitler. His second wife was British, but at this period he was still married to an Austrian *Gräfin*, by then living in America. These two aspects of Kronacker's background – German business associations, Austrian wife – provoked uneasiness, Belgian and British, at a time when an eye naturally had to be kept on the bonafides of everyone entering the United Kingdom.

The Belgians, at least those responsible for such matters, showed the national taste for polemics by disregarding the caution counselled, not only by their own authorities but the British ones too, and almost immediately appointing Kronacker as their assistant military attaché. In neglecting the normal usage of sending a formal letter giving the name of the officer designate to take over an appointment in the military attaché's office, courtesy must be admitted to have been less than conspicuous

on the Belgian side, the sitting Belgian military and air attaché being
taken by surprise as much as the Foreign Office and War Office.

Correspondence between MIL and the military attachés normally
adopted the form of the DO (demi-official or 'Old Boy') letter, in which
rank was dropped in favour of the simple surname or first name. The
current incumbent being, as it happened, an airman, all purely army
matters were left to his subordinate, Kronacker. Accordingly, at the
time I took over Belgian liaison, Kronacker would write direct to me,
but, Kronacker's appointment never having been referred to the British
authorities, I had instructions always to send the answer back to his
boss. This was obviously not a state of affairs to promote good relations,
and naturally Kronacker himself – who had done everything a man
could to show his patriotism and enthusiasm for carrying on active
Belgian antagonism towards the Germans – was furious at being so
treated. He insisted that his case should be investigated to the fullest
extent, the result of this enquiry being that he was totally vindicated
by both Belgian and British authorities in every aspect of what had
been a most unfortunate conjuncture. Kronacker's honour was agreed
to be unassailable. This final clearing up was brought about not long
before the moment when Kronacker's superior officer was promoted
to another job, Kronacker himself becoming Belgian military attaché.

In person Kronacker was small, neat, somewhat severe in manner,
obviously accustomed to getting his own way in whatever he took up.
Two years of existence as assistant military attaché in a somewhat
anomalous state had no doubt left a certain mark. In our earlier dealings Kronacker seemed a little inclined to treat army matters as if
cornering a commodity on the stockmarket, but it was not long before
he showed himself capable of grasping that not being too serious is at
times the best way of dealing with relatively serious army matters. In
fact, notwithstanding this rather sticky start, when we met face to face,
Kronacker and I got on together pretty well. He was not only extremely
efficient where routine affairs were concerned, but quite uncircum-
scribed by a professionally military point of view, often unjustly disparaged in its own field, but at times an impediment to the complex
problems of armies in exile. Of all the Allied officers with whom I
came in contact during the war Paul Kronacker was certainly the outstanding figure.

When I first embarked on Belgian liaison, the Belgian forces included
an artillery battery made up of subjects of the Grand Duchy of Luxembourg. A customs union existed between Belgium and Luxembourg,
but Luxembourgers felt themselves quite separate, detesting the
Germans, not specially drawn towards the French. After invading the
Grand Duchy the Germans annexed that prosperous little state,
declaring its citizens German nationals, therefore liable to be shot as

traitors if found fighting on the side of the Allies. They sent many Luxembourgers to concentration camps, and pillaged the Grand Ducal palace. In short there was nothing funny about the way Luxembourg had been treated, nor the courageous resistance to the Germans that had been put up. Nevertheless something of Comic Opera inescapably attached itself to the affairs of the Grand Duchy, those in charge of them not at all discouraging a certain atmosphere of high spirits and gaiety of tone. 'After all,' as the Prince of Luxembourg once remarked to me, 'As the Austrian Netherlands, we are quite separate from the Spanish Netherlands like Holland and Belgium', a splendidly historical point of view. Prince Felix, the Prince of Luxembourg (a Bourbon-Parma, brother of the ex-Empress Zita of Austria) was consort of the sovereign, Grand Duchess Charlotte, a lady of great distinction of character and bearing.

The demeanour of Prince Felix, a genial figure (who once confided to Carlisle that 'being a consort is a rotten job') by no means diminished the air of opera bouffe that brightened the Grand Duchy's Legation in Wilton Place, off Belgrave Square. If Prince Felix played a kind of *buffo bass*, whose humour with a touch of sentiment sometimes steals the show, the foil was André Clasen, Luxembourg Minister (later Ambassador), the man who did all the work, and lively, witty, with a taste for practical jokes, acted as *raisonneur* in the performance. The two of them might have sung a magnificent comic duet on the subject from opposite corners of the stage.

The Allied landings in North Africa of 1942 greatly changed French political circumstances. The special mission with the Free French in the UK was now dissolved, MIL dealing directly with the French army authorities, the liberation of France in due course bringing about the return to St James's of a French Ambassador and military attaché. I was once more promoted major, and, with two captains to help, added France to an existing empire of Belgium, Czechoslovakia, Luxembourg. When Italy left the Axis and joined the Allies, two Italian liaison officers were sent to London to undertake military contacts there. Owing to the exceptional nature of their position – neither former Allies, nor former Neutrals – no one had been deputed to look after them. They were offered to me. I should greatly have liked to take them on, but existing pressures of work made that impossible, something I have always regretted. I do not remember what finally happened to the Italians, but one of the problems was what they should wear – if anything – when they appeared in London. The terms of the capitulation laid down that Italian military personnel must not wear uniform out of Italy, while former enemy nationals, who had borne arms against the Allies, were forbidden to appear in civilian clothes in the United

Kingdom. If not precisely that, the difficulty of dress was in those areas. During the interim period between the dissolution of the special mission and return of a French military attaché, liaison was held together not so much by various officers of more senior rank as by Captain Jean Kéraudren (Kérnevel in *The Military Philosophers*), a convivial Breton in his fifties, long chief-clerk in the pre-war French military attaché's office, who, on the Fall of France, had been one of the first to volunteer for the Free French Forces.

In November, 1944, the Allies having penetrated about two miles beyond Germany's frontiers, it was decided to take the military attachés on a Continental tour to see something of the progress of the campaign. The Allies, fourteen in number, were shepherded by Carlisle and myself. In Normandy a night was spent at Cabourg, one model for Proust's Balbec, Carlisle and most of the party being billeted in the Grand Hotel, which had meant so much to Marcel, while, with four of the other military attachés, I was accommodated in the smaller Hôtel de Paris, a more modest affair. Although at the time I was struck by an indefinable charm the resort possessed even in wartime, I attributed that to the moving feelings that overwhelmed one on this return to France in such circumstances; not very discerningly, failing to grasp the Proustian significance of the town itself and the hotel. Only on return to England did the experience suddenly crystallize into appropriately Proustian shape in memory.

Main Headquarters, 21 Army Group gave the feeling of entering the precincts of a minor public school which had just defeated its chief rival on the football field. Everyone seemed young, aggressive, enormously pleased with himself, so much that normal army courtesies were sometimes forgotten. From Main HQ the military attachés' party, inspecting various things on the way, proceeded to the Army Commander's Tactical HQ. In *Dance* the Narrator passes through units of his former Division, no literary contrivance, actual personnel of The Welch Regiment being seen en route. It was also true – as I was able to remind Field-Marshal Montgomery, when he mistook my cap-badge for that of the Prince of Wales's Volunteers (a South Lancashire regiment) – that an officer of The Welch had recently been awarded a VC. Having attempted in *Dance* to convey something of Montgomery I have little to add here about the man himself. The atmosphere of his Tactical HQ was far less swaggering than Main HQ, though the two caravans (over which the military attachés were given a personally conducted tour), the brace of yapping dogs, the smiling sergeant suddenly materializing out of thin air with a camera, had all the marks of a set-piece.

Montgomery was then at the peak of a triumphant advance still just short of universally acknowledged victory. Already a stylized figure (which to some extent Montgomery had no doubt been throughout his career), he had not yet hardened into an exhibit, the immensely energetic mobile waxwork that his outward appearance seemed instantly to resemble after accomplishing the task appointed by history. On arrival the military attachés were drawn up in single rank (in order of their appointment, Kalla the senior), and presented one by one, as Carlisle accompanied Montgomery down the line. Lechat (Kronacker, soon to join the Belgian Government as Minister of Economics, having been summoned to Brussels), the most junior, was next to me at the far end. On hearing Lechat was Belgian, Montgomery spoke the words recorded in the novel, to the effect that, if the Belgian Resistance groups gave trouble (as they were showing signs of doing), he would 'shoot 'em up'. Lechat, dissatisfied with much that he found on return to his own country, was not in the least disposed to disagree with this principle. Kronacker would certainly not have dissented either, but I should have liked to witness Kronacker's confrontation with Montgomery. The question of the Belgian Resistance groups was soon to arise again in London in an acute form.

I have always found a certain fascination in the style of individual generals, even at the rank's lower levels, far more so those destined to find a place in the annals of war. On this very superficial contact Montgomery seemed to me to inspire confidence rather than admiration or devotion, but (tactical skills apart) no doubt his own instinct for what was required in our age for the army he was to command, the war to be fought, was substantially a sound one. There was something incongruous about the two badges in his béret, the battle-dress cut from smooth service-dress khaki cloth. Montgomery's personality was not well adapted to military chic. He looked better in an old pair of flannel trousers, pullover deliberately shown beneath battle-dress blouse, a fashion several of the military attachés had followed, then, seeing the mode had changed, hastily tucked up pullover ends. Yet the badges, the service-dress cloth, seemed to suggest in Montgomery a yearning for sartorial panache that some hiatus in taste precluded.

One used to hear of Montgomery's quirks when he had been a mere Corps Commander, but I do not remember him spoken of as inevitably marked out for great things. He was as far from being a rough diamond (displaying petty envy of officers close to him) as cutting a figure as *beau sabreur*; in some ways a very 'typical' soldier, in others never fitting comfortably into the extensive range of military eccentricity. There were unexpected sides to him. Nancy Mitford told me that Montgomery had expressed a wish to meet her at dinner in Paris, when he had revealed a perfectly competent knowledge of her novels.

Montgomery, his own consummate ad-man, was as different in exterior from such few other Great Captains of the time I have had opportunity to observe superficially, as they from each other. I have recorded in *Dance* how, as he burst through the hall of the War Office, the bare shout of 'Good-morning' on the part of Field-Marshal Sir Alan Brooke (later Viscount Alanbrooke) released a galvanizing out-give of energy. There too is recorded the tongue-tiedness of Field-Marshal Viscount Slim. A contrast to all of these was Marshal of the Royal Air Force Sir Charles Portal (Viscount Portal by the time I came across him after the war), who some have supposed the outstanding leader of all. For some years after the war he was Chairman of The Travellers' General Committee, on which I myself for a time sat. Even if club committees are likely to be composed of those who know how best to get quickly through the work required, occasionally an indivi-dual will speak too long, fail to grasp an obvious point, ride some hobbyhorse of his own. With the immense prestige Portal had acquired in the war, he also possessed an infallible ability for summarizing the needs of the Club. At the same time I never saw him by the flicker of an eyelid show impatience, much less crush a speaker who was stupid or prosy. Portal was indeed a leader for whom one guessed it would have been easily possible to feel devotion, though I never knew him personally. The only conclusion seems to be that all sorts are required at the top if a war is to be won.

When Kronacker returned to London after his Brussels consultations he telephoned at once, asking me to come over to Eaton Square. When I arrived at his office he said immediate danger was threatened by the Belgian Resistance groups, some of which were getting daily more out of hand. These groups were chiefly recruited from young men of ex-emplary patriotism, grown up under four and a half years of German occupation, now desperately needing some sort of active employment. Few had been in action against the invaders, and naturally a great deal of frustration was felt, even though members of the Resistance had by now been cadred into some sort of army. More sinister was the fact that some of these groups were dominated by Communist elements, whose aim was to spread confusion with a view to revolution. One form of doing that was by inciting antagonisms (at best a chronic Belgian problem) between Flemish-speakers and French-speakers. The King's abdication was demanded in some quarters. In short, obstruction to the sorting out in a peaceful manner of the many difficulties arising from the liberation, indeed actual threats to democratic government, were very serious indeed.

The Belgian Government's suggested solution to the Resistance Question was that about 30,000 of those who made up this irregular force – say two Divisions – should be sent to the United Kingdom for training. On the face of it that seemed an excellent idea. The point was how soon such a proposal could be first agreed, then implemented.

Clearly the importation of 30,000 Belgians into the UK would have to be a Cabinet decision. Speedy arrangement of the move was not so much menaced at this height, as by details which would have to be worked out lower down. Senior civil servants at the War Office were capable of acting without delay; at lower levels, on the other hand, a love of obstruction was in places deeply rooted on the civil side.

Kronacker was clearly very worried. In any case it looked as if nothing could be done until Monday, because this was the end of the week; as it happened, the Friday before I went away for a fortnightly two days of leave. The normal process to set things in motion would be for a War Office File (a more portentous affair than a mere Branch File) to be opened. I should draft the minute (memorandum) – to be approved by Carlisle and one of the two Brigadiers of the MI Directorate – which would then be signed by the Director of Military Intelligence, and circulated at major-generals' level. Brussels might well be in flames, the Belgian Cabinet hanging from lamp-posts, while the Finance Branch of the War Office was still discussing the monetary minutiae of the proposal.

Then I remembered that, some months before this, Kronacker – who went about more in London than most of the military attachés – had mentioned as worthy of note that on some social occasion he had come across 'Major Morton'. At that we both smiled. Major (later Sir) Desmond Morton, Personal Assistant to the Prime Minister, was universally regarded as a powerful figure, not less so because a certain aura of mystery surrounded his activities. This seemed an excellent opportunity to test the authenticity of Morton's reputation.

'Ring up Morton and say you would like an interview with him as soon as he can possibly give you one. Tell him it's vital. He won't object. That's what he's there for. Repeat to him exactly what you've just told me. Say the War Office has been informed through the usual channels, and your contacts there are at once putting forward the Belgian Government's suggestion. Ask Morton to consider setting the matter before the Prime Minister himself as soon as possible.'

'Shall I tell Colonel Carlisle?'

'No – certainly not.'

Carlisle would have been horrified by the notion of approaching Morton, not because in principle he himself objected in the least to backstairs intrigue, but on account of the enormous respect he felt for his superiors in rank. Kronacker turned the matter over in his mind for a minute or two. 'Very well,' he said. 'I'll get in touch with Major Morton, if you really recommend that.' I returned to the War Office, and reported to Carlisle (leaving out Morton) the situation Kronacker had outlined. Carlisle went at once to the appropriate Brigadier, the two of them then conferring with the DMI. The consequence was, as envisaged, that a War Office File was put into circulation on the subject. That night I went off to Dunstall for the weekend.

Soon after my arrival in the M I L room on Monday morning, Carlisle rang down to say I was to see him at once. I found him in a state of some excitement. A message had been transmitted direct from the Prime Minister (in itself calculated to make Carlisle assume what Dru called 'his religious face') to the effect that movement of the Belgian Resistance Force to Great Britain was to take place forthwith, and be treated as a matter of urgent priority. Accordingly, said Carlisle, a meeting presided over by the Director of Staff Duties (major-general of branch deciding, so to speak, which bit of the army does what) would take place in an hour's time. I was to be there.

'This is an extraordinary thing to have happened, Tony,' said Carlisle. 'I can't understand it. Somebody very high up must have spoken the right word.'

At the meeting the D S D announced that 30,000 Belgian troops were to be transported as soon as possible to Northern Ireland, quarters vacated not long before by the U S Expeditionary Force. The Belgians were installed in Northern Ireland within a very creditably short space of time. Neither Kronacker nor I ever spoke of our initial collusion in the matter.

One of the dramas witnessed in slow motion by M I L – though not, I am glad to say, an affair in which I was compelled personally to be involved – was British disengagement from Allied support of General Mihailovich's Nationalist partisans in Jugoslavia, in favour of transferring all assistance to the Communist forces headed by Tito, later Marshal Tito. Jugoslav liaison was in the charge of Ker, who was responsible for a laughable byproduct of what was in itself an essentially tragic turn of events.

John Plamenatz, rather unexpectedly for a Fellow of All Souls, was a Montenegrin. His family had emigrated from Montenegro at the end of the first war. In due course Plamenatz himself grew up to be an academic of some distinction at Oxford. When the second war broke out in 1939, Plamenatz, who must have been a British subject by this time, joined the Royal Artillery in the ranks, but when Jugoslavia came in on the side of the Allies, was transferred to the Free Jugoslav Forces, in which he became an officer. I confess that I am not quite clear how this could have happened. I should have supposed him to have been given a commission in the Intelligence Corps, and sent to the Jugoslavs as an attached liaison officer, but no doubt there were conveniences in such matters as pay, for example, to approve otherwise. Plamenatz was employed, so far as I remember, in the King's Office of the Jugoslav Government in exile.

When the unedifying transference of British patronage from Mihailovich to Tito took place – after which Mihailovich was judicially murdered by his Communist compatriots – Plamenatz, without giving the least thought as to what would happen to him in a changed military status, simply resigned from the Free Jugoslav army. This left him in his earlier condition of being a gunner in the British Royal Artillery. By this stage of the war Plamenatz's original unit was in Burma. It is unlikely that he would have been posted back to them – though one can never tell in the army – more probably sent to some draft-supplying centre of the RA. He had behaved honourably in joining the army in the first instance (which as an academic, not to mention an academic of Montenegrin parentage, he could certainly have side-stepped), and it was not unreasonable that he should feel less than disposed once more to revert to the ranks. For the moment he had been granted extended leave, but the prospect of being recalled to the British army hung over him. He asked me whether M I L could do anything to remedy his case.

I consulted Ker. Cupping his ear occasionally, Ker listened to the Plamenatz story. At its end his expression did not change. He nodded his head several times sagely.

'I'll go into the matter,' he said.

Some days later Ker invited me over to the table where he sat. He did not speak at first, merely shaking his head from side to side.

'I can't get your man out of the British army,' he said at last. 'No. I can't do that. There's no machinery to do that. He's bound to be called up sooner or later, if no further action is taken about him. That's what we don't want. Don't want that, do we? I've thought about his position a lot, talked it over with several of the Sections concerned, or those who might be concerned. It's a difficult question. Seems no way out. Still we'll have to do our best. This is what I consider the most hopeful course to follow. I'll get a file circulating on him, setting out his position from both the British point of view and the Jugoslav point of view. I'll send that file off to all branches that might be interested – there are a good number of those in the case of a man like that – circulating it in such a way that the question can never, if you understand me, be disentangled. The file, with all the facts about him in it, from the manner in which I've worded my minute, can't avoid going backwards and forwards from Section to Section. Questions not at all possible to sort out. No action can really ever be taken. So long as nothing is decided, he can't be called up. If you agree, I'll go ahead. Would that suit him, do you think? Sorry I haven't been able to do better than that.'

I said that seemed an admirable solution. Ker nodded gravely, and returned to his many other files. I passed on the information to Plamenatz. He was delighted. Now he could earn a living by lecturing on Political Science, a vocation he followed undisturbed until peace came.

While Violet was living at Dunstall she came to know a widow in her late fifties, Margaret Behrens, who was a very good friend to us at about this time. Just before the flying-bombs began Margaret Behrens invited Violet, with Tristram, to stay in a cottage she had taken at Lee, a seaside village three or four miles from Ilfracombe. This was of some consequence in our lives, as we not only decided later to go to Lee for a month or so after I left the army, but often subsequently revisited its bay with the children. During this stay in North Devon the flying bombs settled down to a regular twenty-four hour transit over Shoreham on the way to London. Violet had already done her share of standing up to bombardment from the air, and it seemed wise to delay return to Kent until this infliction had at least lessened. Accordingly she led a nomadic life for some months. We then moved once more into Chester Gate, where the worst of the bomb damage had been more or less repaired. For a time we were joined there by Alick and Gabriel Dru.

Through Margaret Behrens, during the later years of the war we first met T. S. Eliot. Eliot was also an old friend of her great crony, Hope Mirrlees, unmarried, with Bloomsbury associations in early life, though now settled down to a less exacting intellectual condition of comfortable upper-middlebrowdom. Hope Mirrlees lived with her mother, a well-off widow, and a disgruntled spinster aunt. The aunt was for some reason supposed not to smoke. When Eliot called at the Mirrlees house, the aunt (like Harold Brookenham borrowing a sovereign from his parents' guests in *The Awkward Age*) would waylay the poet as he passed through the hall in an effort to scrounge cigarettes. Tom Eliot, a goodnatured man, would bestow a few, but, being also strait-laced, assuaged his conscience by never releasing quite so many cigarettes as were demanded by the aunt.

By the time of the Thanksgiving Service for Victory at St Paul's, 19 August, 1945, Carlisle, Ker, Bradfield, Dru, the Old Guard of MIL, had returned to civil life. This erosion brought me, so far as seniority went, into the position of second-in-command of the Section, which had been taken over some months before by a mild Regular, who had spent most of the war as a prisoner.

One of Dru's letters (21 February, 1947) says: 'For years I have owned most of Péguy's work, and am running through it with the greatest possible interest. The titles bear no relation to the subject which is annoying enough, but the style is a nightmare of heavy repetition. But he is the only man I have ever read who makes sense of French history, and (most flatteringly) confirms all my suspicions about the nineteenth century. Orwell (superficially) has some links. Indeed, I have wondered several times whether he has not read him.' During my War Office association with Dru I had brought him and Orwell together, but the meeting of the three of us at lunch was not a great success. That was not, so far as might be guessed, because either Dru or Orwell took a dislike to the other, but, each possessing an intermittent tendency to withdraw into his own shell, this happened almost the whole time throughout luncheon. There was no apparent antipathy; equally no communication. Dru's suggestion that Orwell had read Charles Péguy (1873–1914), French essayist and poet, whose earlier socialist convictions turned to patriotic enthusiasm and mystical Catholicism, is interesting in the light of a letter (10 July, 1948, *Orwell Letters IV*) from Orwell to Julian Symons, sent about eighteen months later than Dru's remarks to me on the subject. Orwell (at that time in a Lanarkshire hospital) wrote: 'He [Léon Bloy] irritates me rather, and Péguy, whom I also tried recently, made me feel unwell.' This seems to indicate that Orwell's reading of Péguy must have been subsequent in time to Dru's finding some resemblance between the two of them; suspicion of some such similarity perhaps additionally fretting Orwell.

A work Dru caused me to read was Amiel's *Diary*, celebrated on the Continent, inexplicably little known in this country, even among professional intellectuals. Indeed Cyril Connolly's lively squib – in a sense Connolly's swan-song – about Logan Pearsall Smith in *The Evening Colonnade* (1973) invokes Amiel (with Joubert, Vauvenargues, and Logan Pearsall Smith himself) as typification of literary oblivion. The interest that Dru aroused in me for the *Journal intime* of Henri-Frédéric Amiel (1821–1881) had a small public repercussion after the war, which may be recorded out of chronological order. It also made me reflect on Amiel's possible influence on Joseph Conrad, something which, so far as I know, has never been investigated.

Amiel, a professor of philosophy at Geneva, fits into Dru's canon of 'psychological' writers who seem to anticipate Proust and Freud in observations about human character, in Amiel's case notably his own. A somewhat ineffective heterosexual, Amiel was perfectly conscious of a lack of enterprise with women, treating with deprecatory humour the fact that he was verging on forty before acquiring a mistress. Conrad visited Geneva more than once. In 1891, after the Congo experiences embodied in *Heart of Darkness* (1902), he recuperated at a sanatorium in that neighbourhood, where he wrote some of *Almayer's Folly* (1895). *Almayer's Folly* has for epigraph a sentence from Amiel's *Journal intime*: '*Qui de nous n'a eu sa terre promise, son jour d'extase et sa fin en exil?*' This strikingly Conradian rhetorical question makes me wonder if Conrad had already come across the *Journal* before these Swiss visits, or was introduced to Amiel when staying at Geneva. At all events he places most of the action of *Under Western Eyes* in Geneva. *Under Western Eyes* again shows Conrad's familiarity with Amiel's *Journal*. The narrative revolves round a group of Russian refugees in Switzerland, one of whom, Peter Ivanovitch has made an incredible escape across Asia from imprisonment in Siberia. Peter Ivanovitch's adventures, somewhat satirically recalled by Conrad, seem based on Amiel's reference to memoirs the diarist had been reading, written by a Polish political prisoner, who had made a similar flight from a Russian prison.

Conrad may well have seen his own compatriot's book, but the tone in which he writes – making fun of Peter Ivanovitch's pretentiousness, while not denying the genuineness of the experience – suggests that he borrowed Amiel's recorded amazement as a reader in order to strengthen the picture of the character in *Under Western Eyes*. Indeed Amiel's reference could have started Conrad's train of thought in using the whole Genevan connexion. Amiel, without Conrad's painful knowledge, as a Pole, of Russian political attitudes, was himself free of illusion on that subject. The *Journal intime* (1 July, 1856) comments: 'What terrible masters the Russians would be if ever they should spread the might of their rule over the countries of the South! They would bring us a Polar despotism – tyranny such as the world has never known, silent as darkness, rigid as ice, insensible as bronze, decked with an outer amiability and glittering with the cold brilliance of snow, slavery without compensation or relief; this is what they would bring us.'

Towards the close of my army service I wrote a couple of pieces about Amiel (*The Cornhill*, December, 1945: April, 1946), quoting Amiel's views on the Russian political character. The article appeared at a moment when the Soviet Union's policies were hardening into unconcealed antagonism towards the West, in short the beginnings of what was to be called the Cold War.

In one of Mr Attlee's speeches aimed at a more realistic approach to Soviet attitudes, the Prime Minister, attributing the words to a 'wise old Swiss philosopher', quoted Amiel's reflections on Russian political characteristics quoted above. They seem likely to have been brought to his notice by what was in *The Cornhill*; something that might have surprised Amiel, but in which he would have found quiet satisfaction as a diary-entry.

My three months leave, routine period preceding final demobilization, began in September, 1945. At one time or another Violet had put up at various houses in Lee in North Devon. She was now established at Chapel Cottage, belonging to Miss Maud Armstrong, where I joined her. Maud Armstrong was a preponderant figure in Lee's social hierarchy. She was indeed generally recognized as its summit. Then in her early seventies (she lived to ninety or thereabouts) an attractively gnomelike appearance made her seem, in the best and most complimentary sense, a witch. Her life had known romantic aspects. She was a doctor's daughter without much in the way of prospects. Then the young and beautiful widow of a well-to-do parson had unexpectedly bequeathed to her a small but comfortable sufficiency.

Soon after our own arrival at Lee, T. S. Eliot turned up there. He lodged at a farm, but spent most of the time with the Mirrlees family, mother and daughter, who had also taken rooms in the neighbourhood. Eliot was known to us then only from one or two meetings in London, and a dinner at Chester Gate. Now we saw a certain amount of him, usually in the company of Margaret Behrens and Hope Mirrlees.

When I had first set eyes on Eliot in 1927 or 1928, dining by himself at The Étoile, a Charlotte Street restaurant, Eliot (no doubt on his way to a party) was wearing a dinner-jacket. Someone remarked: 'They say Eliot is always drunk these days.' I found that fascinating too, though he seemed perfectly sober when, walking rather quickly, he made his way out into the street. After one came to know him better Tom Eliot was inscrutable only in his mild amiability. The undemanding chit-chat of tea-time and cream cakes (if procurable) seemed the stimulants he needed, giving a rest from poetry, high thinking, very genuine 'good works'. He was the incarnation of his own pronouncement (made in the context of writing rather than behaviour) that 'no artist produces great art by a deliberate attempt to express his own personality'. Eliot, encountered in the Mirrlees household, drinking a pint or two of cider in the pub, dropping in at our bungalow on the cliffs at the end of one of his long solitary walks (wearing a cap and carrying a stick), always kept conversation to light topics, making fun of *The New Statesman* about as far as seriousness was allowed to stray.

Eliot must, I think, have been rather different as a young man: the violent enthusiasms; the boxing; the attempt (precluded by ill health) to join the navy in the first war. No doubt forces from which such elements had taken shape were still active enough within, but they were now concealed. I used to wonder what impression would have survived after an encounter with him during which for some reason Eliot's name and identity had remained unrevealed. Would one, for instance, have guessed American origins? His faint accent was not exactly English, at the same time not recognizably American, anyway to an English ear used to the general run of Americans who come to England. Friendly,

easy, picking up instantaneously the most lightly suggested nuance in
conversation, Eliot had also just a touch of the headmaster, laying aside
his dignity for a talk with the more intelligent boys, boys from whom
he was quite prepared to pick up something for his own use; indeed
a headmaster who had learnt deep humility from shattering experiences.
None the less the façade of buttered scones and toasted crumpets –
both representing a perfectly genuine taste in Eliot – was by this time
all but impenetrable.

> I smile, of course,
> And go on drinking tea.

This amalgam of tea-party cosiness with a cold intellectuality, the
more menacing because strictly implicit rather than explicit, gave Tom
Eliot's personality that very peculiar flavour, which even the most high-
powered of his contemporaries seem at times to have found, if not
exactly intimidating, at least restraining.

Eliot could be entertaining about embarrassments suffered by himself
as a famous poet. Discussing with Violet the restorative effects of
massage, he described how his own masseuse, at a moment when he
could not escape from her clutches, said: 'Mr Eliot, I dreamt last night
that I saw a child drawing with a reed on the water. I knew this child
must be the spirit of William Blake. Do you know why Blake revealed
himself to me, Mr Eliot? It was so that I should tell you to write more
poetry than you have been doing lately.'

'Although I look at everything from an English point of view now,'
Eliot said, 'at times my Americanness returns like a flash. That's when
I hear someone over here assume as a matter of course that, if an
American is described as a gentleman, he must of necessity come from
the South.'

Eliot liking ghost stories, I told about the haunted bungalow in which
I had lived as a child. He responded with a story I record with diffidence, being neither my own, nor anything to do with me, but seeming
to deserve preservation in giving support to the existence of hauntings
lacking what vintners call bottle-age. Eliot had not known personally
the member of the Faber family concerned, but had been told the story
by the publisher of that name, in whose firm Eliot himself worked.

In the 1930s Mr Faber, hero of the anecdote, had been one of a fishing
syndicate renting a house in Scotland for the season. He travelled north
to take over this house, a comparatively modern one, before the others
arrived. A severe attack of toothache developing in the train, he had
a painful night at the house, but managed to find a dentist the following day, who sufficiently put things right for a satisfactory fishing
holiday to follow. Some years later this Mr Faber (or possibly another
member of the syndicate) was talking to a fellow fisherman in a club

or on a train; one of those classic encounters which provide the dénouement of so many ghost stories. The stranger turned out not only familiar with the sport as practised in that corner of Scotland, but revealed himself as having been member of a fishing syndicate renting that very same house.

'Did you catch a lot of fish?'

'The fishing was all right. Very good. There was one drawback, rather an unusual one. The house was haunted. Did none of your party notice that when you stayed there? Several of ours saw the ghost. It was a man walking up and down in one of the rooms, holding his face, as if he had terrible toothache.'

In about 1952, just before we moved to the country, the *Times Literary Supplement* gave a party for its contributors in the 'private house' at Old Printing House Square. Tom Eliot was there, and John Hayward in his wheelchair. About halfway through the party Hayward beckoned me.

'The Bard's accountant has been complaining that he doesn't get sufficient documentary evidence for the Inland Revenue that the Bard spends money entertaining other writers and publishers, so Tom's asking a few friends to dinner at the Savoy Grill tonight, and hopes you'll both join us.'

Hayward's passion for parties caused him almost always to remain until what was often no empty phrase in being termed the bitter end. As someone had to wheel out the chair before his own withdrawal was possible Hayward was in an exceptionally strong position with all but the most ruthless. At the close of the *TLS* assemblage there might have been two or three guests over and above the half-dozen or so making up Eliot's dinner-party (Violet the only woman), these remnants unlikely to hold out on their own, if supporting elements represented by Eliot, Hayward, the auxiliaries, retired in a body. Meanwhile the host and proprietor of *The Times*, Colonel John Jacob Astor (later Lord Astor of Hever), had no means of knowing that the retreat of the Eliot/ Hayward forces would terminate the jollification. Colonel Astor's face, drawn with anxiety at the prospect of apparent unending festivity, suddenly brightened and beamed into a happy smile, as Eliot turned and firmly took hold of the back of Hayward's wheelchair.

Return to London from North Devon shortly before Christmas, 1945, opened up a régime of working on Aubrey at Oxford during the middle of the week, spending only long weekends at Chester Gate. In the second week of January I found a telephone message at Balliol (accepted, it seems, rather unwillingly at the porter's lodge, where it was assumed I was in hiding at the College), instructing me to return to London. When I rang up the nursing-home the following morning (11 January) I was told Violet had given birth to our second son, John.

This was a grisly period, in some respects – fortitudes now relaxed – harder to put up with than the war. At Chester Gate, the house next door, with which we shared a water-main, had been gutted in the blitz, so that every time its roofless frozen pipes were systematically unfrozen during the day, they froze again at night. For three weeks baths depended on the charity of friends whose taps still ran hot water. Apart from work on Aubrey, I was reviewing for *The Daily Telegraph*, *The Spectator*, anywhere else available. *The Spectator*'s literary editor, W. J. Turner, poet ('Chimborazo, Cotopaxi, took me by the hand') and music critic, was an Australian. Turner (whose accent Bloomsbury found 'distressing') had known D. H. Lawrence and kindred writers and painters of the pre-1914 world. He and his wife had been staying at Garsington on one of my visits there in undergraduate days, but naturally enough no contacts had been made. Turner must already have been brooding on his Peacockian dialogue, *The Aesthetes* (1927), where guests gathered in a country house discourse on art and letters, in which Lady Ottoline Morrell is herself caricatured. *The Aesthetes* gave great offence at Garsington, a bad situation being made worse by W. B. Yeats, one of Lady Ottoline's most prized lions, writing in praise of the book. Walter Turner, sallow, slight in build, his movements quick and nervous, gave the impression of being eternally fed up with the human race. He had a name for antagonizing people, especially in the musical sphere, but I found him not at all unsympathetic. I should have liked to hear something of his early days in London, but that was prevented by Turner suddenly dying in his late fifties. He was followed on the paper by a much younger literary editor, barely thirty, one of only two or three persons I have known to be murdered.

Within about a year of returning to civil life Malcolm Muggeridge, with all his family, moved into a flat just round the corner from us in Cambridge Gate. Muggeridge was then leader-writing for *The Daily Telegraph*, of which newspaper he was later to become Washington Correspondent and Deputy Editor. Seeing a good deal of him led as a matter of course to meeting again Hugh Kingsmill, Muggeridge's lifelong friend, whom I had come across years before when Duckworth's published some of his books, though never known well. Kingsmill was now literary editor of the *New English Review*, to the book pages of which I became a contributor. This magazine, which had its eccentric side, was edited by Douglas Jerrold, whose more substantial position was as chairman of Eyre & Spottiswoode, the publishing firm of which Graham Greene, soon after the end of the war, had become managing director.

The Eyre & Spottiswoode/*New English Review* axis largely revolved on the Authors Club, an odd little backwater housed in Whitehall Court, the massive block of flats standing between the Old War Office building and the River, in the restaurant of which I had read aloud to Mrs Syrie Maugham my film 'treatment' about her father, Dr Barnardo. Kingsmill, Muggeridge, Greene, myself for a short period, were all members of The Authors, from the smoking-room of which Kingsmill virtually edited the book pages of the *New English Review*. If consultation was necessary – or talk about literature, love, marriage, the meaning of life, anything but politics – Kingsmill was always to be found asleep every afternoon in one of the upright chairs; a coma from which he would emerge for tea at about four o'clock.

Greene, like Muggeridge, had spent the latter years of the war in the Secret Service. A man of very considerable practical ability, his nervous energy, organizing faculty, taste for conflict, sudden bursts of rage, would have made him successful in most professions; indeed I can think of few in which he might not have made a mark. He soon set humming the veteran engine of Eyre & Spottiswoode. As an actor on this stage-set, Douglas Jerrold seemed in certain respects to have strayed in from another play. He belonged to Kingsmill's generation, was a Roman Catholic convert like Greene, took a vehement interest in politics as did Muggeridge, but at the same time could hardly be said to belong to the accustomed world of any of those three.

If Kingsmill's demeanour always suggested a touch of Victorian moral complacency, a far more pervasive whiff of another form of Victorianism was habitually borne in the wake of Jerrold, the Victorian Englishman's determination to stand up for his rights. Jerrold's life was a perpetual round of making paper mountains out of political molehills, and breaking literary butterflies on the wheels of publishing. Muggeridge used to call him Mr Forcible Feeble. Large, sombrely dressed, immensely gloomy (sounding on the telephone as if already in Purgatory) Jerrold had been employed as a young man in the Treasury. One cannot help wondering sometimes about those recruited for the Treasury. Does it explain otherwise incomprehensible aspects of how we are governed? Jerrold, for instance, could bring instantaneous and inextricable confusion to the simplest transaction.

When *John Aubrey and His Friends* was finished I took Muggeridge's advice, and gave the biography to Graham Greene to read. A contract was signed with Eyre & Spottiswoode in May, 1946, undertaking that the book would appear within nine months from that date. The publication was continually postponed, until at last, two and a half years after the delivery of the manuscript, the biography was scheduled to appear in the late autumn of 1948. Not very long before this projected publication date, Greene, Muggeridge and I, all three lunched at The

314 *Faces in My Time*

Authors. In the course of the meal Greene revealed that Eyre & Spottiswoode's had decided once more to delay publication, this time until some
unstated moment in the New Year. I had raised no difficulties at all
about previous deferments, knowing something of current publishing
difficulties involved, but 1946 to 1949 was too much. I made a fairly
vigorous demur. There was a brisk exchange, in the course of which
Greene said: 'It's a bloody boring book anyway.'

Having myself worked in a publisher's office, I know how tiresome
authors can be, especially when – showing complete disregard for a
publisher's carefully worked out programme – they merely fuss about
the precise date on which their own (indeed often bloody boring) book
is due to appear. At the same time, even in post-war conditions, nearly
three years might be looked on as approaching a near Olympic record
in making an author wait. In addition to that Greene's comment, perfectly acceptable as the bluff judgment of some friend not much conversant with the 17th century, or salutary criticism of a fellow novelist
dissatisfied with the technical arrangement of biographical material,
was, to say the least, discouraging from the managing director of the
firm responsible for marketing the book in question. This scene now
strikes me as hilarious. At the time I was ruffled.

I said it was to be presumed that Greene's words implied release
from a contract that offered further books of mine to Eyre & Spottiswoode. Greene agreed that consequence was implicit in the view he
had expressed. The rest of the luncheon passed without incident. A
disharmony of this kind was one calculated to motivate an absolute
torrent of verbiage in Jerrold. Letters poured from him. One of these
included the piquant image: 'Graham has no more power to release
you from your contract with this firm than I have to sell the company's furniture.' I was, however, unaware of the Second Act of the
drama, the First Act of which had been played in the Authors Club
dining-room. Greene's brusqueness with me on account of the dissatisfaction I had expressed about his firm had been followed apparently at the office by a row about the firm's treatment of myself.
That at least is the impression given by his own subsequent letters.
The antithetical gestures would not be out of character. No doubt
there were many other reasons why Greene no longer wished to
remain a publisher; my own case, at least to some extent, seems to
have provided a *casus belli* for resignation from the Eyre & Spottiswoode board.

In the end all terminated comparatively happily, because *John Aubrey
and His Friends* (a very respectable piece of book production in the
light of the difficulties of that moment) was after all published late
in 1948. The biography sold well for a study of that sort, going into
a second printing. A revised edition, in which a certain amount in the

way of correction and new information was incorporated, was issued by Heinemann in 1963.

Just before taking over the editorship of the *Times Literary Supplement* Alan Pryce-Jones suggested I should come in two or three days a week to supervise novel-reviewing. I accepted the offer, remaining for several years, during which I reviewed a novel myself most weeks, sometimes other books, and from time to time wrote (features now abolished) 'fronts' and 'middles'. In one sense, at least outwardly, Pryce-Jones continued to pursue a professional path that appeared the reverse of strenuous. When parties began slowly to come into being again there were truancies from the office. At the same time *TLS* reviewers seemed to become a shade less stodgy overnight, a faint but perceptible odour of chic sometimes drifting through the dusty caverns of Printing House Square.

In 1947 the second volume of Jean-Paul Sartre's trilogy, *The Roads to Freedom* (*Les Chemins de la Liberté*), *The Reprieve* (*Le Sursis*), arrived at the *TLS*. Communist in flavour, forgoing the humour of which Sartre later showed himself capable, though not, as things turned out, without all touch of impishness, the style was influenced by the experimental schools of twenty or thirty years before whose language was usually English. When the episodes took place at different levels of the narrative, sentences and paragraphs were sometimes dovetailed together by a colon, in a manner to disregard time and space in the course of events there described. I reviewed *The Reprieve* for the *TLS*. The action takes place in late summer 1938, the week of Neville Chamberlain's negotiations with Adolf Hitler at Munich. The *dramatis personae* of the book include the major political figures of the meeting, certain members of their entourage, together with characters of the author's invention. In order to illustrate the intricate nature of the style employed by Sartre I quoted towards the end of my review:

Messrs. Hubert Masaryk and Mastay, members of the Czechoslovak delegation, were waiting in Sir Horace Wilson's room in the company of Mr Ashton-Gwatkin. Mastay was pale and perspiring, with dark circles under his eyes. Hubert Masaryk paced up and down. Mr Ashton-Gwatkin sat on the bed: Ivich had slipped away to her own side of the bed, she wasn't touching him, but she could feel his warmth and hear his breathing: she couldn't sleep, and she knew he wasn't asleep either.

This paragraph of the novel terminated with these further sentences, which I did not quote:

Electric discharges sped through her legs and thighs, she longed to turn over on her back, but if she moved he would touch her: so long as he thought her asleep he would leave her alone. Mastay turned to Ashton-Gwatkin and said: 'It's lasting a long time.'

I closed my review with the comment: 'But what purpose is served by suggesting to the reader's mind that Ivich was taking this silent share in the negotiations?'

F. T. A. Ashton-Gwatkin, CB CMG, was in fact Counsellor in the Diplomatic Service from which he had that very year retired. He did not take Sartre's mention of himself in at all good part. In fact a lawyer's letter imputing libel speedily arrived at the offices of *The Times* and to Sartre's London publisher. Under threat of legal action both publisher and newspaper capitulated at once. Ashton-Gwatkin received an apology and 'sum which recognized the force of his complaint and emphasized the sincerity of their regret' for what was defined as 'the unconventional literary style adopted by the author'. The trouble was the colon. If there had been a full-stop, had all the sentences in the book – even in the paragraph – terminated with a colon, things might have been different.

Ashton-Gwatkin, a clergyman's son, had been at Eton (by odd coincidence at the same house as my own years before), proceeding to Balliol, where he had won that laurel, sometimes fairly lightly proffered, the Newdigate Prize Poem: the subject that year (1909) being *Michelangelo*. As the Newdigate suggests, Ashton-Gwatkin himself aspired to literary ambitions, which he did not abandon in later life. He wrote several novels under the pseudonym John Paris, also producing a volume of verse with the title *A Japanese Don Juan*. I have read only *Kimono* (1921), a work put into paperback only a few months before publication of *The Reprieve* in England. The story opens in 1913, with the fashionable marriage of Captain the Honourable Geoffrey Barrington (a peer by the end of the book) at St George's, Hanover Square, to a Japanese girl, beautiful, rich, orphaned. The photograph of the author on the cover makes one suspect that Barrington, a huge bearlike simple-hearted Englishman, is a self-portrait. Barrington (apparently even after marriage) 'had never gazed on a naked woman except idealized in marble or on canvas', but in Tokyo licentious friends take him to brothels, where 'against the yellow skin the violet nipples glowed like poisonous berries'. Barrington, profoundly disturbed, becomes preoccupied with the evils of prostitution in Japan.

Although his wife's income is £20,000 a year neither Barrington nor she have ever bothered to explore the sources of this money. At a moment when other matrimonial tribulations beset them, her riches turn out to be derived from a chain of Japanese brothels. Violet-coloured nipples like poisonous berries are by no means the only gaudy images of sex, conjured up with a good deal of relish, in *Kimono*. If, as it was rumoured he planned, Sartre had come to London to defend his novel in court, a great legal comedy – not to say farce – was missed.

*

I had been turning over in my mind the possibility of writing a novel composed of a fairly large number of volumes, just how many could not be decided at the outset. A long sequence seemed to offer all sorts of advantages, among them release from the re-engagement every year or so of the same actors and extras hanging about for employment at the stagedoor of one's creative fantasy. Instead of sacking the lot at the end of a brief run – with the moral certainty that at least one or two of the more tenacious will be back again seeking a job, if not this year or next, then in a decade's time – the production itself might be extended, the actors made to work longer and harder for much the same creative remuneration spread over an extended period; instead of being butchered at regular intervals to make a publisher's holiday.

There were many objections to setting out on such a hazardous road, chiefly the possibility of collapse, imaginatively speaking; simply dying (something bound to happen sooner or later) before completing the book. The eighty-thousand-word fetters would not be entirely struck off, if normal processes of commercial publication were accepted but such disciplining of the writing might have advantages in checking too diffuse a pattern, by imposing a series of shorter sections each more or less complete in itself. Certain technical matters had to be settled at once for early establishment of a sufficiently broad base at the start from which a complex narrative might arise; fan out; be sustained over a period of years. This meant that undeveloped characters, potential situations, must be introduced, whose purpose might be unresolved throughout several volumes of the sequence. Perhaps understandably, only very few critics of the opening volumes showed themselves capable of appreciating that, in reality, quite simple principle. An essential point to decide, from the opening sentence, was whether to use a first-person or third-person narrative. I concluded that the first-person narrative was preferable in dodging the artificiality of the invented 'hero', who speaks for the author.

At a fairly early stage in tackling this matter, I found myself in the Wallace Collection, standing in front of Nicolas Poussin's picture there given the title *A Dance to the Music of Time*. An almost hypnotic spell seems cast by this masterpiece on the beholder. I knew all at once that Poussin had expressed at least one important aspect of what the novel must be. The precise allegory which Poussin's composition adumbrates is disputed. I have accepted the view that the dancing figures (three female, one male) are the Seasons, though some suppose they represent the Destiny of Man, as conditioned by Pleasure and Riches, Poverty and Work, an explanation perhaps now more fashionable. The young man, lightly clad, wears a crown of laurel, so he may be Fame. Wealth (if she is Wealth), in a yellow petticoat, does no more than touch the wrist of her sister, Poverty (if she is Poverty), whose head is crowned with a turban. Phoebus drives his horses across the heavens; Time plucks the strings of his lyre. There is no doubt a case for asserting that the dancers are not easily identifiable as Spring, Summer, Autumn, Winter. They seem no less ambiguous as Pleasure, Riches, Poverty, Work, or perhaps Fame. In relation to my own mood, the latter interpretations would be equally applicable. The picture was painted (probably between 1637 and 1639) for Clement IX, and its subject may have been based on personal fantasies chosen by that Rospigliosi pope. The one thing certain is that the four main figures depicted are dancing to Time's tune.

When *A Question of Upbringing*, the first volume of the sequence, was finished – and I was free to find another publisher – Malcolm Muggeridge, at that moment literary adviser to Heinemann's, persuaded me to go there (as formerly to Eyre & Spottiswoode), where I have remained for more than thirty years. At Heinemann's I first met Roland Gant, then recently emerged from a notable war career (which had included digging his own grave, at the end of which the Germans thought better of shooting him), who had a period of infidelity to Heinemann's with another publishing firm, but, reconciliation taking place, returned there to look after me and my books with untold devotion over the years.

Two friends dating from this period of the late 1940s were Osbert Lancaster and Harry d'Avigdor-Goldsmid, who both belonged to the Oxford generation following my own, a less fruity undergraduate vintage perhaps than its antecedent, but one with plenty of bouquet.

Lancaster enjoys the comparatively rare advantage (instanced in the case of Constant Lambert) of being at home not only in the graphic arts he practises, but also in writing and music. His early training as an architect, imposing an academic preoccupation with the Orders of Architecture, has left its mark in a similarly firm adherence to the Orders of Human Society (inescapable whatever the political régime); in the delineation of which Lancaster is one of the few cartoonists who can handle military uniform at once satirically and correctly.

Not long before the *Annus Sanctus* of 1949/1950 was inaugurated by the Pope – naturally an occasion for pilgrimage to Rome – Cyril Connolly (according to himself) saw Evelyn Waugh in White's Club, of which both were by that time fellow-members. Waugh said: 'I am thinking of going to Rome for the Holy Year. I shall be staying in an *hôtel*. I wondered whether you would care to join me? If there were likely to be money difficulties, I could arrange.'

Had Connolly ever flirted with the Roman Church – of which sounder proof than any known to me would be required to speak affirmatively – that flirtation had remained in every sense Platonic. Connolly declined

Waugh's offer to 'stand' him a visit to The Eternal City during the Holy Year, but did not hesitate to dine out on the story. The news of the Waugh/Connolly interchange had scarcely reached me, when a Lancaster drawing arrived by post. It is captioned: *Rough sketch for a gigantic mural to be placed in the coffee-room at White's by public subscription celebrating the theme 'Connolly at Canossa'*. The biretta-capped ecclesiastic standing behind Pius XII (easily recognizable) seems a generalized Vatican functionary, but the bare-headed cleric of lean and hungry look is undoubtedly Fr Martin D'Arcy SJ, celebrated for his conversions in the beau monde. The helmeted Swiss Guard, grasping a halberd, has every air of being a self-portrait by the artist. When Waugh was once in our house I showed him Lancaster's picture, by then framed on the wall. He gazed for a long time, finally saying: 'Not in the least like.' Connolly was never given the chance of expressing an opinion. Opportunities arose, but courage failed me.

When in 1948 we took Evelyn Gardner's cottage in Kent for a few weeks, Somerhill, the d'Avigdor-Goldsmids' house near Tonbridge, was not far away. Violet had known Rosie Goldsmid (*née* Rosemary Nicholl) since deb days. We dined at Somerhill, the beginning of a long series of visits. Hospitality was already on an heroic scale. After six years of wartime austerity one could feel very grateful for a bucket or two of champagne.

Harry Goldsmid (whose family had owned the house for about a century, and traditionally derived from the 2nd century BC Maccabees) had served with great dash in the local Territorials, being profusely decorated. He returned from the war to be a banker and bullion broker in London; later becoming an MP (Con) for a North Midland constituency. Goldsmid's knowledge of the City, the complexities of financial dealings, especially on their comic side, was of incalculable value to me where such matters played a part in my novel. He would give advice, read proofs before publication, make suggestions that were not only well informed about the City, but showed grasp of the literary exigencies that govern writing a novel. In this last respect he was a rare friend, somehow seeming himself to share the life of the novel's characters, without at the same time imposing too much exterior influence in what he recommended.

Harry d'Avigdor-Goldsmid had, in short, brilliant gifts: courage, physical and moral; generosity; a keen and independent intelligence in both intellectual matters and business affairs; an individual wit; and – something that can perhaps at times prove an inconvenience to certain temperaments – a great deal of money. He was also (as Isaiah Berlin observed at the West London Synagogue Memorial Service in 1976) the most easily bored man he, Berlin, had ever met. No one who knew Goldsmid is likely to dissent from that assessment. Almost in the middle of a sentence in which he had been laughing about something (quite likely sparked off by his own wit), boredom would strike him down, melancholy descend like an unwanted guest impossible to exclude from the table. Gloom might easily take over for the rest of the evening. Latterly, there was reason enough for the Goldsmids to be sad. They had two daughters, beautiful, intelligent, wellbehaved, whom they adored. In 1963, the Fates enacting one of their dreadful rôles, tragedy came. The elder girl was lost in a sailing accident. Harry Goldsmid's life was utterly, irretrievably, laid waste.

Goldsmid entered the House of Commons with plenty of enthusiasm and ambition. He was Parliamentary Private Secretary to a Minister, chaired many important committees on financial matters, took a keen interest (uncommon among MPs) in promoting art and letters, including grants for indigent writers. Nevertheless, in the political dog-fight, Goldsmid's critical intelligence, his impatience with bores, humbugs, knaves, was a fatal impediment. He once showed me a letter he had written, rapping the knuckles of a Minister in his own Party for answering a question with a jumble of half-baked pompous clichés. Such an attitude is refreshing in an MP, but unlikely to appease ministerial stupidity. In short, Goldsmid's years in Parliament were useful and honourable but a disappointment to himself. He character-istically expressed his own feelings by quoting a story taken, I imagine, from Sir Richard Burton's translation of *The Arabian Nights*. The tale concerns a man who is brought by some magical means to a magnificent house, the door of which is guarded by a gigantic Nubian. He is admitted. Within, among luxurious surroundings, gorgeous women are playing chess. The man is invited to play with them. It is explained that, if he wins the game, he will enjoy the favours of his beautiful opponent – but, if he loses, he will be buggered by the Nubian.

'That's the House of Commons,' said Goldsmid. 'I lost. I'm being buggered by the Nubian.'

If this was a decade when new friends were made, its close was saddened by the loss of two old ones; George Orwell and Constant Lambert. They belonged to very different areas of my life, and never, I think, came across each other.

Orwell had been seriously ill for months before the end came in January, 1950. He had expressed a wish to be buried in the rites of the Church of England (constituting, in the view of Frazer of *The Golden Bough*, adherence, anthropologically speaking, to a given religion), and the Revd W. V. C. Rose, kindly vicar of Christ Church, Albany Street, took on Orwell's funeral service at short notice. It fell to me to choose the hymns: *All people that on earth do dwell* (I felt Orwell would have liked the Old Hundredth, if only for the name); *Guide me, O thou great Redeemer* (chiefly for my own wartime associations, though *Jehovah* is more authentic); *Ten thousand times ten thousand* (Why, I can't remember, perhaps Orwell himself had talked of the hymn, or because he was in his way a sort of saint, even if not one in sparkling raiment bright). The Lesson was from Ecclesiastes, the grinders in the streets, the grasshopper a burden, the silver cord loosed, the wheel broken at the cistern. For some reason George Orwell's funeral service was one of the most harrowing I have ever attended.

Constant Lambert's first marriage had gone wrong a short time before the outbreak of war in 1939. He was in The Hague the following year, on tour with the Sadler's Wells Ballet Company, when the Germans launched their attack on Holland. Bombs and parachutists descended wholesale from the sky, the city was in flames, but the Company managed to get back to England without casualty. During the war years Lambert had a fairly gruelling time keeping the Sadler's Wells dancers going, something for which, it has often been said, he never received as much credit as he deserved. In 1947 he married again, this time to the painter and stage-designer, Isobel Nicholas, who had herself been model for many well-known painters and sculptors. She executed the sets of Lambert's last ballet, *Tiresias*. After their marriage Constant and Isobel Lambert took part of a house, 197 Albany Street, only a short way up the road from Chester Gate. I had come across Lambert only a few times during the war, but now began to see him again more regularly. By this period he was in rather a shaky condition. In general his drinking had not diminished, but he would have interludes when he hardly drank at all – that happened once when the Lamberts came to dinner, again when they themselves gave a party – but during such abstinences he would be in an odd state, sometimes silent, sometimes convulsed with laughter.

Our chief exchanges, anyway most coherent ones, began to settle into a pattern of Lambert making long telephone calls relatively late at night. He would ring up between half-past eleven and midnight, discussing at great length things which had amused him during the day. This would happen especially on Sunday evenings, when Lambert liked to go through what had appeared on the book pages of the Sunday papers. Sacheverell Sitwell (an old friend of both of us) was then contributing an unsigned column to one of the Sunday papers, in which he wrote of anything that had caught his attention, no intellectual or aesthetic holds barred, resulting in a panorama of esoteric items altogether unfamiliar to most newspaper readers. A wide field was usually covered by Lambert's telephone conversations too, but these were likely to begin with the words: 'I say, *have* you read Sachie this Sunday?'

Lambert was making these calls two or three times a week, when, at the beginning of August, 1951, Violet and I went with the children to Lee; returning a fortnight later. My mother rang up Chester Gate the same evening, 21 August, asking if we had seen in the paper that Constant Lambert had died. We had no knowledge of it, nor that he had been in a bad way for some days, then seemed to recover, followed by a terrible relapse that killed him. The next night an old Oxford friend, Matthew Ponsonby, with his wife, Bess, turned out to be in London, and came at short notice to dinner at Chester Gate. I mention their presence there as witness of what happened. At about a quarter to twelve the telephone-bell rang.

'It's Constant,' said Violet.

I went downstairs and picked up the receiver.

'Hullo?'

There was no sound for an appreciable moment, then a click, followed by the dialling tone.

PART FOUR

The Strangers All Are Gone

Nurse   Anon, anon!
Come, let's away; the strangers all are gone
Romeo and Juliet I5

✳ I ✳

The second war (as the first had done at an earlier age) drew a hard line across the story of one's days. Those six years not only concentrated into a short span of time contacts and experiences that could not otherwise have come my way, but by drastically altering normal routines penetrated almost every area of existence. Total abstinence from writing undoubtedly had the consequence of storing away material, past and current, that might otherwise have been dissipated piecemeal. To that extent the war had a stimulating effect, something new jobs and changed scenes can never guarantee a writer. Meanwhile an untidy scrawl of death and disjunction had been traced by Time across the pages of our address-book: a toll of names that showed no very marked sign of decreasing now that peace was restored. War casualties might have ceased, but on the upward grade were natural causes, the occasional suicide, madness among the once relatively sane, not to mention mere passing into oblivion. Such wastage among friends and acquaintances is one of the liabilities of middle-age. At the same time new names were to some extent taking the place of these deletions, often those of a younger generation of writers and poets just released from the Services.

As one picks one's way between the trees of Dante's dark wood of middle life its configuration becomes ever less discernible. All one can say of the trees is that most are gnarled, some hollow, not a few struck by lightning. Alick Dru used to complain that one of the least supportable things about later life was the fact that you began to see almost everyone else's point of view. I had to agree that tolerance becomes an increasing burden with age. A slowing up of former antagonisms perhaps accounts to some extent for lessening in the sense of pattern. Fallibilities of reportage become only too apparent after reaching an age when biographies begin to appear dealing with personal friends, or even individuals known slightly. I reflect on the extraordinary views and remarks attributed to myself from time to time by newspaper interviewers. Pilate certainly had a point.

One of the strangest figures to surface after the war was Julian Maclaren-Ross. He was produced in the first instance by Bobby Roberts in 1946. Roberts, just returned from India as demobilized squadron-leader from the Public Relations branch of the RAFVR, was himself soon to disappear from sight into an amorphous underworld of backstage provincial theatre undertakings. He may still have drawn a trickle of income from hiring out camp-stools to pit queues, but was probably existing for the most part on an RAF gratuity.

Roberts would sometimes turn up, rather self-consciously sober, at Chester Gate in order to gossip about friends in common; above all to ventilate the ever complex problems set in motion by his determination to get married again. At times he would bring with him for inspection one or other of the candidates docketed as potential bride. These were never insignificant. Like Bagshaw in *Dance*, for whom (as for Fotheringham in *Afternoon Men*) Roberts was to some extent model (showing how a good one may be used more than once), he was a guest never unendurably to overstay his welcome, since an iron law of self-discipline ordained that every night of his life the words 'Last orders, please – time, gentlemen, time' had to ring in his ears. No matter where Roberts found himself, the day's intake of alcohol must categorically include at least one drink in a pub – no matter what pub – to hear the angelus of closing time.

If Roberts went out of his way to exhibit some individual, male or female (including wives designate) encountered on a devious and almost consistently intoxicated pilgrimage through life such persons – not necessarily types with whom one wanted to spend a great deal of time again – were nevertheless always of authentic interest in one direction or another. He possessed acute, if vagrant, perceptions as to human character. Among *convives* warmly canvassed by Roberts (who was surprisingly strong-willed where his own whims were concerned) was a certain Maclaren-Ross, whom he propagated as a writer of excellent short stories, and – very acceptable recommendation after nearly eight years without publishing a book – a fan of my own pre-war novels. Roberts positively insisted on the introduction. Violet and I gave in, and agreed to meet this Roberts literary discovery at a pub in Great Portland Street.

In due course I took some liberties with the theatrically projected personality of Maclaren-Ross – elaborating the scope a little – in constructing the character of X. Trapnel, who (like Bagshaw) appears in the later volumes of *Dance*. I was to continue to see Maclaren-Ross intermittently until within a few years of his death in 1964. 'I warn you,' said Roberts, when we arrived at the rendezvous. 'He's rather an egotist.' This prefigurement turned out no less than the truth, even the first few minutes making plain the colossal ego that Maclaren-Ross wielded. At the same time one was immediately impressed by the unusual texture of this tall, dark, good-looking, faintly foreign figure (then about thirty-two), with an unstemmable flow of talk. That was about books (chiefly novels of the past twenty years but capable of extension backwards in time), and movies (chiefly gangster films though not exclusively), a running commentary delivered in a rasping authoritative stylized tone of voice that defied either class or professional identification.

During any evening's performance indication that the machine was creaking ominously, if not actually breaking down, was introduction of the name of Sidney Greenstreet. Greenstreet announced the need for eviction in as friendly a manner as possible of the protagonist (surely here legitimate use of that much abused figure of speech) as soon as Maclaren-Ross gave pause in the imitation that always followed of the rotund middle-aged film-star (said himself to possess intellectual leanings), master in his own particular line of quietly villainous rôles.

An habitual *tenue* of semi-tropical suit, ancient suede shoes, teddy-bear overcoat (in winter), stick with silver knob, gave the air of a broken-down dandy, though just what brand of dandyism was not easy to define. There was something Mediterranean about the get-up, hints even of more distant climes, Conrad or Maugham islands, Gauguin in the South Seas, though the walking-stick seemed to denote *boulevardier* rather than beachcomber. The equally invariable dark green sun-spectacles (their lenses latterly of a kind to reflect the vis-à-vis) belonged to much the same geographical regions, at the same time hinting of security agent or possibly terrorist.

All this swagger did not entirely mask the hard-up literary man of the post-war London epoch. Maclaren-Ross personified that too, even quintessentially; perhaps as much by leaving his own mark on the times as the times leaving a mark on himself. He wrote as J. Maclaren-Ross, was addressed by friends as Julian, though indications (an old passport once produced) suggested that he had been christened James, the Apostate's name substituted or added as less commonplace. Never in the least insistent on religion in his writings or manner of life, Maclaren-Ross was in fact not himself apostate, remaining the Roman Catholic he had been born. When we first met he had already published three collections of short stories (those about the army in general the best), also a novel. Another (fairly brief) novel had reached proof stage, then – becoming in some manner bedevilled – lay frozen in a publishing limbo from which the author was unable to summon up sufficient will or dexterity to extract this work. A third novel was due to appear the following year.

His origins, unusual ones, are touched on in a lighthearted piece called *My Father was born in Havana*, then rather more fully in a volume of memoirs *The Weeping and the Laughter*. The father in question was half-Scotch, half-Latin American; a grandfather (possibly great-grandfather), on one side or the other, came from the Southern States of North America. Maclaren-Ross *père*, son of an engineer and shipowner, had fought as an officer of Imperial Yeomanry in the South African War, afterwards knocking about all over the world. He came to rest in the South of France where his family (two sons and a daughter) had been largely brought up. There were inevitable hints of a Secret Service connexion – irresistible in the circumstances – which seemed mainly based on a certain amount of translating books from French into English which took place in the home. Maclaren-Ross himself spoke fluent French. Presumably on his father's death he had inherited a little money just before the second war. This was quickly run through, and he found himself uncompromisingly on the rocks. At one moment he had attempted to earn a living as door-to-door salesman of vacuum-cleaners, a vocation bitingly but good humouredly recalled in the then forthcoming novel *Of Love and Hunger* (1947). For a time he was in the army, where – rare for an intellectual – he served three weeks detention in the Glasshouse (not the celebrated Aldershot military lock-up but a slightly milder one) for Absent-Without-Leave.

Maclaren-Ross would often give spirited and unselfpitying accounts of this incarceration. Three minutes were allowed for performing natural functions in the morning, after which period of time a soldier-warder would thrust his face in that of the prisoner attempting to evacuate, shouting: 'Come on, man, come on! What do you think you are? A woman having a baby?' At the sound of the air-raid warning at night the whole prison would be roused for turn-out in battle order including wearing a gas-mask. It was no wonder that men returned to their unit from the Glasshouse immensely smartened up. This im-provement in military bearing does not seem to have taken place in the case of Maclaren-Ross, who was invalided out on psychiatric grounds fairly soon after the Glasshouse interlude; not unreasonably since he was highly neurotic. He passed the latter part of the war as member (with Dylan Thomas) of a documentary film unit.

When first encountered, Maclaren-Ross had been married and divorced at least once. Considering the world in which he lived he was not temperamentally promiscuous, tending to stick to whatever girl (usually an unequivocally pretty one) who made up his establishment, until she herself moved off. He liked to boast of deep drinking, together with superhuman powers of remaining sober whatever the intake, and the strength of his head has been confirmed by one or two of those who knew him. In my own experience Maclaren-Ross potations were never excessive. In decline he would refer to 'my pills', and, whether on account of these or from lack of them, he did turn up once at a Chancery Lane pub where we had a rendezvous in a less than coherent state. That was a unique default in the course of our meetings.

The Maclaren-Ross ménage tended to be accommodated in an hotel, preferably a large one in Russell Square – 'Something I could never afford myself,' once commented Henry Yorke. Maclaren-Ross greatly admired Yorke's novels (written as Henry Green), and at a much later date wrote an accomplished parody of them in a *Punch* series on con-temporary novelists he undertook. I brought Yorke and Maclaren-Ross together. This delighted Maclaren-Ross but on Yorke's side the introduction was less of a success. Yorke had by then already become rather crotchety about new acquaintances, in any case did not care for too strong whiffs of bohemian life, indeed could scarcely tolerate such social levels at all. It had to be admitted that the barrage of Maclaren-Ross conversation was not to every taste. There was no enthusiastic follow-up, though I think the two writers did meet again by arrangement at least once.

Since hotel existence was perforce maintained in terms not much short of utter penury, crises such as laundry being held in hock until the bill was paid were not infrequent. At like junctures loans from friends would sometimes tide over an awkward week or two until an article or story was sold and paid for. During a very brief period some sort of a household was maintained in a decidedly seedy furnished flat in the Holland Park area, but even that comparative domesticity palled. The caravan was soon back on the road, another hotel circuit littered with unpaid accounts and summonses for obtaining credit by methods more or less unsanctioned. Somehow the worst retributions were always sidestepped. Chronically on the brink of disaster, Maclaren-Ross never, I think, was so drastically reduced as in the pre-war years when nights had been spent on the Embankment.

In the end this nerve-racking routine, both precarious and demanding, took its revenge. Books produced never lost a certain degree of competence, but the standard fell off in quality as their author travelled steadily downhill. Nor did he ever fail to find a woman to love and look after him. The battle fought as a writer was an increasingly losing one to keep contact (certainly hard enough for any writer whatever the circumstances) with things worth writing about. At his best – the army stories, the vacuum-cleaner novel, the parodies – there is a touch that remains individual to this day. *Memoirs of the Forties* (1965), of which he himself had high hopes, remained uncompleted at his death in the year previous to its publication. The book contains several amusing close-ups of fellow-writers (Cyril Connolly, Graham Greene), together with a certain amount of less interesting material. Nonetheless, had time allowed, jotted notes suggest that further memoirs might have been worth reading.

The Maclaren-Ross ménage used sometimes to dine with us at Chester Gate, and once – a publisher's advance denoting that life must be lived *en prince* for at least twenty-four hours – he insisted that we should be his guests for dinner at the Café Royal. The occasion was marked by John Heygate and his most recent girl-friend joining our table later in the evening. Heygate, like his old crony Bobby Roberts, had spent most of the war in India, the former as bombardier in the Royal Artillery. He had gone to Ceylon for one of his leaves, where inevitably he ran into Roberts. Harold Acton, like Roberts in the

RAFVR, also turned out to be in Ceylon, and for some reason Hey-gate had to apply to Acton (an Eton and Oxford contemporary) to arrange for being put up at the Services Club in Colombo. Acton said that all would have been well had not an impediment arisen in the shape of Heygate's diminutive Indian mistress, for whom he had paid a lump sum. Coming from one of the more primitive races of the Subcontinent, she was something under four foot high, always insisted on walking behind Heygate, and utterly refused to eat with him. How this delicate social problem was adjusted I do not know.

By the time Heygate arrived back from India, the war now drawing to a close, he was in very poor shape. On the way home he had cele-brated the coming of peace unrestrainedly, was physically ill, and in a highly nervous condition. He must, however, have made some sort of temporary recovery that night at the Café Royal, because he seemed to have regained much of his old capacity for enjoyment. Heygate had mesmerized the authorities of UNRRA (United Nations Relief and Rehabilitation Administration) to take him on as an officer. He was sporting the UNRRA uniform in the Café Royal. A certain irony attached to the organization's resounding name and all-embracing duties embroidered on Heygate's shoulder, as the phrases only too well described what only a short time before he had been in need of himself at the receiving end, and was very soon desperately to need again. Heygate's girl, who was in a flirtatious mood, kept sending him little notes under the table. Maclaren-Ross, who possessed that peculiar skill some have of being able to read handwriting upside down, deciphered one of these affectionate missives – evidently referring to himself – as commenting: *He is too esoteric.* The occasion may have been an infelicitous one to record that judgment, but its truth was undeniable. Maclaren-Ross was too esoteric; certainly too esoteric to find life easy. For a few years he walked his own unique tight-rope above the by-ways of Charlotte Street and Soho, his gifts as a writer never quite allowing the headlong descent for ever threatened by his behaviour as a man. At times, though rarely, he showed signs of grasping that a great deal of the chaos that surrounded him could have been avoided by even a little more restraint on his own part. Such glimpses of self-criticism never lasted long enough for substantial improvement to take place. In the end balance on the tight-rope was not adequately main-tained. A life which with all its absurdities had been in many ways courageous and productive came to an abrupt termination.

Alan Ross, then working for the British Council, was a friend met at this period, who was later to marry Jennifer Fry, niece of Evelyn Gardner, and edit *The London Magazine*. He had just been demobilized as a naval officer (having had some lively war experiences), and already possessed a name as a poet. He used occasionally to review books for the *Times Literary Supplement*, introduced there by the new editor Alan Pryce-Jones. He had also been an Oxford cricket 'blue', and wrote very elegantly about the game. In spite of the attraction cricket exercises over many contemporary writers (Amis, Fuller, Larkin, Pinter, to name only a few) – something all but unknown at anything but a middle-brow level formerly – its mystique holds no spell for me, nevertheless I read Alan Ross on the subject if I come across his articles because, analytical and romantic, they give meaning to the players.

Alan Ross composed one of the most penetrating obituary notices of Maclaren-Ross in which he spoke of that quirkiness that prevented the earning of a standard of living that should have been a right: 'The hidalgo, the author, the man on National Assistance, all spoke with the same resonant voice' well summarized his subject. Maclaren-Ross was certainly familiar with the Labour Exchange, but I believe never in fact drew the dole; probably his personal administration in any case was not sufficiently in order for him to do so. The obituary went on to say that in spite of deep rooted inability to adapt himself to other people's ways Maclaren-Ross was always the first to draw attention to books by his own contemporaries which he thought undervalued. On the whole a reliable critic (as early as 1957 he wrote that Roy Fuller was that rarity, a good poet who also wrote good novels), he had a true passion for the art of writing, always preferring to recommend rather than be dismissive or malicious. Certainly he could display violent dislikes – these quite unaffected by current fashion – but in the literary world, surrounded by lesser talents that were achieving far more commercial success than his own, Maclaren-Ross was one of the least envious of men.

Among other posthumous memoranda left in relation to *Memoirs of the Forties* was a note: *Anthony Powell plays Happy Families*. This refers to an afternoon when Maclaren-Ross turned up at Chester Gate, probably to discuss some article or book to review for the *TLS*. After that was settled we had tea, followed by the card game Happy Families (Mr Bones the Butcher, etc), played with our elder son Tristram, then about six years old. I regret the piece about myself was never written as it would undoubtedly have been funny, and told me things about my own behaviour of which I was quite unaware. Maclaren-Ross must have recalled that game in the year of his own death, because Tristram, by then a television producer, mounted a programme in 1964, *Writers during the War*, with contributions by John Betjeman, Cyril Connolly, Alan Ross, Julian Maclaren-Ross himself. It was one of those unforeseen turns of the wheel. This programme of Tristram's was introduced by another friend, Jocelyn Brooke, of whom now a word.

Jocelyn Brooke really belongs to the period after our move from London, but I first heard of him about the time of which I have been speaking as author of *The Military Orchid* (1948), a book which received very approving notices. I did not read it, partly because I was busy with Aubrey, partly because (being in that respect like Wyndham Lewis's Tarr, for whom 'the spring was anonymous') I thought a book which seemed largely concerned with botany would be out of my line. Quite fortuitously I reviewed Brooke's next book *A Mine of Serpents* (1949) for the *TLS*, treating it more or less as a novel. There was some excuse for that as certain ostensibly fictional characters seemed intended for future development, a note at the beginning saying this work was 'complementary' to *The Military Orchid*, rather than a sequel. I did not grasp that here was the second volume of a loosely constructed autobiographical trilogy. The review now strikes me as rather pompous, but I recognized Brooke's talent at once, and remarked (at the moment about to come to grips with *Dance*) that the epigraph used by Brooke from Sir Thomas Browne's *Christian Morals* – 'Some Truths seem almost Falsehoods and Some Falsehoods almost Truths' – contains 'in a sense the justification of all novel writing'.

I knew nothing of Jocelyn Brooke himself except what was to be gathered from *A Mine of Serpents*. He was in fact then about forty, and had recently emerged from the ranks of the Royal Army Medical Corps, in which he had re-enlisted two years after the end of the second war. A collection of his poems had appeared in 1946, but *The Military Orchid* was his first published prose work. By the time I reviewed Brooke's Kafka-like novel *The Image of a Drawn Sword* in the spring of 1950 I must have read *The Military Orchid*, and by that autumn, when *The Goose Cathedral*, third volume of the trilogy, came out, I had marked Brooke down as one of the notable writers to have surfaced after the war. I wrote an Introduction to these three books when they appeared in one volume as *The Orchid Trilogy* in 1981, another to *The Image of a Drawn Sword* in 1982.

In those days reviewing in the *TLS* was unsigned so there was no question of Brooke having known of my liking for his work when, in 1953, a laudatory article by him appeared in one of the weeklies on the subject of my first novel *Afternoon Men*, published more than twenty years earlier. *Afternoon Men* had, as it happened, been reprinted in a new edition about a year before, but when I sent a letter to Brooke expressing appreciation of this unexpected bouquet he turned out to be unaware of the republication. He had merely reread his own 1931 copy, on impulse rung up a literary editor and asked if he might write a piece on the subject. In due course we lunched together, met from time to time afterwards (though never often), and continued to correspond fitfully until Brooke's death in 1966.

All writers, one way or another, depend ultimately on their own lives for the material of their books, but the manner in which each employs that personal experience, interior or exterior, is very different. Jocelyn Brooke used both elements with a minimum of dilution, though much imagination. However far afield he went physically – which included the Middle East and Italy – he remained morally from birth to death in his own part of Kent, the childhood days which for him never lost their fascination. He was by nature keenly interested in himself (as suggested earlier in these memoirs, apropos of Cyril Connolly, a comparatively rare preoccupation in its truest sense), though (unlike some aspects of Maclaren-Ross) without vanity or the smallest suggestion of exhibitionism. He had been born in 1908 and came on both sides of his family from wine merchants, the paternal business at Folkestone, with a residence at Sandgate. His parents also possessed an inland holiday cottage at Bishopsbourne in the Elham Valley, a favourite setting for imaginary adventures. Brooke's nanny (from some early mispronunciation always known as Ninny) was a preponderant figure in Brooke myth. Latterly – a circuitous but effective reconstruction of childhood – Ivy Cottage, Bishopsbourne, was shared with his mother and Ninny, until their deaths took place only a few years before Brooke's own demise. The passion for botany seems to have begun by the age of four years old, the taste for fireworks soon developing with almost equal strength; the name of a firework providing the title for *A Mine of Serpents*.

After running away twice in the first fortnight of his first term at King's School, Canterbury (alma mater of Marlowe, Pater, Somerset Maugham, Hugh Walpole, Patrick Leigh Fermor), Brooke was sent to Bedales, of which he has left an amusing account, where he decided he was a disillusioned Aldous Huxley character. At Bedales sex was decried as 'silly' – the novelist Julia Strachey told me that one girl there with her was so 'silly' she had a baby – which did not solve all Brooke's problems, though he was reasonably contented. Of Worcester College, Oxford, he afterwards retained only dim memories, and seems to have been a fairly typical Proust-Joyce-Firbank-reading undergraduate. *The Isis*, then edited by Peter Fleming, accepted an article called *Oxford Decadence*, but regrettably Fleming and Brooke never met, which might have given one or both an anecdote.

On coming down there were the endemic employment difficulties. For a time work was found in a bookshop. This must have been about the same moment as George Orwell's bookshop assistant period in Hampstead. Incidentally a correspondent who remembered the Orwell shop told me it was a gloomy cave of a place which sold all sorts of other odds and ends as well as books. The Brooke bookshop in the City was at rather a higher professional level, one imagines. It was followed by a spell in the family wine business, and attempt to grow a moustache, neither a success. Then Brooke suffered some sort of breakdown. When the second war came he at once joined the RAMC. The army recurs throughout most of his works, providing some of their best material. Though much of Brooke's service must have been far from comfortable he felt after a time that his life was too easy, and volunteered for the branch treating venereal disease. He again served in the VD branch – in army parlance the Pox-Wallahs – when he rejoined the Corps a year or two after the war. By that time the Brooke family had moved to Blackheath, and he managed to get a posting conveniently near them at Woolwich Military Hospital.

Brooke always seemed to me to have resolved pretty well his homosexuality in life. I may be mistaken, because David Cecil, who saw something of him soon after *The Military Orchid*'s publication, had the impression that Brooke was going through painful experiences on that account. In his 'straight' novels he never appears wholly at ease with the subject, which is usually treated satirically. This is perhaps to say no more than that Brooke was more skilful in his own particular art, one not altogether definable, than in the give-and-take of traditional novel form. The hint of mutual homosexual attraction, faint but perceptible, is better handled in *The Image of a Drawn Sword*, unquestionably to be categorized as a novel, though set in Brooke's familiar Kentish landscape. There is a touch of Kipling as well as Kafka in this haunting book, though Brooke was not on the whole well disposed towards Kipling, and told me he had not read Kafka at the time of writing it. *The Military Orchid* contains the phrase 'a curious paranoid quality, like a story by Kafka', so that either *The Image* was written before *The Orchid*, or – more probably – Brooke, like many others, invoked Kafka's name before he read him. Perhaps Brooke's best book is *The Dog at Clambercrown* (1955), its title the odd name of a Kentish pub and village, a work that contains all the essential Brooke myth. In it the author reflects on his feelings about the army.

'Anyone'd think you *liked* the Army.'

'As it happened, Pte Hoskins' unlikely hypothesis was perfectly correct: I did like the Army – though 'like' is hardly an adequate word to describe my feelings about it. 'Love' would perhaps be nearer the mark, though here again the word required qualification, for my liaison with the armed forces (and I use the word in its erotic rather than military sense) was by no means a starry-eyed, spontaneous affair the word love suggests. It resembled, rather, the kind of relationship described by Proust, in which love is apprehended, so to speak, only in its negative aspects – the pain of loss, the absence or infidelity of the loved one, the perverse satisfaction of possessing (like Swann) some woman who isn't one's type, whom one doesn't even like, but with whom one has become so fatally obsessed that life without her is unendurable.'

A good deal of acute criticism is scattered through the pages of *The Dog at Clambercrown*. Of *Ulysses*: 'It is, I suppose, the most fascinating and the most devastatingly boring novel ever written.' Of *The Rainbow*: 'A genius for evoking landscape, a sense of character, a marvellous apprehension of human relationships. Yet after a further chapter or two I was finally bogged down ... Lawrence's secret – if one can call it that – was, I suppose, that he was profoundly homosexual.' Lawrence, however, like Shakespeare and Proust, comes well out of Brooke's investigation of the capabilities of writers invoking botanical images.

As already remarked, I cannot claim to have known Brooke well, but we quite often corresponded, and he was one of those people to whom I always wrote with a sense of ease. He speaks more than once of his own liking for the sort of relationship which did not make him feel hemmed in. In his books are several incidents in which the narrator, from his own awareness of being 'different', refuses an invitation from someone with whom he has been getting on pretty well. It came therefore as no very great surprise, after we had lunched together several times, and Brooke had stayed with us for the weekend, when he politely excused himself from another visit on grounds of work. That may also have been true enough. 'Writing time' is a kind of Old Man of the Sea for ever exerting a strangling grip. Nonetheless one suspected an unwillingness to cope too often with face-to-face cordialities that might be acceptable in letters. David Cecil told me later that he himself had a very similar experience in Brooke dealings.

Brooke liked a fair amount to drink, and after luncheon was inclined to say: 'Shall we be *beasts*, and go to *my* club now, and have another glass of port.'

In 1964, when Violet and I were staying with Harry and Rosie Goldsmid at Somerhi.. we drove over to Bishopsbourne to see Brooke in his own realm. By that time his mother and Ninny were no longer alive, and he himself had only a couple of years more. Writing somewhere of the Beatrix Potter books he had remarked that as a child 'the world of *Mr Todd* and *Jemima Puddleduck* seemed indistinguishable from our village'. Brooke was absolutely right. Ivy Cottage, however snugly furnished and full of books, was uncannily like Mr Jeremy Fisher's 'little damp house', and in wet weather the resemblance must have been even closer. The three of us lunched at the Metropole in Folkestone, only slightly less hallowed ground than Bishopsbourne itself in the Brooke Legend.

In appearance Jocelyn Brooke was tall, pale, not bad looking, with an air of desperate melancholy that would suddenly lift when he laughed.

Photographs, especially those he used for his books, are apt to give
him a haggard stare, as of one mesmerized or mesmerizing, an expression perhaps assumed before the camera for fun and hardly doing
him justice. He often reminded me of Orwell, not so much in feature
as by a kind of hesitancy of manner, as if thinking for a second about
the true meaning of what had been said before committing himself,
but he was altogether without Orwell's burning desire to set the world
right, and Brooke's laughter was quite unOrwellian. In spite of having
died comparatively young Jocelyn Brooke realized himself as a writer,
I think. He said what he had to say in the form he wished. No doubt
his critical views would always have been of interest, but he had
already achieved his own particular method of self-expression; an art
not like that of any other writer known to me in its manner of marking
out a region, both actual and imagined, a magical personal kingdom.
Brooke quite often invokes A. E. Housman in his books, half-respect-
fully, half-deprecatingly, recognizing the poetic mastery, the shared
rural images, the homosexuality in common, yet at the same time keenly
aware of a certain over-lushness in Housman directed towards both
fields. Nonetheless one feels a suitable epitaph might be provided by
only the smallest adaptation of Housman's much quoted lines:

> Far in a Kentish Brookeland
> That bred me long ago
> The orchids bloom and whisper
> By woods I used to know.

Circumstances making desirable and possible a move to the country,
we began to look for somewhere not much more than a hundred miles
from London, where a day or two each week would still have
to be spent. Violet had two sisters living in Wiltshire: Pansy married to
Henry Lamb, Julia to Robin Mount. I knew Wiltshire to some extent
myself, having lived at Salisbury as a boy; a more theoretical acquaintance with that county coming from 17th century research into Aubrey's
life there. Wiltshire seemed the answer. After inspecting properties all
over the place, dozens of them, the photograph of one called The
Chantry, a few miles into Somerset, seemed to hold out hope. It was
only twenty miles from where Julia Mount lived in a village 'under the
Plain', so she was asked to make a preliminary report.
Pretty, goldenhaired, plump, Julia was a mixture of energy and

lethargy, withdrawn shyness and neatly ironic phrase. For a report on a house for sale she was unlikely to be stampeded into ill-judged enthusiasm as she did not go in much for enthusiasms. Her reserve, a kind of weapon in her hands, is well illustrated by an incident before her own marriage, when the Lambs had taken her over to luncheon with the Augustus Johns at Fordingbridge. Mutual hospitalities between Coombe Bissett and Fryern Court, always a little delicate in the light of Henry Lamb's former close association with Dorelia John, were nevertheless regularly exchanged. Lamb died in 1960; John in 1961. At some moment between these dates John said to me: 'I saw you at that very enjoyable funeral the other day ... who was it? ... I can't remember ...' It had in fact been Lamb's, attended by both the Johns. John had braced himself for Lamb's obsequies with a few drinks, his deep voice echoing on and off throughout the service. At John's own funeral the clergyman caused an audible intake of breath among the congregation by reminding them in his address that in the Next World 'at His Right Hand are pleasures for ever more'.

At the Johns' it was apt to be assumed that everyone present knew everyone else; indeed might easily know them pretty well. John himself in his latter days found habitual difficulty in remembering, particularly among the younger persons present, who were his children, who his grandchildren, who his current girl-friends, who his sons' current girl-friends, who guests brought to the house for the first time. On this particular occasion, before the assembled party entered the dining-room, a little man unknown to Julia Pakenham (as she then was) showed signs of feeling that he was insufficiently appreciated. That may easily have been true as guests at the Johns' were expected to look after themselves. When the meal was announced, and Julia passed through the door beside him, it became apparent that (very unwontedly) name-cards had been set out in each place. The little man remarked:

'I wonder whether they have put Shaw on my card.'

'Why do you wonder that?' asked Julia.

'Because I have several names.'

'Oh, have you?' said Julia.

There the matter rested, as she saw no reason to pursue this some-what self-regarding opening. On leaving the Johns' house Henry Lamb (who must often have met their fellow luncheon guest, and felt no great affection for him) remarked on the presence of T. E. Lawrence, probably then approaching the close of his RAF period. Lawrence's had been the ego Julia refused to propitiate.

Julia Mount gave a restrained but favourable report on The Chantry. We ourselves paid a couple of visits. I made an offer. Another bidder put up a larger sum. The property passed out of our field of vision, and the search for somewhere to live began again. Some months after this The Chantry's owner, Wing Commander (later Air Chief Marshal Sir John) Barraclough, got into touch and said he would like a talk. On coming to Chester Gate he explained that the other potential buyer became too exigent about minor matters. Negotiations had been broken off. For a very small increase of the original offer I could have the house. The hand of fate seemed at work. A deal was made.

The Chantry, a Regency structure in the classical style of the Italianate villas of Bath (about sixteen miles away), indeed probably designed by a Bath architect, had been completed in 1826. Although not in the direst decay the house, surrounded by undergrowth hardly short of jungle, was far from spick and span. The interior still recalled use during the second war as a refuge for the bombed-out, a school (an establishment apparently attended by no pupils), and briefly a chocolate factory. Only a little time before we took over, all domestic water was pumped up by a giant wheel from the reservoir made by an artificially created pond or lake two fields away to the south. Electric light had been even more recently installed. I have seen a bill of sale for The Chantry in the 1890s which did not overstate the case in saying the property would be a nice one if it had been kept up. Sixty years later that estimate remained no less true.

The Chantry had been built for the Fussells (a name widespread in the West Country), this branch being ironmasters, more specifically welders of agricultural implements. The sheet of water had been contrived to provide power to the Fussell works. Beyond this lake the country rises again, a steeply wooded slope, then more gently ascending fields with hills in the distance. The unsightly outlines of two limestone quarries to the south-west are at times obscured by mist; their effluents intermittently immolate fish in the lake. Though rather late in the day for Romantick fancies, the Fussells also brought into being two grottoes (possibly designed to give labour in the Hungry Forties), one of these cavernlike follies marking the entrance to a small secret garden, ingress to which was so hidden by laurel when we came to the house that it was discovered only after three weeks. One evening a cow found its way into this small enclosed grotto, and the cow's owner felt too uneasy about the presence of ghosts there to extract his beast until the light of morning. The further grotto, more grandiose in conception, was made round a channel feeding the lake from a much lesser pond on higher ground. The surface of water had through some defect in the flow sunk at about the turn of the century; bringing into being a Lost World of trees and shrubs rising from a marshland of reeds, now a nature reserve of tangled thickets and stagnant pools.

The Fussell-endowed church at Chantry (1845) is said to be the first built by Gilbert Scott. Another Fussell benefaction was a school over the road from their house, which included a Boarding School for training teachers and governesses. One of the pupils was Helen Mathers (1853–1920), a novelist whose bestseller *Comin' Thro' the Rye* gives a glimpse of life at The Chantry in the 1860s. As it happened I had seen one of the two (possibly three) silent films made from the book. *Comin' Thro' the Rye* (1875) seems to have been the first novel, of which there were to be so many later examples, dealing with a large family dominated by a domestic tyrant of a father.

The dialogue used by Helen Mathers to describe her heroine's large family and dictatorial father could hardly be in stronger contrast with Ivy Compton-Burnett's novels, also teeming with brothers, sisters, domestic tyrants of both sexes, but the same sort of family is nevertheless being described. I now regret that I never asked Miss Compton-Burnett (as one instinctively thinks of her) whether she had dipped into the works of this pioneer in her own genre.

Some years before I met Ivy Compton-Burnett I spoke of her books to Roger Hinks, putting the accent on the last syllable of the hyphenated surname. Hinks, an accomplished mimic, remarked: 'Búrnett, we call it.' The icy coldness of his tone, one of quiet reduction to powder, made evident that he reproduced the voice of Miss Compton-Burnett herself. Before saying more of her, a word about Hinks. He was son of A. D. Hinks, from the nature of his job at the Royal Geographical Society popularly known as the Geographer Royal, a distinguished and rather crusty old gentleman, who was my fellow member at The Travellers. He once observed to me of the club secretary (who did not in fact stay very long): 'I don't like the new secretary – he is so rude.' I answered that I had not yet spoken with the new secretary. 'Neither have I,' said old Hinks, 'but he *looks* so rude.' This no doubt true of certain countenances, a categorization not without all validity.

Roger Hinks, remembered chiefly – if unjustly – for his too rigorous spring-cleaning of the Elgin Marbles when employed in the British Museum, was one of the accomplished talkers belonging to Ivy Compton-Burnett's little court. Some of Hinks's best anecdotes referred to Sir Edgar Bonham-Carter (with whom he had, I think, an official contact), an *haut fonctionnaire* noted for his vagueness. At some social gathering Sir Edgar had once said to Hinks (who temperamentally preferred his own sex): 'Will you give this cup of tea to your wife – I mean *my* wife.' His words were even odder once at a moment during the second war when Hinks, off on a wartime assignment, had called to take leave. He found Sir Edgar lying on a sofa in the drawing-room with his eyes closed.

'I've come to say goodbye,' said Hinks.

'Goodbye,' said Sir Edgar without opening his eyes.

Hinks was about to depart when Sir Edgar raised the lids of his eyes. 'Have some rubber,' he said. 'I mean butter.'

But to return to Miss Compton-Burnett, I first heard of her as a writer – I. Compton-Burnett – perhaps as early as my Oxford period. I could not be sure about that, but certainly Henry Yorke introduced her name to me as 'the only young novelist Bloomsbury thinks any good. She's about twenty-eight, and lies on a sofa all day long scribbling her novels in an exercise book.' Ivy Compton-Burnett (b. 1884, though accustomed to advance that date a few years) must in fact have been considerably older than twenty-eight. Yorke's comment probably had reference to *Pastors and Masters* (1925). I read that novel some years after publication, finding it obscure, but the absolutely individual manner impressed me. That was more or less where I settled in relation to the Compton-Burnett books, which (like those of P. G. Wodehouse in a very different context) I admire for their wit and *aperçus*, though never found easy to read. Nonetheless I regard Compton-Burnett as one of the most gifted novelists of her generation; a writer of much deeper understanding than, say, Virginia Woolf.

Hilary Spurling (to whom I must be ever grateful for her *Handbook to Dance*, 1977) has treated admirably of Compton-Burnett's life biographically (which has much bearing on her books), and Violet's *A Compton-Burnett Compendium* (1973) provides a series of clear outlines of what are usually complex narratives. This summarizing is of enormous help in relieving the reader from too much concentration on the bearing of conversation on plot, thereby allowing unobstructed enjoyment of the brilliantly stylized dialogue. The scene of all Compton-Burnett stories is laid towards the end of the 19th century, a large upper-middle class family, moderately rich, living in a country house. These persons, all at odds with each other, lack contact with any world but their own. My reason for supposing the Compton-Burnett world not wholly extinct rests both on the vitality of the novels themselves (if there were ever people so credible as that, such people will always exist), also because from time to time one's ears are assailed – in railway carriages or public rooms of hotels – by sudden bursts of pure Compton-Burnett dialogue.

I first met Miss Compton-Burnett in 1947 at a party. There was an appropriateness in seeing her some years later at another, given for the Oxford and Cambridge Boat Race. Although sport has no place in her novels this event belongs so profoundly to Victorian myth (still retaining a touch of those days) that it could be inserted without doing her plots damage. Margaret Jourdain, Ivy Compton-Burnett's lifelong friend and sharer of their South Kensington flat, was by that time dead. No doubt Miss Jourdain's expert knowledge of Regency furniture explained connexion with the host on this occasion, who was Ralph Edwards, head of the Woodwork Department at the Victoria and Albert Museum. Ralph and Marjorie Edwards had a riverside house in

Chiswick Mall. Ralph Edwards was a polemical Welshman always prepared to give his opinions – usually worth hearing – on all matters in a voice calculated to penetrate the furthest corner of any room; more especially if he had something to say of an outrageously indiscreet nature. Edwards was himself by no means inconceivable as a Compton-Burnett character, though the directness of his spoken views would have become more involuted in manner to tone down their brisk delivery without losing any of the biting content. I did not meet her on this particular occasion, but marked the severe expression and black tricorn hat.

I think it would be true to say that she was severe. She saw life in the relentless terms of Greek Tragedy: its cruelties, hypocrisies, injustices, ironies – above all its passions – played out against a background of triviality and ennui. Seduction, adultery, bastardy, incest, homosexuality (male and female), not to mention embezzlement and murder, haunt her pages. Such things are deeply discussed by her characters, though never explicitly, always within the muted terms of the period; indeed precisely as they would have been discussed in, say, my own grandparents' house, a thoroughly Compton-Burnett ménage playing a game that all the players understood. Miss Compton-Burnett and Miss Jourdain always declared themselves very fond of eating, their sensuality, as sometimes happens, perhaps sublimated in this pleasure. According to Ralph Edwards they decided to expend a sizeable proportion of their capital in undergoing a certain medical treatment which would allegedly make possible for them to eat as much as they liked without ever growing fatter. Whether or not this Edwards story was to be believed, it was generally admitted that the treatment, had it indeed taken place, was in outward effects less than successful in the case of Miss Jourdain.

Ivy Compton-Burnett had expressed a liking for my books (though she could not read the war trilogy within *Dance,* finding any reference to war unbearable after the death in action of a much beloved brother), and after exchange of letters we met several times. I liked her, while always feeling some of the constraint experienced by a child talking with an elder person, a grown-up who, though sympathetic, will never fully apprehend the complexities of one's own childish problems. That was absurd because she and I shared many unexpected likes and dislikes where books were concerned. For instance, she too felt lukewarm about *Wuthering Heights,* writing to me (29 November 1963): 'Posterity has paid its debt to her [Emily Brontë] too generously, and with too little understanding.'

Close to where we now lived was Mells, its Manor House owned for four centuries by the Horners, the first of them by tradition steward

to the Abbot of Glastonbury at the time of the Dissolution, when the
lands were acquired by the family. Like many of the rather loosely
termed 'new men' of that time the Horners in question appear already
to have been fairly well-to-do locally. When the Fussells built The
Chantry, they, as a later form of 'new men', had many skirmishes with
the Horners as neighbours.

In 1917 the heir to Mells, Edward Horner, died in action unmarried.
His sister Katharine was by then wife of Raymond Asquith, son of
Herbert Henry Asquith the Prime Minister, created 1st Earl of Oxford
and Asquith in 1925. Raymond Asquith was also killed in the first war.
Mells accordingly passed in due course to Katharine Asquith's son,
Julian Asquith, 2nd Lord Oxford and Asquith (succeeding his grand-
father), who, after coming out of the army at the end of the second
war, held a succession of appointments abroad under the Colonial
Office. Accordingly Mrs Raymond Asquith (who had refused the
accession of rank available to her on the death of her father-in-law)
lived at Mells with her unmarried daughter. After the death of her
husband, Katharine Asquith had been converted to Roman
Catholicism, and since 1947 the Mells household had also included
Monsignor Ronald Knox as chaplain.

Considering the comparatively long residence of four centuries at
Mells of the Horners as lords of the manor the family had raised surprisingly few monuments in the church, a large one, and, so far as earlier
centuries are concerned, these few are of no special interest. On the
other hand three memorials, one belonging to the late 19th century,
two to the first war, are not only exceptional in themselves, but convey,
so it seems to me, a haunting sense of their time, making Mells church
in its way a unique sanctuary of the world leading up to the first war
and that war itself. In all three memorials I know none elsewhere which
imparts quite the same feeling.

Although true that changes in art and letters conveniently styled the
Modern Movement are set well back in the 19th century, the Eighties
and Nineties (if not the Fifties) heralding the explosion, the earlier
assumptions were still operating vigorously while the modernists were
gathering force. The one was not displacing the other, Latin quotations
running parallel with Free Verse. A somewhat far-fetched comparison
might be drawn between these Edwardian, Georgian, Great War
Cultures, and the early years of the (inappropriately styled) Dark Ages,
when classically named high civil servants of the disintegrating
Roman Empire governed side by side with chieftains of Barbarian
nomenclature. Mells church provides striking examples of the early
20th century cultural mélange; both of the civilization in retreat, and
hints of changes soon to come. The three memorials that catch the attention are those to Laura Lyttelton, Raymond Asquith, Edward Horner;

while for good measure Siegfried Sassoon lies under a tombstone in the churchyard. The Lyttelton and Asquith memorials face each other at the west end of the church under the belfry tower; the Horner memorial in a small chapel at the east end.

The mural tablet to Laura Lyttelton, eight or nine foot high, is a bas relief in gesso on wood, executed in 1886 by none other than Edward Burne-Jones. The design, an effective one, represents a peacock, emblem of resurrection. The bird's ornate tail trails down towards the base of the tablet, beside its length a Latin inscription to the effect that she there commemorated lies in the North, yet her friends in the South love and remember her. Laura Lyttelton (née Tennant), married only a year, had died in childbirth in her early twenties. She had been one of that group of young people, rather self-consciously gifted with beauty and wit, called in derision The Souls. The designation did not altogether fit those to whom it was applied, suggesting the current Aesthetic Movement rather than the ambitious young politicians and far from unworldly ladies who tended to be recruited to The Souls. The Souls might affect to sit on cushions placed on the floor of their drawing-rooms, and show devotion to parlour games, but they were not soulful in any unpractical sense. All the same Burne-Jones's peacock does suggest an inner melancholy, not only a search for less material things, but also an inexplicable yet pervasive fear for the future.

This last response in the beholder is no doubt largely induced by the memorial's association with that on the opposite wall, one so peculiarly expressive of what was to be visited on the next generation; a record of mortality that was to fall with especial grimness on the sort of people The Souls had been; indeed directly on some who have been termed 'second generation Souls'. Here again is an overpowering sadness, though sadness of a very different mood from that of the peacock. This memorial is Raymond Asquith's. A notable figure of the group to which he belonged, he had learnt aristocratic arrogance in a single generation, but learnt the aristocratic virtues too. His published *Letters* provide an absorbing example of that parting of the ways between the new things and the old; a scholar treating the classicists with irony, while at the same time himself hesitating as to which way to move forward.

Below a wreath of laurel cast in greenish bronze hang (or rather hung) the sword in leather scabbard and steel helmet that were Raymond Asquith's actual army equipment. On this memorial too the inscription, quite a lengthy one, is in Latin. The tall capital letters are carved on the wall of the church itself with avoidance of too much appearance of ornamental finish, almost with roughness, the concavities picked out in now faded dark blue and dark red.

I find hard to define the powerful effect of this memorial. It seems to me, remembering the period as a child, perfectly to express the emotions of that moment in history, the manner anyway the intellectuals wanted those emotions recorded. Something about the whole conception of the memorial – which would have been different a few years earlier or a few years later, one could almost say a few months in each case – bringing back with a force comparable to no other monument I can think of an overwhelming sense of the first war, its idealisms, its agonies, its tragedies. The Latin inscription still appeals to a classical past, yet sensibilities at once more dramatic and more down to earth strain forward to some modern form of expression, though perhaps dimly understood. There is the same fretting towards a less traditional aesthetic that thirty years before applies to the Laura Lyttelton tablet.

No such hint of uneasy stirrings, indeed the very reverse, belongs to the equestrian statue of Edward Horner in the small chapel at the other end of the church. This memorial is by (Sir) Alfred Munnings, better known for pictures of horses and race-course scenes than as a sculptor, later President of the Royal Academy and blusteringly antagonistic towards 'modern art'. The dimensions of the statue itself, naturalistic within its idealized terms, firmly academic in technique, are not happy. Although less than life-size (perhaps three-quarters) the magnitude still seems too great for the chapel's interior. There is a suggestion of crampedness in addition to the sculptor's less than sensitive viewpoint. The bareheaded saintly young horseman, an Arthurian knight from the pages of Tennyson, rides out on his charger. Here is no reminder, as in Raymond Asquith's memorial, of the brutal realities of war. Even Edward Horner's cavalry gauntlets that lie beneath on the plinth recall the parade ground rather than the barrage. This is quite another approach to honouring the fallen in battle.

Yet the equestrian figure, the Burne-Jones peacock, the Roman capitals incised on the stone of the church wall, together complete the picture of a span of years given over to mixed and changing symbols.

After the Edward Horner gauntlets were stolen from their place in Mells church further despoliation was intercepted by removal of Raymond Asquith's helmet and sword. In short the ensemble described is no more to be seen in its most effective form. All the same much remains to ponder, and, even if robbing tombs stretches back to the earliest antiquity, the fact that such measures have been found necessary emphasizes changes in the English countryside. It would be a pity if such pilfering made the churches of England difficult of access. Their idiosyncrasies of furnishing possess an individuality and charm to be found nowhere else in Europe. Wyndham Ketton-Cremer was always full of stories about the churches and clergy of his native country of Norfolk, where a tradition of eccentricity had long and obstinately flourished.

Ketton-Cremer's own incumbent, about to take a service in a neigh-bouring parish where the parson was ill or absent, moved a candlestick on the altar of the dark and untidy church and caught his finger in a mousetrap. His experience was less disturbing than that of another clergyman friend of Ketton-Cremer's, also officiating for a congre-gation not his own. This Norfolk parson, not knowing the church, had arrived early for a funeral in order to have a short time to look round. In an embrasure over a tomb he saw a mediaeval or renaissance helmet. Helmets, even whole suits of armour, were dedicated to churches in the past, but I believe those to be seen in country churches have not always been worn in war or even for tilting, but come to rest in their surroundings after being used, like hatchments, merely to display at his funeral the coat-of-arms of a local nobleman or squire. Whichever type, Ketton-Cremer's parson friend lifted the helmet down, and as there remained time to kill before the service, tried it on. Assuming this iron head-dress was easy enough, but when the moment came to replace the helmet the clergyman was unable to extract himself. All efforts failed. When the mourners, followed by the undertakers and coffin, arrived at the church they were surprised to be received by a cleric wearing a knight's bascinet. Presumably he had contrived to lift the vizor, though of that Ketton-Cremer was uncertain. All he knew was that the burial service had to be pronounced by a priest thus accoutred.

The village of Stiffkey, at one time famous owing to the goings-on of its vicar (referred to earlier), was comparatively near Felbrigg, Ketton-Cremer's house, and he was a friend of one of the church-wardens of its combined parishes. Ketton-Cremer used to call this versatile and somewhat choleric figure (who united the status of country gentleman with that of dealer in secondhand furniture) 'the old pirate', a type our host undoubtedly resembled when we dined at his house. The Old Pirate, together with the rest of the neighbourhood, had long been exasperated by the behaviour of their vicar, who had some ecclesi-astical commitment with the Stage and was always in London. Once or twice a year the vicar of Stiffkey would arrive on a motor-bicycle, preach a hurried sermon while eating a sandwich in the pulpit, then deal as best he could with the administrative needs of the parish in the time left for getting back to London from the northern parts of East Anglia.

Ketton-Cremer was one day lunching with the Pirate, who had been complaining that it was impossible to be baptized, married, or buried locally on account of the irregularities of the vicar, when a dramatic incident took place. Ketton-Cremer's seat at the luncheon table was facing the window and the drive of the house. A very ramshackle car drove up to the door in which sat a clergyman, and a personage who looked like a bookmaker, wearing a bowler hat and exceptionally loud check suit. The clergyman stepped out of the car, disappearing from sight as he walked towards the front-door. The bell rang. The Pirate's face went crimson.

'Continue with luncheon,' he said. 'I'll deal with this.'

Ketton-Cremer did as he was told. He heard some altercation in the hall. A moment later – as in a slapstick comedy – the clergyman staggered past the window again, this time clutching the seat of his trousers where he had evidently just received a hearty kick. He managed to reach the car, and drove off with the man in the check suit and bowler hat. The Pirate returned to the dining-room.

'I settled that,' he said.

Luncheon continued with conversation about other rural matters. Inevitably there was a row later, which received a fair amount of publicity. The Pirate was fined, in consequence having to resign from the Bench as a magistrate. Cheques and postal-orders poured in to pay his fine, a Yorkshire miner sending a pair of clogs with the recommendation that they be worn on the next occasion when the Vicar had to be admonished. The Vicar himself, as is well known, was in due course unfrocked for relations with prostitutes, earned a living by appearing at fairs in a coffin being consumed by the fires of Hell (where he was inspected by the young Roy Fuller), and finally succumbed to a circus lion.

After moving to the country we used for many years to bottle some of the wine we drank. A hogshead would be ordered from a shipper in Bordeaux, a bill of lading arriving from Bristol about twenty-five miles away, whence the wine would be delivered at the house. In early days we would share the hogshead (about two hundred and eighty bottles) with the Drus, once with the Mells household, but in the end organized the operation on our own, easier to undertake as our sons grew older and could be used in Dickensian child labour. On the occasion when the wine was divided between ourselves and Mells, that is to say Katharine Asquith and Ronnie Knox, we had hoped Knox might assume for the ceremonial broaching of the hogshead the elegant monsignor's cassock with purple piping and sash which he wore in the evening; thereby recreating those 19th-century pictures of cardinals carousing. That was not to be, though, when after the bottling we bathed in Mells swimming-pool, his bathing pants were of a light and decidedly ecclesiastical green.

In appearance Knox – called Ronnie by most of those who knew him, Ronald by Katharine Asquith and a few close friends – had a long thin face, longish nose, and was usually smoking a pipe. He looked very straight at you when he talked. Evelyn Waugh, who wrote Knox's biography, greatly revered him. Waugh's book gives a good impression of the circle associated with Mells in which Knox's wit and intellectual brilliance had brought him; a Youth if golden, also aggressive in its self-confidence, represented by those two commemorated in the church, the Grenfells, Patrick Shaw-Stewart, Charles Lister, several others, most of them killed in the war, of whom much has been written.

'Evelyn looks on Ronnie as Bossuet', Alick Dru used to say. 'I myself don't go as far as that. I think he's just a nice intelligent man.'

Although in general two more different personalities could scarcely be conceived, there was something in Knox's early career that resembled Cyril Connolly's emergence from obscurity at Eton to become, through similar powers of wit and intelligence, a popular figure among a crowd of hearty ambitious school contemporaries. College at Eton had been a launching-pad for both. Connolly's worldly schoolboy friends can claim none of the dazzling legend (though perhaps some also dignified by death in battle) of Knox's group, and Connolly himself turned to literature rather than religion, but the early promise, the attraction towards dashing types, the humour tinged with disappointment, find some parallel.

Katharine Asquith, in her day a beauty, had been one of those to be called 'second generation Souls'. When young she had moved much in the beau monde, but for many years now lived in comparative retirement. From existence under the same roof she and Knox had both developed some of those mild mutual asperities with one another to be associated with a couple long and happily married. I never saw much of Ronnie Knox, but always found him a man of delightful humour. Waugh had written that he could be chilly if surroundings were in the least unsympathetic. I said I had never noticed that. 'You were at Eton and Balliol,' Waugh replied. Knox's disappointment – sometimes voiced in so many words – was that 'They won't make me a bishop'.

Violet once asked whether, when Katharine Asquith was a débutante, gentlemen paying a formal call had still brought top-hat and walking stick with them into the drawing-room. This was a fashion just beginning to change when my father was a young man, and he used to recall one of the social tortures of his younger days being whether or not to leave hat and stick in the hall. I don't remember Katharine Asquith's answer on this grave point, but she must have mentioned the question to Knox (who for some reason had not as usual accompanied her), because he telephoned to Violet later in the evening to add a footnote.

Knox said: 'A French priest wrote a book to try and make English priests more chic and less middle-class. He was very insistent that one of the most important rules of behaviour to bear in mind was that when a priest visited the sick he must above all not lay his hat and umbrella on the bed.'

Ronnie Knox was fond of telling stories to illustrate the vicissitudes of clerical life (the background of his own family), one of which described how he had been booked to preach in an outer London suburb. On approaching the neighbourhood of the church he lost his way. No one was about on Sunday morning. He was in despair when suddenly he saw a man advancing quickly towards him. The man was in fact running at breakneck speed down the hill in front. Knox thought twice about delaying anyone in such a hurry, but there seemed no alternative to stopping the runner and asking the way.

'I'm so sorry to trouble you, but can you by any chance direct me to the Catholic church?'

The man took a second or two to recover his breath.

'Straight up the hill,' he said. 'At the top on the right – but if you come with me we've just time to reach the other Catholic church quite near here *where there's no sermon this Sunday*.'

Although Knox has become one of the legendary figures of the pre-1914 generation, in one sense typical of that vintage, he was quite unlike Ivy Compton-Burnett in making me feel that he belonged to a period made utterly remote from my own. In that respect he also differed from Siegfried Sassoon, although the ages of the three of them were enclosed by about four or five years, and Knox in fact enjoyed talking of former ways of life. Siegfried Sassoon is buried at Mells, beside Knox who about ten years before his death had played some part in Sassoon's conversion to the Roman Church. I had been no more than introduced to Siegfried Sassoon by Osbert Sitwell years before, but never came across him again until the early 1960s, although he lived now only about fifteen miles away at Heytesbury House. This was quite near Robin and Julia Mount at Chitterne, who used often to speak of him. Then he became a member of the dining-club to which I belonged occasionally referred to again in the memoirs.

Sassoon's *Diary* (1981) of the 1920s contains many references to 'Burton'; that is to say Nellie Burton, who let rooms to 'single gentlemen' at 40 Half Moon Street, Piccadilly. It was customary to drop in on her for tea, and Osbert Sitwell once took me to see Burton, who deserves to be recorded as a figure who must have played a part not wholly unlike that of Rosa Lewis, proprietress of The Cavendish. Perhaps a dozen years younger than Rosa Lewis, a very different type within those terms of reference, Burton had a touch of the same suggestion that something a shade *louche* was taking place in the background of her premises; though compared with The Cavendish that was faint and diluted. Burton herself, respectful, chatty, infinitely understanding, had the air of a nanny or ladysmaid (more the latter, possibly explaining the chic use of only her surname), retired after long service in a very 'good' family. Wilde's friend Robert Ross had spent his declining years in Burton's rooms, where among others Lord

Berners lodged, already renowned for his *diableries*; also (Sir) Roderick Meiklejohn, utterly unlike Gerald Berners, but eccentric too for a distinguished civil servant (Private Secretary with the art patron Eddie Marsh to Asquith). Meiklejohn had a curious manner of mumbling and gesturing that was often imitated by the young men who attracted him.

When reviewing Sassoon's *Diary* I mentioned that Burton catered only for single gentlemen, in consequence of which an anonymous correspondent wrote saying that his (or her) mother, then a young Canadian VAD, had stayed in an attic at 40 Half Moon Street during the first war, when Burton had been very kind to her. One of Burton's then frequent comments was that things must be 'shushed up'; no doubt wise. I was surprised at this account of a woman having been accommodated in Burton's rooms, because Osbert Sitwell told me that some years before someone had attempted to introduce a female element, which had greatly annoyed Burton, who had shouted: 'I won't have any Tondelayos here'; Tondelayo being a dusky seductress in *White Cargo*, a play about young men going to pieces in a remote African trading station, which had made rather a hit.

One of Sassoon's habits was to take midnight rides in the darkness through the woods of his quite extensive property at Heytesbury. He must on those occasions have given the appearance of a spectral figure like Herne the Hunter. No doubt a shared interest in horses had connected Sassoon and Robin Mount in the first instance, and the pair of them would sometimes go out hacking together on the Wiltshire downs.

It is of note that both Siegfried Sassoon and Robert Graves served as officers of the Royal Welch Fusiliers, a regiment that also produced from its 'other ranks' Frank Richards, who wrote an excellent book of war reminiscences *Old Soldiers Never Die* (1933), and the poet-painter David Jones, mentioned earlier. The RWF's Medical Officer, J. C. Dunn, also wrote a war book said to be of merit, *The War the Infantry Knew*. In contrast, The Welch Regiment (now incorporated with the South Wales Borderers as the Royal Regiment of Wales, 24th/41st Foot) seems to have produced only two novelists from its temporary officers, Ford Madox Ford and myself. When I met Ford he told me that his Commanding Officer had written on some report for which Ford had been responsible, the note: 'If the illiterate subaltern with the illegible handwriting will etc., etc.' The Welch Regiment regular battalions can however claim an interesting writer, a figure who should not be forgotten, A. J. B. Wavell, a contemporary of my father's as subaltern in the South African War. Wavell left the army in 1906, and, disguised as a Zanzibari, made the pilgrimage to Mecca, giving an account of the experience in *A Modern Pilgrimage to Mecca* (1912), a good book in its

genre. He settled near Mombasa. When the first war came he raised a
force locally known as Wavell's Own, a private army of Arabic-speaking
water-carriers (as it were a battalion of Gunga Dins), which held up a
superior German force trying to cut off the road to Mombasa. Wavell
was decorated, then shortly afterwards killed.

Siegfried Sassoon talked very much the army idiom of my father's
generation, but with a gentle, remote, almost embarrassed air. He was
only a few years from eighty when I met him, and looked like a ghost
haunting the fields of Passchendaele or Bapaume. Unusually tall,
gauntly thin, an apparent frailty made him seem almost transparent,
though even in later life I suspect this outward unsubstantiality concealed a powerful will. When Sassoon heard where we lived he suggested that Violet and I should visit him, come to tea. That was in
the autumn of 1963.

'Ring up one day,' he said. 'I'm always there.'

I did so about a week later. By that time Sassoon seemed a shade
nervous, worried at his own recklessness in having issued such an invitation. The *Diaries* show him even in early days to have felt such uncertainties.

'It's just you and your missus?' he asked apprehensively.

'Just us – but only if that's all right?'

'Yes, come along, of course, of course.'

All the same he sounded a little disturbed; disturbed rather than
inhospitable.

'You know where it is – there's a long stone wall. Just before you
get to that hutted army camp.'

Heytesbury House is said to occupy the site of a palace used by the
Empress Matilda, mother of King Henry II. Several centuries after
her time one of the Lords Hungerford began to build a house there
in the reign of Henry VIII, a project brought to a close when Hungerford, attainted for sodomy, forcing his own daughter, and invoking
devils by black magic, was executed for these alleged irregularities. The
present house, mainly of late 18th century or early 19th century architecture, was completed by the Wiltshire family of à Court, MPs for
the former 'rotten borough' of Heytesbury, one of whom was raised
to the peerage as Baron Heytesbury shortly before the First Reform
Bill. Sassoon had bought the place in the 1930s on making a marriage
that had later come adrift.

On that crisp luminous autumn afternoon the grey façade of Heytesbury House, dignified and massive, like its owner looked also a little
sombre and ghostly. The gardens and background of woods with rolling
downs beyond were absolutely still. These were evidently the grounds
of an enchanted castle. We drove round to the entrance which was at the
back of the building. Nobody answered the front-door bell. Hammering

at the knocker had no effect either. We strolled round to the front of the house, completing this circle a couple of times. A long sash-window had been left half-open. Stepping through we found ourselves in a large drawing-room. Croquet mallets leant against sofas, books lay open on tables. Life seemed to have stopped perhaps half a century before. If the outside of the house had suggested enchantment the interior seemed to confirm some such scene as the Sleeping Beauty's palace; the Sleeping Beauty's rather than that of the Empress Matilda, who was probably always on the look out for an unfriendly visit from King Stephen. Then Sassoon suddenly appeared from nowhere. He showed no surprise at finding us in his drawing-room. We made some apology for forcing an entrance. He seemed to walk in a dream through a dream world.

'How beautiful this place looks on an autumn afternoon.'

'Tennysonian?'

He murmured the question.

'Yes.'

'That's what I always think. Tennysonian. Absolutely Tennysonian. I say, let's have some tea.'

Sassoon had now lost all earlier anxieties about the visit. He chattered away about Mells, the Mounts, local nuns he sometimes went to see. An electric kettle was attached to a plug in the skirting of the wall. Sassoon, evidently too stiff to bend from the waist, leant forward towards the kettle at an ominously acute angle. It seemed impossible that he would be able to maintain his balance, then straighten himself, but he brought about that manoeuvre successfully, and made the tea. As I have said, like Ivy Compton-Burnett, though not like Ronnie Knox, Siegfried Sassoon belonged to another era, another civilization than one's own. He was less brisk than either of those, perhaps just more tired. So far as mannerisms were concerned Miss Compton-Burnett was as if the first war had never taken place; Monsignor Knox, perhaps by an act of will, seemed to be living in the present; for Captain Sassoon, though no longer himself involved in it, the first war was still in progress.

3

Not long after moving to the country I lunched at the Authors' Club with Malcolm Muggeridge, then Deputy Editor of *The Daily Telegraph*. The job seemed to suit him pretty well, his heart being in 'news' journalism, while the particular gradation of rank – so to speak third in command – represented a reasonably powerful sphere of influence not oppressively incommoded by too much responsibility. During the course of luncheon Muggeridge told me that he had been offered the editorship of *Punch*. Foreseeing amusing possibilities he had decided to accept, notwithstanding the satisfactory nature of his position at the *DT* and its good prospects. He suggested that I might follow him to Bouverie Street as Literary Editor. We talked this over at the time, and after further discussions about detail it was settled that I should begin work on *Punch* in the spring of 1953.

I had scarcely opened *Punch* – among highbrows a byword for phil-istinism and stuffy conformity – for years, while retaining a certain affection for the 19th-century volumes that had once been such a solace. In short I was well informed about past *Punch*, wholly ignorant as to the current paper. I liked the idea of working with Muggeridge, the job would not be badly paid, some days in the week would remain free for my own writing. At this period *Punch*, still owned by Bradbury, Agnew & Co, was more or less a family concern. The offices were housed in a dignified and relatively historic building, 10 Bouverie Street, which runs south from Fleet Street. Its proprietors, hoping for some magical formula which would halt its postwar decline, had now taken the hitherto unprecedented step of recruiting an editor – in short Malcolm Muggeridge – from outside the *Punch* staff, rather than make the traditional promotion from within. This innovation was naturally looked on without much enthusiasm on the part of anyone on the spot who saw himself as a potential editor; being almost equally disesteemed by members of the staff not aspiring to such heights.

I think the sole *Punch* figure I had ever come across in the flesh, that only once or twice, was A. P. Herbert. Then in his sixties, Alan Herbert, though his name appeared from time to time in the paper's pages, could no longer be called a very active contributor. To have met only him among the *Punch* group was no mere chance. Herbert, author, publicist, MP, with connexions at the Bar, in the Theatre, even with certain forms of academic life, moved through a wide orbit very different from the restricted beat of his contemporary *Punch* colleagues; yet more from the generation (one tending to be in their early forties) succeeding those. Few of these younger people – so I found – cared to mix with anyone except other members of the *Punch* staff. The younger *Punch* journalists were inclined (not wholly without cause) to find Herbert's general demeanour at Bouverie Street something of an embarrassment; especially on such supposedly festive occasions as the *Punch* Christmas Dinner, when without the least provocation Herbert would rise from his seat at the port-and-brandy stage to sing a lengthy old-time comic song. Indeed after one such Yuletide reunion the *Punch*

Christmas Dinner was abolished out of hand by Muggeridge, to whom in any case all traditional or collective merrymaking of whatever nature was utterly abhorrent.

Herbert's fullblooded unconventional toryism was also inimical to these younger *Punch* colleagues, most of whom (B. A. Young one of the few exceptions), so far as politics played any part in their lives, being mildly Leftish. They had never questioned the virtues of such institutions as the United Nations or the British Commonwealth, far less satirized their humbug. Muggeridge's anarcho-anti-Left-anti-Churchill-anti-intellectual-nihilistic-sex is fun/sex is sinful-diatribes against everything and everybody, expressed in a copious flow of political paradox, and four-letter-word imagery, naturally caused some astonishment, even dismay, at first onset. In short so far from hearty Falstaffian mirth setting the tone at Bouverie Street the immediate impression given by the *Punch* ambience was one of lowish vitality sustained by a fairly dogged and longstanding complacency. That at least was my own first judgment; not an altogether fair one, because without much direction from above a coherent magazine was at least coming out every week, something that in itself required a certain degree of energy.

Nevertheless others as well as myself were struck by the peculiarly muted atmosphere of the *Punch* office, the apparent physical enervation, the inward-looking personal exchanges; a surrounding despondency alleviated only by an unusually charming team of girl secretaries. John Raymond, for instance (whose taste for the bottle and early death prevented him from fulfilling his promise as a literary journalist), observed that when he entered the *Punch* office he had the impression of arriving in a convalescent ward; no one seriously ill or crippled, indeed all likely to be out and about fairly soon, but still none of them quite A.1 at the moment.

One might compare a paper like *Punch* with a human body subject to a recurrent weekly deficiency in certain essential cell-tissues, organisms only to be nourished by an inoculation of jokes: preferably good ones, but even indifferent or actively bad ones better than none at all. The more powerful the restorative, the better the patient feels in any given week, but, from the nature of the disease, even the utmost stringency of tonic injection can be calculated to last no more than seven days; when once again the ghastly symptoms of inanition begin to make themselves plain. This incurable malady persists as long as the body's circulation shows a flicker of movement. The strain on practitioners called in to remedy the case can be severe.

Except for a few minor changes among out-of-office contributors in specialized fields Muggeridge retained the staff that had been producing *Punch* under the previous editorship. At the same time he introduced – a fairly mixed blessing – the practice of using a sprinkling of comparatively wellknown extraneous writers to sharpen up the tone of the paper. So far as new blood in the actual office was transfused, apart from myself as Literary Editor, the only addition was Leslie Marsh, an old colleague of Muggeridge's on *The Evening Standard*, a veteran journalist brought in to collate and administer *Punch* 'copy'. The cartoonists – using the term loosely to denote all *Punch* draughtsmen rather than limiting it to those who executed the weekly cartoon – did not present quite the same potential for making drastic change as the various forms of writer. There are of necessity fewer capable comic artists from whom to choose. A high proportion of the best of these are bound to be under contract to daily newspapers, organs in a position to pay much higher rates than any weekly magazine. The *Punch* 'Table' (an inner circle of the staff, promotion to which was often achieved only after long years of hard service) met at Bouverie Street for luncheon once a week. The Agnews, father and son, partook of this weekly luncheon. Although not precisely skeletons at the feast – that would be going too far in speaking of a repast that was fairly lugubrious anyway – they inevitably constituted a faintly alien element among professional journalists who were their employees. The Agnews themselves never joined the debate to any noticeable extent, far less attempted to influence politically or otherwise. I was on appointment to my job created a member of the Table.

The literary editorship of *Punch* – anyway in my eyes – carried with it no obligation to be 'funny', although at first I had to resist certain pressures, internal and external, from those who assumed the book pages of the paper were principally dedicated by prescriptive right to humour. My view was – and is – that very little doubt exists each week as to which books ought to be noticed. Naturally length and manner of treatment must vary a good deal from paper to paper, but (except in specialized periodicals) not the books themselves. So far as space allowed, the books I myself thought deserved attention would in future be reviewed in *Punch*. This meant imposing a relatively highbrow standard on a magazine with a long and obstinate tradition of active philistinism. Such a tradition, anyway so far as book notices went, was now to undergo a change. In fact *Punch* book reviews, short and few in number, had been for many years on the whole tolerably if un-adventurously written. The book pages, almost universally a poor relation of the main body of any periodical, now gained a little status by the institution of a full-page weekly review. I usually wrote that myself, though from time to time Muggeridge would want to deal with a volume of political memoirs or something of that sort, while R. G. G. Price might suggest some book he preferred to discuss at greater length. A few others also appeared on this opening page of the literary section.

Short notices were normally constricted to one hundred and eighty words. That just gave room to say what the book was about, express a coherent opinion as to worth, and – ideally – make some sparkling comment. Such notices were accommodated in a manner to convenience the printer (rather than the Literary Editor) when the paper was 'made up'.

Let me give an example of a literary editor's hazards. After glancing through the pages of the review copy of L. P. Hartley's novel *A Perfect Woman* (1955) I decided the theme would not attract very sympathetic notices. Accordingly (conforming to the worst suspicions of those who denounce all literary criticism as a racket) I sent this friend's book to another friend (of mine not Hartley's) Jocelyn Brooke, who would, I supposed, feel well disposed towards Hartley as a writer; and let down an indifferent novel fairly lightly. My judgment proved wholly at fault. *A Perfect Woman* received rapturous notices on all sides. Jocelyn Brooke, unusual in him, did not send his review within a week or ten days. On the contrary he delayed so long that I was about to dispatch a reminder, when it arrived with a covering letter. The note enclosed said that Brooke was sorry to be late with his 'copy', had thought Hartley's novel ridiculously over-praised, and done his best to redress the balance by pointing out some of the faults. In short *Punch* was practically the only paper to give *A Perfect Woman* a shabby welcome. Two years later when Hartley's *The Hireling* (1957) appeared I thought the sinister undercurrents of the story might appeal to Maclaren-Ross as showing a more robust development; Maclaren-Ross allowing Hartley's abilities but demurring at the mildness of the plots. That also turned out a misjudgment. Apart from differences in style, Brooke's review of *A Perfect Woman* was repeated in a slightly varied form by Maclaren-Ross's treatment of *The Hireling*. Such can be the consequences (and a good thing too some will mutter) of attempting to accommodate one's friends in the literary world.

Maclaren-Ross himself raised yet another problem. His daily life was in general designed in a manner to dodge a voracious pack of creditors, whose legal representatives in the form of bailiffs were for ever on his track. When the comparatively regular visits of Maclaren-Ross to Bouverie Street to collect review copies became known, a covey of bailiffs came into being outside, where they hung about ominously on the steps of the *Punch* office. At last Agnew *fils*, with some justification as he had found physical difficulty in pushing his way through the mob of debt-collectors at, so to speak, his own front-door, came to me to complain. He asked if Maclaren-Ross could be dispensed with as a reviewer so that free egress might once more be established. My answer was that I perfectly saw his point. As part of the proprietorship he was clearly in a position to lay down that Maclaren-Ross was no longer

persona grata at Bouverie Street owing to the inconvenience his intermittent presence brought about. If Agnew *fils* stated that as an instruction from above, I was prepared to bow to the ruling without raising
objection. But it must be an order. I was not going to abandon a good
reviewer on my own initiative. There the matter rested.

'St Agnew's Eve – Ah, bitter chill it was!' Leslie Marsh used often
to lament on the day of the Table luncheon, but if the Agnews did
not enfold the assembled company conversationally in a blaze of wit,
they did their best to be co-operative, and were patient about voicing
disquiets that must from time to time have afflicted their minds during
the birth-pangs of Muggeridgian *Punch*. It was indeed nearly five years
before the Agnews became visibly restive, heralding Muggeridge's own
resignation. I liked Marsh, with whom I shared a large room, but if the
Beadsman's fingers were numb, his breath frosted from the chilly
atmosphere of the office, that was just as likely to have resulted from
contact with Marsh's own cosmic despair as any frost-bound demeanour imputed by Marsh to St Agnew.

Severely conventional in outward appearance, Marsh was not without
his own inner fads. Like not a few journalists he nourished within him
a passionate hatred of Fleet Street, every cranny of which was long
familiar to him. I have been told (though cannot confirm the truth of
the story) that – showing more enterprise than most romanticizers of
rural life – Marsh had actually abandoned journalism for a time in
favour of working in the fresh air as a hedger-and-ditcher or some such
category of bucolic employment. This rustic calling, whatever its
nature, turned out less attractive in practice than to muse upon in Fleet
Street, and, having naturally lost professional headway by the experiment, Marsh returned to journalism an embittered man. On that
account there were those at *Punch* who found him hard to get on with.
Marsh's gloomy humours were not decreased by his job, the truly
Herculean labour of bringing a modicum of order to the administrative
chaos which had hitherto prevailed in an office where, for instance, some
of the old hands had been accustomed to dispatch their 'copy' direct to
the printer without its passing under any editorial supervision what-
soever. In this area – or rather pre-Adamite formless void – Marsh did
a great deal to pull *Punch* together.

What Marsh did not cover in the way of administration was mostly
dealt with by Peter Dickinson, a young man who also had his being
in our room. A poet and Old Etonian he too sometimes contributed
to the paper, usually verse. Later Dickinson escaped to earn an independent living as a successful writer of detective stories. Years afterwards
he told me that, as one might have nightmares that one were back at
school, he sometimes dreamt that he was still in Bouverie Street trying
to straighten things out. Among the ablest of the *Punch* staff was

B. A. Young. He had remained in the army after the war, completing some ten years service in all, three years of which had been in different parts of Africa. Young possessed a capacity to write readably and knowledgeably about almost every subject required by journalism: politics, painting, music, books, sport, economics, naval and military matters. He was as at home at a NATO exercise as at a Prokoviev concert or an exhibition of Braque. When Muggeridge left, Young would have made a talented – for once unphilistine – editor of the paper, but the management took another choice. Freddie Young, incidentally, provided some useful hints in defining the music likely to be played by General Conyers on his 'cello.

Another adroit *Punch* writer to help with specialized information for *Dance* was Basil Boothroyd, who, having worked in a Lincolnshire bank in his early days, could supply just that smattering of professional jargon necessary for indicating the civil life employment of Territorial officers nearly all of whom came from banks. For a novelist to obtain such arcane trimmings, anyway in just the form needed, can be unbelievably difficult. Boothroyd himself always retained a touch of the *Three Men in a Boat* trio, escaped from their London bank for a weekend, having a high old time on the upper reaches of the Thames. One could well imagine him in the straw boater and high straight collar of the period. It was a book for which we both had an affection, with its extraordinary mélange of knock-about farce combined with Walter Pater's most Pateresque prose. Like Freddie Young, Basil Boothroyd possessed musical aptitudes; once humming for me Vinteuil's 'little phrase', which, isolated and interpreted in such an imaginative rendering, deserved at least a few thousand additional words of Proustian analysis.

On the book pages Richard Price was an auxiliary with an unusually sure touch in undertaking the fairly thankless task of writing short notices; managing to convey what a novel was about (an essential sometimes disregarded by seasoned novel reviewers), make a joke, convey a word of warning to the potential reader without egregiously insulting the author; an action only rarely required. I once discussed newspaper interviewers with Price, remarking on the sameness of their questions whatever writer was being interviewed, particularly the invariable enquiries about routine: 'Do you write with a pen or a typewriter, do you sit down at 9 o'clock every morning, etc?' Price replied: 'All people have a fantasy they could write a novel if only they knew the trick. They think that cunning interrogation might take a novelist off guard – cause revelation of the secret – a particular sort of pen, brand of typewriter, format of paper. Once that is accidentally divulged, the interviewer, all shrewd readers of the article, will themselves be able to become novelists.' On this matter of interviews a military parallel strikes me. In the army it is not uncommon for a soldier to keep certain items of kit purely for the eye of the inspecting officer. Small odds and ends that are a trouble to clean or to assemble are stowed away for daily use, an unsullied example presented. That is rather like what writers usually hand out at interviews.

Muggeridge acquired Michael Cummings, a cartoonist with a keen political grasp, to draw for the Parliamentary pages. That was not easy owing to Cummings's other commitments. The next Editor on taking over at once sacked this very capable commentator. Increased space was also given to the work of another excellent cartoonist, Ronald Searle. Nonetheless – so it seemed to me – not enough was done to reorganize the 'art' side of the paper in the manner *Punch* required. Muggeridge was by temperament not sufficiently interested in drawing, as such, but even in pictures too the Muggeridge years provide at least some meat between the pretty dry crusts of bread that make the sandwich enclosing them.

The main political cartoonist was Leslie Illingworth, who had worked for *Punch* for many years and was then in his fifties. An efficient draughtsman in the John Tenniel/Bernard Partridge tradition, Illingworth brought something of his own to a dying convention of cartooning that could have become hopelessly wooden, and was at best old-fashioned enough. Although of Yorkshire extraction Illingworth had been brought up in South Wales, thereby having become a complete South Walian in appearance, manner, sentiment, humour, and passionate attachment to the Vale of Glamorgan. Wholly apolitical in outlook himself, Illingworth was in a chronic state of having to illustrate political contingencies of every kind both for *Punch* and *The Daily Mail*, which also employed him as main cartoonist. *The Daily Mail* by no means necessarily propagated the same political gospels as Muggerid-gian *Punch*, indeed often took a precisely antithetical standpoint. Illingworth, who liked to be instructed down to the smallest detail as to what he should draw (directions that he would follow with consummate attention, always adding a certain development of his own) used to laugh about this appearance of double-facedness. He would ask people if they thought it mattered advocating one policy in one paper, its converse in another, but I don't think the problem ever kept him awake at night. There was something very sympathetic about Illingworth's gnomelike features, body, and demeanour. I used often to sit next to him at Table luncheons. He was not a great talker, but his opinions were always worth hearing, at moments unexpectedly phrased.

Illingworth once remarked to me: 'You can take it from a comic artist that, if any artist turns to comic drawing, something has *always* gone wrong in his life.'

I have often wondered what Illingworth blamed in his own case.

If the proprietors of *Punch* did not attempt to interfere on the editorial side of the paper, the same could not be said for some of the heads of department other than editorial. These, making up a convocation of perhaps a dozen souls, sat down together once a month at the same table where the weekly editorial luncheons were held, this time to discuss 'business' matters. At first, as Literary Editor, I was required to attend these joyless gatherings, but in due course Muggeridge decided that the Literary Editor's presence was not needed – something only too clear – and I was thankfully released.

Members of the editorial staff, indeed all writers and cartoonists contributing to any periodical, may – almost certainly will – disagree to a greater or lesser extent with some of the decisions of their editor. At the same time Editor and editorial staff are likely to find some common basis from which to debate disagreements if these are voiced. Such common ground was often patently lacking during these 'business' talks round the *Punch* dining-table, where certain of those present appeared wholly unaware (some readers might have urged justifiably) that the magazine was at least intended to make people laugh. I remember, for example, one head of department firmly putting forward the opinion that a stimulating effect on sales would be achieved by a series of articles (practical rather than humorous) on such subjects as *How to Build a Boat*. Similar textures of thought were given expression by discussions preceding the abandonment of the celebrated *Punch* cover, executed by Richard Doyle more than a century before, and continuously used since that period.

Arguments against Doyle's cover, however unappealing such might be to persons with any sense of continuity or appreciation of versatile design, were by no means out of reach; the most cogent being that a contemporary public for a comic paper had grown insensitive to the potency of Doyle's phantasmagoria (surprisingly erotic when closely examined), notwithstanding its long and popular reign. That such obtuseness could exist was made painfully clear by the comments of those sitting round the table. Public indifference, however, was not urged as primary motive for supplanting Doyle's picture. Indeed sheer lack of interest one way or the other might have been advanced as a reason for retention. Muggeridge himself – in whom nostalgia for tradition would have been hard to detect with even the most delicate instrument – felt, I think, without *parti pris* in the matter; neither anxious for a new cover nor objecting to the old.

The proposition put forward by the adherents of change was a far more extraordinary one than allegation of public torpidity. On the contrary it was insisted that the Doyle cover was 'not popular' with bookstall assistants, because, being uncoloured, the magazine 'could not be seen' alongside other periodicals lying on the counter. This – if, which seems highly unlikely, based on any form of enquiry over and above the hungovered daydreams and fevered nocturnal reveries of ad-men, running counter as it did to the simplest and most basic principles of camouflage – was extremely hard to swallow. At that particular moment, doubtless in response to the ad-man doctrine being currently preached, multicoloured covers for weekly illustrated papers had become almost universal, *Punch* perhaps alone in sticking to its black-and-white (occasionally lightly tinted) cover. At the same time the *Punch* cover, a century or more old, was quite a different matter. If those at Bouverie Street in favour of jettisoning Doyle had said: 'We cannot hold up our heads among our fellows because our illustrated weekly does not look exactly like every other illustrated weekly', they would at least have been nearer the truth. As it was, the argument put forward was manifestly absurd. The fact was that Doyle was too good and had to be got rid of.

The postscript was that some *Punch* writer – possibly Richard Price – undertook a rough survey among bookstall assistants in his own neighbourhood some months after the change was made. He found none of them in the least aware that an alteration in *Punch*'s outward appearance had taken place.

Muggeridge showed himself perfectly capable of dealing with snipers from behind his own lines. Indeed, with his ingrained political instinct for bypassing an awkward problem, he was possibly more at ease in such extraneous spheres than in editing proper, when editing came to tedious weekly routines. He had a far keener sense of what was 'funny' than his predecessor or successor, indeed stratospherically outdistancing either, but bees buzzed with increasing fury in his bonnet; public affairs and political personalities tending more and more to cause insensate rage than satirical laughter.

Although he never ceased to inveigh against the Press and the 'Media', Muggeridge believed devoutly (to use one of his own favourite adverbs) that everyone truly thought and acted as Press and Media represented them to think and act. The notion of an individual wholly uninterested in politics was inconceivable to him, and – although he might have denied this – he would be irritated by the view that such sources of information were themselves often wildly misinformed and conspicuously wrong in judgment about what the public thought. I remember him being quite incensed by George Orwell saying that the depressing thing about political canvassing was not that people wanted the opposite party to be elected, but that they did not know that an election was taking place, what an election was, nor what happened in the House of Commons when you got there.

Meanwhile an exterior element loomed. This was the moment when television was developing at headlong pace, calling into being as it did so a new genus of popular figure, the 'TV personality', something now as familiar as – though much more powerful than – what used to be called a matinée idol. The rôle of television personality – one judges merely by a row of striking examples – seems to impose an intense strain on its virtuosos. Perhaps (to adapt Lord Acton) all publicity is disturbing to the nervous system of the individual, total publicity totally disturbing. The peculiar characteristic of the television personality is freedom from responsibility, that apparently providing its own peculiar and acute pressures. The actor is governed by the disciplines of art, the politician by the exigencies of political survival. The television personality is positively encouraged by the condition of existence to be answerable to no one but self, under no sort of restraint other than remaining a recognised 'personality'. The impression often given is that prolonged expenditure in that manner of the personality (as the Victorians used to suppose of masturbation) is cruelly hard on mind and body.

As television bounded into popularity Muggeridge, a born commentator in that medium, found himself more and more in demand. To invoke the image of Hercules – a potential television personality if ever there was one – the serpents so easily strangled in TV infancy finally gave place to a Hydra-headed monster, which, with its ferocious and multiple attacks on time and energy, might be said to have got the best of the battle so far as Muggeridge's (no less than Herculean) labours at *Punch* were concerned. In short a rather different Muggeridge was now coming into being, a metamorphosis finally resulting in a parting of the ways with the proprietors.

Muggeridge was one of the most agreeable of men to work with; easygoing; quick on the uptake; aware of the absurdities of human life and human beings, most of all when concerned with journalism. Perhaps this latter perception became a little blurred as time went on, anyway if journalism be held to include television. His nature had formerly seemed to me dual, indeed not much more complicated than the comparatively common dichotomy in many individuals between the frivolous and the serious. Now it appeared visibly (or rather televisibly) more nearly to approach triune form: the three persons making up the Muggeridgian Trinity each pulling violently in a different direction from the other as they took on an increasingly separate state.

In the beginning (such my own experience of the demiurge) was the sceptical wit mocking all, and the wit was with Muggeridge and the wit was Muggeridge. This First Muggeridge – never wholly exorcised but undergoing long terms of banishment from the Celestial City of the personality – would sometimes support, sometimes obstruct, what then seemed his sole fellow, Second Muggeridge. Second Muggeridge, serious, ambitious, domestic (in fits and starts and when not led away by First Muggeridge's insatiable leaning towards licence), with a strain of Lawrentian mysticism (albeit D. H. Lawrence himself always coming in for Muggeridgian obloquy), had a spell-weaving strain and violent political or moral animosities (animosity rather than allegiance being essential expression of Second Muggeridge's teachings), both forms of vituperation in the main aimed at winning a preponderant influence in public affairs. Third Muggeridge – doubtless always present in the spirit even when in the past invisible (as best faultily transmitted) to the eye of sinful man – was effectively made flesh during the later *Punch* period; a time when Second Muggeridge had initially seemed to be gaining in stature at the expense of First Muggeridge.

In due course, more than ever after *Punch* had been left behind, Third Muggeridge became manifest at full strength, hot-gospelling, near-messianic, promulgating an ineluctable choice between Salvation and Perdition. He who was not with Third Muggeridge was against him, including First and Second Muggeridge. In this conflict without quarter First Muggeridge, who treated life as a jest – now so to speak a thief crucified between two Christs – came off worst (anyway for the moment, alternative avatars always possible), ending as a mere shadow of his former self. The inner tensions of this trio of Muggeridgian personalities coursed like electricity through the *Punch* office during the last days of the Muggeridge reign at Bouverie Street. Indeed latterly I could sense an immediate buzzing in my own nerves on crossing the threshold of the Editor's door, so galvanic were they.

I stayed on a year after Muggeridge abdicated, being sacked at the end of 1959; release from a routine that was becoming increasingly unsympathetic, indeed decidedly irksome.

The actor-director Erich von Stroheim had long interested me, and while I was on *Punch* Stroheim came to London in 1954 to launch a showing of his own pictures at the National Film Theatre. A party for the Press was held at The Savoy to which I went as *Punch* representative, not an ideal manner of being brought face to face, even then only for a short moment, but better than nothing. Erich von Stroheim (1885–1957) was then nearly seventy. To this day much of his early life remains obscure in spite of many books about him. He was certainly Jewish, his father, owner of a straw-hat factory, could have been rich enough to buy a 'von' and put his son into the Imperial and Royal cavalry, but (as I understand from a reliable source)

Austrian army-lists 1900–1913, including Landwehr (militia) and Gendarmerie, do not show his name. A photograph, however, exists, and has been reproduced, showing Stroheim with his parents. His father wears some civil uniform, possibly consular, Stroheim that of a cadet, more probably conscript. It has also been suggested as within the bounds of possibility that Stroheim was educated at Weisskirchen, that socially smart, otherwise somewhat gruesome military school, so hated by Rilke, vividly written of by Musil in *Die Verwirrungen des Zöglings Törless* (1906: tr. *Young Törless*, 1955). Weisskirchen would suitably complete the Portrait of the Artist as a Junker.

There seems no reason to disbelieve the accepted story that Stroheim left Austria under a cloud, perhaps as a cadet, although the date he arrived in America (traditionally 1909, but placed by some as early as 1906 or late as 1913) is in dispute. Early methods of earning a living in the US included dish-washing, selling fly-papers, being a riding-master, the last consistent with the military background. After a few years he found his way to Hollywood, where he seems to have impressed his personality on the film world almost from the start.

Stroheim's art is a striking offshoot on the far side of the Atlantic of Vienna's *belle époque*, which lasted until 1914: the Secession painters; the Viennese school of architecture; the coming of age of psychoanalysis. The Oedipus complex was after all as much Vienna's gift to the world as Strauss waltzes or *Sachertorte*. In Stroheim's version of *The Merry Widow* (operetta, 1905: movie, 1925) both elements are combined, so to speak, in the elderly millionaire who has a stroke on his wedding night (thereby leaving the heroine a *lustige Witwe*), and is a shoe-fetishist. Stroheim may be titillating the public, he is also expressing a new attitude towards sex in the arts. *Foolish Wives* (1921), which was intended to run for some three and a half hours, introduces this new approach with a cascade of shocks.

Stroheim's method has about it something of Toulouse-Lautrec's power to impart, by wit, flourish, a sense of design, beauty and universality to themes in themselves sinister and tawdry. Lautrec had in fact been an acknowledged influence on the Viennese Secessionist painters, notably Egon Schiele. Another Secessionist artist, the proto-Surrealist Gustav Klimt, in his designs for the ceiling of Vienna University (the picture called *Jurisprudence*) represents an octopus about to swallow a bound and naked prisoner, a figure physically not at all unlike Stroheim himself in one of his sadomasochistic rôles. These frescoes, burnt by the German authorities in 1945, can now be seen only in reproduction. Stroheim's gifts as an actor make one wish he had tried his hand in those Shakespearian parts (Macbeth, Othello, Antony) which give scope for that mixture of dominating brutality combined with inner weakness at which he excels. He would also be interesting as a director of classical drama.

The colossal sums Stroheim spent on production finally brought about banishment from Hollywood, and withdrawal to France, where he continued to make some excellent pictures. In the American movie world Irving Thalberg, sentimentalized by Scott Fitzgerald in *The Last Tycoon*, was one of Stroheim's bitterest adversaries; a group whose wanton malice destroyed the residue of Stroheim's unshown film art after he had withdrawn from Hollywood. Not long before I left Duckworth's the American edition of Stroheim's novel *Paprika* (1935) came in on offer. The novel was essentially not his medium. I could not recommend its publication, though I believe the book, much bowdlerized, did eventually appear in England. So far as I can remember the seventeen-year-old heroine was raped at least six times in as many opening pages describing her journey from Budapest to Vienna to seek her fortune.

Just as there are many roles one would have liked to see Stroheim play, there are certain novels (*Les Liaisons Dangereuses*, *A Hero of Our Time*, *Ulysses*, for instance) which he ought to have adapted for the screen. Two books by fellow Austrians come to mind: Robert Musil's great panorama on the eve of the first war *The Man Without Qualities* (more correctly the man without *parti pris*), and a writer less wellknown in this country, Alexander Lernet-Holenia (1897–1976), poet and playwright as well as novelist. The first of Lernet-Holenia's novels to be rendered into English (both admirably translated by Alan Harris) was published by Duckworth's. Lernet-Holenia and I exchanged letters at that time. After reading *Venusberg*, he said he thought we wrote in rather the same manner. I think, in fact, *A Young Gentleman in Poland* (1933) is perhaps more like early Evelyn Waugh; light-hearted, savage, approaching fantasy. *The Standard* (1936) is quite different, a genre of novel of which I can recall no precise equivalent in British writing: romantic; realistic; satirical; moving.

As ever with film stars Stroheim was smaller than expected, additionally dwarfed by a statuesque blonde lady standing beside him. Acting as hostess to the mob of journalists, she introduced them one by one as they moved forward in a queue. Stroheim had not looked particularly young in the photograph I had seen of him in unidentified military uniform; now, trim, unsmiling, even sad, he did not look particularly old. I muttered my name and the paper I represented.

'From *Punch*,' said the blonde, after speaking the name.

Stroheim looked worried. *Punch* evidently did not strike a chord. The blonde offered a helpful word or two as to the magazine being a comic one well known in England.

'What will you drink, Mr Powell?'

The voice was deep, guttural, profoundly melancholy.

'A glass of dry sherry, please.'

Dry sherry seemed no more reassuring than *Punch*. Stroheim, this time almost in despair, glanced again at the blonde for help. Once more she elaborated, and dry sherry was brought. This failure in communication was becoming disconcerting. I took the initiative.

'At the close of the Monteblancan manoeuvres in *The Merry Widow* I was much impressed by your very individual touch in showing a group of foreign military attachés talking together. They gave absolute authenticity to the scene.'

I chose *The Merry Widow* on impulse, though Stroheim himself was said to be not at all proud of his version of Lehar's operetta, which, a box-office success, had been as usual savagely cut. This time he nodded vigorously. The observation had got home. I told him that I had myself served as liaison officer with the Allied military attachés during the second war. He took the point at once. The confrontation was saved.

'In those sequences,' said Stroheim, 'I also arranged for two military chaplains to appear, Roman Catholic and Greek Orthodox, because both religions were officially recognized in the Montenegrin army. I was considered quite crazy on account of those two chaplains.'

Montenegro – model for Monteblanco in *The Merry Widow* libretto – had been the Balkan country in which the story was placed. We talked for a minute or two about disregard shown by most film directors for correctness in detail, especially military detail.

'For them it is just Horse Opera,' Stroheim said.

I tried to explain how long I had admired his art, both as director and actor. Regarding the last he sighed.

'I no longer look like the *Oberleutnant* I once was.'

He was infinitely sad. I remembered how much that individual melancholy had struck me in a comparatively early photograph showing Stroheim standing among a row of other Hollywood notables. I should have liked to hear more of his views, spoken of Musil and Lernet-Holenia, but circumstances were not favourable to an extended talk. In the queue behind the waiting journalists were getting restive for a drink. The blonde began to cast glances towards us hinting that others too must have a chance. I saw I must take my leave. Nevertheless the impact of the putative *Oberleutnant* with a genius for the art of the cinema had been worth experiencing.

When the publisher of D. H. Lawrence's novel *Lady Chatterley's Lover* was prosecuted I was one of those asked to appear if required as witness for the Defence. I agreed, being in principle firmly against censorship, but remained uncalled. Potential witnesses were given access to the Court so that I found myself spectator of some of the scenes in this singular extravaganza, something between a morality play and a pantomime. It was no doubt just as well that my evidence was dispensed with. I should certainly have found anything like enthusiastic support of the novel on purely literary grounds far from easy; while merely to express conviction of the author's honesty of purpose, which I was quite prepared to underwrite, carried no weight in law.

My feelings about Lawrence are that he is a good poet, talented short story writer, author of some first-rate fragments of autobiography (notably his Introduction to Maurice Magnus's memoir of the Foreign Legion), and a brilliant writer of letters. So far as his novels are concerned my reservations are much those quoted earlier made by Jocelyn Brooke. Even the keenest Lawrence fans at the Trial inclined to begin their evidence by stating that they did not consider *Lady Chatterley's Lover* by any means the author's best work. One would heartily agree.

The character who refuses to come to life is a flaw no novelist, even those in the top class, can ever wholly guard against; conversely, a single credible figure occasionally becomes incarnate in an otherwise indifferent novel. It might be argued that in 'real life' too the all but unbelievable individual is not unknown, but that does not excuse the novelist, who has to carry the reader into anyway momentary belief. The miracle must take place; the spirit descend; the blood of St Januarius liquefy. The blood of Mellors does not liquefy. Although the personification of Marie Lloyd's song: 'Everything he does is so artistic', Mellors remains an author's self-identification never galvanized into life: Lawrence, a few labels added or subtracted, as he would like to have been.

The surname Chatterley (like Mellors apparently a fairly common one in Lawrence's neighbourhood) is in itself not without interest, occurring in Surtees, a novelist whose books would almost undoubtedly have been covered in Lawrence's wide and receptive reading; although also true that Chatterley is a Staffordshire place-name, and has a row of entries in the London Telephone Book. Nonetheless it seems to me possible that Lawrence returned to Surtees after deciding on a gamekeeper hero. Among the comparatively rare occasions when Surtees writes of shooting rather than hunting he speaks of gamekeepers wearing the 'green velveteens' attributed to Mellors by Lawrence, while the following comparison is worth noting:

He [Facey Rumford] returned the keeper's semi-military salute with a how are you?

Facey Rumford's Hounds (1865)

The man Mellors faced lightly round, and saluted with a little gesture, a soldier's.

Lady Chatterley's Lover

Moreover Chatterley occurs as the name of a 'county family' in *Plain or Ringlets* (1860), when the Duke of Tergiversation is discussing with his steward Mr Cucumber the routine ducal party given from time to time for the neighbours:

'Well what are the Chatterleys queried for?' asked the Duke.

'The Chatterleys are queried, your Grace, because you struck them off before the last fête. Mr Chatterley voted the wrong way.'

'Then if they were struck off before, what occasion is there to put them back on the list?' asked the Duke.

'They have been presented at Court since then,' replied Mr Cucumber.

The indictment took place at the Old Bailey in October 1960. Making my way there on a bus I overheard a conversation which has no bearing on the Chatterley Trial, but I record for its sheer oddness. Two men sitting behind me were talking English, plainly their natural language, but with a peculiar accent I could not place. They were evidently on a visit to London and seeing the sights. When we passed the Law Courts at the east end of The Strand one of them said:

'What is that building? Is it a church?'

'No, it's not a church,' his companion replied. 'I went in and had a look round yesterday. I rather think it's a sort of hotel.'

If the Law Courts gave the air of an hotel the Old Bailey when I arrived there was like a theatrical First Night with all sorts of literary figures wandering about its corridors. Based – like much of the best comedy – on material not in itself intended to be comic, the Trial was played by a cast of character-actors almost without exception accomplished in their individual roles. In this aspect a high standard was set by leading counsel on each side: Gerald Gardiner QC for the Defence: Mervyn Griffith-Jones for the Prosecution; a couple who could not have been more aptly chosen.

Gerald Gardiner (Harrow, Magdalen College Oxford, later Lord Chancellor in a Labour Government, Garrick Club) spoke quietly and persuasively, without the smallest touch of bombast, indeed scarcely raising his voice. Tall, goodlooking, distinguished, Gardiner was just sixty. He belonged to the Oxford post-first-war undergraduate generation just before my own, and left something of a legend as President of the Union, President of the OUDS, and suchlike. There had been an afterglow of rather showy brilliance. For the moment anyway all showiness had been eliminated.

Mervyn Griffith-Jones (Eton, Trinity Hall Cambridge, later a judge, White's Club) also possessed a good appearance. In contrast to Gardiner's air of sweetness and light Griffith-Jones was saturnine, swashbuckling, standing no nonsense with witnesses, indeed not above settling down to old-fashioned Serjeant Buzfuz legal bullying. He was fifty. After the second war (in which he had won an M C serving with The Coldstream, Gardiner having also been briefly a Coldstreamer in the first war), Griffith-Jones had been one of the Prosecuting Counsel at the Nuremberg Trials of War Criminals, where no doubt a savagely ironical manner had been easy to develop. He must, however, have had his less severe side, because *Who's Who* listed 'painting' as one of his recreations, and recorded the fact of his having notched up half-a-dozen one-man shows of his pictures.

Evelyn Waugh, who contrived to watch some of the Nuremberg Trials, told me he had stayed with Griffith-Jones during the visit. I asked what he was like. 'Not a very nice man,' said Waugh, but did not elaborate. It must be most emphatically added that no one was to be condemned out of hand on Waugh's evidence in that sort of connexion. Griffith-Jones may well have taken reasonable exception to something Waugh had done or said. Nonetheless I should have expected approbation from Waugh for a man of Griffith-Jones's outward complexion. It was currently rumoured, I don't know with how much truth, that even apart from the professional role he was playing Griffith-Jones felt strongly as to the necessity of suppressing Lawrence's novel. I found him on the whole most enjoyable of the actors in the Old Bailey *mise en scène*. Once in Court, for the moment off duty and listening to the case from a faraway seat at the back, he winked at someone on the opposite side of the judge. I could not pin down Griffith-Jones's vis-à-vis, but, Dickens already in my mind from his demeanour, that deliberate closing and opening of the eyelid set up another train of thought.

Might not Sydney Carton have transformed himself into a counsel very like Griffith-Jones had he tired of devilling for Mr Stryver, given up drink instead of wasting his life, decided to make a career at the Bar? A reformed Carton (Shrewsbury School, Law studies in Paris, Inns of Court, Fleet Street taverns) was quite imaginable with a good war record and membership of White's. He had the same peremptory manner as Griffith-Jones. Carton's romantic attitude towards Miss Manette, the essence of propriety, by no means ran counter to disapproval of coarse language and irregular sexual relations. Presumably Carton had learnt his bilingual French at the Sorbonne, knowledge of the language greatly facilitating the Far, Far Better Thing. To round off the parallel perhaps Griffith-Jones (the Welsh name not inappropriate to an Old Salopian) might have changed clothes with one of the War Criminals at Nuremberg; the latter now in consequence leading for the Prosecution in the Chatterley case.

Dismissing such fantasies from the mind one noted Griffith-Jones's emphasis was as much on adultery itself as on the 'four letter Anglo-Saxon words' (as with rather rough-and-ready etymology Lawrence's terms were usually called) used for describing Constance Chatterley's 'bouts' (another favourite designation); the last often accentuated as 'thirteen in number'; the baker's dozen somehow implying a particular viciousness.

Even in private among persons in general agreement about books, familiar with accepted modes of discussing them, literary criticism, especially when complicated by sexual ethic, may arouse violent argument. In a Court of Law, where much regarded as more or less axiomatic by those habituated to literary matters can be made to sound ridiculous under cross-examination, the simplest principles of writing are hard to affirm with credibility. Judges are apt to glory in their own ignorance of art and letters – no doubt often arid enough – and an atmosphere of unrelieved philistinism hangs by their very nature over all legal proceedings. In consequence of these endemic handicaps in putting forward in Court arguments based on widely accepted intellectual standards evidence for the Defence had perforce to take a line scarcely less in the nature of humbug than that of the Prosecution. Indeed the Defence's testimony well illustrated an innate aspect of British puritanism whereby some formerly condemned practice, once vindicated in the eyes of the Law and public opinion, cannot remain a matter of toleration only, but must be propagated as something actively beneficial. What is allowed must be good. Accordingly the supporters of the book were some of them constrained by this national idiosyncrasy to plead that not only should Lawrence's novel remain uncensored, but that *Lady Chatterley's Lover* should be taught in schools and made the subject of organized discussion in youth clubs.

Lawrence, capable of an occasional joke in his letters, is consistently without humour in his books, a failing rarely if ever to be found in novelists of the highest class from Petronius to Proust. There was therefore a certain justice in the rights and wrongs of *Lady Chatterley* being hammered out without a vestige of humour on either side. The Prosecution was hindered from laughing at some of the patently absurd assertions of the Defence, because to show jocularity might have cast doubt on the alleged harmfulness of the novel; while the Defence was equally in no position to allow any laughter at the Prosecution's ineptitudes of understanding, since the Defence's intention was to prove the high seriousness of the book.

Gardiner examined a long string of witnesses, comparatively few of whom were re-examined by Griffith-Jones. Griffith-Jones, on the other hand, produced no 'expert' witnesses for the Prosecution (doubtless sagacious, a pity so far as pure comedy went), and kept masked the batteries of his most deadly anti-personnel weapon until his own closing speech. Quite early on in the proceedings Griffith-Jones asked his now famous question: 'Is it a book which you would even wish your wife or your servants to read?' The enquiry has now passed into history;

together with the equally well remembered comment (attributed to a
peer during the subsequent debate in the House of Lords): 'I should not
object to my wife or daughter reading the book, but have the strongest
objection to it being read by my gamekeeper.'

One of the most dramatic moments of the Trial I witnessed was when
Francis Cammaerts (son of the Belgian poet Emile Cammaerts), Headmaster of a grammar-school in England, was giving evidence for the
Defence. This was to be chiefly in connexion with his experience as a
schoolmaster in the attitude of growing boys towards sex. As with all
such witnesses Gardiner's examination opened with a series of questions calculated to illustrate the credentials of the man or woman in the
box to speak authoritatively of the matter in hand. Gardiner's first
question was an unexpected one:

'At the beginning of the war you were a conscientious objector?'

'Yes,' said Cammaerts.

The temperature of the Court perceptibly fell.

'Then you changed your mind after the war had been going on for
two years?'

'Yes.'

'And you joined the army?'

'Yes.'

'And were parachuted into France?'

'Yes.'

'And later awarded the D S O?'

'Yes.'

'Together with the Légion d'Honneur and Croix de Guerre?'

'Yes.'

'And the American Medal of Freedom?'

'Yes.'

The list of awards may have continued even longer. This bit of staging
was wonderfully effective. Cammaerts went on to declare his approval
of *Lady Chatterley*. One might well ask why personal gallantry in war
should be a recommendation for reliable literary or moral judgments,
but that is the manner in which things are ventilated in open court;
perhaps thereby providing some counterbalance to the often unjust and
boorish reception of a purely intellectual approach.

Several clergymen appeared for the Defence. One of these, Canon
Milford, Master of the Temple, made an interesting point. In principle
well disposed towards the novel, he thought several of the scenes would
have been 'indecent' had someone been watching Constance Chatterley
and Oliver Mellors from behind a tree. In short Canon Milford considered that a reader of *Lady Chatterley* should not assume the individuality of a third party, but 'identify' with one or other of the lovers.
This optional approach to the narrative had not hitherto occurred to me.

Professional novelists are more apt to reflect on how they themselves would have dealt with technical problems, rather than escape into a daydream of the imagination while they read another novelist's book. It is indeed one of the disadvantages of being a novelist that professionalism in that field is hard to shake off even temporarily; something that James and other writers have spoken of.

I saw at once that Canon Milford's distinction was an important one, although – speaking not so much morally as erotically – so far as making a choice between the two attitudes, not absolutely plain sailing. The force of what the Canon asserted was vested not only in openly accepting the popular self-identifying approach of most novel-readers, but also in recognizing that important division of the human race between voyeurs and exhibitionists. In such a crude apportionment of temperament (in life rather than sex) I should, for example, grade myself as a voyeur, though, say, most of my Oxford contemporaries as exhibitionists.

Canon Milford's moral judgment on this differentiation might be thought even more pertinent in regard to those curious passages in *Lady Chatterley* where Lawrence appears to describe Mellors committing an act of buggery on his mistress; also suggesting that the gamekeeper had fomerly been in the habit of behaving in a similar fashion with his ex-wife. Although the language used to narrate these incidents (far from Lawrence's writing at its best) is less explicit than in recording more usual sexual intercourse, the actual term (admittedly not Anglo-Saxon nonetheless of respectable antiquity) not being employed, there seems little doubt the author intended this deviation to be understood; while at the same time momentarily abandoning his view that plain speech purified sexual action.

So far as Lawrence himself is concerned, both as novelist and sex reformer, no aspect of *Lady Chatterley* seems more a case of special pleading than these vague phrases that seem to indicate buggery. They possess all the highflown unstraightforward imagery that elsewhere he so strongly condemns. As to the practice itself, one can be sure that had Lady Chatterley's first lover Michaelis preferred this method of approach he would certainly have earned Lawrence's favourite epithet of sexual contumely 'doggy'; used not only in *Lady Chatterley*, but when speaking of Galsworthy's physically unexhibited pair of adulterers in *The Forsyte Saga*.

Griffith-Jones made no reference to sodomitical passages until his closing speech. At first this strategy seemed a miscalculation, since their innuendo would have been hard to defend in open court by those who put forward *Lady Chatterley* almost as a textbook for the young in learning about sexual relations. The comparative hesitancy of the Prosecution in pressing this line of attack early on had perhaps something in common with similar avoidance of deriding recommendation of the novel as an instructional work. In short the Jury might have been alienated by the overplaying of insinuations too oblique to be defined with absolute certainty to the layman.

Another question only lightly touched on by the Prosecution was how extended a research on Constance Chatterley's part would Lawrence have approved had Mellors, notwithstanding his attractive exterior, proved a less than perfect lover. Was the implication that all wives whose sexual relations were not ideal should (as some do) leave their husbands? Lawrence, no doubt sincerely, averred that he was against promiscuity, passionately on the side of marriage. All the same it is hard to see how the ideal Lawrentian spouse could be found without risking a process of trial and error. What would Constance Chatterley have done, for example, if Mellors, soon after the affair was begun, had in the course of his duties as gamekeeper at a shooting-party sustained from the gun of some unskilful guest a similar injury to that of Sir Clifford?

Lawrence himself would have been surprised, perhaps far from gratified, by the consequences of the Trial's verdict being defined in Philip Larkin's celebrated lines as 'Sexual intercourse began/In nineteen sixty-three ... Between the end of the *Chatterley* ban/And the Beatles' first LP'; the conclusion drawn that the young go to bed with each other *ad lib*. Certainly since that moment sex has been investigated in novel and on screen from every conceivable angle with the greatest frankness. How far that has advanced writing is another matter. Equally there is no turning back. Art is the true adjudicator, in its complicated relationship with taste. In the Courts of Art and Taste I should have thought Lawrence lost the case.

A footnote to the Chatterley Trial may be recorded. In 1967 a letter arrived from the Director of Public Prosecutions asking if I would give views on the propriety of publishing *My Secret Life*, an erotic Victorian work known to me by name but never sampled. On my replying that I was prepared to pass an opinion about *My Secret Life* I received a copy enclosed in a huge and all but impenetrable brownpaper envelope, marked in large letters *On Her Majesty's Service*. The book turned out to be some 900,000 words long, that is to say more than half the twelve volumes of *À la recherche*; a bulk for which I had been altogether unprepared. Written anonymously, the narrative chronicles every sexual action undertaken over certain periods of years by Walter, an upper-middle class Englishman born apparently towards the end of the first quarter of the 19th century. The manuscript is represented as having been bequeathed on Walter's death to a friend, who arranged to have half-a-dozen copies printed in Holland about the year 1882.

The bibliographer and art connoisseur Henry Spencer Ashbee (1834–1900) has been put forward as author of *My Secret Life*, chiefly on the strength of having compiled, under the pseudonym Pisanus Fraxi, a catalogue of Erotica called *Notes on Curious and Uncommon Books*, a work designed in three volumes. In less exotic fields Ashbee was an art historian, traveller, collector, who left works by many artists to the National Gallery and Victoria & Albert Museum. Ashbee was in short a man of taste, and one would suspect by no means without humour. From this external evidence identification of Ashbee with Walter of *My Secret Life* is in the highest degree improbable, indeed ludicrous. So far as datable chronology exists there the narrative refers to the Great Exhibition (1851), friends of Walter killed in the Crimean War (1853/56), the battle of Solferino (1859), all of which were contemporary with Ashbee certainly, but seem viewed through the eyes of one born at least ten years earlier, which would mean that Walter died in his late fifties or early sixties.

My Secret Life is not included in Ashbee's own register of Erotica, to be expected both from an author's natural self-esteem, and requirements of completeness; an omission unthinkable in a man of Ashbee's scholarship. No erotic book is mentioned by Walter except the hackneyed *Fanny Hill*, indeed he indicates that he is not much interested in pornography. Ashbee wrote fluently on all sorts of subjects; Walter's style, pedestrian to a degree, shows not the smallest literary facility. Finally, in an unremitting chronicle of casual sexual encounters none takes place in a bookshop or art gallery; unmatched locations for a pick-up. Nonetheless, in spite of an appalling banality of outlook, and concerns other than sexual that never seem to have taken him further afield than his stockbroker's, Walter must in his way have been an unusual person. He lacked all inspiration, his humour was the least subtle imaginable, he had no turn for expressing himself, yet he recognized his own exceptional sexual urges, and felt an inner need to set them down in terms that Lawrence might very reasonably have stigmatized as 'doggy'.

The vast majority of the bouts (Griffith-Jones's term is appropriate) are with domestic servants or prostitutes. From time to time a few sexual deviations are touched on, but *My Secret Life* never begins to be anything like a pharmacopoeia designed to excite by description of out-of-the-way practices. On the contrary the unsatisfactoriness, even repulsion, of some of these when tried at the suggestion of women with whom he was on terms (e.g. flagellation) is commented upon quite objectively by Walter from the point of view of a man with few sexual fetishes. Walter has interesting observations to make about decrease in availability of *maisons de rendezvous* as the century wore on. These houses of assignation (one was in Blenheim Street off New Bond Street), where impatient arrivals were perpetually knocking on the door to enquire if current occupants had finished, seem at best to have been remarkably uninviting even for a relatively well-to-do fornicator.

After plodding through *My Secret Life* I sent the DPP a report of about a thousand words or more saying that the narrative seemed on the whole true, presented a most unalluring picture of promiscuity as there recorded, though one not without documentary interest, socially and sexually. I added that personally I had no wish to dip into the book again, and thought it unlikely to 'deprave and corrupt'; if anything calculated to have the opposite effect owing to the squalor of the picture. This view was not, I think, followed, and *My Secret Life* was banned. At the close of our correspondence the DPP asked if I would consider accepting an honorarium for my trouble. The sum named, not insultingly small, was far from commensurate with time taken up. I replied that the amount mentioned would be agreeable to me, but – since in the first instance that department of the Law had come to me for guidance on literary matters – it was only right that the Director of Prosecutions should know for future reference that the honorarium represented at best half the amount an author in a position to be consulted on so vital a matter might be expected to receive were mere commercial dealings in question. The DPP thanked me for this information when sending his cheque. Like Stroheim's White Russian Count in *Foolish Wives* pocketing the savings of the unprepossessing housemaid, I felt that it was not much for a man who, in ploughing through *My Secret Life*, had come within measurable distance of giving all for his country.

Like most of his opinions, whether one agrees with them or not, George Orwell's views on censorship are worth hearing. His response to what were often pent-up feelings of his time makes him a kind of Byron (less the sexual exhibitionism) of the Century of the Common Man; dragging through Europe the pageant of his washing-up at The Ritz; fighting in Spain instead of Greece and shedding a tear for the behaviour of Left Wing Spaniards, as Byron had done for that of Greeks in insurrection. In both cases 'thousands counted every groan/and Europe made his woe her own'. In his younger days Orwell had written vigorously deploring British prudery, certainly laughable enough at the time where books were concerned. At his death nothing like the zenith (or nadir) of outspokenness in print had been reached, though laboured descriptions in novels of sexual goings-on were more common than formerly. Orwell used to say that the problem of what might or might not be said would disappear, when these sexually explicit passages took their place in literary history with the lusciously sentimental set-pieces demanded by the Victorians such as the passing of Little Nell or Paul Dombey. The parallel seems apt, but there is small sign of persuasion that in many if not most circumstances in the arts restraint, anyway severe discipline, is more effective – if you like, even more erotic – than pedantically reciting the functioning of every organ and every emission. I don't think Orwell himself, any more than Lawrence, would at all have welcomed future developments. Nowadays not only is Erotica less hard to come by, but many more people can afford to indulge the taste; which turns out to be by no means limited to a few decadent and ageing bourgeois furtively glancing each way before making the purchase. On the contrary the 'affluent society' has shown that pornography can appeal to the population at large, the younger groups at that. Does that matter? Should not grown-ups be allowed to decide what they want to read? Yet those who object to over lavish window displays seem reasonable enough; while not all social side-effects of pornographic big business can be dismissed as absolutely harmless. But how to prevent the puritans from banning *Ulysses*? To declare that any person of intelligence can tell the difference between a 'serious writer' and a pornographer is not as easy as all that; indeed rendered even more difficult by the former sometimes deliberately usurping the functions of the latter.

Guillaume Apollinaire, poet *par excellence* of romantic love, produced a couple of volumes of the hardest of hard porn. He did that at a moment when he was earning a meagre living as clerk in a dubious Paris bank, and (if the metaphor is not contradictory) trying to keep the wolf from the door. Even for a poet who might be called the St Paul of Cubism, Surrealism's John the Baptist, pornography's imaginative bounds are soon set, notwithstanding inclusion of material that (unless the reader's particular 'thing') the least prudish would have to admit to be fairly unappetizing: a sadistic Pelion piled on a scatological Ossa. Even so Apollinaire is not able to suppress all trace of himself and his intelligence. In *Les Onze Mille Verges où les amours d'un Hospodar* (1907) no hack pornographer would have brought in references to the recent murder by Serbian officers of the wanton Queen Draga in the Royal Palace at Belgrade (another incident crying out for Stroheimian treatment), nor the sea battle of Tsushima in the Russo-Japanese War of 1904–5.

Before leaving the subject of books regarded as erotic, a word about a writer I greatly admire whose name is associated with that end of literature; not altogether justly, because, although clinical in some of his descriptions, and not afraid to laugh about sexual matters, he is never deliberately pornographic. The literary standing Giacomo Casanova (1725–1798) has long held on the Continent has never been his in Great Britain, where it is still not generally understood that Casanova is a writer of immense talent who was also an adventurer, and had copious affairs with women; not a professional womanizer and gambler who happened to leave some odds and ends of memoirs which have survived.

The handling of the *Memoirs* is masterly. Casanova has the instincts of a novelist in presenting a succession of autobiographical episodes in such a manner that substance is imparted to the other characters concerned. This is rare in the reminiscences of men of action, usually too egotistical to achieve personal portraits, especially those of women. A dramatic suspense is also imposed on the reader as to what will be the outcome of events with all the ability of a well organized thriller or detective story. This very facility has suggested to some that the *Memoirs* have been invented from start to finish, the whole story imagined. To do that for a million words in Casanova's manner would be an even more extraordinary achievement. In fact modern research has established the truth of all sorts of incidents that might have been supposed, to say the least, highly improbable.

He was probably bastard son of a Venetian nobleman, not the actor supposedly his father. That does not altogether explain the three rather sinister old gentlemen (of whom the chief was Matteo Giovanni Bragadin, a Senator), who kept Casanova going by paying him a small allowance. In return he operated for them a bogus system of fortune-telling which he invented; a form of sortilege which sometimes surprised Casanova himself by producing answers that fell out to be true. We still do not know the motive for Casanova's perpetual flittings backwards and forwards across Europe, nor often for his frequent expulsions. It has been suggested that he was a spy. For whom? The Freemasons? The Jesuits? How did he find time to acquire his undoubted knowledge, say, of metals? He was put in charge of the French lottery, a job others must have coveted. He came to England (a country he admired but never quite got the hang of) with the idea of setting up a similar system of public lotteries there. Casanova may also have collaborated in writing the libretto of Mozart's *Don Giovanni*.

The force of Casanova's work is not to be appreciated by extracts. The *Memoirs* must be read in their entirety like Shakespeare's Sonnets, Ariosto, Proust. They have the coherence of a well-constructed novel, one of the striking features being the manner in which individuals with whom the writer has been involved crop up again in his life. The finely phrased exchanges of stylized dialogue (which often retain their wit) must be accepted as a literary convention of the age; like occasional sententiousness and, it must be acknowledged, intermittent clichés. That may be forgiven in a writer for whom the French Revolution had terminated the epoch in which he had so consciously had his being; a writer who was slowly dying of boredom and irritation as librarian at Count Waldstein's castle of Dux in Bohemia. In this last period of decline he found consolation in his fox terrier Melampyge. The dog's name had been chosen, one presumes, from a surname sometimes given to Hercules on account of the hero's black and hairy back. Casanova must have been on the look-out for visitors sufficiently highbrow to recognize the allusion. Alas, Melampyge died. Casanova wept long, and composed a Latin elegy.

An absorbing sequence in the *Memoirs* is that which deals with the two (mutually lesbian) nuns C C and M M (the first now identified, the second possibly), whom Casanova used to visit in the parlour of the Convent of Santa Maria degli Angeli on the island of Murano; later have fun with them both on the mainland of Venice (sometimes as voyeur) in the company of that broadminded prelate François-Joachim de Bernis, French Ambassador to the Serene Republic, in due course Cardinal. In the spring of 1972 Violet and I made an excursion to Murano. Although the day was wet we found our way to the former conventual church of Santa Maria degli Angeli. Dilapidated to the point of being derelict the buildings retained a crumbling dignity. There was clearly easy access to the water for those clandestine journeys by boat to the love-nest in Venice. One of these trips had nearly cost Casanova his life on account of the storm that had blown up. He often chronicles bad weather in Venice, especially extreme cold. While the rain poured down, making the story of the sudden squall on the lagoon very believable, I reflected that Casanova, in spite of his romanticism, remained on the whole the philosopher—he liked to think himself. Incidentally, when the State Inquisitors impounded his books before incarceration under The Leads, one manuscript volume was entitled *Le Philosophe militaire.*

At the beginning of 1952 the young proprietor of two New York book-shops, The Holliday and The Periscope, wrote to say that he was contemplating a small publishing venture on the side, which he would like to take the form of reissuing one of my pre-war novels. This was Robert Vanderbilt Jr. His project was naturally an extremely agreeable one to myself. With the exception of *From a View to a Death* (republished by John Lehmann in 1948) all these books were out of print even in England. The matter was further discussed in correspondence, then Vanderbilt himself, with his bride Virginia, appeared in London. They were a very congenial couple, and it was arranged that not one but two of these early novels, *Venusberg* (1932), *Agents and Patients* (1936), should be published in one volume, marking in both cases a first appearance in America. The Vanderbilt venture, given the title *Two*

Novels by Anthony Powell (ND), came out in New York a few weeks
before Christmas 1952 under the imprint Periscope-Holliday. Vanderbilt's own energy and enterprise stopped not much short of hawking
Two Novels from door to door on a barrow. He managed to dispose of
nearly three thousand copies, no bad sale at a period when the wartime
boom in reading was over; more especially in disposing of a two-decker
of this kind, emanating from an unorthodox source, and containing a
couple of novels for twenty years wholly defunct as a selling proposition
in the country of their origin. This *jeu d'esprit* of Bob Vanderbilt's
played a part not at all to be disregarded in the lumbering process of
getting my books on the road in America.

Bob Vanderbilt, an admirer of Osbert Lancaster's cartoons, was
anxious that Lancaster should design the wrapper of *Two Novels*. They
met, and it was agreed that two pictures should be executed, one for
the front of the jacket, one for the back, illustrating scenes from
both novels. Vanderbilt told me that when he dined with Lancaster
he learnt from his host that Osbert Sitwell had at first resented that
another Osbert should have entered his *monde*. In due course Sitwell
and Lancaster had become friends, so that when Osbert Burdett, a
man of letters of a somewhat older vintage who wrote of the Nineties,
passed away in the 1930s they lunched *à deux* to celebrate being left
as the sole Osberts (now, alas, reduced to one) in the field.

T. S. Eliot once remarked to Violet that, when you have to do the
washing-up, the vital question to decide is the best moment to drink
coffee. Life is weighed down with such problems, solved by nations
and individuals in different ways. The subject is allied to a comment
of Arthur Mizener's (credentials Princeton, Harvard Business School,
Professorship at Cornell, almost annual visits for many years to Great
Britain) that 'in England there is more formality, in America more
etiquette'. Even in England I would hesitate to speak on the subject
of formality now, but in the US twenty years ago the Mizener precept
was always worth a thought for the traveller there.

Scott Fitzgerald's shade presided over my coming to know Mizener,
whose biography of the novelist, *The Far Side of Paradise* (1951), I reviewed for the *TLS*; subsequent correspondence bringing us together.
Since then Violet and I have been seeing something of Arthur and Rosemary Mizener on and off for the past thirty years. In reply to some now
forgotten observation of mine Mizener once answered: 'I quite see the
logic of what you say, but cannot agree, because if I agreed I should
cease to be an American.' These words much impressed me, confirming
as they did what I had long suspected, that the concept of 'being an
American' inseparably combined a sense of nationality with a kind of
metaphysical creed. This is something of which a European visitor to
the US is often subtly aware, and should always bear in mind.

To undertake a presumptuous investigation into American habits is far from my intention here, but over the years certain of these have inevitably made an impression. For example, another American friend Bill Davis, whose wife Annie was sister to Cyril Connolly's first wife Jean, speaking of Connolly's occasional peevishness about acquaintances who seemed to be doing rather too well, once said: 'But I *like* my friends being successful.' This is, I think, a point worth attention; an engaging counterpart to what is sometimes decried as American success-worship. I don't feel at all confident that I could produce more than a few persons known to me in my own country who could truly echo that sentiment, but here again feelings antipathetic to ambition are not necessarily ignoble ones. How far Bill Davis's remark represents a general American reaction I do not know, but a concrete example of contrast between American and British feelings about failure have been more than once provided by reviewers of these memoirs when they speak, say, of the memorialist having been sacked from a job or otherwise suffered a reverse. American reviewers sometimes sound genuinely shocked and surprised by the admission; British ones, on the other hand, are relieved and diverted by any story of rejection.

After the Hollywood interlude I did not cross the Atlantic again until the autumn of 1961, when I found that even if far from a bestseller, the fact of being not wholly unknown as a writer created a greatly preferable ambience to that attaching to a young man who had published only three or four novels, and was seeking employment as a scriptwriter in the film industry. The second American visit, this time to the Eastern Seaboard, grew out of a letter received from the Vice-President of Dartmouth College, New Hampshire, John Meck, who invited me to visit that foundation, perhaps lecture there. This invitation was expressed in terms that might have flattered King Arthur had he been bidden to the Court of the Yankees rather than the reverse, but I do not care for lecturing, which – unless undertaken in dire need of money – seems no part of a novelist's obligation. Apart from that I foresaw that any such transatlantic jaunt would impose an extortionate toll on 'writing time' mentioned earlier. Accordingly I was at first unwilling to accept this otherwise tempting proposal.

Meck was, however, a man of considerable firmness. He unfolded a prospect from the Arabian Nights in which I should be conveyed by magic carpet (operated through a Dartmouth man in PanAm), and (without reference to myself) arranged that Little, Brown should take me under their wing at The Ritz in Boston, then The St Regis in New York, after the Dartmouth or other commitments were at an end. Recognizing that, if lecturing were to be abjured I should have to substitute an alternative manner of singing for my supper, I agreed to be publicly interrogated about my own books and writing generally (a test of endurance I was also to experience in Japan). Dartmouth was apt to share sporting and other activities with Amherst College over the border in Massachusetts, a foundation I concurred in also visiting with a similar programme. From Amherst I myself arranged to pass on to Cornell University at Ithaca in upstate New York. That was not so much because I wished to prolong what the girl at the US Consulate in London endorsed on my passport as 'informal lectures at Ivy League Colleges' as in order to see the Mizeners, who were in due course kind enough to put me up in their house at Ithaca. It was already in my mind that our younger son John might attend an American university, probably Cornell, and in the event he became an undergraduate there a few years later.

When Violet and I both stayed in Boston (again as guests of Little, Brown) in 1965 the restaurant of our hotel (The Ritz was out of commission being redecorated) was called *The Hungry Pilgrim*. Outside stood an examplar of esurient puritanism dressed in a black-and-white Cromwellian costume with hair in a pigtail, which was a shade anachronistic and had not yet become at all chic for men. From time to time, looking as if he had just landed from *The Mayflower* and was in urgent need of a square meal, this gaunt figure would ring a bell. In general, however, Boston, a city of considerable charm, suggests a date later than the 17th century. The ensemble gives a touch of a more metropolitan Tunbridge Wells. Boston does not disappoint. Even on the briefest visit one can detect layer upon layer of the Bostonianism celebrated in such a long American literary tradition. When I was there in 1961 Little, Brown's, with much other entertaining, gave me luncheon at that haunt of ancient peace, shrine of Boston brahminism, the Somerset Club. The party included Edwin O'Connor, an American novelist I had already come across in England.

The Somerset Club is deservedly famous. I doubt if any club in London could equal – certainly none surpass – the inspissated and enveloping club atmosphere of The Somerset. Ancient armchairs and sofas underpropped one or two equally antiquated members, ossified into states of Emersonian catalepsy in which shadow and sunlight were not only the same, but had long freed them from shame or fame. It was comforting to see so splendid a haunt from the past surviving intact in a widely disintegrating world. I hope the Somerset Club still remains untainted by modern barbarisms. Ed O'Connor, large, talkative, master of a quiet but lively conversational style, was a fellow Little, Brown author. His novels were about Boston political life, and he himself a celebrator of a very different sort of Boston to that surrounding the party at the Somerset Club. He produced a story about Evelyn Waugh which, although turning out to be wholly chimerical, deserves to be put on record for its surrealist overtones.

O'Connor said that a few weeks before he had been chatting with a senior member of the firm, 'old' Mr Thornhill, a publisher very much of a former generation. Mr Thornhill had suddenly expressed aloud to O'Connor what sounded like a long bottled-up grievance.

'You know, Ed, I don't like writers.'

This was a painful admission from a lifelong publisher, one not altogether easy for an author to answer off the cuff. O'Connor temporized.

'You don't, Mr Thornhill?'

Mr Thornhill relented a little. At least he qualified his earlier unmitigated detestation.

'I like you, Ed, and I like Marquand, and I like Thornton W. Burgess, but I don't like most of them – and *I don't like Evelyn Waugh.*'

John P. Marquand (a writer to whom Violet is much addicted) is less known in the UK than in the US, perhaps surprisingly because Marquand more nearly represents an English tradition of writing, the novel of manners, than many American novelists. Marquand books deal with the Harvard end of American society, he also wrote successful detective stories, and it was no surprise to find that Mr Thornhill approved of so respectable, well-informed, patrician, disillusioned, an author. Thornton W. Burgess, unread in Great Britain, but so far as I know still looked on as a popular writer of children's books about animals in his own country, might be compared with Beatrix Potter. Here again Mr Thornhill's approbation gave no cause for surprise. A story no doubt lay behind Mr Thornhill's strongly expressed objection to Waugh. O'Connor pressed the matter further.

'What makes you feel that way about Waugh?'

'He behaved in a very silly manner.'

'Where did that happen?'

'He dined with me.'

'And it didn't go well?'

'He ordered all sorts of ridiculous things.'

'To eat?'

'Yes.'

'I believe he looks upon himself as a gourmet.'

That was too much for Mr Thornhill. He spoke with loud indignation:

'*Three soups!*'

On my return to England I told Waugh this story. He was delighted. At the same time, although Little, Brown's was certainly his American publisher he had no recollection of ever having met Mr Thornhill, still less dined with him and ordered three soups.

'Obviously this is a very important incident in my life,' Waugh said. 'I should like a full record of it for my memoirs. Would it be a great trouble for you to obtain further details about the occasion, and pass them on to me? I should like to know all the circumstances.'

I opened up an investigation. Unhappily it turned out after careful enquiry that Mr Thornhill Sr said he would have very much liked to meet Evelyn Waugh, but had never had the honour of doing so; his certainty that they had never been introduced to each other being even stronger than Waugh's. In short there had been no confrontation. O'Connor must have fabricated the anecdote or forgotten that it was two other people who were concerned. All the same 'Three soups!' must be admitted to be a good pay-off line.

John Meck picked me up at the hotel to continue the journey from Boston to Hanover by road. He was a tall lean New Englander, a figure from a James novel, quiet almost to the point of complete taciturnity, at the same time practical to a degree, and quick to pick up a literary reference. He said we were stopping for luncheon at Andover, one of his sons (aged fifteen, I think) having just entered this well known American boarding-school for boys. Shared two-and-two, the boys' rooms at Andover were remarkably like those of an Eton house; indeed the whole atmosphere of the school reminded me of Eton in what appeared to be its unstrained easygoing tone. The impression could hardly have been more superficial, nor were all Eton houses easygoing. One just had that feeling. A small incident suggested a national difference. Meck asked: 'Are you allowed to drive with us as far as the restaurant?' His son fumbled in a pocket, produced a book of school rules, glanced at them, then said: 'That's OK.' Afterwards I could not decide in my own mind how an English schoolboy would have answered the question; somehow not quite like that.

The pleasing buildings of Dartmouth College date back to the 18th century. A charter was granted by King George III. For six months of the year New Hampshire is under snow; the Dartmouth Winter Carnival a famous institution. Here again Scott Fitzgerald crops up with his calamitous visit to Hanover in February 1939. Fitzgerald and Budd Schulberg the novelist (*What Makes Sammy Run*), then a young script-writer, were to seek local colour for a picture about the Carnival, the 'treatment' for which was already under way. The two of them had stayed at The Hanover Inn, where (while at the same time enjoying a great deal of hospitality at the home of John and Jean Meck) I too put up. The final *Götterdämmerung* of Fitzgerald and Schulberg as employees of the film company concerned (although in fact Schulberg was later rehired) is said to have taken place in the snow on the steps of The Hanover Inn; comic in its parody of oldtime melodrama; tragic in long term consequences for Fitzgerald. This Nemesis was also a happening far more lurid than anything likely to have been achieved by the projected

Winter Carnival picture. I was glad to see the historic spot where banishment had been pronounced by the movie mogul locally in charge.

At one of these public interrogations (I am not sure which college) a professor prefixed a question by saying – rather archly – that he was uncertain how to pronounce my name. As an inspiration of the moment I replied that like the Boston family of Lowell I rhymed it with Noël rather than towel. I was later surprised at the manner in which this off-the-cuff comment spread ahead of me wherever I went, as things do in America. I feel no bigotry as to the usage in which I was brought up, certainly by no means universal, but the practice is not mere affectation. The sound made in Welsh when the names Powell and Howell are spoken in that language is not easy to transliterate into English pronunciation, and the fact that 16th and 17th century documents about Wales and the Marches often spell Powell as Poel must record more or less what the clerk heard.

At Amherst I stayed at The Lord Jeffrey, named after Jeffrey 1st Lord Amherst, much associated with the North American wars against the French, in due course Field Marshal. I was in general looked after by Ben DeMotte, himself a writer, and a man with a proper regard for not always being too serious. Among other things DeMotte took me to an informal talk on Zen philosophy given to a group of star under-graduates by the President of Amherst. The President read aloud some Haiku. He did not include any practical demonstrations of Zen taking a violent form, but the experience was nevertheless an interesting one. Afterwards I tried to imagine which head of an Oxford house known to me would have been most unexpected expounding Zen. Another member of the English Faculty at Amherst was William Pritchard, who has since written several acute critical works. I was having a drink with Pritchard and another of the younger Amherst dons when two elderly professors dropped in by chance. We talked about English writers. I happened to mention my own liking for Surtees. When the two older men left Pritchard and the other young don said almost in the same breath: 'How marvellous that you talked about a Victorian novelist like Surtees. It's always suspected that no one whose books we like reads anything but the latest literary fad. This will do us a lot of good.'

On proceeding to Cornell I stayed in Ithaca with the Mizeners, who were later boundlessly kind to John when he attended the University in 1965. Mizener, as a friend, was in a position to blackmail me into an exertion I had hitherto avoided, that is to say giving a lecture. I fought back to the extent of saying that if I were forced to give a lecture I could do so only by including a reading of certain passages translated from the *Satyricon* of Petronius. A search was made. It turned out that the only English translation of the *Satyricon* to be found in the libraries of Cornell was a comparatively recent one rendered in Twenties gangster slang. I was told afterwards that Petronius read aloud in an English accent, and transferred to the language of an Edward G. Robinson or George Raft gangster movie, was bizarre in the extreme.

At one of the parties I attended at Cornell a lady said: 'There is a very shy girl who wants to meet you, and would never dare, etc. etc.' This was my introduction to Alison Lurie, then married to a Cornell don, Jonathan Bishop, son of the poet John Peale Bishop, contemporary of Scott Fitzgerald at Princeton. Since Alison Lurie is one of the most determined personalities I know, her presentation as the essence of diffidence has always appealed to me. I was not told that she had already written a privately printed work *V. R. Lang: a Memoir* (1959: reprinted in *Poems and Plays by V. R. Lang*, 1975), and that her first novel *Love and Friendship* (1964) must have been on the way to being fixed up with Heinemann (one of the peculiarities of Alison Lurie's literary career being that first publications were in England). After ten minutes' conversation I saw that undoubtedly one would hear more of this supposedly shy girl. I can't remember whether we met again on that visit to Cornell, but we have done so on many subsequent occasions. Though my own favourite is *The Nowhere City* (1965), set in Hollywood but not primarily about movie people, perhaps her most unusual novel is *Imaginary Friends* (1967): two professors set out on a sociological project to study an obscure sect believing itself in touch with beings from Outer Space, one of the investigators himself becoming a convert.

Alison Lurie was with us once on an Hellenic cruise. The ship was sailing by that stretch of Greek coastline ornamented by the monasteries of Mount Athos. She passed when I was standing by the ship's side talking to General Sir John Hackett, one of the guest lecturers. That night at dinner she said: 'I heard the General say to you *Of course the first thing to decide is whether meditation is an action or a condition.* You know that's not the way American generals talk.'

6

After spasmodic comings and goings in the theatrical world extending over about two years a dramatized version of my first novel *Afternoon Men* was given a four weeks' run at the New Arts Theatre Club in the summer of 1963. This fulfilment was principally due to the energy of a young American director Roger Graef, who entered the field after the project of staging *Afternoon Men* had been virtually abandoned, at best postponed *sine die*. By that time an adaptation of the novel had already been made by Riccardo Aragno, an Italian scriptwriter based in London. The presentation of the play was undertaken by a company called J. B. Productions of which I knew nothing.

Riccardo Aragno (who came from Turin), tired of politics after fifteen years of being London correspondent of *La Stampa*, had turned with success to stage and screen. He had complete and fluid command of English, combined with thorough understanding of late 1920s atmosphere, the world the novel depicted, where individual romanticism fights a losing battle in the no-man's-land of sub-intellectual life. Aragno and I had no disagreements whatever about his treatment of the book, and throughout ups and downs of presentation no one could have been a more sympathetic associate. Roger Graef, ardent and tireless in the work he put into the play, never, so it seemed to me, quite got the hang of *Afternoon Men*'s period (naturally before his own), nor the London scene that provided its background; a parallel with which he had probably never run across in American life. Thus the sceptical tone of the characters, perfectly familiar to Aragno, always seemed alien to Graef, who among other misapprehensions inclined to upgrade them all socially. For Graef, for instance, the girls were debs, rather than artists' models and 'mannequins' living on their wits, and a similar tendency took place throughout all the directing. There were also occasional disharmonies between director and hard-worked cast, though no doubt such are far from unknown in most productions. Nonetheless, without Roger Graef *Afternoon Men* would never have been put on at The Arts, an experience I should be sorry to have missed.

Let me repeat that I have never been in the least stage-struck, but as the preliminaries of production began to take shape I became very conscious of the fascination which the Theatre exerts. This was not only in the technical antitheses spoken of above – the contrast of what is dramatic in a novel, what dramatic in a play – but also in the actual physical effervescence generated round one by all that goes with mounting a theatrical performance: the transformation of ideas into the physical actions of men and women; the changes in one's own apprehensions which such visual vitalizings effect; the complicated human relationships which immediately come into being among the various individuals concerned with the whole operation. A pleasant aspect of The Arts as a place of presentation was the personality of the Club's general manager Richard Schulman, an old hand at the Theatre, who knew every move of the game and trick of the trade. Schulman was always goodnatured, always enthusiastic, above all always ready for a good laugh (though confessing that what he really enjoyed at a play was a good cry), particularly a good laugh on the subject of the foibles of actors, directors, anyone else in showbiz, not least at their foibles where sex was concerned.

The cast of *Afternoon Men* – additionally with the passing of time – could reasonably be called distinguished in its names. The anti-hero Atwater, languishing for love of the beautiful Susan Nunnery, but consoling himself with Lola (unsurnamed in the novel) was played by James Fox: Susan by Georgina Ward: Lola by Pauline Boty. James Fox seemed to me everything that was required, and, unlike so many actors, was capable of speaking the throwaway line effectively. Georgina Ward in looks and temperament was ideally suited for the part of Susan. Pauline Boty, immensely funny in the seduction scene, was really too pretty and charming for a character intended to be a trifle grotesque, for whom an actress in, say, the tradition of that incomparable comic film star Zasu Pitts would have been preferable. Harriet's part was taken by Imogen Hassall (rather an unhappy figure later to get a good deal of publicity and die of an over-dose), a beauty undoubtedly, but not *gamine* enough for what she had to do. The rest of the men in the cast have all made names for themselves, indeed were far from unknown then. Peter Bowles played Pringle (also a painter, owner of the country cottage where much of the action takes place). Jeremy Kemp played Barlow (another painter, who seduces Pringle's girl Harriet at the cottage). Alan Howard played Fotheringham (the drunken commentator on life), whose performance specially struck me, though all were admirable.

At an early rehearsal of *Afternoon Men* an incident took place – no doubt common enough in the life of the practised dramatist, but new in my own case as a novelist without theatrical experience, which greatly impressed me. It is one I have often pondered. Alan Howard, trying out a long rambling drunken speech uttered by Fotheringham, said: 'I can do this several ways. Which would you like?' Howard then proceded to demonstrate three altogether different styles which he could adopt in playing the part. I found of absorbing interest that a character I had invented might, by the art of a brilliant actor, be so to speak split into three, perhaps expanded almost indefinitely. The fact that Fotheringham was somewhat modelled on Bobby Roberts added to the interest, as Roberts, the model, might move closer or farther away, but the essentials of Fotheringham remained the same to be variously mimed.

The question at once posed itself: to what extent does the novelist 'realize' the characters created on paper? The dramatist is in rather a different position. Even in the first instance the dramatist knows that an actor (I use the term to include the always slightly suspect noun actress) will add something to what has been specifically written for that medium. Although even in the case of the dramatist differences of opinion can obviously arise with actor or producer, the dramatist's work has something in it of the painter who, knowing colours will slightly fade or change, allows for that in the chiaroscuro. The novelist, on the other hand, sees the characters as complete when the novel is finished. Even with the novel that cannot be so absolutely on account of the deep abyss between writer and reader. This is something often brought home to the novelist; never more so than when readers suppose a character in a novel is based on an existing individual known to the writer, thereby revealing a vision quite other than the author's.

Even in the case of a play written for the stage, when by definition, actor and director have their say before the consumer is reached, how far should these two elements be conditioned to interpret what – perhaps only what – the writer himself is aware of? Should an actor not only develop the part, but perhaps even represent it in opposition to the author's point of view; thereby accepting that a fictional character, as in the case of a 'real human being', is sufficiently alive to make more than one judgment possible? One thinks of Pirandello.

Chekhov opposed any such thing. He knew precisely what he wanted. His aim was to extract from actor and director all that his own intensely professional workmanship had laid down. Most other writers with whom I have discussed the question take in principle the Chekhovian line; characters must be represented as closely as possible to the author's original concept. These writers presuppose an unalterable view of the actor's subordinate role. No doubt that is safer. I myself remain a little uncertain as to whether it is immutable.

When actually writing a novel one is at times conscious of an external agency taking over the job, something beyond the processes of thought, conscious planning, or invention. In a similar manner could not an accomplished actor draw out yet more from a character and situation than the author has been aware of; subtleties of human personality revealed only to an expert practitioner of the actor's art? In saying this I certainly do not mean that (as customary in Hollywood) the structure of a novel should be altered, its tone popularized, but that within the sphere of the relationships laid down by the novelist much may be opened up in another creative field.

In this connexion Aragno used to say that there were certain lines no actor, not even the best, could speak. An author had to face that. The actor's training, designed to get the most out of every word or lack of words, every gesture or rejection of gesture, causes (said Aragno) the representation of various types of individual or throwaway line of speech impossible to obtain on any stage; the very personality of a first-class actor, even before speech, in itself militating against an underplaying that may in fact be required. The cast of *Afternoon Men*, an accomplished and delightful crowd, showed an inflexible loyalty and gaiety throughout what was, from door to door, a far from untroubled run. Their understanding and good sense were a revelation to me. One often reads of the 'sterling qualities' of those usually styled in such eulogies 'theatrical folk'. I had remained unconvinced. Such qualities are sometimes less apparent off the stage on unprofessional occasions, liable to be mistaken for gush. I was now made to feel ashamed of such doubts. The sterling qualities were outstandingly demonstrated in unpropitious circumstances.

By the nature of their job dramatic critics are more powerful than literary critics. The latter can – indeed often do – make foolish misjudgments in the way of praise or blame, but their effect on a book is except in rare cases very relative. Dramatic critics, on the other hand, can, anyway in bulk, wreck a play. The egos of dramatic critics accordingly grow proportionately inflated, their judgments more erratic. Dramatic critics, unlike literary critics, must also make up their minds rapidly, probably dictate an article immediately over the telephone, when at worst a book-reviewer can sleep a night digesting what has been read before the morning excretion of views. There is a certain rightness in this. If the rest of a theatre audience register an immediate reaction, it is putting dramatic critics on the same level as the public for which they are catering in having no opportunity to turn the play over in the mind before passing an opinion; a process in all the arts which can often modify judgment one way or the other.

In the case of the *Afternoon Men* adaptation many of the dramatic critics – while sparing a crumb of praise for the novel itself – deplored the subject of a play dealing with drifting purposeless promiscuous young bohemians. That was not the way young people ought to behave. If they did behave like that plays should not be written about them. This was precisely the condemnation visited on the novel in 1931. Now the novel seemed to have become morally exculpated from this particular form of censure, but in 1963 the play was still reprobated by exactly the same puritanical standards as those of thirty years before. I record this simply as a fact of social rather than aesthetic note, that dramatic critics as a class stubbornly maintained an old fashioned morality that the apparently laxer literary critics had long abandoned. *Qui s'excuse s'accuse* is never more applicable than when writers try to justify their own writings in whatever form. I attempt no 'defence' of *Afternoon Men* as a play (a medium for which it was not written in the first instance) beyond saying that when we returned to London, and I attended several performances, I found myself, admittedly an interested party, amused rather than bored.

The Arts being a club the public could not queue up at the box-office and buy a ticket, to be purchased only by a card-carrying member of at least twenty-four hours' standing. Membership was attainable for some quite modest sum, but one's friends, who would certainly have turned up at any ordinary West End theatre, were on the whole understandably reluctant to make a decision as to how an evening might be spent twenty-four hours in advance. In consequence houses were thin, not to say gaunt. It was then that my admiration for the cast took shape. They played every night with the spirit of a Command Performance at The Haymarket or Drury Lane. One of the two or three critics who spoke warmly of the *Afternoon Men* adaptation was the anonymous representative of the *Times Educational Supplement* (6 September 1963) in a longish piece headed *Latecomer's Luck*. Perhaps I may be forgiven for quoting some of its paragraphs, not so much for the praise, however acceptable, as for the comment on why the show was displeasing to some of the journalists who panned it. The writer began by remarking that he had been unable to attend the play's First Night, having had to cover the Edinburgh Festival. He went on to say:

'In general this [*Afternoon Men*] was given a pretty rough passage from the critics: it did not hang together as a play: it was just a string of inane, empty conversations, which might have some point given the ironic content of the novel but did not begin to stand up by themselves. It was outdated and irrelevant ... So in some trepidation I went along, and to my great surprise found a witty, sophisticated and wholly delightful entertainment, remarkably well acted by everyone and admirably staged ... Far from being dated and irrelevant, it was all too uncomfortably relevant: the horrifying thing is the way that everything Mr Powell wrote thirty years ago is immediately recognizable today ... but nobody is there to say tut-tut or moralize about the Bomb ... no humanist heart is being worn on a liberal sleeve, and that, it seems, is for most of our serious theatre critics the one unforgivable sin in a play about modern society.'

I was grateful for this exposé, however long after the ball it appeared. Another postscript was written fifteen years later.

When we toured India we made two American friends, Bill Robinson and his wife Virginia, who were again in the same party as ourselves in Iran. Bill Robinson once delighted me by repeating a formula used by a fellow Kansas lawyer when lunching with him *à deux*: 'Separate checks, waiter, we ain't romancin'.' The Robinsons, in London in 1978 doing a round of theatres, rang up to say hullo. Almost the first words Robinson spoke were: 'I knew you wrote novels, but I'd no idea you'd had a play running in London that was a great success.' I made some deprecatory remarks as to the dramatization of my first novel having been staged for a week or two at a theatre club, where it had been received without much enthusiasm. I could sense on the telephone that he supposed this comment a piece of typically British understatement.

'But it must have gone pretty well,' he said. 'There was a very complimentary reference to it in our theatre programme last night. I'll send the programme along before we leave.'

He did. Sure enough an item in the magazine part of the programme referred to the 'now celebrated performance of Anthony Powell's *Afternoon Men*'. In some mysterious manner the wine seemed to have matured.

The Kindly Ones (sixth volume of *Dance*, and that which linked the two wars) had been published the year before the staging of *Afternoon Men*. That was a juncture in the sequence when clearly plans had to be made for dealing with the period of the second war. I decided the war would require three volumes of narrative to cover its various aspects and their effect on the characters of the novel. Accordingly, making a rough estimate of the age I should be when the last of the war trilogy had been completed – and not wanting the engine to run down before the end of the journey – I settled at this point that *Dance* should be contained within twelve volumes.

Among the hypnotic influences exercised by the Theatre none is more intoxicating than to hear one's own dialogue spoken on the stage. When *Afternoon Men* was performed I fell an easy victim to this contagion. In the event I wrote two plays. When the show came to an end a nucleus of those who had been involved in *Afternoon Men* continued to meet. Riccardo Aragno was still professionally interested in the play's possibilities, and, with a view to having another shot at placing it in the West End, talked of polishing up his adaptation in the light of what was to be learnt from the staging at The Arts. Richard Schulman always loved to discuss any theatrical venture however remote. Georgina Ward, whose forceful personality had done much to help the production through some of its more troublesome interludes, was not only keen to appear in a new version, but continually urged me to write a play with a good part for herself. She loved to talk about life, her feelings, her relations, her career on the boards, half-consciously creating a dramatic personality, not necessarily her own in truth, but suitable to work over as a character in a play. Her firmness of personal definition was allied to an often acknowledged waywardness, which, in spite of much hard work, would always, I think, have caused her to stop short of that easy malleability, total dedication, required of an actor: the condition of having no other life but the Theatre. In fact her instinct for the Theatre was at least equally an intellectual one, which made her of great assistance in criticizing a script. She had strong opinions, not only experience of acting but of employment on the play-reading side of a literary agency. Her advice about getting the two plays into shape made me want to dedicate them to her. As neither achieved production, nor were they published in book form until 1971, in place of that *The Military Philosophers* had to be the dedication; but the Plays were meant.

The first play *The Garden God* was a fantasy. Priapus, Roman deity of Procreation and Horticulture, is by chance conjured up by a group of archaeologists excavating one of his shrines on a small Greek island. Enraged by their ineptitudes Priapus makes himself manifest. The disturbed god angrily investigates the sexual habits of these intruders, notably their failings in the light of the physical worship they owe him. Richard Schulman, whose opinion was worth having, showed himself well disposed towards *The Garden God*. He set the wheels in motion by introducing me to a friend of his who turned up the very moment after Schulman had read the play. This was William Donaldson, who had been in the past concerned with various theatrical projects, but absented himself from that world for several years. Now he felt a growing desire to return.

Donaldson, a pale fair-haired young man of decidedly raffish appearance, educated at Winchester and Cambridge, had been mixed up with the production of *Beyond the Fringe*, *The Bed-sitting Room*, *An Evening of British Rubbish*, the first of which especially made a hit. Donaldson had for some reason never managed to cash in on these former good connexions, and now hoped to re-establish himself. Schulman suggested that he read *The Garden God*. Donaldson did so, and liked the play. He and Schulman put forward a few minor alterations in the script. These were made without difficulty. An option was arranged through my agent with a company Donaldson knew of. The first step towards staging *The Garden God* had been taken.

As time went on it really looked as if *The Garden God* would be up in lights one day. Before proceeding to its production Donaldson was committed to putting on another show to be called, so far as I remember, *Knights of the Comedy*. This was to be an attempt to revive the glories of the oldtime English music-hall. Before the West End opening a try-out was to take place in Liverpool. Everything was arranged for the First Night when a series of blows began to descend. In the beginning the Liverpool theatre had a much larger stage than The Arts, so that the cast required a day or two's extra rehearsing over and above time allowed. Meanwhile a car containing certain essential props for some of the scenes was stolen on the way up to Liverpool. New props had to be acquired, or some rearrangements of scenes devised. In consequence of these mishaps – there were at least two or three others, including, I think, the leading lady falling sick – the First Night at Liverpool had to be postponed for at least a week.

This delay naturally meant that more money was needed. Donaldson travelled south to see his usual 'angel', who lived far enough from London to necessitate a whole day's visit. After spending morning and afternoon talking things over the angel came to a negative conclusion. He would advance no more money. That was flat. Donaldson, much cast down, left the angel, but with one last trump up his own sleeve. A respectable amount of money was entailed on him at the death of an aged uncle. The Trust in which the capital was vested was controlled by this uncle, with whom Donaldson himself was on the worst of terms. In a crisis such as this delicacies of family feeling had to be disregarded. Donaldson went to see his uncle, to whom he explained what a mess had come about. He asked that in order to be tided over this awkward period a comparatively small sum should be put at his disposal (if necessary to be paid back later) as legatee of funds that he would in any case ultimately inherit. After much persuasion the uncle agreed that the requisite amount should be made available at a Liverpool bank by the time Donaldson returned there.

Donaldson took the train back to Liverpool thinking that anyway for the moment the problem was solved. The following morning he went to the bank named as that from which the money was to be drawn. He was taken in to the manager. The manager explained that Donaldson's uncle had indeed made arrangements the previous day for the sum in question to be advanced. That very morning early – in fact first thing – the uncle had rung up to say that he had changed his mind. He wanted the previous instruction cancelled. This unhappy story was retailed to me by Richard Schulman. Even he, I think, had received it secondhand, possibly from a former girlfriend of Donaldson's. Donaldson himself now withdrew from general circulation. No one seemed to know where he had gone. I never set eyes on him again in the flesh.

A long time later, however, I once or twice saw Donaldson's name in a gossip-column accompanied by a photograph, and in 1975 a firm of publishers unknown to me by name sent a work in paperback entitled: *Both the Ladies and the Gentlemen: the Memoirs of a London Brothel-Keeper in the 1970s*, by William Donaldson. On its blurb the author was quoted in giving an opinion that 'as I might be the only ponce with a pen, it was of some importance that I kept a record of various comings and goings'. Some years after the publication of these autobiographical gleanings Donaldson surfaced once more in print, this time not precisely as author. Under the *nom de guerre* of Henry Root he published two volumes of spoof letters he had written, signed with that equivocal pseudonym, to various persons of eminence or notoriety, together with answers received from them. These collections of Letters were frequently quoted in newspaper Bestseller Lists. On the matter of these Lists I should like to interpolate a reminiscence of my own. When I was at Duckworth's the firm published 'on commission' (i.e. paid for by the writer) a volume of verse in the manner of Swinburne put out after release from prison by a financier called Gerard Lee Bevan, who had in some manner transgressed in City dealings. Bevan's *Poems* appeared at least once if not more in the Bestseller Lists, when in fact Duckworth's had disposed of only three copies. That, however, is by the way, and I am sure did not apply to *The Root Letters*.

The Root Letters seemed to me of less interest than Donaldson's account of life as a souteneur. Everyone who has ever worked in almost any sort of office, let alone a governmental organization, knows that letters from crackpots arrive all the time and have to be given a formally polite answer. Nevertheless Donaldson's literary output up to date does prove that it takes all sorts to create Old Wykehamists; both publications in their different ways emphasizing the truth of the school's motto that *Manners Makyth Man*.

The shipwreck of the show in Liverpool, which took place in 1966, naturally brought on a miscarriage in the state of gestation reached by *The Garden God*'s theatrical pregnancy. In due course other producers and directors read the play, some expressing temperate interest, but nothing material ever resulted. I have myself sometimes wondered whether *The Garden God* might not make the basis of a 'musical'.

The Rest I'll Whistle was written quite soon after finishing *The Garden God*. The title is a quotation from *King Lear* (Kent in the stocks) but borrowed at closer range than Shakespeare, in fact from one of the chapter epigraphs in the Maclaren-Ross novel *Of Love and Hunger*. The play is set in a small rarely visited manor house in remote country, administered by the National Trust or made in some similar fashion more or less a museum. It is looked after by a custodian in late middle-age, an intellectual who has been a failure in life, and is tormented by incestuous feelings towards his hippy daughter. There are other complications such as an alcoholic wife from whom the father is separated, and a bisexual American research student who becomes involved with the girl.

The lady then dealing with plays at my agent's thought *The Rest I'll Whistle* not only 'unpleasant' (shades of what was soon to come in the way of theatrical unpleasantness), but what was more important, unsaleable. She and I were on the best of terms. I saw her point on both issues. It fell out, however, that the young man in principle dealing with film rights in the same firm read *Whistle*, and, while agreeing that some people might be shocked, was by no means convinced of the play's unsaleability. He suggested I hand it over to him with a view to having a look for the right management. I pictured that at best to be something like *Afternoon Men*'s run at The Arts, or perhaps an 'off West End' theatre in Hampstead or the like. This was in the late summer of 1966. That autumn Violet and I went on a trip to the Indian subcontinent. We were staying at Bangalore, in one of those detached

bungalows characteristic of Indian and Pakistani hotels, when very unexpectedly one afternoon I found a cable thrust under the bungalow's
front-door. The cable was from my agent and announced that an option
on *The Rest I'll Whistle* had been taken up by the theatrical management
company of H. M. Tennent.

This news not merely surprised but astonished me. I had scarcely
considered a West End production of *Whistle* in the face of all that
had been said by those calculated to know the form. Here was the most
powerful management in London displaying interest. On return to
England I immediately got in touch with my agent, congratulated him
on this coup, and within a matter of days an interview was arranged
with the redoubtable Binkie Beaumont of Tennent's.

Hugh Beaumont – never referred to as otherwise than Binkie – famous
in song and story throughout the London theatrical world, hero (or
anti-hero) of a thousand stage anecdotes, was virtual dictator of the
West End Stage. Whatever befell I was glad to have an opportunity
to cast an eye on so celebrated a figure, who in the normal course of
events, as one rarely frequenting theatrical circles, I should have been
unlikely to encounter. I set off in the company of the young agent who
had arranged the option. H. M. Tennent's offices were established on
the upper floors of the Globe Theatre. To gain these topmost reaches
of the building it was necessary to ascend in a lift – a legendary lift
I discovered later – that might have been thought not specially roomy
for a service lift in an hotel. My agent and I could only just squeeze
in. We found ourselves at once making apologies for the cramped nature
of our proximity, which seemed to presume on a mere business relationship. In the same breath we both remarked on the convenience of such
a vehicle for Binkie Beaumont to exercise snap judgments on the
potentialities of young and unknown actors suddenly called upon to
show their mettle at the closest of close quarters.

On extracting ourselves one by one from this funicular sardine-tin
we entered Tennent's outer office. A moment later we were ushered
into Binkie Beaumont's room. He was then, I suppose, trembling on
the brink of sixty, the embodiment of brisk genial well-preserved well
turned out theatrical camp. His courtesy was quite overpowering. After
we had sat down Binkie Beaumont began by saying that he had scarcely
looked at the name on the typescript which 'they' had set in front of
him; a faraway state of mind no doubt induced by the weighty responsibilities of showbiz that were his daily lot. He had languidly begun
to scan a page or two.

'After a few lines I asked myself,' said Binkie Beaumont, 'but *who*
has written this dialogue?'

Either he must have turned back to the title-page, or – more probably
– an attendant sprite, hearing the strangled cry of excitement, had

stepped forward apologetically to assist or enlighten the great man. '*Then I read your name* ...'

I bowed some sort of embarrassed and quite inadequate acknowledgment of such commendation from such a source.

'I'm thinking of a *special* director for this play,' said Binkie Beaumont, speaking now very seriously. 'Not one of my usual ones.'

His voice suggested that such prosaic underlings as his 'usual ones' would fall far short of so exalted a task. He then mentioned the name of the director he had in mind. I confess my heart sank. Was he quite the man? I had a twinge of doubt. I had heard more than one disconcerting story about him. Nevertheless who was I to mistrust the opinion of a figure who in theatrical matters was not only omniscient and omnipotent but not far from being omnipresent. By this time Binkie Beaumont was enlarging on the cast of superlative talent that *The Rest I'll Whistle* would need to be at all adequately presented, toying with a series of great names in the Theatre, commending here, disparaging there, jettisoning not a few of both sexes whom he judged wanting in relation to matching their powers in so enviable an opportunity to display histrionic genius.

At last, more than a little overwhelmed, I said goodbye. My agent and I returned to the involuntarily chummy lift, scarcely noticing its restricted confinement after such a reception.

That was the last I ever saw of Binkie Beaumont; the last my agent or myself ever heard of the projected staging by H. M. Tennent of *The Rest I'll Whistle*. Letters remained unanswered; Mr Beaumont was always too momentously engaged to speak on the telephone: no one else in the office seemed to know anything about the negotiation. In the end I put *Whistle* away in a drawer beside *The Garden God*. Both by then had admirable sets designed by Osbert Lancaster, which combined to illustrate when published *Two Plays by Anthony Powell* (1971). Some years before that, indeed not very long after our meeting, Binkie Beaumont himself starred in that widely produced one-man show for which no option has to be arranged, no curtain calls are taken.

❊ 7 ❊

In 1964, four hundredth anniversary of Shakespeare's birth, the Japanese, who possess boundless enthusiasm for the arts of the West, prepared appropriate celebrations. As part of these festivities the British Council in Tokyo organized a Book Exhibition. Also under the

Council's auspices three writers were chosen as anthropological specimens of that trade in the United Kingdom to be dispatched to Japan
for display. I was one of these. The other two examples selected were
Alan Pryce-Jones, an old friend, and Muriel Bradbrook, whom I had
not met (in the event a wholly sympathetic companion for a jaunt of
that sort), Cambridge Professor, authority on Shakespeare and the
Theatre of that period. Pryce-Jones had by then resigned from *TLS*
editorship, and taken up residence in Newport, Rhode Island.

Not long before this our friends and country neighbours Lees and
Mary Mayall had been *en poste* at the British Embassy in Tokyo. They
provided a sheaf of introductions. Through the Mayalls we had already
made a Japanese contact in Ivan Morris and his wife Ayako (Yaki),
a Japanese dancer, both of whom had been with us on an Hellenic cruise
taken in 1963. Ivan Morris (who later parted with Yaki, and died in
1976 at the age of fifty, a tragic loss to Oriental scholarship) was a
remarkable figure. Half-American, half-Swedish, he had been brought
up in Europe, chiefly Great Britain, and become foremost student and
translator of Japanese literature in the generation after Arthur Waley,
whose prize pupil Morris had been. Waley is best known for his rendering of *The Tale of Genji*, 10th century novel by The Lady Murasaki
(*Anglicé*, Lady Violet), and Morris's crowning work, *The World of the
Shining Prince: Court Life in Ancient Japan* (1964) also deals with the
Heian period; roughly that of Aethelred the Unready at home. Good-
looking and convivial, Ivan Morris was a charming friend as well as
scholar, and Yaki too was delightful company. As well as possessing
beauty and a sharp wit, she would produce inimitable malapropisms
in her otherwise fluent English. One of the best of these was to speak
of the ghettos (grottoes) at The Chantry, where the Morrises stayed
more than once.

One of the Mayalls' Japanese friends (who was to turn up years later
staying with them in Wiltshire and come over to see us) was Kenichi
Yoshida, author and critic of some standing, son of a former Ambassador at the Court of St James's. The elder Yoshida had subsequently
become Prime Minister of Japan, pursuing a policy that was anti-war
and pro-British. His son had been up at Cambridge. The Council had
already arranged that Kenichi Yoshida should interview me (in English)
for the Tokyo Radio. This confrontation was to take place at
10.30 a.m., whether 'live' or not I am uncertain. When I arrived in the
studio Yoshida was drinking a large glass of what I supposed, from
its colour and the fact that the glass had a removable base like a *café
filtre*, to be strong tea. He looked like a somewhat battered version of
T. S. Eliot transformed into a Japanese man of letters; an impression
renewed with equal force when we met again long after this in England.
Yoshida held up the glass and asked me to join him in another. At

first I accepted this offer, then withdrew when the beverage turned out to be one of those fine old nut-brown pegs of whisky (no doubt Japanese whisky) measured at a strength that would have knocked one out early for what was to be a day full of engagements. This morning pick-me-up, or perhaps an earlier glass, had already left a perceptible mark on Yoshida's manner. He gave a lively performance, during our duologue pausing in the middle to enquire: 'Well – how do you think it's all going?'

I was told later that Yoshida had a wide reputation for high-spirited toping, being at times deferentially referred to in Tokyo gossip columns as the 'celebrated writer and drunkard', respect thereby paid to his prestige in both spheres. Uninhibited newspaper references to the foibles of the eminent were rarer in those days than they have since become. As Inez Holden predicted in her novel of the future *Born Old: Died Young*: 'No editors would print the dull paragraphs of 1932 ... Gossip writers now referred frankly to sobriety, drunkenness, love affairs, gold-digging, lion-hunting, blackmailing and so on.' When told of such paragraphs proclaiming Yoshida's fame as a tippler I was reminded of a somewhat similar example of taking people as they come retailed by a brother officer during the war who had served in what was then called the Gold Coast. He said that he had read in a local paper the obituary of a popular African clergyman, in which, after listing the many good qualities of the Revd So-and-so, the obituarist added that devotion to religious duties was performed in the face of being 'all his life martyr to gonorrhoea'.

I did not, as I should have liked, meet Yukio Mishima (I rather think he was away at the time), the extravagant combination of writer and man of action less common in England than other countries. Mishima was, however, the subject of a television interview by our elder son Tristram, who was in Japan undertaking a series of such programmes some years after I went there. Watching Tristram's film I was once or twice struck by an odd resemblance that would sometimes cross Mishima's features to those of John Betjeman, his manner too occasionally recalling Betjeman's, though as poets it would be hard to find less similarity, except perhaps a common nostalgia for the past. Possibly all Japanese men of letters possess some sort of visual equivalent in Great Britain. If one of my Oxford contemporaries in the literary field had to be chosen to illustrate Mishima's theory that 'to know and not to act is not to know' a remote parallel might be seen – the approximation pretty far-fetched – in Robert Byron (utterly different from Mishima in personal appearance), though I think Byron would never have taken his own life. Mishima's crazy coup d'état (more truly coup de théâtre) in 1970 was staged with the object of bringing back the absolute rule of the Emperor and other traditions of Old Japan. This melodramatic gesture, doomed to disaster from the start, ended on Mishima's part with *seppuku*, ritual suicide; his salute to death as final work of art. I think Ivan Morris felt his Japanese friend's loss deeply.

At the British Council's Book Exhibition in Tokyo I was presented to the Emperor's sister-in-law, Her Imperial Highness Princess Chichibu, a lady of great charm and beauty, who spoke fluent English. I mentioned that when, as Crown Prince, the Emperor had visited Eton in 1920 I had been among the crowd of boys in School Yard instructed to shout *Banzai!* (alas, without subsequent effect of keeping Japan out of the second war as ally of the Axis Powers). The Princess laughed, and assured me that she would tell the Emperor, who, she said, loved such memories. He may well have felt that those were happy days. In the suite of the Princess, or possibly cruising round on his own, was Admiral Katsunoshin Yamanshi, in his middle eighties, straight out of a drawing by Hokusai. Commissioned as midshipman when Queen Victoria was still on the throne, the Admiral told me that he had served as liaison officer when the British Fleet was in the Far East in 1900. He was clearly very vigorous still, beaming and nodding when I asked whether he had known Violet's cousin Admiral Sir William Pakenham, who – as I suddenly recalled – had been naval attaché at Tokyo during the Russo-Japanese War of 1904–5. Admiral Yamanshi said he well remembered Captain Pakenham. Willie Pakenham (who died the year before Violet and I married, so he and I never met) does indeed seem to have made a strong impression during his time in Japan. He was undoubtedly model for the British naval officer in Claude Farrère's novel about the Russo-Japanese War *La Bataille* (1909), an enjoyable book in its genre, later adapted into a very tolerable movie (Charles Boyer, John Loder, Merle Oberon).

Before going to Japan I had not taken in what could be implied by belonging to the male sex. In Japan – anyway at that period – it was impossible to have a dish set in front of one by a waitress, ascend in a lift worked by a lift-girl, without being made aware of male status as such. At the same time, if apparently submissive (no doubt extremely tough beneath the surface), Japanese women seemed unselfconsciously at ease with men. One had that sense far more than in the West, submission not implying the least sense of inferiority, if anything awareness of power. At several academic functions attended it was literally impossible – short of picking them up and putting them through the door – to persuade distinguished female professors to pass over the threshold first. Among such learned ladies one could not help feeling moved thàt some had been persecuted during the war years for their devotion to Jane Austen. At one of the university 'quizzes' during which I was on the platform replying to questions a Japanese professor asked: 'What do you think of Shakespeare?' Off the cuff that was a tall order, not

least in front of quite a large assemblage of people. Fortunately, on my
setting out for the East, Violet had advised that I should take with me
her own three-volume pocket edition of Shakespeare's Works. This
brilliant suggestion brought a great piece of luck. I had cast my eye over
a page or two of *Richard III* the previous evening before going to sleep.

'Well as a matter of fact I was reading *Richard III* last night, and
it struck me that particular play was etc., etc.'

Moving on from Tokyo to Kyoto, I was shown round that attractive
city by Peter Martin of the British Council and his American wife.
On the last night of my stay the Martins, whose easygoing hospitality
greatly contributed to the Kyoto visit, gave a dinner-party. I found
I was rather too aware of their conviviality on boarding the plane for
Tokyo the next morning, but consoled myself with the thought that
I could sleep at the hotel until about half-past four, when I was seeing
a performance at the Kabuki Theatre. After being airborne for some
little time the Japanese businessman beside me began to grow restive.
He could speak no English, but clearly felt powerfully that fascination
with the oddness of foreigners that is endemic among the Japanese.
He began shyly to finger the camera that I was carrying, seeming to
indicate that I should look out of the window (I was next to it) for
some subject worth photographing. He was right. Quite suddenly from
out of the opaque grey-blue mist of cloud – indeed as if a mountain
were actually standing on a cloud – the snowy apex of Fuji came into
view. This was the sight my neighbour was determined I should not
miss. It was truly magnificent. All at once I felt my eyes fill with tears.

As already mentioned I was suffering from a hangover. I do not deny
that for a moment. The condition may well have had something to do
with such a display of emotion. Nonetheless I had been quite unprepared for this vision of the Holy Mountain (the slopes for ever traversed
by pilgrims), still less selfconsciously expecting to wallow in an aesthetic
experience. Fuji was an utter surprise. To the satisfaction of the
Japanese businessman I quickly took a photograph through the glass
of the aircraft window.

By the time Tokyo Airport was reached I was looking forward more
than ever to that afternoon's sleep. Repose, however, was not to be.
Waiting at the airport was Mr Sunio Saito, Heinemann's smartly turned
out representative in Japan. This courteous attention from one's publisher was not to be ignored. Saito, who spoke excellent English, wanted
me to lunch with him. There seemed no way out. We started luncheon
with a glass of beer each, which was acceptable. Saito then explained
that, since vineyards had only recently been established in the country,
he was anxious that I should try a bottle of Japanese wine. I am always
glad to improve my knowledge of exotic vintages – a hobby only partially
shared by Violet – and although I should have preferred some other

moment to be introduced to the Japanese grape, I agreed to Saito's proposal. The wine turned out to be of claret type. I can unhesitatingly confirm that Japanese red wine is better than Guatemalan (to be sampled on a visit to Central America some years later), beyond that I should not be prepared to make a considered judgment on a single bottle. That particular bottle might have been said to glory in its own lack of pretension. Since then many years have passed, and I don't doubt that Japanese claret has made great strides.

My host told me that when younger he wanted to be a journalist. Instead he had earned a living teaching Judo to US troops during the occupation. He had found that very tolerable. He said he was 'not quite an atheist', and Judo, with its appeal to the will, had become something of a religion with him. I hoped that hospitality to a Heinemann author would not entail a free lesson in elementary Judo, which politeness might make impossible to refuse. I was not really up to it that afternoon. Happily no such offer was made. We did not manage to finish the whole bottle between us, but on top of the beer and the Martins' brandy my share was sufficient to bring immediate sleep for an hour or more on return to the hotel.

The following morning after splitting a final flask of *saké* with Frederick Tomlin, head of the British Council in Japan and philosopher, at the airport I stepped into an Air France Caravelle en route for Manila. Once a picturesque Spanish town of the colonial period, a typical port of call for Conradian schooners, Manila has now only about one church of historic interest left. The place was occupied by the Japanese (greatly detested by Filipinos) during the second war, then badly knocked about when the Japanese forces were ejected. The built-up areas tended to look like the untidier parts of Southern California, though one could see where once might have been the relics of a Spanish past. After dark the sombrely lit boulevards were discreetly illuminated with the electric signs of *louche* nightspots.

The St George's Day Ball, an essentially Somerset Maugham occasion, immediately revealed the beauty of Filipino ladies, who, so I discovered, often look in their twenties when fifteen years or more older than that. They have a national dress they wear in the evening, slightly puffed out shoulders, modification of Nineties leg-of-mutton sleeves, the ensemble very becoming. The men wear white silk shirts with ruffles (no jacket), a style acceptable in the Tropics, though not adapted to London grime. Tables were arranged round the dance-floor with a high table at the top for members of the Government and their wives, Ambassadors and Ambassadresses. Official wives included several superb Asian or possibly African ladies with faces of exotic and baleful beauty. Their unsmiling countenances watching the formal steps of The

Lancers or Sir Roger de Coverley suggested that ritual dances were being performed by the British community prior to mass sacrifice. This impression was not lessened by a speech quoting The Sceptr'd Isle from *Richard II*. I did not leave until 3.0 a.m.; in the light of the previous forty-eight hours feeling that once more I had done my duty by my country.

At the Ball were Ralph and Telly Zulueta da Costa, prominent in the social and intellectual life of Manila, where they also undertook many good works. The Zuluetas were very hospitable to me. A group of young Filipino poets and writers who entertained me to dinner one night in a bamboo-faced room of a Chinese restaurant were as remarkably well up in the writing of the West. Such contacts bring home the luck of European writers, anyway those not too far East and constrained by Communist governments. Books are incomparably easier to obtain in Manila than in the states of Eastern Europe, but even in The Philippines Western books are one of the luxuries of life that require a certain amount of trouble to obtain simply on account of distance.

The last night of my stay I dined with (Sir) John Addis, an authority on Chinese art and agreeably familiar with my own works. Addis, who spoke with some nostalgia of the Duff Cooper régime in Paris when he had been of the Embassy staff, was subsequently aptly posted as Ambassador to Peking. The Zuluetas were among the guests at this dinner-party, and a lively couple from the Embassy, the O'Bryan-Teares, with all of whom I was swept on to La Guardarama, a very dark night-club where a torch-singer flatteringly sang a song of personal welcome to me. The party ended about half-past two.

It was perhaps not surprising that Manila Airport at eight o'clock the following morning seemed a lonely and depressing spot. That was no doubt in some degree consequence of the previous night's festivities, though not entirely. The officially cushioned period of the trip was now over. The next port of call was Saigon, where I should have to look after myself. This was the eve of the Vietnamese War – or rather wars – and the country was already in a fairly ominous condition that had communicated itself to neighbouring states. I felt rather apprehensive as to ways and means of travel. Then a charming thing happened. Mrs Zulueta, before she took her children to school, came to see me off. It was a delightful final gesture. I left greatly cheered, and with the warmest feeling for The Philippines and their lovely ladies.

The object of this journey to Saigon was to see Angkor Wat in Cambodia (a euphonious name I shall contine to use), the country between Vietnam and Thailand. Angkor has often been described. One of the authentic Lost Worlds of Science Fiction, submerged for half a millennium in the creeping oblivion of the jungle, the temples were stumbled upon by a mid-19th century French botanist. Under the French colonial empire (whatever its faults a paradise in the light of what was to come to Indo-China after the French had moved out) much clearing of the six hundred temples had taken place. The Cambodian government still encouraged archaeologists at Angkor. Excavation was at its highest peak when the Communist Khmer Rouge, and their equally bloodthirsty Communist antagonists, were soon to murder the curators, and by the very latest modern equipment devastate one of the Wonders of World. The wonders of Angkor have now been long battered by the guns of warring Communist factions; vandalized by their troops from sheer love of destruction; pillaged by looters for gain; the last detaching bas reliefs from temple walls and decapitating statues for sale to rapacious dealers in works of art. All that had not yet come to pass.

I had always supposed there would be something heavy, brooding, menacing, about the Far East, an atmosphere of which one becomes aware quite strongly in Istanbul, and imagined such an ambience would continue, perhaps increase, after crossing the Bosphorus into Asia. Asia on the whole surprised me by a kind of lightness and buoyancy altogether unexpected. I did not in the least want to spend the rest of my life there; I could now easily understand the hold that 'The East' might exert. In this respect Vietnam lying below brought one up short. As the plane dropped to a lower altitude on approaching the coastline a flat ochre-coloured landscape of paddy fields could be seen bordering the delta of the Mekong river. Something about this country was infinitely threatening. A little of the apprehension felt earlier that morning now returned, I could not say why. We touched down.

In the customs hall a bearded Englishman approached. He said his name was Leonard Downes, British Council representative in Saigon, and he had come to meet me. That was kind because I was no longer a Council responsibility. He had a car. Downes drove me to my hotel, and asked me to dine with himself and his family that evening, saying he would pick me up. On the way to the Downes house I asked why there were so many police about the streets. It was almost as if they were lining the way for a procession.

'Tomorrow is the First of May. The results of the university examinations will be published. If there is a single failure there will be student riots.'

'I see.'

Saigon had always been Constant Lambert's dream city (probably induced by Farrère's *Les Civilisés* which is placed there), and it was through Lambert that I first heard Saigon's name as well as Farrère's.

'Oh, God,' he used to say. 'What cosmic gloom. I wish one was in Saigon. That's the place I should like to be at the moment.'

This first sight of Lambert's Promised Land of oriental radiance was not disappointing. One descended into a pageant of tiny ladies all apparently dazzlingly beautiful, all wearing hats like large shallow saucers, black (occasionally white) divided silk skirts or trousers. In due course one found that although in principle a goodlooking race, not every Vietnamese woman was necessarily the goddess of Indo-Chinese elegance they all seemed at first sight. Even so there was plenty to captivate Lambert's romantic imagination. The sense of danger inspired earlier, diminished in this musical comedy setting, still lay beneath the surface. The two main boulevards might easily have passed architecturally for streets of a French provincial town in the Midi. As soon as one left them all touch with France immediately vanished. I discovered that in the afternoon.

When I had eaten lunch I thought I would take a look round. As soon as one abandoned the boulevards and entered a labyrinth of narrow lanes and alleyways the throng enormously multiplied. Even on the boulevards people were preparing meals on the pavement and sitting about selling things, activities greatly extended in the areas beyond. Within about two minutes of leaving *centre ville* I was lost. I enquired in French from a middle-aged passer-by wearing a city suit, collar and tie, who looked conventional enough. He only barked back at me furiously in an unknown tongue as if being importuned, and hurried on. After a few turnings I struck the right road; otherwise I should have had to await the arrival of the U S Expeditionary Force.

Downes took me the following morning to see the British Council's premises. He said his real subject was Romance languages. A vacancy had turned up at Saigon so he had not much choice except to go there. When we reached the Council's offices the flight of steps leading up to them was cluttered with members of the local population sitting or lying supine. We stepped over the recumbent ones.

'I must apologize for these people,' said Downes. 'The other day when the town was being bombarded they were dreadfully frightened, so I allowed a few of them to come into our place. They've been very grateful ever since – do anything for us in the way of odd jobs.'

'Is Saigon often shelled?'

'Oh, yes, it is from time to time. Not frequently though.'

Downes took bombardment with the most creditable *sang froid*. I was unaware that the Viet Cong forces were so near. It was not the first time that being a British Council representative had been revealed as a potentially risky business. Before the Martins had come to Japan their experiences in Malaysia had often been far from tranquil. The British Council has sometimes been attacked as a medium for giving readings to Lapps of Gerard Manley Hopkins or demonstrations of Cornish folk-dancing to Patagonians, and it was true the higher up officials I reported to in London after this trip did not strike me as particularly inspiring. The people on the spot, on the other hand, gave the impression of doing a first-rate job. One heard that everywhere I went; the same later in the Indian subcontinent.

When I set off for Saigon Airport the following morning the town was fuller than ever of police. No violence was to be seen, so presumably all students had passed their exams. The next staging point was the Cambodian capital of Phnom Penh; thence to Angkor. The flight (Royal Cambodian Airways) went on to Bangkok. I was one of only two or three passengers for Cambodia.

On alighting at Phnom Penh Airport one passed through a narrow passage on one side of which behind a counter sat a row of pistol-toting Security Officials on high stools. I handed the first of these my passport open at the Cambodian visa. He flipped back to the front of the passport, read what turned out to be those fatal words: *Profession*: author and journalist. Speaking reasonably good American-English he announced that I must re-embark in the plane. At that moment no foreign journalists were allowed into the country. This was something quite unenvisaged. I pointed out that the Royal Cambodian Embassy had read that description of myself less than a week before, and seen no objection to granting a visa. I explained that my journalism was not political but literary; that I did not write travel books but novels about love. It was no good. The Cambodian Security man was unmoved. Novel writing seemed to disturb him as much as journalism, if not more. After prolonged argument there was no alternative but return to the aircraft. I did my best to conceal the rage and disappointment I felt at being done out of Angkor by a little Cambodian jack-in-office dressed like a golf-caddy. When I was once more settled in my seat, the plane about to take off, the Captain's voice came on with an announcement:

'We are sorry for the delay but police enquiries were being made into one of the passengers.'

I must have smiled. At some subsequent point in the journey to Bangkok, probably while hanging about in the customs shed there after arrival, an elderly man of indeterminate nationality, who had been on the plane, accompanied by a young girl of Mediterranean good looks, came up to me:

'You're English, aren't you?'

'Yes.'

'I thought you must be because you laughed when they made that announcement about your not being allowed to land at Phomn Penh. Any other nation would have been sore.'

I was relieved that inner fury had not been too apparent. The elderly man settled down to tell me his life story. He was Greek by origin, had emigrated to the US as a young man, done pretty well there.

Recently he had returned to Greece with the object of finding a bride. He had achieved that. They were on their honeymoon.

'I married this young lady. Now I'm giving her a just *wonderful* time.'

The girl was decidedly pretty. There must have been at least forty years between them, perhaps fifty. She was wandering about looking at the windows of the airport shops, closed because of the First of May holiday. It had to be admitted that her demeanour did not transmit unqualified conviction that she was having a just wonderful time; but then – as everyone is given an opportunity to learn sooner or later in life – wonderful times are always apt to be relative.

Bangkok was a hot ugly distended modern city, with a few palaces and temples, mostly of the 18th century. The traffic made the Japanese seem comparatively careful drivers. On the way from the airport I saw only one taxi upside-down by the highway. At first it was touch and go whether the hotel could offer a vacant room. After a long and nerve racking delay accommodation was found. After dinner (Thai food very tolerable) I retired to bed early. I must have been asleep for two or three hours when the telephone bell rang. It was Pryce-Jones. He too had just arrived in Bangkok from goodness knows where, and staying at another hotel. He had learnt of my own presence through the British Council. His company greatly cheered the next two or three days. Thai temples and palaces have a temporary look, as if put up as huge kiosks at a festival or fair. The bright colours, crimson, yellow, sage green, all set against dead white, give an oddly Scandinavian impression. One could imagine the buildings in Norway.

The 'magic circle' of Conrad's melancholy hero Heyst in *Victory* 'just touched Manila, and he had been seen there. It just touched Saigon, and he had likewise been seen there once.' One now knew something of his beat.

When housekeeping was still difficult after the second war we used to lunch fairly often at The Chester Arms, which stood nearly opposite our house. The pub was run by a very nice family, a handsome widow and her two pretty daughters. Possibly because the staff was prepossessing, also no doubt because the place was comparatively remote from frequented scenes, an occasional acquaintance might choose The Chester for lunching someone not his wife. One would look the other way, or give a myopic nod before returning to rationing and bomb

damage. Among those who appeared there from time to time with a guest evidently not his wife was Rupert Hart-Davis. He was unique among these couples with a faintly clandestine air in boldly underlining his presence within the pub by parking outside the entrance a pub-lisher's van on the side of which was inscribed in large letters the words:
RUPERT HART-DAVIS.
In those days I hardly knew him; certainly did not know him enough to have the faintest sense of unease at inadvertently happening on a friend's equivocal situation – if it were an equivocal situation – far less did I have any notion of the story behind the Hart-Davis luncheons *à deux*. I can't remember when Hart-Davis and I first met. Not at Eton, where, two years younger than myself, he was latterly absent for long periods owing to ill health. I did not even know him by sight. He went up to Balliol the term after I came down. I never saw him perform as an actor, earliest of his incarnations. We may have run across each other in pre-war days, when (as he records in *Who's Who*) he was working as office-boy, like myself, in a publishing firm. In the war he served with The Coldstream; when demobilized founding the small lively publishing house advertised on the side of the van. By the time his biography of Hugh Walpole came out in 1952 I seem to have known Hart-Davis scarcely less than I do now; now perhaps scarcely more than then. I say that on account of the hither-to unguessed tracts of Hart-Davis's life that his autobiographical writings have from time to time revealed, even though he has corrected the proofs of many of my own books with precision and severity.

To bury one's friends is notoriously an easier undertaking than to praise them: the latter, anyway in print, a delicate even potentially em-barrassing business. Nonetheless I am prepared to say that the virtues of *Hugh Walpole* as a biography seem peculiarly to exemplify Hart-Davis's individual mixture of tact, humour, instinct for dealing with a tricky subject in a no-nonsense style – a style apparently simple to the point of heartiness, while concealing a good deal of undercover subtlety. I never met Hugh Walpole, though he once flicked towards my first novel a scrap of implied praise. Hart-Davis liked him as a man, even found his works 'easy reading', but had few illusions as to Walpole's standing as a writer. At a period when plain speaking was far less allowable than today he dealt openly with an exacting brand of homosexuality which drew Walpole towards middle-aged married men. Hart-Davis's offices were in Soho Square. Someone said it had the atmosphere of a schooner, the master bawling down the hatchway: 'Below, there . . .' The veteran courtier Sir Alan Lascelles (1887–1981) – always for some reason known as Tommy Lascelles – an old friend of Hart-Davis and key-figure in the dining-club to which we all three belonged, was nearer the mark in observing almost to himself: 'Rupert's more like a Life Guards officer than a publisher.'

The Letters of Oscar Wilde (1962) constitute an achievement altogether unusual in the field of editorship. Hart-Davis admits to a passion for fossicking out information to provide the exhaustive notes which make the *Wilde Letters* an unmatched repository of biographical material, a kind of encyclopaedia of the Nineties always worth consulting for obscure individuals impossible to run to earth elsewhere. *The Lyttelton/Hart-Davis Letters* had their origin towards the close of a dinner-party which included both Rupert Hart-Davis and George Lyttelton (1883–1962), a retired Eton housemaster. By then seventy-two and living in Suffolk, Lyttelton complained that no one any longer wrote discursive letters to cheer the boredom and loneliness of later years. Accordingly Hart-Davis, then aged forty-eight, characteristically promised that he would write Lyttelton a letter once a week.

George Lyttelton (with whom as it happens I had no dealings at school), notable athlete when a boy at Eton, had returned as assistant master. Hart-Davis was up to him for 'English Extra Studies', a not particularly onerous aspect of the work programme as a specialist. Lyttelton's reputation for teaching English in an inspiring manner is to some degree supported by the careers of pupils: Aldous Huxley, J. B. S. Haldane, George Orwell, Cyril Connolly, Peter Fleming, John Bayley, forming a literary *macédoine* to which other names could be added.

Apropos of the *Letters*, a story comes to mind told me years ago by Sacheverell Sitwell. Sitwell said that when he was at Eton a boy threw a lighted firework (something Jocelyn Brooke would have enjoyed) into the aisle during a service in chapel. The Lower Master, F. H. Rawlins (runner-up for the Headmastership when Lyttelton's Uncle Edward was appointed in 1905), rose at once from his stall. Above the echoing crepitations and showers of sparks exploding between the rows of boys facing each other from their respectively *decani* and *cantoris* knifeboards, he pronounced anathema:

'The boy who has done this thing has disgraced himself as an Etonian, as a gentleman, as a Christian, and as a man.'

The Lower Master went on to foretell that a disastrous future would be the lot of the instigator of so sacrilegious an act. I don't know whether the delinquent was incriminated at the time by the school authorities, but these calamitous predictions were in some degree fulfilled in due course, because when the firework thrower grew up he was sentenced to a term of imprisonment for sending fraudulent betting telegrams. That, however, is by the way. I quote the anecdote for Sachie Sitwell's comment: 'The Lower Master's descending order of values was so good.'

More than one reviewer of *The Lyttelton/Hart-Davis Letters* complained that a somewhat similar scale of absolutes was adhered to by the correspondents. That was a little unjust. Since Lyttelton's working life had been spent at Eton it was not surprising that much of his interests in individuals and happenings is connected with the school. If a few of these may seem cabalistic Lyttelton must also be credited with the illuminating item of noncollegiate lore that 'the hero of *The Ballad of Reading Gaol* had cut the throat of the Eton postmistress who had jilted him'.

At the very beginning, the reader's attention is caught by a mysterious reference to a cottage in Yorkshire to which – so Hart-Davis tells Lyttelton – he retires from time to time to work undisturbed at his editing, while at the same time taking the sort of holiday he likes in the Yorkshire dales. He hints that there is more than this; a secret that will some day be revealed. One cannot help wondering how far Lyttelton's curiosity was aroused. Lyttelton's own personality, although growing clearer (especially the melancholy) as he gets into his letter-writing stride, is never, like Hart-Davis's, rounded off into what amounts to a lightly drawn self-portrait. We appreciate that on Lyttelton's side no remotely comparable disclosure is easy of belief, but at the same time (if only as father of Humphrey Lyttelton the musician) he might have allowed himself to be a little less buttoned up.

In his acting days Hart-Davis had been very briefly married to a fellow mime (to use Beerbohm's term), and, though remaining friends, they quickly parted. After a while he had married again, a wife who was partly American, settled down in Oxfordshire, become father of a family, gone into the army when the second war came. After the war, so Hart-Davis tells Lyttelton, his second wife indicated that not only did she prefer to bear no more children, but wished to bring physical relations between herself and her husband to an end. This was not combined with an immediate desire in other respects to break up the household; at least not until the children had grown up.

Hart-Davis explains to Lyttelton that by temperament he had no taste for casual affairs (a subject upon which it might have been interesting to hear Lyttelton's own views, even if from observation rather than experience). Hart-Davis goes on to relate how, not long after this domestic disjunction, he himself fell in love. His feelings were returned. He told his wife, who accepted the contingency, and a place was found in the Hart-Davis office for this new attachment; which was why Violet and I used to see the two ι ˙ʰem lunching together at The Chester.

In short – to speak with his accustomed plain language – for many years Hart-Davis had two wives; one at home in their house in Oxfordshire; the other in Soho Square and in the Yorkshire cottage. The really remarkable thing is that he seems to have run this conjugal troika in a manner acceptable to both parties concerned; something that not every man could have brought off. In due course, when the children grew up, Hart-Davis parted from his second wife; then retired to an Old Rectory in the Dales, the country long associated with the other side of his life. Unhappily there were only a few years to be enjoyed before the sudden and tragic death of Ruth Hart-Davis, as she had by then become.

During these happy Hart-Davis years we were in the North in 1966, and stayed with them at Marske-in-Swaledale, a very attractive spot looking across a kind of gully or coomb with a Georgian manor house among trees on the opposite slope. The other guest was Tommy Lascelles, then close on eighty, who was to live on to ninety-four. I had first heard from Lascelles seven or eight years earlier in connexion with election to the already mentioned dining-club. His writing paper heading 'St James's Palace. S W. 1.' had been crossed out, 'Kensington Palace, W. 8.' scrawled in. This had something stylish about it, but like all his generation (no doubt a habit developed during the paper shortage of the first war) Lascelles liked economizing in stationery. I once received a letter from him with my own name and address pasted over a re-stamped reply-paid Football Pools envelope; a postscript saying: 'I don't do Pools myself. But one of our former cooks did, & they still send these lovely envelopes, which I can't bear to throw away.'

Lascelles had been assistant private secretary to the Duke of Windsor when Prince of Wales, and later as King Edward VIII; assistant private secretary to King George V; Private Secretary to King George VI; Private Secretary, though only for a short time, to Queen Elizabeth II. I found that in fact it had been Lascelles who had accompanied the royal party at the Victory Day Service in St Paul's in 1945, the courtier who is called Colonel Budd in *The Military Philosophers*.

'I like that name,' said Lascelles, when I drew attention to this. 'I'm glad to figure there.'

Although a man of exceptional influence in public affairs he possessed a genuine detestation for being in the limelight, even to an extent of what was necessary professionally. On the other hand he was utterly unpompous about his duties in various royal households, making no bones whatever on the subject of the deep disapproval he felt for the Duke of Windsor's selfishness, conceit, triviality, irresponsibility. While on the subject of monarchs and courts, I myself attended an investiture at Buckingham Palace in 1956 to receive a CBE. When the Queen was hanging a decoration on the man in front of me in the queue of recipients she asked what he did.

'I kill mosquitoes, ma'am.'

'Oh, *good*,' said Her Majesty.

If George Lyttelton had lived on into his nineties he would not only have seen his old friend Hart-Davis married happily again for the fourth time, but would once more have been required to show imperturbability – it is hard to think an inward effort would not have been needed – when he read *The Arms of Time* (1979), Hart-Davis's memoir of his mother. She was born Sybil Cooper, sister of Alfred Duff Cooper (created 1st Viscount Norwich 1952), so that Lady Diana Cooper became his aunt; he Lady Diana's publisher. On the maternal side Sybil Cooper was descended from King William IV through his mistress Mrs Jordan, a celebrated actress in her day. It is not, I think, altogether illusory to see in this blood cause for Hart-Davis's own inclination towards the Stage, with traces in him of the Sailor King's Hanoverian bluffness. Hart-Davis's maternal grandmother (née Lady Agnes Duff), having run away from her husband and been ostracized by her family, found herself in considerable financial straits when the lover to whom she was by then married almost immediately died. Lady Agnes, trying to earn a living as a hospital nurse was seen (allegedly scrubbing the floor) by the subsequently eminent surgeon (Sir) Alfred Cooper, who not long after married her. One of their daughters was Sybil Cooper, Hart-Davis's mother.

Sibbie Cooper was a beauty. At the age of seventeen, staying in a house-party in Hampshire, she was seduced by a fellow guest Richard Hart-Davis, a stockbroker. He also possessed unusual talent as a musician, but no interest whatever in the other arts. As it happened Sibbie Copper was devoted to books and pictures, but entirely un-musical. They were married, settled down to an unhappy life together, though the marriage was never dissolved. Before she died, at the age of forty, Sibbie Hart-Davis took a long succession of lovers. Her son states in the memoir that he is fairly certain Richard Hart-Davis was not his father. Attendant circumstances, a shared physical appearance, suggest the true paternal relationship belonged to a Yorkshire land-owner (perhaps accounting for the lifelong pull towards Yorkshire) named Gervase Becket, a banker and M P.

Rupert Hart-Davis was by no means the only child to be drawn by Augustus John, but he must surely have been the only small boy for whom Wyndham Lewis preserved cigarette-cards. Incidentally, it is a remarkable coincidence that both Hart-Davis's mother, and his second mother-in-law (an American), had affairs with Lewis. Sibbie Hart-Davis adored her son. Throughout the whole of his schooldays they wrote to each other every day. A stifling connexion with his mother; an uncomfortable paternity; parents mutually at odds; poorish health; the silver spoon was not altogether missing certainly, but after all Henry Yorke described himself as a mouth-breather. It is a fairly omi-nous picture. Yet this is a man who became adjutant of a Guards battalion, founded a vigorous publishing firm, wrote an accomplished biography, is perhaps our foremost editor of writers' Letters. There is a temptation to shout that all very loud and clear to any passing psychoanalyst.

But to return for a moment to life at Chester Gate where this chapter began, one of the regulars at The Chester Arms was our butcher Mr Cutts, a man of great ironic humour. In earlier life he had kept a butcher's shop in a tough part of London (whether Shoreditch or a quarter like the New Cut I can't remember), where pease pudding was a popular item. If the pease pudding was thought not to be up to scratch (connoisseurs were very particular) buyers were accustomed to return in the evening and plaster the shop-window with below-standard puddings. In winter Mr Cutts would heat the poker of the saloon bar fire red-hot, then mull his beer by plunging it into the mug.

The story of The Chester ends a little sadly. The handsome widow married again, an ex-policeman rather younger than herself. She was very anxious to carry a white prayer-book at their wedding. As it happened I possessed one that had belonged to my mother. It was bound in vellum, her name *Maud* engraved on the corner in my father's handwriting. I lent it for the ceremony, the true owner's name covered by a white satin marker. We did not go to the Albany Street church (where Orwell's funeral also took place), but attended the festivities after in the pub. Alas, the marriage was not a success. Within a year, on my way home one evening, I met the disconsolate bridegroom lugging two huge suitcases down through the Park. His face showed that he was leaving for good.

Late in 1953, after we had moved to the country and I had begun work on *Punch*, a press-cutting agency sent a short extract from one of the weeklies (probably *The New Statesman*), either a review of someone else's book in which my own name had been mentioned or a piece about writing in general the context of which I don't remember. The remark about myself was well disposed, but not in the least fulsome. It was signed 'Kingsley Amis'. The name was unfamiliar. The style seemed so assured that I suspected a *nom de guerre* masking an experienced contributor, possibly even a vehicle for several persons to write anonymously. The second half might be intended to suggest friends (*amis*) of Kingsley Martin (name of the then editor of *The New Statesman*), on the analogy of the art historian Berenson's invented – subsequently liquidated – Amico di Sandro, imaginary painter in the manner of Botticelli. On the other hand the tone of the cutting did not sound at all like a declared friend of Kingsley Martin; equally far from the Victorian writers Charles and Henry Kingsley. Perhaps the pseudonym was used satirically. Something about the phrasing aroused my curiosity. I addressed a letter to the paper for forwarding, asking 'Kingsley Amis' if he would lunch with me one day when I was in London.

In due course a reply arrived from Swansea, again signed Kingsley

Amis – evidently a perfectly genuine name – saying the signatory could not be in London for a month or two, but when next there would be happy to accept the invitation. The letter gave nothing away. It did not, for example, hint that one of the reasons for being in London during the New Year would be to keep an eye on the publication of a first novel. Although the date on the title-page of *Lucky Jim* says 1953, review copies did not reach the shelves of the *Punch* office until January of the following year. On glancing through Amis's novel I saw at once that I had guessed right in marking down from a dozen lines of journalism a new and notable writer. I take some credit for this. As already observed, *Punch* short notices did not leave much room for manoeuvre, but, dealing with *Lucky Jim* myself, I managed to include a statement that the author was 'the first promising young novelist who has appeared for a long time'.

We did not meet until March, when Amis – who had asked that he might bring his wife with him – lunched with me at The Ivy. In appearance, as I have said, Scott Fitzgerald and Kingsley Amis had a look in common, though naturally Amis was younger and less battered. I don't think I noticed that similarity until a long time after. Amis's wife (the first) Hilary – more usually Hilly – was a lively blonde, hair very yellow, looking about eighteen. She made me laugh by asking for sherry-and-tomato juice as an aperitif; then being indignant at my thinking that drink funny. I don't remember much of the occasion except that Amis, revealed as having been up at St John's College, Oxford, was now a don (EngLit) at the National University of Wales. From the first I greatly liked both of them. Probably conversation started off about the reception of *Lucky Jim* at the hands of reviewers, a mixture of ecstatic praise and shocked horror. No doubt also as a matter of routine I suggested in the course of luncheon that Amis, after return to Swansea, should write something for *Punch*, which he did only much later.

Amis's emphatic personality was at once apparent, although on this first encounter I did not grasp how public a form that would soon take, indeed to some extent had already taken. The first hundred pages of *Lucky Jim* move with unsurpassed gaiety and force, effortlessly introducing – with the author's own *persona*, to remain an essential part of his stock-in-trade – an entirely individual style. I had laughed a lot over the book (as I do today), not in the least – like many readers by no means all of them stupid and humourless – appalled by what seemed to some an unforgivable attack on (the phrase must be forgiven, no other quite covering the nature of the complaint) civilized cultural values. Rupert Hart-Davis's correspondent George Lyttelton had been one of those outraged by *Lucky Jim*, a state of mind not improved by his friend, Eton contemporary, fellow athlete, Sir Lawrence Jones, who had himself written cranky but readable memoirs, and was regarded by Lyttelton as an amiable bore, finding *Lucky Jim* exceedingly funny. Even Wyndham Ketton-Cremer, admittedly prim but a capable critic, while agreeing that he had been amused quite often, was unable to forgive some of Jim Dixon's reflections on the arts.

For my own part, so far from being taken aback by the more abrasive overtones of the novel, I had scarcely noticed them, apart from their being the angle from which the narrative was launched. After all every novel is written from a given point of view, which, as such, has to be accepted. To object would be like hissing the villain in a melodrama; though true that action is said to denote enjoyment of the play. Nevertheless I found that in certain quarters *Lucky Jim* was looked on quite simply as a shower of brickbats hurled by a half-educated hooligan at the holiest and most fragile shrines of art and letters, not to mention music. That such altars could be so easily demolished was an odd point of view, though one quite widely held at the time. There were also those who, so far from decrying Amis as an iconoclast, hailed him as foremost representative of a young (he was just in his thirties) and rebellious generation, 'angry' and anxious to remake the world without delay in a manner to omit its many unsatisfactory elements. The people who thought that turned out to be just as much at sea as those who were scandalized by the novel.

Certain other young writers were happy enough to see themselves in such terms when pointed out to them, and it was Amis's misfortune to be lumped with one or two of these lacking a particle of his talent. I do not by any means subscribe to every statement uttered by Jim Dixon (nor to many of the literary judgments of his creator), but *Lucky Jim* seems to me to represent something not far distant from the precise reverse of the attitudes so deprecated. Far from being a professionally philistine book it is one that could only come from a writer who had thought a great deal about the arts – notably the art of writing – and a novelist who himself possessed more than a touch of Swiftean horror (later illustrated by *Jake's Thing*) at the goings-on of human beings, particularly their sexual antics. The Ivy luncheon led in due course to an exchange of visits: the Amises coming to Somerset: ourselves to Swansea.

Among those who never accommodated themselves to Amis's writing (although someone as unexpected as Edith Sitwell had written a fan letter about *Lucky Jim*) was Evelyn Waugh. At the same time Waugh had a kind of obsession about 'Little Kingsley', whose surname he always pronounced as Ames. This factious misnaming of people of whom he disapproved was a tease going back to Waugh's Oxford period. He would, for instance, always refer to Dylan Thomas as Dilwyn Thomas. Waugh himself had often been victim of such misnomers himself in earlier days, not only those rhyming his surname with 'buff', or supposing his first name feminine (like the *T L S* reviewer of his first book), but also straight misprints, as when the announcement in *The Times* of his second child's birth in 1939 designated the father as Emlyn Waugh. During the Swansea visit the three Amis children were in some skilful manner relegated so that the house was entirely free from them throughout our stay. Since Waugh was very keen on the doctrine that children should neither be seen nor heard, Violet mentioned to him the adroitness of the Amises in having so resourcefully disposed of their family. The story fell very flat. In fact thoroughly annoyed Waugh.

When Amis left Swansea to become a don at Peterhouse (where he remained only very briefly) we also stayed with the Amises at Cambridge. Not long before he had shown round the University a young Russian poet Yevgeny Yevtushenko, then doing a well advertised tour of Great Britain. Yevtushenko was regarded as a shining example of the comparative outspokenness allowed in the supposedly inhibited intellectual climate of the Soviet Union. Amis gave some account of acting as guide to Yevtushenko, and their meeting remained in my mind, leading to a droll incident many years later.

When we first met I did not know that Amis belonged to that comparatively small group of novelists equally at ease with poetry; indeed thought of himself principally as a poet. Celebrity as a novelist has undoubtedly tended to obscure that role (just as Roy Fuller's as poet has to some extent veiled Fuller's novels), although giving a glance at dates one sees indications that *Lucky Jim*'s success actually stimulated Amis's poetry. A critical misapprehension about one group of poems is worth a moment's pause on account of the general principle involved. A sequence in the Amis *Collected Poems* (1979) is called *The Evans Country*. These verses adumbrate the experiences of a Glamorganshire Don Juan, a South Walian depicted as more dexterous than edifying in his chosen pursuit.

A reviewer of the *Collected Poems* (a competent poet himself, now deceased) remarked that Amis had a peculiar hatred of the South Walians. This comment – trivial in the context of a favourable review – is perfect example of a critic being unable to distinguish between realistic observation (if you prefer, knockabout banter) on the subject of an individual or a community, and a malicious attack. Having chanced to see Amis living in South Wales I happen to be in a position to state unequivocally that no one could get on better with the South Walians, nor show less of a tendency to dislike them. Quite the contrary. The fact that Evans and his seductions come most creditably alive in the poems does not indicate like or dislike. To suggest the reverse is to lapse into the principle (one no doubt dating back to the birth of half-baked literary criticism, but peculiarly prevalent today) that a novel about an adulterous stockbroker represents an attack on the City's morals, a limerick celebrating a pederastic bus-conductor must be intended to undermine London Transport. One of the basic human rights is to make fun of other people whoever they are. That now seems threatened on all sides.

Speaking of limericks, Amis – like Constant Lambert – is something of a master in that art-form. So too is Robert Conquest, another poet, whom I met through Amis. This was about the moment when I was writing the latter volumes of *Dance*, on the subject of which Conquest from time to time gave me valuable advice. Conquest, during the years that followed coming out of the army, played a main part in launching the new approach to poetry that is sometimes known as The Movement, with which Amis was also associated, Philip Larkin the monitor. Conquest is probably better known for *The Great Terror* (1968), that scholarly and judicial work recording the fearful post-Revolution innovations in Russia under Stalin.

In attempting a thumbnail sketch of Alick Dru earlier in these memoirs I suggested that transplantation of nationality can add force and subtlety by imparting faculties to an individual which do not seem to be home-grown in the country of birth and upbringing. It would not be difficult to find instances in history. In the case of Dru one saw certain French characteristics, pre-eminently in his methods of thinking and reasoning, processes taking place in an otherwise entirely English system of understanding. Bob Conquest, wholly unlike Dru in almost every other respect, has sometimes given hints of a similar variation in species brought about by regrafting of the plant, more specifically by change of soil. In both cases the mother was English, and the father came to live in England: Dru's father French; Conquest's of a family settled in Virginia since the 17th century, having emigrated to America from Houghton Conquest in Bedfordshire. Both were educated in England, but Conquest (Winchester, Magdalen Oxford), unlike Dru in early familiarity with France, did not set eyes on the US until his early thirties. Nonetheless one sees in Conquest an English point of view, English individuality, linked with characteristically American forms of energy and resilience. He has also the American capacity for taking enormous pains in relation to any enterprise in hand; particularly in the concerns of friendship. This inner Americanism in Conquest seems to me also observable when, as a poet, he passes effortlessly into transatlantic themes, and he is of the few – as one gets older one realizes how few there are – to take an interest in extraneous things (e.g. Roman Britain) for their own sake.

Quite early on during my time at *Punch* I met V. S. Naipaul, then

about twenty-three or twenty-four, already mature, and married to his
English wife Pat. An Indian of Brahmin family from the borders of
Nepal (with which land his name records association), he was third
generation in Trinidad, furthest south of The Antilles, only a mile
or two off the coast of Venezuela. From his Trinidad school he won
a scholarship to Oxford, where he was in residence at University College
for four years. He was now trying to earn a living by writing.

Vidia Naipaul's early novels naturally rely on a Trinidadian background, but from the very first he had none of the marks of a 'regional'
writer. Quite the contrary. Then and later he always liked to emphasize
his own rootlessness, the condition of being a man without a country.
In one sense Naipaul seems to me an 'English' writer, even in preference
to being a 'British' writer, possessing none of those tricks of language
or style that have to be covered by the more inclusive national epithet.
Still less could Naipaul be called 'American', in spite of coming from
so near the South American continent. There is, however, a directness,
a naturalism (can one ever get away from that tricky label?), ability
to stick to the point (all increasing in Naipaul's writing as he developed),
that English writers, as such, do not always find easy; one eye always
swivelling in the direction of fantasy. In the fantasy area Naipaul's
very funny first novel *The Mystic Masseur*, notwithstanding the
Trinidad setting essentially English in humour, just skirts the allowable
unrealities of comedy without ever becoming farce; even when the
Trinidadian Indian hero Ganesh Ramsumair ends up as a Scotchman –
G. Ramsay Muir, MBE. I once suggested that in the very unlikely
event of its author ever wishing to undertake a similar metamorphosis,
Naipaul might become a Welsh writer, Nye Powell.

On my own first reading of *The Mystic Masseur* I did not appreciate
some of the inherently serious comments interpolated in an apparently
lighthearted manner; which is just what good writing should achieve
if that is the aim. Nor did I sufficiently grasp Naipaul's deeply rooted
melancholy; though perhaps melancholy should be taken for granted
in any writer with a true gift for comedy. I make this first point because
when Naipaul's sixth novel *The Mimic Men* (1967) appeared I thought
(after one reading) that the hero, a young local politician in exile from
the Caribbean, showed over much sensibility, too wide a literary imagination, to be the sort of man who would have chosen politics for
a career. I mentioned this to Naipaul. He had an interesting answer
to such objections. He explained that for a bright young man born
on a Caribbean island politics (were he not a cricketer) offer pretty
well the sole route to substantial advancement.

What had been adumbrated in a frivolous manner in *The Mystic
Masseur* was illustrated in a different (if you like more serious) tone
of voice in *The Mimic Men*, though there too always with lightness

of touch. I now grasped the correlation of theme. In Europe – more especially in England – the intellectual might choose to take up politics, prefer to leave politics alone. In Trinidad that alternative was scarcely available. In one sense Naipaul could hardly be less 'committed' (to use an old-fashioned term); in another his political interests, in the deeper meaning of the phrase, are intensely alive. *The Mimic Men* can be looked on as the bridge between the serio-comedy of the earlier and the severe satirical investigations of the more recent books; incidently an extremely difficult personal transmutation for a writer to undertake.

The title of the novel announces Naipaul's searching and bitter individual observation of those countries of the world who possess only 'mimic' civilizations; countries pretending that – politically, socially, industrially – they are living as civilized people live, while unable to govern themselves without secret police and torture, or to produce by their own efforts the goods required for economic existence at the levels to which they aspire; incapable of even such civilization as attempts to survive in our disillusioned epoch. Under much humour, understatement, irony, Naipaul's excoriation is pitiless; a stinging call to order for a world still partly bemused by 19th century sentimentalities and optimisms, to which it has added some of its own yet more futile. Perhaps not surprisingly Naipaul's strong potions have not always been appreciated locally. Even *An Area of Darkness* (1964), Naipaul's absorbing book describing a visit to India, a country about which he feels profoundly on account of his own Indian origins, caused some offence in the subcontinent.

In the British edition of *An Area of Darkness* he speaks of 'my companion', in fact Pat Naipaul, who on that trip was providing support for her husband's work. For some inexplicable reason – possibly a late in the day atavistic puritanism – the American publisher jibbed at the phrase, and 'my wife' was substituted.

'*My wife* sounds too cosy,' Naipaul remarked to me on this subject.

That is perfectly true; one of those special sorts of difficulty in autobiographical writing that are often misunderstood by those to whom writing is not a profession. Indeed we are back with Jocelyn Brooke's epigraph from Sir Thomas Browne: 'Some Truths seem almost Falsehoods and some Falsehoods almost Truths.' The autobiographical writer, with problems enough as to what actually happened, has also to pick a way between right and wrong impressions given by the words themselves.

Vidia Naipaul had bought a house in Stockwell Park Crescent, which, when the Naipauls moved to the country, Tristram and his wife Virginia took over. When Naipaul had contemplated buying this Stockwell house he had asked me to look at it with him before making a final decision. Together we examined the place, discussing advantages and disadvantages of living in that particular house, and in South London generally; this carried out in the very individual Naipauline manner, forceful, penetrating, unexpected. One of the aspects upon which Naipaul felt vehemently was the possibility of neighbours making a noise. On the face of it the quiet respectability of the Crescent was reassuring. Naipaul, however, remained apprehensive. All angles must be studied.

'The house opposite is scheduled as an Old People's Home.'

'Does that matter?'

'*But will they make a noise?*'

I had a sudden vision of those scenes of riotous carousal on the part of intoxicated geriatrics that seem to have preoccupied the painters of the Netherlands: the Stockwell Kermesse, so dreaded by the younger parishioners for the deafening hubbub created by Bacchanalian pensioners. I also remember a tradition I had come on when writing *Aubrey* that ten Morris dancers whose accumulated ages added up to more than a thousand had performed before King James I at Hereford Races.

When Europe had begun to recover a little from the second war the age of Writers' Conferences began. I was invited to one or two gatherings of this kind, but always returned a negative answer, since I was trying to get the earlier volumes of *Dance* under way. This urgency had slightly abated when the Société Européenne de Culture issued an invitation to a meeting in Venice in 1958. It was the year of the *Biennale*. The Venetian authorities had announced that they would co-operate in entertaining the guests of the Conference. In short the enchantments of Venice were too strong to be denied. The occasion was thoroughly enjoyable; incidentally providing a background (much adapted) for some of the scenes in *Dance*.

The only compatriot I knew at all well who was present at the Conference was Alan Pryce-Jones, fellow literary exhibit in the Far East. In Venice local opportunities for conviviality were much enhanced by the influence of Pryce-Jones, a man of unsurpassed social energy. Among other rules laid down by him (one with which I readily fell in) was that in order to avoid a sense of guilt in accepting the hospitality of the Conference without doing anything in return, a just man – anyway a just writer – ought to sit in on either the morning or the afternoon session. To be present at both – unless irresistible to registered Conference addicts – was supererogatory.

I feel fairly sure that Pryce-Jones must have been the intermediary to fling wide the portals (one uses the high-flown phrase advisedly) of the Palazzo Labia, a setting which was to provide in literary terms for *Dance* what is called in music and painting a *capriccio*; the painting sense being the one I have in mind. The Palace was then occupied by Charles Bestigui, a Latin American Old Etonian, whose considerable fortune was said to derive from large profits in guano, those valuable droppings of seabirds associated with the islands off Peru; about which the Baronet in Tennyson's *The Princess* had written pamphlets for which he is commended. I can't remember the precise circumstances of going to the Palazzo, but, arriving at the entrance from the canal (in Venice likely to be the main one), I left a pair of ancient and wet bathing pants in the outer hall. In the course of the visit Bestigui himself showed me the magnificent frescoes in the Palace executed by Gianbattista Tiepolo. On leaving by the street entrance I forgot to reclaim the bathing pants.

The following day a message was conveyed to my hotel to the effect that, if I presented myself at twelve o'clock the following morning in Harry's Bar, the bathing pants would be returned by Lady Diana Cooper. I was overjoyed at this kindness (especially as I did not then know Lady Diana), fearing this venerable and favourite garment had passed out of my life for good. Diana Cooper's memoirs *The Rainbow Comes and Goes* (1958) refer to a bib worn by her in childhood inscribed with the stern words *Don't be Dainty*. Willingness to handle so unalluring a burden must have been an extension of that well learnt lesson.

Charles Bestigui himself, middle-aged but retaining an undiminished zest for entertaining, had that buttoned-up anxious air that some international playboys seem to develop when first youth is passed. He looked particularly worried while displaying the frescoes, which had been restored but remained splendid enough. They depict *The Meeting of Antony and Cleopatra: The Banquet of Antony and Cleopatra*. These scenes are represented as if taking place in an area beyond the room in which the onlooker stands, each fresco placed between real doors, three marble steps below painted in perspective as if leading up into a magical land of Egypt. The first shows a courtyard or quay where Cleopatra has been waiting to greet Antony on disembarkation from the ship which has brought him to her realm: the second, a pillared hall in the foreground of which the Egyptian Queen – a glorious Venetian beauty – entertains Antony (still wearing his helmet no doubt to set himself off to best advantage) to dinner. One other guest is at the table. Attendants stand by. Among this surrounding retinue –

which includes a Beardsleyan dwarf and small dog disporting themselves on the steps – *The Banquet* offers one of the self-portraits Tiepolo would sometimes insert in his works. Clad in a robe the painter stands in the background watching the proceedings rather sardonically. Another self-portrait (familiar to me only in reproduction) figures on the frescoed ceiling of the Residenz at Würzburg, this time with open neck and a cap, the face ill and worried. Behind appears his son Domenico (who followed the same profession) in a tie-wig. Tiepolo's features, to some extent his son's too, are distinctly Sitwellian in cast. In the two Labia frescoes, more especially the scene at the dinner table, the suggestion of mutual sexual expectancy on the faces of Antony and Cleopatra is marvellously conveyed.

The Conference in Venice had been held in the shadow of writers being given a bad time in Eastern Europe generally since the war and Communist takeover; more specifically Soviet persecution of the poet and novelist Boris Pasternak. After *Doctor Zhivago* found its way to publication in the West, an event followed by the Soviet authorities putting pressure on Pasternak to refuse the Nobel Prize, the régime must have felt some sort of counterblast was needed to dispel, at least by distracting attention reduce in volume, the poor impression this tyrannical course of action had created all over the world where books were still allowed to be read.

The only officially approved novelist in the Soviet Union possessing anything to be called an international reputation was Mikhail Sholokhov, whose name was known to English-speaking readers from *And Quiet Flows the Don* (1933), a novel which had received a certain amount of acclaim on publication in the West. Sholokhov, Cossack by origin, had accordingly been dispatched in the spring of 1958 on a promotional tour through Europe beginning in London. In Russian, Sholokhov's book was simply entitled *Quiet Don*, but the London publisher rightly judged that a direct translation would immediately suggest to English ears a novel, probably satirical in character, with a setting of university life.

Almost from the start when Sholokhov's first volume of trilogy appeared in translation odd rumours were in circulation. It was suggested that *Quiet Don*, anyway most of it, had been lifted from the memoirs of another Cossack writer somewhat older than Sholokhov, killed fighting in the army of the Whites rather than the Bolsheviks during the Civil War. This imputation – certainly never authenticated – was raised again many years later in 1974 by Alexander Solzhenitsyn, who identified the author he regarded as the genuine one as Fyodor Krykov, a Cossack officer who had already produced several books about the Don country before his own death. The fact that Sholokhov's name has never been associated with any other work so competently written as *Quiet Don* has sometimes been advanced as an argument in support of Solzhenitsyn's diagnostic attack.

When he arrived in London the British Council arranged a dinner party for Sholokhov at the Savoy Hotel. At this C. P. Snow, novelist, scientist, subsequently Life Peer, was to act as host. Snow, it appeared, was a personal friend of Sholokhov, and accustomed with his novelist wife, Pamela Hansford Johnson, to stay from time to time at the Sholokhov country house in South Russia. I had just met both the Snows, but knew neither at all well. I was invited to the Savoy dinner party, also to a luncheon given the following day at the Soviet Union's Embassy in Kensington Palace Gardens.

On my appearance at The Savoy the British Council lady overseeing arrangements for dinner received me with the words: 'I'm afraid we've had to put you next to the Secret Police man. He doesn't speak very good English, and is in any case not specially easy to get on with. We are sorry about this, but there seemed no other way of arranging the places round the table. I thought we ought to warn you, and hope you will forgive us.' I replied that so far from forgiveness being required I welcomed the assignment. The mere hint of bad English put me on my mettle, apart from this promising contact with the KGB (which I think that department of Soviet administration had already begun to be called). Wartime duties in Military Liaison had developed in me, an incompetent speaker of foreign languages, a certain mastery of broken English. The Secret Police man would be a challenge. The more the Beria.

When Sholokhov entered the room accompanied by the Soviet Ambassador and various members of his staff I was reminded of old Hinks's comment quoted earlier: 'The man *looks* rude.' That was just the impression made by Sholokhov. He looked rude before he opened his mouth. Stocky, unsmiling, with a small fair toothbrush moustache, he had the bearing of a morose taxi-driver dissatisfied with his tip. His air did not at all belie frequent former outbursts against fellow writers, Russian or foreign, who had not seen eye to eye with Soviet methods. Sholokhov offered no English, but conversation with him was not totally reduced to use of an interpreter at this party because the Oxford philosopher Isaiah Berlin was to sit on one side at dinner. Berlin was not only a Russian speaker, who had left Russia at the age of ten, but a conversationalist to be relied upon not to dry up whatever the lack of response in a neighbour. On Sholokhov's other side was a compatriot, probably the Ambassador.

My own next door neighbour the KGB man, as wonted in his profession, looked a little different from the rest of the Embassy staff, all of whom possessed that superficial uniformity imposed by diplomatic life that can make nationality barely distinguishable. The KGB man, probably in his middle to late forties, wore a dark silky mandarin moustache that curled down into the corners of his mouth like an 1880 officer of the Brigade of Guards. His manner, if not particularly genial, was perfectly correct; his English wholly intelligible, indeed much better than I had been led to expect. By about halfway through dinner the KGB man and I were on sufficiently matey terms for him to have confided to me that he was by race Armenian, and, although no longer in the first flush of youth, only comparatively recently married. He was rather arch about this middle-aged marriage, even blushing slightly, and very proud of his two little daughters aged about two and three. The name of the elder daughter escapes me, some very usual one like Catherine or Natasha, but the younger – he strongly emphasized this – was Marië – not Maria but Marië – the Armenian version of Mary. By the end of dinner we were really getting on splendidly.

Toasts were drunk. Snow made a speech. He drew attention to the fact that 1905 had been a Vintage Year for writers, having produced Sholokhov, Powell, and Snow himself. This tribute was translated sentence by sentence. Sholokhov, whose sullen features had not for a moment relaxed under what I don't doubt had been a cascade of wit from Berlin, showed no particular pleasure on learning of this auspicious nativity. Eventually came that always gruelling routine on such occasions as this of being led up to the guest of honour for a word of two; in this case promising to be even less enjoyable than usual on account of Sholokhov's demeanour and the fact that that conversation had to be conducted through an interpreter.

When my turn came I took the Cossack bull by its Communist horns in going straight to the quintessence of Sholokhov's image by saying to the interpreter, a mild bespectacled young man evidently Jewish, that I understood Cossacks were not in themselves a separate race, but in the first instance had been a nomadic tribe of horsemen, principally Turkish in origin. I would like to hear Sholokhov's comments on that subject. Sholokhov listened impatiently while a translation of this not very sparkling item of small talk was being rendered intelligible to him by the young man in spectacles. Then he spat out a word or two. His last angry sentence, uttered with much vehemence, for some reason made the interpreter smile; perhaps because Sholokhov had seemed to aim the words at himself rather than me:

'Mr Sholokhov says Turks – anyone – can be Cossacks. All peoples. Everybody can be Cossack except Jews. Jewish peoples cannot be Cossack.'

I did not prolong this dialogue, and in due course the party broke up. The following morning on waking up and thinking over the dinner I had one of the worst attacks of *l'esprit de l'escalier* (from which I am a congenital sufferer) that I have ever experienced. Why had I not countered Sholokhov's disclaimer that Jews were not allowed to be Cossacks with the words:

'*What about Babel?*'

The unmindfulness was all the more inexcusable because I actually possessed a copy of *Cavalerie Rouge*, a French translation of Babel's best known collected short stories. Babel, a Jew if ever there was one, had fought in a Cossack detachment of Bolshevik cavalry under Budenny, former Tsarist NCO who became a Marshal of the USSR. Later Babel's too realistic writing had given offence to the Marshal, whose thickheadedness was famous throughout Russia, and had probably saved his life as one of the few Old Bolsheviks not executed by Stalin. Budenny complained to Stalin about Babel. The writer had been liquidated in his early forties.

That was the day of luncheon at the Soviet Embassy. I had for some reason, now forgotten, to visit that morning the Reading Room of the British Museum. Passing through one of the small Bloomsbury streets leading to the front of the Museum I paused to look in the window of an arty-crafty shop displaying all sorts of odds and ends. These included a couple of small dolls about six inches high and probably handmade: two little blonde girls, one wearing shorts, the other check trousers. I stepped in and bought these. Saying they need not be wrapped up, I slipped them into a breast pocket. After leaving the British Museum I arrived a minute or two early for the invitation at Kensington Palace Gardens. When I was shown into the Embassy's long drawing-room the only other guests as over punctual as myself turned out to be the celebrated Negro singer Paul Robeson and his wife. As luck would have it they were sitting at the far end of the room talking to the only member of the Embassy staff present, the KGB man. After introduction to Mr and Mrs Paul Robeson, and a moment or two's conversation, I produced the two little dolls from my pocket.

'I brought a small present for Natasha and Marië.'

The effect of making this trifling gift was absolutely galvanic. The KGB man sprang to his feet. He looked all at once greatly disturbed. Had he suddenly remembered something other than his children of which the dolls reminded him? Muttering a word or two that might or might not have been perfunctory thanks he literally snatched the dolls from me, turned away and walked fast – indeed almost ran – down the length of the long lofty room; disappearing from sight among the crowd of guests who were now beginning to flow in from a door some little way from where we were sitting. The Robesons and I settled down again without him. I mentioned to Paul Robeson that I had been fortunate enough to see his Othello which he had played in London a long time before. I would have liked to discuss with him the Black

WPA *Macbeth* watched in Los Angeles, but new introductions had begun to take place. In fact, Robeson's Othello had been interesting rather than impressive. He had seemed to tackle the role with a sense of grievance alien to Shakespeare's selfconfident Moor. The Black WPA players had been infinitely less tense. By this time everyone had arrived; perhaps forty or fifty people, including all who had been at the previous night's Savoy dinner party. I did not set eyes on the KGB man again, though he must have been at the table somewhere, one would have expected.

When on some later occasion I ran across Isaiah Berlin I asked what sitting next to Sholokhov had been like.

'Hates everybody,' said Berlin. 'Touch of Muggeridge. A bad-tempered version of Muggeridge. Distinct touch of Muggeridge.'

All but twenty years passed after the Venice gathering before I attended another Writers' Conference. Then, in the spring of 1977, the Bulgarian Embassy sent a letter announcing an invitation from the Bulgarian Writers' Union to an international conference in Sofia. I excused myself on grounds mentioned earlier – the grip of writing-time's Old Man of the Sea if anything tightening as one grows older – and, as we were soon off to Italy for a fortnight, thought no more about the matter. The Bulgarians, however, refused to take no for an answer, enquiring by telephone whether I would not reconsider the decision. I said we were going to Italy in three days' time, and I would think the matter over on return. At this reply the Embassy official asked if they might send down a representative right away to explain the attractions of this particular conference. They wanted me to come; they also wanted an early answer. June, the month of the Conference, would soon be here. It seemed discourteous to refuse this request.

A Bulgarian diplomat arrived. Over coffee I asked who were likely to be present from the United Kingdom. The answer was: C. P. Snow certainly; Iris Murdoch perhaps (when I rang her up she had heard nothing, and did not appear in the event); two or three other writers of varying note; Peter Elstob, secretary-general of the PEN club. One of the names, known to me as that of a Communist writer, but perhaps not very familiar to many of the London literary world, made me laugh. In fact the Bulgarian diplomat and I both had a good laugh about him. Nevertheless the Bulgarian diplomat continued to insist I ought to come. Scenting indications of weakening, he said it was written that God had asked the Virgin Mary whether there was any corner of the world she would specially like for her own. The Virgin had at once replied that she would like Bulgaria. No doubt in remembrance of her partiality the Virgin Mary still appears from time to time on the Bulgarian postage stamps. This must have clinched matters. In short

I agreed to go; but only on the understanding that I was neither expected to make a speech, nor sign any Resolutions; not even broadly-worded Resolutions, such as those which express pious sentiments about the establishment of World Peace. We laughed about these stipulations too, and I was assured that nonetheless I should be welcome.

In one of the Lyttelton/Hart-Davis letters Hart-Davis quotes those evocative lines of the Cavalier poet Sir John Denham:

> All on a weeping Monday
> With a fat Bulgarian sloven.

On the way to the airport the words came into my head (Denham being one of the people Aubrey records), I hoped not prophetically. C. P. Snow, whom I had hardly seen since the Sholokhov jollifications, was the only person on the plane (a Bulgarian one) known to me. We sat next to each other for three and a half hours in rather cramped conditions, the aircraft being a Spartan model, Snow a big man. He told me that he quite often visited Bulgaria, and gave some account of what lay ahead. He was serious, not in the least afraid of being thought pompous, essentially good-natured and obliging, did not himself deal much in jokes, but had no objection to them. At Sofia Airport, we were allotted interpreters for the Conference. Far from being fat Bulgarian slovens they were slim and decidedly pretty. It was not in the least like Denham's Monday.

On the drive to the hotel my own interpreter – who was to shepherd me through the whole of the Conference – turned out to speak really excellent English. When I told her my son had done a television programme on Beckett she asked whether Samuel or Thomas (it was the former), thereby setting a high standard of literary and historic grasp. She also charmed me by turning out to be an addict of one of my favourite books, Lermontov's *A Hero of Our Time*; while knowing in addition about J. D. Bourchier, the unsuccessful Eton master, hero of Maurice Baring's novel *Friday's Business*, who still has a boulevard named after him in Sofia.

The second night in the skyscraper hotel, feeling a trifle exhausted after the journey, introductions, spate of interviews by Bulgarian and other journalists, I retired to bed early. Sounds of revelry were coming from remote parts of the building (which appeared to include a certain amount of more or less governmental office accommodation as well as the bedrooms), whether carousing on the part of Conference delegates or locals I neither knew nor greatly cared. In spite of these I fell asleep at once. Between two and three o'clock in the morning a great hammering reverberated on my bedroom door. This, I thought, must undoubtedly be the Secret Police. On his arrest Dostoevski had at least been aroused quietly from his slumbers. Assuming, so far as possible in pyjamas, the air of Bulldog Drummond, I opened the door. The man on the threshold, to all appearances a Bulgarian, must have seen, pyjamas or no, that I was English. He adapted to that language at once:

'Excuse me – you have a bottle-opener?'

'Alas, no.'

'Thank you, excuse me.'

He rambled off down the corridor to try some other likely number. I wondered how he chose probable bottle-opener owners; possibly a system of numerology connected with the numbers on the doors adding up to a magical combination. Continuing sounds of festivity in the distance suggested that at least some inmates of the hotel had possessed themselves of means to open a bottle, even several. He may have moved in their direction. I returned to bed.

The main life of the Conference took place in several interconnected lobbies on the ground floor of the hotel, where delegates would sit and talk with each other or their individual interpreters, be interviewed or televised. As with engaged couples, all meals were taken with one's interpreter. The scene would have made a good setting for a play. On one occasion an Italian sent a message by his interpreter to congratulate me on the brilliance of my speech at one of the morning sessions. I never traced with certainty to whom this compliment should rightly have been addressed, British or American. One of the Soviet delegates was Yevgeny Yevtushenko, mentioned earlier in connexion with our Cambridge visit to the Amises fifteen years or so before. He was big, fairhaired, wearing a blue open shirt covered with white lace embroidery, sometimes crowned with a Tolstoyan peaked cap. The Soviet poet was always surrounded by a group of hangers on of varying nationality, and appeared to entertain them with a few words of almost every language. I was introduced to Yevtushenko just as we were both about to enter the hall in which sessions took place. Being unprepared for the meeting at that particular moment I suffered one of those mental hiatuses which link a name to an earlier rather than later connexion. In fact my mind went back to Cambridge and Amis's account of showing Yevtushenko round.

'I believe you know Kingsley Amis,' I said.

'Unfortunately I do,' replied Yevtushenko. 'The shit.'

He remarked that quite genially. Almost before the words were out of his mouth I was aware that I had committed a piece of monumental tactlessness, unless I wanted deliberately to provoke a row. Indeed Yevtushenko could hardly be blamed if he supposed that. There had been plenty of things other than Yevtushenko to think about at the Conference. Some trick of memory had caused me to forget later developments after Yevtushenko's tour of England and well advertised outspoken views. Since then he had been toeing the line obsequiously enough; for instance after Pasternak's former mistress Olga Ivinskaya was sent to a labour camp for four years Yevtushenko later dutifully joined in the general campaign to blacken her reputation and Pasternak's. Consequently, when in 1968 Yevtushenko stood for the Oxford Professorship of Poetry he was given official backing by the Soviet Embassy. Amis and others had vigorously opposed this (unsuccessful) candidature on grounds that poets and writers can keep out of politics – indeed are often better doing so – but if they dabble with politics, as Yevtushenko had, they must be expected to behave differently from the manner in which he had behaved. I should have remembered all that in Sofia. Even at that moment I could recall no more than that Yevtushenko's conduct had been regrettable. The whole episode of the Poetry Professorship had gone out of my head. I could do no more than reply with geniality equal to his own that he must not speak like that about my friends. While this exchange was taking place we were all moving forward into the auditorium.

The following day I was waiting for the lift to take me up to my room when a voice beside me said:

'Thinking of your friends?'

It was Yevtushenko. There was nothing to do but laugh. I explained that I had forgotten about subsequent Amis/Yevtushenko developments.

'I don't like professional Westerners,' said Yevtushenko, this time rather sulkily.

No doubt that statement was perfectly true, though far from reassuring. I took it to mean that he had abandoned any pretence of even mild dissent from what was laid down by the régime, and would in future confine himself to those vapid generalities that a satisfied but humorous official poet might be expected to make in public. Later Yevtushenko asked me to see a film he was showing more or less privately, but I had to refuse on account of an invitation received from the British Embassy.

I was struck with the extent to which Yevtushenko, both in outward appearance and demeanour, exemplified that favourite type in the classical Russian novel, the buffoon; the man always playing the fool, not only for his own amusement and love of exhibitionism, but also with the object of keeping everyone in the dark as to his own inner views and intentions. One thought of all those clowns in Dostoevski whose mental and physical antics sometimes make the reader laugh aloud; characters with a clear eye to the main chance, who not uncommonly play a momentous if not particularly alluring role in the development of the plot. That was how Yevtushenko was behaving at the Conference. When the American writer John Cheever remarked (in an interview) that Yevtushenko's ego would crack crystal at twenty feet I think he underestimated the potential.

Cheever himself, and his wife, were at the Conference. I had an occasional word with them. They seemed to know quite well a lot of the people there. Another American writer present was William Saroyan, who wore a long Mexican-type moustache, and had an unusually penetrating voice. Saroyan would potter about the lobbies imparting maxims of homespun wisdom in a rasping tone that effortlessly echoed above the buzz and whine of international writers' chatter. An acceptable touch of light relief was brought by Gore Vidal. I found myself next to him looking at some of the pictures taken of the sessions, which were stuck up on the walls outside the auditorium. In several of these Vidal was shown beside an Indian delegate.

'I always sit next to a man in a turban,' he said. 'You get photographed more.'

I was wearing a red shirt, and Vidal was kind enough to add: 'Your shirts at this Conference are the envy and admiration of the American delegation.'

When Violet and I had been in Florence some years before we had dined at La Pietra with Harold Acton.

'Gore Vidal turned up here the other day,' Acton said. 'He had a suitcase with him containing the body of his dog which had died in Rome. He wanted to bury it in the garden here.'

'Which you arranged for him?'

'Of course – so like Gore.'

I was struck by the idea of the formal grounds of this Medicean villa being turned into a Pets' Cemetery, a kind of animals' Happy Hunting Ground, but one out of Ariosto; and was surprised when not so very long after that a distinctly tart piece written by Vidal about Acton appeared in the *New York Review of Books*.

'I heard from Harold Acton a year or two ago that you arrived on his doorstep with the remains of your dog for burial.'

'The dog had defenestrated itself,' Vidal said. 'I had to find somewhere for its interment.'

'You were rather sharp with Harold afterwards.'

Vidal laughed.

'Harold made me cross,' he said.

There had been some incident about a goodlooking young man in Naples, so far as I can remember from the paper. Vidal had given at length his own version of the story. He readily agreed that he had run the risk of a riposte from Acton:

> 'That corpse you planted last year in my garden
> *Has* begun to sprout. It will bloom this year.
> Oh keep the Man from hence, that's friend to dog
> Or with his nails he'll dig it up again.'

Throughout the Conference it had not been at all uncommon to find Bulgarians who talked good English, and their passion for books, especially English ones (hard to obtain though a few trickled through the permitted secondhand shop) can only be called phenomenal. At one of the official parties a young man pouring out a glass of Bulgarian wine for me said: 'When in Rome do as the Romans do.'

He had evidently drunk a glass or two of wine himself.

'When in Sofia do as the sophisticates do,' I suggested.

We had another on the strength of that. There are many varieties of Bulgarian wine, only two previously known to me. I find them very drinkable, Violet, however, complaining of a touch of the Black Sea. Snow – sometimes addressed as Lord Charles by Bulgarians – had been very helpful through the Conference, having no doubt attended many such gatherings and knowing *les détours*. On the day of departure I was instructed to be ready at 7.15 a.m., and understood Snow was taking the same flight. I descended about ten minutes before time. No one from the Conference was about in the hall of the hotel. I waited alone for about half an hour. Then a young man arrived in a car and asked for me. We drove off together at great speed. On reaching the gates of the airport all formalities were ignored, and we dashed straight on to the tarmac among the waiting aircraft. A man appeared. Some sort of altercation with my driver took place. This seemed to be on the question of whether or not sufficient time remained for me to be embarked on a given plane. Finally the official turned to me.

'Do you want to go to London, please?'

'Yes.'

The answer at once caused relief.

'In that case get back into the car, please.'

I wondered where I should have been taken had he not bothered to ask about my preferred destination. We returned and I was shown into what was evidently the VIP lounge of the airport. There drinking coffee were the Bulgarian Deputy Prime Minister (stated also to be a poet), a Bulgarian writer (who later kindly presented me with a bottle of *mastik*, a drink like *ouzo* or *raki*), Snow, our respective interpreters. Snow, whose train fever must have been even more acute than my own, had risen an hour earlier than instructed, and been whisked off immediately to the airport. We had a lot of strong black coffee and two double brandies, an admirable *petit déjeuner* in the circumstances. The Deputy Prime Minister said through my interpreter:

'The Bulgarians are sometimes called the English of the Balkans.'

'The English are undoubtedly the Bulgarians of Northern Europe.'

I think it was then that we got on to the subject of drink, and I was given the *mastik* as a souvenir. In the plane Snow and I once more crowded in with each other. After we had dished up the Conference he remarked on Sholokhov not having turned up at Sofia as billed. I asked about Snow's visits to the Sholokhov stately home in the Don country. Snow said that by Russian standards it was all very luxurious.

'Sholokhov is in Soviet terms a rich man?'

'Sholokhov's son once remarked to me,' said Snow. 'You know when my old man dies I shall be *very* well off.'

'But won't it all be taken away from him?'

'No.'

'What does the son do?'

'He's a meteorologist.'

The idea of a Cossack meteorologist was engaging.

'Could he just live on the income he inherited?'

'That would arouse social disapproval.'

Snow returned to the subject of the Conference.

'You know,' he said, 'you were a great success. They had never seen anybody like you before. There was an argument as to whether you looked like a professor or a soldier.'

He fell into silence, seeming to ponder the strangeness of the personality with which I had lived so long, and was still elusive to Bulgarians. I had often wondered about it myself.

❊ 10 ❊

On our first Hellenic cruise in 1960 one of the guest lecturers on board had been Sir Mortimer Wheeler. I had seen him once, before the second war, at a party of Bumble Dawson's, but we did not meet. He already possessed considerable fame as an archaeologist and director of museums, also moving to some extent in the Augustus John world, where he had a certain reputation as a womanizer. After the war his celebrity on television was so great that, boarding an empty bus late one rainy night when in a white tie with rows of medals, a conductress arranged with the driver to take him to the door of Wheeler's small house off Haymarket. Mortimer Wheeler – Rik to his friends, one of his names being Eric – had wanted to be a painter in early life, and was capably equipped in several fields. A powerful dramatic sense supported an appropriately histrionic appearance: height well over six foot; sweeping grey hair (worn longish even before the male fashion for flowing locks came in); moustache well-kept and bristling; an air of command. There was a hint of C. Aubrey Smith playing the Colonel in a film about the North-West Frontier. That did not mean that

Wheeler was without ironic humour nor ability to laugh at things. This military appearance was justified by a dashing career in both wars; in the second, promotion to the rank of brigadier, rare command for a civilian in operations.

When it was announced that Wheeler was undertaking a guided tour of Pakistan and Northern India in 1966 Violet and I thought this a chance not to be missed. Although in a general way anxious to see the Subcontinent, I was unprepared for the emotional impact. India has a moving tragic quality that creates an unforgettable impression; splendours; squalors; an overwhelming awareness that remains of two centuries of British rule; the last, in one sense, belonging to the past as completely as Roman rule in Britain; in another, leaving behind the sort of atmosphere that can almost be felt, as one looks north towards the hills from Hadrian's Wall. For some reason Ceylon, a beautiful country with extraordinary monuments of the past, imposes none of the Subcontinent's haunting grip on the imagination. Violet had often spoken of *On the Face of the Waters* (1896) by Flora Annie Steel (1868–1929), a novel with a background of The Mutiny that had much impressed her. This trip renewed her interest, resulting in her writing a biography *Flora Annie Steel: Novelist of India* (1981), which makes plain the immense influence Mrs Steel had on subsequent novelists tackling Indian subjects.

After the Northern tour we again accompanied Wheeler to Southern India and Ceylon in 1969. I was prepared for an anticlimax. On the contrary the South is no less enthralling, though very different. On these two trips I sharply revised my own estimate of Wheeler. I had always enjoyed his company on Greek cruises, at the same time his inordinate love of showing off was not to be denied. The tours in the Subcontinent convinced me that his gifts rose well above being an unusually talented archaeologist with a flair for catching popular attention and cutting a figure in the press or on the media; an amusing talker who liked drink and girls. In short Wheeler was rather a great man. No one without a degree of greatness about them could have satisfied both countries so thoroughly at the moment of Indian Partition, retained the personal popularity that was Wheeler's in both Pakistan and India. For a number of years after the second war he was Director General of Archaeology in India; Archaeological Adviser to the Government of Pakistan. Possibly more impressive was an incident in a garden we visited. The old gardener, suddenly recognizing Wheeler, knelt down and kissed the hem of his garment; the only occasion when I have witnessed that biblical tribute being paid.

Like most persons of strong natural ebullience Wheeler suffered bouts of black melancholy. When assailed by these he would sit alone at a table deep in thought. He was always withering if asked silly questions by the unwary; disapproved of those who drank Coca Cola whatever the heat of the day; could never believe that either sex had a need to urinate however long sustained the journey. The phrase: 'Nice again this morning', especially if used at 5.30 a.m. on the way to catch a plane for the day's sightseeing, always indicated that small talk was unacceptable. Not every traveller recognized at first sight such storm signals. Equally (though in his eightieth year during the South India itinerary) he was not unknown to exclaim at breakfast: 'Had a marvellous time with some old friends last night. Lots to drink. Didn't get to bed till two.'

Rather unexpectedly Wheeler was by no means opposed to those rambles through bazaars, silk factories, and the like, towards which local guides with an eye to a rake-off love to divert the traveller of otherwise serious intent. This was understandable in Wheeler, for instance, at a fairly sinister smugglers' market visited not far from The Khyber (we traversed the Pass), the wares there often strange items percolated across the Afghan and Soviet frontiers or from even further afield. Wheeler bought a fire-arm (with ammunition) shaped like a large fountain-pen, which could be carried in the breast pocket. On account of his devotion to the opposite sex he was equally entranced by more humdrum emporia, in spite of his professional dedication spending hours trying to decide on just the right individual textile for a string of girlfriends at home.

Wheeler's love of flirtation (no doubt more if available) remains enshrined in an unforgettable vignette when one cruise had ended at Venice. The ship had not gone alongside and passengers were being taken off in open boats with short rows of seats facing each other. Wheeler had been making great going during the cruise with a girl who could not possibly have been less than half a century younger than himself and was travelling with her mother. The girl and Wheeler sat side-by-side in the boat holding hands, their locked fingers hidden under a floppy grey hat which rested on his knees; the girl's mother, a little wistful, tight lipped, glassy eyed, sitting opposite them almost knee-to-knee, gazed out over Wheeler's shoulder towards the waters of the lagoon.

Another side (Wheeler by that time deceased) was illustrated by a story told me by a nonagenarian traveller who had served as brother officer in Wheeler's battery on the Italian front in the first war. The veteran had not in fact greatly cared for his battery commander, but acknowledged that he was an undoubted card. Soon after this officer (as a regular Gunner) had reported for duty in the line Wheeler had arrived in his dugout one night after dinner wearing a tin hat, mackintosh, and carrying a walking stick.

'Get yourself up like me,' he ordered. 'We're going hunting. Remember to move very quietly.'

The two of them went out together into the night, taking a course away from the line. After proceeding a short distance Wheeler whispered:

'Don't make a sound. Here's our quarry.'

In the gloom it was just possible to make out the figure of an Italian soldier advancing slowly towards them. The Italian paused, and seemed to be examining the ground round about him. Then, having apparently settled on a suitable spot, he began to make preparations that were evidently prelude to relieving himself. Wheeler, followed by his subordinate, crept forward. When the Italian's intention had reached an all but critical stage Wheeler advanced swiftly. On coming level with the crouching figure he dealt a sharp whack with the stick he carried. The victim, giving a loud yell, disappeared into the darkness in the direction of his own trenches. The explanation of this bizarre encounter was that Wheeler's sector of the line had been troubled by the Italian unit on its flank omitting to construct any proper latrines; in consequence Italian military personnel sensing an urge for evacuation merely moved out of range of their comrades' immediate vicinity for that purpose; with the result that Wheeler's battery area was becoming increasingly encumbered. Wheeler – by that time widely known along that part of the Front as the Mad Major – had taken upon himself to enforce sanitary discipline. Even the teller of the story had to admit that his battery commander, like him or not, had achieved that limited objective with complete success.

One of the places visited on both Indian tours was the holy city of Benares, where stands the red-ochre stained façade of the temple of Durga, sometimes loosely known as the Monkey Temple. Durga, a goddess also designated Kali in myth, like her consort Shiva has terrible moods of destruction. Her more compassionate side, however, is glorified in one of the bells hanging in the Temple's porch, which was presented by a British official of the Honourable East India Company. The boat carrying himself and his family had been caught in a whirlpool of the river. Death seemed imminent. The boatmen made supplication to Durga, their prayer was answered, the party at last with much stress reaching the shore in safety.

The monkeys after which the Temple is sometimes called reside in the trees nearby. They loiter for ever in the precinct, listening to the drum musicians beat three times a day within the walled courtyard, and affecting the air of bigoted testy worshippers waiting for all human beings to withdraw, so that pious monkeys can devote themselves in peace to their own formal and clandestine religious observances. In spite of this assumed irritation the monkeys pass the time pleasurably enough, watching the intruders who thus invade their parish church, at times mimicking the grotesqueness of human behaviour, or accepting it and trying to join in. On these two visits, separated by about three years, the demeanour of individual monkeys at the Durga Temple particularly struck me on both occasions.

A kind of causeway runs round the upper exterior of the pillared building along which visitors can traverse the roof and look down on those enclosures of the temple more or less open to the sky. In one of these small chapels or oratories a young woman in a yellow robe was holding in her arms a new-born baby over whom a priest was pronouncing some benediction; the ceremony watched by a small group of spectators that included a monkey. As the ritual appeared to be reaching its climax the monkey could no longer bear the tension of remaining a mere onlooker. Feeling himself unjustly excluded from spiritual benefits being bestowed, he tugged at the woman's dress to show that monkeys too could be moved by religious rites; then, unable to control his fervour, tried to climb on to her arm and substitute his own body for the baby's. This unrestrained conduct provoked embarrassed resistance. The monkey, expelled from the congregation, hurried off loudly cursing the priest and others ejecting him; no doubt bent on spreading the story of his discourteous treatment in a place of worship, indeed in the monkeys' own meeting house. Here, one felt, was much to ponder.

Another incident also seen from the roof of the Durga Temple on our second visit struck me even more forcibly. A long way below in a less enclosed, perhaps less sanctified, area of the temple a monkey was seated on the floor gazing at the middle opening of a tattered newspaper. He held the pages stretched out before him as if reading the leading article with close attention. This concentration of thought continued for perhaps half a minute. Then suddenly – as if all at once uncontrollably exasperated with the world as it is today – he jumped up, cast the paper from him, leapt from where he was sitting. Bounding upward he made a steep ascent, flying from buttress to buttress, projecting point to projecting point, higher and higher, always gaining altitude, until he had reached the topmost ledge where a secluded niche could still be found in which to rest, meditate, regain lost composure.

In that parade of utter dissatisfaction with things I became at once aware of a strong fellow feeling. How often do the papers report some item that seems to demand just such energetic and immediate form of self-release – had one the monkey's agility – as the only practical means of discharging inward discontents, rage, contempt, despair, at what one reads in the papers. But – especially for those lacking simian flexibility of physique – it is better to remain calm; try to remember that all epochs have had to suffer assaults on commonsense and common decency, art and letters, honour and wit, courage and order, good manners and free speech, privacy and scholarship; even if sworn enemies of these abstractions (quite often wearing the disguise of their friends) seem unduly numerous in contemporary society.

In Webster's *The White Devil* a character is mentioned who 'prepared a deadly vapour in a Spaniard's fart that should have poisoned all Dublin'. It appears from other 17th century plays (a fact to which Kingsley Amis drew my attention) that in Ireland to break wind was a recognized insult. The invention would find a welcome, morally and physically, among many disturbers of the world today. Indeed this ambitious project seems to have been largely realized on an international scale, fumes extruded from uncounted human organs rather than one solely Spanish individual outlet; so much that one's own inward conviction begins to increase that retirement from such an ambience might not be too bad.

Even after reaching one's early sixties letters start to arrive from insurance firms and the like opening with the words: 'You will soon be sixty-five, etc., etc.', causing the recipient to reflect: 'Well, it's been kind to allow me to stay so long.' As the eighth decade gradually consumes itself, shadows lengthen, a masked and muffled figure loiters persistently at the back of every room as if waiting for a word at the most tactful moment; a presence more easily discernible than heretofore that exhales undoubted menace yet also extends persuasive charm of an enigmatic kind.

> Death is the mother of beauty, hence from her,
> Alone, shall come fulfilment of our dreams
> And our desires

Anyway that was what Wallace Stevens thought; others too. Again – as with loudly decrying the world and its ways – a tranquil approach is probably to be preferred, rather than accept too readily either Death's attractions or repulsions (contrasted with each other like Durga's attributes); better that the dual countenances of the ubiquitous visitant should not cause too prolonged musings on either the potential relief or potential afflictions of departure. Better, certainly, not to bore other people with the subject.

All the same the presence in the corner – whose mask and domino never quite manage to keep out of sight the ivory glint of skull and bones beneath – seems to imply, even if silently, something of that once familiar cadence, harsh authoritarian knell of the drinker's passing day, to which Bobby Roberts used to attach such mystic significance: 'Last orders, please – time, gentlemen, time', in this case the unspoken sanction: 'Last conclusions, please.'

Henry Adams – 'Little Adams' as Henry James called him a trifle

defensively – remarks that 'only on the edge of the grave can a man con-
clude anything'. Even when the graveyard, if perhaps not the grave
itself, must be admitted to have moved closer into the foreground of
one's local landscape I do not find conclusions at all easy to formulate;
certainly not rules for life. By no means everybody takes that view.
For many years now acquaintances have been standing conclusions
generously in the all too crowded bar of this masquerade; a bar made
warm by argument like that warmed by the Blessed Damozel's bosom
pictured in the imagination of Rossetti; a bar by now attended so long
that to offer a final round of conclusions at one's own expense seems
almost superfluous. It would be easy to pass out simply from a
surplus of conclusions. Hesitation in paying one's round is not due to
parsimony so much as a sense of my own conclusions seeming to sound
too humdrum a note; when not humdrum, pretentious; sometimes
both.

For instance there seems a lot to be said for that mystic precept of the
19th-century magician Éliphas Lévi (quoted more than once in *Dance*):
'To know, to will, to dare, to be silent'; but I'm not sure the Mage's
words make a very refreshing draught at so late an hour. It can be said
for his recommendations, however, that they leave options wide open;
are certainly not to be taken as aiming at a mere success story. Again,
one might offer (Bowra would not in principle have refused) a double
Kipling's *If* on the rocks without soda. Once more those daunting pre-
requisites are more likely to be an embarrassment than a restorative;
especially if topped up with a dash of Apollinaire's *Marizibill*, the
closing lines of which are worth bearing in mind in most human
dealings:

> Je connais gens de toutes sortes
> Ils n'égalent pas leurs destins
> Indécis comme feuilles mortes
> Leurs yeux sont des feux mal éteints
> Leurs coeurs bougent comme leurs portes

I'm never quite sure whether this final stanza of the poem is spoken
by the little Cologne tart – 'offerte à tous en tout mignonne' – or the poet
himself is asserting that her nightly experience parallels his own in life.
I suppose the former. It doesn't much matter. In either case such raw
spirits are rough on the palate as a nightcap. In fact, if procurable at the
bar, a packet of literary prejudice however dry might be preferable to
general conclusions; possibly even more revealing.

How, for example, should I rightly have answered the Japanese
professor's question: 'What do you think of Shakespeare?'; bearing in
mind that, even if one manages to remain the right side of sanity, Shake-

speare provides possibly the easiest subject upon earth about which to become a bore.

In the first place I find inexplicable the difficulty so many eminent persons have found (especially American ones as Cyril Connolly once pointed out) in believing that the plays and poems were written by the actor-manager of Stratford. Allowing for an undoubted sprinkling of aristocratic poets, a distinct vein of writers of all sorts who began life in submerged conditions, the overwhelming majority of great artists in any field have emerged from backgrounds comparable with Shakespeare's. Indeed Shakespeare might be thought almost ideally situated to encounter most sides of life; especially those experiences trying to the spirit (neatly summarized by Hamlet and in Sonnet 66) from which the art of writing is so largely woven.

Mighty efforts have been made to depress William Shakespeare's social standing, but if his father John Shakespeare had not suffered financial disaster, William not been the genius he was but only possessed his undeniable dexterity in handling real estate, no one would have thought twice about application for a grant of arms. John Shakespeare and his like were just the sort of people on the upward grade who applied for a coat of arms as a matter of course. The several Shakespeares listed as archers at Bosworth (an army branch offering possibilities of social promotion as seen earlier in Sir John Hawkwood the condottiere) may well have been the forebears referred to in the grant who did 'valiant service to King Henry VII'.

As we know the Shakespeare background was darkened by bankruptcy. My Balliol tutor Kenneth Bell used to say that it was impossible to exaggerate the advantages of having a drunken father in forcing a man to think for himself. Possibly a degree of latent Micawberism in John Shakespeare ought to be taken into account in assessing the formation of his son's powers. In the circumstances marriage at eighteen to an older woman certainly suggested sexual impetuosity. On the other hand parallels in contrasted age for both contracting parties would be easy to find in parish registers, and a form of 'hand-fasting' (regarded as binding) may explain the early birth of the first child as much as disregard for convention. Nonetheless impatience for bed does seem indicated in either case; borne out by Sonnet 145, which has no relevance to the rest of the sequence, is rough hewn in style, and seems clearly to include puns on the name Hathaway.

This and much else mark out Shakespeare as heterosexual; then – at what must have been an inconvenient moment in making a career – he fell into the anguished love with a young man that The Sonnets record. That anyone can believe The Sonnets are about other than actual agonized love seems to me, to say the least, strange.

For a writer of supreme insight and sensibility to walk a sexual knife-edge is hardly surprising. What is interesting is that Shakespeare clearly found his condition embarrassing. Had he been congenitally homosexual (like Marlowe), even a practising bisexual (they must have existed then as now) the desperate inner discomfort of The Sonnets would have been differently expressed. The phrase 'one houre mine' (Sonnet 33) can scarcely mean anything other than that some sort of sexual scuffle took place between Shakespeare and The Friend. The poet-critic William Empson has suggested (I quote from memory) that 'rather grudging masturbation' may have been implied. Empson's surmise accords with a tone of voice not without self-contempt. A physical follow up seems to have ensued, anyway for a short time, and Shakespeare's love, as such, appears to have lasted not much less than four years at least.

It is hard to believe that Shakespeare's tone in The Sonnets – still less the sexual liberties evidently taken – could have been applied to any patron who was not only a 'Great Prince' but himself heterosexual. The Friend was undoubtedly a social superior from what is said, but even apart from sexual aspects could Pembroke or Southampton be spoken of as having a 'budding name' (Sonnet 95)? The Dark Lady seems to me less interesting. She is a female figure easily imaginable in any society. Mrs Shakespeare too is not hard to conceive, fascinating as it would be to know more of her. At moments The Friend's name seems Will (Sonnets 135, 136), yet Hew is often punned upon (Sonnets 20, 67, 82, 98, 104), giving rise to Wilde's ingenious short story about an imagined young actor called Willie Hughes. Could it be that Hew was a private joke, a symbol for the male organ? I have never heard this put forward, but Sonnet 104 would not contradict that meaning, nor for that matter the famous Master Mistress Sonnet 20.

In spite of unsolved enigmas I lean towards Leslie Hotson's William Hatcliffe as The Friend: not only for Hotson's cogent reasoning that the recurrent poetic imagery recalls Hatcliffe's ceremonial instalment as Prince of Purpoole, but – more strongly and in fact taking a contrary view to Hotson – from what little is known of Hatcliffe, who seems to me just the kind of figure to fulfil the part The Friend plays. William Hatcliffe, son of a Lincolnshire squire, was studying Law at Gray's Inn. The Hatcliffes were related (through the Clintons, Earls of Lincoln) to the Dymokes of Scrivelsby. Sir Edward Dymoke was an early patron to Samuel Daniel, sometimes canvassed as the Rival Poet in The Sonnets. The last fact catches the attention but need not be material. In 1587 William Hatcliffe, only four years and a few months younger than Shakespeare, was chosen to be Prince of Purpoole, the title given to the elected Lord of Misrule who headed the carnival at the lawyers'

Christmas revel held by the Inns of Court. In short Hatcliffe had won a kind of charm-and-beauty competition that made him a male Miss Inns of Court. Most people can recall some such goodlooking popular Steerforth type, possibly with a touch of bisexuality, who filled the bill in university days or the equivalent.

Hotson – showing it seems to me naivety in psychology – expresses surprise that a young man who had been the most hero-worshipped student of his year (not to mention the possibility of having stirred Shakespeare to the depths) should in later life have disappeared into an obscurity that is only less than absolute because documentation survives to show that Hatcliffe frittered away his Lincolnshire inheritance. Surely (I can use the adverb in the British interrogative sense rather than the American usage of 'certainly') what happened to Hatcliffe is the fate of many if not most of the young men who in early life become Princes of Purpoole. That is just how I see The Friend.

What effect did this crisis (whether or not caused by Hatcliffe) have on Shakespeare as a writer? How far are personal experiences in emotion required? The answer seems to be that variety sometimes produces literary results; sometimes that is achieved without participation. I feel pretty sure, incidentally, that Shakespeare would not refer to venereal infection in the terms he does without firsthand knowledge. The Friend could have added a dimension, uncomfortable and painful, on which to draw, simply on account of Shakespeare being temperamentally un-homosexual. An aspect of Shakespeare's keen appreciation of relation-ships between the sexes that seems to me often missed is that of *The Taming of the Shrew*, admittedly a lesser play. Shakespeare rises above the artificiality of the plot and conventions of the period by showing how two narcissists (possibly known to him) might hit it off in marriage.

Enough conjecturing about The Bard: what are your conclusions? I have remarked earlier in these memoirs that learning what to avoid from reading the works of the ungifted is often an easier method of finding out about writing than trying to pin down the genius of the great. In that last respect Shakespeare is no exception. Again and again one asks oneself how he brings off his effects; sometimes with effortless sim-plicity; sometimes with masterful elaboration. Shakespeare was, how-ever, no perfectionist. If not feeling at the top of his form, or when committed by a particular play to tedious material, he forges ahead, forcing himself to write. The choice between perfectionism and getting something down at all costs is one that writers have to make. Among the great writers it is not easy to find examples of the former. Flaubert, perhaps; Joyce, perhaps; Balzac and Dickens very much on the other side. Dostoevski was a great artist who took enormous pains to research his material, he was hardly a perfectionist; nor for that matter was Proust. A long list of contrasts could be drawn up.

It seems to me that the choice for or against perfectionism must be decided by personal energy, the crux lying in individual strength of creative vitality. If you have the powers of Balzac or Dickens (Joyce, for instance, didn't) a certain amount of poor stuff mixed up with all the invention, action, poetry, does not greatly matter. Plod on and hope for something better, which always turns up in the case of the giants sooner or later. If that inner energy is lacking a writer cannot afford to take risks, let up on the standard already set. Perfectionism must be the aim. Naturally Shakespeare had the energy to behave as he liked in that respect. He rarely loses touch with reality of one kind or another, and always refuses to be tied down by theory. In this last respect he had been censured, especially by the French, for disregarding set rules. Accordingly, let the French be refuted by one of themselves, their greatest novelist and greatest rule-breaker:

'Saint-Loup n'était pas assez intelligent pour comprendre que la valeur intellectuelle n'a rien à voir avec l'adhésion à une certaine formule esthétique ... ne jugeant chaque chose qu'au poids d'intelligence qu'elle contient, ne percevant pas les enchantements d'imagination que me donnaient certaines qu'il juge frivoles.'

Shakespeare would have agreed with Proust on this point, both of them appreciating that 'great' themes are not necessary for great art; while neither would have underrated the sheer difficulty of 'writing well', whatever that may mean. Perhaps chiefly stimulating the reader's imagination in a new way, while at the same time keeping the writer's own imagination under control. Most if not all the great writers have been well supplied with humour, lack of which (not uncommon in critics) should put the reader on guard where excessive claims are made. At the same time satire and irony are to be employed with care. They are elements that can get out of hand. Lady Mary Wortley Montagu spoke sagely on that point:

> Satire should, like a polished razor keen,
> Wound with a touch that's scarcely felt or seen:
> Thine is an oyster knife, that hacks and hews:
> The rage, but not the talent to abuse;
> And is to hate, what love is in the stews.

But if the consolation for life is art, what may the artist expect from life? An incident mentioned quite casually in Vasari's *Lives of the Most Excellent Italian Architects, Painters and Sculptors* always seems to me worth recalling. It teaches several lessons: that if you want something done get the best executant available to do it; that minor jobs are often worth taking on; that duration in time should not necessarily be the criterion in producing a work of art. Vasari says that on a winter day in Florence, when snow was deep on the ground, one of the Medici sent for Michaelangelo to build a snowman in the courtyard of the Medici palace. Notwithstanding those (like Constant Lambert) who dislike the High Renaissance one can scarcely doubt that the finest snowman on record took shape.

Index

INDEX